MW00527660

JOHN P. ARTHUR.

WESTERN

NORTH CAROLINA

A HISTORY
(FROM 1730 TO 1913)

BY

JOHN PRESTON ARTHUR

PUBLISHED 1914 By
The Edward Buncombe Chapter of the Daughters of the
American Revolution, of Asheville, NC

The Overmountain Press
JOHNSON CITY, TENNESSEE

ISBN 1-57072-062-2
Copyright 1914 by E.H.D. Morrison
Reprinted 1996 by The Overmountain Press
Printed in the United States of America

2 3 4 5 6 7 8 9 0

BIBLIOGRAPHY

The references are to the names of authors or works as follows:

Allen: means "A History of Haywood County," by W. C. Allen, Waynesville, 1908.

Asheville's Centenary: means an article by that name which was published in the Asheville Citizen in February, 1898, by Foster A. Sondley, Esq., of the Asheville Bar.

Balsam Groves: means "The Balsam Groves of the Grandfather Mountain," by Shep. M. Dugger of Banner Elk, Watauga county.

Byrd: means the "Writings of Col. Wm. Byrd of Westover," 1901.

Carolina Mountains, by Margaret W. Morley, 1913

Col. Rec.: means Colonial and State Records of North Carolina.

Draper: means "Kings Mountain and Its Heroes," by Dr. L. C. Draper.

Dropped Stitches: means "Dropped Stitches in Tennessee History," by Hon. John Allison, Nashville, 1896.

Dugger: means "The Balsam Groves" named above.

Fifth Eth. Rep.: means the Fifth Annual Report of the Bureau of Ethnology, 1883-'84.

Foote's Sketches: means "Foote's Sketches of North Carolina."

Hart: means "Formation of the Union," by A. B. Hart, 1901.

Heart of the Alleghanies: means a work of that name by Zeigler & Grosscup, 1879.

Herndon: means "Abraham Lincoln," by W. H. Herndon and J. W. Weik, 1892. Vol. I.

Kerr: means W. C. Kerr's Report of the Geological Survey of North Carolina, 1875.

McClure: means "The Early Life of Abraham Lincoln," by Ida M. Tarbell, 1896.

McGee: means "A History of Tennessee," by R. G. McGee, American Book Company, 1900.

Nineteenth Eth. Rep.: means the Nineteenth Annual Report of the Bureau of Ethnology, 1897.

Polk: means "North Carolina Hand-Book," by L. L. Polk, 1879, Raleigh.

Ramsey: means "Annals of Tennessee," by Dr. J. G. Ramsey.

Roosevelt: means "The Winning of the West," by Theodore Roosevelt, 1905, Current Literature Publishing Company.

Tarbell: means "Life of Abraham Lincoln," by Ida M. Tarbell, Vol. I, 1900.

Thwaites: means "Daniel Boone," by Reuben Gold Thwaites.

Waddell: means the "Annals of Augusta County, Va., " by Joseph A. Waddell, 1886, or the second volume, 1902.

Wheeler: means "Historical Sketches of North Carolina," by John H. Wheeler, 1851.

Woman's Edition: means the "Woman's Edition of the Asheville Citizen," published by the women of Asheville, November 1895.

Zeigler & Grosscup: means "The Heart of the Alleghanies," by them, 1879.

CONTENTS

WESTERN NORTH CAROLINA

A HISTORY

CHAPTER I

INTRODUCTORY

OUR LORDLY DOMAIN. Lying between the Blue Ridge on
the East and the Iron, Great Smoky and Unaka mountains
on the West, is, in North Carolina, a lordly domain.   It
varies in width from about forty miles at the Virginia line to
about seventy-five when it reaches Georgia on the Southerly
side.   Running Northeast and Southwest it borders the State
of Tennessee on the West for about two hundred and thirty
miles, following the meanderings of the mountain tops, and
embraces approximately eight thousand square miles.   Nowhere within that entire area is there a tract of level land
one thousand acres in extent; for the mountains are everywhere, except in places where a limpid stream has, after ages
of erosion, eaten out of the hills a narrow valley.   Between
the Grandfather on the east and the Roan on the west, the
distance in a straight line is less than twenty miles, while
from Melrose mountain, just west of Tryon, to the corner of
North Carolina, Georgia and Tennessee, is over one hundred
and fifty miles.

THE APPALACHIANS. According to the Smithsonian Institution, the name Alleghany is from the language of the Delaware Indians, and signifies a fine or navigable river. [1]   It is
sometimes applied to the mountain ranges in the eastern part
of the United States, but the Appalachians, first applied by
De Soto to the whole system, is preferred by geographers. [2]

THE GRANDFATHER MOUNTAIN. The Blue Ridge reaches
its culmination in this hoary pile, with its five-peaked crown
of archæan rocks, and nearly six thousand feet of elevation.

(7)

Of this mountain the following lines were written in 1898:

TO THE GRANDFATHER MOUNTAIN. [3]

Oldest of all terrestrial things—still holding
 Thy wrinkled forehead high;
Whose every seam, earth's history enfolding,
 Grim Science doth defy—
Teach me the lesson of the world-old story,
 Deep in thy bosom hid;
Read me thy riddles that were old and hoary
 Ere Sphinx and Pyramid!
Thou saw'st the birth of that abstraction
 Which men have christened Time;
Thou saw'st the dead world wake to life and action
 Far in thy early prime;
Thou caught'st the far faint ray from Sirius rising,
 When through space first was hurled,
The primal gloom of ancient voids surprising,
 This atom, called the World!
Gray was thy head ere Steam or Sail or Traffic
 Had waked the soul of Gain,
Or reed or string had made the air seraphic
 With Music's magic strain!
Thy cheek had kindled with the crimsoned blushes
 Of myriad sunset dyes
Ere Adam's race began, or, from the rushes,
 Came Moses, great and wise!
Thou saw'st the Flood, Mount Arrarat o'er-riding,
 That bore of old the Ark;
Thou saw'st the Star, the Eastern Magi guiding
 To manger, drear and dark.
Seething with heat, or glacial ices rending
 Thy gaunt and crumbling form;
Riven by frosts and lightning-bolts—contending
 In tempest and in storm—
Thou still protesteth 'gainst the day impending,
 When, striving not in vain,
Science, at last, from thee thy riddles rending,
 Shall make all secrets plain!

THE PECULIARITIES OF THE MOUNTAINS. Until 1835 the
mountains of New Hampshire had been regarded as the
loftiest of the Alleghanies; but at that time the attention of
John C. Calhoun had been drawn to the numerous rivers
which come from all sides of the North Carolina mountains
and he shrewdly reasoned that between the parallels of 35° and
36° and 30', north latitude, would be found the highest pla-

teau and mountains of the Atlantic coast. The Blue Ridge is a true divide, all streams flowing east and all flowing west having their sources east or west of that divide. The Linville river seems to be an exception to this rule, but its source is in Linville gap, which is the true divide, the Boone fork of the Watauga rising only a few hundred feet away flowing west to the Mississippi. There are two springs at Blowing Rock only a few feet apart, one of which flows into the Yadkin, and thence into the Atlantic, while the other goes into the New, and thence into the Gulf of Mexico; while the Saddle Mountain Baptist church in Alleghany county is built so exactly on the line that a drop of rain falling on one side of the roof goes into the Atlantic, while another drop, falling on the opposite side ultimately gets into the Gulf.

WHEN THE ALLEGHANIES WERE HIGHER THAN THE ALPS. What is by some called The Portal is the depression between the Grandfather on the East and the Roan mountain on the West. When it is remembered that the Gulf of Mexico once extended further north than Cairo, Illinois, and that both the Ohio and the Mississippi once emptied into that inland sea without having joined their waters, it will be easy to understand why these mountains must have been much higher than at present, as most of their surface soil has for untold ages been slowly carried westward to form the eastern half of the valley of the Mississippi from Cairo to New Orleans. Thus, the Watauga first finds its way westward, followed in the order named by the Doe, the Toe, the Cane, the French Broad, the Pigeon, the Little Tennessee and last by the Hiwassee. The most northerly section of this western rampart is called the Stone mountains, and then follow the Iron, the Bald, the Great Smoky, the Unaka, and last, the Frog mountains of Georgia. The Blue Ridge, the transverse ranges and the western mountains contain over a score of peaks higher than Mount Washington, while the general level of the plateau between the Blue Ridge and the mountains which divide North Carolina from Tennessee is over two thousand feet above sea level. Where most of these streams break through the western barrier are veritable canons, sometimes so narrow as to dispute the passage of wagon road, railroad and river. For a quarter of a mile along the Toe, at Lost Cove, the railroad is built on a concrete viaduct in the very bed of the river itself. The mountains are wooded to their crests, except where those crests are covered by grass, frequently forming velvety mountain meadows. The scenery is often grand and inspiring. It is always beautiful; and Cowper sings:

"Scenes must be beautiful that, daily seen,
Please daily, and whose novelty survives
Long knowledge and the scrutiny of years."

THE ABORIGINES. This region was, of course, inhabited from time immemorial by the Indians. The Catawbas held the country to the crest of the Blue Ridge. To the west of that line, the Cherokees, a numerous and warlike tribe, held sway to the Mississippi, though a renegade portion of that tribe, known as the Chicamaugas, occupied the country around what is now Chattanooga. [4]   Old pottery, pipes, arrow- and spear-heads are found at numerous places throughout these mountains; and only a few years ago Mr. T. A. Low, a lawyer of Banner Elk, Avery county, "picked up quite a number of arrow-heads in his garden, some of which were splendid specimens of Mocha stone, or moss agate, evidently brought from Lake Superior regions, as no stones of the kind are found in this part of the country." [5]   None of the towns of these Indians appear " to have been in the valleys of the Swannanoa and the North Carolina part of the French Broad." [6] Parties roamed over the country. Since many of the arrow-heads are defective or unfinished, it would seem that they were made where found, as it is unlikely that such unfinished stones would be carried about the country. The inference is that many and large parties roamed through these unsettled regions. [7] Numbers of Indian mounds, stone hatchets, etc., are found in several localities, but nothing has been found in these mounds except Indian relics of the common type. [8]

ASHEVILLE ON AN OLD INDIAN BATTLE–GROUND?   "There is an old tradition that Asheville stands upon the site where, years before the white man came, was fought a great battle, between two tribes of aborigines, probably the Cherokees and the Catawbas, who were inveterate enemies and always at war. There is also a tradition that these lands were for a long while neutral hunting grounds of these two tribes." [9]

INDIAN NAMES FOR FRENCH BROAD. According to Dr. Ramsey this stream was called Agiqua throughout its entire length;

but Zeigler & Grosscup tell us that it was known as the Agiqua to the Over Mountain Cherokees [erati] only as far as the lower valley; and to the Ottari or Valley Towns Indians, as Tahkeeosteh from Asheville down; while above Asheville "it took the name of Zillicoah." But they give no authority for these statements.

ORIGIN OF THE NAME "FRENCH BROAD." Mr. Sondley[10] states that "as the settlement from the east advanced towards the mountains, the Broad river was found and named; and when the river, whose sources were on the opposite or western side of the same mountains—which gave rise to the Broad river [on the east]—became known, that . . . its course traversed the lands then claimed by the French, and this new-found western stream was called the French Broad."

ORIGIN OF THE NAME "SWANNANOA." The same writer (Mr. Sondley), after considering the claims of those who think Swannanoa means "beautiful", and of those who think it is intended to imitate the wings of ravens when flying rapidly, is of opinion that the name is but a corruption of Shawno, or Shawnees, most of whom lived in Ohio territory, and he seems to think that Savannah may also be a corruption of Shawno, which tribe may have dwelt for a time on the Savannah river in remote times. He then quotes Mr. James Mooney, "that the correct name of the Swannanoa gap through the Blue Ridge, east of Asheville, is Suwali Nunnahi, or Suwali trail," that being the pass through which ran the trail from the Cherokee to the Suwali, or Ani-Suwali, living east of the mountains. He next quotes Lederer (p. 57) to the effect that the Suwali were also called Sara, Sualty or Sasa, the interchange of the l and r being common in Indian dialects.

THE FIRST WHITE MEN. It is difficult to say who were the first white men who passed across the Blue Ridge. There is no doubt, however, that there are excavations at several places in these mountains which indicate that white men carried on mining operations in years long since passed. This is suggested by excavations and immense trees now growing from them, which when cut down show rings to the number of several hundred. It is true that these excavations may have been made by the Indians themselves, but it is also possible that they may have been made by white men who were wandering through the mountains in search of gold, silver or precious stones. Roosevelt (Vol. i, 173–4) says that unnamed and unknown hunters and Indian traders had from time to time pushed their way into the wilderness and had been followed by others of whom we know little more than their names. Dr. Thomas Walker of Virginia had found and named Cumberland river, mountains and gap after the Duke of Cumberland in 1750, though he had been to the Cumberland in 1748 (p. 175). John Sailing had been taken as a captive by the Indians through Tennessee in 1730, and in that year Adair traded with the Indians in what is now Tennessee. In 1756 and 1758 Forts Loudon and Chissel were built on the headwaters of the Tennessee river, and in 1761 Wallen, a hunter, hunted near by . . . In 1766 James Smith and others explored Tennessee, and a party from South Carolina were near the present site of Nashville in 1767.

De Soto. It is considered by some as most probable that De Soto, on the great expedition in which he discovered the Mississippi river, passed through Western North Carolina in 1540.[11] In the course of their journey they are said to have arrived at the head of the Broad or Pacolet river and from there to have passed "through a country covered with fields of maize of luxuriant growth," and during the next five days to have "traversed a chain of easy mountains, covered with oak or mulberry trees, with intervening valleys, rich in pasturage and irrigated by clear and rapid streams. These mountains were twenty leagues across." They came at last to "a grand and powerful river" and "a village at the end of a long island, where pearl oysters were found." "Now, it would be impossible for an army on the Broad or Pacolet river, within one day's march of the mountains, to march westward for six days, five of which were through mountains, and reach the sources of the Tennessee or any other river, without passing through Western North Carolina."[12] But the Librarian of Congress says: "There appears to be no authority for the statement that this expedition [Hernando De Soto's] entered the present limits of North Carolina."[13] In the same letter he says that Don Luis de Velasco, "as viceroy of New Spain, sent out an expedition in 1559 under command of Luna y Arellano to establish a colony in Florida. One of the latter's lieutenant's appears to have led an expedition into northeastern Alabama in 1560." Also, that the statement of Charles C. Jones, in his "Hernando De Soto" (1880), that Luna's expedition penetrated into the Valley river in Georgia and there mined for gold is questioned by Woodbury Lowery in his "Spanish Settlements within the present limits of the United States" (New York, 1901, p. 367).[14] There are unmistakable evidences of gold-mining in Macon and Cherokee counties which, apparently, was done 300 years ago; but by whom cannot now be definitely determined. However, there is no Valley river in Georgia, and the probability is that the Valley river of Cherokee county, N. C., which is very near the Georgia line, was at that time supposed to be in the latter State.

THE ROUNDHEADS OF THE SOUTH. Towards this primeval wilderness three streams of white people began to converge as early as 1730.[15] They were Irish Presbyterians, Scotch Saxons, Scotch Celts, French Huguenots, Milesian Irish, Germans, Hollanders and even Swedes. "The western border of our country was then formed by the great barrier-chains of the Alleghanies, which ran north and south from Pennsylvania through Maryland, Virginia and the Carolinas." Georgia was then too weak and small to contribute much to the backwoods stock; the frontier was still in the low country. It was difficult to cross the mountains from east to west, but easy to follow the valleys between the ranges. By 1730 emigrants were fairly swarming across the Atlantic, most of them landing at Philadelphia, while a less number went to Charleston. Those who went to Philadelphia passed west to Fort Pitt or started southwestward, towards the mountains of North Carolina and Virginia. Their brethren pushed into the interior from Charleston. These streams met in the foothills on the east of the Blue Ridge and settled around Pittsburg and the headwaters of the Great Kanawha, the Holston and the Cumberland. Predominent among them were the Presbyterian Irish, whose preachers taught the creed of Knox and Calvin. They were in the West what the Puritans were in the Northeast, and more than the Cavaliers were in the South. They formed the kernel of the American stock who were the pioneers in the march westward. They were the Protestants of the Protestants; they detested and despised the Catholics, and regarded the Episcopalians with a more sullen, but scarcely less intense, hatred. They had as little kinship with the

Cavalier as with the Quaker; they were separated by a wide gulf from the aristocratic planter communities that flourished in the tidewater regions of Virginia and the Carolinas. They deemed it a religious duty to interpret their own Bible, and held for a divine right the election of their own clergy. For generations their whole ecclesiastic and scholastic systems had been fundamentally democratic. The creed of the backwoodsman who had a creed at all was Presbyterianism; for the Episcopacy of the tidewater lands obtained no foothold in the mountains, and the Methodists and Baptists had but just begun to appear in the West when the Revolution broke out. Thus they became the outposts of civilization; the vanguard of the army of fighting settlers, who with axe and rifle won their way from the Alleghanies to the Rio Grande and the Pacific. "They have been rightly called the Roundheads of the South, the same men who, before any others, declared for American independence, as witness the Mecklenburg Declaration."[16] "They felt that they were thus dispossessing the Canaanites, and were thus working the Lord's will in preparing the land for a people which they believed was more truly His chosen people than was that nation which Joshua led across the Jordan."[17]

A NEW ENGLANDER'S ESTIMATE. In her "Carolina Mountains," (Houghton, Mifflin Co., 1913) Miss Margaret W. Morley, of New England, but who has resided about a dozen years in these mountains (Ch. 14) says that although North Carolina was originally settled "from almost all the nations of Europe," our mountain population, in "the course of time, became homogenious"; that many had come to "found a family," and "formed the 'quality' of the mountains"; while others, "at different times drifted in from the eastern lowlands as well as down from the North." Indeed, the early records of Ashe county, show many a name which has since become famous in New York, Ohio and New England—such as Day, Choate, Dana, Cornell, Storie and Vanderpool. Continuing, Miss Morley says (p. 140) : "Most of the writers tell us rather loosely that the Southern mountains were originally peopled with refuges of one sort and another, among whom were criminals exported to the New World from England, which, they might as well add, was the case with the whole of the newly discovered continent, America being then the

open door of refuge for the world's oppressed . . . but
we can find no evidence that these malefactors, many of
them 'indentured servants', sent over for the use of the colonists, made a practice of coming to the mountains when their
term of servitude expired. . . . The truth is, the same
people who occupied Virginia and the eastern part of the
Carolinas, peopled the western mountains, English predomi-
nating, and in course of time there drifted down from Virginia large numbers of Scotch-Irish, who, after the events of
1730, fled in such numbers to the New World, and good
Scotch Highlanders, who came after 1745. In fact, so many
of these staunch Northerners came to the North Carolina
mountains that they have given the dominant note to the
character of the mountaineers, remembering which may help
the puzzled stranger to understand the peculiarities of the
people he finds here today. . . . The rapid growth of
slavery, no doubt, discouraged many, who, unable to suc-
ceed in the Slave-States, were crowded to the mountains, or
else became the "Poor White" of the South, who must not
be for a moment confounded with the "Mountain White,"
the latter having brought some of the best blood of his nation to these blue heights. He brought into the mountains
and there nourished, the stern virtues of his race, including
the strictest honesty, an old-fashioned self-respect, and an
old-fashioned speech, all of which he yet retains, as well as
a certain pride, which causes him to flare up instantly at any
suspicion of being treated with condescension. . . ." She
gives the names of Hampton, Rogers, McClure, Morgan,
Rhodes, Foster and Bradley as indicative of the English,
Scotch and Irish descent of our people—names that "are
crowned with honor out in the big world." It is also a well-
known fact that Andrew Jackson, Abraham Lincoln, Admiral
Farragut and Cyrus T. McCormick came from the same
stock of people. She adds, very justly : "Bad blood there
was among them, as well as good, and brave men as well as
weak ones. The brave as well as the bad blood sometimes
worked out its destiny in Vendetta and "moonshining," although there *never existed* in the North Carolina mountains
the extensive and bloody feuds that distinguish the annals of
Virginia and Kentucky." (P. 144).

THE MOONSHINER, she declares, (p. 201) is "a product of conditions resulting from the Civil War, before which time the moutnaineer converted his grain into whiskey, just as the New Englander converted his apples into cider. The act of distilling was not a crime, and became so only because it was an evasion of the revenue laws. . . . At the beginning of the Civil War for the sake of revenue a very heavy tax was placed on all distilled alcoholic liquors. After the war was over the tax was not removed, and this is the grievance of the mountaineer, who says that the tax should have been removed; that it is unjust and oppressive, and that he has a right to do as he pleases with his own corn, and to evade the law which interferes with his personal freedom." But, she adds : "Within the past few years the moonshiner, along with many time-honored customs, has been rapidly vanishing.

AN APPRECIATION. Such just, truthful, generous and sympathetic words as the above, especially when found eminating from a New Englander, will be highly appreciated by every resident of the Carolina mountains, as we are accustomed to little else than misrepresentations and abuse by many of the writers from Miss Morley's former home. Her descriptions of our flowers, our gems, our manners and customs, our scenery, our climate and the character of our people will win for her a warm place in the affections of all our people. "The Carolina Mountains" is by far the best book that has ever been written about our section and our people. The few lapses into which she has been betrayed by incorrect information will be gladly overlooked in view of the fact that she has been so just, so kind and so truthful in the estimate she has placed upon our virtues and our section.

POOR COMFORT. Very little comfort is to be derived from the fact that some writers claim ("The Child That Toileth Not," p. 13) that a spirit of fun or a "great sense of humor" among the mountain people induces them to mislead strangers who profess to believe that in some sections of the mountains our people have never even heard of Santa Claus or Jesus Christ; by pretending that they do not themselves know anything of either. Indeed, a story comes from Aquone to the effect that a stranger from New England who was there to fish in the Nantahala river once told his guide, a noted wag, that he had heard that some of the mountain people had not heard of God or Jesus Christ. Pretending to think that the visitor was referring to a man, the guide asked if his questioner did not mean Mike Crise, a timber-jack who had worked on that river a dozen years before, and when the stranger replied that he meant Jesus of Bethlehem, the wag, with a perfectly straight face, answered : "That's the very p'int Mike came from"—meaning Bethlehem, Pa. Therefore, when we read in "The Carolina Mountains (p. 117) that "The mountaineer, it may be said in passing, sells his molasses by the bushel," and (p. 220) that "Under the Smoky mountain we heard of a sect of 'Barkers,' who, the people said, in their religious frenzy, run and bark up a tree in the belief that Christ is there," we are driven to the conclusion that Miss Morley, the author, was a victim of this same irresistible "sense of humor."

NOTES.

[1]Letter of R. D. W. Connor, Secretary N. C. Hist. Com., January 31, 1912.
[2]Zeigler & Grosscup, p. 9.
[3]This mountain is said to be among the oldest geological formations on earth, the Laurentian only being senior to it.
[4]Roosevelt, Vol. III, 111–112.
[5]T. A. Low, Esq.
[6]Asheville Centenary.
[7]Ibid.
[8]Ibid.
[9]Ibid.
[10]Ibid.
[11]Zeigler & Grosscup, p. 222.
[12]Asheville Centenary.
[13]His letter to J. P. A., 1912.
[14]Ibid.
[15]Roosevelt, Vol. I. p. 137. This entire chapter (ch. 5, Vol. I), from which the following excerpts have been taken at random, contains the finest tribute in the language to the pioneers of the South.
[16]Ibid., 214.
[17]Ibid.

CHAPTER II

BOUNDARIES

A DIGRESSION. The purpose of this history is to relate facts concerning that part of North Carolina which lies between the Blue Ridge and the Tennessee line; but as there has never been any connected account of the boundary lines between North Carolina and its adjoining sisters, a digression from the main purpose in order to tell that story should be pardoned.

UNFOUNDED TRADITIONS. It is said that the reason the Ducktown copper mines of Tennessee were lost to North Carolina was due to the fact that the commissioners of North Carolina and Tennessee ran out of spirituous liquors when they reached the high peak just north of the Hiwassee river, and instead of continuing the line in a general southwestwardly course, crossing the tops of the Big and Little Frog mountains, they struck due south to the Georgia line and a still-house. The same story is told as to the location of Asheville, the old Steam Saw Mill place on the Buncombe Turnpike about three miles south of Asheville, at Dr. Hardy's former residence, being its chief rival; but when it is recalled that two Indian trails crossed at Asheville, and the legislature had selected a man from Burke as an umpire of the dispute, it will be found that grave doubts may arise as to the truth of the whiskey tradition. [1] It was the jagged boundary between North and South Carolina and the stories attributing the same to the influence of whiskey that called forth the following just and sober reflections:

ABSTEMIOUS OR CAPABLE IN STRONG DRINK? Hon. W. L. Saunders, who edited the Colonial Records, remarks in Vol. v, p. xxxviii, that "there is usually a substantial, sensible, sober reason for any marked variation from the general direction of an important boundary line, plain enough when the facts are known; but the habit of the country is to attribute such variations to a supposed superior capacity of the commissioners and surveyors on *the other side* for resisting the power of strong drink. Upon this theory, judging from prac-

(18)

tical results, North Carolina in her boundary surveys, and they have been many, seems to have been unusually fortunate in having men who were either abstemious or very capable in the matter of strong drink; for, so far as now appears, in *no instance* have we been overreached." [2]

A SANCTUARY FOR CRIMINALS. Prior to the settlement of these boundary disputes grants had been issued by each colony to lands in the territory in controversy; which, according to Governor Dobbs, "was the creation of a kind of sanctuary allowed to criminals and vagabonds by their pretending, as it served their purpose, that they belonged to either province." [3] "But," adds Mr. W. L. Saunders, "who can help a feeling of sympathy for those reckless free-lances to whom constraint from either province was irksome? After men breathe North Carolina air for a time, a very little government will go a long way with them. Certainly the men who publicly 'damned the King and his peace' in 1762 were fast ripening for the 20th of May, 1775." [4]

THE FIRST GRANT OF CAROLINA. Charles the Second's grant of Carolina in 1584 embraced only the land between the mouth of the St. Johns river in Florida to a line just north of Albemarle Sound; but he had intended to give all land south of the settlements in Virginia. This left a strip of land between the Province of Carolina and the Virginia settlements. [5] In 1665 the King added a narrow strip of land to those already granted. This strip lay just north of Albemarle Sound, and its northern boundary would of course be the boundary line between Carolina and Virginia. It was about fifteen miles wide, and had on it "hundreds of families," which neither colony wished to lose. [6]

THE FIRST SURVEY. In 1709, both colonies appointed commissioners to settle this boundary. North Carolina appointed Moseley and John Lawson; but Lawson left his deputy, Colonel Wm. Maule, to act for him. [7] In 1710 these commissioners met Philip Ludwell and Nathaniel Harrison, commissioners from Virginia, but our commissioners insisted that the surveying instruments used by the Virginians were not to be trusted, and the meeting broke up without having accomplished anything except the charge from the Virginians that Moseley did not want the line run because he was trading in disputed lands. [8] When the commissioners from these two colonies did meet in March 1728, it was found that our commissioners had been right in 1710 as to the inaccuracy of the Virginia instruments, and the Virginians frankly admitted it. [9]

NORTH CAROLINA AND VIRGINIA BOUNDARY. [10] On the 27th of February, 1728, William Byrd, Will Dandridge, and Richard Fitzwilliam, as commissioners from Virginia, met Edward Moseley, C. Gale, Will Little and J. Lovick, as commissioners from North Carolina, at Corotuck Inlet, and began the survey on the 27th day of March, and continued it till the weather got "warm enough to give life and vigor to the rattlesnakes" in the beginning of April, when they stopped till September 20, when the survey was renewed; and after going a certain distance beyond their own inhabitants the North Carolina commissioners refused to proceed further, and protested against the Virginia commissioners proceeding further with it. [11] In this they were joined by Fitzwilliam of Virginia. This protest was in writing and was delivered October 6, when they had proceeded 170 miles to the southern branch of the Roanoke river "and near 50 miles without inhabitants," which they thought would be far enough for a long time. To this the two remaining Virginia commissioners, Byrd and Dandridge, sent a written answer, to the effect that their order was to run the line "as far towards the mountains as they could; they thought they should go as far as possible so that "His Majesty's subjects may as soon as possible extend themselves to that natural barrier, as they are certain to do in a few years;" and thought it strange that the North Carolina commissioners should stop "within two or three days after Mr. Mayo had entered with them near 2,000 acres within five miles of the place where they left off."

BYRD AND DANDRIDGE CONTINUE ALONE. The North Carolina commissioners, accompanied by Fitzwilliam of Virginia, left on October 8th; but Byrd and Dandridge continued alone, crossing Matrimony creek, "so called from being a little noisy," and saw a little mountain five miles to the northwest "which we named the Wart." [12]

On the 25th of October they came in plain sight of the mountains, and on the 26th, they reached a rivulet which "the traders say is a branch of the Cape Fear." Here they stopped. This was Peters creek in what is now Stokes county. [13]

It was on this trip that Mr. Byrd discovered extraordinary virtues in bear meat. This point [14] was on the northern boundary of that part of old Surry which is now Stokes county.

THE "BREAK" IN THE LINE ACCOUNTED FOR. A glance at the map will show a break in the line between Virginia and North Carolina where it crosses the Chowan river. This is thus accounted for: [15] Governors Eden of North Carolina and Spottswood of Virginia met at Nansemond and agreed to set the compass on the north shore of Currituck river or inlet and run due west; and if it "cutt [sic] Chowan river between the mouths of Nottoway and Wiccons creeks, it shall continue on the same course towards the mountains; but it it "cutts Chowan river to the southward of Wiccons creek, it shall continue up the middle of Chowan river to the mouth of Wiccons creek, and from thence run due west." It did this; and the survey of 1728 was not an attempt to ascertain and mark the parallel of 36° 30′, but "an attempt to run a line between certain natural objects . . . regardless of that line and agreed upon as a compromise by the governors of the two States." [16]

THE REAL MILK IN THE COCOANUT. Thus, so far as the Colonial Records show, ended the first survey of the dividing line between this State and Virginia, which one of the Virginia commissioners has immortalized by his matchless account, which, however, was not given to the world until 1901, when it was most attractively published by Doubleday, Page & Co., after careful editing by John Spencer Bassett. But Col. Byrd does not content himself in his "Writings" with the insinuation that the North Carolina commissioners and Mr. Mayo had lost interest immediately after having entered 2,000 acres of land within five miles of the end of their survey. He goes further and charges (p. 126) that, including Mr. Fitzwilliam, one of the Virginia commissioners, "they had stuck by us as long as our good liquor lasted, and were so kind to us as to drink our good Journey to the Mountains in the last Bottle we had left!" He also insinuates that Fitzwilliam left because he was also a judge of the Williamsburg, Virginia, court, and hoped to draw double pay while Byrd and Dandridge continued to run the line after his return. But in this he exultantly records the fact that Fitzwilliam utterly failed.

THE NINETY-MILE EXTENSION IN 1749. In October, 1749, the line between North Carolina and Virginia was extended from Peters creek, where it had ended in 1728—which point is now in Stokes county—ninety miles to the westward to Steep Rock creek, crossing "a large branch of the Mississippi [New River], which runs between the ledges of the mountains"—as Governor Johnston remarked—"and nobody ever drempt of before." William Churton and Daniel Weldon were the commissioners on the part of North Carolina, and Joshua Fry and Peter Jefferson on the part of Virginia. "It so happens, however, that no record of this survey has been preserved, and we are today without evidence, save from tradition, to ascertain the location of our boundary for ninety miles."[17]

This extension carried the line to within about two miles east of the Holston river; and we know from the statute of 1779 providing for its further extension from that point upon the latitude of 36° 30′ that it had been run considerably south of that latitude from Peters creek to Pond mountain, from which point it had, apparently without rhyme or reason, been run in a northeastwardly direction to the top of White Top mountain,[18] about three miles north of its former course, and from there carried to Steep Rock creek, near the Holston river, in a due west course. The proverbial still-house, said to have been on White Top, is also said to have caused this aberration; but the probability is that the commissioners had a more substantial reason than that.

THE LAST EXTENSION OF THIS LINE. In 1779 North Carolina passed an act[19] reciting that as "the inhabitants of this State and of the Commonwealth of Virginia have settled themselves further westwardly than the boundary between the two States hath hitherto been extended, it becomes expedient in order to prevent disputes among such settlers that the same should be now further extended and marked." To that end Orandates—improperly spelled in the Revised Statutes of 1837, Vol. ii, p. 82, "Oroondates"—Davie, John Williams Caswell, James Kerr, William Bailey Smith and Richard Henderson should be the commissioners on the part of North Carolina to meet similar commissioners from Virginia to still further extend it. But it was expressly provided that they should begin where the commissioners of 1749 had left off, and first ascertain if it be in latitude 36° 30′, "and if it be found to be truly in" that latitude, then they were "to run from thence due west

to the Tennessee or the Ohio river; or if it be found not truly
in that latitude, then to run from said place, due north or due
south, into the said latitude, and thence due west to the said
Tennessee or Ohio river, correcting the said course at due
intervals by astronomical observations."[20] Colonial Records.
Vol. iv, p. 13.)

THE LINE RUN IN 1780. Richard Henderson was appointed on the part of North Carolina, and Dr. Thomas Walker
on that of Virginia, to run this line, and they began their task
in the spring of 1780; and on the last day of March of that
year Col. Richard Henderson met the Donelson party on its
way from the Watauga settlements to settle at the French
Lick, in the bend of the Cumberland. (Roosevelt, Vol. iii,
p. 242.) But nine years before, in 1771, Anthony Bledsoe,
one of the new-comers to the Watauga settlement, being a
practical surveyor, and not being certain that that settlement
was wholly within the borders of Virginia, extended the line
of 1749 from its end near the Holston river far enough to the
west to satisfy himself that the new settlement on the Watauga
was in North Carolina.[21]

DISPUTED CAROLINA BOUNDARY LINES. From the Prefa-
tory Notes to Volume V, Colonial Records, p. 35, etc., it
appears that the dispute between the two Carolinas as to
boundary lines began in 1720 "when the purpose to erect a
third Province in Carolina,[22] with Savannah for its northern
boundary," began to assume definite shape, but nothing was
done till January 8, 1829–'30, when a line was agreed on "to
begin 30 miles southwest of the Cape Fear river, and to be
run at that parallel distance the whole course of said river;"
and in the following June Governor Johnson of South Carolina recommended that it run from a point 30 miles southwest of the source of the Cape Fear, shall be continued "due
west as far as the South Sea," unless the "Waccamaw river
lyes [sic] within 30 miles of the Cape Fear river," in which
case that river should be the boundary. This was accepted
by North Carolina until it was discovered that the "Cape
Fear rose very close to the Virginia border,"[23] and would
not have "permitted any extension on the part of North Carolina to the westward." Meanwhile, both provinces claimed
land on the north side of the Waccamaw river."[24] In 1732
Gov. Burrington [of North Carolina] published a proclama-

tion in Timothy's *Southern Gazette*, declaring the lands lying
on the north side of the Waccamaw river to be within the
Province of North Carolina, to which Gov. Johnson [of South
Carolina] replied by a similar proclamation claiming the same
land to belong to South Carolina; and also claiming that when
they [the two governors] had met before the Board of Trade
in London to settle this matter in 1829–'30, Barrington had
"insisted that the Waccamaw should be the boundary from
its mouth to its head," while South Carolina had contended
that "the line should run 30 miles distant from the mouth of
the Cape Fear river on the southwest side thereof, as set forth
in the instructions, and that the Board had agreed thereto,
unless the mouth of the Waccamaw river was within 30 miles
of the Cape Fear river; in which case both Governor Barrington and himself had agreed that the Waccamaw river should
be the boundary." The omission of the word "mouth" in
the last part of the instructions Governor Johnson thought
"only a mistake in wording it."[25]

THE LINE PARTIALLY RUN IN 1735. In consequence of
this dispute commissioners were appointed by both colonies,
who were to meet on the 23d of April, 1735, and run a due
west line from the Cape Fear along the sea coast for thirty
miles, and from thence proceed northwest to the 35th degree
north latitude, and if the line touched the Pee Dee river before reaching the 35th degree, then they were to make an
offset at five miles distant from the Pee Dee and proceed up
that river till they reached that latitude; and from thence
they were to proceed due west until they came to Catawba
town; but if the town should be to the northward of the line,
"they were to make an offset around the town so as to leave
it in the South government." They began to run the line
in "May, 1735, and proceeded thirty miles west from Cape
Fear . . . and then went northwest to the country road and
set up stakes there for the mearing[26] or boundary of the
two provinces, when they separated, agreeing to return on the
18th of the following September." In September the line was
run northwest about 70 miles, the South Carolina commissioners not arriving till October. These followed the line run
by the North Carolina commissioners about 40 miles, and
finding it correct, refused to run it further because they had
not been paid for their services. A deputy surveyor, how-

ever, took the latitude of the Pee Dee at the 35th parallel
and set up a mark, which was from that date deemed to be
the mearing or boundary at that place.

LINE EXTENDED IN 1737 AND IN 1764. In 1737 the line
was extended in the same direction 22 miles to a stake in a
meadow supposed to be at the point of intersection with the
35th parallel of north latitude.[27] In 1764 the line was extended from the stake due west 62 miles, intersecting the
Charleston road from Salisbury, near Waxhaw creek[28] at a
distance of 61 miles.

THE "LINE OF 1772." In 1772, after making the required
offsets so as to leave the Catawba Indians in South Carolina
in pursuance of the agreement of 1735, the line was "extended in a due west course from the confluence of the north
and south forks of the Catawba river to Tryon mountain."
But North Carolina refused to agree to this line, insisting
that "the parallel of 35° of north latitude having been made
the boundary by the agreement of 1735, it could not be changed
without their consent. . . . The reasons that controlled the
commissioners in recommending this course . . . were that
the observations of their own astronomer, President Caldwell of the University, showed there was a palpable error in
running the line from the Pee Dee to the Salisbury road,
that line not being upon the 35th parallel, but some 12 miles
to the South of it, and that "the line of 1772" was just about
far enough north of the 35th parallel to rectify the error, by
allowing South Carolina to gain on the west of the Catawba
river substantially what she had lost through misapprehen-
sion on the east of it." North Carolina in 1813 "agreed that
the line of 1772" should be recognized as a part of the boundary.[29] "The zig-zag shape of the line as it runs from the
southwest corner of Union county to the Catawba river is
due to the offsets already referred to, and which were necessary to throw the reservation of Catawba Indians into the
Province of South Carolina."

NORTHERN AND SOUTHERN BOUNDARIES. The peace of
1783 with Great Britain did nothing more to secure our western limits than to confirm us in the control of the territory
already in our possession; for while the Great Lakes were recognized as our northern boundary, Great Britain failed to
formally admit that boundary till the ratification of the Jay

treaty, on the ground that we had failed to fulfill certain promises; and while she had likewise consented to recognize the 31st parallel as our southern boundary, it had been secretly agreed between America and Great Britain that, if she recovered West Florida from Spain, the boundary should run a hundred miles further north than the 31st parallel. For this land, drained by the Gulf rivers, had not been England's to grant, as it had been conquered and was then held by Spain. Nor was it actually given up to us until it was acquired by Pinckney's masterly diplomacy. (Roosevelt, Vol. iii, p. 283 *et seq.*)

FRANCE'S DUPLICITY. The reasons for these reservations were that while France had been our ally in the Revolutionary war, Spain was also the ally of France both before and after the close of that conflict; and our commissioners had been instructed by Congress to "take no steps without the knowledge and advice of France." It was now the interest of France to act in the interest of Spain more than in that of America for two reasons, the first of which was that she wished to keep Gibralter, and the second, that she wished to keep us dependent on her as long as she could. Spain, however, was quite as hostile to us as England had been, and predicted the future expansion of the United States at the expense of Florida, Louisiana and Mexico. Therefore, she tried to hem in our growth by giving us the Alleghanies as our western boundary. The French court, therefore, proposed that we should content ourselves with so much of the trans-Alleghany territory as lay around the head waters of the Tennessee and between the Cumberland and Ohio, all of which was already settled; "and the proposal showed how important the French court deemed the fact of actual settlement." But John Jay, supported by Adams, disregarded the instructions of Congress and negotiated a separate treaty as to boundaries, and gave us the Mississippi as our western boundary, but leaving to England the free navigation of the Mississippi. [2]   (Roosevelt, Vol. iii, p. 284.)

INCHOATE RIGHTS ONLY UNDER COLONIAL CHARTERS. "In settling the claims to the western territory, much stress was laid on the old colonial charters; but underneath all the verbiage it was practically admitted that these charters conferred merely inchoate rights, which became complete only after conquest and settlement. The States themselves had already by their actions shown that they admitted this to be the case. Thus, North Carolina, when by the creation of Washington county—now the State of Tennessee,—she rounded out her boundaries, specified them as running to the Mississippi. As a matter of fact the royal grant, under which alone she could claim the land in question, extended to the Pacific; and the only difference between her rights to the regions east and west of the river was that her people were settling in one, and could not settle in the other." (Roosevelt, Vol. iii, p. 285.)

WESTERN LANDS AN OBSTACLE. One of the chief objections to the adoption of the Articles of Confederation, which Congress formulated and submitted to the States November 15, 1777, by some of the States was that each State had considered that upon the Declaration of Independence it was possessed of all the British lands which at any time had been included within its boundary; and Virginia, having in 1778, captured a few British forts northwest of the Ohio, created out of that territory the "County of Illinois," and treated it as her property. Other States, having small claims to western territory, insisted that, as the western territory had been secured by a war in which all the States had joined, all those lands should be reserved to reward the soldiers of the Continental army and to secure the debt of the United States. Maryland, whose boundaries could not be construed to include much of the western land, refused to ratify the articles unless the claim of Virginia should be disallowed. It was proposed by Virginia and Connecticut to close the union or confederacy without Maryland, and Virginia even opened a land office for the sale of her western lands; but without effect on Maryland. At this juncture, New York, which had less to gain from western territory than the other claimants, ceded her claims to the United States; and Virginia on January 2, 1781, agreed to do likewise. Thereupon Maryland ratified the articles, and on March 1, 1781, the Articles of Confederation were duly put into force. From that date Congress was acting under a written charter or constitution. (Hart, Sec. 45.)

CESSION OF WESTERN TERRITORY. When, at the close of the Revolution, it became necessary that Congress take steps to carry out the pledge it had given (October 10, 1780) to see that such western lands should be disposed of for the common benefit, and formed into distinct republican States under the Union, it urged the States to cede their western territory to it to be devoted to the payment of the soldiers and the payment of the national debt. The northern tier of States soon afterwards ceded their territory, with certain reservations; but the process of cession went on more slowly and less satisfactorily in the southern States. Virginia retained both jurisdiction and land in Kentucky, while North Carolina, in 1790, granted "jurisdiction over what is now Tennessee," but every acre of land had already been granted by the State. (Hart, Sec. 52). This, however, is not strictly true, much Tennessee land not having been granted then.

THE CAROLINAS AGREE TO EXTEND "THE LINE OF 1772." In 1803 the Legislature of North Carolina passed an act (Rev. Stat. 1837, Vol. II, p. 82) for the appointment of three commissioners to meet other commissioners from South Carolina, to fix and establish permanently the boundary line between these two States "as far as the eastern boundary of the territory ceded by the State of North Carolina to the United States. This act was amended in 1804, giving "the governor for the time being and his successor full power and authoriy to enter into any compact or agreement that he may deem most advisable" with the South Carolina and Georgia authorities for the settlement of the "boundary lines between these States and North Carolina." But this act seems only to have caused confusion and necessitated the passage of another act in 1806 declaring that the act of 1804 should "not be construed to extend or have any relation to the State of Georgia." (Rev. Stat. 1837, p. 84.)

COMMISSIONERS MEET IN COLUMBIA IN 1808.[30] Commissioners of the States of North and South Carolina, however, met in Columbia, S. C., on the 11th of July, 1808, and among other things agreed to extend the line between the two States from the end of the line which had been run in 1772 "a direct course to that point in the ridge of mountains which divides the eastern from the western waters where the 35° of North latitude shall be found to strike it nearest the termination of said line of 1772, thence along the top of said ridge to the western extremity of the State of South Carolina. It being understood that the said State of South Carolina does not mean by this arrangement to interfere with claims which the

United States, or those holding under the act of cession to the United States, may have to lands which may lie, if any there be, between the top of the said ridge and the said 35° of north latitude."

AGREEMENT OF SEPTEMBER, 1813.[31] But, although the commissioners from the two States met at the designated point on the 20th of July, 1813, they found that they could not agree as to the "practicability of fixing a boundary line according to the agreement of 1808," and entered into another agreement "at McKinney's, on Toxaway river, on the fourth day of September, 1813," by which they recommended that their respective States agree that the commissioners should start at the termination of the line of 1772 "and run a line due west to the ridge dividing the waters of the north fork of the Pacolet river from the waters of the north fork of Saluda river; thence along the said ridge to the ridge that divides the Saluda waters from those of Green river; thence along the said ridge to where the same joins the main ridge which divides the eastern from the western waters, and thence along the said ridge to that part of it which is intersected by the Cherokee boundary line run in the year 1797; from the center of the said ridge at the point of intersection the line shall extend in a direct course to the eastern bank of Chatooga river, where the 35° of north latitude has been found to strike it, and where a rock has been marked by the aforesaid commissioners with the following inscription, viz.: lat. 35°, 1813. It being understood and agreed that the said lines shall be so run as to leave all the waters of Saluda river within the State of South Carolina; but shall in no part run north of a course due west from the termination of the line of 1772." The commissioners who made the foregoing agreement were, on the part of North Carolina, John Steele, Montfort Stokes, and Robert Burton, and on the part of South Carolina Joseph Blythe, Henry Middleton, and John Blasingame. Rev. Stat. 1837, Vol. ii, p. 86).

COMMISSIONERS APPOINTED IN 1814. Pursuant to the above provisional articles of agreement North Carolina in 1814 appointed General Thomas Love, General Montfort Stokes and Col. John Patton commissioners to meet other commissioners from South Carolina to run and mark the boundary line between the two States in accordance with the recommenda-

tion of the commissioners who had met and agreed, "at Mc-
Kinney's, on Toxaway river, on the 4th of September, 1813."
(Rev. Stat. 1837, Vol. ii, p. 87).

AROUND HEAD SPRINGS OF SALUDA RIVER.[32] But these
commissioners met and found, "by observations and actual
experiments that a course due west from the termination of
the line of 1772 would not strike the point of the ridge dividing the waters of the north fork of Pacolet river from the
waters of the north fork of Saluda river in the manner contemplated, . . . and finding also that running a line on top of
the said ridge so as to leave all the waters of Saluda river
within the State of South Carolina would (in one place) run
a little north of a course due west from the termination of the
said line of 1772," agreed to run and mark a line "on the ridge
around the head springs of the north fork of Saluda river,"
and recommended that such line be accepted by the two
States.

TERMINATION OF 1772 LINE STARTING POINT OF 1815 LINE.
Therefore the Legislature of North Carolina passed an act
(Rev. Stat. 1837, Vol. ii, p. 89) fixing this line as "beginning
on a stone set up at the termination of the line of 1772" and
marked "N. C. and S. C. September fifteenth, eighteen hundred and fifteen," running thence west four miles and ninety
poles to a stone marked N. C. and S. C., thence south 25°
west 118 poles to the top of the ridge dividing the waters of the
north fork of the Pacolet river from the north fork of the
Saluda river . . . thence to the ridge that divides the Saluda
waters from those of Green river and thence along that ridge
to its junction with the Blue Ridge, and thence along the
Blue Ridge to the line surveyed in 1797, where a stone is set
up marked N. C. and S. C. 1813; and from this stone "a direct
line south 68¼° west 20 miles and 11 poles to the 35° of north
latitude at the rock in the east bank of the Chatooga river,
marked latitude 35 AD: 1813, in all a distance of 74 miles
and 189 poles."

CONFIRMATION OF BOUNDARY LINES. In 1807 the North
Carolina Legislature passed an act (Rev. Stat. 1837, Vol. ii, p. 90)
which "fully ratified and confirmed" these two agreements,
and another act (Rev. Stat. Vol. ii, p. 92) reciting that these
two sets of commissioners "in conformity with these articles
of agreement" had "run and marked in part the boundary

line between the said States." This act further recites that
the North Carolina commissioners "have reported the running and marking of said boundary line as follows:

"To commence at Ellicott's rock,[33] and run due west on the 35° of
north latitude, and marked as follows: The trees on each side of the line
with three chops, the fore and aft trees with a blaze on the east and west
side, the mile trees with the number of miles from Ellicott's rock, on the
east side of the tree, and a cross on the east and west side; whereupon the
line was commenced under the superintendance of the undersigned commissioners jointly: Timothy Tyrrell, Esquire, surveyor on the part of
the commissioners of the State of Georgia, and Robert Love, surveyor
on the part of the commissioners of the State of North Carolina—upon
which latitude the undersigned caused the line to be extended just thirty
miles due west, marking and measuring as above described, in a conspicuous manner throughout; in addition thereto they caused at the end of
the first eleven miles after first crossing the Blue Ridge, a rock to be set
up, descriptive of the line, engraved thereon upon the north side, September 25, 1819, N. C., and upon the south side 35 degree N. L. G.; then
after crossing the river Cowee or Tennessee, at the end of sixteen miles,
near the road, running up and down the said river, a locust post marked
thus, on the South side Ga. October 14, 1819; and on the north side, 35
degree N. L. N. C., and then at the end of twenty-one miles and three
quarters, the second crossing of the Blue Ridge, a rock engraved on the
North side 35 degree N. L. N. C., and on the south side Ga. 12th Oct.,
1819; then on the rock at the end of the thirty miles, engraved thereon,
upon the north side N. C. N. L. 35 degrees, which stands on the north side
of a mountain, the waters of which fall into Shooting Creek, a branch of the
Hiwassee, due north of the eastern point of the boundary line, between
the States of Georgia and Tennessee, commonly called Montgomery's
line, just six hundred and sixty-one yards."

The Legislature then enacted "That the said boundary
line, as described in the said report, be, and the same is hereby
fully established, ratified and confirmed forever, as the boundary line between the States of North Carolina and Georgia."

The last section of the act confirming the survey of the line
from the Big Pigeon to the Georgia line, as run and marked
by the commissioners of North Carolina and Tennessee in
1821, (Rev. Stat. 1837, Vol. ii, p. 97) provides "that a line run
and known by the name of Montgomery's line, beginning
six hundred and sixty-one yards due south of the termination
of the line run by the commissioners on the part of this State
and the State of Georgia, in the year one thousand eight hundred and nineteen, ending on a creek near the waters of Shooting Creek, waters of Hiwassee, then along Montgomery's

line till it strikes the line run by commissioners on the part
of North Carolina and Tennessee in 1821, to a square post
marked on the east side N. C. 1821, and on the west side
Tenn. 1821, and on the south side G. should to be the dividing line between North Carolina and Georgia, so soon as the
above line shall be ratified on the part of the State of
Georgia."

ORIGIN OF THE WALTON WAR.

"North Carolina claimed for her southern boundary the 35th degree
of north latitude. The line of this parallel, however, was at that time
supposed to run about twelve miles north of what was subsequently
ascertained to be its true location. Between this supposed line of 35°
north latitude and the northernmost boundary of Georgia, as settled
upon by a convention between that State and South Carolina in 1787,
there intervened a tract of country of about twelve miles in width, from
north to south, and extending from east to west, from the top of the
main ridge of mountains which divides the eastern from the western
waters to the Mississippi river. This tract remained, as was supposed,
within the chartered limits of South Carolina, and in the year 1787 was
ceded by that State to the United States, subject to the Indian right of
occupancy. When the Indian title to the country therein described
was ceded to the United States by the treaty of 1798 with the Cherokees,
the eastern portion of this 12-mile tract fell within the limits of such
cession. On its eastern extremity near the head-waters of the French
Broad river, immediately at the foot of the main Blue Ridge Mountains,
had been located, for a number of years prior to the treaty, a settlement
of about fifty families of whites, who, by its ratification became occupants
of the public domain of the United States, but who were outside of the
territorial jurisdiction of any State. These settlers petitioned Congress
to retrocede the tract of country upon which they resided to South Carolina, in order that they might be brought within the protection of the
laws of that State. A resolution was reported in the House of Representatives from the committee to whom the subject had been referred,
favoring such a course, but Congress took no effective action on the subject, and when the State boundaries came finally to be adjusted in that
region the tract in question was found to be within the limits of North
Carolina."[34]

THE WALTON WAR. That there should have been great
confusion and uncertainty as to the exact boundary lines
between the States in their earlier history is but natural,
especially in the case where the corners of three States come
together, and still more especially when they come together
in an inaccessible mountainous region, such as characterized
the cornerstone between Georgia, South and North Caro-

lina. And that renegades and other lawless adventurers should take advantage of such a condition is still more natural. It is, therefore, not surprising to read in "The Heart of the Alleghanies," (p. 224-5) that: "In early times, criminals and refugees from justice made the fastnesses of the wilderness hiding places. Their stay, in most cases, was short, seclusion furnishing their profession a barren field for operation. A few, however, remained, either adopting the wild, free life of the chase, or preying upon the property of the community."

WALTON COUNTY. Such a community existed at the commencement of the last century on the head waters of the French Broad river in what are now Jackson and Transylvania counties. Some even claimed that this territory belonged to South Carolina. But Georgia, about December, 1803, created a county within this territory and called it Walton county. Georgia naturally attempted to exercise jurisdiction over what it really believed was its own territory, and North Carolina as naturally resisted such attempts. Consequently, there were "great dissentions, . . . the said dissentions having produced many riots, affrays, assaults, batteries, woundings and imprisonments."

THE NORTH CAROLINA AND GEORGIA LINE. On January 13, 1806, Georgia presented a memorial to the House of Representatives of Congress, complaining that North Carolina was claiming lands lying within the State of Georgia, and asking that Congress interpose and cause the 35th degree of north latitude to be ascertained and the line between the two States plainly marked.

THE TWELVE MILES "ORPHAN" STRIP. This was referred to a committee which, on February 12th, reported that "between the latitude of 35° north, which is the southern boundary claimed by North Carolina, and the northern boundary of Georgia, as settled by a convention between that State and South Carolina, intervenes a tract of country supposed to be about twelve miles wide, from north to south, and extending in length from the western boundary of Georgia, at Nicajack, on the Tennessee, to his northeastern limits at Tugalo, and was consequently within the limits of South Carolina, and in the year 1887 it was ceded to the United States, who [sic] accepted the cession." This territory remained in the possession of the United States until 1802, when it was ceded to the

State of Georgia, when the estimated number of settlers on it
was 800. It was not known where these settlers came from;
but the land had belonged to the Cherokees until 1798 when
a part of it was purchased by the whites by treaty held at
Tellico.[35]

WALTON COUNTY, GEORGIA. At the earnest entreaty of
these inhabitants Georgia in 1803 formed the inhabited part
of this territory into Walton county and appointed commissioners to meet corresponding commissioners to be appointed
by North Carolina to ascertain and mark the line. But
Congress took no definite action on this report.

A SURVEY AGREED UPON. The two States, in 1807, came
to an agreement as to the basis of a survey. In a letter dated
at Louisville, Ga., December 10, 1806, Gov. Jared Irwin to
Gov. Nathaniel Alexander of North Carolina, enclosed sundry resolutions adopted by the legislature of Georgia, and
announced that that body had appointed Thomas P. Carnes,
Thomas Flournoy and William Barnett as commissioners to
ascertain the 35th° of north latitude "and plainly mark the
dividing line between the States of North Carolina and Georgia." On January 1, 1807, Gov. Alexander enclosed to Gov.
Irwin a copy of an act of the legislature passed at the preceding session assenting to the proposition of Georgia and appointing John Steele, John Moore and James Welbourne
commissioners on the part of North Carolina. It was subsequently agreed that the commissioners from both States
should meet at Asheville June 15, 1807; Rev. Joseph Caldwell,
president of the North Carolina University, was the scientist
for North Carolina, while Mr. J. Meigs represented Georgia
in that capacity.

THE RECORD. In the minute docket of the county court
of Buncombe, pp. 104 and 363, the proceedings of these commissioners are set forth in full, showing that Thomas Flournoy, one of the Georgia commissioners, did not attend but
that on the 18th of June, 1807, the others met at Buncombe court house and agreed on a basis of procedure, the
most important point being that the 35th parallel was to be
first ascertained, after which it was to be marked and agreed
on as the line. This they proceeded to do, with the result that
on the 27th of June, at Douthard's gap on the summit of the

Blue Ridge, they signed a supplemental agreement to the effect that they had discovered by repeated astronomical observations that the 35th degree of north latitude is not to be found on any part of said ridge east of the line established by the general government as the temporary boundary between the white people and the Indians, and having no authority to proceed over that boundary "in order to ascertain and mark that degree," they agreed that Georgia had no right to claim any part of the territory north or west of the Blue Ridge and east or south of the present temporary line between the whites and Indians; and would recommend to the Georgia Legislature that it repeal the act which had established the county of Walton on North Carolina soil. Both sets of commissioners then agreed to recommend amnesty for all who had been guilty of violating the laws of either State under the assumption that it had no jurisdiction over that territory.

Following is the story as to how they had reached this agreement:

THE "ASTONISHMENT" OF THE GEORGIANS. [36] These scientists made their first observations at the house of Mr. Amos Justice, which they supposed to be on or near the dividing line of 35° north latitude, but discovered that it was "22 miles within old Buncombe," which astonished them; for Mr. Sturges, the Surveyor General of Georgia, had previously ascertained this meridian to be at the junction of Davidson's and Little rivers. But, said the Georgia commissioners in their report to their governor, they were "accompanied by an artist [sic] appointed by the government [of the United States] whose talents and integrity we have no reason to doubt," whose observations accorded very nearly with their own; they "were under the necessity of suspending our astonishment and proceeding on the duty assigned us."

SUPPLEMENTARY AGREEMENT AT CÆSAR'S HEAD. When they got to the junction of Davidson and Little rivers and found that they were still 17 minutes north of the 35th meridian, they "proceeded to Cæsar's Head, a place on the Blue Ridge about 12 horizontal miles directly south and in the vicinity of Douthet's Gap, which was from 2' 57" to 4' 54" north of the 35th parallel. They then signed the supplementary agreement of June 27.

GEORGIA'S SPORTING BLOOD. On December 28, 1808, Gov. Irwin of Georgia wrote to Governor Stone of North Carolina, asking for the appointment of a new commission on the part of North Carolina to meet one already appointed by the legislature of Georgia; but Gov. Stone declined in a communication of March 21, 1809, in which he states that it "does not readily occur to us on what basis the adjustment is to rest, if not upon that where it now stands—the plighted faith of two States to abide by the determination of commissioners mutually chosen for the purpose of making the adjustment those commissioners actually made". On December 7, 1807, North Carolina had adopted and ratified the joint report of the commissioners of the two States and on December 18 "passed an act of amnesty for offenders within the disputed territory." [37]

GEORGIA IS SNUBBED. [37] But Georgia sent still another petition to Congress by way of appeal, and its legislature on December 5, 1807, "put forth an earnest protest against the decision arrived at by their own commissioners." But although on April 26, 1810, Mr. Bibb of Georgia, asked the United States to appoint some person to run the dividing line, and it was referred to a select committee on the 27th of the following December, that committee never reported. Georgia must have become reconciled, however, for in 1819 its legislature refused relief to certain citizens who had claimed land in this disputed territory.

CONTOUR MAP AND 35TH PARALLEL. The late Captain W. A. Curtis, for a long time editor of the Franklin Press, said, in "A Brief History of Macon County," (1905) p. 23, [38] that "it has long been accepted as a fact that the southern boundary of Macon and Clay counties, constituting the State line between North Carolina and Georgia, is located on the 35th parallel of north latitude. This is either a mistake or else the latest topographical charts are incorrect. According to the charts a straight line starts from the top of Indian Camp mountain on the southern boundary of Translyvania county, 6¾ miles north of the 35th parallel, and dips somewhat south of west until it reaches the Endicott (Ellicut) Rock at the corner of South Carolina exactly on the 35th parallel, and, instead of turning due west at this place, it continues on a straight line for about twenty miles, or to 83½ degrees west longitude, which is near the top of the Ridge Pole, close by the southwest corner of Macon county; then it turns due west, running parallel with the 35th, and about one mile south of it, on towards Alabama. One peculiarity of this survey is that Estatoa, or Mud Creek Falls, which has long been considered as being in Georgia, are, according to the map, in North Carolina. Mud creek crosses the State line a few yards above the falls into North Carolina, and at about half way between the falls and the Tennessee river passes back into Georgia. But, by examining some old records belonging to the State Library at Raleigh in 1881, I am convinced that the line between the States of Georgia and North Carolina has never been correctly surveyed."

THE NORTH CAROLINA AND TENNESSEE BOUNDARY. By the Cessions Act, Revised Statutes, 1837, Vol. ii, p. 171, North Carolina authorized one or both United States Senators or any two members of Congress to execute a deed or deeds to the United States of America of the lands west of a line beginning on the extreme height of the Stone mountain, at the place where the Virginia line intersects it, running thence along the extreme height of the said mountain to the place where Watauga river breaks through it, thence a direct course to the top of the Yellow Mountain, where Bright's road crosses the same, thence along the ridge of said mountains between the waters of Doe river and the waters of Rock creek to the place where the road crosses the Iron mountain, from thence along the extreme height of said mountain, to where Nolechucky river runs through the same, thence to the top of the Bald mountain, thence along the extreme height of the said mountain to the Painted Rock, on French Broad river, thence along the highest ridge of the said mountain to the place where it is called the Great Iron or Smoky mountain, thence along the extreme height of said mountain to the place where it is called Unicoy or Unaka mountain, between the Indian towns of Cowee and Old Chota, thence along the main ridge of the said mountain to the southern boundary of this State."

The 10th section provided that "this act shall not prevent the people now residing south of French Broad, between the rivers Tennessee and Pigeon, from entering their pre-emptions on that tract, should an office be opened for that purpose under an act of the present general assembly."

To Pay Debts and Establish Harmony. The reasons
for making this cession are set out in the act itself and are to
the effect that Congress has "repeatedly and earnestly recommended to the respective States . . . claiming or owning
vacant western territory," to make cession to part of the
same, as a further means "of paying the debts and establishing the harmony of the United States;" "and the inhabitants
of the said western territory being also desirious that such
cession should be made, in order to obtain a more ample protection than they have heretofore received." The act also
provides that neither the land nor the inhabitants of the ceded
territory shall be estimated in ascertaining North Carolina's
proportion of the common expense occasioned by the war for
independence. Also that in case the lands laid off by North
Carolina for the "officers and soldiers of the Continental line"
shall not "contain a sufficient quantity of lands fit for cultivation to make good the quota intended by law for each, such
officer or soldier who shall fall short of his proportion may
make up the deficiency out of lands of the ceded territory."
Having been admonished by the claim of the citizens of Watauga
that until Congress should accept the ceded territory they
would be in a state "of political orphanage," the legislature,
later in the session of 1784, had been careful to pass another
act by which North Carolina retained jurisdiction and sovereignty over the land west of the mountains, and continued
in force all existing North Carolina laws, "until the same shall
be repealed or otherwise altered by the legislative authority
of said territory." The act ordering the survey is ch. 461,
Potter's Revisal, p. 816, Laws 1796.

The First Tennessee Boundary Survey. From the
narratives of David Vance and Robert Henry of the battles
of Kings Mountain [39] and Cowan's Ford, as well as from the
dairy of John Strother, can be gathered a fine account of the
survey from Virginia to the Painted Rock on the French
Broad and the Stone on the Cataloochee Turnpike. The survey began on the 20th of May and ended Friday the 28th of
June, 1799. The original of Strother's diary is filed in the
suit of the *Virginia, Tennessee & Carolina Steel and Iron Company vs. Newman*, in the United States court at Asheville, N. C.
The actual survey began May 22d, "at a sugar-tree and beech
on Pond mountain, so called from two small ponds on it."

Both trees are now gone, and a stone four feet by two feet by sixteen inches in thickness, is buried in the ground where they stood, with a simple cross, east and west, chiseled upon it. Its upper surface is level with the ground, and it was placed there in 1899 or 1900 by a Mr. Buchanan of the United States coast survey. Marion Miller and John and Alfred Bivins assisted him. Mr. Miller still lives within a mile and a half of the corner rock. Strother's party set out from Asheville May 12, and reached Capt. Robert Walls on New River, where Strother arrived on the 17th, and met with Major Mussendine Mathews, of whom Judge David Schenck says [40] that he "represented Iredell county in the House of Commons from 1789 to 1802 continuously. He was either a Tory or a Cynic, it seems." They were awaiting the arrival of Col. David Vance and Gen. Joseph McDowell, but as they did not come, Strother went to the house of a Mr. Elsburg on the 18th.

THE PARTY GATHERS. Col. Vance and Major B. Collins arrived on the 19th, and they all went to Captain Isaac Weaver's. They were General Joseph McDowell, Col. David Vance, Major Mussendine Mathews, commissioners; John Strother and Robert Henry, surveyors; Messers. B. Collins, James Hawkins, George Penland, Robert Logan, Geo. Davidson, and J. Matthews, chain-bearers and markers; Major James Neely, commissary; two pack-horse men and a pilot. They camped that night on Stag creek. On the night of the 23d of May they camped "at a very bad place" in a low gap at the head of Laurel Fork of New river and Laurel Fork of Holston at the head of a branch, "after having passed through extreme rough ground and some bad laurel thickets." A road now runs through that laurel thicket, built since the Civil War, and runs from Hemlock postoffice, where there is now a narrow gauge lumber railroad and an extract plant, to Laurel Bloomery, in Tennessee. A small hotel now stands half on the North Carolina and half on the Tennessee side of the line those men then ran, and the gap is called "Cut Laurel" gap because it is literally cut through the laurel for a mile or more. [41] Thousands of gallons of blockade whiskey used to be carried through that gap when there was nothing but a trail there. It is called by Mr. Strother a low gap, but it is one of the highest in the mountains. On the 28th they went to a Mr. Miller's and got a young man to act as a pilot. Strother went from Miller's "to Cove creek, where I got a Mr. Curtis and met the company in a low gap between the waters of Cove creek and Roan's creek where the road crosses the same," on Wednesday night, the 29th.

CROSSED BOONE'S TRAIL. This, in all probability, is the gap through which Daniel Boone and his party had passed in 1769 on their way to Kentucky. It is between Zionville, N. C. and Trade, Tenn., and the gap is so low that one is not conscious of passing over the top of a high mountain. Tradition says that an Indian trail went through the same gap, and traces of it are still visible to the north of the present turnpike. The young man who had been employed as a pilot at Mr. Miller's house on the 28th was found on the 29th not to be a "woodsman and of course he was discharged." On June 1st they came to the "Wattogo" river, where they killed a bear, "very poor," upon which and "some bacon stewed together, with some good tea and johnny cake we made a Sabbath morning breakfast fit for a European Lord." There is a tradition among the people living near the falls of the Watauga at the State line, that the line between the peak to the north of the falls and the Yellow mountain was not actually run and marked; but the field notes of both Strother and Henry show that the line was both run and marked all the way. The reason the line was run from the peak north of the Watauga to the bald of the Yellow was because the act required it to be run in precisely that way; the language being "to the place where Watauga river breaks through it [the mountain], thence a direct course to the top of the Yellow Mountain where Bright's road crosses the same." As it is impossible to see the Yellow from the river at the falls where the river breaks through, it was necessary to get the course from the top of the peak north of the river.

RATTLEBUGS. On Saturday, June 1st, they came upon "a very large rattlebug," which they "attempted to kill, but it was too souple in the heels for us." On the night of May 31st they had had "severe lightning and some hard slaps [sic] of thunder."

LAUREL AND IVY. There are some who, nowadays, contend that ivy and laurel did not grow in these mountains while the Indians occupied them, and cite as proof that it is almost impossible to find a laurel log with rings indicating more than a hundred years of growth. But Bishop Spangenburg mentions having encountered laurel on what is supposed to have been the Grandfather mountain in 1752, and John Strother, in his diary of the survey between Virginia and North Carolina in 1799, repeatedly mentions it, both before and after crossing the ridge which divides the waters of Nollechucky from those of the French Broad. What are now known as the "Ivory Slicks," is a tunnel cut through the otherwise impenetrable ivy on the slope between the Hang Over and Dave Orr's cabins on Slick Rock, south of the Little Tennessee.

TWO WAGON ROADS ACROSS THE MOUNTAINS. Even at that early date there seem to have been two roads crossing the mountains into Tennessee, for the very next call of the statute is "thence along the ridge of said mountain between the waters of Doe river and the waters of Rock creek to the place where the road crosses the Iron mountain." Bright used to live at the Crab Orchard, long known as Avery's Quarters, about a mile above Plum Tree, and where W. W. Avery now lives. [42] On the 5th of June Major Neely "turned off the line today and went to Doe river settlements for a fresh supply of provisions," and was to meet them at the Yellow mountain, where on that day the trees were "just creeping out of their winter garb," and where "the lightning and thunder were so severe that they were truly alarming." From "the yellow spot" on the Yellow, whither they had gone to take observations, but were prevented by the storm, "we went back and continued the line on to a low gap at the head of Roaring or Sugar creek of Towe [sic] river and a creek of Doe river at the road leading from Morganton to Jonesborough, where we encamped as wet as we could be." This fixes the main road between North Carolina and the Watauga settlement, which had been finished in 1772, and over which Andrew Jackson was to pass in the spring of 1788. [43] Robert Henry mentions a Gideon Lewis as one of the guides from White Top mountain, and it is remarkable that a direct descendant of his and having his name is now living at Taylor's Valley, near Konarok, Va., and that several others now live near Solitude or Ashland, N. C.

WAS THIS EVER "NO MAN'S LAND"? When the surveying party came to the Yellow they found that the compass had been deflected when it had been sighted from the peak just north of Watauga Falls, caused doubtless by the proximity to the Cranberry Iron mountain, of whose existence apparently they then had no knowledge. Of late years some have supposed that the "territory between the Iron mountain and the Blue Ridge, after the act of cession, was left out of any county from 1792 or 1793 till 1818 or 1822, and was without any local government till it was annexed to Burke county." L. D. Lowe, Esq., in the *Watauga Democrat* of July 3d, 1913, gave the following explanation: "It is quite true that there was no local government, but it was not for the reason that this part of the territory was not claimed by Burke county; but it was because the lands had been granted to a few, and there were only a limited number of people within the territory to be governed, hence there was very little attention paid to it." In previous articles in the same paper he had shown that "the reason this territory had not been settled at an earlier date" was because "the State had been paid for more than three hundred thousand acres embraced within the boundaries of six grants," but had failed to refer to the fact that "these grants or some of them had especially excepted certain other grants within their boundaries—for example, certain grants to Waightstill Avery, Reuben White, John Dobson and others. Within the past twenty-five years it has been clearly demonstrated that some of the Cathcart grants run with the Tennessee line for 14 miles."

HOME COMFORTS. "Mr. Hawkins and myself went down to Sugar creek to a Mr. Currey's, where we got a good supper and a bed to sleep in," continues the diary. Evidently the food in the camp had about given out, for we hear nothing more of meals "fit for a European Lord;" but, instead, of the comforts of good Mr. Currey's bed and board. Here too they "took breakfast with Mrs. Currey, got our clothes washed and went to camp, where Major Neely met us with a fresh supply of provisions. It rained all day [and] of course we are still at our camp at the head of Sugar creek."

PLEASANT BEECH FLATS. The next day they crossed "high spur of the Roan mountain to a low gap therein where we encamped at a pleasant Beech flat and good spring."

Any one who has never seen one of these "pleasant beech flats" would scarcely realize what they are like. As one ascends any of the higher mountains of North Carolina, the size of all the trees perceptibly diminish, especially near the six thousand feet line, to be succeeded, generally, on the less precipitous slopes, by miniature beech trees, perfect in shape, but resembling the so-called dwarf-trees of the Japanese. They really seem to be toy trees.

JOHN STROTHER'S FLOWERS OF RHETORIC. It was here that they "spent the Sabbath day in taking observations from the high spur we crossed, in gathering the fir oil of the Balsam of Pine which is found on the mountain, in collecting a root said to be an excellent preventative against the bite of a rattle-snake, and in visioning the wonderful scene this conspicuous situation affords. There is no shrubbery grows on the tops of this mountain for several miles, say, and the wind has such a power on the top of this mountain that the ground is blowed in deep holes all over the northwest sides. The prospect from the Roan mountain is more conspicuous [extensive?] than from any other part of the Appelatchan mountains."

CLOUDLAND. A modern prospectus of the large and comfortable hostelry, called the Cloudland hotel, which has crowned this magnificent mountain for more than thirty years, the result of the ardor and enterprise of Gen. John H. Wilder of Chattanooga, Tenn., could not state the charms of this most charming resort, now become the sure refuge of hundreds of sufferers from that scourge of late summer and early autumn and known as hay fever, more invitingly.

UNSURPASSED VIEW. Of the magnificence of this view a later chronicler has this to say: "That view from the Roan eclipses everything I have ever seen in the White, Green, Catskill and Virginia mountains." This is a statement put into the mouth of a Philadelphia lawyer in 1882 by the authors of "The Heart of the Alleghanies," p. 253.

MOUNTAIN MOONSHINE. On Monday they "proceeded on between the head of Rock creek and Doe river, and en-camped in a low gap between these two streams. The next day they went five or six miles to the foot of the Iron mountain to a place they called Strother's Camp, where they had some good songs, "then raped [wrapped] ourselves up in our blankets and slep sound till this morning." Here "Cols. Vance and Neely went to the Limestone settlements for a pilot, returned to us on the line at two o'clock with a Mr. Collier as pilot and two gallons whiskey, we stop, drank our own health and proceeded on the line. Ascended a steep spur of the Unaker mountain, got into a bad laurel thicket, cut our way some distance. Night came on, we turned off and camped at a very bad place, it being a steep laurelly hollow," but the whiskey had such miraculous powers that it made the place "tolerably comfortable."

BAD LUCK ON THE THIRTEENTH. On Thursday the 13th, if they were superstitious, the expected bad luck happened; for here they were informed that for the next two or three days' march the pack-horses could not proceed on the line— that is, could not follow the extreme height of the mountain crest. This was a calamity indeed; but what was the result? How did these men meet it? We read how:

BETWEEN HOLLOW POPLAR AND GREASY COVE. "Myself [John Strother] together with the chain-bearers and markers packed our provisions on our backs and proceeded on with the line, the horses and rest of the company was conducted round by the pilot a different route. We continued the line through a bad laurel thicket to the top of the Unaker mountain and along the same about three miles and camped at a bad laurelly branch." On Friday, however, they came "to the path crossing [the Unaker mountain] from Hollow Poplar to the Greasy Cove and met our company. It rained hard. We encamped on the top of the mountain half a mile from water and had an uncomfortable evening."

DEVIL'S CREEK AND LOST COVE. It seems that the information Mr. Collier had given "respecting the Unaker mountain was false," and Mr. Strother prevailed upon the commissioners to discharge him on Saturday the 15th of June. They then crossed the Nolechucky "where it breaks through the Unaker or Iron mountain." Here it is that that matchless piece of modern railroad engineering, the C. C. &. O. R. R., disputes with the "Chucky" its dominion of the canon and transports from its exhaustless coal mines in Virginia hundreds of tons of the finest coal to its terminus on the Atlantic coast.

ROBERT HENRY MEETS HIS FATE. Here, too, it being again found "impracticable to take horses from this place on the line to the Bald mountain, Mr. Henry, the chain-bearers and markers, took provisions on their backs [and] proceeded on the line and the horses went round by the Greasy Cove and met the rest of the company on Sunday on the top of the Bald mountain, where we tarried till Tuesday morning."

"TARRYING" IN THE GREASY COVE. One cannot help wondering why they "tarried" here so long; but no one who has ever visited that "Greasy Cove" and shared the hospitality of its denizens need long remain without venturing a guess; for it is a pleasant place to be, with the "red banks of Chucky" still crumbling in the bend of the river and the ravens croaking from their cliffs among the fastnesses of the Devil's Looking Glass looming near. [44] The C. C. & O. have their immense shops here now, covering almost a hundred acres of land.

VANCE'S CAMP. From the Bald mountain, now in Yancey county, it seems that Col. Love became their pilot; and five or six miles further on in "a low gap between the head of Indian creek and the waters of the south fork of Laurel, we encamped and called it Vance's Camp." The richness of the mountains is noted.

THE GRIER BALD. This Bald is sometimes called the Grier Bald from the fact that David Grier, a hermit, lived upon it for thirty-two years. [45] Grier was a native of South Carolina who, because one of the daughters of Col. David Vance refused to marry him, built himself a log house here in 1802, just three years after Colonel Vance had passed the spot, and it is probable Grier first heard of it through this gentleman. In a quarrel over his land he killed a man named Holland Higgins and was acquitted on the ground of insanity "and returned home to meet his death at the hands of one of Holland's friends."

BOONE'S COVE. On Wednesday the 19th of June, after having suffered severely the previous night from gnats, they went to "Boone's Cove, between the waters of Laurel and Indian creeks," while on the 20th they had to pass over steep and rocky and brushy knobs, with water scarce and a considerable distance from the line. All day Friday their horses suffered from want of water and food, part of the way being impassable for horses; while on Saturday it took them "four hours and 23 minutes" to cut their way one and one-fourth miles to the top of the mountain, where, after getting through the laurel, they "came into an open flat on top of Beech mountain where we camped till Monday at a good spring and excellent range for our horses."

A RECRUIT OF BACON. On Monday, the 24th of June, their provisions began to fail them again, but they proceeded on the line six miles and "crossed the road leading from Barnett's Station to the Brushy Cove and encamped in a low gap between the waters of Paint creek and Laurel river."[46] They had a wet evening here; but as they "suped on venison stewed with a recruit of bacon Major Neely brought in this day from the Brushy Cove settlement," we may hope their lot was not altogether desolate; for it is possible that this enterprising commissary, Major Neely, might have brought them something besides that "recruit of bacon"; for it will be recalled that on a former occasion he went for a pilot and returned not only with a pilot but with two gallons of a liquid that "had such marvelous powers" that it made a very "bad place" "tolerably comfortable."

BARNETT'S STATION. At any rate, they knew they were nearing the end of their long and arduous journey, for they had now reached the waters of Paint creek, which they must have known was in the neighborhood of the "Painted Rock," their destination. The Barnett Station referred to above was probably Barnard's old stock stand on the French Broad river, five or six miles below Marshall.

OFF THE TRACK FOR AWHILE. After losing their way on the 25th and "having a very uncomfortable time of it" on Paint creek, they got on the "right ridge from the place we got off of it and proceeded on the line five miles and encamped between the waters of F. B. R. [French Broad river] and Paint creek."

"HASEY" AND "ANCTOOUS." Thursday 27. This morning is cloudy and hasey. The Commissioners being anctoous to get on to the Painted Rock started us early"; but they took a wrong ridge again and had to return and spend an uncomfortable evening.

DROPPING THE PLUMMET FROM PAINT ROCK. However, on Friday, the 28th day of June, 1799, they reached the Painted Rock at last and measured its height, finding it to be "107 feet three inches high from the top to the base," that "it rather projects out," and that "the face of the rock bears but few traces of its having formerly been painted, owing to its being smoked by pine knots and other wood from a place at its base where travellers have frequently camped. In the year 1790 it was not much smoked, the pictures of some humans, wild beasts, fish and fowls were to be seen plainly made with red paint, some of them 20 and 30 feet from its base."

ANIMAL PICTURES HAVE DISAPPEARED. How much more satisfactory this last sentence would have been if he had only added: "I saw them." For, as the rock appears today, the red paint seems to be nothing more or less than the oxidation of the iron in the exposed surfaces, while all trace of "some humans, wild beasts," etc., mentioned by him have entirely disappeared.

THE REAL "PAINTED ROCK." However, he leaves us in no doubt that they had reached the real Painted Rock called for by the Act of Cession, ceding "certain lands therein described"; for he goes on to say that, while "some gentlemen of Tennessee wish to construe as the painted rock referred to" another rock in the French Broad river "about seven miles higher up on the opposite or S. W. side in a very obscure place," that "it is to be observed that there is no rock on French Broad river that ever was known as the painted rock but the one first described, which has, ever since the River F. Broad was explored by white men, been a place of Publick Notoriety."

SURPASSES A "BEST SELLER" OF TO-DAY. This is the next to the concluding sentence in this quaint and charming narrative—a narrative that one hundred and fifteen years after it was penned can still be read with more interest than many of the so-called "best sellers" of the present day.

"We then went up to the Warm Springs where we spent the evening in conviviality and friendship."

THE LONELINESS OF BACHELORHOOD. But it is in the very last sentence that one begins to suspect that John Strother was at that time a bachelor, for we read:

"Saturday, 29th. The Company set out for home to which place I wish them a safe arrival and happy reception, as for myself I stay at the Springs to get clear of the fatigue of the Tour."

One wonders whose bright eyes made his "fatigue" so much greater than that of the others and kept him so long at the springs.

TO THE "BIG PIGEON." The line from the Painted Rock to the Big Pigeon was run a few weeks later on by the same commissioners and surveyors; but we have no narrative of the trip, which, doubtless, was without incident, though the way, probably, was rough and rugged.

SECOND TENNESSEE BOUNDARY SURVEY. North Carolina having acquired by the treaty of February 27, 1819, all lands from the mouth of the Hiwassee "to the first hill which closes in on said river, about two miles above Hiwassee Old Town; thence along the ridge which divides the waters of the Hiwassee and Little Tellico to the Tennessee river at Talassee; thence along the main channel to the junction of the Cowee and Nanteyalee; thence along the ridge in the fork of said river to the top of the Blue Ridge; thence along the Blue Ridge to the Unicoy Turnpike road; thence by straight line to the nearest main source of the Chastatee; thence along its main channel to the Chattahoochee, etc.,"[47] it became necessary to complete its boundary line from the Big Pigeon at the Cataloochee turnpike southwest to the Georgia line. To that end it passed, in 1819 (2 R. S. N. C., 1832), an act under which James Mebane, Montford Stokes and Robert Love were appointed commissioners for North Carolina for the purpose of running and marking said line. These commissioners met Alexander Smith, Isaac Allen and Simeon Perry, commissioners representing Tennessee, at Newport, Tenn., at the mouth of the Big Pidgeon, July 16, 1821; and, starting from the stone in the Cataloochee turnpike road which had been set up by the commissioners of 1799, they ran in a southwestwardly course to the Bald Rock on the summit of the Great Iron or Smoky mountain, and continued along the main top thereof to the Little Tennessee river. The notes of W. Davenport's field book give as detailed an account of the progress of these commissioners and surveyors as did John Strother's in 1799; but as they met no one between these two points there was little to relate. The same or another party might follow the same route to-day and they would meet no one. But Mr. Davenport does not call the starting point a "turnpike." He calls it a "track," which was quite as much as it could lay claim to, the present turnpike having been built from Jonathan's creek up Cove creek, across the Hannah gap, passing the Carr place and up the Little Cataloochee, through Mount Sterling gap, as late as the fifties.[48] At twenty miles from the starting point they were on "the top of an extreme

high pinnacle in view of Sevierville." At 22 miles they were at
the Porter gap, from which, in 1853, Eli Arrington of Waynesville carried on his shoulders W. W. Rhinehart, dying of
milk-sick, three miles down the Bradley fork of Ocona Luftee
to a big poplar, where Rhinehart died. Near here, although
they did not know it then, an alum cave was one day to be
discovered, out of which, in the lean years of the Southern
Confederacy, Col. William H. Thomas and his Indians were
to dig for alum, copperas, saltpeter and a little magnesia to
be used in the hospitals of this beleaguered land, in default of
standard medicines which had been made contraband of war.

ARNOLD GUYOT AND S. B. BUCKLEY. Here, too, Arnold
Guyot, the distinguished professor of geology and physical
geography of Princeton college, came in 1859, following Prof.
S. B. Buckley, and made a series of barometric measurements,
not alone of the Great Smoky mountain chain, but also of that
little known and rugged group of peaks wholly in Tennessee,
known as the Bull Head mountains.

DOUBTFUL OF A ROAD EVER CROSSING THE SMOKIES.
Surveyor Davenport noted a low gap through which "if there
ever is a wagon road through the Big Smoky mountain, it
must go through this gap." Well, during the Civil War,
Col. Thomas, with his "sappers and miners," composed of
Cherokee Indians and Union men of East Tennessee, did make
a so-called wagon road through this gap, now called Collins
gap; and through it, in January, 1864, General Robert B.
Vance carried a section of artillery, dragging the dismounted
cannon, not on skids, but over the bare stones, only to be
captured himself with a large part of his command at Causbey
creek two days later. But no other vehicle has ever passed
that frightful road, save only the front wheels of a wagon,
as it is dangerous even to walk over its precipitous and rock-
ribbed course. No other road has ever been attempted, and
this one has been abandoned, except by horsemen and footmen, for years. Not even a wagon track is visible. On the
7th of August they came at the 31st mile to Meigs' Post.
At the 34th mile they came in view of Brasstown; and next
day, at the 45th mile, they reached the head of Little river, and
must have been in plain view of Tuckaleechee Cove and near
Thunderhead mountain, both immortalized by Miss Mary
N. Murfree (Charles Egbert Craddock) in her stories of the

Tennessee mountains. On the 11th they were at the head of Abram's creek, which flows through Cade's Cove into the Little Tennessee at that gem of all mountain coves, the Harden farm at Talassee ford. On the 13th they came to a "red oak . . . at Equeneetly path to Cade's cove." This is only a trail, and is at the head of one of the prongs of Eagle creek and not far from where Jake and Quil Rose, two famous mountaineers, lived in the days of blockade stills. Of course they did not still any! On this same unlucky 13th, they came to the top of a bald spot in sight of Talassee Old Town, at the 57th mile. This is the Harden farm spoken of above, and is a tract of about 500 acres of level and fertile land. On the 16th they passed over Parsons and Gregory Balds. On this day also they crossed the Little Tennessee river "to a large white pine on the south side of the river at the mouth of a large creek, 65th mile." From there on to the Hiwassee turnpike the boundary line is in dispute, the case being now before the Supreme Court of the United States. One of the marks still visible is that made on the 19th, at the 86th mile, "a holly tree . . . near the head of middle fork of Tellico river." They were then close to what has since been known as State Ridge, on which in July, 1892, William Hall, standing on the North Carolina side of the line, was to shoot and kill Andrew Bryson; and if these surveyors had not done their work well, Hall might have suffered severely; for, all unconsciously, this man was to invoke the same law Carson and Vance and other noted duellists had relied on, when they "fought across the State line."[49] Zim. Roberts, who lives under the Devil's Looking Glass, says that a healthy white oak tree, under which Hall was standing when he fired at Bryson, began to die immediately and is now quite dead. On the 20th of August they were at "the 89th mile, at the head of Beaver Dam" creek of Cherokee county, N. C., and not far from the Devil's Looking Glass," an ugly cliff of rock, where the ridge comes to an abrupt and almost perpendicular end. On that day, at the 93d mile, they came to "the trading path leading from the Valley Towns to the Overhill settlements," reaching the 95th mile on that path before they paused.

THAT SAHARA–LIKE THIRST. On the 24th, at the 96th mile, they were on the top of the Unicoy mountain, and on the same day they reached "the hickory and rock at the wagon road, the 101st mile, at the end of the Unicoy mountain." It was here that tradition says that the Sahara-like thirst overtook the party; as from the 101st mile post their course was "due south 15 miles and 220 poles to a post oak post on the Georgia line, at 23 poles west of the 72d mile from the Nick-a-jack Old Town on the Tennessee river."

TRYON'S BOUNDARY LINE. "In the spring and early summer of 1767 there were fresh outbreaks on the part of the Indians. Governor Tryon had run a boundary-line between the back settlements of the Carolinas and the Cherokee hunting-grounds. But hunters and traders would persist in wandering to the west of this line and sometimes they were killed."[50]

INDIAN BOUNDARY LINES. Almost as important as the State lines were the Indian boundary lines; but most of them were natural boundaries and have given but little trouble. There was one notable exception, however, and that is the

MEIGS AND FREEMAN LINE. According to the map of the "Former Territorial Limits of the Cherokee Indians," accompanying the Fifth Annual Report of the Bureau of Ethnology, 1883-84, there were three lines run to establish the boundary between the Cherokees and the ceded territory under the treaty of October 2, 1798; the first of which was run by Captain Butler in 1798, and extending from "Meigs' post on the Great Stone mountain to a fork of the Keowee river in South Carolina known as Little river. But, according to the text[51] the line was not run till the summer of 1799, and is described as "extending from Great Iron mountain in a southeasterly direction to the point where the most southerly branch of Little river crossed the divisional line to Tugaloo river." However, "owing to the unfortunate destruction of official records by fire, in the year 1800, it is impossible to ascertain all the details concerning this survey, but it was executed on the theory that the "Little River" named in the treaty was one of the northermost branches of Keowee river."[52]

RETURN J. MEIGS AND THOMAS FREEMAN. But, "this survey seems not to have been accepted by the War Department, for on the 3d of June, 1802, instructions were issued by the Secretary of War to Return J. Meigs, as commissioner, to superintend the execution of the survey of this same portion of the boundary. Mr. Thomas Freeman was appointed surveyor."[53] "There were three streams of that name in that vicinity. Two of these were branches of the French Broad and the other of the Keowee."

EXPEDIENCY GOVERNED. "If the line should be run to the lower of these two branches of the French Broad, it would leave more than one hundred white families of white settlers within the Indian territory. If it were run to the branch of the Keowee river, it would leave ten or twelve Indian villages within the State of North Carolina." It was, therefore, determined by Commissioner Meigs to accept the upper branch of the French Broad as the true intent and meaning of the treaty, and the line was run accordingly; whereby "not a single white settlement was cut off or intersected, and but five Indian families were left on the Carolina side of the line."

LOCATION OF THE "MEIGS POST." In a footnote (p. 181-2) Commissioner Meigs refers to the plat and field-notes of Surveyor Freeman, but the author declares that they cannot be found among the Indian office records.[54] Also that there is "much difficulty in ascertaining the exact point of departure of the 'Meigs Line' from the great Iron Mountains. In the report of the Tennessee and North Carolina boundary commissioners in 1821 it is stated to be "31½ miles by the cource of the mountain ridge in a general southwesterly course from the crossing of Cataloochee turnpike; 9½ miles in a similar direction from Porter's gap; 21½ miles in a northeasterly direction from the crossing of Equovetley Path, and 33½ miles in a like course from the crossing of Tennessee river."

. . . It was stated to the author by Gen. R. N. Hood, of Knoxville, Tenn., that there is a tradition that "Meigs Post" was found some years since about 1½ miles southwest of Indian gap. A map of the survey of Qualla Boundary, by M. S. Temple, in 1876, shows a portion of the continuation of "Meigs Line as passing about 1½ miles east of Quallatown." Surveyor Temple mentions it as running "south 50° east (formerly south 52½° east)." Meigs' Post should have stood at the eastern end of the Hawkins Line which had been run by Col. Benj. Hawkins and Gen. Andrew Pickens in August, 1797, pursuant to the treaty of July 2, 1791, commencing 1000 yards above South West Point (now Kingston) and running south 76° east to the Great Iron Mountain.[55] "From this point the line continued in the same course until it reached the Hopewell treaty line of 1785, and was called the "Pickens line."[56] The Hopewell treaty line ran from a point west of the Blue Ridge and about 12 miles east of Hendersonville, crossed the Swannanoa river just east of Asheville, and went on to McNamee's camp on the Nollechucky river, three miles southeast of Greenville, Tenn. "The supposition is that as the commissioners were provided with two surveyors, they separated, Col. Hawkins, with Mr. Whitner as surveyor, running the line from Clinch river to the Great Iron Mountains, and Gen. Pickens, with Col. Kilpatrick as surveyor, locating the remainder of it. This statement is verified so far as Gen. Pickens is concerned by his own written statement."[57]

COL. STRINGFIELD FOLLOWS THE LINE. George H. Smathers, Esq., an attorney of Waynesville, says there is a tradition that the Meigs and Freeman posts were really posts set up along this line, and not marks made on living trees; but Col. W. W. Stringfield of the same place writes that he measured nine and one-half miles southwestwardly of Porter's gap "and found Meigs' post, a torn-down stone pile on the top of a smooth mountain. . . . Meigs' and Freeman's line was as well marked as any line I ever saw; I traced this line south 52½ ° east, from Scott's creek to the top of Tennessee mountain, between Haywood and Transylvania counties, a few miles south of and in full view of the Blue Ridge or South Carolina line . . . I found a great many old marks, evidently made when the line was first run in 1802. I became quite familiar with this line in later years, and ran numerous lines in and around the same in the sale of the Love "Speculation" lands. . . . Many of these old marked trees can still be found all through Jackson county, on the waters of Scott's creek, Cane or Wurry-hut, Caney Fork, Cold or Tennessee creek, and others."[58] When he was running the line he was told by Chief Smith of the Cherokees, Wesley Enloe, then over 80 years old, Dr. Mingus, then 92 years old, Eph. Connor and others, that he was on the Meigs line.

RETURN JONATHAN MEIGS. "He was the firstborn son of his parents, who gave him the somewhat peculiar name

Return Jonathan to commemorate a romantic incident in their own courtship, when his mother, a young Quakeress called back her lover as he was mounting his horse to leave the house forever after what he had supposed was a final refusal. The name has been handed down through five generations."⁵⁹ . . .

TREATY OF 1761.⁶⁰ The French having secured the active sympathy of the Cherokees in their war with Great Britain, Governor Littleton of South Carolina, marched against the Indians and defeated them, and in 1760, concluded a treaty with them, under which the Cherokees agreed to kill or imprison every Frenchman who should come into their country during the war. But as the Cherokees still continued hostile South Carolina sent Col. Grant, who conquered them in 1761, and concluded a treaty by which "the boundaries between the Indians and the settlements were declared to be the sources of the great rivers flowing into the Atlantic ocean." As the Blue Ridge is an unbroken watershed south of the Potomac river, this made that mountain range the true eastern boundary of the Indians. This treaty remained in force till the treaty of 1772 and the purchase of 1775 to the northern part of that boundary, or the land lying west of the Blue Ridge and north of the Nollechucky river. It remained in force as to all land west and south of that territory till 1785 (November 28), called the treaty of Hopewell.

TREATY OF 1772 AND PURCHASE OF 1775. The Virginia authorities in the early part of 1772 concluded a treaty with the Cherokees whereby a boundary line was fixed between them, which was to run west from White Top mountain, which left those settlers on the Watauga river within the Indian limits, whereupon, as a measure of temporary relief, they leased for a period of eight years all the country on the waters of the Watauga river. "Subsequently in 1775 (March 19) they secured a deed in fee simple therefor," . . . and it embraced all the land on "the waters of the Watauga, Holston, and Great Canaway [sic] or New river." This tract began "on the south or southwest of the Holston river six miles above Long Island in that river; thence a direct line in nearly a south course to the ridge dividing the waters of Watauga from the waters of Nonachuckeh (Nollechucky or Toe) and along the ridge in a southeasterly direction to the Blue Ridge

or line dividing North Carolina from the Cherokee lands;
thence along the Blue Ridge to the Virginia line and west along
such line to the Holston river; thence down the Holston to the
beginning, including all waters of the Watauga, part of the
waters of Holston, and the head branches of the New river
or Great Canaway, agreeable to the aforesaid boundaries." [61]

TREATY OF HOPEWELL, 1785. Hopewell is on the Keowee
river, fifteen miles above its junction with the Tugaloo. It was
here that the treaty that was to move the boundary line west
of the Blue Ridge was made. This line began six miles southeast
of Greenville, Tenn., where Camp or McNamee's creek empties
into the Nollechucky river; and ran thence a southeast course
"to Rutherford's War Trace," ten or twelve miles west of
the Swannanoa settlement. This "War Trace" was the route
followed by Gen. Griffith Rutherford, when, in the summer
of 1776, he marched 2,400 men through the Swannanoa gap,
passed over the French Broad at a place still known as the
"War Ford"; continued up the valley of Hominy creek,
leaving Pisgah mountain to the left, and crossing Pigeon river
a little below the mouth of East Fork; thence through the
mountains to Richland creek, above the present town of
Waynesville, etc. From the point where the line struck the
War Trace it was to go "to the South Carolina Indian boundary." Thus, the line probably ran just east of Marshall,
Asheville and Hendersonville to the South Carolina line,
though its exact location was rendered "unnecessary by reason of the ratification in February, 1792, of the Cherokee
treaty concluded July 2, 1791, wherein the Indian boundary
line was withdrawn a considerable distance to the west." [62]

NORTH CAROLINA'S INDIAN RESERVATION. Meantime, however, North Carolina being a sovereign State, bound to the
Confederation of the Union only by the loose articles of
confederation, in 1883, set apart an Indian reservation of its
own; which ran from the mouth of the Big Pigeon to its source
and thence along the ridge between it and the waters of the
Tuckaseigee (Code N. C., Vol. ii, sec. 2346) to the South
Carolina line. This, however, does not seem to have been
supported by any treaty. The State had simply moved the
Indian boundary line twenty miles westward to the Pigeon
river at Canton.

TREATIES OF 1791 AND 1792. The treaty of 1791 was not satisfactory to the Indians and another treaty supplemental thereto was made February 17, 1792, which in its turn was followed by one of January 21, 1795, and another of October 2, 1798. They all call for what was afterwards run and called the Meigs and Freeman line, treated fully under that head. [63]

TREATY OF FEBRUARY 27, 1819. This treaty cedes all land from the point where the Hiwassee river empties into the Tennessee, thence along the first ridge which closes in on said river, two miles above Hiwassee Old Town; thence along the ridge which divides the waters of Hiwassee and Little Tellico to the Tennessee river at Talassee; thence along the main channel to the junction of the Nanteyalee; thence along the ridge in the fork of said river to the top of the Blue Ridge; thence along the Blue Ridge to the Unicoy Turnpike, etc. This moved the line twenty miles west of what is now Franklin. [64]

TREATY OF NEW ECHOTA, DECEMBER 29, 1835. By this treaty the Cherokees gave up all their lands east of the Mississippi river, and all claims for spoliation for $5,000,000, and the 7,000,000 acres of land west of the Mississippi river, guaranteed them by the treaties of 1828 and 1833. This was the treaty for their removal, treated in the chapter on the Eastern Band. [65]

THE RAINBOW COUNTRY. During the year 1898 while Judge H. G. Ewart was acting as District Judge of the U. S. Court at Asheville, some citizens of New Jersey obtained a judgment against the heirs of the late Messer Fain of Cherokee county for certain land in the disputed territory, known as the Rainbow Country because of its shape. The sheriff of Monroe county, Tennessee, armed with a writ of possession from the Tennessee court, entered the house occupied by one of Fain's sons and took possession. Fain had him arrested for assault and trespass, and he sued out a writ of *habeas corpus* before Judge Ewart, who decided the case in favor of Fain; but the sheriff appealed to the Circuit Court of Appeals for the 4th circuit, and Judge Ewart was reversed. Thereupon Fain sued out a writ of *certiorari* before the Supreme Court of the United States; but after the writ had been granted Fain decided not to pay for the printing of the large record, and the case was dismissed for want of prosecution. This was one of the forerunners to litigation with Tennessee.

RECENT BOUNDARY DISPUTES. There is now pending before the Supreme Court of the United States a controversy between the State of Tennessee and the State of North Carolina over what is known as the "Rainbow" country at the head of Tellico creek, Cherokee county. Tennessee claims that the line should have followed the main top of the Unaka mountains instead of leaving the main ridge and crossing one prong of Tellico creek which rises west of the range. This is probably what should have been done if the commissioners who ran the line in 1821 had followed the text of the statute literally; but they left the main top and crossed this prong of Tellico creek, and their report and field-notes, showing that this had been done were returned to their respective States and the line as run and marked was adopted by Tennessee as well as by North Carolina. [66]

LOST COVE BOUNDARY LINE. In 1887, Gov. Scales, under the law providing for the appointment of a commission to meet another from Tennessee to determine at what point on the Nollechucky river the State line crosses, appointed Captain James M. Gudger for North Carolina, J. R. Neal being his surveyor; but there was a disagreement from the outset between the North Carolina and the Tennessee commissioners. The latter insisted on going south from the high peak north of the Nollechucky river, which brought them to the deep hole at the mouth of lost Cove creek, at least three quarters of a mile east of the point at which the line run for the North Carolina commissioner reached the same stream, which was a few hundred yards below the mouth of Devil's creek. The North Carolina commissioner claimed to have the original field-notes of the surveyors, and followed them strictly. Neither side would yield to the other, and the line remains as it was originally run in 1799. The notes followed by Captain Gudger were deposited by him with his report with the Secretary of State at Raleigh. See Pub. Doc. 1887, and *Dugger v. McKesson*, 100 N. C., p. 1.

MACON COUNTY LINE. The legislature of North Carolina provided for a survey between Macon County, N. C., and Rabun county, Ga., in 1879, from Elliquet's Rock, the corner of North Carolina, South Carolina and Georgia, to the "Locust Stake", and as much further as the line was in dispute. L. Howard of Macon county was the commissioner for North Carolina. (Ch. 387, Laws 1883.)

TENNESSEE LINE BETWEEN CHEROKEE AND GRAHAM. The line between these two counties and Tennessee was ordered located by the county surveyors of the counties named according to the calls of the act of 1821. See Ch. 202, Pub. L. 1897, p. 343.

NOTES.

[1]Asheville's Centenary.
[2]Col. Rec., Vol. V, p. xxxix.
[3]Ibid.
[4]Ibid.
[5]Hill, p. 31-32.
[6]Ibid., p. 33.
[7]Ibid., p. 89.
[8]Ibid., p. 88.
[9]Ibid., 89.
[10]Col. Rec., Vol. III, p. 23 et seq.
[11]Ibid., Vol. II, p. 790.
[12]Ibid., p. 794.
[13]"The line thus run was accepted by both Colonies and remains still the boundary between the two states." Hill, 89.
[14]Byrd, 190.
[15]Col. Rec., Vol. II, p. 223.
[16]Ibid., Vol. I, p. xxiv.
[17]Col. Rec., Vol. IV, p. xiii.
[18]The large green, treeless spot on the top of this mountain, covered with grass, is surrounded by a forest of singular trees, locally known as "Lashorns." From a sketch of Wilborn Waters, "The Hermit Hunter of White Top," by J. A. Testerman, of Jefferson, Ashe Co., N. C., the following description of these trees is taken: "They have a diameter of from 15 to 30 feet, and their branches will hold the weight of several persons at one time on their level tops. They resemble the Norway Spruce, but do not thrive when transplanted." The diameter given above refers to that of the branches, not of the trunks.
[19]Ch. 144, Laws 1779, 377, Potter's Revisal; W. C. Kerr in Report of Geological Survey of N. C., Vol. I, (1875), p. 2, states that this survey carried the line beyond Bristol, Tenn.-Va.
[20]A glance at any map of Tennessee reveals the fact that the line does not run "due west" all the way; but that does not concern North Carolina now.
[21]Roosevelt, Vol. I, 217.
[22]Oglethorpe did not sail for Savannah till November 17, 1732.
[23]Its head waters are in Rockingham and Guilford counties.
[24]The mouth of the Waccamaw river must be 90 miles southwest from that of the Cape Fear.
[25]Col. Rec., Vol. IV, 8.
[26]Mear means a boundary, a limit.
[27]Col. Rec., Vol. IV, p. vii, and W. C. Kerr's Report of the Geological Survey of N. C., (1875).
[28]It was in the Waxhaw settlement that Andrew Jackson was born, March 15, 1767.
[29]Potter's Revisal, p. 1280.
[30]Potter's Revisal, 1131.
[31]Ibid., 1280.
[32]Ibid., 1318.
[33]Ellicott's Rock is on the west bank of Chatooga river. Rev. St. N. C., Vol. II, 145. Andrew Ellicott had been previously appointed to survey the line under the Creek treaty of 1790, according to Fifth Eth. Rep., p. 163.
[34]Fifth Eth. Rep., p. 182.
[35]N. C. Booklet, Vol. III, No. 12.
[36]Ibid.
[37]Ibid.
[38]By the late C. D. Smith, 1905.
[39]Draper, 259.
[40]In the Narrative of Vance and Henry of the Battle of Kings Mountain, published in 1892 by T. F. Davidson.
[41]Ambrose gap is a few miles southwest, and is so called because a free negro of that name built a house across the State line in this gap, and when he died his grave was dug half in Tennessee and half in North Carolina, according to local tradition.
[42]Draper, 176.
[43]Allison, p. 4.

[44]Robert Henry had gone to get Robert Love as a pilot; and a few years later he married Love's daughter Dorcas.

[45]Zeigler & Grosscup, pp. 271-2-3.

[46]Bishop Asbury's diary shows that he was at Barnett's Station, November 4, 1802.

[47]Fifth Eth., 219, 220.

[48]Laws 1850-51, ch. 157. But there was a road of some kind, for Bishop Asbury mentions crossing Cataloochee on a log in December, 1810. "But O the mountain—height after height, and five miles over!"

[49]114 N. C. Rep., 909, and 115 N. C., 811. Also Laws 1895, ch. 169.

[50]Thwaite, 69.

[51]Fifth Eth., 181.

[52]Ibid.

[53]Ibid.

[54]Ibid., 181.

[55]Ibid., 168.

[56]Ibid.

[57]Ibid., 168.

[58]154 N. C. Rep., 79.

[59]Nineteenth Eth., 214.

[60]Fifth Eth., 146.

[61]Ibid.

[62]Ibid., 156-157.

[63]Ibid., 158-159, 169.

[64]Ibid., 219.

[65]Ibid., 253.

[66]Rev. St. N. C., Vol. III, 96-97.

CHAPTER III

COLONIAL DAYS

Though the mountains were not settled during colonial days except north of the ridge between the Toe and Watauga rivers, the people who ultimately crossed the Blue Ridge lived under colonial laws and customs, or descended from those pioneers who did. Therefore, colonial times in North Carolina, especially in the Piedmont country, should be of interest to those who would know how our more remote ancestors lived under English rule. This should be especially true of those venturesome spirits who first crossed the Blue Ridge and explored the mountain regions of our State, whatever may have been the object of their quest. For "when the first Continental Congress began its sittings the only frontiersmen west of the mountains and beyond the limits of continuous settlement within the old thirteen colonies were the two or three hundred citizens of the Little Watauga commonwealth. [1] For they were a commonwealth in the truest sense of the word, being beyond the jurisdiction of any government except that of their own consciences. In these circumstances they voluntarily formed the first republican government in America. "The building of the Watauga commonwealth by Robertson and Sevier gave a base of operations and furnished a model for similar commonwealths to follow." [2]

> For the first written compact that, west of the mountains,
> Was framed for the guidance of liberty's feet,
> Was writ here by letterless men in whose bosoms,
> Undaunted, the heart of a paladin beat.

EARL OF GRANVILLE. There were eight Lords Proprietors to whom Carolina was originally granted in 1663. Among them was Sir George Carteret, afterwards Earl of Granville. [3] On the 3d of May, 1728, the king of England bought North Carolina and thus ended the government of the Lords Proprietors. But he did not buy the interest of the Earl of Granville, who refused to sell; though he had to give up his share

in the government of the colony. Hence, grants from Earl
of Granville are as valid as those from the crown; for in 1743
his share was given him in land. It included about one-half
of the State, and he collected rents from it till 1776, his dis-
honest agents giving the settlers on it great trouble.

MORAVIANS. The Moravians were a band of religious
brethren who came to America to do mission work among
the Indians and to gain a full measure of religious freedom.
Their plan was to build a central town on a large estate and
to sell the land around to the members of the brotherhood.
The town was to contain shops, mills, stores, factories, churches
and schools. After selecting several pieces of lowlands,
Bishop Spangenberg bought from the Earl of Granville a
large tract in the bounds of the present county of Forsyth,
and called the tract Wachovia, meaning "meadow stream." [4]
On November 17, 1753, a company of twelve men arrived at
Wachovia, and started what is now Salem. This Bishop
Spangenberg is spoken of in Hill's "Young People's History
of North Carolina" as Bishop Augustus G. Spangenberg;
while the Spangenberg whose diary is quoted from extensively in the next few pages signs himself I. Spangenberg.
He will be called the Bishop, nevertheless, because he "spake
as one having authority." [5]

FIRST TO CROSS THE BLUE RIDGE. Vol. V, Colonial Records (pp. 1 to 14), contains the diary of I. Spangenberg, of the
Moravian church. He is the first white man who crossed
the Blue Ridge in North Carolina, so far as the records show,
except those who had prolonged the Virginia State line in
1749. He, with his co-religionist, Brother I. H. Antes, left
Edenton September 13, 1752, for the purpose of inspecting
and selecting land for settling Moravian immigrants. The
land was to have been granted by Earl Granville, and the
surveyor, Mr. Churton, who accompanied the expedition, had
instructions from that proprietor to survey the lands, and as
he was to be paid three pounds sterling for each 5,000-acre
tract, he was averse to surveying tracts of smaller acreage.
His instructions limited him also to north and south and east
and west lines, which frequently compelled the good Bishop
to include mountains in his boundaries that he did not particularly desire. Having run three lines this surveyor declined
to run the fourth, and the Bishop notes that fact in order

to save his brethern the trouble of searching for lines that
were never run or marked.   The surveyor, however, did survey for the Bishop smaller tracts than those containing 5,000
acres, though reluctantly.

QUAKER MEADOWS.   In Judge Avery's "Historic Homes"
(N. C. Booklet, Vol. IV, No. 3) he refers to the fact that these
meadows were so called from the fact that a Quaker (Moravian) once camped there and traded for furs.   This Quaker
was Bishop Spangenberg.   He reached on November 12,
1752, the "neighborhood of what may be called Indian Pass.
The next settlement from here is that of Jonathan Weiss,
more familiarly known as Jonathan Perrot.   This man is a
hunter and lives 20 miles from here.   There are many hunters
about here, who live like Indians: they kill many deer, selling their hides, and thus live without much work."   On the
19th of November he reached Quaker Meadows, "fifty miles
from all settlements and found all we thought was required
for a settlement, very rich and fertile bottoms. . . .   Our
survey begins seven or eight miles from the mouth of the 3d
river where it flows into the Catawba.   What lies further
down the river has already been taken up.   The other [west-
ern] line of the survey runs close to the Blue Ridge. . . .   This
piece consists of 6,000 acres.   We can have at least eight settlements in this tract, and each will have water, range, etc.
. . . I calculate to every settlement eight couples of brethren
and sisters."

BUFFALO TRAILS.   There were no roads save those made
by buffaloes.   The surveyor was stopped by six Cherokees on
a hunt, but they soon became friendly.   November 24th they
were five miles from Table Rock, which with the Hawk's Bill
is so conspicuous from Morganton, where they surveyed the
fifth tract of land, of 700 or 800 acres.

MUSICAL WOLVES.   "The wolves, which are not like those
in Germany, Poland and Lapland (because they fear men
and do not easily come near) give us such music of six different cornets, the like of which I have never heard in my life.
Several brethren, skilled in hunting, will be required to exterminate panthers, wolves, etc."

OLD INDIAN FIELDS.[6]   On November 28th they were
camped in an old Indian field on the northeast branch of
Middle Little river of the Catawba, where they arrived on

the 25th, and resolved to take up 2,000 acres of land lying on two streams, both well adapted to mill purposes. That the Indians once lived there was very evident—possibly before the war which they waged with North Carolina—"from the remains of an Indian fort: as also the tame grass which was still growing about the old residences, and from the trees." On December 3d they camped on a river in another old Indian field at the head of a branch of New river, "after passing over frightful mountains and dangerous cliffs."

WHERE MEN HAD SELDOM TROD. On the 29th they were in camp on the second or middle fork of Little river, not far from Quaker Meadows "in a locality that has probably been but seldom trodden by the foot of man since the creation of the world. For 70 or 80 miles we have been traveling over terrible mountains and along very dangerous places where there was no way at all." One might call the place in which they were camped a basin or kettle, it being a cove in the mountains, rich of soil, and where their horses found abundant pasture among the buffalo haunts and tame grass among the springs. The wild pea-vines which formerly covered these mountains, growing even under the forest trees most luxuriantly for years after the whites came in, afforded fine pasturage for their stock. It also formed a tangled mat on the surface of the earth through which it was almost impossible for men to pass. Hence, the pioneers were confined generally to the Indian and buffalo trails already existing. These pea-vines return even now whenever a piece of forest land is fenced off a year or two.

ON THE GRANDFATHER? It would seem that they had been misled by a hunter whom they had taken along to show them the way to the Yadkin; but had missed the way and on December 3d came "into a region from which there was no outlet except by climbing up an indescribably steep mountain. Part of the way we had to crawl on our hands and feet, and sometimes we had to take the baggage and saddles from the horses, and drag them up, while they trembled and quivered like leaves. The next day we journeyed on: got into laurel bushes and beaver dams and had to cut our way through the bushes. Arrived at the top at last, we saw hundreds of mountain peaks all around us, presenting a spectacle like ocean waves in a storm." The descent on the western side was "neither so steep, nor as deep as before, and then we came to a stream of water, but no pasture. . . . The next day we got into laurel bushes and beaver dams and had to cut our way through the bushes. . . ."

WANDERING BEWILDERED IN UNKNOWN WAYS. "Then we changed our course—left the river and went up the mountain, where the Lord brought us to a delicious spring, and good pasturage on a chestnut ridge. . . . The next day we came to a creek so full of rocks that we could not possible cross it; and on both sides were such precipitous banks that scarcely a man, certainly no horse could climb them . . . but our horses had nothing—absolutely nothing. . . . Directly came a hunter who had climbed a mountain and had seen a large meadow. Thereupon, we scrambled down . . . and came before night into a large plain. . . .

CAUGHT IN A MOUNTAIN SNOWSTORM. "We pitched our tent, but scarcely had we finished when such a fierce windstorm burst upon us that we could scarcely protect ourselves against it. I cannot remember that I have ever in winter anywhere encountered so hard or so cold a wind. The ground was soon covered with snow ankle deep, and the water froze for us aside the fire. Our people became thoroughly disheartened. Our horses would certainly perish and we with them."

IN GOSHEN'S LAND. "The next day we had fine sunshine, and then warmer days, though the nights were 'horribly' cold. Then we went to examine the land. A large part of it is already cleared, and there long grass abounds, and this is all bottom. Three creeks flow together here and make a considerable river, which flows into the Mississippi according to the best knowledge of our hunters." There were countless springs but no reeds, but "so much grass land that Brother Antes thinks a man could make several hundred loads of hay of the wild grass. . . . There is land here suitable for wheat, corn, oats, barley, hemp, etc. Some of the land will probably be flooded when there is high water. There is a magnificent chestnut and pine forest near here. Whetstones and millstones which Brother Antes regards the best he has seen in North Carolina are plenty. The soil is here mostly limestone and of a cold nature. . . . We surveyed this land and took up 5,400 acres. . . . We have a good many mountains,

but they are very fertile and admit of cultivation. Some of
them are already covered with wood, and are easily accessible. Many hundred—yes, thousand crab-apple trees grow
here, which may be useful for vinegar. One of the creeks
presents a number of admirable seats for milling purposes.
This survey is about 15 miles from the Virginia line, as we
saw the Meadow mountain, and I judged it to be about 20
miles distant. This mountain lies five miles from the line
between Virginia and North Carolina. In all probability this
tract would make an admirable settlement for Christian Indians, like Grandenhutten in Pennsylvania. There is wood,
mast, wild game, fish and a free range for hunting, and admirable land for corn, potatoes, etc. For stock raising it is also
incomparable. Meadow land and pasture in abundance."
After "a bitter journey among the mountains where we were
virtually lost and whichever way we turned we were literally
walled in on all sides," they came on December 14, 1752,
to the head of Yadkin river, after having abandoned all
streams and paths, and followed a course east and south, and
"scrambling across the mountains as well as we could."
Here a hunter named Owen, "of Welch stock, invited us
into his house and treated us very kindly." He lived near
the Mulberry Fields which had been taken up by Morgan
Bryant, but were uninhabited. The nearest house was 60
miles distant.

THE FIRST HUNTERS. The hunters who assisted the Bishop
in finding the different bodies of suitable land were Henry
Day, who lived in Granville, John Perkins, who lived on the
Catawba, "and is known as Andrew Lambert, a well-known
Scotchman," and Jno. Rhode, who "lives about 20 miles
from Capt. Sennit on the Yadkin road." John Perkins was
especially commended to the Brethren as "a diligent and true
worthy man, and a friend to the Brethren." The late Judge
A. C. Avery said he was called "Gentleman John," and that
Johns river in Burke was named for him. [7]

SETTLERS FROM PENNSYLVANIA. "Many of the immigrants were sent to Pennsylvania, and they had traveled as
far west as Pittsburg early in the 18th century. The Indians
west of the Alleghanies were, however, fiercer than any the
Quakers had met; but to the southwest for several hundred
miles the Appalachians "run in parallel ranges . . . through

Virginia, West Virginia, the Carolinas and East Tennessee
. . . '' and through these "long, deep troughs between these
ranges . . . Pennsylvanians freely wandered into the South
and Southwest . . . '' and "between the years 1732 and 1750,
numerous groups of Pennsylvanians—Germans and Irish largely, with many Quakers among them—had been . . . gradually pushing forward the line of settlement, until now it had
reached the upper waters of the Yadkin river, in the northwest corner of North Carolina.'' [8] "Thus was the wilderness tamed by a steady stream of immigration from the older
lands of the northern colonies, while not a few penetrated
to this Arcadia through the passes of the Blue Ridge, from
eastern Virginia and the Carolinas.'' [9]

NICK-A-JACK'S CAVE. Almost the first difficulties those
who first crossed the mountains encountered was from the
depredations of renegade Indians and desperate white men
defiant of law and order. There was at this time (1777-78)
a body of free-booters, composed of "adventurous and unruly
members from almost all the western tribes—Cherokees,
Creeks, Chickasaws, Choctaws, and Indians from the Ohio,
generally known as Chickamaugas. Many Tories and white
refugees from border justice joined them and shared in their
misdeeds. Their shifting villages stretched from Chickamauga creek to Running Water. Between these places the
Tennessee twists down through the somber gorges by which
the chains of the Cumberland range are riven in sunder.
Some miles below Chickamauga creek, near Chattanooga,
Lookout mountain towers aloft into the clouds; at its base
the river bends round Moccasin Point, and then rushes through
a gap between Walden's Ridge and the Raccoon Hills. Then,
for several miles, it foams through the winding Narrows
between jutting cliffs and sheer rock walls, while in its boulder-
strewn bed the swift torrent is churned into whirlpools, cata-
racts, and rapids. Near the Great Crossing, where the war
parties and hunting parties were ferried over the river, lies
Nick-a-jack's cave, a vast cavern in the mountain-side. Out
of it flows a stream up which a canoe can paddle two or three
miles into the heart of the mountain. In these high fastnesses,
inaccessible ravines, and gloomy caverns the Chickamaugas
built their towns, and to them they retired with their prisoners
and booty after every raid on the settlements.''

FRENCH AND INDIAN WAR LAND WARRANTS. [10] The Chickamaugas lived on Chickamauga creek and in the mountains about where Chattanooga now stands; they were kinsmen of the Cherokees. In 1748 Dr. Thomas Walker and a
party of hunters came from Virginia into Powell's Valley,
crossing the mountains at Cumberland gap, and named it
and the river in honor of the Duke of Cumberland, Prime
Minister of England. In 1756-7 the English built Fort Loudon, 30 miles from Knoxville, as the French were trying to
get the Cherokees to make war on the North Carolina settlers. After the treaty of peace between France and England
in 1763 many hunters poured over the mountains into Tennessee; though George III had ordered his governors not to
allow whites to trespass on Indian lands west of the mountains, and if any white man did buy Indian lands and and the
Indians moved away the land should belong to the king.
He appointed Indian commissioners; but the whites persisted,
some remaining a year or more to hunt and were called Long
Hunters. Land warrants had been issued to officers and
soldiers who had fought in the French and Indian wars and
those issued by North Carolina wanted to settle in what is
now Tennessee. The Iroquois complained that whites were
killing their stock and taking their lands, and at a great Indian
council at Fort Stanwix, at Rome, N. Y., the northern tribes
gave England title to all their lands between the Ohio and
Tennessee rivers in 1767. But the Indian commissioners for
the southern tribes called a council at Hard Labor, S. C., and
bought title to the same land from the Cherokees. These
treaties were finished in 1768. William Bean in 1769 was
living in a log cabin where Boone's creek joins the Watauga.
In 1771 Parker and Carter set up a store at Rogersville, and
people from Abingdon (called Wolf's Hill) followed, and
the settlement was called the Carter's Valley settlement.
In 1772 Jacob Brown opened a store on the Nollechucky river,
and pioneers settling around, it was called Nollechucky settlement. Shortly before Bean had settled the Cherokees had
attacked the Chickasaws and been defeated, and the settlers
got a ten years' lease from Indians for lands they claimed.
In May 1771, at Alamance, Tryon had defeated the Regulators and many of them had moved to Tennessee. Most
settlers in Tennessee thought they were in Virginia, but either

Richmond or Raleigh was too far off, so they formed the
Watauga Association in 1772 and a committee of 13 elected
five commissioners to settle disputes, etc., with judicial powers
and some executive duties also. It was a free government
by the consent of every individual. When the Revolutionary War began Watauga Association named their country
Washington District and voted themselves indebted to the
United Colonies for their share of the expenses of the war.

THE WATAUGA SETTLEMENT AND INDIAN WARS. This
caused the British government to attempt the destruction
of these settlements by inciting the Cherokees to make war
upon them. Alexander Cameron was the Indian commissioner for the British and he furnished the Indians with guns
and ammunition for that purpose; but in the spring of 1776,
Nancy Ward, a friendly Indian woman, told the white settlers
that 700 Cherokee warriors intended to attack the settlers.
They did so, but were defeated at Heaton's Station and at
Watauga Fort. In these battles the settlers were aided by
Virginia. James Robertson and John Sevier were leaders
in these times. It was after this that Virginia and North
Carolina and South Carolina sent soldiers into the Cherokee
country of North Carolina for the extermination of the savage Cherokees.[11] In August 1776 the Watauga Settlement
asked to be annexed by North Carolina, 113 men signing
the petition, all of whom signed their names except two, who
made their marks. There seems to be no record of any formal
annexation; but in November, 1776, the Provisional Congress
of North Carolina met at Halifax and among the delegates
present were John Carter, John Sevier, Charles Robertson
and John Haile from the Washington District. It is, therefore, safe to conclude that Watauga had been annexed, for
these men helped to frame the first free constitution of the
State of North Carolina. But this Watauga Association
seems to have continued its independent government until
February, 1778; for in 1777 (November) Washington District became Washington county with boundaries cotermi-
nous with those of the present State of Tennessee. Magistrates or justices of the peace took the oath of office in February, 1778, when the entire county began to be governed
under the laws of North Carolina. Thus, the Watauga Association was the germ of the State of Tennessee, and although

there is on a tree near Boone's creek an inscription indicating
that Daniel Boone killed a bear there in 1760, William Bean
appears to have been the first permanent settler of that section. Indeed, this author states that Col. Richard Henderson, of North Carolina, induced Boone to make his first visit
to Kentucky in the spring of 1769, and that James Robertson,
afterwards "The Father of Middle Tennessee," accompanied
him; but stopped on the Wautaga with William Bean and
raised a crop, removing his family from Wake county in 1770
or 1771.

FORTS LOUDON AND DOBBS. Fort Loudon was on the Little
Tennessee. It was attacked and besieged by the Indians,
and surrendered August 9, 1760, after Indian women had
kept the garrison in food a long time in defiance of their own
tribesmen.[12] In 1756 Fort Dobbs was constructed a short
distance south of the South Fork of the Yadkin.[13] For
the first few years Fort Dobbs was not much used,[14] the
Catawbas being friendly; but in 1759 the Yadkin and Catawba valleys were raided by the Cherokees, with the usual
results of ruined crops, burned farm buildings, and murdered
households. The Catawbas, meanwhile, remained faithful
to their white friends. Until this outbreak the Carolinas had
greatly prospered; but after it most of the Yadkin families,
with the English fur-traders, huddled within the walls of
Fort Dobbs, but many others fled to settlements nearer the
Atlantic.[15] In the early winter of 1760 the governors of
Virginia and North and South Carolina agreed upon a joint
campaign against the hostiles, and attacked the Cherokee
towns on the Little Tennessee in the summer of 1760, completely crushing the Indians and sent 5,000 men, women and
children into the hills to starve.[16] With the opening of 1762
the southwest border began to be reoccupied, and the abandoned log cabins again had fires lighted upon their hearths,
the deserted clearings were again cultivated, and the pursuits
of peace renewed.[17]

REMAINS OF FORT LOUDON. In June, 1913, Col. J. Fain
Anderson, a noted historian of Washington College, Tenn.,
visited Fort Loudon, and found the outline of the ditches and
breastworks still visible. The old well was walled up, but
the wall has fallen in. He says there were twelve small iron
cannon in this fort in 1756, all of which had been "packed

over the mountains on horses," and that a Mr. Steele who
lives at McGee's Station—the nearest railroad station to
the old fort—has a piece of one of them which his father
ploughed up over forty years ago.   The land on which the
fort stood now belongs to James Anderson, a relative of J. F.
Anderson, near the mouth of Tellico creek.   But no tablet
marks the site of this first outpost of our pioneer ancestors.

WESTWARD THE COURSE OF EMPIRE TAKES ITS WAY.
From Judge A. C. Avery's "Historic Homes of North Carolina" (N. C. Booklet, Vol. iv, No. 3) we get a glimpse of the
slow approach of the whites of the Blue Ridge :   "According
to tradition the Quaker Meadows farm near Morganton was
so called long before the McDowells or any other whites
established homes in Burke county, and derived its name
from the fact that the Indians, after clearing parts of the
broad and fertile bottoms, had suffered the wild grass to
spring up and form a large meadow, near which a Quaker
had camped before the French and Indian War, and traded
for furs."   This was none other than Bishop I. Spangenberg,
the Moravian, who, on the 19th of November, 1752, (Vol. v,
Colonial Records, p. 6) records in his diary that he was encamped near Quaker Meadows "in the forest 50 miles from
any settlement."

THE McDOWELL FAMILY.   Judge Avery goes on to give
some account of the McDowells :   Ephraim McDowell, the
first of the name in this country, having emigrated from the
north of Ireland, when at the age of 62, accompanied by two
sons, settled at the old McDowell home in Rockbridge county, Virginia.   His grandson Joseph and his grandnephew
"Hunting John" moved South about 1760, but owing to the
French and Indian War went to the northern border of South
Carolina, where their sturdy Scotch-Irish friends had already
named three counties of the State, York, Chester and Lancaster.   One reason for the late settlement of these Piedmont
regions was because the English land agents dumped the
Scotch-Irish and German immigrants in Pennsylvania, from
which State some moved as soon as possible to the unclaimed
lands of the South.

"HUNTING JOHN" AND HIS SPORTING FRIENDS.   "But as
soon as the French and Indian war permitted the McDowells removed to Burke.   'Hunting John' was so called be-

cause of his venturing into the wilderness in pursuit of game, and was probably the first to live at his beautiful home, Pleasant Gardens, in the Catawba Valley, in what is now McDowell county. About this time also his cousin Joseph settled at Quaker Meadows; though 'Hunting John' first entered Swan Ponds, about three miles above Quaker Meadows, but afterwards sold it, without having occupied it, to Waightstill Avery. . . . The McDowells and Carsons of that day and later reared thorough-bred horses, and made race-paths in the broad lowlands of every large farm. They were superb horsemen, crack shots and trained hunters. John McDowell of Pleasant Gardens was a Nimrod when he lived in Virginia, and we learn from tradition that he acted as guide for his cousins over the hunting grounds when, at the risk of their lives, they, with their kinsmen, James Greenlee and Captain Bowman, [who fell at Ramseur's Mill in the Revolutionary War] traveled over and inspected the valley of the Catawba from Morganton to Old Fort, and selected the large domain allotted to each of them."

Log–Cabin Ladies' Whims. "They built and occupied strings of cabins, because the few plank or boards used by them were sawed by hand and the nails driven into them were shaped in a blacksmith's shop. I have seen many old buildings, such as the old houses at Fort Defiance, the Lenoir house and Swan Ponds, where every plank was fastened by a wrought nail with a large round head—sometimes half an inch in diameter. From these houses the lordly old proprietors could in half an hour go to the water or the woods and provide fish, deer or turkeys to meet the whim of the lady of the house. They combined the pleasure of sport with the profit of providing their tables. . . . 'Hunting John' probably died in 1775."

Living Without Law or Gospel? William Byrd, the Virginia commissioner who helped to run the boundary between North Carolina and Virginia in 1728, wrote to Governor Barrington, July 20, 1731, [18] that it "must be owned that North Carolina is a very happy country where people may live with the least labor that they can in any part of the world," and "are accustomed to live without law or gospel, and will with great reluctance submit to either." This is still true of North Carolina, except the statement—which was never true—that

we were accustomed to live without law or gospel in 1731; for
when this identical gentleman was seeking to get paid for his
services as a commissioner to run the boundary line in 1728,
he wrote the Board of Trade that the Reverend Peter Fountain, the chaplain of that survey "christened over 100 children among the settlers along the line in North Carolina."

A "BIRD" WHO SPELT HIS NAME IMPROPERLY.   In spite
of his animadversions upon the pioneer settlers of the eastern
part of our State, we must always incline to forgive Col. William Byrd of Westover after reading his piquant and learned
disquisitions upon many matters in the "Dividing Line."   He
must truly have been what we of more modern times call a
"Bird," although he spelt his name with a y.

WHERE EVERY DAY WAS SUNDAY.[19]   Following are Col.
Byrd's Pictures of Colonial Days: "Our Chaplain, for his
Part, did his Office, and rubb'd us up with a Seasonable Sermon.   This was quite a new Thing to our Brethren of North
Carolina, who live in a climate where no clergyman can Breathe
any more than Spiders in Ireland.   For want of men in Holy Orders, both the Members of the Council and Justices of the Peace
are empowered by the Laws of that Country to marry all
those who will not take One another's Word; but for the
ceremony of Christening their children, they trust that to
chance.   If a parson come in their way, they will crave a
Cast of his office, as they call it, else they are content their
Offspring should remain Arrant Pagans as themselves.   They
account it among their greatest advantages that they are
not Priest-ridden, not remembering that the Clergy is rarely
guilty of Bestriding such as have the misfortune to be poor.
. . .   One thing may be said for the Inhabitants of that Province, that they are not troubled with any Religious Fumes,
and have the least Superstition of any People living.   They
do not know Sunday from any other day, any more than
Robinson Crusoe did, which would give them a great Advantage were they given to be industrious.   But they keep so
many Sabbaths every week, that their disregard of the Seventh
Day has no manner of cruelty in it, either to servants or
cattle."

NYMPH ECHO IN THE DISMAL SWAMP.[20]   Once, when separated from their companions, Col. Byrd "ordered Guns to
be fired and a drum to be beaten, but received no Answer,

unless it was from that prating Nymph Echo, who, like a loquacious Wife, will always have the last word, and Sometimes return three for one."

THEY BROUGHT NO CAPONS FOR THE PARSON.[21] Some of the people were apprehensive that the survey would throw their homes into Virginia. "In that case they must have submitted to some Sort of Order and Government; whereas, in North Carolina, every One does what seems best in his own Eyes. There were some good Women that brought their children to be Baptiz'd, but brought no Capons along with them to make the solemnity cheerful. In the meantime it was Strange that none came to be marry'd in such a Multitude, if it had only been for the Novelty of having their Hands Joyn'd by one in Holy Orders. Yet so it was, that tho' our chaplain Christen'd above an Hundred, he did not marry so much as one Couple during the whole Expedition. But marriage is reckon'd a Lay contract, as I said before, and a Country Justice can tie the fatal Knot there, as fast as an Archbishop."

GENTLEMEN SMELL LIQUOR THIRTY MILES.[22] "We had several Visitors from Edenton [who] . . . having good Noses, had smelt out, at 30 Miles Distance, the Precious Liquor, with which the Liberality of our good Friend Mr. Mead had just before supply'd us. That generous Person had judg'd very right, that we were now got out of the Latitude of Drink proper for men in Affliction, and therefore was so good as to send his Cart loaden with all sorts of refreshments, for which the Commissioners return'd Him their Thanks, and the Chaplain His Blessing."

GETTING UP AN APPETITE FOR DOG.[23] "The Surveyors and their Attendants began now in good earnest to be alarmed with Apprehensions of Famine, nor could they forbear looking with Some Sort of Appetite upon a dog that had been the faithful Companion of their Travels."

POVERTY WITH CONTENTMENT.[24] The following is Col. Byrd's idea of some of our people who lived near Edenton in 1728:

"Surely there is no place in the world where the Inhabitants live with less labor than in North Carolina? It approaches nearer to the description of Lubberland than any other, by the great felicity of the Climate, the easiness of raising provisions, and the Slothfulness of the People. . . .

The Men, for their Parts, just like the Indians, impose all the Work upon the poor Women. They make their Wives rise out of their Beds early in the morning, at the same time that they lye and Snore, till the sun has run one third his course, and disperst all the unwholesome damps. Then, after Stretching and Yawning for half an Hour, they light their Pipes, and, under the Protection of a cloud of Smoak, venture out into the open Air; tho', if it happens to be never so little cold they quickly return Shivering into the Chimney corner. When the weather is mild, they stand leaning with both their arms upon the corn-field fence, and gravely consider whether they had best go and take a Small Heat at the Hough; but generally find reasons to put it off till another time. Thus they loiter away their lives, like Solomon's Sluggard, with their arms across, and at the Winding up of the Year Scarcely have Bread to Eat. To speak the truth, 'tis aversion to Labor that makes People file off to N. Carolina, where Plenty and a warm Sun confirm them in their disposition to Laziness for their whole Lives."

OUR COMMISSIONER TREATS THE PARSON TO A FRICASSEE OF RUM. [25] The chaplain went once to Edenton, accompanied by Mr. Little, one of the North Carolina commissioners, "who to shew his regard for the Church, offer'd to treat Him on the Road with a fricassee of Rum. They fry'd half a Dozen Rashers of very fat Bacon in a Pint of Rum, both of which being disht up together, served the Company at once for meat and Drink."

THE DEMOCRACY OF THE COLONISTS. [26] "They are rarely guilty of Flattering or making any Court to their governors, but treat them with all the Excesses of Freedom and Familiarity. They are of opinion their rulers wou'd be apt to grow insolent, if they grew Rich, and for that reason take care to keep them poorer, and more dependent, if possible than the Saints in New England used to do their Governors."

THE MEN OF ALAMANCE. Meantime the exactions of the British tax collectors had brought on the Regulators War, and the battle of Alamance in May, 1771, resulted in the departure of a "company of fourteen families" from "the present county of Wake to make new homes across the mountains. [27] The men led the way and often had to clear a road with their axes. Behind the axmen went a mixed procession of women, children, dogs, cows and pack-horses loaded with kettles and beds." These settled in Tennessee on the Watauga river. James Robertson, "a cool, brave, sweet-natured man was the leader of the company." Then came John Sevier and many others. In the language of the

Hon. George Bancroft, historian and at that time minister
to England, "it is a mistake if anyone have supposed that
the Regulators were cowed down by their defeat at Alamance.
Like the mammoth, they took the bolt from their brow and
crossed the mountains." Of them and those who followed
them, Hon. John Allison in his "Dropped Stitches of Tennessee History" (p. 37) says:

"The people who made it possible for Tennessee to have a centennial
were a wonderful people. Within a period of about fifteen years they
were engaged in three revolutions; participated in organizing and lived
under five different governments; established and administered the first
free and independent government in America, founded the first church
and the first college in the Southwest; put in operation the second
newspaper in the 'New World West of the Alleghanies'; met and
fought the British in half a dozen battles, from Kings Mountain to the
gates of Charleston, gaining a victory in every battle; held in check,
beat back and finally expelled from the country four of the most powerful tribes of Indian warriors in America; and left Tennesseans their fame
as a heritage, and a commonwealth of which it is their privilege to be
proud."

THE FREEST OF THE FREE. The historian, George Bancroft, exclaims: "Are there any who doubt man's capacity
for self-government? Let them study the history of North
Carolina. Its inhabitants were restless and turbulent in their
imperfect submission to a government imposed from abroad;
the administration of the colony was firm, humane and tran-
quil when they were left to take care of themselves. Any
government but one of their own institution was oppressive. North Carolina was settled by the freest of the free."[28]

THE FIRST PUBLIC DECLARATION OF INDEPENDENCE. This
was made at Halifax, N. C., by the Provisional Congress,
April 12, 1776, when its delegates to the Continental Congress were authorized to concur with other delegates in
"declaring independence and forming foreign alliances,"
reserving the right of forming a constitution and laws for
North Carolina.

THE SCOTCH-IRISH; THEIR ORIGIN AND RELIGION.[29] "Men
will not be fully able to understand Carolina till they have
opened the treasures of history and drawn forth some few
particulars respecting the origin and religious habits of the
Scotch-Irish and become familiar with their doings previous
to the Revolution—during that painful struggle—and the

succeeding years of prosperity; and Carolina will be respected as she is knwon."

IN PIONEER DAYS.[30]   The men and boys wore moccasins, short pantaloons and leather leggings, hunting shirts, which were usually of dressed deerskin, cut like the modern shirt, open the entire length in front and fastened by a belt.   In this belt were carried a small hatchet and a long, sharp hunting knife.   They wore caps of mink or coon skin, with the tail hanging behind for a tassel.   The rifles were long, muzzle-loading, flint-locks, and in a pouch hung over one shoulder were carried gun-wipers, tow, patching, bullets, and flints, while fastened to the strap was a horn for powder.   The women and girls wore sun bonnets, as a rule, and had little time to spend on tucks and ruffles.   There was no place at which to buy things except the stores of Indian traders, and they had very few things white people wanted. . . .   The pioneer moved into a new country on foot or on horse back and brought his household goods on pack horses.   They were about as follows : The family clothing, some blankets and a few other bed clothes, with bed ticks to be filled with grass or hair, a large pot, a pair of pothooks, an oven with lid, a skillet, and a frying pan, a hand mill to grind grain, a wooden trencher in which to make bread, a few pewter plates, spoons, and other dishes, some axes and hoes, the iron parts of plows, a broadax, a froe, a saw and an auger.   Added to these were supplies of seed for field and vegetable crops, and a few fruit trees.   When their destination was reached the men and boys cut trees and built a log house, split boards with the froe and made a roof which was held on by weight poles, no nails be-ing available.   Puncheons were made by splitting logs and hewing the flat sides smooth for floors and door shutters. Some chimneys were made of split sticks covered on the in-side with a heavy coating of clay; but usually stones were used for this purpose, as they were plentiful.   The spaces between the log walls were filled in by mortar, called chinks and dobbin.   Rough bedsteads were fixed in the corners of the rooms farthest from the fire place, and rude tables and benches were constructed, with three-legged stools as seats. Pegs were driven into the walls, and on the horns of bucks the rifle was usually suspended above the door.   Windows were few and unglazed.   Then followed the spinning wheel, the reel, and the hand loom. Cards for wool had to be bought. The horses and cattle were turned into the woods to eat grass in summer and cane in winter, being enticed home at night by a small bait of salt or grain. The small trees and bushes were cut and their roots grubbed up, while the larger trees were girdled and left to die and become leafless. Rails were made and the clearing fenced in, the brush was piled and burnt, and the land was plowed and planted. After the first crop the settler usually had plenty, for his land was new and rich. Indeed, the older farmers of this region were so accustomed to clearing a "new patch" when the first was worn out, instead of restoring the old land by modern methods, that even at this time they know little or nothing of reclaiming exhausted land. Cooking was done on the open hearths by the women who dressed the skins of wild animals and brought water from the spring in rude pails, milked the cows, cut firewood, spun, wove, knit, washed the clothing, and tended the bees, chickens and gardens. When the men and boys were not at work in the fields they were hunting for game. After the first settlement time was found for cutting down the larger trees for fields, and the logs were rolled together by the help of neighbors and burned. The first rude cabin home was turned into a stable or barn and a larger and better log house constructed. When the logs had been hewed and notched neighbors were invited to help in raising the walls. The log-rollings and house-raisings were occasions for large dinners, some drinking of brandy and whiskey, games and sports of various kinds. There were no schools and no churches at first, and no wagon roads; but all these things followed slowly.

OTHER EARLY EXPLORERS. In the case of *Avery v. Walker*, (8 N. C., p. 117) it appears that Col. James Hubbard and Captain John Hill had "been members of Col. George Dohorty's party" and explored "the section of country around Bryson City, Swain county, shortly before April. 22, 1795"; that Col. John Patton, the father of Lorenzo and Montreville Patton of Buncombe, and who owned the meadow land on the Swannanoa river which was sold to George W. Vanderbilt by Preston Patton, and the "haunted house" at the ford of that river, when the stage road left South Main street at what is now Victoria Road and crossed the Swannanoa, there, instead of at Biltmore, was then county surveyor of Buncombe, and refused to survey land on Ocona Lufty for Waightstill Avery because it was "on the frontier and the Indian boundary had not then actually been run out, and it might be dangerous to survey near the line." Also that Dohorty's party had a battle with the Indians at the mouth of Soco creek, and that what is now Bryson city was then called Big Bear's village. In *Eu-Che-Lah v. Welch* (10 N. C., p. 158) will be found an exhaustive study of the laws of Great Britain in colonial days regarding the granting of Indian lands and of the various treaties made by the State with the Cherokee Indians since July 4, 1776.

NOTES.

[1]Roosevelt, Vol. III, 276 to 280.
[2]Ibid.
[3]Hill, pp. 32, 116.
[4]Ibid., p. 121
[5]Ibid., pp. 89, 90, 116.
[6]There were other Old Fields, doubtless made by Indians years before America was discovered, at the mouth of Gap creek in Ashe; at Valle Crucis in Watauga, at Old Fields of Toe in Avery, at "The Meadows" in Graham, and at numerous other level places.
[7]There is a family of Perkinses living at Old Field now, 1912, the descendants of Luther Perkins.
[8]Thwaites, p. 14.
[9]Ibid., p. 15, and Col. Rec., Vol. IV, p. 1073.
[10]From R. G. McGee's "A History of Tennessee."
[11]Ibid.
[12]Thwaites, pp. 46–47.
[13]Ibid., p. 37.
[14]Ibid., p. 41.
[15]Ibid., p. 42.
[16]Ibid., p. 48.
[17]Ibid., p. 59.
[18]Col. Rec., Vol. III, pp. xii and 194. Thwaite also says: "There was for a long time neither law nor gospel, upon this far-away frontier. Justices of the Peace had small authority. Preachers were at first unknown." "Daniel Boone," p. 33.
[19]Byrd, 60–61.
[20]Ibid, 62.
[21]Ibid, 63.
[22]Ibid.
[23]Ibid., 66–67.
[24]Ibid., 75–76.
[25]Ibid., 76.
[26]Ibid., 80–81.
[27]McGee, p. 214.
[28]Asheville's Centenary.
[29]Foote's Sketches, p. 83.
[30]Condensed from G. R. McGee's "A History of Tennessee."

CHAPTER IV

DANIEL BOONE

Just as seven cities contended for the honor of having been the birthplace of Homer; so, too, many states are proud to boast that Boone once lived within their borders. But North Carolina was the home of his boyhood, his young manhood and the State in which he chose his wife. From his home at Holman's Ford he passed to his cabin in the village of Boone on frequent occasions, making hunting trips from that point into the surrounding mountains. From there, too, he started on his trips into Kentucky.

From an address read by Miss Esther Ransom, daughter of the late U. S. Senator Matt. W. Ransom, to Thomas Polk Chapter, D. A. R., the following is copied :

"It has been argued that Boone did not fight in the Revolutionary war. This is true. He was too busy fighting Indians in Kentucky, the 'dark and bloody ground.' Let me impress it upon you that but for Boone and Clark and Denton and the other Indian fighters there wouldn't have been any Revolutionary war; no Kings Mountain, no Guilford Court House, no Yorktown. The Indians were natural allies of the British. British money supplied them with arms and ammunition and King George III was constantly inciting them through his officers, to murder and destroy the Patriots.

"Just suppose for a moment if, at Kings Mountain where the mountain men surrendered Ferguson they, in their turn, had been surrounded by five hundred or a thousand Indians. The day would have ended in dire disaster and it would have taken another Cæsar to have rescued the Patriots from that terrible predicament.

"Daniel Boone did as much or more service for our country in fighting Indians and keeping them back as if he had served in the war with Washington and Green.

"Like Washington, Boone was a surveyor. He surveyed nearly all the land in Kentucky. He was a law maker. He passed a law for the protection of game in Kentucky and also one for keeping up the breed of fine horses.

"Roosevelt in his vigorous English calls him 'Road-Builder, town-maker and Commonwealth founder,' and when Kentucky had representation in Virignia, Boone sat in the house of commons as a Burgess.

"He might be styled the 'Nimrod' of the United States, for truly 'He was a mighty hunter before the Lord.'"

JOHN FINLEY.   Finley was the Scotch-Irishman who had descended the Ohio river as far as Louisville in 1752; and who, after Boone's return from his trip to the Big Sandy in 1767, turned up at Boone's cabin at Holman's Ford in the winter of 1768–69.[1] He had suggested when on the Braddock expedition that Boone might reach Kentucky "by following the trail of the buffaloes and the Shawnese, northwestward through Cumberland gap."[2] "Scaling the lofty Blue Ridge, the explorers passed over Stone and Iron mountains and reached Holston Valley, whence they proceeded through Moccasin gap of Clinch mountain and crossed over intervening rivers and densely wooded hills until they came to Powell's Valley, then the furthest limits of white settlement. Here they found a hunters' trail which led them through Cumberland gap."[3] If they did this by the easiest and shortest route, they passed up the Shawnee trail on the ridge between Elk and Stony forks through Cooks gap, down by Three Forks of New river, through what is now Boone village and Hodges gap, across the Grave Yard gap down to Dog Skin creek, following the base of Rich mountain to State Line gap between Zionville and Trade to the head of Roan creek to the crossing of the two Indian trails at what is now Shoun's Cross Roads, and thence over the Iron mountains. Any other route would have been deliberately to go wrong for the sake of doing so. From any eminence that route seemed to have been marked out by nature.

BENJAMIN CUTBIRTH.   This name was pronounced Cutbaird according to the recollection of Cyrus Grubb, a prominent citizen of Watauga, and Benjamin Cuthbirth's name appears on the records of Ashe county as having conveyed 100 acres of land on the South Fork of New river to Andrew Ferguson in 1800. This is the same "Scotch-Irishman" who had married Elizabeth Wilcoxen, a neice of Daniel Boone, at the close of the French and Indian war, and when he was about twenty-three years old. In 1767 he and John Stuart, John Baker and John Ward, crossed the mountains and went to the Mississippi river, where they spent a year or two, going even to New Orleans.[4]

HOLMAN'S FORD.   About this time Daniel Boone moved sixty-five miles west from the Yadkin settlement near Dutchman's creek, "choosing his final home on the upper Yadkin, just above the mouth of Beaver creek. [5] Col. James M. Isbell's grantfather, Martin, told him that Daniel Boone used to live six miles below James M. Isbell's present home near the bank of the Yadkin river, on a little creek now known as Beaver creek, one mile from where it flows into the Yadkin river, near Holman's ford. The Boone house was in a little swamp and canebrake surrounding the point of a ridge, with but one approach—that by the ridge. The swamp was in the shape of a horse-shoe, with the point of the ridge projecting into it. The foundations of the chimney are still there, and the cabin itself has not been gone more than 52 years. Alfred Foster who owned the land showed Col. Isbell the cabin, which was still there during his boyhood, and he remembered how it looked. His grandmother, the wife of Benjamin Howard, knew Boone well as he often stayed with her father, Benjamin Howard, at the mouth of Elk creek, now Elkville. [6]

BOONE'S TRIP TO KENTUCKY. There is no evidence except the inscription on the leaning beech at Boone's creek, nine miles north of Jonesboro, Tenn., that Boone was at that spot in 1760. Thwaite's life of Boone, compiled from the Draper manuscript in the Wisconsin State library, says that in the spring of 1759, Boone and two of his sons went to Culpepper county, Virginia, where he was employed in hauling tobacco to Fredericksburg, and that he was again a member of Hugh Waddell's regiment of 500 North Carolinians, when, in 1761, they fought and defeated the Cherokees at Long Island on the Holston. He cites the inscription but gives no other facts. [7] As 1769 is generally considered the date of his first trip across the mountains, it becomes important to state that Thwaite (p. 69) says that, in 1767, Boone's brother-in-law, John Stewart, and Benjamin Cutbirth, who had married Boone's niece, and several others, went west as far as the Mississippi, crossing the mountains and returning before 1769; and that Boone himself, and William Hall, his friend, and, possibly, Squire Boone, Daniel's brother, in the fall of 1767, still desiring to get to Kentucky—of which he had been told by John Finley, whom he had met in the Braddock expedition—crossed the mountains into the valleys of the Holston, and the Clinch, and reached the headwaters of the west fork of the Big Sandy, returning to Holman's Ford in the spring of 1768.

COLONEL JAMES M. ISBELL. According to the statement made by this gentleman, in May, 1909, Benjamin Howard, his grandfather, owned land near the village of Boone, and used to range his stock in the mountains surrounding that picturesque village. He built a cabin of logs in front of what is now the Boys' Dormitory of the Appalachian Training School for the accommodation of himself and his herders whenever he or they should come from his home on the head waters of the Yadkin, at Elkville. Among the herders was an African slave named Burrell. When Col. Isbell was a boy, say, about 1845, Burrell was still alive, but was said to have been over one hundred years of age. He told Col. Isbell that he had piloted Daniel Boone across the Blue Ridge to the Howard cabin the first trip Boone ever took across the mountains.

BOONE'S TRAIL. [8] They went up the ridge between Elk creek and Stony Fork creek, following a well-known Indian trail, passed through what is now called Cook's gap, and on by Three Forks church to what is now Boone. There is some claim that Boone passed through Deep gap; but that is six miles further north than Cook's gap, and that much out of a direct course. If Boone wanted to go to Kentucky he knew his general course was northwest; and having reached the town of Boone or Howard's cabin, his most direct route would have been through Hodge's gap, down Brushy Fork creek two miles, and then crossing the Grave Yard gap to Dog Skin creek; then along the base of Rich mountain, crossing what was then Sharp's creek (now Silverstone) to the gap between what is now Zionville in North Carolina and Trade in Tennessee. He would then have been at the head of Roan's creek, down which he is known to have passed as far as what is now known as Shoun's Cross Roads. There, on a farm once owned by a Wagner and now by Wiley Jenkins, he camped. His course from there in a northwesterly direction would have led him across the Iron and Holston mountains to the Holston river and Powell's Valley. There is also a tradition that he followed the Brushy Fork creek from Hodge's gap to Cove creek; thence down Cove creek to Rock House branch at Dr. Jordan B. Phillips'—also a descendant of Benjamin Howard—across Ward gap to the Beaver Dams; then across Baker's gap to Roan's creek; thence down it to its mouth in the Watauga at what is now Butler, Tenn. Also, that when he got to the mouth of the Brushy fork he crossed over to the Beaver Dams through what has for many years been called George's gap; and thence over Baker's gap. [9] If he took either of these routes he preferred to cross two high mountains and to follow an almost due southwest course to following a well-worn and well-known Indian trail which was almost level and that led directly in the direction he wished to go. A road now leaves the wagon road nearly opposite the Brushy Fork Baptist church, about three miles from Boone, and crosses a ridge over to Dog Skin creek, and thence over the Grave Yard gap to Silverstone, Zionville, and Trade, thus cutting off the angle made by following Brushy Fork to its mouth. [10] Tradition says the Indian trail also crossed Dog Skin and the Grave Yard gap. Yet, while this seems to be the most feasible and natural trail, the venerable Levi Morphew, now well up in ninety, thinks Boone had a camp on Boone's branch of Hog Elk, two miles east of the Winding Stairs trail, by which he probably crossed the Blue Ridge, which would have taken him four miles northeast of Cook's gap, and Col. Bryan states that there is a tradition that Boone passed through Deep gap, crossed the Bald mountain and Long Hope creek, through the Ambrose gap and so into Tennessee. No doubt all these routes were followed by Boone during his hunting trips through these mountains prior to his first great treck into Kentucky; but on that important occasion it is more than probable that, as his horses were heavily laden with camp equipage, salt, ammunition and supplies, he followed the easiest, most direct, and most feasible route, and that was via Cook's gap, Three Forks, Hodges' gap, across Dog Skin, over the Grave Yard gap, to Zionville and Trade and thence to what is now known as Shoun's Cross Roads.

BOONE'S CABIN MONUMENT. The chimney stones of the cabin in which it is said that Boone camped while hunting in New river valley are still visible at the site of that cabin where it is said Boone was found one snowy night seated by a roaring fire when the young couple who had occupied it the night before and had allowed their fire to go entirely out, returned

from a trip to the Yadkin for a "live chunk" with which to
rekindle it; but which they had dropped in the snow when
almost at Boone's cabin, thus putting it out, and leaving them
as badly off as when they had set out that morning.   Boone
had struck fire from his flint and steel rifle and caught the spark
in tow, from which he had kindled his blaze.   Upon this site,
that public-spirited citizen, the venerable and well-informed
Col. W. L. Bryan, now in his 76th year, has erected an imposing stone and concrete monument, whose base is seven by
seven feet, with a shaft 26 feet in height.   On the side facing
the road is the following inscription, chiseled in white marble:
"Daniel Boone, Pioneer and Hunter; Born Feb. 11, 1735;
Died Sep. 26, 1820."   On the opposite side of the monument
on a similar stone is the following: "W. L. Bryan, Son of
Battle and Rebecca Miller Bryan; Born Nov. 19, 1837; Built
Daniel Boone Monument, Oct. 1912.   Cost $203.27."

BOONE'S WATAUGA RELATIVES. William Coffey married
Anna Boone, a sister of Jesse Boone and a neice of Daniel
Boone. She had another brother called Israel Boone. Jesse
Boone undoubtedly lived in a cabin which used to stand in a
field four miles from Shull's mills and two miles from Kelsey
post office, where he had cleared a field. The chimney foundation is still shown as his. On the 8th of July, 1823, Jesse
Boone conveyed to William and Alexander Elrod for $600
350 acres of land on Flannery's fork of New River and on
Roaring branch, about two miles southeast of Boone village;
adjoining land then being owned by John Agers, Jesse Council
and Russell Sams, and now owned in part by J. W. Farthing.
This deed was registered in Book M, page 391, of Ashe county
records, July 2, 1841. When Jesse Boone's sister, Anna Coffey, was nearly one hundred years old she talked with Mr.
J. W. Farthing while he was building a house for her grandson Patrick Coffey, on Mulberry creek, Caldwell county, in
1871. Mr. Mack Cook of Lenoir is a direct descendant of
Daniel Boone's brother, Israel, Boone and has a rifle and powder horn that used to belong to him. Arthur B. Boone of
Jacksonville, Fla., claims direct descent from Daniel Boone,
and his son Robbie E. Boone, has a razor said to have been the
property of Daniel Boone. There are many others who are
related to the Boone family. Col. W. L. Bryan thinks that
Thwaites is mistaken in stating that Rebecca Boone was the

daughter of Joseph Bryan, as her father's name was Morgan, from whom he himself and William Jennings Bryan are directly descended. [11] Smith Coffey was born in 1832 in Caldwell county, and says that Jesse was a brother of Daniel Boone, and had three daughters; Anna, who married William Coffey; Hannah, who married Smith Coffey, and Celie, who married Buck Craig. The Smith Coffey who married Hannah Boone was the present Smith Coffey's grandfather. Smith Coffey's father moved to Cherokee in 1838 and settled on Hiwassee river four miles above Murphy, after which he moved to Peach Tree creek where he died a year later, his family returning to Caldwell. In 1858 Smith returned to Cherokee and lived on a place adjoining the farm of George Hayes on Valley river, and had a fight with that gentleman concerning a sow just before the Civil War. Nevertheless he joined Hayes' company, when the war began, which became Company A in the Second N. C. Cavalry. After the battle before New Bern, Hayes resigned and returned to Cherokee, and William B. Tidwell of Tusquitte, now Clay county, was elected captain from the ranks, and retained that place till the close of the war.

THE HENDERSON PURCHASE. Although the purchase of Indian lands by white men had been prohibited by royal proclamation [12] as early as October 7, 1763, and although much of the territory was in the actual possession of the Indians, Richard Henderson and eight other private citizens determined to buy a large tract of land in Kentucky and the northern part of Middle Tennessee. To anticipate somewhat, it may be here stated that this intention was carried out but afterwards repudiated by both Virginia, which claimed the Kentucky portion, and North Carolina, which claimed the Tennessee tract, and Henderson and his associates were partially compensated by grants of much smaller bodies of land; [13] nevertheless, at the treaty of Hopewell, S. C., on the Keowee river, fifteen miles above its junction with the Tugaloo, on the 18th of December, 1785, Benjamin Hawkins, Andrew Pickens, Joseph Martin and Lachlan Campbell, commissioners representing the United States, had the face to deny the claim of the Indians to this identical territory— contending that they had already sold it to Henderson and associates. [14]

BOONE'S SPLIT-BULLET. About 1890 John K. Perry and another were felling trees in Ward's gap on Beaver Dams, Watauga county, when Perry's companion cut a bullet in two while trimming a young poplar. He remarked that it might have been fired there by Daniel Boone, as it was on his old trail. Perry said that whether Boone fired it or not it should be a Boone bullet thereafter. So, he filed two corners off a shingle nail and pressing the point of the nail thus filed on to the clean surface of the split bullet made the first part of a B. Then he finished the second part by pressing the nail below the first impression, and found he had a perfect B. Filing a larger nail in the same way he made the impression of a D, which completed Boone's initials. This was shown around the neighborhood for a number of years, and most people contended that the bullet really had been fired from Boone's rifle. But in June, 1909, Mr. Perry disclosed the joke rather than have the deception get into serious history.

DANIEL BOONE, THE PATH FINDER. From Chief Justice Walter Clark's "The Colony of Transylvania," (N. C. Booklet, Vol. iii, No. 9) we learn that Boone was a wagoner under Hugh Waddell in Braddock's campaign of 1755, when Boone was 21 years old; and that "in the following years he made the acquaintance of Col. Richard Henderson, who, struck with Boone's intelligence, and the opportunity for fortune offered by the new lands south of the Ohio, since known as Kentucky, organized a company, and employed Boone in 1763 to spy out the country[15] . . . Years passed before it took final shape. Boone is known to have made one of his visits to Kentucky in 1769, and was probably there earlier.[16] In 1773 he again attempted to enter Kentucky, carrying his family, but was driven back with the loss of six men killed by the Indians, among them his eldest son at Wallen's gap." But in 1768 Henderson had been appointed a judge, which position he held till 1773 and which probably delayed his land scheme; but in 1774 Nathaniel Hart, one of Henderson's partners, journeyed to the Otari towns to open negotiations with the Cherokees for the grant of suitable territory for a colony of whites. On March 17, 1775, the Overhill Cherokees assembled at the Sycamore Shoals of the Watauga, pursuant to an order of their chief, Oconostata, where a treaty

was made and signed by him and two other chiefs, Savanoo-
koo and Little Carpenter (Atta Culla Culla), by which, in
consideration of £12,000 in goods, the Cherokees granted the
lands between the Kentucky and Cumberland rivers, embracing one-half of what is now Kentucky and a part of Tennessee. But Dragging Canoe, a chief, had opposed a treaty
for four days, and never consented to it. The share of one
brave was only one shirt. But, the Cherokees had no title
to convey, as this land was a battle-ground where the hostile
tribes met and fought out their differences. Besides, this conveyance of the land by Indians was unlawful under both the
British and colonial laws. Henderson called this grant Transylvania.

As soon as Henderson thought this treaty would be signed
he started Boone ahead on March 10, 1775, with 30 men, to
clear a trail from the Holston to Kentucky—the first regular
path opened in the wilderness.

THE BOONE FAMILY. Many people of the mountains
claim descent or collateral relationship with Daniel Boone.
His father was Squire Boone, who was born in Devonshire,
England and came to Pennsylvania, between 1712 and 1714,
when he was about 21 years old. He maried Sarah Morgan
July 23, 1720. Their children were Sarah, Israel, Samuel,
Jonathan, Elizabeth, Mary, Daniel, George, Edward, Squire
and Hannah, all born at Otey, Penn. Daniel was the sixth
child and was born November 2, 1734. Edward was killed
by Indians when 36 years old, and Squire died at the age of
76. Daniel married Rebecca Bryan, daughter of Joseph, in
the spring of 1756. Daniel's children were James, Israel,
Susannah, Jemima, Lavinia, Rebecca, Daniel Morgan, John
B. and Nathan. The four daughters married. The two
eldest sons were killed by Indians, and the three younger
emigrated to Missouri.[17] None of Daniel's children was
named Jesse, but there was a Jesse Boone who lived just
west of the Blue Ridge, about four miles east of Shull's Mills
and one mile west of Kelsey postoffice in Watauga county,
N. C. This was on what has been called "Boone's Fork"
of Watauga river.

THE CALLOWAYS. Among the Kentucky pioneers was
Col. Richard Calloway[18]. Two of his daughters, Betsy and
Fanny, were captured with Jemima, Boone's second daugh-

ter, in a boat at Boonesborough, Ky., on the 17th of July, 1776. They were recovered unharmed soon afterwards;[19] and in the following August Betsy was married to Samuel Henderson, one of the rescuing party.[20] Jemima Boone afterwards married Flanders Calloway, a son of Colonel Calloway.[21] It was this Colonel Calloway who accused Boone of having voluntarily surrendered 26 of his men at the Salt Licks; that when a prisoner at Detroit he had engaged with Gov. Hamilton to surrender Boonesborough, and that he had attempted to weaken the garrison at Boonesborough before its attack by the Indians by withdrawing men and officers, etc.;[22] but Boone was not only honorably acquitted, but promoted from a captaincy to that of major. Related to this Colonel Calloway was Elijah Calloway, son of Thomas Calloway of Virginia, who "did much for the good of society and was a soldier at Norfolk, Va., in the War of 1812."[23] John Calloway represented Ashe county in the House in 1800, and in the Senate in 1807, 1808, 1809; and Elijah Calloway was in the House from 1813 to 1817, and in the Senate in 1818 and 1818, and 1819. One of these men is said to have walked to Raleigh, supporting himself on the way by shooting game, and in this way saved enough to build a brick house with glass windows, the first in Ashe, near what is now Obid. He was turned out of the Bear creek Baptist church because he had thus proven himself to be a rich man; and the Bible said no rich man could enter the kingdom of heaven. The church in which he was tried was of logs, but the accused sat defiantly during the trial in a splint-bottomed chair, which he gave to Mrs. Sarah Miller of that locality. This may have been Thomas Calloway, whose grave is at Obid, marked with a long, slender stone which had marked one of the camping places of Daniel Boone.[24]

AN IMPORTANT HISTORICAL CONTRIBUTION. Dr. Archibald Henderson, a descendant of Richard Henderson, published in the Charlotte (Sunday) *Observer*, between the 16th of March and the 1st of June, 1913, a series of articles entitled "Life and Times of Richard Henderson," in which much absolutely new matter is introduced, and numerous mistakes have been corrected in what has hitherto been accepted as history. It is especially valuable regarding the Regulators' agitation and the part therein borne by Richard Henderson.

Dr. Henderson is a member of the faculty of the University of North Carolina, of the State Library and Historical Association, and of the American Historical Association, and in the forthcoming volume, soon to appear, he will put the result of years of study and research into permanent form. He may be relied on to give adequate authority for every statement of importance concerning his remarkable kinsman and the times in which he lived.

HENDERSON'S SHARE IN BOONE'S EXPLORATIONS. Roosevelt, Ramsey and other historians have related the bare fact that Boone went on his first trip into Kentucky in 1764 at the instance of Richard Henderson; but in these papers the details of the association of the two men are set forth. Certainly as early as 1763, Boone and Henderson, then a lawyer, met, and discussed the territory lying to the west of the mountains. Henderson was seated as a Superior Court judge at Salisbury, March 5, 1868, and ceased to represent Boone as attorney in litigation then pending before the Superior Court of Rowan county; but in March, 1769, when the distinguished Waightstill Avery, then fresh from his birthplace, Norwich, Conn., and from Princeton College, where he had graduated in 1766, made his first appearance before the bar of that county, we are told that he might have seen also "the skilled scout and hunter, garbed in hunting shjrt, fringed leggings and moccasins, the then little known Daniel Boone," who attended that term of court in defence of a lawsuit, and must have (as shown by the sequel) conferred with Judge Henderson at this time about his contemplated trip into Tennessee and Kentucky in the interest of himself, John Williams and Thomas Hart, Henderson's first associates in the colonization enterprize he contemplated even at that early date, and while holding a commission as judge of the colony. [25]

THE SIX NATIONS' CLAIMS TO "CHEROKEE." Before Richard Henderson's appointment as judge by Governor Tryon in 1768, he and Hart and Williams had engaged Boone to spy out the western lands for them as early as 1764, though the proclamation of George IV, in 1763, forbidding the Eastern Colonists to settle on lands west of the Blue Ridge, may have retarded their plans for "securing title to vast tracts of western lands, and no move was made by Henderson to that end until after the treaty of Fort Stanwix in 1768, by which Great Britain had acquired by purchase from the Six Nations their unwarranted claim to all the territory east and southeast of the Ohio and north of the Tennessee rivers, which territory had always been claimed by the Cherokees, and that country was then known as "Cherokee." [26]

TITLE OF THE CHEROKEES. "The ownership of all the Kentucky region, with the exception of the extreme northeastern section, remained vested absolutely in the tribe of Cherokee Indians. Their title to the territory had been acknowledged by Great Britain through her Southern agent of Indian Affairs, John Stuart, at the Treaty of Lochaber in 1770." [27]

KING GEORGE'S PROCLAMATION MADE TO BE BROKEN? Dr. Henderson insists that the King's proclamation forbidding the acquisition of Indian lands by the settlers was universally disregarded by the settlers of the east. And while he points out that Richard Henderson obtained an "opinion, handed down by the Lord Chancellor and the Attorney General," which "cleared away the legal difficulties" in the way of securing "an indisputable title from the Indian owners and . . . to surmount the far more serious obstacle of Royal edict against the purchase of lands from the Indians by private individuals, he would doutbless have been justified in his purchase by the popular sentiment of the day in view of the universal disregard of the Royal Proclamation of 1763." Dr. Henderson points out that "George Washington expressed the secret belief of the period when he hazarded the judgment that the Royal Proclamation of 1763 was a mere temporary expedient to quiet the Indians, and was not intended as a permanent bar to Western Civilization. . . . George Washington, acquiring vast tracts of western land by secret purchase, indirectly stimulated the powerful army that was carrying the broadax westward. . . . It is no reflection upon the fame of George Washington to point out that, of the two, the service to the nation of Richard Henderson in promoting western civilization was vastly more generous in its nature and far-reaching in its results than the more selfish and prudent aims of Washington." [28]

HENDERSON'S TITLE. "The valid ownership of the territory being [now] actually vested in the Cherokees, Henderson foresaw that the lands could be acquired only by lease or by purchase from that tribe, and he forthwith set about acquiring an accurate knowledge of the territory in question. To get this information the services of Daniel Boone were secured, and the latter must have "conferred with Judge Henderson at Salisbury where he was presiding over the Superior Court, and plans were soon outlined for Boone's journey and expedition. At this time Boone was very poor and his desire to pay off his indebtedness to Henderson [lawyer's fees] made him all the more ready to undertake the exhaustive tour of exploration in company with Finley and others"; but "at the time of Boone's return to North Carolina Judge Henderson was embroiled in the exciting issues of the Regulation. His plan to inaugurate his great western venture was thus temporarily frustrated; but the dissolution of the Superior Court (under the judiciary act of 1767) took place in 1773," and left Richard Henderson free to act as he saw fit. [29]

HENDERSON AND DANIEL BOONE. "In the meantime, Daniel Boone grew impatient over the delay . . . and on September 25, 1773, started from the Yadkin Valley . . . for Kentucky, with a colony numbering eighteen men, besides women and children;" but, being attacked by Indians, and some of Boone's party, including his own son, having been killed, "the whole party scattered and returned to the settlements. This incident is significant evidence that Boone was deficient in executive ability, the power to originate and execute schemes of colonization on a grand scale . . . Boone lacked constructive leadership and executive genius. He was a perfect instrument for executing the designs of others. It was not until the creative and executive brain of Richard Henderson was applied to the vast and daring project of Western colonization that it was carried through to a successful termination." [30]

HENDERSON'S SCHEME DENOUNCED. "When, on Christmas Day, 1774, there was spread broadcast throughout the colony of North Carolina 'Proposals for the encouragement of settling the lands purchased by Messrs. Richard Henderson & Co., on the branches of the Mississippi river from the Cherokee tribe of Indians,' a genuine sensation was created." Archibald Neilson, deputy auditor of the colony, asked : "Is Richard Henderson out of his head?" and Governor Josiah Martin issued "a forcible-feeble proclamation against Richard Henderson and his confederates in their daring, unjust and unwarrantable proceeding.   In letters to the Earl of Dartmouth, Martin speaks scathingly of 'Henderson, the famous invader,' and of 'the infamous Henderson and his associates' whom he dubs 'an infamous company of land Pyrates.'   He denounced their project as a 'lawless undertaking,' and 'an infraction of the royal prerogative.'   But these 'fulminations' were unheeded and 'the goods already purchased were transported over the mountains in wagons to the Sycamore Shoals.' " [31]

FAILURE OF THE TRANSYLVANIA COLONY. "Serious dangers from without began to threaten the safety and integrity of the colony.   While the Transylvania legislature was in session, Governor Josiah Martin of North Carolina ingloriously fled from his 'palace', and on the very day that his emissary, a British spy, arrived at Boonesborough, Lord Dunmore, the royal governor of Virginia, escaped to the protection of the British vessel, the 'Fowey' . . .   At Oxford, N. C., on September 25, 1775, the proprietors of the Transylvania company drew up a memorial to the Continental Congress, then in session at Philadelphia, for the recognition of the Transylvania company as the fourteenth American colony; but this was refused "until it had been properly acknowledged by Virginia."   Application was then made to the Virginia convention at Williamsburg for recognition, but the effort of Henderson, assisted by Thomas Burke, was "defeated chiefly through the opposition of two remarkable men : George Rogers Clark, who represented the rival settlement of Harrodsburg in Kentucky, and Patrick Henry, who sought to extend in all directions the power and extent of the 'Ancient Dominion of Virginia.'   Under pressure of Henderson's representations, Virginia finally acknowledged the validity of the Transylvanians' claims against the Indians; but boldly confiscated the purchase, and made of Transylvania a county of Virginia.   Instead of the 20,000,000 acres obtained by the treaty of Sycamore Shoals, Virginia granted the company 200,000 acres between the Ohio and Green rivers, and North Carolina later granted to the company a like amount on Powell and Clinch rivers in Tennessee." [32]

HENDERSON AND JAMES ROBERTSON.   Dr. Archibald Henderson claims for his kinsman the honor of "having accom-

plished for Tennessee, in the same constructive way as he had
done for Kentucky [at Boonesborough], the pioneer task of
establishing a colony in the midst of the Tennessee wilderness, devising a system of laws and convening a legislature
for the passage of those laws." This was nothing less than
the settlement of Nashborough (now Nashville) and the country surrounding it; for he claims that "under Henderson's
direction Robertson made a long and extended examination
of the region in the neighborhood of the French Lick, just as
Boone in 1769–1771 had made a detailed examination under
Henderson's direction of the Kentucky area. Upon his return to the Watauga settlements on the Holston, Robertson
found many settlers ready and eager to take the great step
towards colonization of the new lands, inspired by the promise of Henderson and the enthusiastic reports of Robertson
and his companions." It was while Henderson was engaged
in surveying the line between Virginia and North Carolina—
"the famous line of latitude of 36° 30' "—"that the Watauga
settlers set out for the wilderness of the Cumberland. Part
of these settlers went by water—down the Tennessee and up
the Cumberland rivers—under the leadership of Col. John
Donelson, father of Mrs. Andrew Jackson, and the others,
under Robertson, overland. Donelson's diary records the
meeting of Richard Henderson on Friday, March 31, 1780.
Henderson not only supplied the party with all needed information but informed them that "he had purchased a quantity of corn in Kentucky to be shipped at the Falls of Ohio
(Lousville) for the Cumberland settlement. . . . James
Robertson's party had already arrived and built a few log
cabins on a cedar bluff above the 'Lick', when Donelson's
party arrived by boat, April 24,1780. Henderson himself arrived soon afterwards, and, assisted by James Robertson,
drew up and adopted a plan of civil government for the colony. A land office was established; the power to appoint
the entry-taker was vested in Henderson, as president of the
Transylvania company, and the Transylvania company was to
be paid for the lands at the rate of 26 lbs., 13 shillings and 4
pence, current money, a hundred acres, as soon as the company could assure the settlers a satisfactory and indisputable
title. This resulted in perpetual non-payment, since in 1783,
North Carolina, following Virginia's lead, expropriated the

lands of the Transylvania company, granting them in compensation a tract of 200,000 acres in Powell's Valley." Henderson returned to North Carolina, and died in 1785, aged fifty; and although memorials in his honor have been erected in Tennessee and Kentucky, his grave at Nutbush creek in North Carolina is unmarked; "and North Carolina has erected no monument as yet to the man who may justly be termed the founder of Kentucky and Tennessee." [33]

THE SHADOW OF COMING EVENTS. [34] "One sentence of this backwoods constitution [of Nashborough], remarkable in its political anticipation, is nothing less than that establishing for the first time in America the progressive doctrine of which so much is heard today, the recall of judges . . . and must forever be associated in American history with the names of Henderson and his coadjutor, Robertson : 'As often as the people in general are dissatisfied with the doings of the judges or triers so to be chosen, they may call a new election in any of the said stations, and elect others in their stead, having due respect to the number now agreed to be elected at each station, which persons so to be chosen shall have the same power with those in whose room they shall or may be chosen to act.'"

BOONE'S TRAIL. The North Carolina Society of the Daughters of the American Revolution marked Boone's trail in North Carolina by planting iron tablets bolted to large boulders at Cook's Gap, Three Forks' Church, Boone Village, Hodge's Gap, Graveyard or Straddle Gap, and at Zionville, in October, 1913. Addresses were made at Boone courthouse October 23, 1913, by Mrs. W. N. Reynolds, State Regent, Mrs. Lindsay Patterson, chairman of committee on Boone's trail, and Mrs. Theo. S. Morrison, Regent of Edward Buncombe Chapter.

RECORD EVIDENCE OF THE RESIDENCE OF THE BOONES. Jonathan Boone sold to John Hardin (Deed Book No. 5, p. 509, Ashe county) 245 acres on the 15th of September, 1821, for $600—on the North side of New river and on both sides of Lynches' Mill creek, adjoining Jesse Councill's line, and running to Shearer's Knob. This was near the town of Boone. The John Hardin mentioned above was the father of John and Joseph Hardin of Boone, and his wife was Lottie, the daughter of Jordan Councill, Sr., and the daughter of Benjamin Howard. On the 7th of November, 1814, Jesse Boone entered

100 acres on the head waters of Watauga river, beginning on a
maple, Jesse Coffey's corner, and obtained a grant therefor
on the 29th of November, 1817. (Deed Book "F," Ashe
county, p. 170.)

NOTES.

[1]Thwaites' "Daniel Boone," pp. 22, 69.
[2]Ibid., 23.
[3]Ibid., 73.
[4]Ibid., p. 66.
[5]Statement of James M. Isbell to J. P. A. in May, 1909, at latter's home.
[6]It "could still be seen, a few years ago, at the foot of a range of hills some seven and
a half miles above Wilkesboro, in Wilkes county." Thwaites' "Daniel Boone," p. 68.
[7]That inscription is not legible now. The picture of it opposite page 56 of Thwaites'
"Daniel Boone" shows that. If it had been made in 1760 it would not have been legible
in 1856 when Captain W. T. Pritchett of Jonesboro, Tennessee, was a boy, as he stated was
the case in June, 1909, to J. P. A.
[8]Some think Boone went down Brushy Fork to Dr. Phillips's present home on Cove
creek and crossed Phillips' gap to Beaver Dams and thence by Baker's gap to Roan's
creek. This, however, would not have brought him to Shoun's Cross Roads, below which
about three-fourths of a mile he is said to have made a camp on the old Wagner farm,
now owned by Wiley Jenkins.
[9]Dr. Jordan B. Phillips has always heard that George's gap is so called from George
Finley who so often hunted with Boone.
[10]Holland Hodges says Dog Skin creek is so called because settlers on it used to kill
all stray dogs to get their skins for tanning.
[11]Thwaites, 25.
[12]Martin's North Carolina, Vol. II, p. 339, cited in Fifth Annual Report of the Bureau
of Ethnology, 1883–84, p. 149.
[13]Ramsey's Annals of Tennessee, p. 204, cited in Fifth Annual Report of the Bureau of
Ethnology, 1883–84, p. 149.
[14]Fifth Annual Report of the Bureau of Ethnology, 1883–84, p. 153.
[15]Thwaites' "Life of Boone," p. 21.
[16]The only evidence of that is the inscription on the beech tree nine miles north of
Jonesboro, Tennessee, about killing a bear on that tree in 1760.
[17]Thwaites, pp. 1, 2, 25, 43.
[18]Thwaites' "Daniel Boone," p. 117.
[19]Ibid., p. 1356.
[20]Ibid., p. 143.
[21]Ibid., p. 158.
[22]Ibid., p. 165-7.
[23]"Footprints on the Sands of Time," by Dr. A. B. Cox, p. 106.
[24]Statement of T. C. Bowie, Esq., to J. P. A., in September, 1912.
[25]"Life and Times of Richard Henderson," Charlotte Observer, April 6, 1913.
[26]Ibid., May 11, 1913.
[27]Ibid.
[28]Ibid.
[29]Ibid.
[30]Ibid.
[31]Ibid.
[32]Ibid.
[33]Ibid., June 1.
[34]Ibid.

CHAPTER V

REVOLUTIONARY DAYS

OUR PART IN THE REVOLUTION.[1] In the summer of 1880 "the British were making a supreme effort to dismember the colonies by the conquest of the Southern States." "They thought," says Holmes, "that important advantages might be expected from shifting the war to the rich Southern colonies, which chiefly upheld the financial credit of the Confederacy in Europe, and through which the Americans received most of their military and other supplies." "The militiaman of Western North Carolina was unique in his way. Regarded by his government, in the words of Governor Graham, as 'a self-supporting institution,' he went forth to service generally without thought of drawing uniform, rations, arms or pay. A piece of white paper pinned to his hunting cap was his uniform; a wallet of parched flour or a sack of meal was his commissariat; a tin-cup, a frying-pan and a pair of saddle-bags, his only impedimenta; his domestic rifle—a Deckard or a Kutter—and sometimes a sword, made in his own blacksmith shop, constituted his martial weapons; a horse capable of 'long subsisting on nature's bounty' was his means of rapid mobilization or 'hasty change of base'; a sense of manly duty performed, his quarter's pay. Indeed, his sense of propriety would have been rudely shocked by any suggestion of reward for serving his endangered country. . . An expert rider and an unerring shot, he was yet disdainful of the discipline that must mechanaze a man into a soldier or convert a mob into an army . . . he was so tenacious of personal freedom as to be jealous of the authority of officers chosen by his vote."

THE MECKLENBURG RESOLVES. Alamance was but the forerunner of the declaration of independence at Mecklenburg, the proof of which follows :

Hon. George Bancroft, the historian, and at the time Minister to England, wrote to David L. Swain, at Chapel Hill, July 4, 1848, as follows : "The first account of the Resolves 'by the people in Charlotte Town, Mecklenburg County,' was

(93)

Robert Henry

(From a daguerreotype taken when he was in his 94th year.)

sent over by Sir James Wright, then Governor of Georgia, in a letter of the 20th of June, 1775. The newspaper thus transmitted is still preserved, and is in number 498 of the *South Carolina Gazette and Country Journal.* [1] Tuesday, June 13, 1775. I read the Resolves, you may be sure, with reverence, and immediately obtained a copy of them, thinking myself the sole discoverer. I do not send you the copy, *as it is identically the same with the paper you enclosed to me*, but I forward to you a transcript of the entire letter of Sir James Wright. The newspapers seem to have reached him after he had finished his dispatch, for the paragraph relating to it is added in his own handwriting, the former part being written by a secretary. . . . It is a mistake if any have supposed that the Regulators were cowed down by their defeat at Alamance."

THE MEN OF ASHE AND BUNCOMBE. As many of those who had taken part in the Mecklenburg Resolves bore their part in the Revolutionary War which followed, and then moved into Ashe and Buncombe counties, west of the Blue Ridge, the interest of their descendants in the reality of that heroic step is intense. As, also, many of these men were with Sevier and McDowell in the expedition to and battle of Kings Mountain, the following account of their experiences through the mountains of Western North Carolina and of the landmarks which still mark their old trails must be of equal importance.

WESTERN NORTH CAROLINIANS WON THE REVOLUTIONARY WAR. [3] After the battle of Alamance, the defiance declared at public meetings, the declaration of independence at Mecklenburg and at Halifax; after Gates' defeat at Camden, August 16, 1780, and Sumter's rout at Fishing creek, Cornwallis started northward to complete the conquest of Virginia and North Carolina. "At this dark crisis the Western North Carolinians conceived and organized and, with the aid which they sought and received from Virginia and the Watauga settlement [the latter being then a part of North Carolina] now in Tennessee, carried to glorious success at Kings Mountain on October 7, 1780, an expedition which thwarted all the plans of the British commander, and restored the almost lost cause of the Americans and rendered possible its final triumph at Yorktown on October 19, 1781. This

expedition was without reward or the hope of reward, undertaken and executed by private individuals, at their own
instance, who furnished their own arms, conveyances and
supplies, bore their own expenses, achieved the victory, and
then quietly retired to their homes, leaving the benefit of
their work to all Americans, and the United States their
debtors for independence."

VANCE, McDOWELL AND HENRY. "The white occupation
of North Carolina had extended only to the Blue Ridge when
the Revolution began"; but at its close General Charles
McDowell, Col. David Vance and Private Robert Henry were
among the first to cross the Blue Ridge and settle in the new
county of Buncombe. ⁴ As a reward for their services, no
doubt, they were appointed to run and mark the line between
North Carolina and Tennessee in 1799, McDowell and Vance
as commissioners and Henry as surveyor.   While on this work
they wrote and left in the care of Robert Henry their narratives of the battle of Kings Mountain and the fight at Cowan's
ford.   After his death Robert Henry's son, William L. Henry,
furnished the manuscript to the late Dr. J. F. E. Hardy, and
he sent it to Dr. Lyman C. Draper, of Wisconsin.   On it is
largely based his "King's Mountain and its Heroes" (1880).

DAVID VANCE.   He was the grandfather of Governor and
General Vance; "came south with a great tide of Scotch-Irish
emigration which flowed into the Piedmont country from
the middle colonies between 1744 and 1752, and made his
home on the Catawba river, in what is now Burke, and was
then Rowan county, where he married Miss Brank about
1775; and here, pursuing his vocation as a surveyor and teacher,
the beginning of the Revolutionary war found him.   He was
one of the first in North Carolina to take up arms in support
of the colonies, and in June, 1776, was appointed ensign in
the second North Carolina regiment of Regular Continental
troops, and shortly thereafter was promoted to a lieuten-
ancy, and served with his regiment until May or June, 1778,
"when the remnant of that regiment was consolidated with
other North Carolina troops. He served at Brandywine,
Germantown, Monmouth, and was with Washington at Valley Forge through the terrible winter of 1777-78.   In command
of a company he fought at Ramseur's Mill, Cowpens, and
King's Mountain in 1780-81.   His son David was the father

of Zebulon and Robert B. Vance, the United States senator
and Confederate general respectively, was a prominent and
influential citizen of his time, and a captain in the War of
1812, which, however, terminated before his regiment reached
the theater of war.

CAPTAIN WILLIAM MOORE. He was from Ulster county,
Ireland, and was the first white man to settle west of the
Blue Ridge in Buncombe. He was with his brother-in-law,
Griffith Rutherford when that officer came through Buncombe
in 1776 on his way to punish the Cherokees, and was struck
with the beauty and fertility of the spot on which he afterwards settled, six and a half miles west of Asheville, the present residence, remodeled and enlarged, of Dr. David M.
Gudger. He was a captain of one of Rutherford's companies. He returned in 1777 and built a fort on the site
above referred to, obtaining a grant for 640 acres from Governor Caswell soon afterwards, for "land on Hominy creek,
Burke county." But he had to leave his new home for the
Revolutionary War, in which he served gallantly, returning
at its close with his own family—his wife being Gen. Rutherford's sister—and five others. He had three sons, William,
Samuel, and Charles, and three daughters, all of whom married Penlands, brothers. William and Samuel moved to
Georgia, and Charles, the youngest, fell heir to the home
place. Of him Col. Allen T. Davidson says in *The Lyceum* for
April, 1891, page 24, that he had been born in a fort on Hominy creek "and was one of the most honorable, hospitable,
open-hearted men it was my good fortune to know, whom
I was taught by my parents to revere and respect; and I can
now say I never found in him anything to lessen the high estimate placed upon him by them."

MOUNTAIN TORIES. There was a man named Mills mentioned in "The Heart of the Alleghanies" as living in Henderson county during the Revolutionary War; local tradition says there was a Tory named Hicks who at some time
during the Revolutionary War built himself a pole cabin on
what is now the Meadow Farm near Banners Elk; but which
was for years known as Hick's Improvement. Benjamin Howard built what is known as the Boone cabin for the accommodation of himself and his herders when they were looking after
the cattle grazing on the mountains near what is now the

town of Boone. Howard's Knob, where he is said to have
had a cave, and Howard's creek are named for him. His
daughter Sarah married Jordan Council, Sr., a prominent
citizen, and they lived near the oak tree that has buck-horns
embedded in its trunk, near Boone village. There is also here,
at the spring, a large sycamore tree which grew from a switch
stuck in the moist soil by Jesse Council, eldest son of Jordan
Council, about one hundred years ago. Howard was a Tory.
Some of the Norris family are said to have been Tories also;
and two men, named White and Asher, were killed by the
Whigs near Shull's Mills during the Revolutionary War. [5]
There were, doubtless, other Tories hidden in these mountains
during those troublous times. Daniel Boone himself was not
above suspicion, and escaped conviction under charges of disloyalty at Boonesborough, Ky., by pleading that his acts of
apparent disloyalty were due to the fact that he had been
"playing the Indians in order to gain time for getting rein-
forcements to come up." [6]

THE NORRIS FAMILY. William Norris settled on Meat
Camp, and his brother Jonathan on New river, about 1803,
probably, as William was less than ninety when he died in 1873.

THOMAS HODGES came to Hodges' gap one, and a half miles
west of what is now Boone, during the Revolutionary War.
He came from Virginia, and brought his family with him. He
was a Tory and was seeking to keep out of taking up arms
against Great Britain when he came to his new home. There
was a Norris in this section who was also a Tory. Thomas
Hodges' son Gilbert married a daughter of Robert Shearer who
lived on New River, three miles from Boone, and died there
about 1845. Robert Shearer was a Scotchman who had fought
in the American army. In 1787 Gilbert was born, and lived at
the place of his birth in Hodges' gap till his death in December,
1862. Hollard Hodges, a son of Gilbert, was born there
July 18, 1827, and is still there. He still remembers that
about 1856 he and Jordan McGhee in one day killed 432
rattlesnakes on a rocky and cliffy place on the Rich mountain
about three miles from Boone; and that he has always heard
that Ben. Howard had entered all the land about Hodges gap.
His wife was born Elizabeth Councill, and is a grand-doughter
of Jordan Councill, Sr., whose wife was Sallie, daughter of
Ben. Howard.

HENDERSON COUNTY HEROES. In her history of Henderson county, written for this work, Mrs. Mattie S. Candler says, "here are unquestionably numbers of quiet sleepers in the little old and neglected burying grounds all over the county who followed Shelby and Sevier at Kings Mountain," and mentions the grandfather of Misses Ella and Lela McLean and Mrs. Hattie Scott as having fought against his immediate relatives in the British army on that occasion, receiving a severe wound there. Elijah Williamson is said to have lived in Henderson county on land now owned by Preston Patton, his great grandson. Williamson was born in Virginia, moved to Ninety-Six, S. C., and afterwards settled on the Patton farm, where he planted five sycamore trees, naming each for one of his daughters. They still stand. Samuel Fletcher, ancestor of Dr. G. E. Fletcher and of Mrs. Wm. R. Kirk and Miss Estelle Edgerton of Hendersonville, owned an immense tract adjoining the Patton farm, to which it is supposed he came about the time that Elijah Williamson did.

DESCENDANTS OF REVOLUTIONARY HEROES. Representatives of several Revolutionary soldiers reside in these mountains, among whom are the Alexanders, Davidsons, Fosters, McDowells, Coffeys, Bryans, Penlands, Wisemans, Allens, Welches, and scores of others, who fought in North Carolina. Others are descendants of Nathan Horton, who was a member of the guard at the execution of Major Andre, when he carried a shot-gun loaded with one ball and three buckshot. J. B. Horton, a direct descendant, has the gun now. J. C. Horton, who lives on the South Fork of the New River, near Boone, has a grandfather's clock which his ancestor, Nathan Horton, brought with him from New Jersey over one hundred years ago. The late Superior Court Judge, L. L. Greene of Boone, and the Greenes of Watauga generally, trace their descent directly from General Nathanael Greene, who conducted the most masterly retreat of the Revolutionary War, when he slowly retired before Cornwallis from Camden to Yorktown, and won the applause of even the British. [7]

THE OLD FIELD. Where Gap creek empties into the South Fork of New River is a rich meadow on which, according to tradition, there has never been any trees. It has been called the "old field" time out of mind. It was here that Col. Cleveland was captured by a notorious Tory named Riddle

and his followers during the Revolutionary War. [8]   The apple
tree under which it is said he was seated when surprised and
captured is still standing in the yard of the old Luther Perkins home, [9] now occupied by a son of Nathan Waugh.   The
tree is said to be 180 years old.   It is three feet in diameter six feet from the ground, and still bears fruit.   It is
said that Mrs. Perkins sent her daughter to notify Ben Greer
and Joseph Calloway of Cleveland's capture and that they
followed him by means of twigs dropped in the river as he
was led up stream, having joined the party of Captain Cleveland, who had gone in pursuit.   Greer lived four miles above
Old Field and Calloway two miles below.   It is said that
Greer shot one of the captors at Riddle's knob, to which
point Cleveland had been taken, and that the rest fled, Cleveland himself dropping behind the log on which he had been
seated while slowly writing passes for his captors.   It is also
claimed that Ben. Greer fired the shot which killed Col. Ferguson at Kings Mountain.   [10]Roosevelt says Ferguson was
pierced by half a dozen bullets.   (Vol. iii, 170).

THE WOLF'S DEN.   Riddle's knob is ten miles north of
Boone, and is even yet a "wild and secluded spot, being very
near the noted Elk Knob, the place where this noted Tory
had his headquarters.   It is known as the "Wolf's Den," and
is the place where the early settlers caught many young
wolves."   About 1857 Micajah Tugman found Riddle's
knife in the crevices of the Wolf's Den.   It was of peculiar
design, the "jaws" being six inches long, and the handle was
curved. [11]

BENJAMIN CLEVELAND.   This brave man was born in Virginia May 26, 1738.   When thirty-one years of age he came
to North Carolina to live, settling in Wilkes county.   In 1776
he became a Whig.   He was himself somewhat cruel, as it is
related of him that "some time after this (his capture at Old
Field) this same Riddle and his son, and another was taken,
and brought before Cleveland, and he hung all three of them
near the Mulberry Meeting House, now Wilkesborough." [12]
Cleveland weighed over three hundred pounds, and his men
called him "Old Roundabout," and themselves "Cleveland's
Bull Dogs."   The Tories, however, called them "Cleveland's
Devils."   He was a captain in Rutherford's expedition across
the mountains to punish the Cherokees in 1776, for which

service he was made a colonel, and as such rendered great service in suppressing Tory bands on the frontier. He raised a regiment of four hundred men in Surry and Wilkes counties and with them took part in Kings Mountain fight. Before he died he weighed over 450 pounds, but was cheerful and witty to the end, which came in October, 1806. [13]

DR. DRAPER'S ACCOUNT. In his "Kings Mountain and Its Heroes," Dr. Draper tells us (Ch. 19, p. 437, *et seq.*) that the Old Fields belonged to Colonel Cleveland, and served, in peaceful times, as a grazing region for his stock, and there his tenant, Jesse Duncan, resided. On Saturday, April 14, 1881, accompanied only by a negro servant, Cleveland rode from his "Round About" plantation on the Yadkin to the Old Fields, where he spent the night. Captain William Riddle, a son of Col. James Riddle of Surry county, both of whom were Royalists, was at that time approaching Old Field from Virginia, with Captain Ross, a Whig captive, and his servant, enroute to Ninety Six, in South Carolina. Captain Riddle's party of six or eight men, reached the home of Benjamin Cutbirth, some four miles above Old Field, on the afternoon of the day that Cleveland arrived at Jesse Duncan's, and abused Cutbirth, who was a Whig and suffering from wounds he had but recently sustained in the American cause. Riddle, however, soon left Cutbirth's and went on to the upper end of Old Fields, where Joseph and Timothy Perkins resided, about one mile above Duncan's. Both these men were absent in Tory service at the time; but Riddle learned from their women that Cleveland was at Duncan's "with only his servant, Duncan and one or two of the Calloway family." Riddle, however, was afraid to attack Cleveland openly, and determined to lure him into an ambush the next morning. Accordingly, that night, he had Cleveland's horses secretly taken from Duncan's to a laurel thicket "just above the Perkins house," where they were tied and left. But, it so happened, that on that very Saturday, Richard Calloway and his brother-in-law, John Shirley, went down from the neighboring residence of Thomas Calloway, to see Col. Cleveland, where they remained over night. On the following (Sunday) morning, discovering that his horses were missing, Cleveland and Duncan, each with a pistol, and Calloway and Shirley, unarmed, went in pursuit, following the

tracks of the stolen horses, just as Riddle had planned.
"Reaching the Perkins place, one of the Perkins women,
knowing of the ambuscade, secretly desired to save the Colonel from his impending fate, and detained him as long as she
could, while his three companions went on, Cleveland following some little distance behind." She also followed, retard-
ing Cleveland by enquiries, until his companions had crossed
the fence that adjoined the thicket, where they were fired
upon by Riddle's men from their places of concealment.
Calloway's thigh was broken by the shot of Zachariah Wells,
but Duncan and Shirley escaped. Cleveland "dodged into
the house with several Tories at his heels." There he surrendered on condition that they would spare his life; but
when Wells arrived he swore that he would kill Cleveland
then and there, and would have done so had not the latter
"seized Abigal Walters and kept her between him and his
would-be assassin." Riddle, however, soon came upon the
scene and ordered Wells to desist; after which, "the whole
party with their prisoner and his servant were speedily
mounted and hurried up New river," traveling "mostly in
its bed to avoid being tracked, in case of pursuit." Two
boys, of fourteen and fifteen, "Daniel Cutbirth and a youth
named Walters," had resolved to waylay Riddle on his return
to Benjamin Cutbirth's, and rescue whatever prisoners he
might have with him; but they were deterred from their purpose by the size and noise of Riddle's party as they passed
their place of concealment that Sunday morning. Riddle's
party got dinner at Benjamin Cutbirth's where one of Cutbirth's daughters was abused and kicked by Riddle because
of her reluctance in serving Riddle's party. After dinner
Riddle's party proceeded up the bed of New river to the
mouth of Elk creek, where the new and promising town of
Todd now flourishes at the terminus of a new railroad now
building from Konarok, Va., Cleveland meanwhile breaking
off overhanging twigs and dropping them in the stream as a
guide to his friends who, he knew, would soon follow in pursuit. "From the head of the south fork of Elk, they ascended up the mountains in what has since been known as
Riddle's Knob, in what is now Watauga county, and some
fourteen miles from the place of Cleveland's captivity,"
where they camped for the night. Meantime, early that

Sabbath morning, Joseph Calloway and his brother-in-law, Berry Toney, had called at Duncan's, and hearing firing in the direction of Perkins's home, hastened there; but, meeting Duncan and Shirley in rapid flight, they learned from them that Richard Calloway had been left behind for dead and that Cleveland was either dead or captured. Duncan, Shirley and Toney then went to notify the people of the scattered settlements to meet that afternoon at the Old Fields, while Joseph Calloway rode to Captain Robert Cleveland's place on Lewis Fork of the Yadkin river, a dozen miles distant. His brother, William Calloway, started forthwith up New river and soon came across Benjamin Greer and Samuel McQueen, who readily joined them, and together they followed Riddle's trail till night overtook them ten miles above the Old Fields, where Calloway and McQueen remained, while Greer returned to pilot whatever men might have gathered to engage in the pursuit of the Tories. Greer soon met Robert Cleveland and twenty others at the Old Fields, and all started at once, reaching Calloway and McQueen before day Monday morning. John Baker joined Calloway and McQueen to lead the advance as spies or advance guards; and, soon after sunrise, the nine men who were in advance of the others fired upon Riddle's party, while Cleveland tumbled behind the log on which he was slowly writing passes for his Tory captors. But Wells alone was shot, being hit as he scampered away by William Calloway, and was left as it was supposed that he had been mortally wounded. Riddle and his wife mounted horses and escaped with the others of his band. "Cleveland's servant, who had been a pack-horse for the Tory plunderers," was rescued with his master. Captain Ross, Riddle's Virginia prisoner, was also rescued. Shortly after this Riddle captured on Kings creek at night two of Cleveland's noted soldiers, David and John Witherspoon, who resided with their parents on Kings creek, and spirited them many miles away in the mountain region on Watauga river. Here they escaped death by taking the oath of allegiance to the King of England, and were released; but as soon as they reached their home, David hastened to notify Col. Ben. Herndon, several miles down the Yadkin, who with a party of men, under the guidance of the Witherspoon brothers, returned and captured Riddle and two of his noted associates,

Reeves and Gross, who were taken to Wilkesboro and "executed on the hill adjoining the village on a stately oak. . . . Mrs. Riddle," who seems to have accompanied her husband on his wild and reckless marauds, "was present and witnessed his execution." Wells had been captured and hanged by Cleveland a short time before. (P. 446.)

DAVID AND JOHN WITHERSPOON. Of these heroes Dr. Draper says (p. 461), "David was a subordinate officer—perhaps a lieutenant— in Cleveland's regiment at Kings mountain, and his younger brother John was a private." They were of Scotch origin, but natives of New Jersey. David was born in 1758 and John in 1760. They were collateral relatives of John Witherspoon, president of Princeton college, and a signer of the Declaration of Independence. Each afterwards represented Wilkes in the legislature. David died in May 1828 while on a visit to South Carolina, and John in Wayne county, Tenn., in 1839. Captain William Harrison Witherspoon, of Jefferson, was descended from John Witherspoon, and was born near Kings creek, January 24, 1841. He was a sergeant major of the 1st N. C. Infantry, was shot in the leg at Seven Pines in 1862, and in the forehead at Spottsylvania Court House, May 12, 1864, returning for duty in less than two months. He surrendered with Lee at Appomattox, after serving four years and nine days in the Confederate army. His wife was born Clarissa Pennell in Wilkes county. In the Spring of 1865, while seven of Stonemen's men—three negroes and four white men—were trying to break into her father's stable near Wilkesboro, for the purpose of stealing her father's horses and mules, she warned them that if they persisted she would shoot; and as they paid her no heed, she did actually shoot and kill one of the white robbers, and the rest fled. Gen. Stoneman, when he heard of her conduct, sent her a guard and complimented her highly for her courage and determination.

THE PERKINS FAMILY. J. D. Perkins, Esq., an attorney at Kendrick, Va., in a letter to his brother, L. N. Perkins, at Boone, N. C., of date December 1, 1913, says that his ancestors Joseph and Timothy Perkins were tax gatherers under the colonial government of Massachusetts about the commencement of the Revolutionary War, but removed to Old Fields, Ashe county on account of political persecution. They remained loyal to the King during the whole of the Revolutionary War, and Timothy was killed somewhere in Ashe in a Tory skirmish. Timothy left several sons and one daughter, Lucy, J. D. Perkin's great grandmother, who married a man named Young. Joseph also left sons and daughters. "I have forgotten the names of most of our great grand uncles," wrote J. D. Perkins in the letter above mentioned, "but I remember to have heard our mother tell about seeing 'Granny Skritch,' a sister to our great-great-grandfather, and who was very old at that time, and living with one of her Perkins relatives up on Little Wilson. Our mother was then quite small and the old lady (Granny Skritch) was very old and confined to her bed; but our mother was impressed with Granny Skritch's loyalty, even then, to King George, and the manner in which she abused the Patriot soldiers in her talk."

OTHER IMPORTANT FACTS. Dr. Draper says (p. 435), "In the summer of 1780 he (Cleveland) was constantly employed in surpressing the Tories—first in marching against those assembled at Ramsour's mill, reaching them shortly after their defeat; then in chasing Col. (Samuel) Bryan from the State, and finally in scouring the region of New River including the Tory rising in that quarter, capturing and hanging some of their notorious leaders and outlaws."

CLEVELAND'S CHARACTER. Dr. Draper tries to temper the facts of Benjamin Cleveland's career as much as possible, but that this hero of the Revolutionary War was inhumanly cruel, cannot be disguised. His compelling a horse-thief, socalled— for he had not been tried—to cut off his own ears with a case knife in order to escape death by hanging, was inexpressibly revolting. (P. 447). Cleveland lost his "Round About Farm" "by a better title" at the close of the war, and moved to the "fine region of the Tugalo on the western border of South Carolina" and "though the Indian title was not yet extinguished," he resolved to be among the early squatters of the country, and "removed to his new home in the forks of the Tugalo river and Chauga creek in the present county of Oconee" in 1785. He served many years as a "judge of the Court of Old Pendleton county, with General Pickens and Col. Robert Anderson as his associates, . . . 'frequently taking a snooze on the bench' says Governor B. F. Perry, while the lawyers were making long and prosy speeches." He was defeated for the legislature in 1793 by seven votes. "He had scarcely any education," and "was despotic in his nature" declares Dr. Draper; but "North Carolina deservedly commemorated his services by naming a county after him." Here he died and was buried; but "no monument—no inscription—no memorial stone—point out his silent resting place." (P. 453-4.)

ASHE A BATTLE GROUND. From Robert Love's pension papers it appears that the first battle in which he took part was when he was in command of a party of Americans in 1880 against a party of Tories in July of that year. This band of Tories was composed of about one hundred and fifty men, and they were routed "up New River at the Big Glades, now in Ashe county, North Carolina, as they were on the way to join Cornwallis." "In the year 1780 this declarent was engaged against the Torys at a special court first held on Toms creek down the New river, and afterwards upon Cripple creek; then up New river . . . then, afterwards at the Moravian Old Town . . . making an examination up to near the Shallow Ford of the Yadkin . . . routing two parties of Tories in Guilford county, hanging one of the party who fell into his hands up the New River, and another, afterwards, whom they captured in Guilford." This activity may explain the presence of the mysteriuos battle ground in Alleghany county. (See ch. 13, "A Forgotten Battlefield.")

THE BIG GLADES. This may be the Old Field, and it is most probable that this is the spot reached and lauded by Bishop Spangenberg in 1752. (See ch. 3, "In Goshen's Land.")

But whether they are identical with that locality or not, the following is an account of that well-known spot:

SHORT STORY OF AN OLD PLACE. This land was granted to Luther Perkins by grant No. 599, which is recorded in Ashe county July 28, 1904, Book WW, page 254. But the grant itself is dated November 30, 1805, while the land was entered in May, 1803. This tract is the one on which the apple tree stands under which Cleveland is said to have been captured; but it is probably not the first tract nor the best, which was conveyed by Charles McDowell, a son of Gen. Charles McDowell of Revolutionary fame, to Richard Gentry for $1,000 in

1854. There seems to be several hundred acres in that boundary, beginning on a Spanish oak in the line of Joseph Perkins's
Old Field Tract, and crossing Gap creek. There is no record in
Ashe county, of how Charles McDowell got this place, though
he probably inherited it. Richard Gentry divided his property
into three parts, two in land and one in slaves. Adolphus
Russeau, who married one of Gentry's daughters got the land
now owned by Arthur Phillips. Nathan Waugh got the other
tract, while James Gentry, a son, took the slaves. It was on
this tract that the first 100 bushels of corn to the acre of land
in Ashe county was raised by Richard Gentry. He was a member of the family of whom Dr. Cox said in his "Foot Prints,"
(p. 110): "The Gentry family have been distinguished for
their principles and patriotic love of constitutional liberty and
justice." Of Hon. Richard Gentry himself he said (p. 116):
"He married a Miss Harboard and his residence was at Old
Field. He was a Baptist preacher, justice of the peace and
clerk of the Superior Court and a member of both branches
of the legislature."

SWORD-TILT BETWEEN HERNDON AND BEVERLY. "The
depredations of the Tories were so frequent, and their conduct
so savage, that summary punishment was demanded by the
exigencies of the times. This Cleveland inflicted without
ceremony. General Lenoir relates a circumstance that occurred at Mulberry Meeting-house. While there, on some public occasion, the rumor was that mischief was going on by the
Tories. Lenoir went to his horse, tied at some distance from
the house, and, as he approached, a man ran off from the opposite side of the horse. Lenoir hailed him, but he did not stop;
he pursued him and found that he had stolen one of the stirrups of his saddle. He carried the pilferer to Colonel Cleveland, who ordered him to place his two thumbs in a notch for
that purpose in an arbor fork, and hold them there while he
ordered him to receive fifteen lashes. This was his peculiar
manner of inflicting the law, and gave origin to the phrase,
'To thumb the notch.' The punishment on the offender
above was well inflicted by Captain John Beverly, whose
ardor did not stop at the ordered number. After the fifteen
had been given, Colonel Herndon ordered him to stop, but
Beverly continued to whip the wincing culprit. Colonel
Herndon drew his sword and struck Beverly. Captain Bev-

erly drew also, and they had a tilt which, but for friends, would have terminated fatally." [14]

SHAD LAWS' OAK. There is a tree on the public road in Wilkes, which to this day bears the name of "Shad Laws' Oak," on which the notches, thumbed by said Laws under the sentence of Cleveland, are distinctly visible. [15]

SEVIER, THE HARRY PERCY OF THE REVOLUTION. When "General Charles McDowell, finding his force too weak to stop Ferguson," "crossed the mountains to the Watauga settlements, he found the mountaineers ready to unite against the hated Ferguson. . . . These hardy men set out to search for Ferguson on September 25 (1780). They were armed with short Deckard rifles, and were expert shots. They knew the woods as wild deer do, and from boyhood had been trained in the Indian ways of fighting. They furnished their own horses and carried bags of parched flour for rations." [16]

According to Dr. Lyman C. Draper's "Kings Mountain and Its Heroes," page 176, Sevier followed the Gap creek from Mathew Talbot's Mill, now known as Clark's Mill, three miles from Sycamore Shoals, "to its head, when they bore somewhat to the left, crossing Little Doe river, reaching the noted 'Resting Place,' at the Shelving Rock, about a mile beyond the Crab Orchard, where, after a march of some twenty miles that day, they took up their camp for the night. . . . Here a man named Miller resided, who shod several of the horses of the party." The next morning, Wednesday, the twenty-seventh (of September, 1880,) . . . they reached the base of the Yellow and Roan mountains and ascended the mountain by following the well-known Bright's Trace, through a gap between the Yellow mountain on the north and the Roan mountain on the south. The sides and top of the mountain were "covered shoe-mouth deep with snow." On the 100 acres of "beautiful table land" on top they paraded and discharged their short Deckard rifles; "and such was the rarity of the atmosphere, that there was little or no report." Here two of Sevier's men deserted. They were James Crawford and Samuel Chambers, and were suspected of having gone ahead to warn Ferguson of Sevier's approach. Sevier did not camp there, however, as there was still some hours of daylight left after the parade and refreshments, but "passed on a couple of miles, descending the eastern slope of the mountains into Elk Hollow, a slight depression between the Yellow and Roan mountains, rather than a gap; and here, at a fine spring flowing into Roaring creek, they took up their camp for the night. Descending Roaring creek on the 28th four miles they reached its confluence with the North Toe river, and a mile below they passed Bright's place, now Avery's; and thence down the Toe to the noted spring on the Davenport place, since Tate's, and now known as the Childs place, a little distance west of the stream."

HAYWOOD IN THE REVOLUTIONARY WAR.

"Long before white people had come into the mountain country, all the land now included in Haywood county was occupied by the warlike Cherokees. As the western frontier of civilization, however, approached the Indian territory, the simple natives of the hills retired farther and farther into the fastnesses of the mountains. While the Regulators were resisting Tryon at Alamance and the patriots under Caswell and Moore were bayonetting the Tories at Moore's Creek Bridge, the Cherokees of what is now Haywood county were smoking their pipes in peace under the shadows of Old Bald or hunting along the banks of the murmuring Pigeon and its tributaries.

"When, however, the tide of western immigration overflowed the French Broad and began to reach the foothills of the Balsams the Cherokees, ever friendly as a rule to the white man, gave up their lands and removed to the banks of the Tuckaseigee, thus surrendering to their white brothers all the land eastward of a line running north and south between the present town of Waynesville and the Balsam range of mountains. Throughout the period of the early settlement of Haywood county and until the present the most friendly relations have existed between the white people and the Cherokees.

"Only one incident is given by tradition which shows that any hostile feeling existed at any time. It is related that a few Indians from their settlement on the Tuckaseigee, before the close of the eighteenth century, went across the Smoky mountains into Tennessee and stole several horses from the settlers there. A posse of white men followed the redskins, who came across the Pigeon on their way home, encamped for the night on Richland near the present site of the Hardwood factory in Waynesville. While encamped for the night, their white pursuers came up, fired into them, recaptured the horses, and began their journey back to Tennessee. The Indians, taken by surprise, scattered, but soon recovered themselves and went in pursuit of the white men. At Twelve Mile creek they came upon the whites encamped for the night. Indian fashion they made an attack, and in the fight which ensued one white man by the name of Fine was killed. The Indians, however, were driven off. Before leaving their camp next morning the white men took the body of their dead comrade, broke a hole in the ice which covered the creek, and put him in the ice cold water to remain until they could return for the body. A big snow was on the ground at the time, and it was bitter cold. From this story Twelve Mile creek came to be called Fines creek.

"Haywood county's citizenship has always been at the front in times of war. From the best information obtainable it is quite certain that most of the earliest settlers had been in the Continental army and fought through the entire war of the Revolution, and later on many of them were in the war of 1812. Still later a number of these veterans of two wars moved to the great and boundless West, where the hazardous life might be spent in fighting savage tribes of Indians.

"As best it can be learned, only seven of these grand old patriots died and were buried within the confines of Haywood county, to-wit: at Waynesville, Colonel William Allen and Colonel Robert Love; at Canton, George Hall, James Abel, and John Messer; at upper Fines creek, Hughey Rogers; at Lower Fines creek, Christian Messer. There were doubtless others, but their names have been lost.

"All of these old soldiers were ever ready to fight for their homes. They came in almost daily contact with the Cherokee Indians, once a great and warlike tribe controlling the wilderness from the glades of Florida to the Great Lakes. While these savages were friendly to the settlers it was ever regarded as not a remote possibility that they might go upon the warpath at any time. Hence our forefathers had them constantly to watch while they were subduing the land."[17]

NOTES.

[1]N. C. Booklet, Vol. I, No. 7, p. 3.
[2]Dropped Stitches, 2, p. 17.
[3]Asheville's Centenary.
[4]McDowell entered land and settled his children near Brevard.
[5]Captain W. M. Hodge's statement to Col. W. L. Bryan of Boone, 1912, in letter from latter to J. P. A., November 26, 1912.
[6]Thwaites, p. 167.
[7]N. C. Booklet, Vol. I, No. 7.
[8]Wheeler's History of North Carolina, p. 444.
[9]He was probably related to "Gentleman George" Perkins who had piloted Bishop I. Spangenberg's party in 1752. Col. Rec., Vol. V, pp. 1 to 14.
[10]This tradition is also preserved in the family of Prof. Isaac G. Greer, professor of history in the Appalachian Training School, Boone.
[11]From Col. W. L. Bryan's "Primitive History of the Mountain Region," written in 1912 for this work.
[12]Wheeler's History of North Carolina, p. 444.
[13]N. C. Booklet, Vol. I, No. 7, p. 27.
[14]Wheeler's History of North Carolina, p. 445.
[15]Ibid., citing Mss. of General Wm. Lenoir.
[16]Hill, p. 189.
[17]Allen, p. 21.

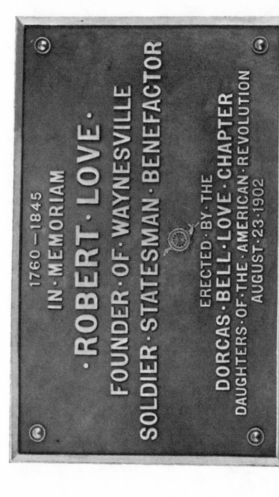

ROBERT LOVE MEMORIAL TABLET.

CHAPTER VI

THE STATE OF FRANKLIN

THE ACT OF CESSION OF TENNESSEE. As Congress was heavily in debt at the close of the Revolutionary War, North Carolina, in 1784, "voted to give Congress the twenty-nine million acres lying between the Alleghany mountains and the Mississippi river."[1] This did not please the Watauga setlers, and a few months later the legislature of North Carolina withdrew its gift, and again took charge of its western land because it feared the land would not be used to pay the debts of Congress. These North Carolina law makers also "ordered judges to hold court in the western counties, arranged to enroll a brigade of soldiers, and appointed John Sevier to command it."[2]

FRANKLIN. In August, 1784, a convention met at Jonesboro and formed a new State, with a constitution providing that lawyers, doctors and preachers should never be members of the legislature; but the people rejected it, and then adopted the constitution of North Carolina in November, 1785, at Greenville. They made a few changes in the North Carolina constitution, but called the State Franklin. John Sevier was elected governor and David Campbell judge of the Superior court. Greenville was made the capital. The first legislature met in 1785; Landon Carter was the Speaker of the Senate, and Thomas Talbot clerk. William Gage was Speaker of the House, and Thomas Chapman clerk. The Convention made treaties with the Indians, opened courts, organized new counties, and fixed taxes and officers' salaries to be paid in money, corn, tobacco, whiskey, skins, etc., including everything in common use among the people.[3]

TENNESSEE'S VIEW OF THE ACT OF CESSION. "The settlers lived and their public affairs were conducted under the jurisdiction of the County Court of Pleas and Quarter Sessions for a period of about six years, in a quiet and orderly manner; but ever since that May day of 1772 when they organized the first "free and independent government," their dream had been of a new, separate and independent commonwealth, and they began to be restless, dissatisfied and disaffected toward the government of North Carolina. Many causes seemed to conspire to increase their discontent. The first constitution of North Carolina had made provision for a future State within her limits, on the western side of the Alleghany mountains. The mother State had persistently refused, on the plea of poverty, to establish a Superior Court and appoint an attorney general or prosecuting officer for the inhabitants west of the mountains. In 1784, many claims for compensation for military services, supplies, etc., in the campaigns against the Indians, were presented to the State government from the settlements west of the Alleghanies. North Carolina was impoverished; and, notwithstanding the fact that these claims were just, reasonable and honest, it was suggested, and perhaps believed, 'that all pretenses were laid hold of (by the settlers) to fabricate demands against the government, and that the industry and property of those who resided on the east side of the mountains were become the funds appropriated to discharge the debts contracted by those on the west.' Thus it came about that, in May, 1784, North Carolina, in order to relieve herself of this burden, ceded to the United States her territory west of the Alleghanies, provided that Congress would accept it within two two years. At a subsequent session, an act was passed retaining jurisdiction and sovereignity over the territory until it should have been accepted by Congress. Immediately after passing the act of cession, North Carolina closed the land office in the ceded territory, and nullified all entries of land made after May 25, 1784.

"The passage of the cession act stopped the delivery of a quantity of goods which North Carolina was under promise to deliver to the Cherokee Indians, as compensation for their claim to certain lands. The failure to deliver these goods naturally exasperated the Cherokees, and caused them to commit depredations, from which the western settlers were of course the sufferers." (McGhee's History of Tennessee).

"At this session the North Carolina Assembly at Hillsboro laid taxes, or assessed taxes and empowered Congress to collect them, and vested in Congress power to levy a duty on foreign merchandise.

"The general opinion among the settlers west of the Alleghanies was that the territory would not be accepted by Congress   .   .   .   and

that, for a period of two years, the people in that territory, being under
the protection neither of the government of the United States nor of
the State of North Carolina, would neither receive any support from
abroad nor be able to command their own resources at home—for the
North Carolina act had subjected them to the payment of taxes to the
United States government. At the same time, there was no relaxation
of Indian hostilities. Under these circumstances, the great body of
people west of the Alleghanies concluded that there was but one thing
left for them to do, and that was to adopt a constitution and organize a
State government of their own. This they proceeded to do."

(McGhee's History of Tennessee.)

SEVIER AND NORTH CAROLINA. In this condition of affairs
the State of Franklin had been organized. The cession act
was repealed and a judge sent to Tennessee to hold court;
but there were two rival governments attempting to exercise power in the Watauga settlement, and there were, in consequence, frequent clashes, between Col. John Tipton's forces,
representing North Carolina, and those of John Sevier. According to Roosevelt, from whose history [4] the balance of this account has been taken, the desire to separate from the Eastern
States was strong throughout the west owing to the unchecked
ravages of the Indians and the refusal of the right to the settlers to navigate the Mississippi. The reason the Watauga
settlers seized upon the first pretext to separate from the
mother State was because most of them were originally from
Virginia, and in settling where they did, supposed they were
still on Virginia soil. Then, too, North Carolina had a weak
government, and Virginia was far more accessible to the
pioneers than the Old North State. While Kentucky had
settled up after the Revolutionary War with "men who were
often related by ties of kinship to the leaders of the Virginia
legislatures and conventions," the North Carolina settlers
who came to Watauga "were usually of the type of those who
had first built their stockaded hamlets on the bank of the
Watauga, and the first leaders of Watauga continued at the
head of affairs." Many of these, including Robertson and
Sevier, had been born in Virginia, where there was intense
State pride, and felt little loyalty to North Carolina. It is,
however, but just to say that James Robertson had no part
in this attempt to set up a separate State government, he
having already gone to the French Licks where he had established a government which was as loyal to North Carolina as

its remoteness admitted. North Carolina herself wished to be rid of the frontiersmen, because it was poor and felt the burden of the debts contracted in the Indian wars of the border. Then, too, the jurisdiction of the State courts had not been extended over these four western counties, Davidson, Washington, Sullivan and Greene, although they sent representatives to the State legislature at Hillsborough. Consequently, those counties became a refuge for outlaws, who had to be dealt with by the settlers without the sanction of law. In June 1784 the legislature passed an act ceding all the western lands to the Continental Congress, to be void in case Congress did not accept the gift within two years; but continuing its sovereignty and jurisdiction over the ceded lands. Even the members from these four counties then in the legislature of the mother State voted for the cession. It was a time of transition between the weakness of the Confederation and the adoption of the constitution of 1787; but North Carolina did not propose to allow this new State to set up for itself without her formal and free consent. It therefore set about reducing the recalcitrants to submission, and soon the last vestige of the Sevier government had become extinct.

COLONEL JOHN TIPTON. Although this gentleman had at first favored the separation, he had opposed putting the act of independence into force till North Carolina could be given an opportunity to rectify the wrongs complained of, and it was he who became the leader in the suppression of Sevier's government. About March, 1788, a writ was issued by North Carolina courts and executed against Sevier's estate, the sheriff seizing his negroes, and taking them to the house of Col. Tipton on Sinking creek for safe keeping . . . Sevier, with 150 men and a light field-piece, marched to retake them, and besieged Tipton and from thirty to forty of his men for a couple of days, during which two or three men were killed or wounded. Then the county lieutenant of Sullivan with 180 militia came to Tipton's rescue, surprised Sevier at dawn on the last of February, 1788, killing one or two men and taking two of Sevier's sons prisoners. Tipton was with difficulty dissuaded from hanging them. This scrambling fight marked the ignoble end of the State of Franklin. Sevier fled to the uttermost part of the frontier, where no writs ran, and the rough settlers were devoted to him. Here he speedily

became engaged in the Indian war, during which some ma-
rauding Indians killed eleven women and children of the family of John Kirk on Little river, seven miles south of Knoxville while Kirk and his eldest son were absent.

A BLOT ON SEVIER'S ESCUTCHEON. Later on young Kirk
joined about forty men led by Sevier to a small Cherokee
town opposite Chilhowa. These Indians were well known to
have been friendly to the whites, and among them was Old
Tassel, or Corn Tassel, "who for years had been foremost in
the endeavor to keep the peace and to prevent raids on the
settlers. They put out a white flag; and the whites then
hoisted one themselves. On the strength of this, one of the
Indians crossed the river, and on demand of the whites ferried them over. Sevier put the Indians in a hut, and then a
horrible deed of infamy was perpetrated. Among Sevier's
troops was young John Kirk, whose mother, sisters and brothers had been so foully butchered by the Cherokee, Slim Tom
and his associates. Young Kirk's brutal soul was parched
with longing for revenge, and he was, both in mind and heart,
too nearly kin to his Indian foes greatly to care whether his
vengeance fell on the wrong-doers or on the innocent. He
entered the hut where the Cherokee chiefs were confined, and
brained them with his tomahawk, while his comrades looked
on without interfering. Sevier's friends asserted that he was
absent; but this is no excuse. He knew well the fierce blood-
lust of his followers, and it was criminal negligence to leave
to their mercy the friendly Indians who had trusted to his
good faith; and, moreover, he made no effort to punish the
murderer."

THE HORROR OF THE FRONTIERSMEN. Such was the indignation with which this deed was received by the better class
of backwoodsmen that Sevier's forces melted away, and he
was obliged to abandon a march he had planned against the
Chickamaugas. The Continental Congress passed resolutions
condemning such acts, and the justices of the court of Abbeville, S. C., with Andrew Pickens at their head "wrote to the
people living on Nollechucky, French Broad and Holstein"
denouncing in unmeasured terms the encroachments and outrages of which Sevier and his backwoodsmen had been guilty.
"The governor of North Carolina, as soon as he heard the
news, ordered the arrest of Sevier and his associates [for trea-

son] doubtless as much because of their revolt against the
State as because of the atrocities they had committed against
the Indians. . . . The Governor of the State had given
orders to seize him because of his violation of the laws and
treaties in committing wanton murder on friendly Indians;
and a warrant to arrest him for high treason was issued by
the courts."

SEVIER IS ARRESTED FOR HIGH TREASON. Sevier knew of
this warrant, and during the summer of 1788 led his bands of
wild horsemen on forays against the Cherokee towns, never
fighting a pitched battle, but by hard riding taking them by
surprise. As long as he remained on the frontier he was in
no danger; but late in October, 1788, he ventured back to
Jonesborough, where he drank freely and caroused with his
friends. He soon quarreled with one of Tipton's side, who
denounced him for the murder of Corn Tassel and the other
peaceful chiefs. "Finally they all rode away; but when some
miles out of town Sevier got into a quarrel with another man;
and after more drinking and brawling, he went to pass the
night at a house, the owner of which was his friend. Meantime, one of the men with whom he had quarreled informed
Tipton that his foe was within his grasp. Tipton gathered
eight or ten men and early next morning surprised Sevier in
his lodgings. Sevier could do nothing but surrender, and Tipton put him in irons, and sent him across the mountains to
Morganton in North Carolina."

DR. RAMSEY'S ACCOUNT OF THE ARREST. In his Annals of
Tennessee (p. 427) this writer copies Haywood's History of
Tennessee : "The pursuers then went to the widow Brown's,
where Sevier was. Tipton and the party with him rushed
forward to the door of common entrance. It was about sunrise. Mrs. Brown had just risen. Seeing a party with arms
at that early hour, well acquainted with Colonel Tipton, probably rightly apprehending the cause of this visit, she sat herself down in the front door to prevent their getting into the
house, which caused a considerable bustle between her and
Colonel Tipton. Sevier had slept near one end of the house
and, on hearing a noise, sprung from his bed and, looking
through a hole in the door-side, saw Colonel Love, upon which
he opened the door and held out his hand, saying to Colonel

Love, 'I surrender to you.' Colonel Love led him to the place where Tipton and Mrs. Brown were contending about a passage into the house. Tipton, upon seeing Sevier, was greatly enraged, and swore that he would hang him. Tipton held a pistol in his hand, sometimes swearing he would shoot him, and Sevier was really afraid that he would put his threat into execution. Tipton at length became calm and ordered Sevier to get his horse, for that he would carry him to Jonesboro. Sevier pressed Colonel Love to go with him to Jonesboro, which the latter consented to do. On the way he requested of Colonel Love to use his influence that he might not be sent over the mountains into North Carolina. Colonel Love remonstrated to him against an imprisonment in Jonesboro, for, said he, 'Tipton will place a strong guard around you there; your friends will attempt a rescue, and bloodshed will be the result'. . . . As soon as they arrived at Jonesboro, Tipton ordered iron hand-cuffs to be put on him, which was accordingly done. He then carried the governor to the residence of Colonel Love and that of the widow Pugh, whence he went home, leaving Sevier in the custody of the deputy sheriff and two other men, with orders to carry him to Morganton, and lower down, if he thought it necessary. Colonel Love traveled with him till late in the evening.

"Before Colonel Love had left the guard, they had, at his request, taken off the irons of their prisoner. . . . A few days afterwards James and John Sevier, sons of the Governor, . . . and some few others were seen by Colonel Love following the way the guard had gone. . . . The guard proceeded with him to Morganton where they delivered him to William Morrison, the then high Sheriff of Burke county. . . . General McDowell and General Joseph McDowell . . . both followed him immediately to Morganton and there became his securities for a few days to visit friends. He returned promptly. The sheriff then, upon his own responsibility, let him have a few days more to visit friends and acquaintances. . . . By this time his two sons . . . and others, came into Morganton without any knowledge of the people there, who they were, or what their business was. Court was . . . sitting in Morganton and they were with the people, generally, without suspicion. At night, when the court broke up and the people dispersed, they, with the Governor, pushed forward towards the mountains with the greatest rapidity, and before morning arrived at them."

ROOSEVELT REPUDIATES THE SENSATIONAL ACCOUNT. In a foot note on page 226, Vol. iv, Roosevelt says: "Ramsey first copies Haywood and gives the account correctly. He then adds a picturesque alternative account—followed by later writers—in which Sevier escapes in an open court on a celebrated race mare. The basis for this last account, so far as it has any basis at all, lies on statements made nearly half a century after the event, and entirely unknown to Haywood. There is no evidence of any kind as to its truthfulness. It must be set aside as mere fable." The late Judge A. C. Avery, in 1889, published in the *Morganton Weekly Herald* a third account, to the effect that after having been released on bond a few days Sevier surrendered himself to the sheriff of Burke and went to jail; that afterwards, when his case was called the sheriff started with him to the court, but Sevier's friends managed to get him separated from the sheriff and to open a way for him to his horse then being held near by. But this, too, rests upon what old men of thirty years prior to 1889 said their fathers had told them.

SEVIER'S SECOND TREASON AGAINST THE STATE. Miro in New Orleans and Gardoqui in Washington, were the chief representatives of Spain in America in 1778, and the unrest "in the West had taken the form, not of attempting the capture of Louisiana by force, but of obtaining concessions from the Spaniards in return for favors to be rendered to them. Clark and Robertson, Morgan, Brown and Innes, Wilkinson and Sebastian, were all in correspondence with Gardoqui and Miro, in the endeavor to come to some profitable agreement with them. Sevier now joined the number. His new-born State had died; he was being prosecuted for high treason; he was ready to go to any lengths against North Carolina; and he clutched at the chance of help from the Spaniards. At the time North Carolina was out of the Union (not having yet ratified the Constitution) so Sevier committed no offense against the Federal Government." So, when Gardoqui heard of the fight between Sevier's and Tipton's men, he sent an emissary to Sevier, who was in the mood to grasp "a helping hand stretched out from no matter what quarter." He had no organized government back of him, but he was in the midst of his successful Cherokee campaigns, and he knew the reckless Indian fighters would gladly follow him in any movement, if he had a chance of success. He felt that if he were given money and arms, and the promise of outside assistance, he could yet win the day. He jumped at Gardoqui's cautious offers; though careful not to promise to subject himself to Spain, and doubtless with no idea of playing the part of Spanish vassal longer than the needs of the moment required. In July he wrote to Gardoqui, eager to strike a bargain with him, and in September sent him two letters by the hand of his son, James Sevier, who accompanied White [Gardoqui's emissary] when the latter made his return journey to the Federal Capital." In one of these letters he assured Gardoqui "that the western people had grown to know that their hopes of prosperity rested on Spain, and that the principal people of Franklin were anxious to enter into an alliance with and obtain commercial concessions from, the Spaniards. He importuned Gardoqui for money, and for military aid, assuring him that the Spaniards could best accomplish their ends by furnishing these supplies immediately, especially as the struggle over the adoption of the Federal Constitution made the time opportune for revolt. . . . He sent them to New Orleans that Miro might hear and judge their plans, nevertheless nothing came of the project, and doubtless only a few people in Franklin ever knew that it existed. As for Sevier, when he saw that he was baffled, he suddenly became a Federalist and an advocate of a strong central government; and this, doubtless, not because of love of Federalism, but to show his hostility to North Carolina, which had at first refused to enter the new Union. Thus the last spark of independent life flickered out in Franklin proper. The people who had settled on the Indian borders were left without government, North Carolina regarding them as trespassers on the Indian territory. They accordingly met and organized a rude governmental machine, on the model of the Commonwealth of Franklin; and the wild little State existed as a separate and independent republic until the new Federal government included it in the territory south of the Ohio."[5]

Washington county sent Sevier as a representative to the North Carolina legislature in 1789, and late in that session he was reluctantly admitted. He was also a member of the first Congress of the United States from North Carolina, March 4, 1789 to March 3, 1791, and was elected the first governor of Tennessee.

SEVIER AND TIPTON. It must be admitted that Sevier had, upon the repeal of the act of session "counselled his fellow citizens to abandon the movement for a new State"[6] and after the expiration of his term and the collapse of the Franklin government he wrote to one of the opposing party, not personally unfriendly to him, that he had been dragged into the Franklin government by the people of the county; that he wished to suspend hostilities, and was ready to abide by the decision of the North Carolina legislature; but that he was determined to share the fate of those who had stood by him, whatever it might be.[7] John Tipton, on the other hand, while favoring the formation of an independent State at the outset, voted against putting the new government into immediate operation, presumably because he hoped that when the mother State realized the seriousness of the defection in Watauga, she would remedy the wrongs of which the frontiersmen had complained. In this he was right; but when in November, 1785, the convention met at Greenville to provide a permanent constitution for the new State, he favored the adoption of a much more radical charter as a remedy for the ills under which the people suffered than Sevier, whose influence secured the adoption of the constitucion of the very State from which the western people had withdrawn. To some this document favored by Tipton seems absurd, but it had been drawn by no less a man than the redoubtable Sam Houston, afterwards president of the Republic of Texas.

JAMES ROBERTSON. In May, 1771, James Robertson, his brother Charles, and sixteen families from Wake county reached Watauga, preceding Sevier by about one year. Robertson at once became the brains of the settlement—its balance wheel, so to speak. Robertson and Sevier proved themselves to be, "with the exception of George Rogers Clark, the

greatest of the first generation of trans-Alleghany Pioneers,"
for they were the fathers of the first self-governing body in
America.

> For there on the banks of the sparkling Watauga
>   Was cradled the spirit that conquered the West—
> The spirit that, soaring o'er mountain and prairie,
>   E'en on the Pacific shore paused not for rest.

In 1779-1780 he founded the Cumberland settlement where
Nashville now stands, and Roosevelt gives him the chief
credit for the tuition under which those frontiersmen were
governed from the first, [8] though Richard Henderson was
present, counselling and aiding. When, however, Henderson's title proved null, he returned home, while Robertson
remained, and piloted the settlers through the dangers of
that early day. Thus, though he had no share in Kings
Mountain, he was at that time doing a work quite as important as fighting the British; for he was guiding the most remote
of the western settlements in America on the difficult path
of self-government.

SEVIER'S SPRING AT BAKERSVILLE. There is a fine spring
at Bakersville, nearly in front of the old Penland House, now
the Young hotel, at which it is said that Sevier and his party
stopped and rested after leaving Morganton. About 1850 an
old sword was found near this spring, and was supposed to
have been lost by one of these mountaineers. They reached
Cathey's, or Cathoo's, plantation that night, after coming 20
miles from Elk Hollow, at the mouth of a small eastern tributary of the North Toe flowing north from Gillespie's gap, and
called Grassy creek. Here they camped. It is near what is
now Spruce Pine on the line of the Carolina, Clinchfield and
Ohio Railroad. "On Friday the 29th they passed up Grassy
creek and through Gillespie's gap in the Blue Ridge, where
they divided; Campbell's men, at least, going six or seven
miles south to Henry Gillespie's, and a little below to Colonel
William Wofford's Fort, both in Turkey Cove; while the others pursued the old trace in a easterly direction, about the
same distance, to the North Cove, on the North Fork of the
Catawba, where they camped for the night in the woods, on
the bank of that stream, just above the mouth of Honeycutt's
creek."

SYCAMORE SHOALS MONUMENT. Monuments have been placed along this route to mark it permanently; Sycamore Shoals, Tennessee, at Elk Hollow, at the mouth of Grassy creek near Spruce Pine, and at the junction of Honeycutt's creek and the North Fork, near a station on the C. C. & O. Railroad known as Linville Falls. The monument at Sycamore Shoals is beautiful, and was erected September 26, 1909, by Bonny Kate, John Sevier and Sycamore Shoals chapters, D. A. R. Here it was that the patriots on their way to Kings Mountain assembled under Sevier, Shelby and Campbell, September 25, 1780. On the southern face is the inscription: "The Sword of the Lord and of Gideon." Also a statement that Fort Watauga, the first settlers' fort built west of the Alleghanies, was erected here in 1770. Also a statement that "Here was negotiated the Treaty of Sycamore Shoals under which Transylvania was acquired from the Cherokees, March 19, 1775."

ROBERT LOVE. He was born near the Tinkling Spring Meeting house, Augusta county, Va., May 11, 1760. His father was Samuel, son of Ephraim Love, captain of the Colonial Horse; and his mother Dorcas, second daughter of James Bell, to whom had been issued on the formation of Augusta county, October 30, 1745, a "commission of the Peace."[9] Samuel Love and Dorcas Bell were married July 3, 1759. Robert Love was christened by Rev. John Craig, who was pastor of the Tinkling Spring church from 1740 to 1764.[10] It was at this old church that the eloquent James Waddell, afterwards immortalized by Wm. Wirt, was pastor for several years, though he did not become "The Blind Preacher" till after the Revolutionary War and he had removed to Gordonsville, his blindness having been caused by cataract. Robert Love's pension papers show[11] that he was on the expedition under Col. Christie in 1776 against the Cherokees; that he was at Fort Henry on Long Island of the Holston in 1777; that he was stationed in 1778 at the head of the Clinch and Sandy rivers (Fort Robertson), and operated against the Shawnees from April to October; that from 1779 to 1780 he was engaged against the Tories on Tom's creek, New River, and Cripple creek, at Moravian Old Town, and at the Shallow ford of the Yadkin, under Col. Wm. Campbell; that in 1781 he was engaged in Guilford county "and the adjoining county" against Corn-

wallis, and "was in a severe battle with his army at White-
sell mill and the Rudy ford of the Haw river, under Gen.
Pickens; that from this place, with Capt. Wm. Doach, he was
sent back "from the rendezvous at the Lead Mines to collect and bring more men;" that in 1782 he "was again stationed out on the frontiers of the Clinch, at Fort Robertson
.   .   .   from June to October." He was living in Montgomery, now Wythe county, Va., when he entered the service
in 1776, and after the Revolutionary War, his parents being
dead, he moved with Wm. Gregory and his family to Washington county, N. C. (now Tennessee), in the fall of 1782.
Having moved to Greasy Cove, now Erwin Tenn., he married
Mary Ann Dillard, daughter of Col. Thomas Dillard of
Pittsylvania county, Va., on the 11th day of September, 1783;
and on the 5th of April, 1833, he made application for a pension under the act of Congress of June 7, 1832, attaching his
commission signed by Ben. Harrison, governor of Virginia;
but, a question having arisen as to the date of this commission Andrew Jackson wrote from The Hermitage on October
12, 1837, to the effect that he had known Col. Love since the
fall of 1784, and that there "is no man in this Union who has
sustained a higher reputation for integrity than Col. Robert
Love, with all men and with all parties, although himself a
uniform democratic Republican, and that no man stands
deservedly higher as a man of great moral worth than Col.
Love has always stood in the estimation of all who knew him."
Even this endorsement, however, did not serve to secure the
pension; but when E. H. McClure of Haywood filed an affidavit to the effect that the date of the commission was 1781
or 1782, official red-tape had no other refuge, and granted the
pension. He was a delegate to the Greenville convention of
the State of Franklin, December 14, 1784, and voted to adopt
the constitution of North Carolina instead of that proposed
by Sam Houston. [12] In 1778 he was engaged against the Chickamauga Indians as colonel of a regiment operating near White's
fort. [13]

He also drew a pension from the State (Colonial Records,
Vol. xxii, p. 74). He and John Blair represented Washington county (formerly the State of Franklin) in the North
Carolina legislature in November, 1889 (*Ibid.*, Vol. xxi, p.
194). Later in the same session John Sevier appeared and

was sworn in as an additional representative from the same county (*Ibid.*, pp. 584–85). Love was also a justice of the peace for Washington county in October, 1788. (*Ibid.*, Vol. xxii, p. 702); and the journal of the North Carolina State convention for the ratification of the constitution of the United States shows that Robert Love, Landon Carter, John Blair, Wm. Houston and Andrew Green were delegates, and that Robert Love voted for its adoption. (*Ibid.*, Vol. xxii, pp. 36, 39, 47, 48).

He moved to Buncombe county, N. C., as early as 1792, and represented that county in 1793, 1794, 1795[14] in the State Senate. According to the affidavit of his brother, Gen. Thos. Love, Robert Love "was an elector for president and vice-president when Thomas Jefferson was elected, and has been successively elected ever since, down to (and including) the election of the present chief magistrate, Andrew Jackson."[15] This affidavit is dated April 6, 1833. In a letter from Robert Love to William Welch, dated at Raleigh, December 4, 1828, he says that all the electors were present on the 3d "and gave their votes in a very dignified manner and before a very large concourse of people," the State House being crowded.[16] Fifteen cannon were fired "for the number of electoral votes and one for the county of Haywood, and for the zeal she appeared to have had from the number of votes for the Old Hero's Ticket. It was submitted to me to bring forward a motion to proceed to ballot for a president of the United States . . . and of course you may be well assured that I cheerfully nominated Andrew Jackson. . . . I was much gratified to have that honor and respect paid me. From the most authentic accounts . . . Adams will not get a vote south of the Potomac or west of the mountains. Wonderful what a majority! For Jackson 178 and Adams only 83, leaving Jackson a majority of 95 votes. So much for a bargain and intrigue."[17] The reason for firing an extra gun for Haywood county was because that county had cast a solid vote for Robert Love as elector for Andrew Jackson, such staunch Whigs as William Mitchell Davidson and Joseph Cathey having induced their fellow Whigs to refrain from voting out of regard for their democratic friend and neighbor, Robert Love. He carried the vote to Washington in a gig that year. He

named the town of Waynesville for his friend "Mad" Anthony
Wayne, with whom he had served at Long Island during the
Revolution.

In 1821 he was one of the commissioners who ran the boundary line between North Carolina and Tennessee from Pigeon
river south. On the 14th day of July, 1834, he was kicked
on the hip by a horse while in Green county, Tenn., and so
crippled that he had to use a crutch till his death.[18] The gig,
too, had to be given up for a barouche, drawn by two horses
and driven by a coachman. His cue, his blue swallow-tailed
coat, and knee breeches with silver knee-buckles and silk
stockings are remembered yet by a few of the older people.
He died at Waynesville, July 17, 1845, "loved by his friends
and feared by his enemies."[19] He was largely instrumental
in having Haywood county established, became its first clerk,
defeating Felix Walker for the position; and in 1828, he wrote
to Wm. Welch (December 4) from Raleigh: "The bill for
erecting a new county out of the western part of Burke and
northeastern part of Buncombe after severe debate fell in
the house of commons, on its second reading by a majority
against it of three only. The bill for the division of Haywood
county has passed the senate the third and last reading by a
majority of seven; and, I suppose, tomorrow it will be taken
up in the house of commons and in a few days we will know
its fate. I do not like the division line, but delicacy closes
my mouth for fear its being construed that interest was my
motive."[20]

He left an estate which "at one time was one of the largest
estates in North Carolina."[21] "He acquired great wealth
and died respected, leaving a large fortune to his children."
He was the founder of Waynesville. "Besides the sites for the
public square, court-house and jail, land for the cemetery
and several churches was also the gift of Col. Love." Of
him and his brother Thomas, Col. Allen T. Davidson said:[22]
"These two men were certainly above the average of men,
and did much to plant civilization in the county where they
lived, and would have been men of mark in any community."

EDMUND SAMS. In "Asheville's Centenary," Dr. Sondley tells us that this pioneer was "one of the first settlers who
came from Watauga," and established a ferry at the place

where the French Broad is now crossed by Smith's Bridge; had been in early life an Indian fighter, and lived on the western side of the French Broad at the old Gaston place. He was later a soldier in the Revolution. In 1824 his son Benoni Sams represented Buncombe in the House.

GENERAL THOMAS LOVE. He was a brother of Robert Love, and was born in Agusta county, Va., November 15, 1765. The date of his death is not accurately known, as he removed to Maury county, Tenn., about 1833.[23] Prof. W. C. Allen, in his "Centennial of Haywood County", says (p. 55) that he was a soldier of the Revolution, and served under Washington," but this must have been towards the close of that struggle, as he could not have been quite eleven years of age on the 4th of July, 1776.[24] At the close of that war, however, "he went to East Tennessee and was in the Sevier-Tipton war when the abortive State of Franklin was attempted."[25] Ramsey's "Annals of Tennessee" (p. 410) records the fact that on one occasion one of Tipton's men had captured two of Sevier's sons, and would have hanged them if Thomas Love had not argued him out of his purpose. He was one of Tipton's followers, but he showed Tipton the unworthiness of such an act. "He came to what is now Haywood county about the year 1790. When Buncombe was formed in 1791 he became active in the affairs of the new county," continues Prof. Allen. In 1797 he was elected to the house of commons from Buncombe, and was re-elected till 1808, when Haywood was formed, largely through his efforts. There is a tradition[26] that in 1796 he had been candidate against Philip Hoodenpile who represented Buncombe in the commons that year, but was defeated. For Hoodenpile could play the violin, and all of Love's wiles were powerless to keep the political Eurydices from following after this fiddling Orpheus. But Love bided his time, and when the campaign of 1797 began he charged Hoodenpile with showing contempt for the common herd by playing the violin before them with his left hand; whereas, when he played before "the quality," as Love declared, Hoodenpile always performed with his right hand. This charge was repeated at all the voting places of the county, which bore such significant names as Upper and Lower Hog Thief, Hardscrabble, Pinch Stomach, etc. Hoodenpile who, of course, could play only with his left hand, protested and denied; but the virus of class-feeling had been aroused, and Hoodenpile went down in defeat, never to rise again, while Love remained in Buncombe. "From the new county of Haywood General Love was one of the first representatives, the other having been Thomas Lenoir. Love was continuously reelected from Haywood till 1829, with the exception of the year 1816. Who it was that defeated him that year does not appear, though John Stevenson and Wm. Welch were elected to the house and Hodge Raborne to the senate. This Hodge Raborne was a man of influence and standing in Haywood county, he having been elected to the senate not only in 1816, but also from 1817 to 1823, inclusive, and again in 1838; but whether it was he or John Stevenson who defeated Thomas Love, or whether he ran that year or no, cannot now be determined. [27] William Welch was a nephew by marriage of Thomas Love, and it is not likely that he opposed him. Gen. Love moved to Macon county in 1830, where his wife died and is buried in the Methodist church yard of the town of Franklin. He was one of the commissioners for North Carolina who ran the line between this State and South Carolina in 1814. [28] "He resided in Macon for several years, and then removed to the Western District of Tennessee; was elected to the legislature from that State, and was made presiding officer of the senate. He was a man of very fine appearance, more than six feet high, very popular, and a fine electioneer. Many amusing stories are told of him, such as carrying garden seeds in his pocket, and distributing them" with his wife's special regards to the voter's wife. [29] His service in the legislature for such an unprecedented length of time was due more to his genial manner and electioneering methods, perhaps, than to his statesmanship; though, unless he secured what the voters most desired he would most probably have been retired from public life. He never was so retired.

A CURIOUS BIT OF HISTORY. William Blount, a native of this State and brother of John Gray Blount to whom so much land had been granted, was territorial governor of Tennessee until it became a State, and was then elected one of its first senators; but served only from 1796 to 1797. He was charged in the United States senate with having entered into a conspiracy to take Louisiana and Florida from Spain and give them to England in the hope that England would prove a better neighbor than had Spain, which had restricted the use of the Mississippi. Articles of impeachment were brought against him in 1797 by the House, and on the day after he was expelled by the Senate. But the impeachment trial was to have proceeded, and an officer was sent to arrest him. But Blount refused to go, those summoned to aid the officer refused to do so, and the trial would have proceeded without him in December, 1798, if Blount's attorney had not appeared after the Senate had formed itself into a court and filed a plea that Blount had not been an officer of the United States when the offence charged was committed, and it was decided, 14 to 11, that the Senate had no jurisdiction, on the ground that a senator is not a civil officer of the United States. The specific charge was that Blount had made an attempt to carry into effect a hostile expedition in favor of the British against the Spanish possessions in Florida and Louisiana, and to enlist certain Indian tribes in the same. [30]

NOTES.

[1]Hill, p. 215.
[2]Ibid.
[3]Dropped Stitches, 28; McGee, p. 80.
[4]Roosevelt, Vol. IV, ch. 4.
[5]Ibid., 231.
[6]Ibid., 182.
[7]Ibid., 211.
[8]Ibid., Vol. III, 26.
[9]Waddell (First Edition), 20, 30, 33, 210, et seq. Ibid. (Second Edition), 288.
[10]Augusta county records.
[11]Pension office files.
[12]Dropped Stitches, 28.
[13]Ramsey, 417, 427.
[14]W. C. Allen's "Centennial of Haywood County," p. 52.
[15]Robert Love's Pension Papers.
[16]Published in Waynesville Courier, but date of publication not known, except that it was about 1895, probably.
[17]This refers to the alleged "puritan and blackleg trade" between Adams and Clay four years before.
[18]W. C. Allen's "Centennial of Haywood County," 1908, p. 51.
[19]Ibid., p. 52.
[20]Private letter.
[21]W. C. Allen's "Centennial of Haywood County," p. 52.
[22]Col. A. T. Davidson's "Reminiscenses" in "The Lyceum," January, 1891.
[23]Prof. Allen says that he died about 1830, but he signed an affidavit on April 6, 1833, in Robert Love's pension matter.
[24]Although but a boy, he was a private in the Continental Line. Col. Rec., Vol. XXII, 73.
[25]Allen, 55.
[26]Statement of Capt. J. M. Gudger, Sr.
[27]Wheeler, 54, 206. There is no other record that approaches this. Col. A. T. Davidson in Lyceum, January, 1891.
[28]Rev. Stat. N. C., 1837, Vol. II, p. 87.
[29]The Lyceum, p. 9, January, 1891.
[30]Manual of the constitution of the United States, by Israel Ward Andrews, pp. 199, 200.

CHAPTER VII

GRANTS AND LITIGATION

PUBLIC LANDS. Immediately upon the declaration of independence the State began to dispose of its immense tracts of vacant lands. It was granted at first in 640-acre tracts to each loyal citizen with one hundred additional acres to his wife and each child at five cents per acre; but for all in addition to that amount, ten cents per acre was charged, if the additional land was claimed within twelve months from the end of the session of the legislature of 1777. [1] The price was expressed in pounds, two pounds and ten shillings standing for the lower and five pounds for the higher price. Ten cents was the charge for all lands in 1818. No person in Washington county, however, could take more than 640 acres and 100 additional for wife and each child, [2] until the legislature should provide further; but the county was ceded as part of Tennessee before this restriction was removed. When the State acquired the Cherokee lands it reduced the price per acre in 1833 to five cents per acre again; but it was afterwards restored to ten cents, where it remained for a long time. There is also a curious proviso in the act of 1779 (ch. 140, s. 5) to the effect that no person shall be entitled "to claim any greater quantity of land than 640 acres where the survey shall be bounded in any part by vacant lands, or more than 1,000 acres between the lines of lands already surveyed and laid out for any other person." Both the provision for the payment of five pounds for all in excess of 640 acres, etc., in any one year, and this last proviso, seem to have been disregarded from the first; for in 1796 the State granted to John Gray Blount over one million acres in Buncombe for fifty shillings a hundred acres. Under a statute allowing swamp lands to be granted in one body land speculators laid their entries adjoining each other in 640-acre tracts, and took out one grant for the entire boundary. [3] These large tracts usually excepted a considerable acreage from the boundary granted, which acreage had been determined by the secretary of state

(131)

from the surveys made upon the warrants; but unless the grants themselves showed upon their faces the number of acres of each tract and the names of the grantees to the excepted lands, the grantees could not show title by proving dehors that their land lay within the limits of the granted tract, as such excepted acreage merely was held to be too vague to confer title; but the boundaries of these excepted tracts could be determined by the Secretary of State and shown by certified copies from his office. [4]

CHEROKEE LANDS. Up to 1826 all lands had been ranked alike; but with the acquisition of the large Cherokee territory, with bottom, second bottom, hill, timber, mountain and cliff lands, a classification was imperative. So in that year commissioners were appointed to ascertain all the Cherokee lands that were worth more than fifty cents an acre, lay them off into sections containing from fifty to three hundred acres, and to note the quality of the land, stating whether it was first, second or third. [5]   But this limited classification was soon found to be inadequate, and in 1836 commissioners were required to ascertain all unsold Cherokee lands as would sell for 20 cents per acre and over, and divide them into sections or districts and expose them for public sale; lands of the first quality to be sold for four dollars per acre; lands of the second quality for two dollars per acre; lands of the third quality for one dollar per acre; lands of the fourth quality for fifty cents per acre and lands of the fifth quality for not less than twenty cents per acre. [6]   The surveyor was also required to note in his field book the mines, mineral springs, mill seats, and principal water-courses; and to make three maps before November 1, 1837, one of which was to be deposited in the governor's office, the second in the office of the secretary of state, and the third in the office of the county clerk of the county of Macon. All the lands worth less than twenty cents per acre were denominated vacant and unsurveyed lands, but they could be entered while those classified could be bought only at auction.

HOW LANDS WERE TO BE SURVEYED. These surveyed and classified tracts were to be bounded by natural boundaries or right lines running east and west, north and south, and to be an exact square or oblong, the length not to exceed double the breadth, unless where such lines should interfere with lands already granted or surveyed, or should bound on navigable water, in which last case the water should form one side of the survey, etc.

PREFERENCES.   Those who had made entries under the crown or Lord Granville, or, who, since his death had made improvements on the lands were to have preference in entering them. [7]

INDIAN BOUNDS. [8]   In 1778 (ch. 132) it was provided that no lands within the Indian boundaries should be entered, surveyed or granted, and those boundaries were described as starting from a point on the dividing line agreed upon between the Cherokees and Virginia where the Virginia and North Carolina line shall cross the same when run; thence a right line to the north bank of the Holston river, at the mouth of Clouds creek, which was the second creek below the Warrior's ford at the mouth of Carter's valley; thence a right line to the highest point of High Rock or Chimney Top; thence a right line to the mouth of Camp or McNamee's creek on the south bank of Nollechucky river, about ten miles below the mouth of Great Limestone; and from the mouth of Camp creek a southeast course to the top of the Great Iron mountain; and thence a south course to the dividing ridge between the waters of French Broad and Nollechucky rivers; thence a southwestwardly course along said ridge to the Blue Ridge, and thence along the Blue Ridge to the South Carolina line.   This excluded from entry and grant all of the mountain region west of the Blue Ridge that was south of the ridge between the French Broad and the Nollechucky rivers; but opened a territory now covered by the counties of Alleghany, Ashe, Watauga, Avery, Mitchell and a part of Yancey; and a good deal of the northeastern corner of what is now Tennessee.

HOUSES OF WORSHIP ON VACANT LANDS. [9]   All churches on vacant lands were given outright to the denominations which had built them, together with two acres adjoining.

OFFICERS AND SOLDIERS OF THE CONTINENTAL LINE.   In 1782 (ch. 173), each soldier and officer of the Continental line, then in service and who continued to the end of the war; or who had been disabled in the service and subsequently all who had served two years honorably and had not re-enlisted or had been dropped on reducing the forces, were given lands as follows :

Privates 640 acres each; Non-commissioned officers 1000 acres each; Subalterns 2560 each; Captains 3840 each; Majors 4800 each; Lieut.-Colonels 7200 each; Lieut.-Colonel Commanders 7200 each; Colonels 7200 each; Brigadiers 12000 each; Chaplains 7200 each; Surgeons 4800 each; and Surgeons Mates 2560 each. Three commissioners and a guard of 100 men were authorized to lay off these lands without expense to the soldiers.

LANDS FOR SOLDIERS OF THE CONTINENTAL LINE. In 1783 (ch. 186), the following land was reserved for the soldiers and officers of the Continental line for three years : Beginning on the Virginia line where Cumberland river intersects the same; thence south fifty-five miles; thence west to the Tennessee river; thence down the Tennessee river to the Virginia line; thence with the Virginia line east to the beginning." This was a lordly domain, embracing Nashville and the Duck river country which was largely settled up by people from Buncombe county, including some of the Davidsons and General Thomas Love, who moved there about 1830. For it will be remembered that in the act of cession of the Tennessee territory it was expressly provided that in case the lands laid off for "the officers and soldiers of the Continental line" shall not "contain a sufficient quantity of lands for cultivation to make good the quota intended by law for each, such officer or soldier who shall fall short of his proportion shall make up the deficiency out of the lands of the ceded territory." But, while preference was given to the soldiers in these lands, they were not restricted to them, but could enter and get grants for any other land that was open for such purposes.

THE FOREHANDEDNESS OF CERTAIN OFFICERS. From Hart's "Formation of the Union," Sec. 51, we learn that although Congress had provided bounty lands for the soldiers of the Revolution, our officers demanded something better for themselves; and, to appease them, Congress, on the 26th of April, 1778, had voted them half pay for life, as an essential measure for keeping the army together. This caused great dissatisfaction; but on the 10th of March, 1783, the so-called "Newburgh Address" appeared. This anonymous document urged the officers of the army not to separate until Congress had done justice to them; and on the 22d of March following,

Washington used his influence to induce Congress to grant
the officers full pay for the ensuing five years. This was
done; but as the treasury was empty, certificates of indebtedness were issued in lieu of cash. These certificates bore
interest. But in June, 1783, 300 mutineers surrounded the
place of meeting of Congress, and demanded a settlement of
the back pay; and the executive council of Pennsylvania
declined to disperse them. This caused Congress to leave
Philadelphia forever.

REVOLUTIONARY PENSIONS.[10] On August 26, 1776, Congress promised, by a resolution, to the officers and soldiers of
the army and navy who might be disabled in the service, a
pension, to continue during the continuance of their disabilities; and on June 7, 1785, recommended that the several
States should make provision for the army, navy and militia
pensioners resident within them, to be reimbursed by Congress.
On September 29, an act was passed providing that the military pensions which had been granted and paid by the States,
respectively, in pursuance of the foregoing acts, to invalids
who were wounded and disabled during the late war, should
be paid by the United States from the fourth day of March,
1789, for the space of one year; and the act of March 26,
1790, appropriated $96,000.72 for paying pensions which may
become due to invalids. The act of April 30, 1790, provides
for one-half pay pensions to soldiers of the regular army disabled while in line of duty; and the act of July 16, 1790, provides that the military pensions which have been granted and
paid by the States respectively shall be continued and paid
by the United States from the fourth of March, 1790, for
the space of one year.

The first general act providing for the pensioning of all
disabled in the actual service of the United States during the
Revolutionary War was the act approved March 10, 1806,
which was to remain in force but six years, but was subsequently extended and kept in force by acts of April 25, 1812,
May 15, 1820, February 4, 1822, and May 24, 1828.[11]

LAND SPECULATION. Immediately after the formation of
Buncombe the rush began, and large grants were issued to
Stokely Donelson, Waightstill Avery, William Cathcart, David
Allison and John Gray Blount, besides many others. The
Flowery Garden tract on Pigeon was regarded as of the finest

quality of land, and was granted to one of the McDowells. As the boundaries of the Cherokees were moved westward the same greed for land continued, and many large boundaries were entered, Robert and James R. Love of Waynesville having obtained tracts—those belonging to the Love speculation in 1865 containing in Haywood two hundred thousand, in Jackson fifty thousand, and one hundred and twenty-five thousand acres, in two tracts in Swain; a total of 375,000 acres in all.

ENLARGEMENT OF THE WESTERN BOUNDARY.[12]   In 1783 (ch. 185) the western boundary was enlarged so as to take in all lands south of the Virginia line and west of the Tennessee river to the Mississippi, then down that stream to the 35th parallel of north latitude; thence due east to the Appalachian mountains, and thence with them to the ridge between the French Broad and the Nollechucky [sic] river, and with that line till it strikes the line of the Indian Hunting grounds, set forth in chapter 132 of the laws of 1778. This, however, was superceded by the Act of Cession, 1789, ch. 299, accepted by Congress, April 2, 1790, Vol. II, p. 85, note on p. 455.

ENTRIES WEST OF THE MISSISSIPPI VOID.[13]   It would seem that some of our enterprising citizens had been entering lands west of the Mississippi river at some time prior to 1783, for there is an act of that year (ch. 185) which declares that all entries of land heretofore made, or grants already obtained, or which may be hereafter obtained in consequence of the aforesaid entries of land, to the westward of the line last above described in this act . . . are hereby declared to be null and void. . . . "

ENTRIES OF INDIAN LANDS VOID.[14]   Section 5 of the act of 1783 (ch. 185) reserves certain of the lands to the Indians, which embrace part of the enlarged western boundary, with the Pigeon river as the eastern boundary, including the ridge between its waters and those of the Tuckaseegee river to the South Carolina line.   All entries of such lands were void and all hunting and ranging of stock thereon were prohibited. But all other lands not reserved to the Indians were subject to entry; but at the price of five pounds per hundred acres.

ENTRY TAKER'S OFFICE CLOSED IN 1784.[15]   By chapter 196 of the laws of 1784 North Carolina passed an act to remove all doubts as to the ceded territory of Tennessee by expressly retaining jurisdiction over it till Congress should accept it; but until Congress did accept it it was considered "just and right that no further entries of lands within the territory aforesaid should be allowed until the Congress [should] refuse the cession." Therefore, it closed the entry taker's office and declared void all entries made subsequent to the 25th of May, 1784, John Armstrong having been the entry-taker; except "such entries of lands as shall be made by the commissioners, agents and surveyors who extended the lines allotted to the Continental officers and soldiers, and the guards and hunters, chain-carriers and markers" who had allotted the lands to the soldiers. This, however, applied only to the ceded territory of Tennessee.

GRANTS TO JOHN GRAY BLOUNT AND DAVID ALLISON. Two of the largest grants of land West of the Blue Ridge were to John Gray Blount of Beaufort, North Carolina, and David Allison. The grant to Blount called for "320,640 acres and is dated November 29, 1796.[16] It began in the Swannanoa gap and ran to Flat creek, and thence to Swannanoa river and to its mouth; thence down the French Broad to the Painted Rock; thence to the Bald mountain, thence to Nolle-chucky river, or Toe, thence to Crabtree creek, and thence to the beginning. The grant to David Allison is for 250,240 acres and is dated November 29, 1796.[17] [18] This land lies on Hominy creek, Mill's and Davidson's rivers, Scott's creek, Big Pigeon and down it to Twelve-Mile creek to the French Broad and to the beginning. These lands were sold September 19, 1798, by James Hughey, Sheriff of Buncombe, for the taxes of 1796, and were purchased by John Strother of Beaufort for £115, 15 shillings, and the Sheriff gave him a deed dated September 29, 1798.[19] Strother sold some of these lands and made deeds to them, and in each deed he recited this Sheriff's deed as his source of title.[20] Strother was the friend and agent of John Gray Blount, and it is not clearly known why this large body of land was suffered to go on sale for the non-payment of taxes, only to be bought in by the man whose duty it had been, presumably, to see that the taxes were paid. But it is certain that, on the 22d of November, 1806, Strother made his last will (describing himself as of Buncombe county) and devised all of the lands he had received through Sheriff Hughey's deed as formerly belonging to John Gray Blount to that gentleman, describing him as his "beloved friend." This will was admitted to probate in Davidson County, Tennessee, March 1, 1816, and later on in Haywood and Madison counties, North Carolina. It was executed according to North Carolina laws of that date; but only one of the two subscribing witnesses to it was examined and he omitted to state that he had subscribed his name in the presence of the other subscribing witness. Chapter 52 of the Private Laws of 1885 validated this defective probate. The constitutionality of the act was questioned nevertheless, in *Vanderbilt v. Johnston* (141 N. C., p. 370) but upheld by the Supreme Court on the ground that only the heirs of Blount or Strother could object to the probate.

LOVE SPECULATION. After the death of Strother, Robert Love became the agent of the executors of J. G. Blount for the sale of these lands, [21] but, on the 10th of December, 1834, these executors conveyed what was left of the Blount lands to Robert and James R. Love of Haywood county for $3,000. This deed, however, was not recorded till October 5, 1842, it having been probated by the late R. M. Henry, a subscribing witness, before Richmond M. Pearson, October 2, 1839, who for years was the Chief Justice of this State. [22]

THE CATHCART GRANTS. Other large tracts were granted to William Cathcart in July, 1796, 33,280 at the head of Jonathan's creek, and covering Oconalufty and Tuckaseegee river; 49,920, on Tuckaseegee river and Cane creek, "passing Wain's sugar house in a sugar tree cove," [23] and a like acreage on Scott's and Cane creeks. Much of this lay west of the divide between the headwaters of Pigeon river and those of Tuckaseegee river in what is now Jackson, and which was not subject to entry and grant in July, 1796, because it had been reserved to the Cherokee Indians by North Carolina by an act of 1783. (Sec. 2347, Code of N. C.) The State being the sovereign, the fee in such lands reverted to it whenever a new treaty with the Indians removed their boundary further west; which had happened by the treaty of Holston made in July, 1791, and that of Tellico, made afterwards. If Cathcart had taken out a new grant to this part of the land after that treaty his title thereto would have been good. But he did not.

JAMES ROBERT LOVE.

LATIMER v. POTEET. The question as to the validity of the
Cathcart grant to land west of that divide came up in *Latimer v. Poteet* (14 Peters U. S. Reports, p. 4), in which it was
decided that while there may have been doubt as to the location of the eastern line of the Cherokees—subsequently known
as the Meigs and Freeman line—the parties to that treaty
had the right to determine disputes as to its location and
remove uncertainties and defects, and that private rights could
not be interposed to prevent the exercise of that power; which
was tantamount to saying that Cathcart's title to that part
of the land was null.

BROWN v. BROWN.[24] But, as land grew more valuable
on account of the timber on it, the same question was brought
up in the State court when a grant was taken to a part of the
land which had been granted to David Allison in November,
1796, and lay west of the reservation divide between Pigeon
and Tuckaseegee. This land had been sold by the heirs of
Robert Love, who held under the deed from Sheriff Hughey
of September 29, 1798. On the trial of the case in the Superior court, the judge held that the last grant was valid and that
the original grant to Allison in 1796 was invalid. On appeal
great consternation was caused in the fall of 1888 by the
decision of the Supreme Court (in *Brown v. Brown*, 103 N. C.,
213) to the effect that all grants of land extending west of the
"dividing ridge between the waters of Pigeon river and Tuckaseegee river to the southern boundary of this State, were
utterly void" (Code N. C., sections 2346-47) because when
granted they were "within the boundary prescribed of the lands
set apart to and for the Cherokee Indians." It was further
held "that the treaty of Holston, concluded on the 2d day of
July, 1791, between the United States and the Cherokee
Indians, did not extinguish the title and right of those Indians
to the territory embracing the lands embraced by the grant
in question"—that to David Allison, of date 29th November,
1796. Immediately there was a rush to enter and secure grants
to all lands to which grants had been issued west of the dividing ridge between the Pigeon and the Tuckaseegee. Where
would the effect of that decision reach? No one knew. But,
on a petition for a rehearing, Chief Justice Merrimon discovered "among a vast number of very old uncurrent statutes"
one (Acts 1784, 1 Pot. Rev., ch. 202) that required surveyors

in the "eastern part of the State" to survey lands that any
person or persons "have entered or may hereafter enter";
which was afterwards extended (Acts 1794, 1 Pot. Rev., ch.
422; Haywood's Manual, p. 188) to apply to "all lands in this
State lying to the eastward of the line of the ceded territory,"
which was construed to mean "all the lands of this State not
specially devoted to some particular purpose, and the impli-
cation intended was, that they should be subject to entry and
survey just as were the lands mentioned in the statutes
amended," it having been the purpose to embrace "the lands so
acquired from the Cherokee Indians." Hence, the words,
"lying to the eastward of the line of ceded territory"; this
was the line separating this State from Tennessee which had
been ceded to the United States in 1789; while the land acquired from the Indians by the treaty of Holston "lay immediately to the eastward of a part of that line." In the language of the chief justice, "it is fortunate that it has been
discovered, as it rendered the land subject to entry and makes
valid and sustains the grant in question, under which, no
doubt, many excellent people derive title to their land."
Upon the rehearing (106 N. C., 451) the Supreme Court held
that by an act of 1777 it was made lawful for any citizen of
the State "to enter any lands not granted before the fourth
of July, 1776, which have accrued or shall accrue to this State
by treaty or conquest"; and that the title of the Indians to
all lands east of the Holston treaty line were extinguished.
This line had been fixed by the Meigs and Freeman survey,
which location the State could not without breach of faith
question; and the land in controversy, while lying west of the
reservation of 1784, was east of the Meigs and Freeman survey. This settled the dispute.

WAIGHTSTILL AVERY GRANTS. About 1785 Hon. Waightstill Avery of Burke took out "hundreds of grants," generally for 640-acre tracts, covering almost the entire valley of
North Toe river, from its source to somewhere below Toecane, there being, here and there, along the valley, some
older grant wedged in between his tracts. He took out grants
also for lands on most all of the tributaries of the North Toe,
including the lower part of Squirrel creek, of Roaring creek,
of Henson's creek and of Three-Mile creek [25] and also along
the lower valley of South Toe and of Linville river, down to

the Falls, and the upper valley of Pigeon in Haywood county and of Mills river in Henderson and Transylvania. . . . William Cathcart took out in 1795 two large grants, one known as the "99,000-Acre Tract," and the other as the "59,000-Acre Tract," which two large boundaries covered practically all of Mitchell county and of Avery county, except some tracts along the Blue Ridge. . . ."[26] They also covered about all that had been previously granted to Waightstill Avery. For the litigation that subsequently ensued see "Cranberry Mine" under chapter on "Mines and Mining." Many grants were also made to William Lenoir and others.

CHEROKEE LANDS. By the act of 1819[27] no portion of the lands recently acquired from the Cherokees was required to be surveyed except such that, in the opinion of the commissioners appointed for that purpose, would sell for fifty cents per acre and over, while the rest was reserved for future disposition to be made by a subsequent legislature, and the act of 1826 required such lands to be classified into three tracts, as we have already seen. This was to be sold at auction, and in the meantime, no land not subject to survey—that is not worth fifty cents an acre or more—was subject to entry. But by the act of 1835[28] all such lands as were not worth fifty cents an acre were made subject to entry. Under the law of 1836[29] the Cherokee lands were required to be laid off into districts, which were to be numbered, and divided into tracts of from fifty to four hundred acres each, the first class of which was to be sold at auction for not less than $4 per acre, the second class for not less than $2, the third class for not less than $1, the fourth class for not less than fifty cents, and the fifth class for not less than 25 cents per acre. All the rest of the Cherokee lands which were not considered by the commissioners to be worth at auction more than 20 cents per acre were subject to entry. The surveyors were to note all the mines, mill sites, etc., on each tract, and three maps were to be made, showing the lands surveyed and the "vacant and unsurveyed lands," one of which was to be deposited in the office of the governor, another in the office of the secretary of state at Raleigh, and the third in the office of the register of deeds in Franklin, Macon county.

ACT FOR THE RELIEF OF PURCHASERS OF LANDS. Under this act of 1836 several purchasers found that they could not pay for the lands bid in by them at the auction sales, and in 1844-45 another act was passed providing that such persons might surrender such lands, after which the lands were to be reassessed by commissioners, when they could be repurchased by the former bidders at the new valuation by giving bonds with good security, if they so desired, and if not, then they could be sold at the new valuation to anyone. This law also provided for the sale of such lands as had not been sold at all under the first appraisment of their value, and for the relief of such poor and homeless people as had settled on the less valuable lands and had made improvements thereon in the hope of being able to pay for them at some future time and had been unable to do so, as well as for insolvent people who had been unable to pay for lands they had bought. New valuations were to be made and certificates given to such persons, which certificates gave them preemption rights for the purchase of such lands upon giving good bonds for the payment of the purchase price. Much of the best lands were subsequently held under these "Occupation Tracts," they having the refusal of the lands they had settled on and improved.

FLOATING ENTRIES. Such entries were those which stated in the entry that land beginning on a natural object in a certain district had been entered, but, without further description, they were void against enterers whose surveys covered it.

NOTES.

¹Potter's Revisal, p. 275.
²Ibid., p. 280.
³*Melton v. Munday* (64 N. C. Rep., p. 295); *Waugh v. Richardson*, 8 Ired. Law (30 N. C., p. 470).
⁴Potter's Revisal, p. 463.
⁵2 Vol. Rev. St. 1837, p. 201.
⁶Ibid., pp. 210-11.
⁷Potter's Revisal, p. 280.
⁸Ibid., p. 355.
⁹Potter's Revisal, p. 356.
¹⁰Potter's Revisal, p. 442.
¹¹From "Dropped Stitches," pp. 71-72.
¹²Potter's Revisal, p. 435.
¹³Ibid., p. 456.
¹⁴Ibid., p. 436.
¹⁵Potter's Revisal, p. 457.
¹⁶Book No. 4, p. 230.
¹⁷Book 2, p. 458.
¹⁸43,534 acres already granted are excepted from this boundary.
¹⁹Book 4, p. 230.
²⁰The lands embraced in this sale aggregated one million and seventy-four thousand acres. The tax title stood all tests. *Love v. Wilbourn*, 5 Ired., N. C. Rep., p. 344.
²¹Will book E, p. 42.
²²Book 22, p. 88.
²³Book 22, p. 393.
²⁴Daniel Webster represented the defendant in this case, and Chief Justice Roger B. Taney filed a dissenting opinion.
²⁵So called because it is almost exactly three miles in length.
²⁶From letter of December 5, 1912, from Hon. A. C. Avery to J. P. A.
²⁷Rev. St. 1837, Vol. II, p. 190.
²⁸Ibid., p. 209.
²⁹Ibid., p. 210.
NOTE : For Forge Bounty grants see ch. 293, laws 1788, Potter's Revisal, p. 592.

CHAPTER VIII
COUNTY HISTORY

BUNCOMBE COUNTY.[1] In 1781 or 1782 settlers from the blockhouse at Old Fort, McDowell county as it is now, crossed the mountains to the head of the Swannanoa river, and became trespassers on the Cherokee territory, the Blue Ridge at that time being the boundary line. Samuel Davidson, his wife and child were among the first. They brought a female negro slave with them, and settled a short distance east of Gudger's ford of Swannanoa river, and near what is now Azalea. He was soon afterwards killed by Indians, and his wife and child and slave hurried through the mountains back to Old Fort. An expedition to avenge his death set out, with the late Major Ben. Burgin, who died at Old Fort in November, 1874, at the age of ninety-five, among the number and conquered the Indians at the mouth of Rock House creek. By this time, however, several other settlements had been effected on the Swannanoa from its head to its mouth by the Alexanders, Davidsons, Smiths and others, the earliest being about the mouth of Bee Tree creek, a little above this being the Edmundson field, the first cleared in Buncombe. Soon another company passed through Bull gap and settled on upper Reems creek, while still others came in by way of what is now Yancey county and settled on lower Reems and Flat creeks. Some of the people who had been with Sevier at Watauga settlement, settled on the French Broad above the mouth of Swannanoa, and on Hominy creek. Some from South Carolina settled still higher on the French Broad.

THE CHEERY NAME OF BUNCOMBE.[2] The Swannanoa was now recognized as the dividing line between Burke and Rutherford counties, from portions of which counties Buncombe was subsequently formed, and named for Edward Buncombe, who had been a colonel in the Revolutionary War.[3] In 1791 David Vance and William Davidson, the former representing Burke and the latter Rutherford, agreed upon the formation of a new county from portions of both these counties west of the Blue Ridge, its western boundary to be the Tennessee line.

First Court at the Gum Spring. [4]   In April, 1792, at the residence of Col. William Davidson on the south bank of the Swannanoa, half a mile above its mouth, subsequently called the Gum Spring place, Buncombe county was organized, pursuant to the act which had been ratified January 14, 1792. On December 31, 1792, another act recited that the commissioners provided for in the first act had failed to fix "the center and agree where public buildings" should be erected, and appointed Joshua Inglish, Archibald Neill, James Wilson, Augustin Shote, George Baker and John Dillard of Buncombe, and Wm. Morrison of Burke, commissioners in place of Phillip Hoodenpile, William Brittain, Wm. Whitson, James Brittain and Lemuel Clayton, who had failed to agree, to select a county seat.   There was rivalry for this position, many contending for the "Steam Saw Mill Place on the road afterwards known as the Buncombe Turnpike Road about three miles south of Asheville, where Dr. J. F. E. Hardy resided at the time of his death," says Dr. Sondley in his Asheville's Centenary. They selected the present site, which at first was called Morristown.   As the Superior court was at this time held at Morganton, five men from Buncombe were required to serve there as jurors, for the July term, 1792.   These were Matthew Patton, Wm. Davidson, David Vance, Lambert Clayton and James Brittain.   The first court house stood in the middle of the street upon the public square at the head of what is now Patton avenue, and was of logs. The first county court held there was on the third Monday in July, 1793.   In January, 1796, commissioners were appointed to lay off a plan for public buildings; but in April, 1802, the grand jury complained that the county had no title to the land on which the jail, etc., stood, and in April, 1805, steps were taken to secure land for a public square.   In April, 1807, the county trustee, or treasurer, was ordered to pay Robert Love one pound for registering five deeds made by individuals for a public square. . . .   The next court house was made of brick, a little further east, in the erection of which the late Nicholas W. Woodfin, while a poor boy, carried brick and mortar.   This gave way to a handsome brick building fronting on Main street, which was destroyed by fire on the 26th day of January, 1865.   Some years later a small one-story brick structure was built nearly in front of W. O. Wolf's storeroom, the late Rev. B. H. Merrimon having been the contractor. In 1876 this gave way to a larger building with three stories, J. A. Tennent being the architect. In the erection of this a workman fell from the southwest corner of the tower to the ground and was killed. His name has been forgotten. The first jail was succeeded by a brick building now a part of the Library building; but a new jail was built afterwards on the site of the present city hall, its site being sold to the city when the Eagle street jail was built some years afterwards. The first jail was a very poor structure, every sheriff from 1799 to 1811 complaining of its insufficiency. In 1867 the county began to sell off portions of the public square on the north and south sides, thus reducing it to its present dimensions.

MORRISTOWN. John Burton's grant was "by private contract laid out . . . for a town called Morristown, the county town of Buncombe county, into 42 lots, containing, with the exception of the two at the southern end, one-half an acre each, lying on both sides of a street 33 feet wide," which runs where the southern part of North Main street and the northern part of South Main street now are. [5] There were two cross streets across the public square. "Nobody seems to know why the name of Morristown was bestowed upon the place . . . but there is a seemingly authentic tradition that it was named for Robert Morris, who successfully financed the American Revolution, yet himself died a bankrupt." [6] About this time he owned large bodies of land in Western North Carolina; indeed it is shown in the record of one case in the Federal Court here (Asheville) that Robert Tate of York county, Pennsylvania, and William Tate, of Burke county, N. C., conveyed to him in one deed 198 tracts of land, only one tract of which, containing 70,400 acres and lying in what are now Yancey, Burke, and McDowell counties, was involved in that litigation. The State grant for these lands was issued to Robert and William Tate on May 30, 1795, and they conveyed the same lands to Morris on August 15 of the same year. "The Tates were evidently the agents of Morris. . . . Morris was one of the heroes of the Revolution, and . . . it is small wonder that . . . the people . . . should name it for him." His will (dated in 1804) was probated in McDowell county on April

21, 1891. In November 1797, the village was incorporated by the legislature as Asheville in honor of Samuel Ashe of New Hanover, governor.

OLD ASHEVILLE. On Thanksgiving Day, 1895, Miss Anna C. Aston, Miss Frances L. Patton and other ladies published a "Woman's Edition" of the *Asheville Daily Citizen*. It contained much valuable and important information of that city. But in February, 1898, Foster A. Sondley, Esq., a descendant of the Fosters and Alexanders of Buncombe county, and a leading member of the Asheville Bar, published a historical sketch of Buncombe county and Asheville, containing practically all that could then be ascertained concerning the early history of this section. Hon. Theo. F. Davidson and the late Albert T. Summey also contributed their recollections. There was a woodcut reproduction of an oil painting of Asheville by F. S. Duncanson, which was taken from Beaucatcher, and it appears that there were not more than twenty five residences in 1850 that were visible from that commanding eminence, all the buildings, including outhouses, not exceeding forty, and they were between Atkin, Market and Church streets. The painting itself, now owned by Mrs. Martha B. Patton, shows five brick buildings, the old Presbyterian church, on the site of the present one, with the cupola on its eastern end, because the street ran there; the little old Episcopal church, on the site of the burned Trinity; the old jail, standing where the city hall now stands; Ravenscroft school, and the Rowley house, now occupied by the Drhumor building. The old jail was three stories high. The other buildings were white wooden structures, and included the central portion of the old Eagle hotel and the old Buck hotel. Mr. Ernest Israel also has a similar picture.

Dr. J. S. T. Baird's facile pen has given us an equally vivid picture of Asheville in his "Historical Sketches of Early Days," published in the *Asheville Saturday Register* during January, February and March, 1905, as it appeared in 1840. He records the facts that the white population then did not exceed 300, and the total number of slaves, owned by eight or nine persons, did not exceed 200. In the 400 acres embracing the northeastern section of the city, between the angle formed by North Main and Woodfin streets, he recalled but two dwellings, those of Hon. N. W. Woodfin and Rev. David

McAnally, both on Woodfin street. There was an old tannery and a little school house near the beginning of what is now Merrimon avenue, the school having been taught by Miss Katy Parks, who afterwards became Mrs. Katy Bell, mother of Rev. George Bell of Haw Creek. This 400-acre boundary, now so thickly settled, was then owned by James W. Patton, James M. Smith, Samuel Chunn, N. W. Woodfin and Israel Baird. There was a thirty-acre field where Doubleday now is, and was called the "old gallows field," because Sneed and Henry had been hanged there about 1835. Standing south of Woodfin and East of North and South Main streets to the southern boundary, there were but eight residences, not including negro and outhouses.

SOUTHWEST ASHEVILLE. Just north of Aston street was the brick store of Patton & Osborne, and later Patton & Summey, adjoining which was the tailor shop of "Uncle" Manuel, one of James W. Patton's slaves. Then came a white house which was kept for guests when there was an overflow crowd at the Eagle hotel. Between this house and the Daylight store, J. M. Smith some years later erected a two-story building for the use of Dr. T. C. Lester, a physician who came from South Carolina and settled here about 1845. He kept a sort of drug store, the first of its kind in Asheville. The negroes called it a shot-i-carry-pop, in their effort to call it an apothecary shop. Hilliard Hall now stands where it stood. Just above was the residence and place of business of James B. Mears, now the Daylight store. Then came Drake Jarrett's place—better known as the Coche[7] place "where for many years the little short-legged 'monsieur' and his 'madam' dealt out that which Solomon says biteth like a serpent and stingeth like an adder." Thus was reached what was the Chunn property, which, beginning at the lower side of T. C. Smith's drug store, ran straight back to Church street. Samuel Chunn had lived in a large brick house which fronted north, and which was later replaced by a building used as a banking house, known as the Bank building. This was about 1845. The Asheville branch of the Bank of Cape Fear occupied it till the Civil War period. The residence of A. B. Chunn stood on the corner now occupied by Pat McIntyre's grocery store. An old stable stood at the corner of Patton and Lexington avenues.

CHURCH STREET. The grounds of the Methodist church extended from Patton avenue and Church street to the Aston property and several rods back, forming an oblong plat of several acres. On the corner of Patton avenue and Church street stood a large brick building used as a boarding house in connection with the school for girls which was taught for many years in the basement of the Methodist church. The late William Johnston afterwards bought and occupied this building as a residence. The land south of the Methodist church was used as a cemetery till long after the Civil War.

The Presbyterian church of that day stood nearly where the one of this day stands, opposite that of the Methodist church, and its cemetery extended down to Aston street. Near where Asheland and Patton avenues join the late James M. Smith had a large barn, which stood in a ten-acre field.

NORTHWEST ASHEVILLE. In the angle formed by North Main street and Patton avenue, in 1840, there were not many houses. Beginning at the north end, Mrs. Cassada—"Granny Cassie"— occupied a one-room house which stood where the Rankin tan house afterwards stood. She baked and sold ginger cakes, and brewed cider. Coming up North Main street was a house built by Israel Baird in 1839, now known as the Brandt property. Israel Baird had lived two and a half miles north of Asheville at what is now the Way place, but about 1838 he bought 40 acres, commencing at the junction of North Main street and Merrimon avenue, running west to the present auditorium, thence to Starnes avenue and thence back to North Main street. The only other building within this area was the wooden store and shoe-shop opposite the old Buck hotel, now occupied by the Langren hotel, and the barns, stables, sheds and cribs of J. M. Smith, which covered a large portion of the lot lying between West College street, Walnut and Water streets. From the foregoing it is evident that the artist Duncanson did not get all the houses into his oil painting of 1850.

EAST AND SOUTH ASHEVILLE. In these sections of the town the land was owned by James M. Smith, James W. Patton, Montraville Patton, Dr. J. F. E. Hardy, Mrs. Morrison and Thomas L. Gaston, principally. The old Buck Hotel, a small frame building near it, what was known as the Dunlap store, the court house, the jail, the office of the *Highland Messenger* on what is now North Pack Square, east of the *Gazette News* office, were then the oldest houses in town. The old jail stood where the new Legal building now stands; the court house stood where Vance's monument stands, with the whipping post and stocks immediately in its rear. Mrs. Rose Morrisons' residence occupied the site now covered by the present court house, while the store of Montraville Patton occupied the corner now used by the Holt Furniture Company. Lower down on South Main street lived William Coleman in a brick building in a part of which the post-office was kept. Later on Col. R. W. Pulliam lived there and Rankin and Pulliam did a large mercantile business. Just below this, embowered in green vines and fragrant flowers, was the stylish wooden dwelling occupied for years by Dr. J. F. E. Hardy, and was later to fall into such disrepute as to be called "Greasy Corner." This, however, was about 1890 after the handsome old residence had for years been used as a negro hotel and restaurant. On it now stands the large Thrash Building.

EAGLE HOTEL. Just below Eagle street stood and still stands the building then and for years afterwards known far and wide as the Eagle hotel, then owned by James Patton and later by his son James W. Patton. There were a large blacksmith shop just below this hotel, where Sycamore street now leaves South Main, and a tannery on the branch back of and below this. Joshua Roberts lived on the hill where Mrs. Buchanan lived until her recent death, and it was the last house on that side of the street.

LARGE LAND OWNERS. In the angle formed by Patton avenue and South Main street, according to Dr. Baird, the lands were owned principally by James M. Smith, Col. James M. Alexander, James W. Patton, and Samuel Chunn, but James B. Mears and Drake Jarrett owned from T. C. Smith's drug store down to and including Mears' Daylight store. The Methodist and Presbyterian churches owned and occupied the land now used by them for their present places of worship. Within this area were eleven residences, two stores, two churches, two stables, one tanyard and one barn. At the corporate line on South Main street, at the forks of the road, lived Standapher Rhodes, and north of him was the blacksmith shop of Williamson Warlick whose sign read: "Williamson Warlick Axes," his axes being especially fine.

He died and was succeeded there by Elias Triplett. Two hundred yards north was the home of Rev. William Morrison, a Presbyterian minister and the father of Mr. Theodore S. Morrison. J. M. Alexander afterwards lived in this house. Then came a tannery of J. M. Smith's, while David Halford occupied a residence at the corner of South Main and Southside avenue, known as the Goodlake curve because of the reverse curve of the street railway tracks at that point. There was a frame house about halfway between the Halford house and Mrs. M. E. Hilliard's residence. Mrs. Hilliard's home site was formerly occupied by a large two-story frame house which stood upon the street, and was occupied at one time by Col. J. M. Alexander before he removed to "Alexander's," ten miles down the French Broad river. Then John Osborne occupied the Alexnader (Hilliard) house for a long time, to be followed by Isaac McDunn, a tailor. It was finally bought by the late Dr. W. L. Hilliard, and occupied as a residence. From his house to Aston street there was no dwelling, though a large stable belonging to the Eagle hotel stood where now stands the Swannanoa-Berkeley Hotel.

GEORGE SWAIN. He was born in Roxborough, Mass., June 17, 1763, and on September 1, 1784, he left Providence, R. I., for Charleston, S. C.; but as a storm had required that much of the cargo be thrown over board, Swain arrived at Charleston penniless. He walked to Augusta, Ga., where he lived a year, and then removed to Wilkes, afterwards Oglethorpe county, where he engaged in hat-making, and was a member of the legislature of Georgia five years, and of the Constitutional convention held at Louisville about 1795, in which year he moved to Buncombe county and settled in or near Asheville, soon afterward marrying Carolina Lowrie, a sister of Joel Lane, founder of the city of Raleigh, and of Jesse Lane, father of Gen. Joseph Lane, Democratic candidate for Vice-President in 1860. She was the widow of a man who had been killed by the Indians. In the early part of his residence George Lane lived at the head of Beaverdam creek, where the late Rev. Thomas Stradley afterwards resided and died, and where, on January 4, 1801, David Lowrie Swain, afterwards judge, governor and president of the University, was born. Here the future statesman saw the first wagon ever in Buncombe brought up the washed out bed of Beaverdam creek in default of a road. At this sight, "he incontinently took to his heels and rallied only when safely entrenched behind his father's house, a log double cabin." "About 1805 a post-route was established on the recently constructed road through Buncombe county. . . . In 1806, the post-office at Asheville was made the distributing office for Georgia, Tennessee and the two Carolinas, and George Swain became postmaster," the commission issuing in 1807. He was a ruling elder in the Presbyterian church. He used to say his father was a Presbyterian and an Arminian, and his mother was a Methodist and a Calvinist. He was a trustee of the Newton academy. He afterwards carried on the hatter's business in the house now called the Bacchus J. Smith place in Grove Park, where his son-in-law, William Coleman, succeeded him as a hatter. For some time before his death he was insane. He died December 24, 1829.

SAMUEL CHUNN. In 1806 he was chairman of the Buncombe county court, having been a tanner for years, his tanyard being where Merrimon avenue crosses Glenn's creek. In 1807 he was jailer, and from him Chunn's Cove took its name. He died in 1855, on the bank of the French Broad in Madison county at what is known as the Chunn place, where he had resided in his old age.

WILLIAM WELCH. He was at one time a member of the Buncombe county court, and in January, 1805, was coroner. He was interested in lands on what are now Haywood and Depot streets. He afterwards removed to Waynesville and married Mary Ann, a daughter of Robert Love. In 1829 he was a senator from Haywood county, a member of the constitutional convention of 1835 and for many years clerk of the court. He was born April 8, 1796, and died February 6, 1865.

COLONEL WILLIAM DAVIDSON. He was a son of John Davidson and first cousin of Gen. Wm. Davidson, who succeeded Griffith Rutherford in the generalship when the latter was captured at Camden. Gen. Davidson was killed February 1, 1781, at Cowan's ford of Catawba river. Col. Davidson was a brother of the Samuel Davidson who was killed by the Indians in 1781-2 at the head of the Swannanoa river, and was the first representative of Buncombe county in the State Senate, taking a prominent part in the preparations made by the

North Carolinians for the Battle of Kings Mountain. He was the father of William Mitchell Davidson of Haywood county, whose son, Col. Allen T. Davidson, was a prominent lawyer and represented this section in the Confederate Congress.

WILLIAM MITCHELL DAVIDSON. He was born January 2, 1780, and died at Rock Island Ferry, on the Brazos river, Washington county, Texas, May 31, 1846, and was buried in the Horse Shoe Bend of that stream in the private burying ground of Amos Gates. On January 10, 1804, he married Elizabeth Vance (who was born on Reem's creek, Buncombe county, North Carolina, March 23, 1787), the ceremony being performed by the Rev. Geo. Newton. She died at the home of her son, Col. Allen Turner Davidson, on Valley river, Cherokee county, April 15, 1861. They settled on a beautiful farm on Jonathan's creek, in Haywood county, where they remained until October 24, 1844, when the family went to Santa Anna, Ill., where they remained until the first of March, 1845, when they again set out for Texas. They settled on Wilson's creek of Collin county in April. From there they moved to Rock Island Ferry, where Mr. Davidson died. The family then returned to North Carolina—April, 1847. One cause of his removal to Texas was an unfortunate mercantile venture which he had made with his sons, W. E., H. H., an A. T., at Waynesville, in 1842. The story of the adventures of this family to and from Texas at that early day, as preserved in a manuscript written by John M. Davidson, one of W. M. Davidson's sons, reads more like a romance than a sober recital of real facts. (See Appendix.)

ISAAC B. SAWYER. Was born on Tuskeegee creek in Macon, now Swain, county in 1810. James W. Patton, John Burgin and 'Squire Sawyer were, for years, the three magistrates composing the Buncombe county court. He was the first mayor of Asheville and was clerk and master for many years before the Civil War and until the adoption of the Code. He was the father of Captain James P. Sawyer, who for years was the president of the Battery Park bank, a successful merchant and a public spirited and enterprising citizen. Isaac B. Sawyer died in 1880.

JAMES MITCHELL ALEXANDER. He was born on Bee Tree creek, Buncombe county, May 22, 1793. His grandfather, John Alexander, of Scotch-Irish descent, was a native of Rowan county, where he married Rachel Davidson, a sister of William and Samuel Davidson, and resided in Lincoln county, during the Revolutionary war. They were afterwards among the first settlers of Buncombe, but moved to Harper's river, Tenn. His son, James Alexander was born in Rowan, December 23, 1756. He fought on the American side at Kings Mountain, and Cornwallis's camp chest, captured by him, was in Buncombe in 1898 when "Asheville's Centenary" was written by F. A. Sondley, Esq. March 19, 1782, he married in York district, South Carolina, Miss Rhoda Cunningham, who had been born in Pennsylvania, October 13, 1763. They then moved to Buncombe with their father and uncle and settled on Bee Tree, where he died in the Presbyterian faith. James Mitchell Alexander was their son, and on September 8, 1814, he married Nancy Foster, oldest child of Thomas Foster, who was born November 17, 1797. In 1816 he removed to Asheville and bought and improved the Hilliard property on South Main street. He was a saddler, and at this house he lived till 1828, carrying on his trade and keeping hotel. In 1828, upon the completion of the Buncombe turnpike, he bought and improved the place on the right bank of the French Broad, ten miles from Asheville, afterwards famous as Alexander's hotel, also carrying on a mercantile business there. In the latter part of his life he turned over this business to his son, the late Alfred M. Alexander, and one of his sons-in-law, the late Rev. J. S. Burnett, and improved the place three miles nearer Asheville called Montrealla, where he died June 11, 1858. His wife died January 14, 1862.

ANDREW ERWIN. He is the man to whom Bishop Asbury referred as "chief man." He was born in Virginia about 1773 and died near the War Trace in Bedford county, Tenn., in 1833. When seventeen years old he entered the employment of the late James Patton, afterwards becoming his partner as inn-keeper and merchant at Wilkesborough. In 1800-01 he was a member of the House of Commons from Wilkes. He was Asheville's first postmaster. In 1814 he moved to Augusta, Ga.

THOMAS FOSTER. He was born in Virginia October 14, 1774. In 1776 his father, William Foster came with his family and settled midway between the road leading to the Swannanoa river by way of Fernihurst from Asheville. He married Miss Orra Sams, whose father, Edmund Sams, was one of the settlers from Watauga. After his marriage Thomas Foster settled on the bank of Sweeten's creek, afterwards called Foster's Mill creek, the first which enters Swannanoa from the south above the present iron bridge on the Hendersonville road. He was a member of the House of Commons from Buncombe from 1809 to 1814, both inclusive, and represented that county in the State senate in 1817 and 1819. He died December 24 (incorrectly on tombstone December 14), 1858. He was a farmer and accumulated a considerable property. A large family of children survived him. His wife died August 27, 1853. He is mentioned in Wheeler's History of North Carolina, Bennett's Chronology of North Carolina and Bishop Asbury's journal.

WEAVERVILLE, BUNCOMBE COUNTY. The greater part of the early settlers of this country was made up of men and women seeking religious liberty. This motive no less prompted the immigrants from Northern Europe than the great body of Scotch-Irish that emigrated to this country from Scotland and Ireland. In Pennsylvania and down through the valley of the Shenandoah we find the Dutch of Holland and the Scotch-Irish, living side by side dominated by a single purpose.

One of the pioneers in Buncombe county came from the valley of Virginia from this large Dutch settlement into what is now Buncombe county, and was the ancester of the large family of Weavers now living in that section.

Previous to 1790 John Weaver and wife, Elizabeth, with their infant son (Jacob), came from Virginia via the Watauga in Tennessee, crossing the Ball mountain in what is now Yancey county, and settled on Reems creek, near the present town of Weaverville. From the first census of the United States 1790 (see page 110) it appears that John Weaver was a resident of Burke county, which then included what is now Buncombe county. His family then consisted of wife, two daughters and one son under sixteen years of age. From this it is evident that he reached North Carolina sometime between 1786 and 1790. In the office of Register of Deeds for Buncombe county, in Book No. 1 at page 100, is recorded a deed from John McDowell of Burke county, conveying to John Weaver of Buncombe county 320 acres of land; consideration 100 pounds; description, "On both sides of Reems creek and

on both sides of the path leading from Green river to Nola-
chuckee." This is interesting inasmuch as it seems to locate
the old Indian trail from the east to the lands west of Unakas.
There is little doubt that this young pioneer brought his
young wife and infant son from the Watauga over this trail
in quest of a permanent home.

John Weaver was born December, 1763, and died December,
1830. In his will, probated April Session, 1831, was found
the following names: wife, Elizabeth; daughters, Susannah,
Christiana, Mary, Elizabeth, Matilda and Catherine; sons,
Jacob, James, John (better known as Jack), Christopher G.,
and Michael Montreville. From this family of six daughters
and five sons sprang the largest number of descendants, or most
numerous group of related families in Buncombe county,
springing from one ancestor. Some of the oldest related
families living in Buncombe county have their origin in more
than one ancestor; for instance, the Baird family sprang from
two brothers, Zebulon and Bedent; the Alexander family,
from James Alexander, followed by a brother, nephew and
other kinsmen; the Davidson family, from Samuel and William. These last named pioneers entered Buncombe county
from the east through the Swannanoa gap. John Weaver,
as stated above, came from Virginia and entered this county
from the northern section and what is now Yancey county.
His oldest son, Jacob, married Elizabeth Siler of Macon county.
From this union were born four sons and three daughters,
John S., Jesse R., William W., and James Thomas, Elizabeth,
Saphronia and Mary. All these children of Jacob Weaver
married and became the heads of families living in Buncombe
county. Their descendants constitute the large majority of
Weavers and Weaver relations now living in this county.
John S. Weaver first married Mary Miller of Bolivar, Ten-
nessee; she died in 1867 and his second wife was Mary Mc-
Dowell of Macon county, daughter of Silas McDowell. Jesse
R. Weaver married Julia Coulter of Greenville, Tennessee.
William Weimer Weaver married Evalin Smith of Buncombe
county, daughter of Samuel Smith. James Thomas Weaver
married Hester Ann Trotter of Macon county. Elizabeth
Weaver married Burdie Gash. Saphronia Weaver married
Jamison McElroy. Mary Weaver married Robert V. Black-

stock. Nearly all of the living descendants of these families now live in Buncombe county, except the McElroy family, which moved to Arkansas shortly after the Civil War.

The next child of the pioneer, John Weaver, was Susannah, who married a Mr. McCarson; from these are descendants living in this and adjacent counties.

The second daughter, Christiana, married Samuel Vance, uncle of Z. B. Vance, who later moved to Bedford county, Tennessee. The third daughter, Mary, married Henry Addington of Macon county, where many descendants from this union still live. The fourth daughter, Catherine, married Andrew Pickens from South Carolina, who settled in Buncombe county. Rev. R. V. Pickens, Tarpley Pickens, Christly Pickens, Mrs. Eliza Gill, and Mrs. Martha Carter, who became the heads of large families in this county, were sons and daughters of Andrew and Catherine Pickens. The fifth daughter, Elizabeth, married Robert Patton Wells. From this union were many sons and daughters, some of whom, known to the writer and living in Buncombe county, were Robert C. Wells, W. F. Wells, Saphronia, who married Capt. R. P. Moore, Jane, who married Dr. Micheaux, and Matilda, who married Mathias Faubion of Tennessee. The sixth daughter of John Weaver, Matilda, married Jefferson H. Garrison. From this union were born sons and daughters in this and adjacent counties. Two sons, William and John, were gallant soldiers in the Civil War.

Referring to the sons of John Weaver, other than Jacob, who has already been referred to, James first married a Miss Barnard. Their daughter, Christiana, married William R. Baird, and these were the parents of Capt. I. V. Baird, William Baird, Zebulon Baird, Dr. Elisha Baird, John R. Baird, Misses Mollie and Catherine Baird, all now living in Buncombe county, except Dr. Elisha and John R. Baird, who died within the last ten years. James Weaver's second marriage was to Mrs. Gilliland. Children were born to James Weaver by both of these unions, but they moved in early life to Tennessee and Missouri.

James Weaver first represented Buncombe county in the lower house of the legislature in 1825, serving with David L. Swain. He was subsequently re-elected to this office in 1830, 1832, 1833 and 1834, serving with William Orr, John Clayton and

Joseph Henry resepectively. Later he moved to Cocke county, Tennessee, died July 28, 1854, and was buried on the old homestead, at the place known as Weaver Bend, just below Paint Rock. Subsequently, one of his daughters removed his remains and re-interred them at Knoxville, Tenn. Overlooking this grave, and on the very apex of a high, steep mountain, at Weaver Bend, is a small white cross set in a rock, by whose hands no one knows. It can be seen from the car window as the train moves through the river gorge 500 feet below. It is a tradition that some Jesuits placed a few of these crosses on conspicuous promontories through the Smoky mountains long before any of the settlements had been made by white men. However, this may be, this little emblem has rested on this western "Horeb" for possibly two centuries, looking out and towards the rolling rivers and alluvial valleys of East Tennessee, which to the early settlers was a real land of promise flowing with milk and honey.

John, or Jack, Weaver married and lived on the French Broad river just above the mouth of Reems creek. Some of his descendants are still living in this county; of those who moved elsewhere little is now known.

Christopher G. Weaver married a Miss Lowry and lived on Flat creek three miles north of Weaverville. He died in early life and has no descendants now living in Buncombe county.

Montreville Michael Weaver was the youngest son of John Weaver. He was born August 10, 1808, married Jane Baird. To this union was born four sons and five daughters. The sons were Fulton, who died unmarried, and Capt. W. E. Weaver, who married Miss Hannah Baird and is now living at Weaverville, N. C. The third son, John, married Miss Garrison, neither of whom is now living. Dr. Henry Bascomb Weaver married Miss Hattie Penland, daughter of Robert Penland of Mitchell county, N. C. Dr. Weaver is now living in Asheville, a practicing physician who possesses the confidence and esteem of those who know him. The daughters of Montreville Weaver: Mary Ann, married Dr. J. A. Reagan; Martha, married Dr. J. W. Vandiver; Margarette, married Capt. Wylie Parker; Catherine, married Dr. I. A. Harris; Eliza, married D. H. Reagan; all of whom have many descendants living in Buncombe county. Montreville Weaver, the last surviving child of the family of John Weaver, died in September, 1882.

Among these people are many strong men and women who have left their impress upon the communities in which they lived and have largely contributed to the upbuilding of the country. John Weaver the First left the information with his children that his father was a Holland gentleman. Other information obtainable indicates that his father came from Holland to Pennsylvania, and in company with other brothers and kinsmen of the same name settled near Lancaster, Pennsylvania, later migrating across Maryland into the valley of the Shenandoah in Virginia. The name of Weaver appears frequently in the public records about Lancaster, Pennsylvania, and in Virginia. From the report of Mr. H. J. Eckerode, the Archivist of the State of Virginia, it appears that there were two men by the name of John Weaver in the Revolutionary War from Virginia. One of these men was from Augusta county. In the same report also appear the following Weavers : Aaron Weaver, Princess Ann county, Tillman Weaver, Captain of Fauquier Militia. From the Pennsylvania Archives, Third Series, Vol. 23, appear the names of Captain Martin Weaver and Captain Jacob Weaver of Fifth and Seventh Companies of the Tenth Pennsylvania Regiment (see pages 314 and 383). The commissions of these men bear date July 1, 1777, and January 13, 1777, respectively. Other Weavers who figured in the Revolutionary history of Pennsylvania are George, Dolshen, Daltzer, Daniel, Henry, Adam, Jacob and Joshua. In fact this name appears in some muster roll of United States forces in every conflict in which the country has been engaged, beginning with the subjugation of the savage tribes, through all the wars with England and down to the Spanish-American war of recent date.

It is easy to believe that these Dutch people found congenial friends and neighbors in the Scotch-Irish people that were thrown together in the valley of the Shenandoah. They were all dominated by a single purpose, to hew out for themselves and their posterity a civil and ecclesiastic system, free from the domination of king or pope. There is no doubt but that the ancestors of these Dutch people were the loyal supporters of William, Duke of Nassau, called "William the

Silent'' who broke the power of Catholic Spain over the Netherlands in his defeat of Philip the Second in the latter part of the Sixteenth Century.

ASHE COUNTY. The act to establish the county of Ashe is one of the shortest on record. It was passed in 1799 (Laws of N. C., p. 98) and provides that "all that part of the county of Wilkes lying west of the extreme height of the Appalachian mountains shall be, and the same is hereby erected into a separate and distinct county by the name of Ashe," followed later by an act to establish permanently the dividing line between Ashe and Buncombe counties, the same to begin at "the Yadkin spring, and thence along the extreme height of the Blue ridge to the head spring of Flat Top fork of Elk creek, thence down the meanders of said creek to the Tennessee line."

The first record of the county court of Ashe is at the May term, 1806, with Alexander Smith, John McBride and Charles Tolliver, esquires, present. The following were the jurors : Sidniah Maxwell, foreman, James Sturgill, Allen Woodruff, Samuel Griffith, Seth Osborn, George Koons, John Green, James Dickson, Levi Pennington, Benjamin Hubbard, Charles Kelly, James Murphy, Wm. Harris, Alex. Lethern, Sciras Fairchilds. Edward King was appointed constable to attend the grand jury. Elisha Collins was excused from road duty "by reason of infirmity." At the February Term, 1807, James Cash recorded his "mark" for stock, being a crop and slit and under keel on the right ear; and Elijah Calloway and Mathias Harmon were qualified as justices of the peace. The jury appointed to "view the road from Daniel Harper's into the Elk spur road" made report that it "was no road."

FROM THE OLD COURT RECORDS. If there was a term of the Superior Court held in Ashe county prior to the March term, 1807, there is no record of it. On the 9th day of March of that year, however, Francis Locke presided as judge, and appointed John McMillan clerk, with bond of £2,000. Thomas McGimsey was appointed clerk and master, but resigned at the September Term, 1807. The grand jurors were Nathan Horton, foreman, James Bunyard, David Earnest, John Brown, Eli Cleveland, Joseph Couch, John Koons, Jonathan Baker, Elijah Pope, Jesse Ray, Samuel C. Cox, John Holman, Joshua Cox, Elijah Calloway, John Judd, Alex. Johnson, Morris

Baker, Wm. Weaver. Henry Hardin, constable, was sworn to
attend the jury. Only two cases were tried, the first of which
was *John Cox v. Isaac H. Robinett and Nathan Gordon,*
debt, judgment for £596, 14–6d and costs. At the September term, 1807, Judge Spruce McCay presided and fined the
delinquent jurors £10 each, but afterwards released them.
Six cases were tried. Judge Francis Locke returned for the
Spring Term, 1808, and Judge Samuel Lowrie followed him
at the Fall term. At the September term, 1810, on motion
of Robert H. Burton, who was to become judge and preside
at a future term, Samuel Cox, sheriff, was amerced, *nisi,* for
not returning execution in the case of *Robert Nall v. Jno.
Burton* and others. At the March term, 1811, Peter Hart
was committed to jail for 24 hours and fined 40 shillings for
making a noise and contempt of court, and Gideon Lewis and
John Northern were fined 20 shillings each for not answering
when their names were called. Judge Henderson presided at
the March term, 1812, when John A. Johnson resigned his
appointment as clerk and master. John Hall presided at the
September term, while at the March term, 1813, the jury
acquitted Wm. Pennington of rape. At this term Waugh
& Findlay recovered judgment for $55.06½ against Elizabeth
Humphries, but judgment was arrested and a new trial ordered. Duncan Cameron presided at the March term, 1814,
while at the September term, 1815, the jury found that Wm.
Lambeth, indicted for malicious mischief (Betty Young pros-
scutrix) had taken "a mare from his cornfield to a secret
place and stabbed her to prevent a repetition of injuring his
crop, but were unable to say whether he was guilty or not
and the judge, Hon. Leonard Henderson, ordered that a transcript of the bill of indictment and verdict be sent to the
Conference court. At the September term, 1817, Judge Lowery did not get to court on Monday, but arrived the following Tuesday, and ordered Thomas Calloway, county surveyor,
to survey the land in dispute between Thomas McGimsey
and Elisha Blevins. There is a grant to Gideon Lewis to 200
acres on Spring branch, entered September 16, 1802, of date
November 27, 1806, and a grant to Reuben Farthing for 200
acres on Beaver Dams, entered July 4, 1829, of date December 5, 1831. Benjamin Cutbirth conveyed 100 acres on South
Fork of New river to Andrew Ferguson, the execution of

which deed was proven by the oath of Joseph Couch at the May term, 1800, of the county court.

SECOND JAIL WEST OF THE BLUE RIDGE. The first jail stood behind what is now the Jefferson Bargain store, conducted by Dr. J. C. Testerman, from which some of the logs were removed to and made into the old stable in east Jefferson, where they are still visible. The next jail was of brick and stood on the site of the present jail on Helton road, and was built, probably, about 1833. It was burned in the spring of 1865 by men in the uniform of the United States army. A prisoner set the jail on fire about 1887 and Felix Barr repaired it.

JEFFERSON. A tract of fifty acres was deeded to Ashe county on which the town of Jefferson was built early in the 18th century; but the records of the grantor and grantee are lost. A map in the possession of G. L. Park, Esq., is supposed to have been made about 1800. It was made by J. Harper and shows the location of all lots, the court house and the crossing of the Helton road. The first court house was of logs and stood at the intersection of this road and the road running east and west, and now known as Main street. The next court house was of brick, and stood flush with Main street, in front of the present structure, and was built about 1832 or 1833, according to statement of Edmund C. Bartlett to Felix Barr, who also remembers seeing the date on a tin gutter, the tin work having been done by Lyle & Wilcox of Grayson county, Va. The present court house was built in 1904, the old road for Helton still going by it, but passing on both sides now, in narrow alleys or lanes, but coming together again before crossing the gap of the Phœnix mountain, nearly two miles to the north. There is a conflict of opinion as to where the first court was held, some claiming that it was in an old log church in the meadow immediately in front of the present court house and known as the McEwen meadow, and others that it was held in an old Baptist church half a mile from Jefferson on the Beaver creek road, near which a Mr. and Mrs. Smithdeal kept a tavern and on the opposite side of the road. The three rows of black-heart cherry trees on the main street give not only shade but an air of distinction not noticeable in newer towns, while the colonial style of several of the houses indicates a degree of refinement among the earlier inhabitants sadly missing from many places of equal

antiquity. Like Charleston, S. C., Jefferson has the air of
having been finished years ago; but as the Methodist Conference
has appropriated $20,000 and the citizens of Ashe $10,000
to build a school and college, and Mrs. Eula J. Neal, widow
of the late J. Z. Neal has conveyed eight or ten acres of choice
land for that purpose, and as a railroad from Virginia is expected soon, Jefferson is looking to the future with pride in
her past and a determination to achieve greater and greater
results. Before the coming of railroads Asheville was no
larger than Jefferson is now, nor had it any greater evidences
of culture and education than is here indicated by the citizenship of Jefferson. The large numbers of negroes in and
around Jefferson indicate that the former residents were men
of wealth and leisure. In 1901, the legislature incorporated
the Wilkesboro and Jefferson Turnpike company [7], and five
years later a finely graded road was completed between those
two places. By the terms of this act the State furnished
the convicts while the stockholders furnished the provisions
and paid the expenses. This road has been of greater help
to North Wilkesboro than to Jefferson; but if the town of Jefferson and the county of Ashe would secure trackage rights
over the narrow gauge road now operated for lumber exclusively between Laurel Bloomery, Tenn., and Hemlock, N. C.,
and then secure convicts to complete the line to Jefferson, under
the same terms as were granted for the building of the turnpike, and operate it by electricity, it need not wait for the
pleasure of lumber companies to construct a standard gauge
road at their convenience

OLD BUILDINGS. The building now known as Jefferson
Inn was built in two parts by the late George Bower. The
part used by the Bank of Ashe was built first, but the date cannot be determined definitely, and the eastern part some years
later. The frame building next to the east was George Bower's store, in which the postoffice was kept, and holes in the
partitions are still visible which had been used for posting
letters. James Gentry was killed one snowy Christmas
night about the year 1876, in front of this building while
Mont. Hardin was keeping hotel. Douglas Dixon was tried
for the murder, but was acquitted. It was in this building
also that Judge Robert R. Heath, sick and delirious, inflicted
a wound upon himself from which he afterwards died (May

26, 1871). The hand-forged hinges and window fastenings indicate that the building is old.

WAUGH AND BARTLETT HOUSES. But what is still known as the Bartlett house, east of the present postoffice, is probably the oldest house in town. It was occupied by Sheriff E. C. Bartlett, grandfather of the Professors Dougherty of Boone. Another old building is that still known as the Waugh house, notwithstanding its modern appearance. It is now a part of the Masonic building, apparently, but its main body, like the Bartlett house, is of logs. In it Waugh, Poe and Murchison sold goods in the first part of the nineteenth century. Certain it is that to this firm there were grants and deeds to land at a very early date, and the first map of Jefferson was made by J. Harper for Wm. P. Waugh, the senior member of this firm; Mathias Poe, the third member is said to have lived in Tennessee; but Col. Murchison for years occupied the large old residence which still stands on the hill at the eastern end of town.

EARLY RESIDENTS OF JEFFERSON, ASHE COUNTY. Nathan H. Waugh moved to Jefferson from Monroe county, Tenn., in 1845. He was born April 24, 1822. Among those living in Jefferson in 1845 were Col. George Bower, Rev. Dr. Wagg, a Methodist preacher, and the Rev. William Milam, also a Methodist preacher, and the jailer; also Sheriff E. C. Bartlett, Cyrus Wilcox, a tinner, George Houck, blacksmith, whose daughter married Cyrus Grubb of the Bend of New river; and Wm. Wyatt. Daniel Burkett, who lives one mile South of Jefferson and whose daughter married Rev. Dr. J. H. Weaver of the Methodist Church, South. William Willen, an Englishman and a ditcher, lived one mile east of Jefferson on the farm now owned by D. P. Waugh. Mrs. Lucy A Carson moved to Jefferson in 1870, and remembers as residents at that time S. C. Waugh, Wiley P. Thomas, Mrs. America Bower, Dr. L. C. Gentry, Rev. James Wagg, J. E. and N. A. Foster, E. C. Bartlett. The Fosters delivered salt to Ashe county during the Civil War. Mrs. Milam owned a residence opposite J. E. and N. A. Foster's, but gave the lot to Adam Roberts, colored, who subsequently sold it and built the brick house on the hill to the south of town. The Carson house, brick, was built in 1845, Geo. Bower giving John M. Carson,

his brother-in-law, the lot on which it stands.   Captain Joseph
W. Todd built the house to the west of the Carson residence in 1870, and the Henry Rollins house had been built
long before that time.   The Negro mountain was so called
because a runaway negro, during or before the Revolutionary
War, escaped and hid in a cave on the mountain till his hiding place was discovered and he was recaptured and returned
to his master east of the Blue Ridge.   The Mulatto mountain
is said to have taken its name from the color of the soil, but
no plausible reason was given for the names applied to the
Paddy and Phoenix mountains.

ARAS B. COX.   Aras B. Cox was born in Floyd county,
Va., January 25, 1816, and married Phoebe Edwards, February 23, 1845.   They settled in Ashe county.   In 1849 he was
elected clerk of the Superior Court, and also in 1853.   He
sold his farm in Alleghany county, and bought one seven
miles from Jefferson.   He was in the Confederate War.   He
was a distinguished physician and the author of "Footprints
on the Sands of Time," published at Sparta, N. C., in August,
1900.   He died soon after.

COLONEL GEORGE BOWER.   So higly regarded was Col.
Bower for his wisdom and sagacity that he was almost universally called " Double Headed Bower," or "Two Headed
Bower."   He was born in Ashe county, January 8, 1788.   His
father was John Bower, whose will as recorded in Ashe county
disposed of considerable property. [8]   George was a merchant,
farmer, live-stock raiser and hotellist at Jefferson.   He married a Miss Bryant first, and after her death Miss America
Russeau.   He was elected State Senator when Andrew Jackson was elected president both times. [9]   He became one of
the bondsmen of John McMillan as clerk of the Superior
Court as early as the September term, 1813. [10]   At subsequent terms he was appointed clerk and master and gave
bond as such. [11]   He owned a large number of slaves and
many State bonds.   He was drowned in the Yadkin river,
October 7, 1861.   His will was probated in 1899, Book
E, p. 387.   His widow married Robert R. Heath, who was
born in New Hampshire October 25, 1806, and died at Jefferson, May 26, 1871.   "He was an able lawyer and an upright judge," is engraved on his tomb.   Mrs. Heath then

married Alston Davis. She was born February 26, 1816, and died May 25, 1903. Her will was probated in 1903, Book E, p. 524.

A TRAGIC DEATH. In October, 1861, George Bower followed a runaway slave to the ford of the Yadkin river. He was in his carriage, and the negro driver told him the river was too swollen to admit of fording it at that time. Col. Bower, insisting, however, the colored man drove in. The current took the carriage with its single occupant far beyond the bank. Col. Bower was drowned, but the driver and horses escaped.

STEPHEN THOMAS. This gentleman was a progressive and valuable citizen of Creston, having kept a store and tavern there. He was born in May, 1796, and died in May, 1864. His wife was a daughter of Timothy Perkins. He reared a splendid family. [1] [2]

DAVID WORTH. He was descended from William Worth, who emigrated from England in the reign of Charles the Second. His father had owned considerable property under the Commonwealth, but at the Restoration it had been confiscated, and his family scattered in search of safety. William had a son, Joseph, born in Massachusetts, and Joseph's son Daniel, married Sarah Husey. Daniel Worth was a son of Joseph and was born in Guilford county, October 15, 1810. Daniel Worth was the father of David Worth, who came to Creston about 1828, and died December 10, 1888. He was a tanner by trade. He also was a most valuable citizen and highly respected. He married Miss Elizabeth Thomas, daughter of Stephen Thomas. She was born January 18, 1821, and died October 22, 1895. [1] [3]

ZACHARIAH BAKER. He lived at Creston and was a successful farmer and stock raiser. His wife was Miss Zilphea Dickson. They reared a large family of influential and successful citizens. One of his sons, John, married Delilah Eller, and the other, Marshall, married Mary Eller, a daughter of Luke Eller. [1] [4]

THE GRAYBEALS. They are said to be of Dutch ancestry, are generally thrifty and successful folk, and own much real estate and live stock. They are honest, frugal and among the best citizens of Ashe.

JACOB, HENRY AND JOHN ELLER. They were sons of Christian Eller, once a resident of the Jersey Settlement in Davidson county. The two former came to Ashe and settled on the North Fork of New river, reared large families, and were successful, useful, respected citizens. Their sons were Peter, Luke, William, John, David and Jacob. John settled on the South Fork and later moved to Wilkes. His sons were Simeon, David, Absalom, John and Peter, who reared large families which are scattered over Western North Carolina, Tennessee, Virginia, Iowa and Nebraska.[15]

SOME EARLY SETTLERS OF ASHE.[16] "These noble, self-sacrificing men and women of the early times endangered their lives and braved many hardships in the wild Indian coutry to open the way to happy homes, schools, churches and the blessings of our present civilization. Some of these were Henry Poe, Martin Gambill, Thomas Sutherland, Timothy Perkins, Captain John Cox, Henry Hardin, Canada Richardson, James Douglas, Daniel Dickson and Elijah Calloway. Besides these were many others whose names awaken much unwritten history : Miller, Blevins, Ham, Reeves, Woodin, Barr, Baker, Eller, Goodman, Ray, Burkett, Graybeal, Houck, Kilby, Ashley, Jones, Gentry, Smith, Plummer, Lewis, Sutherland, McMillan, Colvard, Barker, Senter, Maxwell, Calhoun, Sapp, Thomas, Worth, Oliver and others."

HAYWOOD COUNTY.[17] "In the legislature of 1808, General Thomas Love, whose home was near where the 'Brown' house now stands back of the McAfee cottage in Waynesville, and who was that year representative from Buncombe county in the General Assembly, introduced a bill having for its purpose to organize a county out of that portion of Buncombe west of its present western and southwestern boundary and extending to the Tennessee line, including all the territory in the present counties of Haywood, Macon, Jackson, Swain, Graham, Clay, and Cherokee. The bill met with favor, was passed, ratified and became a law December 23, 1808.

"On Richland creek, about the year 1800, the neucleus of a village had been formed on the beautiful ridge between its limpid waters and those of Raccoon creek. The ridge is less than a mile wide and attracted settlers on account of the picturesque mountains on either side and the delightfulness of the climate. At that early time a considerable population was already there. Several men, who were well known in the State and who afterwards became prominent in public affairs, had built homes upon that nature favored spot and were living there. Such men as General Thomas Love, Colonel Robert Love, Colonel William Allen, John Welch, and others of Revolutionary fame were leaders in that community. Without changing his residence General Thomas Love was a member of the State Legislature, with two or three years intermission, from 1797 to 1828, for nine years as a member from Buncombe county and the remainder of the time from Haywood. Most of the time he was in the House of Commons but for six years he was also in the Senate. Colonel Robert Love served three years in the senate from Buncombe county, from 1793 to 1795. William Allen and John Welch were veterans of the Revolution and men of considerable influence in that community.

"As already stated that law was ratified on December 23, 1808, but it did not become operative until early in the year 1809. On the fourth Monday in March of that year the justices of the peace in the territory defined by the act erecting the county met at Mount Prospect in the first court of pleas and quarter sessions ever held in the limits of Haywood county. The following justices were present at that meeting: Thomas Love, John Fergus, John Dobson, Robert Phillips, Abraham Eaton, Hugh Davidson, Holliman Battle, John McFarland, Phillip T. Burfoot, William Deaver, Archibald McHenry, and Benjamin Odell.

"One of the first things the court thus constituted did was to elect officers for the new county. There were several candidates for the different positions, but after several ballots were taken the following were declared duly elected: Clerk of the court, Robert Love; Sheriff, William Allen; register of deeds, Phillip T. Burfoot; constable of the county, Samuel Hollingsworth; entry taker, Thomas St. Clair; treasurer, Robert Phillips; stray master, Adam Killian; comptroller, Abraham Eaton; coroner, Nathan Thompson; solicitor, Archibald Ruffin; standard keeper, David McFarland.

"Thus officered the county of Haywood began its career. The officers entered at once upon their respective duties, and the county became a reality. The first entry in the register's book bears date of March 29th, 1809, signed by Philip T.

Burfoot, and the first in the clerk's book is the same date by Robert Love.

"Until the court house and jail could be built the county officials met at private residences at Mount Prospect and prisoners were carried to jail in Asheville. Such proceedings were inconvenient and the commissioners appointed by the legislature, therefore, made haste to locate and erect the public buildings. It was expected that they would be ready to make their report to the court of pleas and quarter sessions as to the location of the county seat at the March session. Instead, however, they asked at that session to be indulged until the June term, and that request was granted.

"On Monday, June 26, 1809, the court met at the home of John Howell. The old record names the following justices as being present: Thomas Love, Philip Burfoot, Hugh Davidson, John McFarland, Abraham Eaton, John Dobson, William Deaver, Archibald McHenry, and John Fergus. At this meeting the commissioners named in the act of the legislature erecting the county made their report, in which they declared that it was unanimously agreed to locate the public buildings somewhere on the ridge between Richland and Raccoon creeks at or near the point then called Mount Prospect. As the commissioners were clothed with full power to act, it required no vote of the justices, but it is more than probable that the report was cheerfully endorsed by a majority of the justices present.

"At this June term of the court, the first for the trial of causes, the following composed the grand jury: John Welch foreman, William Welch, John Fullbright, John Robinson, Edward Sharteer, Isaac Wilkins, Elijah Deaver, David McFarland, William Burns, Joseph Chambers, Thomas St. Clair, John Shook, William Cathey, Jacob Shock, and John St. Clair. The following grand jurors for the next term of the Superior court that was to be held in Asheville in September: Holliman Battle, Hugh Davidson, Abraham Eaton, Thomas Lenoir, William Deaver, John McFarland, John McClure, Felix Walker, Jacob McFarland, Robert Love, Edward Hyatt and Daniel Fleming. This was done because of the fact that no Superior court was held in Haywood for several years after the formation of the county; but all cases that were appealed from the court of pleas and quarter sessions came up by law in the Superior court of Buncombe county at Asheville. For this court Haywood county was bound by law to send to Asheville six grand jurors and as many more as desired.

"At the June term inspectors of election, that was to take place in August, were also selected. There were then two voting precincts, and this election was the first ever held in the county. For the precinct of Mount Prospect the following inspectors were appointed: George Cathey, William Deaver, John Fergus, and Hugh Davidson. For the precinct of Soco, Benjamin Parks, Robert Reed, and Robert Turner were appointed.

"In the location of the public buildings at Mount Prospect, there was laid the foundation of the present little city of Waynesville. Tradition says and truthfully, no doubt, that the name was suggested by Colonel Robert Love in honor of General Anthony Wayne, under whom Colonel Love served in the Revolutionary War. The name suited the community and people, and the village soon came to be known by it. In the record of the court of pleas and quarter sessions the name of Waynesville occurs first in 1811.

"Some unexpected condition prevented the immediate erection of the public buildings. The plans were all laid in 1809, but sufficient money from taxation as provided for in the act establishing the county had not been secured by the end of that year. It was, therefore, late in the year 1811 before sufficient funds were in hand to begin the erection of the courthouse. During the year 1812 the work began and was completed by the end of the year. Mark Colman is said to have been the first man to dig up a stump in laying the foundation for that building. On December 21, 1812, the first court was held in this first court house."

HAYWOOD'S SIX DAUGHTERS. Formerly belonging to Haywood were Macon, Cherokee, Jackson, Swain, Clay and Graham counties. Of many of the pioneer residents of these counties when they were a part of Haywood Col. Allen T. Davidson speaks in *The Lyceum* for January, 1891. Among them were David Nelson and Jonathan McPeters, Jonathans creek having been named for the latter. David Nelson was the uncle of Col. Wm. H. Thomas, and died at 87 highly respected and greatly lamented. "He was of fine physical form, honest, brave and hospitable." "Then there were

Joshua Allison, George Owens, John and Reuben Moody, brothers, all sturdy, hardy, well-to-do men and good citizens, who, with Samuel Leatherwood constituted my father's near neighbors." "Joseph Chambers of this neighborhood moved to Georgia about the opening of the Carroll county gold mine, say, about 1831–32. He was a man of more than ordinary character, led in public affairs and reared an elegant family. His daughters were splendid ladies and married well. His wife was a sister of John and Reuben Moody." John Leatherwood was well known for his "thrift and industry, fine hounds, fine cattle and good old-time apple brandy; a good citizen who lived to a good old age. James McKee, father of James L. McKee of Asheville, lived on this creek, was sheriff of Haywood for many years, and died at an advanced age at Asheville. Near him lived Felix Walker. . . . He was a man of great suavity of manner, a fine electioneer, insomuch that he was called "Old Oil Jug." He went, after his defeat for Congress in 1824 by Dr. Robert Vance, to Mississippi, where he died about 1835. The manufacture and sale of gensing was begun on Jonathans creek by Dr. Hailen of Philadelphia, who employed Nimron S. Jarrett and Bacchus J. Smith, late of Buncombe county, to conduct the business. It was abundant then and very profitable, the green root being worth about seven cents a pound. A branch of this business was established on Caney river in Yancey county. I well remember seeing great companies of mountaineers coming along the mountain passes (there were no roads then only as we blazed them) with packed horses and oxen going to the "factory," as we called it; and it was a great rendezvous for the people, where all the then sports of the day were engaged in such games as pitching quoits, running foot-races, shooting matches, wrestling, and, sometimes a good fist and skull fight. But the curse and indignation of the neighborhood rested on the man who attempted, as we called it, "to interfere in the fight, or double-team," or use a weapon. The most noted men were John Welch, John McFarland, Hodge Reyburn, Thomas Tatham, Gen. Thomas Love and Ninian Edmundson. The leading families of Haywood were the Howells, being two brothers, John and Henry, who came from Cabarrus about 1818; the Osborns; the Plotts, Col. Thomas Lenoir; the Catheys, Deavers, McCrackens, Penlands, Bryers; David Russell of Fines creek, Peter Nolan, Robert Penland, Henry Brown, James Green, who was born in 1790, and was living in January, 1891, and many others.

JOSEPH CATHEY. He was born March 12, 1803, and died June 1, 1874, was a son of William Cathey, one of the first settlers on Pigeon river; was a delegate to the State convention of 1835, and in the senate and declined further political honors.

NINIAN EDMUNDSON. He was born in Burke, October 21, 1789, of Maryland ancestry, and came with his father to Pigeon Valley prior to 1808, where the family remained. He was in the War of 1812; was four years sheriff of Haywood. He served several terms in the State senate and many in the house. He was a most successful farmer and useful citizen. He died in March, 1868, highly esteemed.

JAMES ROBERT LOVE. He was born in November, 1798, and died November 22, 1863. He represented Haywood county many times in the legislature. He married Miss Maria Williamson Coman, daughter of Col. James Coman of Raleigh, who died January 9, 1842, aged 75 years. This marriage occurred November 26, 1822. Charles Loehr, a German professor of music, taught his children music for years, and Loehr's son afterwards became professor of music at the Asheville Female college. Love was so anxious to encourage the building of a railroad that he set aside a lot for the depot long before he died. He bought large boundaries of vacant and unsurveyed lands, and died wealthy.

DR. SAMUEL L. LOVE. He was born August 5, 1828, and died July 7, 1887. He received his diploma as a physician from the University of Pennsylvania; but was soon elected to the legislature, where he served many terms. He was a surgeon in 1861 on the staff of Gov. Ellis, and a delegate to the Constitutional convention of 1875. In 1876 he was elected State auditor.

THOMAS ISAAC LENOIR. Was born on Pigeon river August 26, 1817, a son of Thomas Lenoir of Wilkes. He went to the State University, and did not return to Haywood till 1847. He was a farmer and stock raiser and a progressive citizen. On June 13, 1861, he married Miss Mary E. Garrett. He died January 5, 1881. His brother, Walter Lenoir, was a captain in the Confederate army, and spent much of his life at Joseph Shull's in Watauga county, where he died July 26, 1890, aged sixty-seven years. He was graduated with high honor at the State University. He studied law and was admitted in 1845. He married Miss Cornelia Christian of Staunton, Va., in 1856, but she died soon afterward. He lost a leg in the Civil War at the battle of Ox Hill, September, 1862.

WILLIAM JOHNSTON was the fourth son of Robert Johnston, Sr., and was born two miles from Druhmore, the county town of Down county, Ireland, July 26, 1807, his ancestors having emigrated from Scotland to Ireland in 1641. He came with his father's family to Charleston, South Carolina, in December, 1818, and settled in Pickens District, South Carolina. About 1828 he moved to Buncombe county and married Lucinda, the only daughter of James Gudger and his wife Annie Love, daughter of Col. Robert Love of Waynesville, March 18, 1830, and settled in Waynesville, where he accumulated a large fortune. About 1857 he moved with his family to Asheville. After the Civil War he, with the late Col. L. D. Childs of Columbia, South Carolina, became the owner of the Saluda factory, three miles from that city. It was burned, however, and Mr. Johnston returned to Asheville, where he died. He was admittedly the most successful business man in this entire section of the State; and some think that the same business ability, if it had been exerted in almost any other field, would have produced results that would have rivaled the fortunes of some of our merchant princes.

JERRY VICKERS was a tinner who worked for Wm. Johnston, and also made gravestones out of locust, paradoxical as that may appear; but his head-boards in Waynesville cemetery, with names and dates neatly carved in this almost indestructible wood, are still sound and legible today.

WM. PINCKNEY WELCH. He was born in Waynesville November 14, 1838, and died at Athens, Ga., March 18, 1896. His mother's father was Robert Love, and his father was William the son of John Welch, one of the pioneers. The Welches came from Philadelphia soon after the Revolutionary War. He attended school at Col. Stephen Lee's school in Chunn's cove, after which he went to Emory and Henry college, leaving there in May, 1861, to join the Confederate army. He was a lieutenant in the 25th N. C. regiment, and took part in the battles of from Gaines Mills to Malvern Hill, Sharpsburg, Fredericksburg and in the campaign near Kinston and Plymouth, Petersburg, Bermuda Hundreds, and surrendered as a captain with Lee at Appomattox. The survivors of that war have named their camp after him. He practiced law after the war, was in the legislature in 1868 and 1870 and helped to impeach Gov. Holden. He was married first to Miss Sarah Cathey, a daughter of Col. Joseph Cathey of Pigeon river, soon after the war, and on the 26th of January, 1875, he married Miss Margaretta Richards White of Athens, Ga., his first wife having died soon after marriage. No braver man ever lived than Pink Welch.

THE PEOPLE OF MACON. Macon was organized into a county in 1828 "and was singularly fortunate in the character of the people who first settled it.[18] It was first represented in the legislature in 1831 by James W. Guinn in the senate and Thomas Tatham and James Whitaker in the house, and was thereafter represented in the senate four times by Gen. Ben. S. Britton, with James Whitaker, Asaph Enloe, James W. Guinn and Jacob Siler and Thomas Tatham in the house." Luke Barnard, Wimer Siler, and his sons William, Jesse R., Jacob and John; John Dobson, John Howard, Henry Addington, Gen. Thomas Love, Wm. H. Bryson, James K. Gray, Mark Coleman, Samuel Smith, Nimrod S. Jarrett, George Dickey, Silas McDowell, George Patton, and William Angel were typical men of the early population. "Wm. and Jacob Siler having married sisters of D. L. Swain, and Jesse R. Siler having married a daughter of John Patton of Buncombe, sister of the late lamented Mont. Patton, it is not difficult to account for the great moral worth of the county that now exists and has from its first settlement. . . .
Samuel Smith was the father of Bacchus J. Smith and Rev. C. D. Smith, and volunteered as a messenger to bear a letter from Gen. McDowell, at the Old Fort, to the principal chief of the Cherokees, at the Coosawattee towns about the close of the Revolutionary War.[19] The undertaking was full of peril, the whole country west of the Blue Ridge being then in the Cherokee Nation, then in arms, and before any white men lived in this country. The Coosawattee towns were on a river of that name in Georgia at least 250 miles away; but the mission was accomplished by this valiant man who aided

largely in bringing these people into peaceable terms with the whites. He moved to Texas, after having raised a family of distinguished sons in North Carolina,—dying in Texas when over ninety years of age." [20]

FRANKLIN. This was called the Sacred Town by the Cherokees [21] and was not named for Benjamin Franklin, as so many think, but for Jesse Franklin, once governor of this State. [22] The county was named for John Haywood, treasurer of the State in 1787. According to Rev. C. D. Smith in his Brief History of Macon county, p. 2, Macon was never a part of Buncombe county, because its western boundary line never extended west of the Meigs and Freeman line of 1802, and the territory embraced in Macon and a portion of Jackson and Swain was acquired from the Cherokees by treaty in 1817-18. In the spring of 1820 the State commissioners, Jesse Franklin and James Meabin, in accordance with an act of the legislature, came to the Tennessee valley and organized for the survey of lands "a corps of surveyors of whom Captain Robert Love, a son of Gen. Thomas Love, who settled the place at the bridge where Capt. T. M. Angel recently lived [23], was chief. Robert Love had been an honored and brave captain in the war of 1812, was much respected on account of his patriotic devotion to American liberty, and was consequently a man of large influence." Watauga plains, where the late Mr. Watson lived, was first settled upon for the county site and 400 acres, the land appropriated for that purpose, was located and surveyed there; but Captain Love favored the present site, and by a vote of all six companies of surveyors then in the field, on the ridge where Mrs. H. T. Sloan resided in 1905, the 400 acres appropriated was located.

FIRST SETTLERS IN FRANKLIN. Joshua Roberts, Esq., built the first house on the Jack Johnston lot, "a small round log cabin;" but Irad S. Hightower built the first "house proper," one built of hewn logs on the lot where stands the Allman hotel. Capt. N. S. Jarrett bought the first house proper, then Gideon F. Morris got it, and then John R. Allman. Lindsey Fortune built a cabin on the lot where the Jarrett hotel stood in 1894, and Samuel Robinson built on the lot occupied in 1905 by Mrs. Robinson. Silas McDowell first built where the residence of D. C. Cunningham stood, and Dillard Love built the first house on the Trotter lot. N. S.

Jarrett built on the lot owned by S. L. Rogers, and John F. Dobson first improved the corner lot owned in 1894 by C. C. Smith. James K. Gray built the second hewn-log house on the lot owned by Mrs. A. W. Bell, and Jesse R. Siler, one of the first settlers, built at the foot of the town hill where Judge G. A. Jones resided. He also built the second house on the Gov. Robinson lot and the brick store and dwelling owned in 1894 by the late Capt. A. P. Munday. James W. Guinn or Mr. Whitaker built the house afterwards owned by Mr. Jack Johnston. John R. Allman opened the first hotel in Franklin, followed soon afterward by a house at the "foot of the hill" built by Jesse R. Siler. [24]

PROMINENT RESIDENTS OF MACON. [25] James Cansler was born February 22, 1820, in Rutherford county, and died in Macon, July 24, 1907. He aided in the removal of the Cherokees in 1836-38, and was a captain in the Civil war. Captain James G. Crawford was born May 6, 1832, and in 1855 was appointed deputy clerk, being elected sheriff in 1858. He was a captain in the Civil War in the 39th regiment, serving till the end. He was in the legislature, and in 1875 was elected register of deeds, which place he held till near the end of his life. He married Miss Virginia A. Butler. One of the early settlers was Henry G. Woodfin, a physician and brother of Col. N. W. Woodfin of Buncombe. He was born December 27, 1811, and was married June 5, 1838 to Miss E. A. B. Howarth. He settled first on Cartoogechaye, but later moved to Franklin. He was a member of the county court, serving as chairman, and was in the legislature two terms. He died in 1881. He stood high as a physician and citizen. Dr. James M. Lyle came to Macon before the Civil War and formed a copartnership with Dr. Woodfin. He married Miss Laura Siler, and after her death, he married Miss Nannie Moore. Dr. G. N. Rush, of Coweta station, was born in 1824, in Rockingham county, Va., and read medicine under Dr. A. W. Brabson, graduated in medicine at University of Nashville in 1854. He served in the legislature in 1876-7. In 1854 he married Miss Elizabeth Thomas. He died December 12, 1897. Dr. A. C. Brabson was born in Tennessee in 1842, served through the Civil War, graduated from the College at Nashville in medicine, 1866-67, married Miss Cora Rush, March 30, 1881. Mark May, son of Frederick and Nellie

May, was born in Yadkin county December 7, 1812, and
married Belinda Beaman at the age of 24.   Early in life he was
ordained a Baptist minister, coming to Macon county after
serving as a minister 17 years in Yadkin and two years in
Tennessee.   He is the father of Hon. Jeff May of Flats, N. C.
Rev. Joshua Ammons was born in Burke, February 14, 1800,
and moved to Macon in 1822, settled on Rabbit creek,
was ordained a Baptist minister at Franklin in 1835, and
died September 27, 1877, after a very useful life.   Logan
Berry was born December 18, 1813, in Lincoln county, and
died February 8, 1910.   He married Matilda Postell of Buncombe, served as county commissioner, and was a useful and
respected citizen.   Stephen Munday was born in Person
county about the beginning of the nineteenth century but
moved to Buncombe county before the Civil War, where he
built a mill at Sulphur Springs.   He then moved to Macon,
and lived with his son, the late Alexander P. Munday at
Aquone, till his death in the seventies. [26] He was a useful
and highly respected citizen.   His son Alexander P. Munday
married Miss Addie Jarrett a daughter of the late Nimrod
S. Jarrett, and they resided first at the Meadows in what is
now Graham county about 1859, where they remained till
after the Civil War, moving thence to Aquone where they
died early in this century.   Captain Nimrod S. Jarrett was
born in Buncombe county in 1800, married a Miss McKee, and
moved to Haywood county in 1830, engaging in the "sang"
business, till he moved to Macon, where he resided at Aquone
in 1835, afterwards at the Apple Tree place six miles down
the river, and still later at Jarretts station on the Murphy
railroad.   He owned large tracts of mountain lands, and the
talc mine now operated at Hewitts.   He was murdered in
September, 1873, by Bayless Henderson, a tramp from Tennessee.   Henderson was executed for the crime, at Webster,
in 1874.

JOHN KELLY.   He was born in Virginia, married a Miss
Pierce, a neice and adopted daughter of Bishop Pierce, and
moved to Buncombe where he lived till about 1819, when he
moved to Macon to what is now known as the Barnard farm,
but soon moved to the Hays place, waiting for the land sale,
at which he bought a boundary of land lying in both Georgia
and North Carolina, including Mud and Kelly's creeks in

Georgia. His third son, Samuel, was born in Westmoreland county, Va., and in 1825 bought land six miles from Franklin, where he lived till his death in 1852. He married Miss Mary Harry. Three of his sons enlisted in the Confederate army, where one was killed in battle, the other two serving till the close of hostilities. They were N. J. and M. L. Kelly.[27]

NATHAN G. ALLMAN.[28] He was born in Haywood, January 5, 1818, and came to Franklin in 1846, where he lived 46 years continuously. He was a merchant and hotel keeper, and died February 17, 1892. He was a useful and influential citizen.

DR. W. LEVY LOVE. He was born in Chautauqua, N. Y., September 30, 1827, and early in life went to Kentucky with his father. There he joined the army and went to the war in Mexico, taking part in several battles. Returning, he was educated at Bacon college, Kentucky, where he also studied medicine, completing his course at Philadelphia. He then moved to Franklin, where, in 1868, he married Miss Maggie, a daughter of N. G. Allman. In this year he was elected to the State senate, where he served six years. He was also a lawyer, enjoying a fine practice. He died July 29, 1884. He was generally known as Levi Love.

JACKSON JOHNSTON. He was born in Pendleton district, S. C., November 25, 1820, and at sixteen years of age removed to Waynesville, where for several years he clerked for his brother William. While there, he married Miss Osborne of Haywood county; late in the forties he removed to Franklin, and became a merchant, accumulating a handsome fortune. His first wife having died he married Miss Eugenia Siler in 1859. She was a daughter of William Siler. His hospitality and humor were famous. He died April 10, 1892. He was charitable, intelligent and of high character.

THOMAS TATHAM. He served in the State senate from Haywood in 1817, removed to Macon and served in the legislature from that county from 1831 to 1834 inclusive, after which he removed to Valley river where he died. He was a good man and left many friends.

JAMES WHITAKER. He was born in Rowan April 3, 1779, one mile from Lexington, now Davidson. He was a justice of the peace in that county and removed to Buncombe in 1817, from which, in 1818 he was elected to the legislature and served till 1823, and removed to Macon in 1828, lived one mile from Franklin, and was elected to the legislature in 1828 and served continuously till 1833. He was appointed Superior court clerk at the first term of Cherokee county, and was elected to the legislature from that county in 1832 and 1842. He died on Valley river November 2, 1871, aged 92 years. He was a man of great intellect, high character and unsullied reputation; a stern man, a strong Baptist and did perhaps as much for his church as any other man in the State.

YANCEY. Yancey county was formed in 1833. It was cut off from Burke and Buncombe. Three counties have since been partly formed out of Yancey. They are: Watauga in 1849; Madison in 1851; and Mitchell in 1861. Yancey county is now bounded on the north by Mitchell county and the State of Tennessee; on the east by Mitchell and McDowell counties; on the south by McDowell and Madison; on the west by Madison and Buncombe counties and the Tennessee line. Mt. Mitchell, the highest mountain in the eastern half of North America, is in Yancey county. It was named for Dr. Elisha Mitchell, a teacher in the University, who explored it. Mt. Mitchell is a part of the Black mountains which extend partly across this county. Yancey county contains eighteen mountain peaks that rise above 6,300 feet. These mountains are very fertile and are covered with great forests of gigantic trees. Cherry trees in Yancey often grow four feet, the walnut eight feet, and the poplar ten feet in diameter.

The county was named for Bartlett Yancey, a native of Caswell county. He was educated at the University of North Carolina, studied law, and became eminent in his profession. He was twice a member of the Congress of the United States, and eight times a member of the senate of North Carolina. He was one of the first men in the State to favor public schools for all the people.

The county seat of Yancey is Burnsville, named in honor of Capt. Otway Burns, of Beaufort, N. C. He won fame in the war of 1812 against England. With his vessel, the "Snap-Dragon," he sailed up and down the Atlantic coast, capturing many English vessels and destroying the British trade. He had many wild adventures, and his name became a terror to British merchants. Finally the English government sent a war vessel, called the "Leopard," to capture Captain Burns.

The "Leopard" succeeded in capturing the "Snap-Dragon" while Captain Burns was on shore sick. After the war he was frequently a member of the legislature. A monument to his memory was recently erected at Burnsville.

Yancey has an approximate area of 193,000 acres, with an average assessed value of $2.60 per acre. Over 40 per cent of the land is held in large tracts of 1,000 acres or more in extent. These holdings are valued chiefly for their timber and are held principally as investments.

The topography is generally rough and the average elevation is high. The Black mountain range in the southern portion of the county contains many peaks more than 6,000 feet high, and Mount Mitchell, the highest peak east of the Rockies, rises to an elevation of 6,711 feet above sea level. In the northern and western sections of the county the ridges have an average elevation of about 4,000 feet above sea level, Bald mountain rising to 5,500 feet.

Four considerable streams, South Toe and Caney rivers, and Jacks and Crabtree creeks, rise within the county, and flowing in a northerly direction empty into Toe river, which forms the northern boundary of the county.

MRS. NANCY ANDERSON GARDNER. There are many old people in these mountains, but Mrs. Nancy Gardner of Burnsville was 98 the 15th of January, 1913. She was in full possession of all her faculties, and in 1912 furnished for this history a list of names of the first settlers of Yancey county. Her husband's father was Thomas Gardner, who was born in Virginia in 1793, and died in Yancey in 1853. He settled on Cane river when a boy. Her father was W. M. Anderson and her mother Patty Elkins, who was born in Tennessee in 1790. Her parents were married in 1809. James Anderson was from Ireland and served in Virginia with the Americans during the Revolutionary War, after which he moved (1870), first to Surry, and then to Little Ivy, where D. W. Angel now lives and where Mrs. Gardner was born, January 15, 1815. Her husband was William Gardner, to whom she was married March 22, 1832. Thomas Dillard, father of the wife of Robert Love, was her mother's uncle. She died early in 1913.

FIRST SETTLERS OF BURNSVILLE. Mrs. Gardner gave the following as the first settlers of Burnsville: John L. Williams and his sons Edward and Joshua; Dr. Job, Dr. John Yancey,

Abner Jarvis, Dr. Jacob Stanley, Samuel Flemming, Gen.
John W. McElroy, James Greenlee, John W. Garland, "Knock"
Boone, Amos Ray, W. M. Westall, J. Bacchus Smith, Joseph
Shepard, Adam Broyles, Mitchell Broyles, W. M. Lewis,
John Woodfin, James Anderson, Milton P. Penland, Jack
Stewart and John Bailey.

FIRST SETTLERS OF YANCEY. Among them Mrs. Gard-
ner mentioned the following, giving also the names of their
wives: Henry Roland, Berry Hensley, Ed. and James
McMahan, Thomas Ray, Edward Wilson, Jacob Phipps, Jerry
Boons, Hiram Ray, John Bailey, John Griffith, Joseph Shep-
ard, Strowbridge Young, James Proffitt, James Greenlee,
Blake Piercy, Thomas Briggs, John McElroy, Wm. Angel,
James Evans, W. M. Angelin, John Allen, Rev. Samuel Byrd.

INTERESTING FACTS ABOUT OLD TIMES. Mrs. Gardner's
grandfather, James Anderson, was said to be the first Methodist
west of the Blue Ridge. She remembered Parson Brownlow and
the "lie bill" suit and the sale of his bridle, saddle and horse;
also that William Angel lived near the present site of Burnsville but moved to Georgia, carrying his family and "One
hundred geese, which they drove." She gave not only the
names of the wives of the first settlers, but their children,
and where the first settlers lived. Also, that John Bailey
married Hiram Ray's daughter and donated the land for the
town of Burnsville; that Joseph Shepard married Betsy Horton, the grandparents of the late Judge J. S. Adams; that
Thomas Ray married Ivey Hensley and lived in Cane river
valley; that Jacob Phipps married Nancy Hampton, and
lived four miles west of Burnsville; that Edward Wilson married Polly Gilbert and lived on Cane river; that Jerry Boone
was a noted blacksmith and married Sallie McMahan. They
lived where Burnsville now stands; also that Hiram Ray
married a Miss Cox and was a wealthy and influential man.
Also that Zepheniah Horton lived one mile west of Burnsville, but none of his descendants now live in Yancey, though
some live in Buncombe and the State of Kansas; that Henry
Roland married Sallie Robinson and lived on Cane river; that
Berry Hensley married Betsy Littleton, among whose descendants were B. S., W., and Jas. B. Hensley. Edward and
James McMahan were the first settlers of Pensacola, and
Strowbridge Young married Patty Wilson. She spoke of

James Proffitt as having lived on Bald creek, and of his direct descendants, but did not give the name of his wife. She also spoke of James Greenlee as having married Polly Poteet and living on Cane river, but having had no children; Blake Piercy who married Fanny Turner, and lived on Indian creek, Thomas Briggs who married Jane Wilson and lived on Bald creek, John McElroy who married Miss Jamison and lived on Bald creek, James Evans who married a Miss Bailey and lived on Jack's creek, W. M. Angelin who married Miss Betsy Austin and lived on Banks creek, John Allen who married Molly Turner, and the Rev. Samuel Byrd who married a Miss Briggs and lived in the northern part of the county, naming many of his descendants.

FINE RIVER BOTTOMS. Those splendid lands, extending from the mouth of Prices creek up Cane river to within two or three miles of Burnsville, were in possession of white people as early as 1787, and were originally granted to John McKnitt Alexander and Wm. Sharp. The 640-acre tract at the mouth of Bald and Prices creeks is owned by descendants of Thomas L. Ray, who was among the first settlers of Yancey county. The Creed Young place, originally the John Griffith farm, on Crabtree, about two miles from Burnsville, is another fine farm. Milton P. Penland was another early settler, and owned valuable land near Burnsville. He was a man of influence and ability.

CELO OR BOLEN'S PYRAMID. What is known on government maps as Celo Peak used to be called Bolen's Pyramid; but why either name should have been given to this northern-most peak of the Blacks is not known, though, as there is a Bolen's creek between it and Burnsville, it is probable that a man of that name once lived near what is now called Athlone.

HENDERSON COUNTY.[30] Until 1838 Henderson was a part of Buncombe, and the story of its first settlement belongs to that county. . . . But in 1838, when Hodge Rabun was in the senate and Montreville Patton and Philip Brittain were in the house, it was erected into a separate county and named in honor of Leonard Henderson, once chief justice of the State, the county seat also having been named in his honor. In 1850 it had only 6,483 population, while in 1910 it contained 16,262.

"The crest of the Blue Ridge, in Henderson county, is an undulating plateau, which will not be recognized by the traveler in crossing. The Saluda mountains, beyond Green river, are the boundary line of vision on the south. The general surface features of the central part of this pearl of counties will be best seen by a glance at the pictorial view from Dun Cragin, near Hendersonville." [3] [1]

With a general altitude about that of Asheville, with broad river bottoms along the French Broad, Mud creek and elsewhere, its agricultural and grazing advantages surpass those of Buncombe; while as a summer and health resort, Hendersonville, its county seat, with its fine and well-kept hotels and boarding houses, surpasses in many important respects the only town that exceeds it in population, the famed city of Asheville. The social charm of this beautiful place, as well as of Flat Rock and Fletcher, is at least not surpassed in Buncombe or in Asheville itself. Hendersonville has everything in the way of hotels, boarding houses, clubs, banks, street railways, parks, lights, water, livery and other advantages that could be wished. The points of interest in the immediate vicinity are numerous and appealing. Last summer there were 15,000 visitors in town and 25,000 in the county. The churches represent every denomination.

John Clayton, of Mills river section, was in the legislature in 1827 and 1828, and in the senate in 1833. Largely through his influence Henderson was formed into a separate county. He was the grandfather of Mrs. Mattie Fletcher Egerton, first wife of Dr. J. L. Egerton and great-grandfather of Mrs. Wm. Redin Kirk. He with his son, John, was among the first jurors of this county. R. Irvine Allen, brother of Dr. T. A. Allen, the latter being the oldest male inhabitant of this county, and Jesse Rhodes were among the chain-bearers when the county lines were first surveyed. A committee, consisting of Col. John Clayton, Col. Killian, and Hugh Johnston, was appointed to select and lay off a county seat, and their first choice was the land at what is now called Horse Shoe in 1839. But there was so much dissatisfaction with this that two factions arose, called the River and the Road parties, the River party favoring the Horse Shoe site, it having been on the French Broad river. In 1839, however, the Road party enjoined the sale in lots of the land selected at Horse Shoe, and the controversy soon waxed so warm that the legislature authorized an election to determine the matter by popular vote, resulting in the success of the Road party. Judge Mitchell King of Charleston, S. C., who had been among the first settlers of this section and owned much of the land where Hendersonville now stands, conveyed fifty acres for the county site; and this was laid off into lots and broad, level right-angled streets, and sold in 1840. Dr. Allen died early in 1914.

HENDERSONVILLE. At the time the Civil War commenced there were on Main street, the Episcopal church, completed save for the spire; the Shipp house, adjoining, which formerly stood where the Pine Grove lodge now stands, and where Lawyer Shipp, father of Bartlett Shipp, Esq., lived. The present Sample home was then owned by the Rev. Collin Hughes, the Episcopal clergyman. The old Virginia House stood on the corner now occupied by the First National bank, and was built by David Miller and William Deaver, the latter having been killed in the Civil War. It was conducted many years by Mr. C. C. Chase; but about eighteen years ago it became the property of Hall Poole. A still older house was the old hotel built by John Mills, and stood on the present site of the St. John. It later became the property of Colonel Ripley, and was known far and wide as the Ripley House. There was nothing south of the court house site except the old Ripley residence, built by the Kings, and the house that is now Col. Pickens' residence. The only two houses standing prior to the formation of Henderson county in the town of Hendersonville, and remaining unchanged now, are the Arledge house on Main street, and the stone office-building in front of the Pine Grove lodge, near the Episcopal church.

BOWMAN'S BLUFF. About forty years ago a small colony of English people came to this section, and bought a vast acreage of land. Among them were the Valentines, well known in Hendersonville for many years, the Thomases, the Jeudweines, the Malletts (who still live on their place) and the Holmeses, still owning the place above referred to. It would be hard to describe this beautiful place. To the south of the old-fashioned house lies a tangle of garden, with its riot of vines, and its numerous overgrown arbors, and old trees trimmed in fantastic shapes. The house is approached by a long winding drive, between great old pines, and just in front of the house is the immense bluff, whereon wild crab-apples bloom in profusion. This falls away, a sheer descent many feet to the river below, and it was here that Mary Bowman was said to have leaped to her death many years ago, desperate over a hopeless love.

Centrally located to what was this English colony and on top of a hill, sits the little Episcopal church where they were wont to worship on Sunday, and which is used irregularly still.

Mr. Frank Valentine, who came to America in this colony, was educated at Cambridge, England, graduated with highest honor, holding several degrees. He went from Bowman's Bluff to Asheville, and later moved to Hendersonville, where he spent his remaining days. He was known as one of the finest educators in Western North Carolina.

FORMER CITIZENS. Peter Stradley lived at Old Flat Rock, and in 1870 died there almost 100 years old, highly respected and loved; Joseph Dotson lived to the age of 104 on his farm near Bat Cave, and made baskets and brooms. He was captured while in the Confederate army but escaped, running 18 miles over the ice. Govan Edney of Edneyville, also lived to a great age, and had a large experience as a hunter. Harvey Johnston and his wife once owned nearly all the land on the west side of South Main street, Hendersonville, and having no horse, managed to make fine crops notwithstanding. Robert Thomas, first sheriff of Henderson county, was killed by bush-whackers during the Civil War. Solomon Jones lived on Mount Hebron, and was known as a builder of roads, having constructed one from Hendersonville to Mount Hebron, and another up Saluda mountain; lived to be nearly 100, and made his own tombstone.

BUSINESS ENTERPRISES. The Freeze Hosiery mills were opened June 15, 1912; the Skyland Hosiery Co., at Flat Rock make silk and cotton hose and have been operating several years; the Green River Mfg. Co., at Tuxedo, six miles south of Hendersonville, was started in 1909. They make combed peelers and Egyptain yarns, their annual output being 350,-000 pounds; employing 250 hands, of whom 200 are skilled. They support an excellent school eight months every year; the Case Canning factory on the Edneyville road six miles from Hendersonville, at Dana, has a capacity of 500,000 cans a season;

the Hendersonville Light & Power Co., 7½ miles east of Hendersonville, have 1,250 horsepower, using only 400 at present; George Stephens operates a mission furniture factory, at Lake Kanuga, six miles out, where also is Kanuga club.

COUNTRY RESORTS. Besides the excellent hotels in Hendersonville, there is a fine hotel at Osceola lake, one mile from town on the Kanuga road; Kanuga club on Kanuga lake; Highland lake club, one and a half miles out on the Flat Rock road, with cottages, is a stock company; Chimney Rock, twelve miles east, is in the Hickory Nut canon; Buck Forest, now the property of the Frank Coxe estate, was for years a summer resort, and the falls in the vicinity are noted; Fletcher, near the Buncombe line is also popular, and the social charms of the neighborhood are well recognized; Buck Shoals is near, and the famous Rugby Grange, the attractive country estate of the Westfelts of New Orleans, is one of the "show-places" of Western North Carolina.

A LITERARY CURIOSITY. A poem written on white satin in quatrain form, into each of which was incorporated a clause of the Lord's prayer, is known to have been written by Mrs. Susan Baring and is now in the possession of a Hendersonville lady.

SETTLING THE GRAHAM BOUNDARY LINE. By ch. 202, Pub. Laws, 1897, 343, the county surveyors of Cherokee and Graham were authorized to locate the line between these two counties and Tennessee, according to the calls of the act of 1821.

CHEROKEE AND MURPHY. As early as 1836 the legislature provided that the Indian lands west of Macon should remain under the jurisdiction of that county till a new county should be formed for them, whose county seat should be named Murphy. (Rev. St. 1837, Vol. ii, p. 213 and p. 214). In 1842 the State granted to A. Smith, chairman of the County court, 433 acres for a court house, etc. (Deed Book A, p. 429, dated March 23, 1842.) [3] [2]

OLD COUNTY BUILDINGS. The old jail was back of the J. W. Cooper residence and the whipping post stood near where a street now runs, and the first court house, a very plain and unpretentious affair, stood at the intersection of the two main roads from the country. The new court house was built where the present one now stands, in 1891, at a cost of about $20,000., but it was burned in 1892. In 1893 and 1894 it was rebuilt, as the marble foundations and brick walls stood intact after the fire, at a cost of $12,000. There was no insurance on the burned building.

PREEMINENT ADVANTAGES. Murphy's location between two clear mountain rivers, its broad and almost level streets, its fine court house, schools and hotels form the nucleus around which a large city should grow. It has two competing railroads, and a climate almost ideal. Its citizens, too, are enterprising and progressive, good streets and roads being appreciated highly

MURPHY'S FIRST CITIZENS. Daniel F. Ramseur kept the old "Long Hotel," with offices, that used to stand near the public square. Felix Axley was the father of the Murphy bar and of F. P. and J. C. Axley. J. C. Abbott lived at the old A. T. Davidson place, and was a leading merchant after the Civil War. Samuel Henry, deceased, was an ante-bellum resident, was U. S. Commissioner for years, and a friend of the late U. S. District Judge R. P. Dick. A. M. Dyche (pronounced Dike) was sheriff, justice of the peace and a good citizen. S. G. R. Mount was postmaster and lived in the southern part of town. Dr. John W. Patton was a leading physician and lived near Hiwassee bridge. Mercer Fain lived where the Regal hotel stands now, and was a merchant, farmer and land speculator. Benjamin S. Brittain lived in East Murphy from the organization of the county till his death, and was register of deeds. Drewry Weeks lived on the northeast corner of the Square and was from the organization of the county till his death clerk of the old county court. Seth Hyatt, sheriff, lived where Capt. J. W. Cooper afterwards resided. Johnson King lived where S. Hyatt had lived, and married his widow. He was a partner of the late Col. W. H. Thomas, and the father of Hon. Mark C. King, several terms in the legislature. Dr. C T. Rogers was another leading physician. Jesse Brooks was a merchant and lived on what is now Church street. G. L. D. McClelland lived first on Church and afterwards on the east side of Main street and lived to be over ninety years of age, being highly esteemed. William Berry was a merchant and farmer; Xenas Hubbard was a tinner; James Grant was a merchant and kept store where the Dickey hotel now stands; John Rolen was a lawyer; J. J. Turnbill was a blacksmith, and a man of unusual sense.

WILLIAM BEALE. This scholarly man came to Murphy from Canada just prior to the Civil War and taught school; was several times sheriff, and lived on the south side of Hiwassee bridge.

DAVID AND JOHN HENESEA. Just after the Civil War they moved from a fine farm at the head of Valley river. John kept a hotel, now the residence of C. E. Wood.

JAMES W. COOPER. He moved to Murphy from Graham soon after the Civil War, and was a most successful lawyer and land speculator.

RESIDENTS OF CHEROKEE COUNTY. Among the more prominent may be mentioned Abraham Harshaw, the largest slave owner, four miles south of Murphy; John Harshaw, his brother; Abraham Sudderth, who owned the Mission farm six miles south of Murphy, where Rev. Humphrey Posey had established a mission school for the Cherokees; William Strange owned a fine farm at the mouth of Brasstown creek; Gideon Morris, a Baptist preacher, who married Yonaguska's daughter; Andrew Moore; David Taylor; David Henesea; James W. C. Piercy, who, from the organization of the county till his death, located most of the land in Cherokee; James Tatham, the father of Purd and Bent, who lived a mile west of Andrews; James Whitaker and his son Stephen, who lived near Andrews; Hugh Collett and his father, who lived just above Old Valley Town and were men of industry and integrity; Buck and Neil Colvard, who lived at Tomotla; Wm. Welch, who lived in the same neighborhood; and Henry Moss, who lived at Marble, Ute Hyatt living on the adjoining farm. Elisha P. Kincaid lived four miles east of Murphy, and above him lived Betty Welch, or Betty Bly or Blythe, the heroine of Judge Strange's romance, "Yonaguska." John Welch was her husband, a half-breed Cherokee, and an "Avenger of Blood." (See ch. 26.) In the western part of the county were Burton K. and George Dickey, Wm. C. Walker, who was killed at the close of the Civil War, having been colonel of the 29th N. C. regiment; Abel S. Hill, sheriff; Calvin C. Vest; and others, who lived on Notla. In the northern part lived Harvey Davidson, sheriff and farmer; and the Hunsuckers, Blackwells, Longwoods, Gentrys and others. Goldman Bryson lived on Beaver Dam, and was said to have been at the head

of a band of banditti during the Civil War, and was followed
into the mountains and killed by a party of Confederates.
Andrew and Jeff Colvard were founders of large and influential families. They were bold and daring frontiersmen and
citizens of character and ability. "Old Rock Voyles," as he
was affectionately called, lived on Persimmon creek, ten miles
from Murphy, and was a man of originality and humor. He
lived to a great age.

A CEMETERY IN THE CLIFFS. All along the crest of the
ridges which terminate in rock cliffs on the bank of the Hiwassee river about one mile below Murphy are large deposits
of human bones, supposed to be the bones of Cherokees. The
number of shallow graves on the crests of these ridges, covered over by cairns of loose stones, indicate that this must
have been the burial place of Indians for many years.

EARLY WATAUGA AND BOONE HISTORY. The first court in
Watauga was held in an old barn near the home of Joseph
Hardin one mile east of Boone, Judge Mitchell presiding,
and E. C. Bartlett being clerk. The first court house was
built in Boone in 1850 by John Horton for $4,000, but was
burned in 1873, with the records. The records were restored
afterwards by legislative authority upon satisfactory evidence
being furnished, and T. J. Coffey & Bro. in 1874 rebuilt the
court house for $4,800, the building committee having been
Henry Taylor, Dudley Farthing and Jacob Williams. The
present fine court house was erected in 1904 by L. W. Cooper
of Charlotte for $19,000. Alex. Green, J. W. Hodges and
George Robbins were the county commissioners. The first
jail was of brick and built by Mr. Dammons for $400, and the
second jail was a wooden building of heavy logs. On the second floor the timbers were twelve inches square, crossed with
iron, and when it was torn away by W. P. Critcher in 1909
the logs were made into lumber of the finest grade. A splendid new jail, with iron cages and rooms, was built in 1889 by
Wm. Stephenson of Mayesville, Ky., for $5,000. The follow-
ing have been sheriffs of Watauga : Michael Cook, John
Horton, Cob McCanles, Sidney Deal, A. J. McBride, John
Horton, A. J. McBride, D. F. Baird, J. L. Hayes, D. F.
Baird, J. L. Hayes, D. F. Baird, W. M. Calloway, W. B. Baird,
J. H. Hodges, D. C. Reagan. The following have been clerks:
Mr. McClewee, J. B. Todd, Henry Blair, W. J. Critcher, J.

B. Todd, M. B. Blackburn, J. H. Bingham, Thomas Bingham, W. D. Farthing.

W. L. Bryan in 1872 started the Bryan hotel and conducted a first class hotel for 27 years. In 1865 T. J. Coffey & Bro. came to Boone, and started the Coffey hotel, where they maintained an up-to-date stopping place for many years. It is now being conducted by Mr. Murry Critcher.

In 1858 Marcus Holesclaw, Thomas Greene and William Horton ran for the legislature upon the issue of moving the court house from Boone to Brushy Fork, and Holesclaw was elected by one vote. This meant that the court house must be moved; and Holesclaw introduced the bill for that purpose; but Joe Dobson represented this district in the senate, and although he was from Surry county, he managed to keep Holesclaw's bill at the foot of the calendar until the legislature adjourned. Of course, Holesclaw was never satisfied that his bill never reached a vote in the senate.

From ordinary circumstances L. L. Green came from the farm, studied law and became a leader in politics; was elected judge and performed his duties well. His portrait hangs in the court room, to the left of the judge's stand, while on the right is a portrait of his friend, Major Bingham, who was a fine lawyer and a great teacher of law. His name and fame went out over the whole State.

E. Spencer Blackburn was one of the most attractive men this section has produced. His father was Edward Blackburn, and his mother Sinthia Hodges. He was one of nine children. He was four times nominated for Congress, was elected twice; was assistant district attorney of the United States court, and died at Elizabethtown early in 1912.

W. B. Councill was a student of the learned Col. G. N. Folk, who after being admitted to the bar was elevated to the position of judge of the Superior court of this judicial district. He declined a renomination.

A FAMILY OF PREACHERS. William Farthing came as a missionary from Wake county to Beaver Dams, now in Watauga county, about 1826, but lived only three months after settling there. He bought what was then known as the Webb farm, about one-half mile from the principal Baptist church of that settlement. He had owned many acres near Durham before going to the mountains. His sons and those of John, his brother, who soon followed him to Watauga, were men of the highest character and standing. Many of them have been preachers, and four brothers of his family were in the ministry. Like the descendants of the original Casper Cable who settled on Dry Run, just in the edge of Tennessee, no drop of rowdy blood ever developed in any of the descendants of the pioneer Farthings. Dudley, son of Wm. Farthing, was for years judge of the county court and chairman of the board of county commissioners.

THE BROWNS OF WATAUGA. Joseph Brown came from Wilkes to Watauga long before the Civil War, and settled at Three Forks, where he married Annie Haigler, and reared eight children. Captain Barton Roby Brown of May Mead, Tenn., was a grandson, and married Callie Wagner in 1864. He was in the Sixth North Carolina cavalry, and a gallant soldier.

THE MAST FAMILY. Joseph Mast, the first of the name to come to Valle Crucis, Watauga county, was born in Randolph county, N. C., March 25, 1764, and on the 30th of May, 1783, married Eve Bowers who had been born between the Saluda and Broad rivers, South Carolina, December 30, 1758. Joseph was a son of John, who was brother of the Jacob Mast who became bishop of the Amish Mennonite church in Conestoga, Pa., in 1788. They had left their native Switzerland together, and sailed from Rotterdam in the ship "Brotherhood," which reached Philadelphia November 3, 1750. John Mast was born in 1740, and shortly after becoming 20 years of age left his brother Jacob, who had married and was living near the site of what is now Elverson, Pa. John wandered on foot through many lonely forests, but finally settled in Randolph county, where Joseph was born. There he married a lady whose given name was Barbara. From Joseph and Eve Mast have descended many of the most substantial and worthy citizens of Western North Carolina, while the Mast family generally are people of influence and standing in Pennsylvania, Ohio, Nebraska, Iowa, Montana, Oregon, Florida, Illinois, Missouri, California, Kansas, and in fact nearly every State in the Union. C. Z. Mast of Elverson, Pa., in 1911, published a volume of nearly a thousand pages all of which are devoted to an excellent record of all the Masts in America. John A. Mast was born on Brushy creek September 22, 1829. He married Martha Moore of Johns river, December 5, 1850. He died February 6, 1892. His paternal grandfather, John Mast, and maternal grandfather, Cutliff Harman, were among the pioneers of this section, and were Germans, settling on Cove creek. His wife, Martha Mast, was born April 13, 1833. She died February 15, 1905.

THE MORETZ FAMILY. John Moretz came from Lincolnton long before the Civil War and settled on Meat Camp, seven miles from Boone, where he built and operated a large mill, which was burned but rebuilt. He prospered greatly, and his descendants are numerous and influential.

THE SHULL FAMILY. Philip P. Shull was born at Valle Crucis, February 15, 1797, and married Phœbe Ward of Tennessee. He died January 9, 1866. His father, Simon Shull was one of the first settlers of this country, having been a German, and settled near Valle Crucis. His wife, Phœbe-was born May 28, 1801, and died September 29, 1882. Joseph Shull, who was desperately wounded in May, 1863, at the Wilderness fight, is a son of Philip P. Shull.

THE COUNCILL FAMILY. Jordan Councill, Sr., was the first of the name to settle in Watauga, then Ashe county. He married Sally, the daughter of Benjamin Howard, and from them have descended a long line of virile men and lovely women, who for years have been the backbone of this section.

OTHER FIRST SETTLERS were Amos and Edward Greene near Blowing Rock; Ransom Hayes at Boone; Jackson, Steven and Abner Farthing at Beaver Dams, James McCanless, Elisha Coffey, Amos Greene, Isaac Greene, Lee Foster and Joel Moody, at and near Shull's Mills; Malden Harmon, Calvin Harmon, Seaton Mast, Lorenzo Whittington, and George Moody, on Cove creek. Henry Taylor came to Valle Crucis long before the Civil War and married a Miss Mast.

FORGOT HOW TO MAKE AN "S." In the graveyard of the old German Reformed church, one mile from Blowing Rock, is an old gravestone which, tradition says, was brought by a Mr. Sullivan from the Jersey settlement in Davidson county for the purpose, as he stated, of "starting a graveyard." On it are carved or scratched the following letters and numbers:

E E S 1794.

This stone is said to mark the grave of the pioneer who brought it to Blowing Rock. But whether he died or was born in the year given, is not known.   It is quite evident that he had forgotten in which way an "S" is turned.

JACKSON COUNTY.   While the late Michael Francis was in the senate and R. G. A. Love was in the house from Haywood in 1850–52, Jackson county was formed with Webster as the county seat.   Daniel Webster had just died, and the naming of this town for him was a graceful concession to the Whig element of the country, while giving to "Old Hickory" the honor of naming the county for him pleased the Democrats. Col. Thaddeus D. Bryson, a son of Daniel Bryson of Scott's creek, was the first representative in the house from Jackson, while Col. W. H. Thomas represented it in the senate.   John R. Dills, a member of the large and influential Dills family of Dillsborough, represented this county in 1856.   Joseph Keener, an influential and valuable citizen represented the county in 1862, followed by W. A. Enloe, a representative of the extensive and leading Enloe family of Jackson.   Following are the names of some of the more prominent legislators :   J. N. Bryson, E. D. Davis, G. W. Spake, F. H. Leatherwood, J. W. Terrell, J. M. Candler, R. H. Brown, W. A. Dills, C. C. Cowan, and John B. Ensley.   The late John B. Love lived near Webster, and kept a store, W. H. Thomas being a partner for a while.   Mr. Love owned much of the land in that section, and his sons settled on Scott's creek from Addie to Sylva.   He also owned the famous "Gold Spring," near the head of Tuckaseegee, in the basin of which a small amount of gold was deposited each morning; but a blast ruined even that small contribution.   He married a Miss Comans of Wake county.   Philip Dills was another pioneer, and was born in Rutherford, January 10, 1808, and came with his father to Haywood soon after his birth, and about the time Abraham Enloe settled on Soco creek.   .   .   .   He was a useful and respected citizen.   Abraham Battle was born in Haywood in 1809, and his father was one of the three men who came from Rutherford to Haywood with Abraham Enloe.   Wm. H. Conley was another important citizen of Jackson before Swain was taken from it, and was born in 1812 within fifteen miles of Abraham Enloe's Ocona Lufty place, his father, James Conley having been the first white man to settle on that stream. James W. Terrell was born in Rutherford county, December 31, 1829, and at sixteen years of age, came to Haywood and lived with his grandfather, Wm. D. Kilpatrick, till 1852, when he went into business with the late Col. Wm. H. Thomas. In 1854 he was made disbursing agent for the Cherokees, was a captain in the Civil War, and in the legislature for several terms. The late Daniel Bryson kept a hotel or stopping place on the turnpike road below Hall's and above Addie, in the turn of the road, where all the judges and lawyers stopped while attending the courts of the wetsern circuit. He was a most excellent and useful citizen, and left several sons who have been prominent and influential citizens. Rev. William Hicks lived in Webster after the Civil War, where he taught school for two years; but in 1868 he was appointed presiding elder and moved to Hendersonville where he remained till 1873, when he returned to Webster and resumed his school. Later he moved to Quallatown where he taught school till he was appointed to a district in West Virginia, where he afterwards died. He was a fine public speaker, a Confederate soldier, a member of the Secession convention from Haywood in 1861, and with Rev. J. R. Long, in 1855, built up a large school near the junction of Richland and Raccoon creeks, giving the place the name of Tuscola. This school flourished till the beginning of the Civil War. Mr. Hicks also edited *The Herald of Truth*, a newspaper in Asheville, for a few years. He was born in Sullivan county, Tennessee, in 1820, became a Methodist preacher and came to Buncombe in 1848, holding that year the first conference ever held in Haywood, the meeting being held at Bethel church.

WEBSTER AND THE RAILROAD. With the coming of the railroad, Webster, the county seat, found itself about three miles from that artery of trade and travel; and, soon afterward, an agitation began for the removal of the court house to Dillsboro or Sylva, and has continued ever since. The question was submitted to the people but they voted to retain Webster as the county site; a new court house was built, and it was supposed that the matter had been settled forever; but in 1913 a more vigorous movement was started to change the county court house to Sylva, which offered a bonus in case it should be done. The legislature of 1913 authorized the people to vote on the proposition, and the result changed the county site to a point between Dillsboro and Sylva, May 8, 1913. Webster is a pretty little town with many attractive and useful citizens. The improvements along the line of railroad from Hall's to Whittier have been remarkable. The talc mine and factory of C. J. Harris at Dillsboro, the nickel mine nearer Webster of W. J. Adams, and the tannic acid plant at Sylva contribute much to the prosperity of these towns and to that of the county generally. With a railroad up Tuckaseegee a large tract of timber will find an outlet, and the copper mine on that stream may come into development. Jackson is a rich and productive county and its people are thriving and energetic. Lake Fairfield and Inn, and Lake Sapphire are in this county on Horsepasture creek. Ellicotte mountain is near the extreme eastern end of the county. Cashiers Valley, Chimneytop, Whiteside Cove and mountain, Glenville, East LaPorte, Cullowhee and Painter are places of interest and importance.

SCOTT'S CREEK. As this creek was on the eastern border of the Cherokee country from which the Indians were removed, and as Gen. Winfield Scott was in charge of their removal in 1835–38, some suppose that the creek took its name from him; but in two grants to Charles McDowell, James Glascow and David Miller, dated December 3, 1795, (Buncombe Deed Book No. 4, p. 104) the State conveyed 300 acres on the waters of Scott's creek, waters of Tuckaseegee river, including the forks of Scotts creek and "what was said to be Scott's old lick blocks," and on the same date there was a further grant to the same parties to 300 acres on the same stream, including a cane brake, with the same reference to Scott's old lick blocks. (Book 8, p. 85.) But a careful search revealed no grant to any Scott in that section at or near that time; and the Scott who gave his name to this fine stream was doubtless but a landless squatter who was grazing and salting his cattle on the wild lands of that day. He probably lived in Haywood county, near the head of Richland creek.

MADISON COUNTY. It was formed in 1851 from Buncombe and Yancey; it was named for James Madison, while its county seat bears the name of the great chief justice, John Marshall.

JEWEL HILL OR LAPLAND? It is almost forgotten that the postoffice at what is now Marshall was called Lapland in 1858, and that it used to be said that pegged shoes were first made there because the hills so enclose the place that it would be impossible for a shoemaker to draw out his thread to the full width of his arms, and consequently had to hammer in pegs, which he could do by striking up and down. It is also uncertain whether the name of Madison's first county seat is Jewel Hill or Duel Hill. One thing, however, is certain, and it is that there once was a spirited contest over keeping the seat of government there. There were several "settlements" which desired to become the county seat of Madison county, Lapland, on the French Broad river, being barred by the act of the legislature (1850–1), which provides that the "county seat is to be called Marshall which is not to be within two miles of the French Broad river. The principal candidates for this honor were "Bryants," Barnards and Jewel Hill. The last named was selected at first and several terms of court were held there.

The location of the county site at Jewel Hill soon proved unsatisfactory, and the legislature of 1852-53 appointed a commission to fix the plan for a county government. They decided on what is now Marshall "on lands of T. B. Vance where Adolphus E. Baird now lives." But a doubt as to the legality of this selection was immediately raised, though the county offices remained at Jewel Hill. But David Vance, in order to comply with the terms of the act, deeded to Madison county fifty acres of land for a town site, by deed dated April 20, 1853. [33]

The location of the county site entered into the politics of that year, and the legislature of 1854-55 (ch. 97, Pr. Laws) passed an act which provided for an election to be held the first Thursday in June, 1855, to determine whether the new location should stand or another location be chosen. In case a new location should be decided on, a commission of nine citizens was named, any five of whom might determine the new location; or if five did not agree, then they were to name two places, one of which should be on the French Broad river, one of which was to be chosen by a majority of the voters at an election to be held at a time to be fixed by the county court.

The act further provided that "if the Supreme court now sitting [February, 1855] should decide that the location of the county seat at Adolphus Baird's" was lawful, then this act should be null and inoperative. Pursuant to this act the question as to whether the location of the county site at Adolphus E. Baird's should stand or a new location be chosen was

decided at a popular election held on the first Thursday in
June, 1855, pursuant to the act of 1852-53, and an order of the
county court made at its April term, 1855.[34]   The votes
for and against the present location, however, is not stated
in the minutes; but there is a tradition that Marshall won
by only one vote.   At the fall term, 1855, of this court, a
building committee was appointed and the building of a brick
court house decided upon, which was ordered to be built in
1856.   The records show, however, that the county court
was still held at Jewel Hill up to the fall of 1859.   There
appears to be no record of any litigation to test the legality of
the selection of the commissioners under the Act of 1852-53,
notwithstanding the allusion to such a suit in the act itself.

OLD RESIDENTS OF MADISON.   Dr. W. A. Askew was born
on Spring creek in August, 1832, his father having been G. C.
Askew, and his mother Sarah H. Lusk, daughter of Wm. Lusk,
and a sister of Col. Virgil S. Lusk of Asheville.   There were
only four men living on Spring creek when G. C. Lusk settled
there in 1820, and they were Wm. and Sam Lusk, a Mr. Crawford and Wm. Garrett.   Later on Wm. Moody and Josiah
Duckett of South Carolina, a soldier of the Revolution, came.
Wm. Woody also lived there, and his son Jonathan H. Woody
moved to Cataloochee and married, first Malinda Plemmons,
and afterwards Mrs. Mary Caldwell, a widow.   The Gaha-
gans and Tweeds lived on Laurel, while on Turkey creek Jacob
Martin, James Alexander, A. M. Gudger, R. L. Gudger, Wm.
Penland, Robert Hawkins, Irwin West and John Alexander
lived and prospered.   Col James M. Lowrie, a half-brother
of Gov. Swain, with John Wells, John Reeves, lived on Sandy
Mush.   Ebbitt Jones also lived on Sandy Mush; and on Little Sandy Mush G. D. Robertson, Jackson Reeves, Jacob
and John Glance and others lived.   Nathaniel Davis, Nathan
Worley and the Worleys lived on Pine creek.   James Nichols
married a Barnard and lived at Marshall.   Robert Farnsworth
lived and died at Jewel Hill, where Mrs. Clark now lives,
and was a son of David Farnsworth who kept a stock stand
on the French Broad.   James Gudger and his wife Annie Love
also lived in this county, and Col. Gudger was a delegate to
the State convention of 1835.

ALLEGHANY COUNTY.[35]   "Alleghany" is, in the language of the
Delaware Indians, "a fine stream."   Up to 1858-59 Alleghany

was a part of Ashe. Wm. Raleigh and Elijah Thompson of
Surry, James B. Gordon of Wilkes, and Stephen Thomas and
John F. Green of Ashe were appointed commissioners by the
act creating the county to locate the county seat, and had
power to purchase or receive as a gift 100 acres for the use of
such county, upon which the county site, to be called Sparta,
should be located. In April, 1859 Wm. C. DeJournett, a
Frenchman, of Wilkes, made a survey and plat locating the
center of the county; James H. Parks and David Evans donated
50 acres where Sparta now stands, near the geographical
center located by DeJournett, but the deed was destroyed
by a fire which burned Col. Allen Gentry's house, and another
deed was executed in 1866. In 1859 the county court appointed commissioners to lay off and make sales of town lots,
but at the next term revoked their appointment and directed
them not to proceed. A mandamus was asked and the Superior and Supreme courts both ordered that it be granted; but
nothing further seems to have been done till the April term,
1866, when the county court appointed F. J. McMillan, Robert Gambill, Sr., James H. Parks, Morgan Edwards and S.
S. Stamper commissioners to lay off and sell lots from the
tract donated for a county seat, etc.; and at the October
term following these commissioners were directed to advertise for bids for building a court house, etc. But, at the January term, 1867, all bids were rejected and the plans altered
so that the court house and jail should be in one and the same
building. This was the first term held in Sparta, and the
court was composed of Morgan Bryan and Wm. L. Mitchell.
The first term of the Superior court was held at Sparta in the
spring of 1868, with Anderson Mitchell as presiding judge,
J. C. Jones, sheriff, and W. L. Mitchell as foreman of the
grand jury. Stephen Landreth was officer in charge of the
grand jury.

BEFORE THE REVOLUTION. It seems that there were no
settlers in Alleghany prior to the Revolutionary War; but
it had been visited by hunters both from Virginia and the central part of this State, among whom were three brothers
named Maynard from what is now Surry, who crossed the Blue
Ridge and built cabins along Glade creek. This was about
1786, and they had lived there about six years when Francis
Bryan, from Orange county, in 1793, located within five miles

of them. About the same time Joel Simmons, Wm. Woodruff and ——— Crouce settled along the top of the Blue
Ridge, thus making seven families in the county. But this
was too much for the Maynard brothers, and claiming that
the country was too thickly settled, they moved to Kentucky.
But who was the first white man to visit this section is unknown; though Wm. Taylor, the Coxes, Gambills and Reeves
probably lived in the borders of what is now Alleghany during
the Revolutionary War. Two men named Edwards settled
here also at an early date, viz: David and William Edwards.
John McMillan came from Scotland in 1790 and was the first
clerk of Ashe court. Joseph Doughton from Franklin county,
Va., was an early settler, and represented Ashe in the House
of Commons in 1877. Joseph Doughton was the youngest
son of Joseph. This family has always been prominent in
the county. H. F. Jones built the present court house for
$3,475, and it was received September 4, 1880, J. T. Hawthorn
and Alex. Hampton, building committee.

PRINCIPAL OFFICE–HOLDERS. The following are the names
of those who have held the principal offices in the county.

Senators: 1879, Jesse Bledsoe; 1880, F. J. McMillan; 1893,
W. C. Fields; 1899, W. C. Fields; 1906, Stephen A. Taylor;
1909, R. L. Doughton; 1911, John M. Wagoner.

Representatives: 1869, Dr. J. L. Smith; 1871, Robert Gambill; 1873, Abram Bryan; 1875, W. C. Fields; 1877, E. L.
Vaughan; 1879 and 1881, E. L. Vaughan; 1883, Isaac W.
Landreth; 1885, Berry Edwards; 1887, R. A. Doughton; 1891,
R. A. Doughton; 1893, C. J. Taylor; 1895, P. C. Higgins;
1897, H. F. Jones, 1899; J. M. Gambill; 1901, J. C. Fields;
1903, R. A. Doughton; 1905, R. K. Finney; 1907, 1909, 1911,
1913, R. A. Doughton.

Clerk of County Court: 1859 to 1862, Allen Gentry; 1862
to 1866, Horton Reeves; 1866 to 1868, C. G. Fowlkes.

Clerk Superior Court: 1864 to 1868, Wm. A. J. Fowlkes;
1868 to October, 1873, B. H. Edwards. Edwards resigned
and J. J. Gambill appointed. October 1873 to March 1882,
J. J. Gambill; Gambill resigned and R. S. Carson appointed.
March 1882 to 1890, R. S. Carson; 1890 to 1898, W. E. Cox;
1898 to 1910, J. N. Edwards; 1910 to 1914, S. F. Thompson.

Sheriff: 1859 to 1864, Jesse Bledsoe; 1864 to 1870, J. C.
Jones; 1870 to 1882, J. R. Wyatt; 1882 to 1884, Berry Edwards;

1884 to 1885, George Bledsoe (died while in office); 1885 to 1888, W. F. Thompson; 1888 to 1894, W. S. Gambill; 1894 to 1898, L. J. Jones; 1898 to 1904, D. R. Edwards; 1904 to 1908, S. A. Choate; 1908 to 1910, John R. Edwards; 1910 to 1914, S. C. Richardson.

Register of Deeds: 1865 to 1868, Thompson Edwards; 1868 to 1880, F. M. Mitchell; 1880 to 1882, F. G. McMillan; 1882 to 1886, F. M. Mitchell; 1886 to 1892, J. C. Roup; 1892 to 1898, J. N. Edwards; 1898 to 1904, S. F. Thompson; 1904 to 1908, John F. Cox; 1908 to 1914, G. D. Brown.

The following is a list of the first Justices of the Peace of the county:

A. B. McMillan, John Gambill, Berry Edwards, John A. Jones, Solomon Jones, W. P. Maxwell, Solomon Long, Nathan Weaver, Wm. Warden, C. G. Fowlkes, F. J. McMillan, John Parsons, Caleb Osborn, Wm. L. Mitchell, C. H. Doughton, James Boyer, Wm. Anders, Thomas Edwards, Thomas Douglass, I. C. Heggins, Hiram Heggins, Morgan Bryan, A. M. Bryan, A. J. Woodruff, Alfred Brooks, Wm. T. Choate, Daniel Whitehead, Goldman Heggins, Absalom Smith, Martin Carico, Ruben Sparks, Spencer Isom, Chesley Cheek.

Of this number, Dr. C. G. Fowlkes and Nathan Weaver are the only ones now living, 1912.

FIRST MARRIAGE CERTIFICATE. This is a copy of the first marriage record in the county:

"This is to certify that I married Calvin Caudill and Sarah Jones the 16th day of March, 1862.

DANIEL CAUDILL."

TWO NOTED LAWSUITS. What is probably the most important lawsuit that ever existed in the county was *W. D. Maxwell v. Noah Long*, for the recovery of the "Peach Bottom Copper Mines" and for about 1000 acres of land. This cause was carried to the United States Circuit Court of Appeals and then to the United States Supreme Court. Polk, Fields, Doughton, Watson & Buxton represented Maxwell. Vaughan, Linney, and Judge Schenk represented Long. Maxwell finally gained the suit, Chief Justice Fuller writing the opinion.

Another historical lawsuit in this county, was one of ejectment, *Wm. Edwards v. Morgan Edwards*. This litigation was begun about the year 1864, and lasted nearly thirteen years. The action was moved to Ashe county at one time, and probably to Watauga at another. It was finally disposed of at Spring term 1877 of Alleghany Superior Court. After a desperate battle, which lasted for nearly a week, the jury gave a verdict in favor of Morgan Edwards. [3] [6]

MITCHELL'S COUNTY SEAT. By ch. 8, Pub. Laws of 1860–61 Mitchell county was created out of portions of Yancey, Watauga, Caldwell, Burke and McDowell; and by chapter 9 of the same laws it was provided that the county court of Pleas and Quarter Sessions should be "held in the house of Eben Childs on the tenth Monday after the fourth Monday in March, when they shall elect a clerk, a sheriff, a coroner, a register of deeds and entry-taker, a surveyor, a county solicitor, constables and all other officers. Thomas Farthing of Watauga, John W. McElroy of Yancey, Joseph Conley of McDowell, A. C. Avery of Burke, David Prophet of Yancey, John Harden of Watauga and James Bailey, Sr., of Yancey, were appointed commissioners to select a permanent seat of justice and secure fifty acres of land, to meet between the first of May and June, 1861. Tilmon Blalock, J. A. Person, Eben Childs and Jordan Harden were appointed commissioners to lay off town lots; "and said town shall be called by the name of Calhoun."

A HITCH SOMEWHERE. But, at the first extra session of 1861 (Ratified September 4, 1861), Moses Young, John B. Palmer of Mitchell, John S. Brown of McDowell, Wm. C. Erwin of Burke, and N. W. Woodfin of Buncombe were appointed commissioners to "select and determine a permanent seat of justice," to meet between October 1, 1861, and July 1, 1862.

STILL ANOTHER HITCH. By chapter 34, Private Laws, second extra session, 1861, the boundary lines of Mitchell were so changed as to detach from Mitchell and re-annex to Yancey all the country between the mouth of Big Rock creek and the Tennessee line, so that the county line of Mitchell should stop on Toe river at the mouth of Big Rock creek and run thence with the ridge that divides Rock Creek and Brummetts creek to the State line at the point where the Yancey and McDowell turnpike road crosses the same.

THE LAND IS DONATED. On the 17th of October, 1861, Lysander D. Childs and Eben Childs conveyed to Tilmon Blalock, chairman of the County Court, fifty acres of land

(Deed Book C, p. 30) the which fifty acres were to be used "for the location thereon of a permanent seat of justice in said county; two acres for a public grave-yard, one acre for the site of a public school building, and one-half acre to be devoted to each of the following denominations for the erection thereon of church buildings; to wit: Episcopalians, Presbyterians, Methodists and Baptists"; the location of lots in the grave-yard and for the school and church buildings to be made by the commissioners charged by law with the duty of laying off the town lots in said seat of justice.

CALHOUN. This town was not far from Spruce Pine and Ingalls, "on a lane leading from the Burnsville and Boone road."[37] It was what was afterwards called Childsville. But, although by chapter 61 of the second session of the laws of 1861, a term of the Superior court was directed to be held "for Mitchell county in the town of Calhoun on the sixth Monday after the fourth Monday each year," the county seat never assumed town-like proportions. The people never liked it; and at the first session of the legislature after the Civil War it was changed to the present site of what is now called Bakersville. But, it seems, it was first called Davis; for by chapter 2, Private Laws of 1868, the name of the "town site of Mitchell county" was changed from Davis to Bakersville.

BAKERSVILLE. On the 27th of July, 1866, for $1,000 Robbert N. Penland conveyed to the chairman of the board of county commissioners 29 acres on the waters of Cane creek "and the right of way to and the use of the springs above the old Baker spring . . . to be carried in pumps to any portion of said 29 acres.[38] This was a part of the land on which Bakersville is situated. In 1868 there was a sale of these lots, and at the December, 1868, session of the commissioners the purchasers gave their notes, due in one and two years for balances due on the lots. The first court house in Bakersville was built by Irby & Dellinger, of South Carolina, in 1867, and on the first of November, 1869, M. P. and W. Dellinger gave notice of a mechanic's lien in the building for work done under a contract for the sum of $1,409.85 subject to a set-off of about $200. The first court held in Bakersville was in a grove near the former Bowman house, when it stood on the top of the ridge above its present site. Judge A. S. Merrimon presided. The next court was held in a log house

built by Isaac A. Pearson.   The present court house was built
by the Fall City Construction Company, of Louisville, Ky.

TRANSYLVANIA.[39]   This county was formed in 1861, while
Marcus Erwin was in the senate and Joseph P. Jordan of
Henderson county was in the house.   M. N. Patton was its
first representative, in 1864.   Court was held in a store room
on what is now Caldwell street, Brevard.   The first regular
court house was a small frame building which stood on site
of present building.   It was built by George Clayton and
Eph. England, contractors, and was not quite complete in
1866.   The first jail was also small and of wood.   Both these
buildings were moved across the street and are still in existence.   The present court house was built about 1874 by
Thomas Davis contractor.   Probit Poore built what is still
known as the "Red House," before the Civil War; but it was
not used as a hotel till William Moore opened it as such, and
this was the first hotel in Brevard.   In 1872 or 1873 Nathan
McMinn built a store and afterwards a hotel where the present
McMinn house stands and opened a hotel there about 1879.
George Shuford, the father of Judge G. A. Shuford, used to
own the Breese or Hume place in Brevard, and sold it to
Meredith D. Cooper who built the present mansion, and sold
it to Mrs. Hume.   George Shuford bought the mill place
from Ethan Davis and built a grist mill there, but when M. D.
Cooper got it he built a flour mill, which was burned.   Cooper
afterwards sold the mill to Mr. Lucas and he sold it to Mrs.
Robert L. Hume, who conveyed it to her daughter, Mrs.
Wm. E. Breese, the mill having been rebuilt.   About 1800
George Shuford moved from Catawba county and bought
land below Shuford's bridge on the French Broad river, and
took up a lot of mountain land, considered valueless, but
which is held today by John Thrash at $25 per acre.   It
is in the Little river mountains.   John Clayton, father of
John, George and Ephriam Clayton, settled on Davidson's
river, above the mill, at the Joel Mackey place.   The Gash
family were originally from Buncombe.   Leander S. Gash
lived for a time in Hendersonville where he died.   He was a
prominent and influential man, having represented Henderson
county in 1866 in the senate; while Thomas L. Gash represented Transylvania in the house in 1874.   Their ancestor
had fought in the Revolutionary War.   The Duckworths are

another large and influential family, John having settled at the mouth of Cherryfield creek on a part of the David Allison grant, which corners there, after following the present turnpike from Boylston creek. It was here, too, that the Paxtons lived. Just prior to the Civil War, while Transylvania was a part of Henderson county, many wealthy and fashionable people from the lower part of South Caroliua bought many of the finest farms and built what were palatial homes for those days. Among them were Frank McKune and William Johnston from Georgetown, S. C. Their fine teams and liveried servants are still remembered. Then, too, Robert Hume built a stone hotel at the foot of the Dunn Rock, about four miles southwest of Brevard, where he kept many summer boarders prior to the Civil War; but, during that awful time, the hotel was burned; the ruins still standing. What is still known as the Lowndes Farm, on the French Broad river, about five miles below Brevard, originally belonged to Benjamin King, a Baptist minister, who married Miss Mary Ann Shuford; but when the Cherokee country was opened to the whites, Mr. King sold it to William Ward, a son of Joshua Ward. William Ward built the fine house which stands on the land still; his father having built Rock Hall, the present home of the Westons. Ephriam Clayton was the contractor who built the Lowndes house for William Ward, and it was then one of the show-places of Transylvania. The Wards were South Carolina rice planters, and quite wealthy; but during the Civil War William got into debt to Mr. Lowndes, a banker of Charleston, who obtained judgments and sold the land after the war, bidding it in, and afterwards placing the farm in charge of a Scotch gardner named Thomas Wood, who immediately put the land in splendid condition— the amount spent for the land and improvements having cost the estate nearly one hundred thousand dollars. Mr. Lowndes was very much attached to this place and spent much of his time there; but after his death, his grandson did not care much for it, and sold it, with stock and farm implements for a small sum to John Thrash, and he in time sold it to Col. Everett, a genial and popular gentleman of Cleveland, Ohio. He has improved the place greatly. The original farm now includes the James Clayton, the Wm. Allison and the Henry Osborne places—all fine farms. The late A. Toomer

Porter, of Charleston, started to build a home on top of a small mountain, three and one half miles down the French Broad river, and a Mr. Clarkson of South Carolina started a summer residence on the opposite side, but the war stopped both enterprises. A relative of the late P. T. Barnum, owns the Hankel place about three miles from Brevard on the French Broad river. He has an extensive chicken farm, containing 5,000 white Leghorns. His name is Clark. Buck Forest, nine miles south of Brevard on Little river, containing the shoals and three picturesque falls or cascades of that stream, graphically described the "Land of the Sky," was originally the property of Micajah Thomas, who after building a hotel there before the Civil War, kept summer boarders when deer hunting was popular; but after the war sold it to Joseph Carson. The late Frank Coxe, Carson's brother-in-law, however, paid for it, and in the litigation which followed retained the title and possession by paying Carson's estate about $12,000 in 1910. The Coxe estate have since bought large tracts of land in that neighborhood and it is said will create a large lake and build a hotel on the property. The Patton family of Transylvania is one of the largest and most influential of that section, the original of that name having owned from Clayton's to the Deaver farm, a distance along the French Broad river of about three miles. They were a large family, but there was land enough to go around to about a dozen children. No better people live anywhere than the Pattons.

CHERRY FIELD. In November, 1787, Gen. Charles McDowell and Willoughby Williams entered 200 acres in Rutherford county (Buncombe county Deed Book A, p. 533), "adjoining the upper end of his Cherry Field survey on French Broad river and extending up to his Meadow Camp survey"; and in November, 1789, the State granted to Charles McDowell 500 acres on both sides of the French Broad river, including the forks of said river where the Path crosses to Estatoe (Deed Book No. 9, p. 200, Buncombe). This old Indian path to Estatoe crossed near Rosman.

BEN DAVIDSON'S CREEK.[40] On the 25th of July, 1788, Charles McDowell entered 500 acres in Rutherford county on Ben Davidson's river, including the Great Caney Cove two or three miles above the Indian Path, though the grant was not issued till December 5, 1798 (Buncombe county Deed Book 4, p. 531), and in November, 1790, Ben Davidson got a grant for 640 acres in Rutherford county on both sides of French Broad river, above James Davidson's tract, including the mouth of the Fork on the north side and adjoining Joseph McDowell's line, "since transferred to Charles McDowell." (Buncombe county Deed Book 1, p. 74.)

CLAY COUNTY AND HAYESVILLE. Clay county was enacted in 1861, but it was organized in 1864. The first sheriff was John Patterson, but he could not give the necessary bond and the commissioners appointed J. P. Chastine in his place. Then came James P. Cherry who was sheriff for many years. Wm. McConnell was the first register of deeds. John C. Moore, G. W. Bristol and Harvey Penland were the first County Commissioners. The county seat was named for George W. Hayes. He lived on Valley river near Murphy and was the father of Mr. Ham Hayes, who is still living. He was an extraordinary man and much respected. He had Clay county cut off from Cherokee while he was in the legislature.

John H. Johnson of Tennessee, Robert Martin of Wilkes county, North Carolina, and Elijah Herbert of Wythe county, Virginia, married three daughters of John Alexander, of Abshers, Wilkes county, North Carolina, about 1823, and afterwards moved to Clay, then Cherokee county, when the Cherokee lands were sold. They settled near Hayesville. Elijah Herbert, who had married Winifred Alexander, died in March, 1875, aged seventy-four years. John H. Johnson died about 1895. Robert Martin died about 1880.

Clay county lands are exceedingly fertile and, with the sparkling Hiwassee river flowing through the center from east to west, with its tributaries, Tusquittee, Brasstown, Sweetwater, Shooting Creek and various other smaller streams and hundreds of clear, sparkling springs, make it a well watered country. It is surrounded on three sides by mountains forming an amphitheatre overlooking a valley that is unexcelled for natural beauty. Its soil is adapted to the production of all the grains and grasses but more especially to the growth of apples. This county has long been noted for the morality of its people and the maintenance of a high school at Hayesville, the county seat, the courts seldom last longer than two days, and often only one day, and the jail is almost always free of prisoners.

This county was settled largely by emigrants from the counties east of it. The Cherokee Indians were removed from this particular territory in the year 1838, but a number of pioneers had settled in the county prior to their removal. G. W. Hayes was the representative in the legislature from Cherokee at that time and the county seat was named in his honor. The minerals of the county are gold, corundum, asbestos, garnet, mica, kaolin, and iron.

George W. Bristol came from Burke county in the spring of 1844 and settled at the Mission Farm on Peachtree creek. The Bristols came to Burke from Connecticut. His son, Thomas B. Bristol, was born in Burke county July 3, 1830, and married Mary Addie Johnson, a daughter of the late John H. Johnson of Tusquittee, January 22, 1852. He died January 19, 1907. His widow survived him till October 8, 1911.

Archibald O. Lyon was born in Tennessee and married Miss M. E. Martin September 14, 1856. She was a daughter of Robert Martin, one of the first and most prominent settlers of Clay county. A. O. Lyon died February 16, 1885. He went to Raleigh soon after the Civil War and obtained a charter for a Masonic lodge at Hayesville, which was organized as Clay Lodge October 2, 1866. He was its Worshipful Master ten years and a faithful member for nineteen years. He was a progressive and successful farmer, and was loved and respected by all who knew him. James H. Penland also married one of John H. Johnson's daughters, Miss Fanny E. Johnson, as did H. G. Trotter of Franklin and Wm. B. Tidwell of Tusquittee two others.

John C. Moore was one of the first settlers of Clay county and lived in an Indian hut which stood near a beech tree near John H. Johnson's house before the land sale. He came from Rutherford county and married Polly Bryson of Mills river. Their daughter, Sarah, married Wm. H. Herbert about the year 1851.

W. P. Moore, universally called "Irish Bill," was a son of Joab Moore and was born in Rutherford county and was a brother of John C. Moore. He married Miss Hattie Gash of Transylvania county. He was a captain in the Confederate

army and "every inch a soldier." He is still living at his
home on Tusquittee aged eighty-three years.

Alexander Barnard settled on Hiwassee river, three miles
above Hayesville. Eli Sanderson was born in Connecticut
and was the father of George W. Sanderson who died some
years ago. He and William Sanderson were among the first
settlers of Clay county. James Coleman was also among
the first settlers and owned a large farm. William Hancock
lived below Hayesville and Richard Pass came early from
Georgia to Clay county. One of his daughters married S. H.
Haigler of Hayesville.

Joshua Harshaw was the original settler at the mouth of
Brasstown creek on a good farm. He came early from Burke
county. Abner Chastine came from Jackson county early
and died about 1874 or 1875, when an old man. He left sev-
eral children, among them having been J. P. Chastine the
first sheriff of Clay county. Byron Brown married Miss
Nancy Parsons and died about 1901. Daniel K. Moore, of
Buncombe county, also lived on Brasstown. He married a
Miss Dickey and was the father of Judge Frederick Moore.
He is still living. Henry Platt, the father of the present
Rev. J. T. Platt of Clay, was also an early settler, and died
many years ago.

George McLure came from Macon county long before the
Civil War and settled near Hiwassee river. He was the father
of W. H. McLure who has represented Clay county in the
legislature. W. H. McLure married one of the daughters of
R. S. Pass and was one of the California Forty-Niners. He
stayed in California till the Civil War, when he returned to
Clay county.

The Mission farm is now partly owned by the heirs of a
Mr. Sudderth, originally of Burke county. He was at one
time sheriff of Clay and a gentleman of fine character. Fort
Embree, one of the collecting forts at time of the removal
of the Cherokees, was on a hill just one mile southwest of
Hayesville. There is an Indian Mound at the mouth of
Peachtree creek on the old Robert McLure farm. It is about
the same size as that near Franklin. There is also a mound
half a mile east of Hayesville which is highest of all these
mounds. It is on the land of W. H. McLure and S. H. Allison, their line splitting the mound.

Among other prominent citizens of Clay should be mentioned Dr. D. W. Killian, Dr. John Duncan, Gailor Bristol and S. H. Allison's father, who came to Clay many years ago. S. H. Allison married Miss Elizabeth Lyon, daughter of A. O. Lyon. John O. Hicks was born in Rutherford county and was among the first school teachers in Clay county. He built up a splendid school at Fort Embree and afterwards moved to Hayesville. He represented Clay in the legislature. He closed his school in 1876 and moved to Walhalla, South Carolina, and then went to Texas, where he died in 1910.

There is now a fine high school at Hayesville. It is in charge of Mr. N. A. Fessenden, who succeeded John O. Hicks. Among those who have distinguished themselves after attending this school are Rev. Ferd. C. McConnell, of Texas, one of the finest preachers of the Baptist church; George Truett, another fine preacher; and Hon. George Bell of the Tenth Georgia Congressional district.

SWAIN COUNTY AND BRYSON CITY. The county was created in 1871. The first court house was a frame building, with the upper floor for a court room and the lower for a jail. The "cage" was a pen of logs, under the front outside stairs, and was used for misdemeanants only. The dungeon was a log room within a log room, the space between being filled with stones. A padlocked trapdoor from the floor above was the only entrance, reached by a ladder let down when required. Bryson City was first called Charleston, which name it retained sixteen years when it was called Bryson in honor of Col. Thad. Dillard Bryson who was instrumental in having the new county formed. Col. D. K. Collins built the first house there, Capt. Epp Everett the next, and James Raby and M. Battle followed. H. J. Beck was first clerk of court, Epp Everett sherriff, D. K. Collins postmaster, and Wm. Enloe, B. McHane, and John DeHart county commissioners.

OCONALUFTY. The first settlers on this creek were Robert Collins, Isaac Bradley, John Beck, John Mingus, Abraham Enloe, after whom came the Hugheses, Connors, Floyds, Sherrills, etc. Col. D. K. Collins' mother had thirteen children, of whom twelve lived to be grown. Seven of her sons took part in the Civil War, one being killed. Their neighbor had eighteen children. The earliest settlers on Deep creek were the Shulers, Wiggins, and Millsaps. Those on Alarka were the Cochrans, Brendels, Welches, and DeHarts.

ROBERT COLLINS. He was the guide and assistant of Professor Arnold Guyot's surveying party in 1858–59, and Col. D. K. Collins was along as a helper, to carry the instruments, chain, stakes, etc. They followed the summit of the Smoky mountains from Cocke county, Tenn., to Blount county, Tenn., breaking up the party at Montvale springs, 16 miles from Maryville. Robert Collins was born on Oconalufty river September 4, 1806, married Elizabeth Beck, December 30, 1830, and died April 9, 1863, when he was an officer in charge of 500 troops, mostly Cherokees, in Sevier county, Tenn.

ELI ARRINGTON. He helped to carry Rhynehart, who was ill of milk-sick in 1855, near Collins gap. Wain Battle was also one of the party who helped carry Rhynehart from the mountains. About two years later he was with Dr. John Mingus, Dr. Davis and a few others going to the Alum cave where Col. Thomas got magnesia and alum during the war, and took sick and died alone in one of the roughest countries in the mountains. He was found by Col. D. K. Collins and taken to his home in Waynesville.

DANGER IN CROSSING THE UNAKAS IN WINTER. Andrew Sherman and ———— O'Neal, two lumbermen, left camp on the head of Tellico creek just before Christmas, 1899, intending to cross the Unaka mountains south of the John Stratton Meadows, near Haw Knob, so as to reach Robbinsville in time for Christmas. They got as far as the Whig cabin where they bought some whiskey from Jim Brooksher; after which they started to cross the Hooper bald. A blizzard and heavy snowstorm began and continued all that night. They were never seen again alive. In September following Forest Denton found their skeletons near the Huckleberry Knob, where Sherman's remains were buried; but some physicians took O'Neal's remains home with them.

ORIGIN OF NAMES. Hazel creek was named from a patch of hazelnut bushes near its mouth; Noland creek was named for Andrew Noland, its first settler; Chambers creek for John Chambers; Eagle creek from a nest of eagles near its head; Twenty-Mile creek is so called because it is just twenty miles from the junction of Tuckaseegee and Little Tennessee rivers.

WILLIAM MONTEITH. He was the father of Samuel and the grandfather of Ellis, John, Robert and Western Monteith. He married Nancy Crawford.

COL. THADDEUS DILLARD BRYSON. He was born near the present railroad station called Beta, Jackson county, February 13, 1829, was married to Miss Mary C. Greenlee of Turkey Cove, McDowell county, April 4, 1871. He died at his home at Bryson City, January 2, 1890. He represented Jackson and Swain a number of years in the legislature. He was appointed colonel-commandant of the Jackson county regiment militia, February 20, 1854, and was commissioned captain in the 20th N. C. Infantry of the Confederate army, September 7, 1861.

BRYSON CITY has one bank, three hotels, several boarding houses, a pump factory where columns and liquor logs are made, a roller mill of 35-barrel capacity, an ice plant, bottling works, a telephone system, a planing mill, lumber yards and builder's supplies, livery stables and a fine retail and wholesale trade with the surrounding country. The town owns its own water system and watershed at Rich gap of 200 acres. The water is from mountain springs and is piped to a fine reservoir on Arlington Heights overlooking the town. There is also a sewerage system. The town owns its own water power plant three miles up Deep Creek which furnishes electricity to operate the ice plant and the roller mill and the electric lights of the town, and has surplus power to sell. It has 140-horsepower capacity.

GRAHAM AND ROBBINSVILLE. Graham was formed in 1872, but it was represented in the legislature by the member from Cherokee till 1883, when George B. Walker, Esq., was elected to the house. The county commissioners-elect met at King & Cooper's store on Cheoah river, October 21, 1872, and were sworn in by J. W. King, J. P.; J. J. Colvard, John Gholey, G. W. Hooper, N. F. Cooper, and John Sawyer, commissioners, all being present. J. J. Colvard was elected chairman, and the official bond of William Carpenter, register deeds, was approved. So were also the bonds of John G. Tatham, as clerk, J. S. Hyde, as sheriff, Reuben Carver, surveyor, all of whom were sworn in. It was then ordered that the first term of the Superior court be held at the Baptist church in Cheoah township, about one mile from Robbinsville. Judge Riley Cannon held this court at that place in March, 1873; and the first court held in the court house in Robbinsville was the fall term of 1874. On the 7th of December, 1872, the commission-

ers considered three sites for the county seat : Rhea Hill, Fort
Hill, and land of C. A. Colvards. They chose the first
named. Junaluska, the Cherokee chief, lived at Robbinsville
and is buried there. A tablet on an immense boulder marks
his grave. Snowbird mountains, the Joanna Bald, the
Hooper Bald, Huckleberry Knob, Laurel Top, the two Stratton
Balds, the Hang Over, the Hay O, the Fodder Stack and the
Swim Bald are the principal mountain peaks. They are the
least known of any of our mountains. In them head the
Santeetla, Buffalo, Snowbird, Sweet Water, the Yellow and
Tallulah creeks, all of which flow into the Cheoah river. One
hundred and fifty Cherokee Indians live on the head of Snowbird
and Buffalo creeks. There is more virgin forest land in this
county than in any other now. It has immense resources in water
power, and the gorge at Rocky Point where the Little Tennessee
goes through has great value as a power site. The Union Development Company has bought up many sites on these streams.
In 1910–11 the Whiting Manufacturing Company bought up
many of the lots and houses in Robbinsville and many thousands
of acres of timber lands. Lafayette Ghormley is the grandson
of the man of that name who lived near the mouth of Mountain
creek, and the son of DeWitt Ghormley. Dave Orr went to
his present home between Bear and Slick Rock creeks in 1866,
and his fame as a hunter and trapper is now secure. Rev.
Joseph A. Wiggins, a distinguished Methodist minister of this
county, was born on Alarka creek in 1832, but moved with his
father to Graham in 1840, when there was but one wagon
road, that from Old Valley Town to Fort Montgomery, just
constructed for the soldiers who removed the Indians in 1838.
Dr. Dan F. Summey of Asheville was in charge of its construction. There were no mills except a few grist mills, and
wheat was "packed" on horses by a trail to a mill five mile
from what is now Bryson City—a distance of about thirty
miles. Indian relics were then plentiful at the head of Tallulah creek at what is called The Meadows. Mr. Wiggins married a daughter of George W. Hayes, after whom Hayesville
was named. There was not a church in the county and but
a few log school houses. He began to preach in 1859, and
served four years as chaplain in the Confederate army, after
which he rode circuits in Tennessee, Southwestern Virginia
and Western North Carolina till stationed in Graham county

His great-grandfather Garland Wiggins served in the Revolutionary War, as did his wife's great-grandfather, Edward Hayes. Andrew Colvard lived on Long Hungry branch, which got its name from the fact that a party of hunters was once detained there by high water till their rations gave out and they were for a long time hungry. The Stewarts of Santeetla came from Georgia and the Lovens from Ducktown, Tenn. John and Robert Stratton came from Monroe county, Tenn., in the thirties and settled on the Unaka mountains between the head of Sassafras ridge and Santeetla creek. John lived on the John Stratton Bald ten years and caught 19 panthers on Laurel Top, making "bacon" of their hams and shoulders. He came with nothing but his rifle, blanket, skillet and ammunition, but made enough herding cattle and selling deer and bear hams and hides, etc., to buy a fine farm in Monroe county, Tenn. On a rude stone on the John Stratton meadow is carved:

A. S.
Was born
1787
Died 1839.

A State Line stone stands about a quarter of a mile away. John Ropetwister, Organdizer, Big Fat Commisseen and others moved from East Buffalo creek to Slick Rock during the Removal of 1838, where they remained in concealment till Col. Thomas arranged to have the remnant remain. They sent their women into Tennessee to swap bear and deer hides for meal. Thomas Cooper, the father of James W. Cooper of Murphy, lived on Tallulah three miles east of Robbinsville. There was a large and influential family of Crisps who settled on Stekoah, of whom Hon. Joel L. Crisp is a distinguished representative. Rev. Isaac Carringer came from the eastern part of this State and lived on Santeetla. He was a Baptist minister and died about 1897, highly respected. John Denton the most picturesque mountaineer in this section, moved from Polk county, Tenn., to Little Santeetla in 1879. In 1900 he was crippled while logging. He stands six feet three in his stockings. Soon after his arrival some of the bullies of Robbinsville tested John's pluck; but he worsted five of them in a fist fight, and since then he has lived in peace. His, wife's mother was Jane Meroney, and a first cousin of Jefferson Davis. She married a Turner, Mrs. Denton's given name being Albertine.

AVERY COUNTY. This was created in 1911, out of portions of Watauga and Mitchell counties, principally.[41] At an election held August 1, 1911, Old Fields of Toe was selected as the county seat. It so happened that this land had been granted to Col. Waightstill Avery November 9, 1783. It was in his honor that this, the 100th county, was named, while the county seat was called Newland, in honor of Hon. W. C. Newland, of Lenoir, then the lieutenant governor of the State. The jail and court house were completed sufficiently to allow court to be held in April, 1913, Judge Daniels presiding. There are two legends concerning the reason this tract was called the Old Fields of Toe. L. D. Lowe, Esq., in the *Watauga Democrat* of June 19, 1913, states that one legend relates that Estatoe, the daughter of one of two rival chieftains, fell in love with the son of the other; but her father refused his consent, which caused a bloody war between the two factions. But Estatoe caused a pipe of peace to be made with two stems of ti-ti so that two could smoke it at once. The two rival chiefs assembled their respective followers on the bank of the river, and smoked till peace was concluded and Estatoe married her lover. The other legend is that found in The Balsam Groves of the Grandfather mountain (p. 221), and in it Estatoe is made to drown herself because she could not wed her Indian lover because of her father's implacable opposition.

AVERY COUNTY'S LONG PEDIGREE. "It was a part of Clarendon in 1729; of New Hanover in 1729; of Bladen in 1734; of Anson in 1749; of Rowan in 1753; of Surry in 1770; of Burke in 1777; of Wilkes in 1777; of Ashe in 1799; of Yancey in 1833; of Caldwell in 1841; of Watauga in 1849; of Mitchell in 1861; so that that portion taken from Caldwell and attached to Avery in 1911 represents the eighth subdivision; and that from Watauga the tenth; which is a record probably unsurpassed."[42] The principal reason for the formation of this new county was the inaccessibility of Bakersville to most of the inhabitants of Mitchell, it being in the northeastern part of that county and only two and a half miles from the Yancey line.[43] Lineville City, two miles from Montezuma and Pinola, is "the cleanest town in the North Carolina mountains east of Asheville, and the only place of the kind where guests have a large, ideal zone for golf."[44]   The same author speaks of the Yonahlossee road, running from Linville City to Blowing Rock, as the Appian Way which ran from Rome via Naples, to Brundesium, and claims that the latter was not more interesting than the former.[45]   The world will one day admit that the fine scenery of North Carolina has its culmination in Avery county.

---

[1]From Asheville's Centenary.
[2]Ibid.
[3]Ibid.
[4]Ibid.
[5]Ibid.
[6]Bourne's Asheville Code, 1909, vi. *Scaife v. Land Co.*, 90 Federal Reporter (p. 238.) The deed from Tate to Morris is on parchment nearly fifteen feet in length. It was written by an English law clerk, and still looks like copperplate. At page 165 of the Colonial Records is found a letter from Robert Morris to the governor of North Carolina in refernece to a settlement of the account between this state and the United States, in which he refers to the proposed arbitration in which this State proposed to appoint one arbitrator and retain power of objecting to the other!
*Pronounced Cochay. He was a Frenchman who had been brought to the Sulphur Springs by Col. Reuben Deaver as a confectionery and pastery cook.
[8]Will Book B, p. 103, September 23, 1844.
[9]Dr. A. B. Cox's "Footprints on the Sands of Time," p. 107.
[10]Record Book Superior Court, not paged.
[11]Ibid.
[12]From information furnished by Hon. A. H. Eller, 1912.
[13]Ibid.
[14]Ibid.
[15]Ibid.
[16]Ibid.
[17]Allen.
[18]Col. Allen T. Davidson, in *The Lyceum*, January, 1891.
[19]Ibid.
[20]Ibid.
[21]Nineteenth Annual Report of Bureau of Ethnology, p. 43.
[22]Vol. II, Rev. St., 1837, p. 195.
[23]"A Brief History of Macon County," by Rev. C. D. Smith Franklin, 1905. "The organization of the county took place nine years after the survey of the lands and the location of the site for the town of Franklin."
[24]Ibid.
[25]Much of the information about the citizens of Franklin and Macon was furnished by Henry G. Robertson, Esq.
[26]In 1852 he represented Macon in the House of Commons.
[27]Henry G. Robertson, Esq., to J. P. A., 1912.
[28]Ibid.
[29]Connor.
[30]Written for this history by Mrs. Mattie S. Candler of Hendersonville.
[31]Zeigler & Grosscup.
[32]The county seat was named in honor of Judge Archibald D. Murphey, who was elected to the Superior court bench in 1818 and resigned in 1819. He spelt his name, however with an "e".
[33]Deed Book G, p. 139, et seq.
[34]Madison county records.
[35]See ante, page 7.
[36]Facts as to Alleghany county furnished by Hon. S. F. Thompson.
[37]Deed Book C, p. 30.
[38]Deed Book E, p. 203.
[39]Facts Furnished by Hon. George A. Shuford.
[40]What used to be called Davidson's River settlement is now known as Pisgah Forest.
[41]Caldwell also contributed to this territory.
[42]L. D. Lowe, Esq., in Watauga Democrat, May 23, 1913.
[43]Ibid.
[44]Balsam Groves, 223.
[45]The same author claims that the Old Fields of Toe, now Newland, was a muster ground before the Civil War, p. 180.

CHAPTER IX

PIONEER PREACHERS

SOLITUDE AND RELIGION. The isolation of the early settlers was conducive to religious thoughts, especially among the uneducated ministry of that day. This is impressively told in the following paragraph:

"There was naught in the scene to suggest to a mind familiar with the facts an oriental landscape—naught akin to the hills of Judea. . . Yet, ignorance has license. It never occurred to Teck Jepson [a local preacher in the novel] that his biblical heroes had lived elsewhere. . . He brooded upon the Bible narratives, instinct with dramatic movement, enriched with poetic color, and localized in his robust imagination, till he could trace Hagar's wild wanderings in the fastnesses; could show where Jacob slept and piled his altar of stones; could distinguish the bush, of all others on the "bald," that blazed with fire from heaven when the angel of the Lord stood within it; . . . saw David, the smiling stripling, running and holding high in his right hand the bit of cloth cut from Saul's garments while the king had slept in a cave at the base of Chilhowie mountain. And how was the splendid miracle of translation discredited because Jepson believed that the chariot of the Lord had rested in scarlet and purple clouds upon the towering summit of Thunderhead that Elijah might thence ascend into heaven?"[1]

EARLY PREACHERS. Staunton, Lexington and Abingdon, Virginia, and Jonesboro, Tenn., and Morganton, N. C., have been largely Presbyterian from their earliest beginning. Not so, however, Western North Carolina in which the Baptists and Methodists got the "start" and have maintained it ever since, notwithstanding the presence almost from the first of the Rev. George Newton and many excellent ministers of the Presbyterian faith since his day. The progress of the Methodists was due largely, no doubt, to the frequent visits of Bishop Asbury.

THE FIRST METHODIST BISHOP. "In the year 1800 Bishop Francis Asbury began to include the French Broad valley in his annual visits throughout the eastern part of the United States, which extended as far west as Kentucky and Tennessee."[2] He was so encouraged by the religious hunger he discovered in these mountain coves that he continued his visits till November, 1813, notwithstanding the rough fare he no doubt frequently had to put up with. Following extracts are from his "Journal":

At Warm Springs in 1800.

(Thursday, November 6, 1800.) "Crossed Nolachucky at Querton's Ferry, and came to Major Craggs', 18 miles. I next day pursued my journey and arrived at Warm Springs, not, however, without an ugly accident. After we had crossed the Small and Great Paint mountain, and had passed about thirty yards beyond the Paint Rock, my roan horse, led by Mr. O'Haven, reeled and fell over, taking the chaise with him; I was called back, when I beheld the poor beast and the carriage, bottom up, lodged and wedged against a sapling, which alone prevented them both being precipitated into the river. After a pretty heavy lift all was righted again, and we were pleased to find there was little damage done. Our feelings were excited more for others than ourselves. Not far off we saw clothing spread out, part of the loading of household furniture of a wagon which had overset and was thrown into the stream, and bed clothes, bedding, etc., were so wet that the poor people found it necessary to dry them on the spot. We passed the side fords of French Broad, and came to Mr. Nelson's; our mountain march of twelve miles calmed us down for this day. My company was not agreeable here—there were too many subjects of the two great potentates of this Western World, whisky, brandy. My mind was greatly distressed."

Curiously Contrived Rope and Pole Ferry.

"North Carolina,—Saturday 8. We started away. The cold was severe upon the fingers. We crossed the ferry, curiously contrived with a rope and pole, for half a mile along the banks of the river, to guide the boat by. And O the rocks! the rocks! Coming to Laurel river, we followed the wagon ahead of us—the wagon stuck fast. Brother O'H. mounted old Gray—the horse fell about midway, but recovered, rose, and went safely through with his burden. We pursued our way rapidly to Ivy creek, suffering much from heat and the roughness of the roads, and stopped at William Hunter's."

At Thomas Foster's.

"Sabbath Day, 9. We came to Thomas Foster's, and held a small meeting at his house. We must bid farewell to the chaise; this mode of conveyance by no means suits the roads of this wilderness. We were obliged to keep one behind the carriage with a strap to hold by, and prevent accidents almost continually. I have health and hard labor, and a constant sense of the favor of God."

Blacksmith, Carpenter, Cobbler, Saddler and Hatter.

"Tobias Gibson had given notice to some of my being at Buncombe courthouse, and the society at Killyon's, in consequence of this, made an appointment for me on Tuesday, 11. We were strongly importuned to stay, which Brother Whatcoat felt inclined to do. In the meantime we had our horses shod by Philip Smith; this man, as is not infrequently the case in this country, makes wagons and works at carpentry, makes shoes for men and for horses; to which he adds, occasionally the manufacture of saddles and hats."

Rev. George Newton at Methodist Service.

"Monday, 10. Visited Squire Swain's agreeable family. On Tuesday we attended our appointment. My foundation for a sermon was Heb. ii, 1. We had about eighty hearers; among them was Mr. Newton, a Presbyterian minister, who made the concluding prayer. We took up our journey and came to Foster's upon Swansico (Swannanoa)—company enough, and horses in a drove of thirty-three. Here we met Francis Poythress—sick of Carolina—and in the clouds. I, too, was sick. Next morning we rode to Fletcher's, on Mud creek. The people being unexpectedly gathered together, we gave them a sermon and an exhortation. We lodged at Fletcher's."

A Lecture at Ben. Davidson's.

"Thursday, 13. We crossed French Broad at Kim's Ferry, forded Mills river, and made upwards to the barrens of Broad to Davidson's, whose name names the stream. The aged mother and daughter insisted upon giving notice for a meeting; in consequence thereof Mr. Davis, the Presbyterian minister, and several others came together. Brother Whatcoat was taken with a bleeding at the nose, so that necessity was laid upon me to lecture; my subject was Luke xi, 13."

Describes the French Broad.

"Friday, 14. We took our leave of French Broad—the lands flat and good, but rather cold. I have had an opportunity of making a tolerably correct survey of this river. It rises in the southwest, and winds along in many meanders, fifty miles northeast, receiving a number of tributary streams in its course; it then inclines westward, passing through Buncombe in North Carolina, and Green and Dandridge counties in Tennessee, in which last it is augmented by the waters of Nolachucky. Four miles above Knoxville it forms a junction with the Holston, and their united waters flow along under the name of Tennessee, giving a name to the State. We had no small labor in getting down Saluda mountain."

Again at Warm Springs. In October, 1801, we find this entry:

"Monday, October 5. We parted in great love. Our company made twelve miles to Isaiah Harrison's, and next day reached the Warm Springs upon French Broad river."

"Man and Beast 'Felt the Mighty Hills.'"

"Wednesday, 7. We made a push for Buncombe courthouse: man and beast felt the mighty hills. I shall calculate from Baker's to this place one hundred and twenty miles; from Philadelphia, eight hundred and twenty miles."

Resting at George Swain's.

"Friday, 9. Yesterday and today we rested at George Swain's."

Quarterly Meeting at Daniel Killon's.

"Sabbath Day, 11. Yesterday and today held quarterly meeting at Daniel Killon's, near Buncombe courthouse. I spoke from Isa. lvii, 6, 7 and I Cor. vii, 1. We had some quickenings."

A Sermon from N. Snethen.

"Monday, 12. We came to Murroughs, upon Mud creek; here we had a sermon from N. Snethen on Acts xiv, 15. Myself and James Douthat gave an exhortation. We had very warm weather and a long ride. At Major Britain's, near the mouth of Mills river, we found a lodging."

At Elder Davidson's.

"Tuesday, 13. We came in haste up to elder Davidson's, refreshed man and beast, commended the family to God, and then struck into the mountains. The want of sleep and other inconveniences made me unwell. We came down Saluda River, near Saluda Mountain : it tried my lame feet and old feeble joints. French Broad, in its meanderings, is nearly two hundred miles long; the line of its course is semi-circular; its waters are pure, rapid, and its bed generally rocky, except the Blue Ridge; it passes through all the western mountains."

At William Nelson's at Warm Springs. Again in November, 1802, we find this entry:

"Wednesday, 3. We labored over the Ridge and the Paint Mountain : I held on awhile, but grew afraid of this mountain, and with the help of a pine sapling worked my way down the steepest and roughest parts. I could bless God for life and limbs. Eighteen miles this day contented us, and we stopped at William Nelson's, Warm Springs. About thirty travelers having dropped in, I expounded the scriptures to them, as found in the third chapter of Romans, as equally applicable to nominal Christians, Indians, Jews, and Gentiles."

Dinner at Barnett's Station.

"Thursday, 4. We came off about the rising of the sun, cold enough. There were six or seven heights to pass over, at the rate of five, two or one mile an hour—as this ascent or descent would permit : four hours brought us to the end of twelve miles to dinner, at Barnett's station; whence we pushed on to John (Thomas) Foster's, and after making twenty miles more, came in about the going down of the sun. On Friday and Saturday we visited from house to house."

"Dear William McKendree."

"Sunday, 7. We had preaching at Killon's. William McKendree went forward upon 'as many as are led by the Spirit of God, they are the sons of God;' my subject was Heb. iii, 12, 13. On Monday I parted from dear William McKendree. I made for Mr. Fletcher's, upon Mud creek; he received me with great attention, and the kind offer of everything in the house necessary for the comfort of man and beast. We could not be prevailed on to tarry for the night, so we set off after dinner and he accompanied us several miles. We housed for the night at the widow Johnson's. I was happy to find that in the space of two years, God had manifested his goodness and his power in the hearts of many upon the solitary banks and isolated glades of French Broad; some subjects of grace there were before, amongst Methodists, Presbyterians and Baptists. On Tuesday I dined at Benjamin Davidson's, a house I had lodged and preached at two years ago. We labored along eighteen miles, eight ascent, on the west side, and as many on the east side of the mountain. The descent of Saluda exceeds all I know, from the Province of Maine to Kentucky and Cumberland; I had dreaded it, fearing I should not be able to walk or ride such steeps; nevertheless, with time, patience, labor, two sticks and above all, a good Providence I came in about five o'clock to ancient father John Douthat's, Greenville County, South Carolina."

AGAIN AT NELSON'S. On October, 1803, we meet with this entry:

"North Carolina. On Monday, we came off in earnest; refreshed at Isaiah Harrison's, and continued on to the Paint Mountain, passing the gap newly made, which makes the road down to Paint Creek much better. I lodged with Mr. Nelson, who treated me like a minister, a Christian and a gentleman."

IVY HAD BEEN BRIDGED IN 1803.

"Tuesday, 25. We reached Buncombe. The road is greatly mended by changing the direction, and throwing a bridge over Ivy."

SISTERS KILION AND SMITH DEAD.

"Wednesday, 26. We called a meeting at Kilion's, and a gracious season it was : my subject was I Cor. xv, 38. Sister Kilion and Sister Smith, sisters in the flesh, and kindred spirits in holiness and humble obedience, are both gone to their reward in glory. On Thursday we came away in haste, crossed Swamoat (Swannanoa) at T. Foster's, the French Broad at the High (Long) Shoals, and afterwards again at Beard's Bridge, and put up for the night at Andrew Mitchell's : In our route we passed two large encamping places of the Methodists and Presbyterians : it made country look like the Holy Land."

HE ESCAPES FROM FILTH, FLEAS, AND RATTLESNAKES.

"Friday, 28. We came up Little River, a sister stream of French Broad : it offered some beautiful flats of land. We found a new road, lately cut, which brought us in at the head of Little River at the old fording place, and within hearing of the falls, a few miles off of the head of Matthews Creek, a branch of the Saluda. The waters foaming down the rocks with a descent of half a mile, make themselves heard at a great distance. I walked down the mountain, after riding sixteen or eighteen miles, before breakfast, and came in about twelve o'clock to father John Douthat's; once more I have escaped from filth, fleas, rattlesnakes, hills, mountains, rocks, and rivers; farewell, western world, for awhile!"

AT FLETCHER'S ON MUD CREEK. Again in October, 1805, we find the following entry:

"North Carolina. We came into North Carolina and lodged with Wm. Nelson, at the Hot Springs. Next day we stopped with Wilson in Buncombe. On Wednesday I breakfasted with Mr. Newton, Presbyterian minister, a man after my own mind : we took sweet counsel together. We lodged this evening at Mr. Fletcher's, Mud Creek. At Colonel Thomas's, on Thursday, we were kindly received and hospitably entertained."

BEDS A BENCH AND DIRT FLOOR OF SCHOOL HOUSE. Again in September, 1806, we find the following entry:

"Wednesday, 24. We came to Buncombe : we were lost within a mile of Mr. Killion's (Killian's), and were happy to get a school house to shelter us for the night. I had no fire, but a bed wherever I could find a bench; my aid, Moses Lawrence, had a bear skin and a dirt floor to spread it on."

HIS FOOD BRINGS BACK HIS AFFLICTION.

"Friday, 26. My affliction returned: considering the food, the labor, the lodging, the hardships I meet with and endure it is not wonderful. Thanks be to God! we had a generous rain—may it be general through the settlement!"

CAMP MEETING ON TURKEY CREEK.

"Saturday, 27. I rode twelve miles to Turkey Creek, to a kind of camp meeting. On the Sabbath, I preached to about five hundred souls : it was an open season and a few souls professed converting grace."

RODE THROUGH SWANINO RIVER.

"Monday, 29. Raining. We had dry weather during the meeting. There were eleven sermons and many exhortations. At noon it cleared up, and gave us an opportunity of riding home : my mind enjoyed peace, but my body felt the effect of riding. On Tuesday I went to a school house to preach: I rode through Swanino River, and Cane and Hooper's Creeks."

LITTLE AND GREAT HUNGER MOUNTAIN.

"North Carolina, Wednesday, October 1. I preached at Samuel Edney's. Next day we had to cope with Little and Great Hunger mountains. Now I know what Mill's Gap is, between Buncombe and Rutherford. One of the descents is like the roof of a house, for nearly a mile: I rode, I walked, I sweat, I trembled, and my old knees failed; here are gulleys and rocks, and precipices; nevertheless the way is as good as the path over the Table Mountain—bad is the best. We came upon Green River."

WARM SPRINGS IN 1807. Again on October, 1807, we find the following entry:

"Friday 16. We reached Wamping's (Warm Springs). I suffered much today; but an hour's warm bath for my feet relieved me considerably. On Saturday we rode to Killon's."

George Newton, an Israelite Indeed.

"North Carolina, Sabbath, 18. At Buncombe courthouse I spoke from 2 Kings, vii, 13–15. The people were all attention. I spent a night under the roof of my very dear brother in Christ, George Newton, a Presbyterian minister, an Israelite indeed. On Monday we made Fletcher's; next day dined at Terry's, and lodged at Edwards. Saluda ferry brought us up on Wednesday evening."

Labored and Suffered, But Lived Near God. Again in October, 1808, we find the following entry:

"On Tuesday we rode twenty miles to the Warm Springs, and next day reached Buncombe, thirty-two miles. The right way to improve a short day is to stop only to feed the horses, and let the riders meanwhile take a bite of what they have been provident enough to put into their pockets. It has been a serious October to me. I have labored and suffered; but I have lived near to God."

Mr. Irwon (Erwin), a Chief Man.

"North Carolina, Saturday, 29. We rested for three days past. We fell in with Jesse Richardson : He could not bear to see the fields of Buncombe deserted by militiamen, who fire a shot and fly, and wheel and fire, and run again; he is a veteran who has learned to 'endure hardness like a good soldier of the Lord Jesus Christ.' On the Sunday I preached in Buncombe courthouse upon I Thess. i, 7–10. I lodged with a chief man, a Mr. Irwon. Henry Boehm went to Pigeon Creek to preach to the Dutch."

Wootenpile Asks Pay in Prayer. In October, 1909, we find:

"We crossed the French Broad and fed our horses at the gate of Mr. Wootenpile (Hoodenpile); he would accept no pay but prayer; as I had never called before he may have thought me too proud to stop. Our way now lay over dreadful roads. I found old Mr. Barnett sick—the case was a dreadful one, and I gave him a grain of tartar and a few composing drops, which procured him a sound sleep. The patient was very thankful and would charge us nothing. Here are martyrs to whiskey! I delivered my own soul. Saturday brought us to Killion's. Eight times within nine years I have crossed these Alps. If my journal is transcribed it will be as well to give the subject as the chapter and the verse of the text I preached from. Nothing like a sermon can I record. Here now am I and have been for twenty nights crowded by people, and the whole family striving to get round me."

James Patton, Rich, Plain, Humble, Kind.

"Sabbath, 29. At Buncombe I spoke on Luke xiv, 10. It was a season of attention and feeling. We dined with Mr. Erwin and lodged with James Patton; how rich, how plain, how humble, and how kind! There was a sudden change in the weather on Monday; we went as far as D. Jay's. Tuesday, we moved in haste to Mud Creek, Green river cove, on the other side of Saluda."

AT VATER SHUCK'S ON A WINTER'S NIGHT. Again, in December, 1810, we find the following entry:

"At Catahouche (Catalouche) I walked over a log. But O the mountain—height after height, and five miles over! After crossing other streams, and losing ourselves in the woods, we came in, about nine o'clock at night, to Vater Shuck's. What an awful day! Saturday, December 1. Last night I was strongly afflicted with pain. We rode twenty-five miles to Buncombe."

GEORGE NEWTON ALMOST A METHODIST.

"North Carolina, Sabbath, December 2. Bishop McKendree and John McGee rose at five o'clock and left us to fill an appointment about twenty-five miles off. Myself and Henry Boehm went to Newton's academy, where I preached. Brother Boehm spoke after me; and Mr. Newton, in exhortation, confirmed what was said. Had I known and studied my congregation for a year, I could not have spoken more appropriately to their particular cases; this I learned from those who knew them well. We dined with Mr. Newton. He is almost a Methodist, and reminds me of dear Whatcoat—the same placidness and solemnity. We visited James Patton; this is, perhaps, the last visit to Buncombe."

SPEAKING "FAITHFULLY."

"Monday. It was my province today to speak faithfully to a certain person. May she feel the force of, and profit by the truth."

THE HOODENPILE ROAD IS OPEN. In December, 1812, we find the following:

"Monday, 30. We stopped at Michael Bollen's on our route, where I gave them a discourse on Luke, xi, 11-13. Why should we climb over the desperate Spring and Paint mountain when there is such a fine new road? We came on Tuesday a straight course to Barratt's (Barnett's), dining in the woods on our way."

BACK AGAIN AT KILLION'S.

"North Carolina, Wednesday, December 2. We went over the mountains, 22 miles, to Killion's."

AT SAMUEL EDNEY'S AND FATHER MILLS'S.

"Thursday, 3. Came on through Buncombe to Samuel Edney's : I preached in the evening. We have had plenty of rain lately. Friday, I rest. Occupied in reading and writing. I have great communion with God. I preached at Father Mills's."

IN GREAT WEAKNESS. Again, in November, 1813, we meet with this entry:

"Sabbath, 24. I preached in great weakness. I am at Killion's once more. Our ride of ninety miles to Staunton bridge on Saluda river was severely felt, and the necessity of lodging at taverns made it no better."

VALEDICTORY TO PRESIDING ELDERS.

"Friday, 29. On the peaceful banks of the Saluda I write my valedictory address to the presiding elders."

Killian's, so often mentioned with different spellings in the foregoing extracts, is the present residence of Capt. I. C. Baird on Beaverdam.[3] When the General Conference of the Methodist Episcopal Church, South, met at Asheville in May, 1910, a gavel made of a portion of the banister of the old Killian home was presented to the presiding bishop.

FIRST CHURCH IN THE MOUNTAINS. According to Col. W. L. Bryan of Boone, the first church established west of the Blue Ridge and east of the Smokies was at what is still called "Three Forks of New river in what is now Watauga county, a beautiful spot." It was organized November 6, 1790. The following is from its records: "A book containing (as may be seen) in the covenant and conduct of the Baptist church of Jesus Christ in Wilkes county, . . . New River, Three Forks settlement" by the following members: James Tomkins, Richard Greene and wife, Daniel Eggers and wife, William Miller, Elinor Greene and B. B. Eggers. "This is the mother of all the Baptist churches throughout this great mountain region. From this mother church, using the language of these old pioneers, they established 'arms' of the mother church; one at what is now known as the Globe in Caldwell county, another to the westward, known as Ebinezer, one to the northeast named South Fork . . . and at various other points. Yet, it should be remembered that the attendance upon the worship of the mother church extended for many, many miles, reaching into Tennessee." After these "arms" had been established "there was organized Three Forks Baptist association, which bears the name to this day, and is the oldest and most venerated religious organization known throughout the mountains. Among the first pastors of the mother church were Rev. Mr. Barlow of Yadkin, George McNeill of Wilkes, John G. Bryan who died in Georgia at the age of 98, Nathaniel Vannoy of Wilkes, Richard Gentry of Old Field, Joseph Harrison of Three Forks, Brazilla McBride and Jacob Greene of Cove creek, Reuben Farthing, A. C. Farthing, John or Jackie Farthing, Larkin Hodges and Rev. William Wilcox, the last named having been the last of the Old Patriarchs of this noted church to pass away. They were all farmers and worked in the fields for their daily bread. To the above list should be added Rev. D. C. Harmon of Lower Cove creek, Rev. D. C. Harmon, Rev. Smith Ferguson, who, though they have been gone for many years, yet speak to some of those left behind."[4]

PROMINENT PIONEER RELIGIOUS TEACHERS.[5] Among these were " Richard Gentry, Aaron Johnson, William Baldwin, Richard Jacks, David Smith, all of whom were Baptists favoring missions; and among the Methodists were James Wagg, Samuel Plumer, A. B. Cox and Hiram and Elihu Weaver."

REV. HUMPHREY POSEY. Of this good man Col. Allen T. Davidson says in *The Lyceum* for January, 1891, p. 11, that James Whittaker of Cherokee "and the Rev. Humphrey Posey established the leading (Baptist) churches in this upland country, to wit: Cane creek, in Buncombe county, and Locust Old Field in Haywood county, where the friends of these two men have worshipped ever since. . . . There they stand, monuments to the memory of these pioneers. . . . Perhaps the most remarkable man in this up-country was Rev. Humphrey Posey, who was born in Henry county, Va., January 12, 1780, was brought to Burke when only five years old and remained there until he reached manhood, was ordained a minister at Cane creek church in 1806. About 1820 he established a mission school at what is now known as the Mission Place on the Hiwassee river, seven miles above Murphy. He removed to Georgia in 1784, and died at Newman, Ga., 28 December, 1846. He was a man greatly endowed by nature to be a leader, of great physical force, with a profile much like that of the Hon. Tom Corwin of Ohio. He had a fine voice and manner, was singularly and simply eloquent. . . . In fact, by nature, he was a great man, and "his works do follow him." The effect of his mission schools have been seen for many years past, and many citizens of Indian blood are left to tell the tale. The Stradley brothers of Asheville were two other pioneer Baptist preachers of note. They had been in the Battle of Waterloo as members of Wellington's army before emigrating to America. Their record is known of all men in Buncombe county, and a long line of worthy descendants attest the sturdy character of the parent stock.

REV. BRANCH HAMLINE MERRIMON. He was born in Dinwiddie county, Va., February 22, 1802, and moved with his parents as far as Rogersville, Tenn., on their way to the Great West, when one member of the family becoming too ill to travel further, they stopped there permanently. He joined the Methodist Conference at Knoxville in 1824 and became an itinerant Methodist preacher, being assigned to this section. In 1829 he married Mary E. Paxton, a daughter of William Paxton and his wife Sarah McDowell, a sister of Gen. Charles McDowell of Revolutionary fame. William Paxton was born in Roxbridge county, Va., and came to Burke county, where at Quaker Meadows he married his wife. William Paxton and wife then moved to the Cherry Fields in what is now Transylvania county, where they bought and improved a large tract of fertile land, whither Mr. Merrimon and his wife followed. William Paxton was a brother of Judge John Paxton of Morganton, a Superior court judge from 1818 to 1826. He was also a near kinsman of Judge John Hall, a member of the first Supreme court of this State. Mr. Merrimon died at Asheville in November, 1886, leaving seven sons and three daughters. Chief Justice A. S. Merrimon was one of his sons, and Ex-Judge J. H. Merrimon of Asheville is another. Rev. Mr. Merrimon was a staunch Union man during the Civil War.

The late Rev. J. S. Burnett was another pioneer Methodist preacher of prominence.

UNITED THEY STOOD. "It is a striking fact in the character of this primitive people," says Col. A. T. Davidson in *The Lyceum* for January 1891, "that they were entirely devoted to each other, clannish in the extreme; and when affliction, sorrow, trouble, vexation, or offence came to one it came to all. It was like a bee-hive—always some one on guard, and all affected by the attack from without. They were the constant attendants around the bed of the sick; suffered with the suffering, wept with those who wept, and attended all the funerals without reward, it never having been known that a coffin was charged for, or the digging of a grave for many long years. Is it a fact that these men were better than those of the present day, or does it only exist in my imagination? When I look back to them I think that they were the best men I ever knew; and the dear old mothers of these humble people are now strikingly engraved upon my memory. The men rolled each others' logs in common; they gathered their harvests, built their cabins, and all work of a heavy character was done in common and without price. The log meeting-house was reared in the same way, and it is

W. N. C.—15

a fact that this was done promptly, without hesitation—regardless of creeds or sect—all coming together with a will. The Baptists, "rifle, axe and saddle-bag men," or the Methodist "circuit rider" supplied the people with the ministry of the word; and it is pleasant to look back and reflect upon the enjoyment and comfort these humble people had in the administration by these humble ministers in the long-ago. Then they came together and held what they called "union meetings," under arbors made with poles and brush, or, at the private residence of some good citizen—often at my father's. I remember distinctly that Nathaniel Gibson, of Crabtree creek, converted the top story of his mill house into one of these places of worship; and Jacob Shook, on Pigeon, the father of the family near Clyde, turned his threshing floor, in his barn, into a place of worship; and near this was established about 1827 or 1828, Shook's Camp Ground. The good old Dutchman contributed or donated to the church ten acres of land, which have ever been kept for a place of public worship.

REV. WM. G. BROWNLOW.[6]   In the year 1832 Rev. Wm. G. Brownlow, a Methodist minister, afterwards better known as Parson Brownlow and Governor of Tennessee, served as pastor of the Franklin circuit in Macon county. These were the days of intense religious prejudices and denominational controversies. Rev. Humphrey Posey, a kinsman of the late Ben. Posey, Esq., was at that time the leading minister of the Baptist church in this section.

"It was impossible for men of the type of Brownlow and Posey to long remain in the same community without becoming involved in controversy. Nor did they. From denominational discussions their controversy degenerated into matters personal, a personal quarrel. Brownlow, as is well known, was a master of invective and his pen was dipped in vitriol. On July 23, 1832, he wrote Rev. Posey a 24-page letter which is still on file among the records of Macon court and which that gentleman regarded as libelous. He thereupon indicted parson Brownlow, as appears from the court records. The first bill was found at fall term 1832. It is signed by J. Roberts, solicitor *pro tem.*, and seems to have been quashed; at any rate a new bill was sent and the case tried at spring term 1833. Wm. J. Alexander was the solicitor when the case was tried. The defendant pleaded not guilty but was found guilty by the jury, whether upon the ground that the "greater the truth the greater the libel" or not does not appear. He was sentenced to pay a fine and the costs. The amount of the fine was not given but the record discloses that it was paid by J. R. Siler, one of the leading citizens and original settlers, and a prominent member of the Methodist church. Execution issued for the costs and the return shows that on July 1, 1833, the sheriff 'levied on dun mare, bridle, saddle and saddle bags. Sold for $65.50. Proceeds into office $53.83.'

"There is a generally accredited story to the effect that when the sheriff went to levy on the Parson's horse, Brownlow was just closing a preaching service at Mt. Zion church—that he saw the sheriff approaching and knew the purpose of his coming. and before the sheriff came up Brownlow handed his Bible to one lady member of his congregation and his hymn book to another and that these books are still in the families of the descendants of these ladies. It is also said that when Brownlow started to conference that fall, J. R. Siler made him a present of another horse in lieu of the one that had been sold."

William Gunnaway Brownlow was born in Virginia in 1805, and became a carpenter first and then a Methodist preacher. In 1828 he moved to Tennessee and in 1839 became a local preacher at Jonesboro and editor of *The Whig*, but moved to Knoxville, taking *The Whig* with him and continued its publication till the beginning of the Civil war. He preached many sermons defending slavery, and was defeated by Andrew Johnson for Congress in 1843. He wrote several books, the most famous of which was called Parson Brownlow's Book, in which he gave his unpleasant experiences with the Confederates and his views on secession and the Civil War. He was a member of the convention which revised the constitution of Tennessee in 1865, and was elected governor in 1865, and again in 1867. He was sent to the United States senate in 1869 where he remained till 1875. He died at Knoxville in April, 1877.[7]

CANARIO DRAYTON SMITH.[8]   He was a son of Samuel and Mary Smith, and was born in Buncombe April 1, 1813. His grandfather, Joseph Smith, was born on the eastern shore of Maryland, April 1, 1730, and his grandmother, Rebecca Dath (Welch), was born near the same place on April 1, 1739. In 1765 they moved to North Carolina, and on the journey C. D. Smith's father was born at a public inn in Albemarle county, Va., August 20, 1765. They first settled at Hawfields in Guilford county, where they were living when the battle was fought in 1780. His maternal grandfather, Daniel Jarrett, was born in Lancaster county, Pa., December 18, 1747. He was of English blood. His grandmother Jarrett, whose maiden name was Catharine C. Moyers, was born in

Lancaster county, Pa., February 9, 1753. She was a German woman. They were married October 25, 1772, moving to North Carolina shortly afterwards and settling in Cabarrus, where his mother, Mary Jarrett, was born June 23, 1775. Soon after the close of hostilities between the Cherokees and whites they moved to Buncombe county, where in 1796 his father and mother were married. They moved to Macon in the winter of 1819-20. At the sale of the Cherokee lands at Waynesville in September, 1820, his father bought the land known as the Tessentee towns, now Smith's Bridge, where C. D. Smith was reared to manhood. He attended the subscription schools of the neighborhood, and in 1832 went to Caney river, then in Buncombe, now in Yancey, to clerk for Smith & McElroy, merchants, where he spent five years, buying ginseng principally, getting in in 1837 over 86,000 pounds which yielded 25,000 pounds of choice clarified root, which was barreled and shipped to Lucas & Heylin, Philadelphia, and thence to China. In the meantime Yancey had been created a county and John W. McElroy had been elected first clerk of the Superior court, making C. D. Smith his deputy. At a camp meeting held at Caney River Camp Ground in 1836, by Charles K. Lewis, preacher in charge, of the Black Mountain circuit, he was converted and joined the church. At the quarterly conference at Alexander chapel the following June he was licensed to preach by Thos. W. Catlett, presiding elder. He continued to preach till 1850 when he went on the supernumerary list on account of bad health. In 1853 he became agent for the American Colonization Society for Tennessee and sent to Liberia two families of emancipated negroes. In 1854 he became interested in mineralogy, and continued this study of mineralogy and geology till his death. He was assistant State Geologist under Prof. Emmons and a co-worker with Prof. Kerr. He is mentioned in Dr. R. N. Price's works on Methodism, and has an article in Kerr's Geology of North Carolina. He died in 1894.

[1] "The Despot of Broomsedge Cove," by Mary N. Murfree.
[2] Asheville's Centenary.
[3] Reference is to 1898.
[4] From "A Primitive History of the Mountain Region," by Col. W. L. Bryan.
[5] Facts Furnished by Hon. A. H. Eller of Ashe county, 1912.
[6] By Fred S. Johnston, Esq., of Franklin, N. C.
[7] McGee, p. 173.
[8] From the "Autobiography of Dr. C. D. Smith," and statements of Henry G. Robertson, Esq.

CHAPTER X

ROADS, STAGE COACHES, AND TAVERNS

BUFFALO TRAILS AND TRADING PATHS. It is probable that buffaloes made the first roads over these mountains, and that the Indians, following where they led, made their trading paths by pursuing these highways. It is still more probable that the buffaloes instinctively sought the ways that were levelest and shortest between the best pastures, thus insuring a passage through the lowest gaps and to the richest lands. The same applies to deer, bear and other wild animals—they wanted to go by the easiest routes and to the countries which afforded the best support. It is still said in the mountains that when the first settlers wanted to build a new road they drove a steer or "cow-brute" to the lowest gap in sight and then drove it down on the side the road was to be located, the tracks made by it being followed and staked and the road located exactly on them. The fact that John Strother mentions no trading paths in the 1799 survey simply indicates that the Indians had not used them for years in the territory north of the ridge between the Nollechucky and the French Broad. No doubt there had been trading paths until the whites came to interrupt their passage over the mountains. But Davenport mentions crossing several on the 1821 survey, viz.: the Cataloochee track at the mouth of Big creek, "the Equeneetly path to Cades cove" at the head of Eagle creek, and at the 60th mile from Pigeon river, in "a low gap at the path of Equeneetly to Tallassee." Seven miles further on they came to another trading path of Cheogee (Cheoah) now known as the Belding trail. At the ninety-third mile they reached "the trading path leading from the Valley Towns to the Overhill Settlements" and reaching the ninety-fifth mile on the path before they paused. On August 24th they passed the white oak, 96th mile, on top of the Unicoi mountain, and on the same day reached the "hickory and rock at the wagon road, the 101st mile, at the end of the Unicoi mountain."

HARD ROADS TO BUILD AS WELL AS TO TRAVEL. Powder was scarce and tools were wanting for the construction of

(229)

roads in the early days.   Dynamite and blasting powder were
then unknown.   Ridges offered least resistance to the construction of a roadway because the timber on their crests
was light and scattered and because, principal consideration,
they were generally level enough on top to allow wagon wheels
to pass up or down them.   But they were frequently too
steep even for the overtaxed oxen and horses of that time.[1]
The level places along creeks and rivers were the next places
where roads could be built with least labor; but these were
always subject to overflow; and cliffs shutting in on one side
always forced the road to cross the stream to get lodgment on
the opposite bank.   Sometimes there were cliffs on both sides
of the stream, and then the road had to run up the nearest
"hollow" or cove to the head of the branch flowing in it and
across the gap down another branch or brook to the stream
from which the road had just parted company.   When there
was no escape from it, "side-cutting" was resorted to; but as
it took a longer road to go by a gentle grade than by a steep
climb, the steeper road was invariably built.

"NAVIGATING WAGONS." James M. Edney, in his Sketches
of Buncombe Men in Bennett's Chronology of North Carolina,
written in 1855, says:

"Col. J. Barnett settled on French Broad seventy years ago, and was
the first man to pilot or navigate wagons through Buncombe by putting
the two big wheels on the lower side, sometimes pulling, sometimes pushing, and sometimes carrying the wagon, at a charge of five dollars for
work and labor done."[2]

THE FIRST ROAD BUILDERS.   "Most of the work done at
the earlier sessions of the county court of Buncombe related
to laying out and working roads.   These roads or trails, rude
and rough, narrow and steep as they were, constituted the
only means of communication between the scattered settlers
of this new country, and were matters of first importance to its
people.   They were located by unlettered hunters and farmers,
who knew nothing of civil engineering, and were opened by
their labor, and could ill afford to spare time from the support
and protection of their families.   Roving bands of Indians
constantly gave annoyance to the white settlers, and frequently
where they found the master of the house absent, would
frighten the women and children into taking refuge in the
woods, and then burn the furniture and destroy the bedding

which they found in the house. Many were the privations incident to a life in a new country suffered by these early setlers, and many were the hardships which they underwent at the hands of these predatory savages. We can scarcely wonder that they saw in the red man none of the romantic feature of character which their descendants are so fond of attributing to him. This state of affairs continued even up into the present century.[3]

THE HARD, UNYIELDING ROCKS. Whenever rock ledges and cliffs were encountered our road-builders usually "took to the woods." That is, they went as far around them as was necessary in order to avoid them. But, in some cases, they had to be removed; and then holes were drilled by driving steel-tipped bars with sledge-hammers as far as practicable, which was rarely over two feet in depth. Into these gunpowder costing fifty cents per pound was poured, and a hollow reed or elder tubes filled with powder were thrust, and the earth tamped around these. A line of leaves or straw was laid on the ground a dozen feet or more from the tube, and slowly burnt its way to the powder. It was a slow and ineffective method, and too expensive to be much used. Another and cheaper way was to build log heaps on top of the ledge of rock and allow them to burn till the rock was well heated, when buckets and barrels of water were quickly poured on the rock after removing the fire, which split the rock and permitted its being quarried.

STAGE-COACH CUSTOMS. In old times there were no reserved seats on stage coaches—first come, first served, being the rule. This resulted, oftentimes, in grumbling and disputes, but as a rule all submitted with good grace, the selfish and pushing getting the choice places then as now. Three passengers on each seat were insisted on in all nine passenger coaches, and woe to that poor wight who had to take the middle of the front seat and ride backwards. Seasickness usually overcame him, but there was no redress, unless someone volunteered to change seats. In dry and pleasant weather, many preferred a seat with the driver or on the roof behind him. Many pleasant acquaintances were made on stage coach journeys, and sometimes friendships and marriages resulted. Stages were never robbed in these mountains, however, as Murrell and his band usually transacted their affairs further west. Heated stones wrapped in rugs and blankets were sometimes taken by ladies during cold weather to keep their feet warm.

OLD TAVERNS. Whenever there was a change of horses, which usually happened at or near a tavern or inn, the passengers would get out and visit the "grocery," either to get warm inside or outside, frequently on both sides. Then, they would walk ahead and be taken up when the coach overtook them. When meals were to be taken there was a rush for the "washing place," usually provided with several buckets of cold spring water and tin basins, with roller towels. Then the rush for the dining room and the well-cooked food served there. Most of these meals were prepared on open hearths before glowing beds of coals, in wide fire-places whose stone hearths frequently extended half across the kitchen floor. But riding at night grew very monotonous, and when possible the ladies remained at these taverns over night, resuming their journeys in the morning.

FIRST ROADS. Boone's trail across the mountains in 1769 was the first of which there is any record, and that seems to be in dispute (see Chapter "Daniel Boone."). The next one was that followed by James Robertson and the sixteen families who left Wake county after Alamance and found their way to the Watauga settlement in Tennessee. They probably followed the Catawba to its head, crossing at the McKinney gap, and followed Bright's trace over the Yellow and thence down to the Doe and so on to the Watauga at Elizabethton.[4] McGee says: "When the Watauga settlement became Washington county, in 1778, a wagon road was opened across the mountains into the settled parts of North Carolina . . . and in 1779 . . . Washington county was divided into . . . Sullivan, etc."[5] The Act of Cession, 1789, calls for the top of the Yellow mountain where "Bright's road crosses the same, thence along the ridge of said mountain between the waters of Doe river and the waters of Rock creek to the place where the road crosses the Iron mountain"; and John Strother, in his diary of the survey of 1799 between North Carolina and Tennessee, mentions that the surveying party crossed "the road leading from Morganton to Jonesborough on Thursday, June 6, 1799." This road was north of the Toe or Nollechucky river and between

it and the Bright road over the Yellow; but, as there are now
two roads crossing between those points, it is important to
ascertain which is the one opened in 1778, as that, undoubtedly,
was the first wagon road crossing the mountains. Chancellor
John Allison speaks of Andrew Jackson crossing this road
from Morganton to Jonesborough, Tenn., in the spring of
1788, as early "as the melting snow and ice made such a trip
over the Appalachians possible."[6] It was "more than one
hundred miles, two-thirds of which, at that time, was without
a single human habitation along its course." Practically all
histories claim that Sevier and his men passed over the Bright
Trace over the Yellow; but Col. W. L. Bryan of Boone, N. C.,
says that Sevier and his men passed through what is now
known as the Carver gap, southwest of the Roan, and down
Big Rock creek.[7] And it does seem more probable that his
men would have followed the wagon road, which Historian
McGee says had been opened in 1778, from Sycamore Shoals,
than a trail which must have taken them considerably further
north than a road nearer the Nollechucky river would have
been. But all these dates referring to that road were prior
to the passing of the first wagon from North Carolina into
Tennessee, mentioned in Wheeler's History of North Carolina
as occurring in 1795.[8] Indeed, John Strother mentions
another "road" at a low gap between the waters of Cove creek
(in what is now Watauga county) and Roan creek (in what is
now Johnson county, Tenn.); but the road over which the first
wagon passed into Tennessee in 1795 was probably the one
Bishop Asbury traveled from 1800 to October, 1803, over
Paint mountain to Warm Springs; and was not the road on
the left side of the river leading down to the mouth of Wolf
creek. This road is a mile and a half southwest of Paint
Rock. Probably no road at that time followed the river
bank there. It is certain, however, that in 1812 Hoodenpile
had charge of a road from Warm Springs to Newport, Tenn.,
and was under contract to keep it in repair from the "top of
Hopewell Hill (now Stackhouse) to the Tennessee line."[9]
William Gillett had built it from Old Newport, Tenn., to the
North Carolina line.[10] It was on the right bank all the way.
The Love road leaves the river six miles below the Hot Springs
at the Hale Neilson house and joins main road 12 miles from
Greenville, Tenn.

PATH CROSSING THE UNAKER MOUNTAIN.[11] John Strother
tells us that about the 13th of May, 1799, they came "to the
path crossing from Hollow Poplar to the Greasy Cove and
met our company." But what kind of a path that was he
does not say. It was probably the road through the Indian
Grave Gap, near the buffalo trail. For they were close to
the Nollechucky river then, and Bishop Asbury's Journal
records the fact that on Thursday, November 6, 1800, he
crossed Nollechucky at Querton's Ferry, and came to Major
Gragg's, 18 miles, arriving at Warm Springs next day. This
road crossed the Small and the Great Paint mountains, for he
mentions an accident that befell his horse after crossing both.
This most probably was the road over which the first wagon
passed in 1795 as recorded in Wheeler's history. In November
1802, the good Bishop "grew afraid" of Paint nountain "and
with the help of a pine sapling worked my way down the
steepest and roughest parts," on his way to Warm Springs
where, at William Nelson's, he found that thirty travelers
had "dropped in," and where he expounded to them the
scripture as found in the "third chapter of Romans as equally
applicable to nominal Christians, Indians, Jews and Gentiles."[12]

WHAT NEW ROAD WAS THIS? In October, 1803, he continued to Paint mountain "passing the gap newly made, which
makes the road down Paint creek much better."

THE HOODENPYLE ROAD. In December 1812, Bishop
Asbury asks "Why should we climb over the desperate Spring
and Paint mountains when there is such a fine new road? We
came on Tuesday a straight course to Barrett's (Barnett's)
dining in the woods on our way." This must have been the
Hoodenpyle road from Warm Springs to Newport, Tenn.,
which he was under contract to keep in order from Hopewell
Hill to the Tennessee line. This road follows Paint creek
one mile and then crosses the mountains.[13] He moved to
Huntsville Landing on the Tennessee river in the territory
of Mississippi, where John Welch of Haywood, agreed to
deliver to him on or before the first of May, 1813, 2,667 gallons
of "good proof whiskey"; and on or before 14 of August,
1814, 1,500 gallons of the same gloom-dispelling elixir, for
value received. No wonder Philip Hoodenpile could play
the fiddle with his left hand![14]

SWANNANOA GAP TRAIL. This, doubtless, was the first road into Buncombe from the east, and led from Old Fort in McDowell county to the head of the Swannanoa river and Bee Tree creek where the first settlers stopped about 1782. How long after this it was before a wagon road was built through this gap does not appear; but it is recorded that the Bairds brought their first wagon through Saluda gap, some miles to the southwest, in 1793. Even that, however, at that date was probably only a very poor wagon road. But a wagon road was finally built through the gap Rutherford and his men had passed through in 1776 to subdue the Cherokees.

THE OLD SWANNANOA GAP ROAD.[15] "The old road through this gap did not cross, as it has often been stated to have done, at the place where the Long or Swannanoa Tunnel is. In later years the stage road did cross at that place. But the old road crossed a half a mile further south. To travel it one would not, as in the case of the later road, leave Old Fort and pass up Mill Creek three miles to where Henry station, so long the head of the railroad, stood. He would leave Old Fort and go across the creek directly west for about a mile before going into the mountains. Then he would turn to the right, ascend the mountain, cross it at about one-half mile south of Swannanoa tunnel, and thence pass down the mountain until the road joined the later road above Black Mountain station."

BUNCOMBE COUNTY ROADS. In his very admirable work, "Asheville's Centenary" (1898), Dr. F. A. Sondley gives a fine account of the building of the first roads in Buncombe county. The first of these ran from the Swannanoa river to Davidson river, in what is now Transylvania county, crossing the French Broad below the mouth of Avery's creek, passing Mills river and going up Boydsteens (now improperly pronounced Boilston) creek; the second ran from "the wagon ford on Rims (now called Reems) creek to join the road from Turkey cove, Catawba, to Robert Henton's on Cane river, after passing through Asheville. In July, 1793, the court ordered a road to be laid off from Buncombe court house to the Bull mountain road near Robert Love's. In 1795 a road was ordered to run from the court house to Jonathan McPeter's on Hominy creek; and at a later period two other roads ran out north

from Asheville to Beaver Dam and Glenn creek. Then followed the Warm Springs road, crossing Reems creek at the
old Wagoner ford and through the rear of the old Alexander
farm, crossing Flat creek" and ran on to the farm of Bedent
Smith near the Madison county line, where it turned west
and ran to the mouth of Ivy, thence to Marshall "and about
one-half mile below that town turned to the east and ran
with the old Hopewell turnpike, built by Philip Hoodenpyle,
later known as the Jewel Hill road, to Warm Springs."

On July 8, 1795, Governor Blount of the territory south of
the Ohio river, now called Tennessee, suggested to the council
of that territory the opening of a road from Buncombe court
house to Tennessee; and Sevier and Taylor were appointed
to act with Wear, Cocke, Doherty and Taylor to consider the
matter, which resulted in the opening of a road from North
Carolina to Tennessee, via Warm Springs, following the right
bank of the French Broad to Warm Springs. In 1793 the
Bairds "had carried up their four-wheel wagon across the
Saluda gap, a road through which had been opened by Col.
Earle for South Carolina for $4,000, and is probably the old
road from Columbia, which passed through Newberry and
Greenville districts," and yet known in upper South Carolina as the old State or Buncombe road. "There was already
a road or trail coming from the direction of South Carolina
to Asheville," crossing the Swannanoa at the Gum Spring,
and known as the "road from Augusta in Georgia to Knoxville." (Record Book 62, p. 361.)

THE NEW STOCK ROAD. This road passes through Weaverville, Jupiter, Jewel Hill and through Shelton Laurel in Madison into Tennessee, and was built when Dr. Wm. Askew,
who was born in 1832, was a boy, in order to escape the delays
of waiting for the French Broad river to subside in times of
freshets, and in winter, of avoiding the ice which drifted into
the road from the river and sometimes made it impassable.
But Bishop Asbury records the fact that on Tuesday, October
25, 1803, in coming from Mr. Nelson's at Warm Springs to
Killian's on Beaver Dam, "the road is greatly mended by
changing the direction and throwing a bridge over Ivy."
This is probably part of the road that runs up Ivy creek from
French Broad and crosses Ivy about a mile up stream, and
then comes on by Jupiter to Asheville. If so, the New Stock

must have started from that bridge across Ivy and run by Jewel Hill to the Tennessee line.

THE BUNCOMBE TURNPIKE.[16] "In 1824 Asheville received her greatest impetus. In that year the legislature of North Carolina incorporated the now famous but abandoned Buncombe Turnpike road, directing James Patton, Samuel Chunn and George Swain to receive subscriptions "for the purpose of laying out and making a turnpike road from the Saluda Gap, in the county of Buncombe, by way of Smith's, Maryville, Asheville and the Warm Springs, to the Tennessee line." (2 Rev. Stat. of N. C., 418). This great thoroughfare was completed in 1828, and brought a stream of travel through Western North Carolina. All the attacks upon the legality of the act establishing it were overruled by the Supreme court of the State, and Western North Carolina entered through it upon a career of marvelous prosperity, which continued for many years.

ASHEVILLE AND GREENVILLE PLANK ROAD.[16] "In 1851 the legislature of the State of North Carolina incorporated the Asheville & Greenville Plank Road Company, with authority to that company to occupy and use this turnpike road upon certain prescribed terms. A plank road was ocnstructed over the southern portion of it, or the greater part of it south of Asheville, and contributed yet more to Ashevilles's prosperity. By the conclusion of the late war, however, this plank road had gone down, and in 1866 the charter of the plank road company was repealed, while the old Buncombe turnpike was suffered to fall into neglect."

ASHEVILLE GETS A START.[16] From the time of the building of the Buncombe Turnpike road, Asheville began to be a health resort and summering place for the South Carolinians, who have ever since patronized it as such.

THE WATCHESE ROAD. In 1813 a company was organized to lay out a free public road from the Tennessee river to the head of navigation on the Tugaloo branch of the Savannah river. It was completed in 1813, and became the great highway from the coast to the Tennessee settlements.[17]

FIRST ROADS OVER THE "SMOKIES." John Strother mentions but two roads as crossing the mountains between Virginia and the Pigeon river, that at "a low gap between the waters of Cove creek—in what is now Watauga county—

and Roans creek—in what is now Johnson county, Tenn.—
and that of "the road leading from Morganton to Jonesborough," Tenn., between the Yellow and the Roan.[18]

FIRST ROADS OVER THE UNAKAS. Of the survey in 1821,
from the end of the 1799 survey on Big Pigeon to the Georgia
line is 116 miles; and yet, as late as 1821 there were but two
roads crossing from North Carolina into Tennessee. They
were "the Cataloochee track" where the 1799 survey ended
and "the wagon road" at the 101st mile post on the Hiwassee
river.[19]

LITTLE TENNESSEE RIVER ROAD. Just when the wagon
road from Tallassee ford up the Little Tennessee river was
first constructed cannot be definitely ascertained. Some
sort of a road, probably an Indian trail, may have existed for
years before the coming of the whites into that section; but
it is not probable, as a road near the river bank is simply
impossible, while on the left side of the Little Tennessee is
what is now known as the Belding Trail. But this name has
only recently been bestowed on an ancient Indian trail which
followed the Cheoah river to what is now Johnson post office
and then cut across the ridges to Bear creek, passing Dave
Orr's house, to Slick Rock creek, and thence down to Tallassee
ford and the Hardin farm.

GEN. WINFIELD SCOTT'S MILITARY ROAD. It is probable,
however, that Gen. Winfield Scott had a military road constructed from Calhoun, his headquarters in Tennessee, up
to the junction of the Little Tennessee with the Tuckaseegee
at what is now Bushnell; for we know that it was down this
road that most of the Cherokees were driven during the
Removal of 1838. But it was impossible for this road to
follow the river bank beyond the Paine branch, where it left
the river and by following that branch, crossed the ridge and
returned to the river again, reaching it at what is now called
Fairfax. For it was at the mouth of the Paine branch that
Old Charley, the Cherokee, and his family made their break
for liberty, and succeeded in escaping in 1838. Beyond
Rocky Point, however, it is impossible even for modern engineers, except at a prohibitive cost, to build a road near the
river bank, and the consequence has been that the road runs
over a series of ridges, which spread off from the end of the
Great Smoky range like so many figures, down to the Little

Tennessee. Gen. Wool's soldiers built the road from Valleytown to Robbinsville in 1836-7.[20]

CRUSOE JACK AND JUDGE FAX. There is a tradition that, when the treaty of Tellico in 1789 was made, Crusoe Jack, a mulatto, got a grant to the magnificent Harden farm and that John Harden traded him out of it. Harden worked about fifty slaves on this farm, among whom was Fax, a mulatto, who bought his freedom from John Harden, whose descendants still own this farm, and settled at Fairfax, where Daniel Lester afterwards lived for many years, and where Jeremiah Jenkins afterwards lived and died. Fax was called Judge Fax and kept a public house where he supplied wagoners and other travelers with such accommodations as he could.

OLD WILKESBOROUGH ROADS. The prinicipal road from Wilkesboro passed through Deep gap and went by Boone. The Phillips gap road was made just before the Civil War and after Arthur D. Cole settled on Gap creek and began his extensive business there it was much used. All freight came from Wilkesboro. The turnpike from Patterson over Blowing Rock gap passed down the Watauga river and Shull's Mills to Valle Crucis, Ward's store, Beech, and Watauga Falls to Cardens' bluff in Tennessee, after which it left the Watauga river and crossed the ridge to Hampton and Doe river, going on to Jonesboro. It was surveyed about 1848 by Col. William Lenoir and built soon afterwards. David J. Farthing and Anderson Cable remember seeing the grading while it was being built, and Alfred Moretz of Deep Gap was present when sections of the road were bid off by residents, the bidding being near the mouth of Beech creek.

THE WESTERN TURNPIKE. In 1848–9 the legislature passed an act to provide for a turnpike road from Salisbury to the line of the State of Georgia. The lands of the Cherokees were later pledged for the building of this "Western Turnpike," as it was officially called, and in 1852–3 another act was passed "to bring into market the lands" so pledged, and this act was later (Ch. 22, Laws 1854–5) supplemented by an act which gave the road the proceeds of the sales of the Cherokee lands in Cherokee, Macon, Jackson and Haywood counties. At the latter session another act was passed making Asheville the eastern terminus and the Tennessee line, near Ducktown, the western terminus of this road, and providing that it should

also extend to the Georgia line; but that the latter road should
be only a branch óf the main road.   It also provided that in
case the bridge across the French Broad river—presumably
Smith's bridge at Asheville—could not be obtained on satisfactory terms, the route of the turnpike might be changed
and a new bridge constructed.   As this was not done, it is
probable that satisfactory terms were made for the use of
Smith's bridge, as it had been sold to Buncombe county
about 1853.   When this road reached the Tuckaseegee river
"the influence of Franklin and Macon county was the principal force which took it across the Cowee and Nantahala
mountains[21].   The survey was made by an engineer by the
name of Fox in 1849.   It was completed over the Valley river
mountains and Murphy in 1856.   The late Nimrod S. Jarrett
was chief of construction.   Chapter 51, Laws of 1854–5 defined
the duties of and powers of turnpike and plankroad companies, and acts incorporating the latter throughout the State
passed at that session extend from page 178 to page 216,
showing their popularity.

SMITH'S BRIDGE.   Long before a bridge had been built
across the French Broad at Asheville Edmund Sams, who had
come from the Watauga settlement and settled on the west
side of the French Broad at what was later known as the
Gaston place about a mile above the mouth of the Swannanoa operated a ferry there.   He had been an Indian fighter,
and later a soldier of the Revolution.   He was also for years
a trustee of the Newton Academy, and died on the farm of
his father-in-law, Thomas Foster, near Biltmore.   John Jarrett afterwards lived at the western terminus of the present
bridge, keeping the ferry and charging toll.   Subsequently he
sold it to James M. Smith, who built a toll bridge there, which
he maintained till about 1853, when he died, after having sold
the bridge to Buncombe county.   After this it became a free
bridge.   In 1881 it was removed to make way for the present iron structure, but its old foundations are yet plainly to be
seen.[22]   That old bridge was a single track affair without
handrails for a long time before the Civil War, and nothing
but log stringers on each side of the roadway.   Col. J. C.
Smathers of Turnpike remembers when, if a team began to
back, there was nothing to prevent a vehicle going over into
the river.   Chapter 313, Laws, 1883, made it unlawful to

drive or ride faster than a walk over the new double-track bridge at Asheville."

CARRIER'S BRIDGE. This was built about 1893, crossing the French Broad at the mouth of the Swannanoa river. It was afterwards sold to the county. Pearson's Bridge, near Riverside Park, was built by Hon. Richmond Pearson about this time, but afterwards taken over by the county. The Concrete bridge below the passenger depot was finished and opened in 1911.

GORMAN'S BRIDGE. This is about five miles below Asheville and was erected long before the war, but was washed away. It was replaced by the present iron structure, about 1900.

THE ANDERSON ROAD. About the year 1858 a road was made from the head of Cade's Cove in Blount county, Tenn., around the Boat mountain to what is now and was probably then the Spence Cabin at Thunderhead mountain. It was finished to this point, in the expectation that a road from the mouth of Chambers creek, below Bushnel, would be built over into the Hazel creek settlement, and thence up the Foster ridge and through the Haw gap to meet it. But North Carolina failed to do its part, and the old Anderson road in a ruinous condition, but still passable for footmen and horsemen, remains a mute witness to somebody's bad faith in the past.

GREAT ROAD ACTIVITY. Between 1848 and 1862, while the late Col. W. H. Thomas was in the legislature, the statute books are full of charters for turnpike and plankroad companies all through the mountains. Many of these roads were not to be new roads but improvements on old roads which were bad; and some of the roads authorized were never built at all. The Jones gap road to Cæsar's head, the road from Bakersville to Burnsville, the road from Patterson to Valle Crucis and on to Jonesboro, the road up Cove creek by trade and Zionville to what is now Mountain City, the road over Cataloochee to Newport, the road up Ocona Lufty, the road through Soco gap, the road up Tuckaseegee river and the Nantahala, through Red Marble gap, etc., were all chartered during that time. And Col. Thomas was especially interested in the road from Old Valleytown over the Snowbird mountain, via Robbinsville (Junaluska's old home) down the Cheowah river to Rocky Point, where he had built a bridge across the Little Tennessee and was confidently awaiting the approach of the Blue Ridge railroad, which has not arrived yet.

OLD STAGE COACH DAYS. "From Greenville to Greenville" was the watchword when bids were made for the mail lines in those days. Each Greenville was sixty miles from Asheville. The stops between Greenville, S. C. and Asheville were, first, at C. Montgomery's, ten miles north of Greenville, then at Garmany's, twenty miles; then at Col. John Davis's, near the State line, where Col. David Vance was taken to die after his duel with Carson in 1827; then at Hendersonville; then at Shufordsville, or Arden, 12 miles, then at Asheville. Col. Ripley sold out to John T. Poole, of Greenville, S. C., about 1855, and he ran hacks till 1865 when Terrell W. Taylor bought him out and continued to run hacks till the Spartanburg & Asheville Railroad reached Tryon, about 1876.

OLD STAGE COACH CONTRACTORS. J. C. Hankins of Greenville, Tenn., used to have the line from that point to Warm Springs, his stages starting out from Greenville nearly opposite the former residence of the late Andrew Johnson, once President of the United States, and whose son, Andrew Johnson, Jr., married Elizabeth, the second daughter of Col. J. H. Rumbough of Hot Springs. He stopped running this line, however, when the railroad reached Wolf Creek in 1868. The late Wm. P. Blair of Asheville, who used to run the old Eagle hotel, also ran the stage line from Asheville to Greenville, Tenn., (this was at the beginning of the Civil War) until his stock and coaches were captured by Col. G. W. Kirk. In July, 1866, Col. Rumbough ran the stage line from Greenville, Tenn., to Greenville, S. C. The "stands," as the stopping places were called, were breakfast at Warm Springs, dinner at Marshall, supper at Asheville. Owing to the condition of the roads Col. Rumbough cut down the toll gate at Marshall in July, 1866, and the matter was compromised by allowing him to apply the tolls to keeping the road in condition, instead of letting the turnpike company do it.

KEEN COMPETITORS. Col. Rumbough ran the line about a year and a half, when Hon. A. H. Jones, congressman, got the contract, but failed to carry it out, and Col. Rumbough took it again.

THE MORGANTON LINE. The stage line from Morganton to the "head of the railroad," as the various stopping place

S

along the line as the road progressed toward Asheville were
called, was running many years before the Civil War. After
that, the late E. T. Clemmons of Salem came to Asheville
and operated the line from Old Fort to Asheville.

THROUGH HICKORY-NUT GAP. In 1834 Bedford Sherrill
secured a four years' contract to haul the mails from Salisbury via Lincolnton, Schenck's Cotton mills, and Rutherfordton to Asheville. He moved shortly afterwards to Hickory Nut gap, for years thereafter famous as one of the old
taverns of the mountains. Ben Seney of Tennessee succeeded
him as mail carrier on this route, but he did not complete his
contract, giving it up before the expiration of the four years.
Old fashioned Albany stage coaches were used.

HACKS TO MURPHY. As the railroads approached Asheville the hacks and stages were taken off. The late Pinckney
Rollins ran a weekly hack line, which carried the mail, from
Asheville to Murphy from about 1870, and shortly afterward
changed it to a daily line. But he failed at it, and lost much
money. The stopping places in 1871 were Turnpike for
dinner, Waynesville for supper, where a stop was made till
next day. Then to Webster for dinner and Josh Frank's,
two miles east of Franklin, for supper and night. The third
day took the mail through Franklin to Aquone for dinner
at Stepp's, at the bridge[23]; and to Mrs. Walker's, at Old Valley Town, for supper. The next day the trip was made to
Murphy for dinner, and back that night to Old Valley Town.
As the railroad progressed toward Waynesville the hacks ran
from the various termini to that town.

FROM SALEM TO JONESBOROUGH. As far back as 1840 stages
or hacks ran from Salem via Wilkesboro, Jefferson, Creston,
through Ambrose gap, Taylorsville, Tenn., to Jonesboro,
Tennessee; but they were withdrawn at least ten years before
the Civil War, after which Samuel Northington ran a line of
hacks from Jefferson to Taylorsville, now Mountain City,
Tennessee. Stages were run from Lenoir via Blowing Rock,
Shulls Mills and Zionville from 1852 to 1861.

MOONLIGHT AND THE OLD STAGE HORN. In 1828, when
"Billy" Vance kept the Warm Springs hotel, old fashioned
stage coaches ran between Asheville and Greenville, Tenn.,
and Greenville, S. C.[24] According to the recollection of Dr.
T. A. Allen of Hendersonville, N. C., "the old stage line back

in 1840 was operated by the Stocktons of Maryland from Augusta, Ga., "via Greenville, S. C., Asheville, N. C., the Warm Springs and across Paint Mountain to Greenville, Tennessee. "The line from Greenville, S. C., to Greenville, Tenn., was sold to the late Valentine Ripley, who bought it and settled in Hendersonville about 1845." They ran Concord coaches—sometimes called Albany coaches—which were swung on leather braces and carried nine passengers inside, with a boot behind for trunks, and space on top and beside the driver for several additional passengers. The driver was an autocrat, and carried a long tin horn, which he blew as stopping places were approached, to warn the inn-keepers of the number of passengers to be entertained. Nothing was lovelier on a moonlit, frosty night than these sweet notes echoing over hill and dale:

> "O, hark, O, hear, how thin and clear,
>   And thinner, clearer, farther going!
> O, sweet and far from cliff and scar
>   The horns of Elfland faintly blowing!"

When the railroad was completed to Greenville, S. C., in 1855, Col. Ripley ran stages from Greenville, Tenn., to Greenville, S. C., daily, though in 1853 he had been limited to the run from Greenville, S. C., to Asheville, N. C."[25]

Jefferson and Wilkesborough Turnpike. In 1901 the Wilkesborough and Jefferson Turnpike company was incorporated. (Private Laws, ch. 286) and the road was completed in five years. The State simply furnished the convicts and the stockholders the provisions and the expenses of the guard.

Other Counties Get Good Roads. In 1911 Hon. J. H. Dillard secured the passage by the legislature of a road law under which Murphy township is authorized to issue $150,-000.00 of six per cent bonds for the improvement of the roads, and the four main streets of the town and roads leading into the country. Haywood had already done much for the improvement of its roads, while Watauga has undoubtedly the best roads west of the Blue Ridge, the roads to Blowing Rock, Shull's Mills, Boone, Valle Crucis and Banners Elk and Elk Cross roads being unsurpassed anywhere.

Carver's Gap Road. Chapter 63 of the Private laws

of 1881 amended chapter 72 of Private laws of 1866-67 by allowing John L. Wilder, John E. Toppan and others to build a turnpike from Wilder's forge on Big Rock creek across Roan mountain to Carver's gap on the Tennessee State line; and to make a turnpike from Carver's gap down the valley of Little Rock creek to the ford of said creek at John G. Burlison's dwelling house.

CONVICTS TO MAKE COUNTY ROADS.   On the 6th of Febraury, 1893, the Buncombe county commissioners approved a bill which had been introduced in the legislature by Gen. R. B. Vance to use convicts for working county roads, which has proven beneficent, except that negroes and whites are crowded together in too small quarters. Convicts prefer work in the open air to confinement in jails and penitentiaries.

END OF TOLL GATES. On the 5th of September, 1881, the old Buncombe Turnpike company surrendered and the commissioners accepted its charter. The turnpike down the French Broad river having been turned over to the Western North Carolina railroad company for stock in that enterprise in 1869, all that was left to be surrendered was the road from the Henderson county line to Asheville, passing through Limestone township. Gradually each county took over the great Western Turnpike from Asheville to Murphy, thus abolishing toll gates along the road, the legislature having authorized this change. There are still toll gates on some roads, but they have been specially authorized by legislative enactment, and are comparatively few, Yonahlossee and Elk Park roads being of the number.

RIP VANWINKLE BUNCOMBE. From 1880 to 1896 Asheville had gone ahead by leaps and bounds, having in that time paved its streets, built electric railroads, hotels and private residences that are still the pride of all; but the county had stood still. Its old court house, jail and alms house were a reflection on the progress of the times. But in 1896, "Cousin Caney" Brown was elected chairman of the board of county commissioners, and graded a good road from Smith's bridge in the direction of his farm, using the county convicts for the work.[26] He had a farm at the end of the road, it is true, and was criticised for building the road; but it was such a well graded thoroughfare and such an object lesson that the people not only forgave him for providing a better road to his home, but all commissioners who have followed him have been afraid not to contribute something to what he began.

MARK L. REED. Profiting by the example set by "Cousin Caney," M. L. Reed spent a lot of good money building other roads which were macadamized, placing good steel bridges over creeks and rivers where they had long been needed, and in replacing the disgraceful old court house by a modern structure, and providing a jail that is ample for the demands of humanity and the times. A decent home was provided for orphan children of the county. The old alms house was given up and better quarters provided for the old and infirm of the county. "Cousin Caney" had set the pace, and soon other good roads and good roads sentiment followed.

BUNCOMBE GOOD ROADS ASSOCIATION. The Good Roads Association of Asheville and Buncombe county was organized March 6, 1899, Dr. C. P. Ambler was the president and B. M. Jones secretary and treasurer. These officers have been continued in their positions ever since. Their object is the construction and improvement of roads. They have succeeded in accomplishing much good—not the least of which are mile posts and sign boards. They raised $5,000.00 to improve the road from Asheville to Biltmore soon after its organization and $550 for the survey of the "crest of the Blue Ridge highway;" and constructed a horse-back trail to Mitchell's Peak. They are advocating the construction of other highways.

YONAHLOSSEE TURNPIKE. About 1890 the Linville Improvement company was formed, having among its stockholders Mr. S. T. Kelsey, formerly of Highlands, N. C., and before his building of that town, of Kansas. Through his instrumentality, largely, assisted by the Messers. Ravenel and Donald Macrae, the latter of Wilmington, there was constructed the most picturesque and durable highway in the mountains or the State. It begins at Linville City, two miles from Montezuma, Avery county, and runs around the eastern base of Grandfather mountain to Blowing Rock, a distance of twenty miles. It cost about $18,000 complete. It gave an impetus to other road-builders. A road was soon thereafter built from Blowing Rock to Boone, and from Valle Crucis to Banners Elk. There are no finer roads in the State, and none

built on more difficult ground.   In 1912 they were the delight
of numerous automobile owners.

NOTES.

[1]Asheville's Centenary.
[2]The first brakes were made of hickory saplings whose branches were twined around
the front axle and bent around the hind wheels; afterwards came "locking chains" attached
to the body of wagons and then passed between the spokes of the wheels to retard the
vehicle's going down steep grades.   Young trees dragged on the road also served at times.
[3]Asheville's Centenary.
[4]Roosevelt (Vol. I, 225) records the fact that on his return from his first visit to Watauga,
in the fall of 1770, James Robertson lost his way, and for 14 days lived on nuts and berries,
and abandoned his horse among impassible precipices. If he followed up the left bank of
the Watauga and did not see that the Doe came into the former stream at what is now
Elizabethton, it is easy to see how he followed up the left bank of the latter and got lost
amid the precipices of what is now Pardee's Point.
[5]Roosevelt, Vol. III, pp. 97–98.
[6]"Dropped Stitches in Tennessee History," p. 4.
[7]Letter from Col. W. L. Bryan of Boone to J. P. A., December 3, 1912.
[8]Asheville's Centenary.   Wheeler's History of North Carolina, p. 476.
[9]Deed Book E., p. 121-2, Buncombe.
[10]Statement of Francis Marion Wells to J. P. A., July 15, 1912.   Old Newport is three
miles above the present town, the railroad does not pass the former at all.
[11]This must have been a local name for this part of the range, for the real Unaka mountains are southwest of Little Tennessee river.
[12]This is spelled Neilson.
[13]Deed Book E, Buncombe, p. 122.
[14]Ibid., p. 123.
[15]Asheville's Centenary.
[16]From Asheville's Centenary.
[17]See chapter on Cherokee Indians.
[18]Deed Book E, Reg. Deeds, Buncombe county, pp. 122–123.
[19]Davenport's Diary quoted in chapter on boundaries.
[20]Sketch of Graham County by Rev. Joseph A. Wiggins, February 3, 1912.
[21]Capt. James W. Terrell in The Commonwealth, Asheville, June 1, 1893.
[22]Condensed from Asheville's Centenary, 1838.
[23]But from 1872 dinner was taken at Capt. A. R. Munday's.
[24]Col. J. H. Rumbough to J. P. A., November 13, 1912.
[25]Dr. T. A. Allen to J. P. A., November 12, 1912.
[26]This was T. Caney Brown.

CHAPTER XI

MANNERS AND CUSTOMS

THEN AND NOW. Probably there was no more difference in the manners and customs of the early days than we should now see in a community of modern people situated as were our ancestors one hundred and fifty years ago. There was a spirit of co-operation then that made conditions much easier to bear than they might otherwise have been. Those who remember the Civil War times in the South will recall that it is possible to get on without many things ordinarily considered indispensible; and that when it is the "fashion" to do without, simplicity becomes quite attractive. Calico gowns and ribbonless costumes used to look well on pretty women and girls during the war, and hopinjon was far better than no hopinjon. We imagine that we are far removed from a state of nature, but when the occasion arises we readily adapt ourselves to primitive manners and customs.

THE RUSH FOR THE MOUNTAINS. Long before the treaty of 1785 white men had passed beyond the Blue Ridge to hunt and trap. Ashe was sparsely settled long before Buncombe; but as soon as the land between the Blue Ridge and the Pigeon river was open for settlement legally, white men began to settle there, too.

WHERE THEY CAME FROM. Most of these early settlers came from east of the Blue Ridge, though many came from the Watauga Settlements in what is now Tennessee. Wolf Hill, now Staunton, contributed its quota, most of them going into what are now Ashe, Alleghany and Watauga counties. The charm of hunting lured many, but most who sought the mountains doubtless came from the mountainous regions of Scotland. After the French and Indian War several families that had gone into the Piedmont region of South Carolina, came through the Saluda gap and settled in what was then Buncombe, though now called Henderson and Transylvania. The Whiskey Rebellion in Pennsylvania late in the Eighteenth century is also credited with having sent many good citizens into the mountains of western North Carolina.

(248)

THE PIONEER SPIRIT PERSISTS. Roosevelt was the first historian that gave to the pioneers of western North Carolina and Tennessee their rightful place in reclaiming from savage Indians the boundless resources of the Great West. Sam Houston, Davy Crockett and Daniel Boone went from our sacred soil, and added Texas and Kentucky to the galaxy of our starry flag; while Joseph Lane of Oregon first saw the light of day through the chinks of a dirt-floor cabin that once stood in the very shadow of what is still called Lane's Pinnacle of the rugged Craggies—a mute, yet eloquent, monument to that spirit of liberty, enterprize and adventure that still fills our army and navy with recruits for the Sandwich and Philippine Islands of the Pacific. Yet, what visitor to that matchless canon beyond Hickory Nut pass, knows that in passing through Mine Hole gap six miles east of Asheville, he was within a stone's throw of the spot where Lane's father in the dawn of the last century spent laborious days while mining for the precious ore that was to furnish horse-shoes, plough-shares and pruning-hooks for those who first tilled the savannahs of the Swannanoa and the French Broad? Did the pearls of Henry Grady's eloquence, erstwhile, drop scintilant, and thrill the nation from the Kennebeck to the Willamette, because his lightest gem was "shot through with sunshine"? Then know, O ye fools and blind, ye who never cast one longing, lingering look behind, that his grandfather was once sheriff of that Buncombe county whose people are classed by such self-styled "national journals" as *Collier's Weekly*, with the scorners of all law and order, because, forsooth, of the sporadic Allen episode in Virginia. Who discovered that wonderland—the matchless valley of the far-famed Yosemite? James M. Roan of Macon county, North Carolina, in March of Fifty-one.[1] He, with the Argonauts of the world, won his way to the Pacific coast, and left to others to dig from the dim records of the past some frail memorial of his heroic deeds. The spirit that drove him forth has never died, and today, the mountains and hills of Idaho, Montana, Washington and Colorado, are dotted with the homes and ranches of those whose feet first trod "where rolls the Oregon." And Onalaska's ice-ribbed hills are peopled with our kin, as will be every frontier region till Time shall be no more. Our ancestors were the Crusaders of American civilization, and "as long as the fame

of their matchless struggle shall linger in tradition and in song
should their memories be cherished by the descendants" of the
peerless "Roundheads of the South." Still, the incredulous
may ask "Can honor's voice provoke the silent dust, or flat-
tery soothe the dull, cold ear of death"? No; but if we will
but heed while yet we may the silent voices of our worthy
dead, and learn the lesson of the days now gone, we, taking
hope, with Tennyson may cry :

> "Forward to the starry track,
> Glimmering up the heights beyond me,
> On, and always on!"

THE FIRST INDIAN MASSACRES. Samuel Davidson was
killed by Indians in 1781 or 1782 at the head of the Swannanoa river, near what is now Gudger's ford; and Aaron
Burleson was killed on Cane creek in what is now Mitchell
county about the same time, probably, though the date has
been lost. He was an ancestor of Postmaster-General Burleson
of President Wilson's Cabinet in 1914. Davidson had belonged
to a small colony of whites which had settled around what is
now known as Old Fort at the head of the Catawba river in
what is now McDowell county. Among those settlers were
the Alexanders, Davidsons, Smiths, Edmundsons, and Gudgers,
from whom have come a long line of descendants now residing
in Western North Carolina. Burleson probably belonged to
the settlers around Morganton, and had ventured beyond the
Blue Ridge to hunt deer. Davidson's purpose, however, had
been permanent settlement, as he had built a cabin where his
family was living when he was killed.[2]

ASHE COUNTY. Except in a few localities, there are few
evidences of Indian occupation by Indians of the territory
west of the Blue Ridge and North of the Catawba. At the
Old Field on New River, near the mouth of Gap creek, in
Ashe county, was probably once a large Indian town, arrow-
heads, spear points, pieces of pottery, etc., still being found
there; but this section of the mountains had not been populated by the red men for thirteen years before the treaty of
1785, the Indians having leased those lands in 1772, and in
1775, conveyed them outright.[3]

BUFFALOES. Thwaite's "Daniel Boone" gives much information as to the buffaloes that once were in this section. "At
first buffaloes were so plenty that a party of three or four men

with dogs, could kill from ten to twenty in a day; but soon the
sluggish animals receded before the advance of white men, hiding themselves behind the mountain wall" (pp. 17, 18). "They
exhibited no fear until the wind blew from the hunters toward
them, and then they would dash wildly away in large droves
and disappear" (p. 90). Buffalo trails led down the French
Broad; and just north of the Toe and near the Indian Grave
gap the trail is still distinctly visible where it crossed the
mountain. The valley of the French Broad was a well recognized hunting ground and probably it had contained many
buffaloes; but as the Cherokees occupied most of the territory
west of the Pigeon, it is more than likely that the bison family
was not so numerous there; although in Graham county there
are two large creeks which have been called Buffalo time out
of mind. Buffalo used to herd at the head of the Yadkin
river, and their trails crossed the mountains into Tennessee
at several places. But this part of the mountains had been
free of Indians for many years before 1750, when the whites
began to settle there. Col. Byrd, in his "Writings" (p. 225),
says that when near Sugar-tree creek when running the Dividing Line that his party met a lone buffalo two years old—a
bull and already as large as an ox, which they killed. He
adds that "the Men were so delighted with the new dyet,
that the Gridiron and Frying Pan had no more rest all night
than a Poor Husband Subject to Curtain Lectures." Roosevelt[4] mentions that "When Mansker first went to the Bluffs
(now Nashville) in 1769, the buffaloes were more numerous
than he had ever seen them before; the ground literally shook
under the gallop of the mighty herds, they crowded in dense
throngs round the licks, and the forest resounded with their
grunting bellows."

ONE VIRTUE IN LEATHER BREECHES. Col. Byrd in his
"Writings" (p. 212) has these observations upon the curing
of skins by means of "smoak," as he invariably spells it :
"For Expedition's Sake they often stretch their Skins over
Smoak in order to dry them, which makes them smell so dis-
agreeably that a Rat must have a good Stomach to gnaw
them in that condition; nay, 'tis said, while that perfume continues in a Pair of Leather Breeches, the Person who wears
them will be in no danger of that Villainous insect the French
call the Morpion"—whatever that may be.

SOME INSECT PESTS OF PIONEER DAYS. This same versatile and spicy writer makes these sage remarks concerning certain wood insects that have since that time cost these United States millions of dollars: "The Tykes (ticks) are either Deertykes, or those that annoy Cattle. The first kind are long, and take a very Strong Gripe, being most in remote woods, above the Inhabitants. The other are round and more generally insinuate themselves into the Flesh, being in all places where Cattle are frequent. Both these Sorts are apt to be troublesome during the Warm Season, but have such an aversion to Penny Royal, that they will attack no Part that is rubbed with the juice of that fragrant Vegetable. And a strong decoction of this is likewise fatal to the most efficient Seedtikes, which bury themselves in your Legs, where they are so small you can hardly discern them without a Microscope. [Surely the man is talking about "chiggers."]

HORSEFLIES AND MUSQUETAS. He says (p. 213) that Dittany "stuck in the Head-Stall of your Bridle" will keep horse flies at a "respectful Distance. Bear's Oyl is said to be used by Indians (p. 214) against every species of Vermin." He also remarks that the "Richer sort in Egypt" used to build towers in which they had their bed-chambers, in order to be out of the reach of musquetas, because their wings are "so weak and their bodies so light that if they mount never so little, the Wind blows them quite away from their Course, and they become an easy prey to Martins, East India Bats," etc. (p. 214).

FIRE-HUNTING. This Gentleman of Old Virginia (p. 223) describes an unsportsman-like practice of the early settlers of setting the woods afire in a circumference of five miles and driving in the game of all kinds to the hunters stationed near the center to slaughter the terrified animals. The deer are said "to weep and groan like a Human Creature" as they draw near their doom. He says this is called Fire-Hunting, and that "it is much practiced by Indians and the frontier Inhabitants." This, however, is not what was later known as firehunting, which consisted in blinding the deer with the light from torches at night only, and shooting at their eyes when seen in the darkness.

PRIMOGENITURE REVERSED. So hateful and unjust to our ancestors seemed the English rule which gave the eldest son the real estate, that a custom sprang up of giving the young-est son the family homestead, which persists till this good hour. Each girl got a cow, a mare and sufficient "house-plunder" with which to set up house-keeping, but they rarely got any land, the husband being expected to provide that. This latter practice still exists, though girls now sometimes get land also.

GAME AND HUNTERS. According to Thwaite's "Daniel Boone" (p. 18), "Three or four men, with dogs, could kill from ten to twenty buffaloes in a day," while "an ordinary hunter could slaughter four or five deer in a day. In the autumn from sunrise to sunset he could kill enough bears to provide over a ton of bear meat for winter use; wild turkeys were easy prey; beavers, otters and muskrats abounded; while wolves, panthers and wildcats overran the country." "Throughout the summer and autumn deerskins were in their best condition. Other animals were occasionally killed to afford variety of food, but fur-bearers as a rule only furnish fine pelts in the winter season. Even in the days of abun-dant game the hunter was required to exercise much skill, patience and endurance. It was no holiday task to follow this calling. Deer, especially, were hard to obtain. The hab-its of this excessively cautious animal were carefully studied; the hunter must know how to imitate its various calls, to take advantage of wind and weather, and to practice all the arts of strategy" (p. 74).

COMMERCIAL SIDE OF HUNTING. "Deerskins were, all things considered," continues Thwaite (p. 74), "the most remunerative of all. When roughly dressed and dried they were worth about a dollar each; as they were numerous and a horse could carry for a long distance about a hundred such skins, the trade was considered profitable in those primitive times, when dollars were hard to obtain. Pelts of beavers, found in good condition only in the winter, were worth about two dollars and a half each, and of otters from three to five dollars. Thus a horse-load of beaver furs, when obtainable, was worth about five times that of a load of deerskins; and if a few otters could be thrown in, the value was still greater. The skins of buffaloes, bears, and elks were too bulky to carry for long distances, and were not readily marketable. A few elk hides were needed, however, to cut into harness and straps, and bear and buffalo robes were useful for bedding."

How Game and Pelts Were Preserved. Thwaite continues (p. 75), "When an animal was killed the hunter skinned it on the spot, and packed on his back the hide and the best portion of the meat. At night the meat was smoked or prepared for 'jerking,' and the skins were scraped and cured. When collected at the camps, the bales of skins, protected from the weather by strips of bark, were placed upon high scaffolds, secure from bears and wolves. Our Yadkin hunters were in the habit, each day, of dividing themselves into pairs for company and mutual aid in times of danger, usually leaving one pair behind as camp-keepers." Tow, rammed into the barrel of a "dirty" rifle took the oder of burnt powder, and was hung in trees near the fresh meat. This oder kept off wolves, wild cats, etc.

The Plott Dogs. The motive which prompted the settlement of most of these mountain counties was the desire of the pioneers to hunt game. To that end dogs were necessary, the long bodied, long legged, deep mouthed hound being used for deer, and a sort of mongrel, composed of cur, bull and terrier, was bred for bear. The Plott dog, called after the famous bear hunter, Enos Plott, of the Balsam mountains of Haywood county, was said to be the finest bear dogs in the State. A few of them still exist and command large prices. Although most of the settlers were Scotch, collies and shepherd dogs did not make their appearance in these mountains till long after the Civil War. They are quite common now.

When Land Was Cheap. Land was plentiful in those primitive times and as fast as a piece of "new ground" was worn out, another "patch" was cleared and cultivated until it, in its turn, was given over to weeds and pasturage. In all old American pioneer communities it was necessary to burn the logs and trunks of the felled trees in order to get rid of them, and the heavens were often murky with the smoke of burning log-heaps. The most valuable woods were often used for fence rails or thrown upon the burning pile to be consumed with the rest. Fences built of walnut and poplar rails were not uncommon. "New ground" is being made now by scientific fertilization.

Crude Cultivation. The ploughing was not very deep and the cultivation of the crops was far from being scientific. Yet the return from the land was generally ample, the seasons usually proving propitious. There was one year, however, that of 1863, when there was frost in every month. There was still another year in which there could not have been very much rain, as there is a record of a large branch near the Sulphur Springs in Buncombe county having dried up completely. This was in August of the year 1830. (Robert Henry's Diary.)

UNERRING MARKSMEN. The flint-lock, long-barreled Kentucky rifle was in use in these mountains until the commencement of the Civil War. Game was abundant. Indeed, if the modern repeating arms had been in use in those days, the game upon which many depended, not only for food but for clothing as well, would have disappeared long before it did. The fact that the hunter could get but one shot from his gun resulted in making every Nimrod a sure marksman, as he realized that if he missed the first shot the game would be out of sight and hearing long before he could "wipe out" his trusty rifle, charge it with powder and with his slim hickory ramrod ram down the leaden bullet encased in buckskin, and "prime" his flint-lock pan with powder.

USEFUL PELTRIES. The hams of the red deer were cured and saved for market or winter use, while the skins of both deer and bears were "dressed" with the hair left on them and made into garments or used as rugs or mats for the children to play upon before the wide fireplace, for bed coverings, or cut into plough lines and bridles, or made into moccasins. Out of the horns and hoofs of cows they made spoons and buttons, while from hollow poplar logs they constructed bee-hives, cradles for their children, barrels for their grain, ash hoppers, gums for their bees and what not.

COTTON. Small patches of cotton were planted and culti-vated in sandy and sheltered spots near the dwellings, which generally reached maturity, was gathered and "hand-picked," carded and made into batting for quilts and cloaks, or heavy skirts for the women and girls.

JACKS OF ALL TRADES. The men were necessarily "handy" men at almost every trade known at that day. They made shoes, bullets and powder, built houses, constructed tables, chairs, cupboards, harness, saddles, bridles, buckets, barrels, and plough stocks. They made their own axe and hoe-han-dles, fashioned their own horseshoes and nails upon the anvil, burnt wood charcoal, made wagon tires, bolts, nuts and everything that was needed about the farm. Some could even make rifles, including the locks, and Mr. John C. Smathers, now (1912) 86 years old, is still a good rock and brick mason, carpenter, shoemaker, tinner, painter, blacksmith, plumber, harness and saddle maker, candle maker, farmer, hunter, storekeeper, bee raiser, glazier, butcher, fruit grower, hotel-keeper, merchant, physician, poulterer, lawyer, rail-splitter, politician, cook, school master, gardener, Bible scholar and stable man. He lives at Turnpike, halfway between Asheville and Waynesville, and brought the huge trees now growing in front of his hotel on his shoulders when they were saplings and planted them where they now stand, nearly seventy years ago. He can still run a foot race and "throw" most men in a wrestle "catch as catch can." He is the finest example of the old time pioneer now alive.

INDUSTRIOUS WOMEN. But it was the women who were the true heroines of this section. The hardships and constant toil to which they were generally subjected were blighting and exacting in the extreme. If their lord and master could find time to hunt and fish, go to the Big Musters, spend Saturdays loafing or drinking in the settlement or about the country "stores," as the shops were and still are called, their wives could scarcely, if ever, find a moment they could call their own. Long before the palid dawn came sifting in through chink and window they were up and about. As there were no matches in those days, the housewife "unkivered" the coals which had been smothered in ashes the night before to be kept "alive" till morning, and with "kindling" in one hand and a live coal held on the tines of a steel fork or between iron tongs in the other, she blew and blew and blew till the splinters caught fire. Then the fire was started and the water brought from the spring, poured into the "kittle," and while it was heating the chickens were fed, the cows milked, the children dressed, the bread made, the bacon fried and then coffee was made and breakfast was ready. That over and the dishes washed and put away, the spinning wheel, the loom or the reel were the next to have attention, meanwhile keeping a sharp look out for the children, hawks, keeping the chickens out of the garden, sweeping the floor, making the beds, churning, sewing, darning, washing, ironing, taking up the ashes, and making lye, watching for the bees to swarm, keeping the cat out of the milk pans, dosing the sick children, tying up the hurt fingers and toes, kissing the sore places well again, making soap, robbing the bee hives, stringing beans, for winter use, working the garden, planting and tending a few hardy flowers in the front yard, such as princess feather, pansies, sweet-Williams, dahlias, morning glories; getting dinner, darning patching, mending, milking again, reading the Bible, prayers, and so on from morning till night, and then all over again the next day. It could never have been said of them that they had "but fed on roses and lain in the lilies of life."

FASHION ON A BACK SEAT. There was little thought of "finery," no chance to display the latest fashions, few drives or rides for pleasure, and only occasionally a dance, a quilting party or a camp meeting. No wonder the sons and daughters of such mothers are the best citizens of the "Old North State"!

PEWTER PLATTERS AND POTTERY. The early settlers "burned their own pottery and delftware,"[5] but most of their dishes and spoons were of pewter, though horn spoons were also in evidence. "They made felt hats, straw hats and every other article of domestic consumption." Most young people never saw a bolster, and pewter plates are tied up with blue ribbons these days and hung on parlor walls as curiosities.

FRONTIER KITCHENS AND UTENSILS.[6] "Dishes and other utensils were few—some pewter plates, forks and spoons; wooden bowls and trenchers, with gourds and hard-shelled squashes for drinking mugs. For knife, Boone doubtless used his belt weapon, and scorned the crock plates now slowly creeping into the valley, as calculated to dull its edge." . . . Grinding corn into meal, or cracking it into hominy, were, as usual with primitive peoples, tasks involving the most machinery. Rude mortars and pestles, some of the latter ingeniously worked by springy "sweeps," were commonly seen;[7] a device something like a nutmeg grater was often used when the corn was soft;[8] two circular millstones, worked by hand, were effective, and there were some operated by water power.

MEDICINE AND SUPERSTITION. "Medicine was at a crude stage, many of the so-called cures being as old as Egypt, while others were borrowed from the Indians. The borderers firmly

W. N. C.—17

believed in the existence of witches; bad dreams, eclipses of
the sun, the howling of dogs, the croaking of ravens, were
sure to bring disasters in their train."[9]   Teas made of bur-
dock, sassafras, catnip, and other herbs are still in use.   Lye
poultices were considered sovereign remedies for wounds and
cuts.   Hair bullets shot from guns against barn doors were
sure to drive away witches.   Tangled places in a horse's mane
or tail were called "witches' stirrups," in which the witches
were thought to have placed their feet when riding the animals
over the hills.[10]   Mullein was cultivated for medicine for horses
and cows.

NAILLESS HOUSES.   Nails were scarce in those days and
saw mills few and far between, rendering it necessary for them
to use wooden pins to hold their ceiling and shelving in place
and to rive out their shingles or "boards" for their roof covering and puncheons for their door and window "shutters"
and their flooring.   Thin boards or shingles were held in position upon the roof rafters by long split logs tied upon them
with hickory withes, or held in place by laying heavy stones
upon them.   There is still standing in the Smoky mountains a
comfortable cabin of one large room, floored and ceiled on the
inside, and rain and wind proof, in the construction of which
not a single nail was used.   This cabin was built in 1859 and
is on the Mill Creek Fork of Noland Creek in Swain county.

FIRST HOUSES.   A single room was as much as could be
built at first, then followed a shed, a spring house, a stable
and crib.   Then would come the "double" log house.   In
some of these houses there might be as many as six rooms,
including two garret or loft rooms above the two main rooms
of the house, and two shed rooms or lean-tos. After saw mills
became more general, frame houses were erected, often of
from eight to twelve rooms, with the kitchens detached from
the main dwelling.   But the log cabin in which Abraham
Lincoln was born, and now enshrined in a marble palace at
Hogdensville, Ky., is a fair sample of the average home of
pioneer days.

"CHINKED AND DOBBED."   The walls of these log houses
were "chinked and daubed."   That is, the spaces between
the logs were filled with blocks or scraps of wood and the
interstices left were filled with plain, undisguised mud—lime
being too expensive to be used for that purpose.

THE GREAT "WAR GOVERNOR'S" HOME. The house in which Hon. Zebulon Baird Vance, the great War Governor and statesman of the Old North State lived for many years is on Reems Creek in Buncombe county. It consisted of a single large room below and a garret or loft above, reached by rude stairs, almost a ladder, running up in one corner near the chimney. There was also a shed room attached to the rear of this house. Some of us are quite "swagger" nowadays, but we are all proud of our log-cabin ancestry.

UNGLAZED WINDOWS. Windows, as a rule, were scarce. The difficulty and expense of glazing them were so great as to preclude the use of many. Most of those which found place in the walls of the house were made by removing about 18 inches from one of the wide logs running the length of the house and usually opposite the huge fire place. It rarely contained any sash or glass and was closed by a sliding shutter running in grooves inside the wall. It was rare that upstairs or loft rooms contained any windows at all.

PRIMITIVE PORTIERS. Privacy was obtained by hanging sheets or counterpanes from the overhead sleepers or "jists," as the joists were almost universally called. Behind these screens the women and girls dressed when "men folks" were present, though their ablutions were usually performed at the "spout" or spring, or in the room after the male element had gone to their work. Sometimes a board partition divided the large down-stairs room into two, but as this made a very dark and ill-ventilated bedroom far removed from the light of the front and back doors and cut off from the heat of the fire place, this division was not popular or general.

THE LIVING ROOM. Usually, in more primitive days, the beds, mostly of feathers, were ranged round the room, leaving a large open space in the middle. The dining table stood there or against a wall near the fireplace. The hearth was wide and projected into the room two feet or more. A crane swung from the back of the chimney on which pots were hung from "pot hooks,"—familiar to beginners in writing lessons— and the ovens were placed on live coals while their lids, or as they were generally called "leds," were covered with other live coals and left on the broad hearth. In the kitchen of the old Mitchell Alexander hotel or "Cattle stand," eleven miles below Asheville on the French Broad, there is still standing and in daily use a deep old fireplace ten feet wide, the hearth of which projects into the room eight or nine feet. The water bucket with a curved handled gourd stood on a shelf just inside the door. Usually there was no wash pan, the branch or spout near by being deemed sufficient for all purposes. A comb in a box under a small and imperfect looking-glass was usually hung on the wall over the water bucket. Around the walls behind the beds on pegs were hung the skirts of the girls and women; and, if the men of the house owned any extra coats or trousers, they hung there, too. On the tops of boxes or trunks, usually called "chists," were folded and piled in neat order the extra quilts, sheets and counterpanes. Some of these counterpanes or "coverlids" were marvels of skill and beauty in color and design and all were woven in the loom which stood at one end of the porch or shed in front of the house. There was also a wooden cupboard nailed against the wall which contained racks for the plates and dishes. Beneath this was a place for the pots and pans, after the cooking was over.

WHERE COLONIAL ART SURVIVES.[11] Mrs. Eliza Calvert Hall has discovered recently that "in the remote mountains of the South, where civilization has apparnetly stood still ever since the colonial pioneers built their homes there," they still make coverlets that are rich "in texture and coloring" and are "real works of art." Of course we are also told that this art was first brought to America through New England; but she fails to state that it was also brought to Philadelphia, Charleston and every other American port through which English, Scotch or Irish women were admitted to America. That it has perished everywhere else, and still survives among us, might indicate that civilization instead of having stood still, in the mountains has at least held its own there, while it has receded in New England. That, however, is immaterial. Certain it is that Mrs. Finley Mast of Valle Crucis is now at work on an order from President Wilson, and expects soon to see specimens of her handiwork in the White House of the nation.

SLANDERS BY THE "UNCO' GUID." Because in the spring of 1912 the Allen family of the mountains of Virginia "shot up" the court at Hillville, the entire "contemporary mountaineer" is condemned as resenting "the law's intrusion," partly, perhaps, because he himself enjoys few of the benefits of civilized society.[12]   We regret the ignorance of this self-styled "national weekly" and others who defame us, and in view of the exploits of the "gunmen" of Broadway a few months later[13] recall with complacency the louse that gave occasion for that immortal prayer :   "Oh, wad some power the giftie gie us to see ourselves as others see us."   Little of good about the mountain whites is ever published North of Mason and Dixon's line.   The *Watauga Democrat* of July 10, 1913, records the fact that a few days before a journalist of New Canaan, Conn., and a photographer and illustrator of New York, had visited Boone, and that they had distinctly stated that their sole object in visiting these mountains was to look up "the destitution, ignorance and vice among the mountain whites." They were surprised to learn that the Applachian Training School was located in Boone, and wanted no facts as to the good it was accomplishing.   Their names were stated in the *Democrat*.   In "The Child That Toileth Not," Thomas R. Dawley, Jr., (1912) has presented many photographs of the most destitute and degenerate of the mountain population, ignoring the splendid specimens of health and prosperity he met every day.   About 1905 a "lady" from New York had two photographs taken of the same children at Blowing Rock. In the first they were dressed in rags and outlandish clothing; in the second, they wore most tasteful and becoming garb. She labeled the first "Before I Began," and the second, "After Three Weeks of Uplift Work."   She had offered a prize to the child who should appear for the first picture in the worst clothing, and another prize for the child who should dress most becomingly for the second.   The work of Miss Prudden and of Miss Florence Stephenson is appreciated by us; but our slanderers only make our blood boil.   For, in the *Outlook* for April 26, 1913, appeared "The Case of Lura Sylva, "showing the filth, destitution, depravity and degrading surroundings of a twelve-year-old girl "which" we are told is "not an unusual" story of similar conditions "in a prosperous farming community of the Hudson river valley."   Nothing worse has ever been written of any of the "mountain whites" than is there recorded of this girl.   Let your charity begin at your own home.   Charles Dudley Warner made a horseback trip from Abingdon, Va., to Asheville in August, 1884.   He saw

absolutely nothing on that trip which he could commend.
("On horseback," 1889) except two pianos he found in the
home of the Worths at Creston. He was, however, lavish
with his fault finding.

EVERY HOME A FACTORY. Manufacture means hand-made.
Therefore, since few homes manufacture anything today, we
have made no progress in manufactures, but have receded
from the time when every home was a factory. We have
instead simply adopted machinery and built factories.

SOME LOST ARTS. Those who never lived in a mountainous country are often surprised at the sight of what we call
sleds, slides or sledges, made of the bodies of small trees with
crooked ends, turning upward like those of sleigh runners,
though much more slumsy and heavy. As these runners wore
down they were "shod" by tacking split saplings under them.
Sleds can be hauled on steep hill-sides where wheeled vehicles
would turn over or get beyond control going down hill. Our
"Union" carpenters of this day could not build a house with
the materials and tools of their pioneer ancestors, nearly all
of whom were carpenters. Modern carpenters would not
know what "cracking" a log was, for instance; and yet, the
pioneer artizans of old had to make their boards by that
method. It consisted in driving the blade of an ax or hatchet
into the small end of a log by means of a maul, and inserting
wooden wedges, called "gluts." On either side of this first
central "crack" another crack was made, and gluts placed
therein. There were usually two gluts placed in each crack
and each was tapped in turn, thus splitting the log uniformly.
These two riven pieces were next placed in "snatch-blocks,"
which were two parallel logs into which notches had been cut
deep enough to hold the ends of these pieces, which were held
in position with "keys" or wedges. The upper side of this
riven piece was then "scored" with a broad ax and then
"dressed" with the same tool, the under edges being beveled.
The length of these pieces, now become puncheons, was usually half the length of the floor to be covered, the two ends
resting on the sleeper running across the middle of the room.
The beveled edges were placed as near together as possible,
after which a saw was run between them, thus reducing the
uneven edges so that they came snugly together, and were air
tight when pinned into place with wooden pegs driven through

augur-holes into the sills and sleepers. Hewed logs were first "scalped," that is the bark was removed with an ax, after which the trunk was "lined" with a woolen cord dipped in moist charcoal, powdered, which had been made from locust bark. This corresponded to what is now called a chalk-line. Then four of these lines were made down the length of the log, each pair being as far apart as the hewed log was to be thick—usually four to six inches—one pair being above and the other pair below; after which the log was "blocked" with an ax, by cutting deep notches on each side about four feet apart. These sections were then split from the sides of the log, thus reducing its thickness to nearly that desired. Then these sides were "scored" and then dressed till they were smooth. The block on which the "Liberty Bell" of Philadelphia rests still shows this "scoring," or hacks made by the broad-ax. Houses were framed on the ground by cutting the ends of the logs into notches called "saddles" which, when placed in position, fitted like joiner work—each log having been numbered while still on the ground. When the logs were being placed in position they were lifted into place on the higher courses by means of what were called "bull's-eyes." These were made of hickory saplings whose branches had been plaited into rings and then slipped over the logs, their stems serving as handles for pulling, etc.

ROOFING LOG HOUSES. Modern carpenters would be puzzled to roof a house without nails or shingles or scantling; but their forbears accomplished this seemingly impossible task with neatness and dispatch. After the main frame or "pen" of the house was up, two parallel poles were laid along and above the top logs, and "gable" logs were placed under these, the gable logs being shorter than the end logs of the house. This was continued till the gable end was reached, when the "ridge pole" was placed in position, being held there with pegs or pins. The frame of the roof was now ready, and "boards," or rough shingles were riven from the "blocks" or sections of chestnut, poplar or white oak, though the latter would "cup" or twist into a curved shape if "laid" in the "light" of the moon. The lower ends of the lowest row of "boards" rested against the flat side of a split log, called the "butting pole," because the boards butted upon it. Upon the lower row of boards, which were doubled in order to cover the cracks in

the under tier, a single row of boards was then laid, the first
row being held in place by a split log laid on them and made
fast by pegs driven through their ends and into the ends of
the poles under the boards. These were also supported by
"knees." The various pieces of roofing were called eve-
bearers, rib-poles, weight poles, etc., etc.

TANNING HIDES AND MAKING SHOES. According to Col.
W. L. Bryan, every farmer had his tan-trough, which was
an excavation dug out of a poplar or chestnut log of large
size, while some had two troughs in one log, separated by
leaving a division of the log in place. Into these troughs
ashes or lime was placed, diluted with water. Skins should
always be salted and folded together a few days till all the
blood has been drawn out; but salt was high and scarce,
and this process was often omitted. When "green" hides
were to be tanned at once, they were first "fleshed," by
being placed on the "fleshing block" and scraped with a
fleshing knife—one having a rounded edge. This block was
a log with the upper surface rounded, the lower end resting on the ground and the upper end, supported on pegs,
reaching to a man's waist. Fleshing consisted in scraping
as much of the fat and blood out of the hide as possible.
When hides were to be dried before being tanned, they
were hung lengthwise on poles, with the flesh side upper-
most, and left under shelter till dry and hard. Hair was
removed from green and dry hides alike by soaking them in
the tan-trough in a solution of lime or wood ashes till the
hair would "slip"—that is, come off easily. They were then
soaked till all the lime or ashes had been removed, after which
they were placed again on the fleshing bench and "broken" or
made pliable, with a breaking-knife. They then went into
the tan-trough, after having been split lengthwise into two
parts, each of which was called a "side." The bottom of
the tan-trough was lined with a layer of bark, after which a
fold of a "side" was placed on the bark and another layer of
bark placed above the upper fold of the side; then the side
was folded back again and another layer of bark placed on
it, and so on till the tan-trough had been filled. Then water
was turned or poured in, and the mass allowed to remain two
months, after which time the bark and water were renewed
in the same manner as before. This in turn remained another

two months, when the bark and water were again renewed. Two months longer completed the process, making six months in all. This was called "the cold-ooze" process, and while it required a much longer time it made better leather than the present hot-ooze process, which cooks and injures the leather. The hide of every animal bearing fur is thicker along the back-bone than elsewhere, and after the tanning process this was cut off for sole leather, while the rest was blacked for "uppers," etc. The under side of the thin or "uppers" leather was then "curried" with a knife, thus making it as smooth as the upper side. Sole leather, however, was not curried ordinarily. "Buffing" was the removal of the "grain" or upper surface of the hide after it had been tanned, thus making both sides alike. Smaller skins were tanned in the same way, and those of dogs, coons, ground hogs, etc., were used for "whang" leather—that is, they were cut into strings for sewing other leather with. Horse collars, harness and moccasins thus joined will outlast those sewed with thread. The more valuable hides of smaller animals were removed from the carcass without being split open, and were then called "cased" hides. This was done by splitting open the hind legs to the body and then pulling the skins from the carcass, fore legs and head, after which they were "stretched" by inserting a board or sticks inside, now the fur-side, and hanging them up "in the dry" till dried. Other less valuable skins were stretched by means of sticks being stuck into the four "corners" of the hide, tacked to the walls of the houses under the eaves and allowed to dry. The women made moccasins for the children by doubling the tanned deer skin along the back, laying a child's stocking along it so that the sole of the stocking was parallel with the fold in the skin, and then marking around the outline of the stocking, after which the skin, still doubled, was cut out around the outline, sewed together with "whang" leather, placed on a last till it was "shaped," after which it was ready for wear. The new moon in June was the best time for taking the bark from trees. White and chestnut oak bark was preferred, the outer or rough part of the bark having been first removed with a drawing knife, which process was called "scurfing" or "scruffing." The bark was then piled, inside up, under shelter, and allowed to dry. Among the personal effects of Abraham

Lincoln's grandfather were "a drawing-knife, a currying-knife, and a currier's knife and barking iron."[14] Lime was scarce in most localities in this section, and ashes were used instead. Every deer's head was said to have enough brains to "dress" its hide.[15] The brains were rubbed into the hair of the hide, after which the hide was folded together till the hair would "slip," when the hide was placed in the tan-trough and tanned, the brains thus taking the place of lime or ashes. After vats came in bark mills came also.

ELIZABETHAN ENGLISH? Writers who think they know, have said that our people have been sequestered in these mountains so long that they speak the language of Shake-speare and of Chaucer. It is certain that we sometimes say "hit" for it and "taken" for took; that we also say "plague" for tease, and when we are willing, we say we are "consent-able." If we are asked if we "care for a piece of pie," we say "yes," if we wish to be helped to some; and if we are invited to accompany anyone and wish to do so, we almost invariably say "I wouldn't care to go along," meaning we do not object. We also say "haint" for "am not" "are not" and "have not," and we invite you to "light" if you are riding or driving. We "pack" our loads in "pokes," and "reckon we can't" if invited "to go a piece" with a passerby, when both he and we know perfectly well that we can if we will. Chaucer and Shakespeare may have used these expressions : we do not know. We are absolutely certain, though, that "molases" is as plural as measles; and ask to be helped to "them" just as con-fident that we shall be understood as people of greater cul-ture hope their children will soon recover from or altogether escape "them," meaning only one thing, the measles. Though we generally say we "haven't saw," it is the rarest thing in the world when we do things "we hadn't ought to," and we never express surprise or interest by exclaiming, "Well, I want to know." On the other hand we have Webster for our authority that "hit" is the Saxon for it; and we know ourselves that "taken" is more regular that "took"; Webster also gives us the primary meaning of "plague": anything troublesome or vexatious; but in this sense applied to the vexations we suffer from men, and not to the unavoidable evils inflicted on us by divine providence; while "tease" means to comb or card, as wool; to scratch, as cloth in dressing, for the purpose of raising a nap; and to vex with importunity or impertinence." Surely one may be in a mood or condition of consent, and when so, why is not he "consentable"? Webster also says that "care" means "to be inclined or disposed; to have regard to; with "for" before a noun, and "to" before a verb;" while "alight" is "to get down or descend, as from horseback or from a carriage," the very sense in which we invariably use it, our only fault consisting in keeping the "a" silent. Webster does not authorize the use of "pack" as a verb transitive, in the sense of bearing a burden, but he gives "burden or load" as the meaning of the noun "pack"; while a "poke" is "a pocket; a small bag; as, a pig in a poke." A "piece" is a fragment or "part of anything, though not separated, or separated only in idea," in which sense going "a piece" (of the way, understood) is quite intelligible to some of us who do not know our letters. Being, in our own estimation, at least, "as well as common," in this respect as in many others,"we still manage to understand and to be understood"; and claim that when we "want in," we generally manage to "get" in, whether we say "get" or not. Still, in these respects, we may "mend," not improve; and who shall say that our "mend" is not a simpler, sweeter and more significant word than "improve"? But we do mispronounce many words, among which is "gardeen" for guardian, "colume" for column, and "pint" for point. The late Sam Lovin of Graham was told that it was improper to say Rocky "Pint," as its true name is "Point." When next he went to Asheville he asked for a "point" of whiskey. We even take our mispronounciation to proper names, and call Metcalf "Madcap"; Pennell "Pinion"; Pilkington "Pilkey"; Cutbirth "Cutbaird"; Mast "Moss"; Presnell "Pressly"; Moretz "Morris"; and Morphew "Murphey." "Mashed, mummicked and hawged up," means worlds to most of us. Finally, most of us are of the opinion of the late Andrew Jackson, who thought that one who could spell a word in only one way was a "mighty po' excuse for a full grown man."

HORSE TRADING.[16] "It is an interesting sight to watch the proceedings of a shooting-match. If it is to be in the afternoon, the long open space beside the creek, and within the circle of chestnut trees, where the shooting is to be done, is empty; but, just as the shadow of the sun is shortest, they begin to assemble. Some of them come on foot; others in wagons, or, as is most generally the case, on horseback galloping along through the woods. The long-haired denizen of the hidden mountain cove drops in, with his dog at his heels. The young blacksmith, in his sooty shirt-sleeves, walks over from his way-side forge. The urchins who, with their fish-rods, haunt the banks of the brook, are gathered in as great force as their "daddies" and elder brothers.

"A unique character, who frequently mingles with the crowd, is the 'nat'ral-born hoss-swopper.' He has a keen eye to see at a glance the defects and perfections of horse or mule (in his own opinion), and always carries the air of a man who feels a sort of superiority over his fellow men. At a prancing gait, he rides the result of his last sharp bargain, into the group, and keeps his saddle, with the neck of his horse well arched, by means of the curb-bit, until another mountaineer, with like trading propensities, strides up to him, and claps his hand on the horse's mane.

"An examination on the part of both swappers always results in a trade, boot being frequently given. A chance to make a change in horseflesh is never let slip by a natural-born trader. The life of his business consists in quick and frequent bargains; and at the end of a busy month he is either mounted on a good saddle horse, or is reduced to an old rack, blind and lame. The result will be due to the shrewdness or dullness of the men he dealt with, or the unexpected sickness on his hands of what was considered a sound animal."

FROLICS.[17] The banjo and the fiddle have been as constant companions of the pioneers of the mountains of North Carolina as the Bible and the Hymn Book. The country "frolics" or "hoe-downs", were necessarily less recherche than the dances, hops and germans of the present day, for, as a rule, the dancing had to take place on the uneven puncheon floors and in a very restricted space, often procured by the removal of the furniture of the kitchen or bed room, for usually a dwelling rarely had more than these two apartments, in the earlier days.

POOR ILLUMINATION. Owing to the fact that kerosene was unknown in the pioneer days, there was but poor illumination for those little mountain homes, generally consisting of but one large room and a shed or lean-to in the rear. Tin candle molds and heavy wicks were used with the tallow of beeves and deer for making of candles, which gave but a poor light. Bear's oil in a saucer, with a spun cotton thread wick also served to light the houses. As there were only a few books, the early settlers did not feel the want of good lights as much as we would at this time. So, when the days grew short and the nights long, our forbears usually retired to their beds soon after dark, which meant almost fourteen hours in bed if they waited for daylight. But, usually, they did not wait for it, arising long before the sun came above the horizon, building huge fires and beginning the day by the light of the blazing logs.

This is one reason so many of those people saw the "falling of the stars" on the early morning of the thirteenth of November, 1833. Twenty years ago there were still living scores of people who witnessed this extraordinary and fearful sight.

DANGER FROM WILD ANIMALS. Panthers, wild cats, wolves and bear were the most troublesome depredators and they were the means of much serious damage to the stock of the settlers, most of which was driven to the mountain ranges, where luxuriant grasses abounded from May till October. Colts, calves and pigs were frequently attacked and destroyed by these "varmints," as the settlers called them. But while there was little or no danger to human beings from these animals, the black bear being a notorious coward, unless hemmed up, the "women folk" were "pestered" by the beautiful and, on occasion, malodorous pole-cat or skunk, the thieving o'possum, the mink, weasel, etc., which robbed the chicken roosts after dark. Moles and chipmunks, also destroyed their "garden truck" in early summer, while hawks and eagles played havoc with their fowls, and crows pulled up the young corn and small grain which had not been sown deep enough.

THE ORIGINAL "HOUN DAWG." Hounds were the principal breed of dogs employed by the pioneer. Crossed with the more savage species, the hound also made a good bear dog, and the Plott bear dogs were famous in the pursuit of Bruin. Some settlers kept a pack of ten or fifteen hounds for deer dogs.

THE DARK SIDE OF THE CLOUD. But from Thwaite's "Daniel Boone" we gather much that robs the apparent charm of pioneer life of something of its attractiveness.

"Among the outlying settlers, much of the family food came
from the woods, and often months would pass without bread
being seen inside the cabin walls" (p. 58).   "For head covering, the favorite was a soft cap of coon-skin, with the bushy
tail dangling behind; but Boone himself despised this gear,
and always wore a hat. The women wore huge sunbonnets
and loose gowns of homemade cloth; they generally went
barefoot in summer, but wore moccasins in winter" (p. 29).
These moccasins were "soft and pliant, but cold in winter,
even when stuffed with deer's hair and leaves, and so spongy
as to be no protection against wet feet, which made every
hunter an early victim to rheumatism." That many prisoners were massacred is also an evidence of the harshness of
these times.

TOUCHSTONE AND TERPSICHORE. There were shooting
matches at which a young steer was divided and shot for,
foot races, wrestling bouts, camp-meetings, log-rollings, house-
raisings and the "Big Musters" where cider and ginger cakes
were sold, which drew the people together and promoted social
intercourse, as well as the usual religious gatherings at the
"church houses." Singing classes and Sunday Schools, now
so common, were not at first known in these mountains, and,
indeed, even Sunday Schools are of comparatively recent origin.
When a young couple were married they were usually serenaded with cow horns, tin pans and other unearthly noises.
This is still the custom in many parts of the mountains. Agricultural fairs were unknown in the olden days. Horse-racing
over ordinary roads, horse-swapping and good natured contests of strength among the men were also in vogue generally.

BEFORE THE DAYS OF "BRIDGE." Among the women and
girls there were spinning, carding, reeling and knitting matches,
and sometimes a weaving match.[18] Quilting parties were
very common, and, indeed, the quilting frame can still be
observed in· many a mountain house, suspended from the
ceiling above, even in the modern parlor or company room.
All sorts of superstitions attended a quilting—the first stitch
given being usually emblematic of the marriage of the one
making it and the last of the death of the person so unfortunate as to have that distinction. Of course the coverlid or
top of the quilt, usually a patchwork of bright scraps of cloth
carefully hoarded and gathered from all quarters, had been

prepared in advance of the gathering of the quilting party, and the quilting consisted in spreading it above the wool or cotton rolls spread uniformly on a white cloth and stitching the upper and lower cloths together. Hence the great convenience of the quilting frame which held the quilt and was lowered to a point about waist high.

THE "CAUSUS BELLI." At school it was customary for the larger boys to bar the teacher out when a holiday was ardently desired. This was accomplished by placing themselves inside the school room and barring the door by placing the rude and backless benches against it and refusing to remove them. As there was but one door and no windows the teacher was helpless, and, after threatening and bullying for a time, usually left the boys in possession of the school house till the following day, when no one was punished. For anyone, be he friend or foe, but especially a stranger to holler "school butter" near a school was to invite every urchin to rush from the room; and the offender had either to treat the scholars or be soundly thrashed and pelted. In Monroe county, Tennessee, near Madisonville, in the year of grace 1893, this scribe was dared and double-dared to holler those talismanic words as he passed a county school, but ignominiously declined.

"ANT'NY OVER." A game almost universal with the children of that day was called "Ant'ny Over." Sides were chosen, one side going to one side of the house and the other to the other. A ball was tossed over the roof by one side, the problem being whether it would reach the comb of the roof and fall on the other side. If it did so and was caught by one on that side, that side ran around the house and tried to hit somebody on the other side with the ball; if they succeeded the one hit had to join the other side, and the side catching the ball had to throw it over the house and so on until one side lost all children. The rule was for the side tossing the ball to cry "Ant'ny!" as they were ready to throw the ball and when the other side hollered "Over!" the ball was thrown.

MOUNTAIN LAGER BEER. Methiglen, a mildly intoxicating drink, made by pouring water upon honey-comb and allowing it to ferment, was a drink quite common in the days of log rollings, house raisings and big musters. It was a sweet and pleasant beverage and about as intoxicating as beer or wine.

LAWFUL MOONSHINE. "Ardent spirits were then in almost

universal use and nearly every prosperous man had his whiskey or brandy still. Even ministers of the gospel are said in some instances to have made and sold liquor. A barroom was a place shunned by none. The court records show license to retail issued to men who stood high as exemplary members of churches. On November 2, 1800, Bishop Asbury chronicles that "Francis Alexander Ramsey pursued us to the ferry, franked us over and took us to his excellent mansion, a stone house; it may not be amiss to mention that our host has built his house, and taken in his harvest without the aid of whiskey."

MOONSHINING. Before railroads were constructed in these mountains there was no market for the surplus corn, rye and fruit; and it was considered right to convert these products into whiskey and brandy, for which there was always a market. When, therefore, soon after the Civil War, the United States government attempted to enforce its internal revenue laws, much resistance was manifested by many good citizens. Gradually, however, illicit distilling has been relegated to a few irresponsible and ignorant men; for the penalty inflicted for allowing one's land to be used as the location for a still, or to grind corn or malt for illicit stillers, or to aid them in any way, is great enough to deter all men of property from violating the law in this regard. Moonshining is so called because it is supposed that it is only while the moon is shining that illicit stilling takes place, though that is erroneous, as much of it is done during the day. But, as these stills are located, usually, in the most out-of-the-way places possible, the smoke arising during the day from the stills attracts attention and final detection. Stills are usually located on small, cold streams, and on wild land little adapted to cultivation. Sometimes, however, stills are situated in the cellar or kitchen or other innocent looking place for the purpose of diverting suspicion. Neighbors, chance visitors, the color the slops give to the streams into which they drain, and other evidence finally lead to the arrest of the operators and the destruction of the stilling plant and mash. The simplest process is to soak corn till it sprouts, after which it is dried and ground, making malt. Then corn is ground into meal, and it and the malt are placed in tubs with water till they sour and ferment, making mash. This mash is then placed in the still and boiled, the steam passing through a worm or spiral metal tube which rests in a cooling tub, into which a stream of running water pours constantly. This condenses the steam, which falls into the "singling keg"; and when a sufficient quantity has been produced, the mash is removed from the still, and it is washed out, after which the "singlings" are poured into the still and evaporated, passing through the worm a second time, thus becoming "doublings," or high proof whiskey. It is then tested or proofed—usually by shaking it in· a bottle—when its strength is determined by the bubbles or "beads" which rise to the top. It is then adulterated with water till it is "right," or mild enough to be drunk without blistering the throat. Apples and peaches are first mashed or ground, fermented and evaporated, thus becoming brandy. Still slops are used to feed cattle and hogs, when practicable, but moonshiners usually have to empty their slops upon the ground, from which it is sure to drain into some stream and thus lead to discovery. Still slop-fed hogs do not produce as firm lard as corn-fed animals, just as mash-fed hogs do not produce as good lard as corn-fed hogs, though the flesh of mast-fed hogs is considered more delicate and better flavored than that of any other kind.

Blockading is usually applied to the illegal selling of moonshine whiskey or brandy.

THE STRENGTH OF UNION. The following account of the cooperation common among the early settlers is taken from " A Brief History of Macon County" by Dr. C. D. Smith, published in 1905, at Franklin:

"It was the custom in those early days not to rely for help upon hired labor. In harvesting small grain crops the sickle was mostly used. When a crop was ripe, the neighbors were notified and gathered in to reap and shock up the crops. The manner was for a dozen or more men to cut through the field, then hang their sickles over their shoulders and bind back. The boys gathered the sheaves together and the old men shocked them up. The corn crops were usually gathered in and thrown in great heaps alongside the cribs. The neighbors were invited and whole days and into the nights were often spent in husking out a single crop. I have seen as many as eighty or ninety men at a time around my father's corn heap. If a house or barn was to be raised the neighbors were on hand and the building was soon under roof. Likewise, if a man had a heavy clearing, it was no trouble to have an ample force to handle and put in heaps the heaviest logs. It was no unusual thing for a man to need one or two thousand rails for fencing. All he had to do was to proclaim that he would have a 'rail mauling' on a given day, and bright and early the neighbors were on the ground and the rails were made before sun-down. This custom of mutual aid, cultivated a feeling of mutual dependence and brotherhood, and resulted in the most friendly and neighborly intercourse. Indeed, each man seemed to be on the lookout for his neighbor's comfort and welfare as well as his own. It made a community of broad, liberal-minded people, who despite the tongue of gossip and an occasional fist-icuff in hot blood, lived in peace and good will one toward another. There was then less selfishness and cold formality than now. . . . I am free to admit that there has been improvement along some lines, such, for instance, as that of education, the building of church-houses, style of dress, etc., but I am sure that there has been none in the sterner traits of character, generosity, manliness, patriotism, integrity, and public spirit."

GIANTS IN THOSE DAYS. It also appears from the same very admirable sketch of Macon county, that when a new road was desired a jury was appointed to lay it off and divide it into sections as nearly equal as possible, the work on each section being assigned by lot to the respective captains of militia companies, and that the work was done without com-pensation. Dr. Smith cites an instance when he saw "men taking rock from the river with the water breast deep to aid in build-ing wharves. They remained until the work was finished."

FIST AND SKULL.
"There was another custom in those bygone days which to the pres-ent generation seems extremely primitive and rude, but which, when an-alyzed, shows a strong sense of honor and manliness of character. To settle minor disputes and differences, whether for imaginary or real per-sonal wrongs, there were occasional fisticuffs. Then, it sometimes oc-curred in affairs of this kind, that whole neighborhoods and communities took an interest. I have known county arrayed against county, and state against state, for the belt in championship, for manhood and skill in a hand-to-hand tussel between local bullies. When these contests took place the custom was for the parties to go into the ring. The crowd of spectators demanded fairness and honor. If anyone was disposed to show foul play he was withheld or in the attempt promptly chastised by some bystander. Then, again, if either party in the fight resorted to any weapons whatever, other than his physical appendages, he was at once branded and denounced as a coward, and was avoided by his former associates. While this custom was brutal in its practice, there was a bold outcropping of character in it, for such affairs were conducted upon the most punctilious points of honor. . . . This custom illustrates the times and I have introduced it more for the sake of contrast than a desire to parade it before the public."

HORN AND BONE. Buttons were made from bones and cow's horns, while the antlers of the red deer were almost indispen-

sable as racks for the long barreled flint-lock rifle, hats, clothing or other articles usually suspended from pegs and hooks.
Dinner and powder horns were from cow's horns, from which
the "picker" and "charger" hung. Ink bottles were made
from the small ends of cow's horns, powder was carried in
these water-proof vessels, while hounds were called in from
the chase or "hands" were summoned from the fields by
toots upon these far-sounding if not musical instruments.
During the Civil War, William Silvers of Mitchell county
made combs from cow's horns, filing out each separate tooth
after boiling and "spreading" the horns into flat surfaces.
He sold these for good prices, and once made a trip to Asheville with a wagon for a full load of horns as the neighborhood did not supply the demand.

GUNPOWDER BOUNTY.[19] " In 1796 Governor Ashe issued
a proclamation announcing that in pursuance of an Act to
provide for the public safety by granting encouragement to
certain manufactures, Jacob Byler, of the county of Buncombe, had exhibited to him a sample of gunpowder manufactured by him in the year 1799 and also a certificate proving that he had made six hundred and sixty-three pounds of
good, merchantable, rifle gunpowder; and therefore, he was
entitled to the bounty under the Act (2 Wheeler's History
of North Carolina, 52). This Jacob Byler, or rather Boyler,
was afterward a member of Buncombe County court, and in
the inventory of his property returned by his administrator
after his death in October, 1804, is mentioned "Powder mill
irons."

ELIZABETHTON'S BATTLE MONUMENT. On a massive monument erected in 1910 at Elizabethton, Tenn., to the soldiers
of all the wars in which Tennessee has participated is a marble
slab to the memory of Mary Patton who made the powder
with which the battle of Kings Mountain was fought. This
was made on Powder Mill branch, Carter county, Tennessee.
On what is still known as Powder Mill creek in old Mitchell,
so long ago that the date cannot now be fixed with certainty,
Dorry and Loddy Oaks made powder near where the creek
empties into Toe River. Zeb Buchanan now owns the land.

WANDERLUST. Alexander Thomas, A. J. McBride, and
Marion Wilson, all of Cove creek, Watauga county, went to
California in 1849, crossing the plains in ox carts, and mined

for gold.   Captain Young Farthing helped to carry the Cherokees to the West in 1838, as did also William Miller, Col.
James Horton and others of Watauga.   They were paid in
land warrants to be located in Kansas, but the warrants were
usually sold for what they would bring, which was little.
Jacob Townsend of near Shull's Mills was a pensioner of the
War of 1812.   Colonel J. B. Todd, Peter Hoffman and Jason
Martin of Watauga were in the Mexican war.   A number of
others volunteered from these mountains, but were never
called out.

FORGE BOUNTY LAND GRANTS.   One of the first needs of
these pioneers was iron, and in 1788 (Ch. 293, Laws of N. C.
as revised by Potter J. L. Taylor and Bart Yancey, Esqs.,
1821) the legislature passed an act by which 3,000 acres of
vacant lands "not fit for cultivation most convenient to the
different seats is hereby granted for every set of iron works,
as a bounty from this State to any person or persons who will
build and carry on the same."   One or more tracts for each
set of works was to be entered and a copy of the entry transmitted to the next court that should be held in the county,
when a jury of twelve persons of good character should view
the land and certify that it was not fit for cultivation.   Iron
works were then to be erected within three years, and when
it should be made to appear to the court that 5,000 weight
of iron had been made the grant was to be issued.   "Three
forges where it was made grew up in Buncombe county, one
on Hominy creek, upon the old Solomon Luther place, which
belonged to Charles Lane; another on Reems creek at the
Coleman mill place, which belonged to the same man, but
was sold by him in 1803, to Andrew Baird; the third was on
Mills river, now in Henderson county on what has ever since
been called the Forge mountain, on which are also the Boilston gold mines.   The iron ore for this purpose was procured
at different places in Buncombe county."[20]   The State
granted to Thomas Calloway, November 21, 1807, 3,000 acres
of land in Ashe county (Deed Book D, p. 88) and to William
Daniel, David Worth, Moses L. Michael and R. Murchison
2,000 acres in Ashe county, in 1854.   (Deed Book U, p. 62.)
Grants were also issued to the late Messer Fain in Cherokee,
and some of the pigs are still in existence there.

DATES OF WORKING OLD IRON MINES.   From " The Iron

Manufacturer's Guide" (1859, by J. P. Lesley) we find that Harbard's Bloomery Forge near the mouth of Helton creek was built in 1807 and washed away in 1817; that the Cranberry Bloomery Forge on Cranberry was built in 1820, and rebuilt in 1856; that North Fork Bloomery Forge eight miles northwest of Jefferson on New river, was built in 1825; abandoned in 1829; washed away in 1840; Ballou's Bloomery Forge, at Falls of North Fork of New river, 12 miles northeast of Jefferson, was built in 1817; washed away in 1832 by an ice freshet; Helton Bloomery Forge, on Helton creek, 12 miles north-northwest of Jefferson, was built in 1829; washed away in 1858; another forge was built one and one-fourth miles further down in 1802, but did not stand long; Laurel Bloomery Forge, on Laurel creek, 15 miles west of Jefferson, built in 1847; abandoned in 1853; Toe river Bloomery Forge, five miles south of Cranberry Forge, built in 1843; Johnson's Bloomery Forge, six miles south of Cranberry Forge, built in 1841; Lovingood Bloomery Forge, on Hanging Dog, Cherokee county, two miles above Fain's Forge, built from 1845 to 1853; Lower Hanging Dog Bloomery Forge, five miles northwest of Murphy, built in 1840; Killian Bloomery Forge one-half miles below Lower Hanging Dog Forge, built in 1843, abandoned 1849; Fain Bloomery Forge, on Owl creek, two miles below Lovingood Forge, built in 1854; Persimmon creek Bloomery Forge, on Persimmon creek 12 miles southwest of Murphy, built in 1848; Shoal creek Bloomery Forge, on Shoal creek, five miles west of Persimmon creek Forge, built about 1854; Palsey Forge, built by John Ballou at mouth of Helton in 1859 and rebuilt by W. J. Pasley in 1871 (it is now abandoned); New River Forge on South Fork of New river, one-half mile above its junction with North Fork; built 1871, washed away in 1878. Uriah Ballou of Crumpler, N. C., has gold medals for the best magnetic iron ore from the Louisiana Purchase Exposition and from the World's Fair at Paris immediately afterwards, which was taken from these mines. The lands are now the property of the Virginia Iron & Coke Company.

PIONEER THORS AND FORGES. Iron was manufactured at these old time forges about as follows : When the ore was in lumps or mixed with rock and dirt it was crushed by "stompers," consisting of hardwood beams 6x6 inches, which were raised and dropped by a cogged horizontal revolving shaft. When the ore was fine enough it was washed in troughs to separate it from as much foreign matter as possible. It was then ready for the furnace, which consisted of a rock base 6x6 feet and two and one-half feet high. On three sides of this base walls of rock were erected two and one-half feet high, leaving one side open. A nest was left in the bottom of this base or hearth, through the middle of which a two inch blast pipe ran, and projecting above it. Air was furnished to this pipe by a stream of water passing through wooden tubes 12x12 inches. A small fire of chips was started in this nest above the mouth of the blast pipe. Over this fire three or four bushels of charcoal was placed and blown into a white heat. Upon this charcoal a layer of ore was spread, and as it was heated, another layer of charcoal was placed above, and on it still another layer of ore. This was gradually melted, the molten ore settling into the nest and the silica remaining on top. Into the mass of melted iron an iron bar would be thrust. This bar was used simply to form a handle for the turning of the ore that adhered to it after it had been withdrawn and placed on the anvil to be hammered. The melted ore thus drawn out was called a "loop."

The hammer and the anvil were about the same weight, 750 pounds each, with an eye through, 6x12 inches. They were interchangeable. The anvil was placed on white-oak beams, about the size of a railroad cross-tie, which spanned a pit dug in the ground in order to give spring to the blow made by the hammer. Through the eye of the hammer a beam of strong wood was fastened, the other end working on a pivot or hinge. Near this hinged end was a revolving shaft shod with four large iron cogs, each about six inches long and five inches square, and each having a rounded corner. These cogs lifted the hammer handle rapidly, while above the handle a wooden "bray" overcame the upward thrust, and gravity drove the hammer downward upon the heated mass awaiting it on the anvil. The blows thus dealt were rapid and heavy and could be heard under favorable conditions ten or more miles.

SILENT FINGER SIGNALS. It was the duty of the "tender," the chief assistant of the hammerman, to withdraw the loop from the furnace and place it on the anvil, when the hammerman took the end of the handle and signaled with his fingers

laid on the handle to the tender to begin hammering, which
was done by the latter allowing the water to strike the wheel
which worked the hammer shaft.   Two fingers indicated more
rapid hammering, three still more rapid hammering, and the
withdrawal of all fingers meant that the hammering should
cease.   When the foreign matter had been hammered out of
the loop, it was divided into two or more loops of 25 to 30
pounds each; a short iron bar, to serve as handles, was welded
to each piece, and they were again placed in the furnace and
re-heated and then hammered into bars from 9 to 12 feet in
length, or divided into smaller pieces for wagon-tires, hoe-
bars, axe-bars, plough-shares, plough-molds, harrow-teeth bars,
horse-shoe irons, and gun "skelps."   There was an extra
charge for "handage" in the case of wagon-tires, because they
were hammered out thinner.   In finishing up each bar or
smaller piece of iron the tender would pour cold water on its
surface to give it a hard and smooth finish.

GIANT "HAMMERMEN."   The hammerman soon became a
veritable giant in his arms, and it is related of one of the older
Duggers that he could insert an arm into the eye of the hammer
and another into that of the anvil and strike the two together.
For miles below the water powers which drove these forges
the streams were muddy with the washings from the ore.
For years iron thus made was the principal commodity of
trade.   The ends of the iron bars were bent like the runners
of a sled, and as many of these bars were bound together by
iron bands as could be dragged over the rough trails by a
single ox.   In this crude fashion many tons of iron found a
market on farms remote from wagon roads.

EXPENSIVE HAULING.   It took from three weeks to a
month to go from Asheville to Charleston or Augusta by
wagon before the Civil War.   The roads were bad, and those
in charge of the wagons camped on the roadside, cooking their
own meals.   No wonder freight rates were high, and that people did without much that seems indispensible now.   It is
said that Waugh, Murchison & Poe, early merchants of Jefferson, hauled their goods from Wilmington, N. C.   The late
Albert T. Summey says that : "goods were hauled from Augusta and Charleston and cost from $1.75 to $2.00 per hundred.   Salt cost in Augusta $1.25 for a sack of 200 lbs.   Add
$4.00 for hauling, and it is easy to understand why people

thought it cheap when they could buy it for $5.00." As
late as the spring of 1850 it took Deacon William Skiles of
Valle Cruces three weeks to ride horseback from Plymouth,
N. C. to Watauga.[21]

RIFLE GUNS.[22] The word "rifle" is too generic a term for
the average mountaineer; but he knows what a "rifle-gun"
is. Some of the older men have seen them made—lock, stock
and barrel. The process was simple : a bar of iron the length
of the barrel desired was hammered to the thickness of about
three-sixteenths of an inch and then rolled around a small
iron rod of a diameter a little less than the caliber desired.
After this, the rolled iron was welded together gradually—
only three or four inches being welded at a time because it
was not practicable to do more at a single "heating" without
also welding the rod which was inside. This rod was withdrawn from the barrel while it was being heated in the furnace and allowed to cool, and when the glowing barrel was
withdrawn from the fire the rod was inserted and the welding would begin and be kept up till the bar inside began to get
too hot, after which it was withdrawn and cooled while the
barrel was being heated again, and then the same process was
repeated till the work was done. The caliber of the barrel
was now smaller than desired, but it was enlarged by drilling
the hole with a steel bit operated by water-power. The spiral
grooves inside the barrel were made by small pieces of steel,
two inches long, with saw-teeth on the edges, which served
the purpose of filing the necessary spiral channels. The caliber was determined by the number of bullets which could be
molded from a pound of lead, and usually ran from 80 to 140.
The caliber of rifles is now measured by the decimels of an
inch, regardless of the number of bullets to the pound of lead.
No hand-made rifle was ever known to burst. The locks,
hammers, triggers, guards, ramrods, etc., were all made on
the common anvil.[23]

PRIMITIVE TOOLS AND METHODS. Dutch scythes for cutting grass have been in the mountains time out of mind, but
English scythes for the same purpose did not come into use
in some of the counties till about 1856–7. Cradles for cutting
small grain were employed about 1846; before which time
reaping hooks had been used entirely. Before thrashing machines arrived small grain was separated from the stems by

means of flails, as in the old Bible days of the threshing floors—
only in western North Carolina a smooth place was made in
the hillside, if there was no level ground elsewhere, cloth was
spread down over it, and the grain beaten out by flails. After
this had been done, what was known as a "riddle" was used
to free the grain of straw and chaff, sheets or coverlids of beds
being used to fan the chaff away as the grain fell. Then
came the sieve to separate the grain from all heavy foreign
matter, after which it was ground in grist mills, and bolted
by sifting it through thin, loosely woven cloth wound over a
cylindrical wooden frame revolved by hand, a labor often imposed by the indolent miller on the boy who had brought the
grist to mill. The miller never made any deduction from his
toll because of this labor, however.

GROUND HOG THRESHERS. When the threshing machine
came, about 1850, it was a seven days wonder. It was what
was known as the "ground-hog" thresher, and required eight
horses to pull it from place to place. It was operated by
horse power also, which power was communicated to the machine by means of a tarred cotton rope in place of a band or
sprocket chain, both of which came later. The grain and
straw came from the machine together and were caught in a
big sheet surrounded by curtains. The straw was raked from
the top of the grain by wooden forks made from saplings or
the limbs of trees. Steel pitchforks did not come into general use in these mountains till about 1850. A ground hog
thresher could thresh out about 100 bushels a day with the
help of about 16 hands, while the modern machine can easily
thresh out over 400 bushels with the assistance of 10 hands;
but as the extra hands of the olden time charged nothing for
their labor, and felt honored by being allowed to take part in
such glorious work, no complaint was ever heard on that score.
Mowing machines did not come into general use in this section till 1869 or 1870. Even the North refused them till
England took them up. [24]

THE HANDY BLACKSMITH. Tools of all kinds were made by
the ordinary blacksmiths of the country at ordinary forges.
They made axes, hatchets, drawing-knives, chisels, augurs,
horse-shoes, horse-shoe nails, bolts, nuts and even pocket
knives!

FISH AND FISH TRAPS. Fish abounded in all mountain

streams, and "a good site for a fish trap" was the greatest recommendation which a piece of land could have.   These places were always the first entered and granted.   In them fish by the barrelful would sometimes be caught in a single night where the trap was well situated and strongly built. Fishing at night in canoes by torchlight with a gig was a favorite sport as well as profitable practice and it was much indulged in." [25]   Above vertical falls trout could not pass.   Elk river, above the Great Falls, had no trout till 1857 (D. L. Low in *Watauga Democrat*, June 26, 1913), when men placed them there.

GRIST MILLS. "The first consideration, however, with these primitive inhabitants, was the matter of grist mills. Hence at the first session of the [Buncombe] county court we find it 'Ordered that William Davidson have liberty to build a grist mill on Swannanoa, near his saw mill, Provided he builds said mill on his own land.' This was in April, 1792. In January, 1793, it was 'Ordered that John Burton have liberty to build a Grist mill on his own land, on a branch of French Broad River, near Nathan Smith's, below the mouth of Swannanoa,' Apparently Davidson's mill was not built, "but John Burton's was on Glenn's creek a short distance above its mouth."

WHEN THE CLOCK STOPPED. There were a few old seven-day clocks brought by the first settlers, but as a rule watches and clocks were few. Men and women learned to guess the time with some accuracy by looking at the sun on clear days, and guessing at it on cloudy. Following is a description of the usual time-piece : "The clock consisted of a knife mark, extending north from one of the door-facings across the puncheon next to it. When the mark divided the sunshine that fell in at the door from the shadow of the facing, it was noon. All other hours were guessed at : on cloudy days the clock stopped." [26]

CULTURE AND MANUFACTURE OF FLAX. The flax seed were sown thick, and when the plant was mature it was pulled up by the roots and spread on the ground to dry. Then it was bound in bundles and placed in a dry place till the envelope surrounding the fiber was decomposed. Sometimes it was scattered over the snow to bleach the lint. It was then rebound in small bundles and when the farmer was ready it was opened and placed on the "brake," which consisted of four or five wooden slats parallel to each other through which wooden knives passed, driving the flax stems between.   After the flax was thus broken a handful of it was placed on the end of an upright board which had been driven into the ground, and struck smartly by a wooden swingling knife in order to knock off the small pieces of straw from the fiber.   Then the fiber was drawn through the hackle, which consisted of a board from whose surface projected five or six inches a row of iron spikes, which served to separate the tow from the flax. The flax was then spun on the low wheels, now sometimes seen in drawing rooms, gilded and beribboned, but never used. Then it was wound on spools from which it was reeled into hanks.   In the elder day the women had to count the revolutions of the reels, but before the Civil War a device was invented by which, after 100 revolutions, the reel would crack, and the housewife thus knew a hank had been reeled off.   The flax thread was then ready to be spooled and placed on the warping bars from which it was wound on the beam of the loom.   From this beam it was put through gears and slays of split reeds, thus making the warp.   After this, other flax thread was reeled off on quills from the hanks and placed in shuttles which were shot through the warp as the tread opened it, and the thread thus placed between the warp was driven back against the first thread by means of the battern, thus making loose cloth.   Wool was shorn, washed, dried, picked, carded, spun, reeled on to brooches with shuck cores from the spinning wheel, when it was ready to be woven or knitted.

CHURCHES AND SCHOOLS.   The early settlers were Scotch-Irish, as a whole, and their descendants are a hardy, hospitable and enterprising pouplation,   They were about equally divided in the War between the States and are still almost equally divided in politics.   Until the coming of the railroads there had been necessarily much of primitiveness in their houses, clothing and manners; but religion has always been a strong and controlling factor in their lives.   Churches have always existed here; but school-houses had been few and small and very little attention had been given to education. But, since the railroads have penetrated into this region, all this has changed, and dwelling houses have improved, clothing and manners have changed, and it is the exception nowadays to find a boy or girl of twelve years of age who cannot read and write.

MILITIA MUSTER DAYS. On the second Saturday of October each year there was a general muster at each county seat, when the various companies drilled in battalion or regimental formation; and each separate company met on its local muster grounds quarterly, and on the fourth of July the commanding officers met at the court house to drill. The Big Musters called most of the people together, and there was much fun and many rough games to beguile the time. Cider and ginger cakes were sold, and many men got drunk. There was also some fighting, but seldom with stones or weapons.

SALABLE PRODUCTS. Apples, hog meat, deer hams, chestnuts, chinquapins, butter, honey, wax, lard, eggs were the commodities they usually took to market, returning heavily laden with salt, yarn, pins, needles, tools, crockery ware, ammunition and a few cooking utensils. They relied principally upon herbs for such medicines as they used; they wove their own cloth upon hand looms, spinning the wool into thread and hetcheling or hatcheling out the flax. As sewing machines had not yet been invented, the women and girls cut out and sewed together all the garments used by themselves, their children and " the men folks" generally.

No MONEY. According to Col. A. T. Davidson in *The Lyceum* for January, 1891, the older people "had no money to buy with. . . . All the necessaries of life were procured from the markets in Georgia and South Carolina. It was a three weeks' trip with a wagon to Augusta, Georgia. For this market the neighborhood would bunch their products, bring their forces together and make trips to Augusta loaded with bacon, peltries and such other marketable articles as would bear transportation in this simple way. The return for these products was sugar, coffee, salt and molasses; and happy was the family on the return of the wagons to be able to have a jugful of New Orleans black molasses. And how happy the children were to meet their fathers and brothers again, and have them recite the many stories of the trip. We then bought salt by the measure, a bushel weighing about seventy pounds. The average price on the return of the wagon was about three dollars per bushel. It was interesting to see the people meet to get from the wagons their portion of the return load; and happy was the small family that got a half bushel of salt, 50 cents worth of coffee and a gallon of molasses. There was a general rejoicing, all going home satisfied and happy, content with their small cargoes, confident that they had enough to do them for the next year. It is remarkable how simply and carefully they lived, and with what earnestness and hope they went to their daily toil, expecting nothing more than this small contribution to their luxury for a year to come.

STOCK RAISING.[27] "The borders in the valley of Virginia and on the western highlands of the Carolinas were largely engaged in raising horses, cattle, sheep and hogs, which grazed at will upon the broad slopes of the eastern foothills of the Alleghanies, most of them being in as wild a state as the great roving herds now to be seen upon the semi-arid plains of the far West." The same occupation was followed by those who passed west of the foothills of the Alleghanies, and is kept up till this day. Those who had bought up the wild lands at low figures encouraged cattle herders to pasture or "range" their stock there. In the first place it gained their good will, and in the second it enabled landowners to become aware of the presence of any squatters who might seek to hold by adverse possession. Two other reasons were that landowners could not have prevented the ranging of cattle except by fencing in their lands, an impossible task at that time, and the suppression of fires in their incipiency. Certain it is, that all sorts of stock were turned into the mountains in May, where they remained till October, with weekly visits from their owners for purposes of salting and keeping them gentle. After awhile a market was found on the coast for the cows, sheep, horses and hogs, and they were driven there in the late summer and during the fall. "There annually passed through Buncombe county an average of 150,000 hogs, driven on foot about eight miles daily, which required 24 bushels daily for each 1,000 and were fed on corn raised in Buncombe."[28]

STOCK "STANDS." There were many "stock stands" along the French Broad river in ante-railroad days, for the turnpike from Asheville to the Paint Rock was a much traveled thoroughfare. Its stockholders made money, so great was the travel.[29] James Garrett had a stand about one mile below

the Hot Springs. Then there was another opposite the Hot
Springs, known as the White House, and kept by the late
John E. Patton. At the mouth of Laurel creek was still
another stand kept by David Farnsworth. Just above the
railroad station now called Putnam's is where Woolsey had
a stand, while Zach. Candler had another at Sandy Bottoms.
Then came Hezekiah A. Barnard's stand at what is still called
Barnards, though it used to be called "Barnetts," and opposite the mouth of Pine creek Samuel Chunn gave bed and
board to the weary drovers and feed to "his dumb driven"
cattle, sheep, hogs, horses, mules or turkeys. At the lower
end of what is now Marshall, Joseph Rice lived and at the
upper end of that narrow village David Vance kept a tavern—a long one—probably 150 feet in length, huddled between the stage road and the mountains. Samuel Smith
accommodated all travelers and their belongings at the mouth
of Ivy, and Mitchell Alexander was the Boniface at Alexander's.

Hezekiah Barnard used to boast that, while David Vance at
Lapland, now Marshall, had fed 90,000 hogs in one month,
he himself had fed 110,000 in the same period of time.
Aquilla Young, of Kentucky, also made his boast—he had
driven 2,785 hogs from Kentucky to North Carolina in a
single drove. [30]

OLD ROAD HOUSES. "The stock stands, as the hotels between Asheville and Warm Springs were called, were generally
'well kept.' They began four miles below Asheville, at five
miles there was another, at seven and a half miles still another, at ten another, and another at thirteen and a half.
After this, at 16, 18, 21, 22, 28, 33, 36, 37, 40 and 47 mile-
posts there were still other hotels. "Many of them have
entirely gone, and actually the ground upon which some of
them stood has disappeared. The road, with a few points
excepted, is but a wreck of its former self. It was once a
great connecting link between Kentucky, Tennessee, South
Carolina and Georgia, and the travel over it was immense.
All the horses, mules, cattle, sheep and hogs were driven over
this route from the first mentioned States to the latter, and
the quantities of each and all used then was very much
greater than now. In October, November and December
there was an almost continuous string of hogs from Paint

Rock to Asheville. I have known ten to twelve droves, containing from 300 to one or two thousand stop over night and feed at one of these stands or hotels. Each drove was 'lotted' to itself, and 'corned' by the wagon-load, the wagon being driven through each lot with ten or a dozen men scattering the corn right, left and rear, the load emptied and the ground literally covered. The drivers of these hogs were furnished large rooms, with immense log-heap fire-places and a blanket or two each, that they furnished themselves. They would form a semi-circle upon the bare floor, their feet to the fire, and thus pass the night; that they slept, I need not tell you. After driving 20 to 50 hogs from daylight to dark they could eat without coaxing and sleep without rocking. The travel over this thoroughfare was the life of the country."[31]

OLD TIME COUNTRY STORES. "Corn, sixty years ago, was 'the staple production'; the culture of tobacco was not thought of. These hotel men, many of them, kept little stores, bartered or sold everything on a credit; and in the fall they would advertise that on certain days they would receive corn in payment of 'store accounts,' and then the farmers would bestir themselves. They would commence delivering frequently by daylight and continue it until midnight. I have seen these corn wagons strung out for a mile and as thick as they could be wedged. They were more anxious to pay accounts then than some of us are now; but it was pay or no credit next year. Each merchant had his 'trade,' and there was no getting in debt to one and then skip to another. The price allowed for corn was almost invariably fifty cents per bushel, the hotel men furnishing it to drovers at about 75 cents. They charged the drovers from twenty to twenty-five cents 'per diet,' meaning per meal for their drivers, asking the whole in lame hogs at so much per pound, or a due-bill from the manager to be paid as he returned home after having made sale of his stock, cash being only rarely if ever paid. These lame hogs taken on bills were kept until a suitable time for killing—a cold spell being necessary to save the meat—when they were slaughtered and converted into bacon and lard."[31]

HOG-KILLIN' TIME. "This hog killin' was a big time, and 'away 'fo' day' as the negroes, who were the principal participants, would say, twenty to thirty hands would build im-

mense log-heap fires; with, first, a layer of wood and then a
layer of stones, which continued till satisfactory dimensions
were reached, when the fire was applied and kept burning
until the stones reached a red-heat. In the meantime, a
platform would have been made out of puncheons, slabs or
heavy plank, at one end of which and very near the fire a
large hogshead (or scalding tub), filled with water, was placed.
Then the hot stones were transferred to the water till a proper
temperature for scalding was reached, and a certain number
of hogs having been shot and 'stuck' (bled by sticking long
knives in the throat), two stout men would plunge each hog
into the hot water and twist and turn it about until the hair
would 'slip,' when it would be drawn out and turned over
to other hands, who, with knives, would remove all the hair
from the hog, and then hang it by its hind legs, head down,
on a long horizontal pole, where it would we washed and
scraped down, opened, the entrails removed, and after cooling, be cut to pieces, thus making hams, shoulders and mid-
dlings. Then it would be salted down, the fat having been
taken from all parts. This fat was stewed into lard, from
which the boy's dainty 'cracklings' was removed. How well
I remember the enjoyment I had on these occasions, in broil-
ing upon the hot stones the 'melts,' making a delicacy that
I think would be relished even now; and in blowing up and
bursting the 'bladders,' frequently saving up a lot of them
for Christmas 'guns.' "[32]

OUR DEPOTS SIXTY YEARS AGO. "Forty years ago Charleston and Augusta were our depots; think of it—thirty to
sixty days in going and returning from market! Our people
then thought little or nothing of hitching up four or six mules,
once or twice a year, and starting to market . . . with
forty to fifty hundred pounds of bacon and lard, flour and
corn meal, dried fruit, apples and chestnuts . . . and
bring back a barrel or two of molasses and sugar, a keg or
so of rice, a few sacks of salt and coffee, a little iron, a hundred or two pounds of nails and a box or so of dry-goods."[33]

ROADS SIXTY YEARS AGO. "But the roads then were
charming. I can remember when the road from Asheville to
Warm Springs, every foot of it, was better than any half-mile
of Asheville streets. Old Colonel Cunningham's 'mule and
cart' and two or three hands traversed it from beginning to

end of year, removing every loose stone and smoothing up
every place. All travel was then by private conveyance or
stage, there being several four-horse coaches out from Asheville daily." [34]

AGRICULTURE AND WIT SIXTY YEARS AGO. Of the farming
along the French Broad between Asheville and Warm Springs
sixty years ago, we read that "the lands were in a high state
of cultivation, exceedingly high a great deal of it, as one would
infer in passing along the foot of many steep hills and looking
up to the top, seemingly almost perpendicular; and yet I have
ploughed over some of the worst of them many a day, and
was often indignant at the surprise expressed and sarcastic
remarks made by the passer-by. One would ask if we did
our planting with 'shot-guns'! Another, when were we going to move, as he saw that we had our land rolled up ready
for a start! The Kentucky horse-drovers would say the water
of the French Broad was so worn out by splashing and dashing over and against the rocks that it was actually not fit
for a horse to drink!"

HERBS AND ROOTS. Ginseng was for years the principal
herb that commanded cash in this section, but at first it
brought, when green, only seven cents a pound. It is now
worth six dollars or more. [35] But gradually a market was
developed for many other native herbs, such as angelico,
blood root, balm of gilead buds, yellow and white sarsaparilla,
shamonium (Jamestown or gympsum weed), corn silk (from
maize), corn-smut or ergot, liverwort, lobelia, wahoo bark,
Solomon's seal, polk root and berries, pepper and spear-mint,
poppy and rose leaves, and raspberry leaves. Dried black-
berries since the Civil War also find a ready market. Arthur
Cole on Gap creek in Ashe county once did an immense business in herbs, and the large warehouses still standing there
were used to store the herbs which he baled and shipped
north. Ferns, galax leaves and other evergreens are gathered
by women in the fall and winter and find ready sale.

A LOW MONEY WAGE. Laborers and lawyers were poorly
paid in the old days, and the doctors of medicine fared little
better. A fee of one hundred dollars in a capital case was
considered the "top notch" by many leaders of the bar, while
the late David Ballard of Ox creek, Buncombe county, who
died about 1905 at the age of eighty-odd years, used to say

that, when he was a young man, he "had worked many a day for 25 cents a day and found himself." But 25 cents in those days would buy more than a dollar would now, and, as most of the trading was by barter, money was not missed as much as might be imagined. Stores were few and most of the things we now consider indispensable were unknown to many of the poorer people. Besides, everything that was indispensable was made at home, and things that were not indispensable were cheerfully dispensed with.

DYES. Madder dyed red; walnut bark and roots dyed brown; bedewood bark dyed purple; dye-flowers and snuff weed dyed yellow; copperas dyed yellow, and burnt copperas dyed nearly red. All black dyes rot wool. Dyes fade unless "set" in the thread—that is, made fast before the thread is placed in the loom. Laurel leaves, copperas, alum, and salt set dyes. The ooze from boiled walnut roots and bark was used to dye the wool before it was spun. It was dipped and dried, and dipped and dried again and again till the proper color had been attained. The dye pot stood on the hearth nearly all the time, as it had to be kept warm. Some dye plants were grown in the gardens, but they usually grew wild.

NOTES.

[1]The Century Magazine for September, 1890.
[2]Asheville's Centenary.
[3]Fifth Eth., Rep. 147.
[4]Roosevelt, Vol. III, p. 225.
[5]Asheville's Centenary.
[6]Thwaites, p. 30.
[7]Hominy creek in Buncombe got its name from a hominy mill with a pestle worked by water.
[8]These graters are still used in many places.
[9]Thwaites, p. 32.
[10]Thwaites, p. 32. The late Col. Allen T. Davidson used to tell of a famous hunter named "Neddy" McFalls who traveled from Cataloochee to Waynesville to have a witch doctor—a woman—remove a "spell" he thought someone had put on his Gillespie rifle.
[11]"Book of Hand-woven Coverlets," by Eliza Calvert Hall.
[12]Collier's Editorial, April 6, 1912. John Fox, Jr.'s novels.
[13]The murder of the gambler, Rosenthal, in August, 1912, on Broadway, New York, N. Y.
[14]Tarbell, Vol. I, p. 5
[15]Byrd, 212.
[16]Zeigler & Grosscup, p. 96.
[17]Ibid., 94–96.
[18]There is a spinning-wheel on Grassy Branch in Buncombe county on which Polly Henry spun more thread than Judge Burton's daughter in 1824.
[19]Asheville's Centenary.
[20]Ibid.
[21]From "A Life of Deacon William West Skiles."
[22]Asheville's Centenary.
[23]Description furnished by Col. David J. Farthing of Butler, Tenn. This applies only to the guns whose barrels were not bored out. The late Col. Allen T. Davidson used to tell of a famous gun-maker, who lived near Cherry Fields at the head of the French Broad river, whose "rifle guns" were much sought. The iron bars from which they were made were called "gunskelps." His name was Gillespie.
[24]Mace's "School History of U. S.," 1904, p. 287.
[25]Asheville's Centenary.
[26]"Balsam Groves," p. 17.
[27]Thwaites, p. 35.
[28]A. T. Summey in Asheville's Centenary.
[29]John A. Nichols' statement to J. P. A., July, 1912.

[30]Upon the organization of the Western Division of the W. N. C. R. R. Co., the stock and property of the Buncombe Turnpike Co. were exchanged for an equal amount of stock in the Western Division. Shipp's Land Com. Report, pp. 284-285.

[31]Col. J. M. Ray in Lyceum, p. 16, December, 1890.

[32]Ibid., p. 17.

[33]Ibid., p. 16.

[34]The reference was to a time shortly before any paving had been done in Asheville.

[35]In the "Autobiography of Rev. C. D. Smith," p. 2, we find that ginseng was "manufactured," and Col. A. T. Davidson in the Lyceum for January, 1891, p. 5, speaks of the "factory." Dr. Smith also says this herb was gathered "in Madison, Yancey, a portion of Buncombe, Mitchell, Watauga, Ashe, and Alleghany counties." Col. Davidson speaks of Dr. Hailen and Dr. Smith, of Lucius & Heylin of Philadelphia, as the merchants to whom it was shipped.

CHAPTER XII

EXTRAORDINARY EVENTS

JUNALUSKA. In the fall of 1910 the General Joseph Winston Chapter, D. A. R., unveiled at Robbinsville, Graham county, a metal tablet, suitably inscribed, to Junaluska and Nicie his wife. The tablet was attached to a large boulder which had been placed on the graves of these two Cherokees. Mrs. George B. Walker of Robbinsville read a paper in which was given the chief facts of the career of this noted Indian chieftain; among which was the recovery by him of an Indian maiden who had been sold into slavery and taken to Charleston, S. C., by proving by microscopic tests that her hair had none of the characteristics of the negro's. He also, on separate occasions, saved the lives of Rev. Washington Lovingood and Gabriel North, whom he found perishing from cold in the mountains. He went with the Cherokees to the west in 1838, but returned, and was allowed to remain, the legislature of North Carolina of 1847 having, by special act, made him a citizen and granted him 337 acres of land near what is now Robbinsville. The Battle of the Horse Shoe was fought August 27, 1814, according to Alfred M. Williams' Life of Sam Houston (p. 13), and on March 27th, according to others. It was called the Battle of To-ho-pe-ka, and was fought in a bend of the Tallapoosa river, Alabama, by Gen. Andrew Jackson in the Creek War. It was fortified across the neck of the peninsula by a fort of logs against which Jackson's small cannon were ineffective. But in the rear there were no fortifications except the river itself, so that Gen. Coffey, Jackson's coadjutor, could not cross. But Junaluska swam the river and stole the canoes of the Creeks, strung them together and paddled them to the opposite shore, where he filled them with a large number of Cherokees, recrossed the river, led by himself, and attacked in the rear while Jackson attacked in front, Sam Houston and his Tennesseans scaling the walls and grappling the Creeks hand to hand. The Creeks asked and received no quarter, Houston himself being desperately wounded. This ended the last hope of the Creeks as a nation. I-su-nu-la-hun-ski, which has been improved into Junaluska, is Cherokee for "I tried but failed," and was given this chief because at the outset of the Creek War he had boasted that he would exterminate the Creeks, but, at first, had failed to keep his promise. The following is the inscription on the tablet: "Here lie the bodies of the Cherokee chief Junaluska, and Nicie, his wife. Together with his warriors, he saved the life of General Jackson, at the Battle of Horseshoe Bend, and for his bravery and faithfulness North Carolina made him a citizen and gave him land in Graham county. He died November 20, 1858, aged more than one hundred years. This monument was erected to his Memory by the General Joseph Winston Chapter, D. A. R., 1910." Before his death Junaluska conveyed his land to R. M. Henry. But Sheriff Hayes administered on the estate of the deceased Indian and got an order from the court for the sale of the land to make assets. Under the sale Gen. Smythe of Ohio became the purchaser, and took possession. The case was carried to the United States court, where Henry won. But Judge Dick held that it was a case in equity, and set aside the verdict of the jury, heard the evidence himself and decided it in favor of Smythe. Henry did not appeal. See record in office of clerk of United States court, Asheville. It was decided in the seventies.

PEYTON COLVARD. This pioneer was of French extraction, the name originally having been spelt Calvert, according to the Rev. Mr. Verdigans of the Methodist Church, South. Peyton Colvard came to Ashe county after the Revolutionary War. The Colvards of Cherokee and Graham are descendants, as is also Dr. J. W. Colvard of Jefferson, Ashe county.

PART OF NEGRO MOUNTAIN FALLS. About the year 1830 Peyton Colvard lived in a log building which stood on the site of the present Jefferson Cash store of Dr. Testerman, and on the morning of February 19, 1827, the day his daughter Rachel, now the wife of Russell Wilbar of Texas, was born, a huge mass of rock fell from the top of Negro mountain and ploughed a deep furrow, still visible, down its side for a quarter of a mile. The main mass of this rock, almost intact, is still visible, with a small tree growing on it, while large trees have since grown in the ravine left by the fall of this immense boulder.

THE FALLING OF THE STARS. Several people still living remember this wonderful and fearful event. Col. John C. Smathers, who then lived on Pigeon river above Canton, remembers it distinctly. He remembers hearing women wailing and men praying. Francis Marion Wells, still living on Grass creek in Madison county, remembers it also. He is now over ninety-two years of age. Mrs. Eliza Burleson, still living on the head of Cane creek in Mitchell county, remembers the occurrence. She also is over ninety-two years of age.

FRANKIE SILVER'S CRIME AND CONFESSION. According to Mrs. Lucinda Norman, the only living sister of Charles Silver, now (1912) 88 years of age and residing at Ledger, Mitchell county, N. C., Frances Stewart Silver murdered her husband, Charles Silver, at what is now Black Mountain Station on the Carolina, Clinchfield and Ohio Railroad—the mouth of the South Toe river—on the night of December 22, 1831.[2] She was tried before Judge Donnell, June Term, 1832, and convicted at Morganton, where she was executed July 12, 1833. On appeal her conviction was affirmed by Judge Ruffin (14 N. C., 332). She escaped from jail but was recaptured. She cut her husband's head off with an ax, and then dismembered the body, after which she tried to burn portions of it in the open fireplace of her home. She left a poem lamenting her fate, in which she refers to "the jealous thought that first gave strife to make me take my husband's life." She also pleads that her "faults shall not her child disgrace." She also relates in the poem that

> "With flames I tried him to consume
> But time would not admit it done."

She must have been educated better than the average woman of that day. Finding that she could not get rid of the body by burning it, she concealed portions of it under the floor, in rock cliffs and elsewhere, claiming that he had gone off for whiskey with which to celebrate Christmas, and had probably fallen into the river, which had soon thereafter frozen over. A negro with a "magic glass" was brought from Tennessee, and as the glass persisted in turning downward, the floor was removed and portions of the body found. The weather growing warmer other parts of the remains revealed themselves, a little dog helping to find some.

TWO BAIRD FAMILIES. Indicative of the almost utter desolation of these early scattered mountain communities is the story of the two Baird families. On the 20th of April,

1795, John Burton sold to Zebulon and Bedent Baird all his lots in Asheville "except what lots is [already] sold and maid over."[3] In 1819 Bedent Baird represented Ashe county in the House of Commons. He was not the Bedent who had bought the lots from John Burton.[4] Certain it is that another Bedent Baird lived at Valle Crucis in what is now Ashe county, and his descendants constitute a large and influential family in that county at this time, just as the Bairds of Buncombe do in that county. But these two families seem never to have heard of the existence of the other till the 28th of January, 1858, when Bedent E. Baird wrote to Adolphus E. Baird at Lapland, now Marshall, in answer to Baird's note of enquiry, which he had penciled on the margin of a newspaper. In that note he had claimed Bedent as a relative and stated that he resided at Lapland; but he failed to sign his name or state the county in which Lapland was situated. A. E. Baird received the letter promptly, but seems never to have answered it. In it Bedent gave a full family history; and the letter was published in full in the Asheville *Gazette News* on February 20, 1912. This letter was read and preserved by the numerous Bairds in Buncombe but no one seems to be able to trace the exact relationship between the Buncombe and the Watauga Bairds. That they are the same family no one who knows them can doubt, as they look, and, in many things, act alike, besides having the same given names in many cases.[5]

THE COLD SATURDAY. This date is fixed in Watauga by the fact that John Hartley was born on that day, which is set down in his family Bible as February 8, 1835. On June 5, 1858, a freeze killed corn knee-high, and all fruits, vegetables and white oak trees between Boone and Jefferson, according to the recollections of Col. W. L. Bryan of Boone. There was a slight frost at Blowing Rock on the night of July 26, 1876. There was snow on the Haywood mountains June 10, 1913.

"THE BIG SNOW." Just when occurred what old people call the "big" snow cannot be determined to the satisfaction of everyone. Mrs. Eliza Burleson, of Hawk, Mitchell county, and the mother of Charles Wesley Burleson of Plum Tree, was born on the 5th of April, 1820, on Three Mile creek, her father having been Bedford Wiseman. She married Thomas Burleson, now deceased, in 1840, and *after* the Big Snow, and

still remembers the hunters who came to her father's house
from Morganton with guns and dogs and well nigh exterminated the deer, which could not run on the frozen surface
of the deep snow, their sharp hoofs plunging through the crust,
thus rendering locomotion impossible. Strange to say, near
this very place is now the largest private collection of deer in
the mountains—Bailey's deer-park being well stocked, while
a small number of deer still wander wild in the neighborhood
and are hunted every fall. George W. Vanderbilt's and the
Murchison deer parks also contain a number of these animals,
as well as several other smaller collections.

"SNEW, BLEW AND FRIZ." T. L. Lowe, Esq., of Banner
Elk, thinks that two hundred years ago elk, moose or caribou
roamed these mountains, and that there was little or no underbrush or laurel or ivy then. He speaks of a big snow which
fell during the Fifties which recalled Dean Swift's great snow
in England, when he said "first it blew, then it snew and then
it friz." A large number of deer were killed at this time for
the same reason, the frozen crust. In Watauga they still tell
of a big snow which entirely obliterated all evidence of fences
and shrubbery; but the year seems to have been prior to 1850.

OTHER WEATHER EXTRAVAGANCIES. From Robert Henry's
diary we learn that in "the summer of 1815 no rain fell from
the 8th of July till the 8th of September. Trees died." Also
that, "on the 28th day of August, 1830, Caney branch (which
runs by Sulphur spring five miles west of Asheville) ceased to
run. Tom Moore's creek and Ragsdale's creek had ceased
to run some days before; the corn died from the drouth. This
has been the driest summer in sixty years to my knowledge.
Our spring ceased to run for some weeks previous to the above
date." Again: "The summer of 1836 was the wettest
summer in seventy years in my remembrance." This is the
climax: "Thursday, Friday, and Saturday next before
Christmas, 1794, were the coldest days in seventy years,"
though as he had been born in 1765 he could not then have
been quite thirty years of age himself.

A MODERN "BIG SNOW." On the 2d and 3d of December,
1886, a snow three feet in depth fell in Buncombe and adjoining counties. On December 6th the newly elected officers of
Buncombe county were required by law to present their official bonds to the county commissioners for approval; but,

owing to the snow, it was impossible to travel very far. As a consequence R. H. Cole, who had been elected register of deeds, and J. V. Hunter, who had been elected treasurer, could not provide bonds acceptable to the commissioners, and J. H. Patterson who had been defeated was appointed register of deeds, and J. H. Courtney, who had also been defeated, was appointed treasurer.

Two Recent Cold Snaps. On the night of February 7, 1895, there was a dangerous fire on Pack Square, Asheville, threatening for awhile the entire southeastern section of the city. The thermometer was seven degrees below zero. On the morning of February 13, 1899, the thermometer was 13½ below zero at Asheville.

Mount Mitchell.[6] In 1835 Prof. Elisha Mitchell made the first barometrical measurements of our mountains, and his report was the first authoritative announcement of the superior altitude of the highest southern summit to that of Mount Washington in New Hampshire. In 1844 he and Gen. T. L. Clingman took observations in the Balsam, Smoky and Black mountains, and Gen. Clingman subsequently published a statement to the effect that he had found a higher peak in the Blacks than the one measured by Dr. Mitchell. "It was admitted that Gen. Clingman had measured the highest point, the only question being whether that peak was the same as that previously measured by Dr. Mitchell."

Discoverers Dispute. To settle the matter Dr. Mitchell ran a series of levels from the terminus of the railroad near Morganton to the half-way house built by Mr. William Patton of Charleston, S. C., in 1856. From this place Dr. Mitchell started alone to Big Tom Wilson's in Yancey by the route he had followed in 1844. He intended to meet his son Charles at an appointed place on the Blacks the following Monday, he having left the half-way house Saturday, June 27, 1857. His son waited and searched for him till Friday following, when news of the professor's disappearance reached Asheville, and many men set out to search for him. On the following Tuesday Big Tom Wilson, who had been the professor's guide in 1844, discovered his trail and found the body in a pool of water at the foot of a waterfall, since called Mitchell's creek and Mitchell's fall. The body was taken across the top of the Blacks to Asheville and there interred in the Presbyterian church yard; but a year later it was taken back to the Peak and buried there.[13]

THE MERITS OF THE CONTROVERSY. Dr. Arnold Guyot of Princeton College, in an article published in the Asheville *News*, July 18, 1860: "The statements Dr. Mitchell made, at different times, of the results of his measurements failed to agree with each other, and, owing to unfavorable circumstances and the want of proper instruments, the precise location of the points measured, especially of the highest, had remained quite indefinite, even in the mind of Dr. Mitchell himself, as I learned it from his own mouth in 1856. .   .   . I may, perhaps, be permitted to express it as my candid opinion (without wishing in the least to revive a controversy happily terminated) that if the honored name of Dr. Mitchell is taken from Mount Mitchell and transferred to the highest peak, it should not be on the ground that he first made known its true elevation, which he *never did*, nor himself ever *claimed* to have done; for the true height was not known before my measurement of 1854, and the coincidence made out quite recently may be shown, from abundant proofs furnished by himself, to be a mere accident.   Nor should it be on the ground of his having first visited it; for, though, after his death, evidence which made it probable that he did [came out,] he never could convince himself of it.   Nor, at last, should it be because that peak was, as it is alleged, thus named long before; for I must declare that neither in 1854, nor later, during the whole time I was on both sides of the mountain, did I hear of another Mount Mitchell than the one south of the highest, so long visited under that name; and that Dr. Mitchell himself, before ascending the northern peak, in 1856, as I gathered it from a conversation with him, believed it to be the highest.   Dr. Mitchell has higher and better claims, which are universally and cheerfully acknowledged by all, to be forever remembered in connection with the Black Mountain. .   .   . From these facts it is evident that the honorable senator [T. L. Clingman] .   .   .   could not possibly know when he first ascended it that anyone had visited or measured it before him, nor have any intention to do any injustice to Dr. Mitchell. .   .   . As to the highest group in the Great Smoky Mountains, however, I must remark that, in the whole valley of the Tuckaseegee and Oconaluftee, I heard of but one name applied to the

highest point, and it is that of Mount Clingman. The greatest authority around the peak, Robert Collins, Esq., knows
of no other. . . . Gen. Clingman was the leader of a party
which made, in 1858, the first measurement, and the party
was composed, besides himself, of Mr. S. P. Buckley and Dr.
S. L. Love. He caused Mr. Collins to cut a path six miles to
the top, which enabled me to carry there the first horse . . .
ever seen on these heights. . . . The central or highest peak
is therefore designated as Clingman's Dome, the south peak,
the next in height, as Mount Buckley, the north peak as
Mount Love."

THE MONUMENT. The monument to Professor Elisha
Mitchell, on the crest of the highest peak east of the Rocky
mountains, was completed August 18, 1888. It is bolted to the
bed-rock itself, is of white bronze—an almost pure zinc—
treated under the sandblast to impart a granular appearance, cause it to resemble granite, and prevent discoloration;
and was made by the Monumental Bronze Company, of
Bridgeport, Conn. It was erected by Mrs. E. N. Grant, a
daughter, and other members of Prof. Mitchell's family. Its
dimensions are about two and one-half feet at the base and
about twelve feet high. It is a hollow square and without any
ornamentation. Vandals have shot bullet holes in it and an
ax blade has been driven into one of its sides. Professor W.
B. Phillips, now the professor of Geology at the University
of Texas, had charge of its erection. It contains the following inscriptions:

Upon the western side, in raised letters is the single word:

" MITCHELL"

On the side toward the grave is the following:

"Erected in 1888.
"Here lies in hope of a blessed resurrection the body of Rev. Elisha
Mitchell, D.D., who, after being for 39 years a professor in the University of North Carolina, lost his life in the scientific exploration of this
mountain in the 64th year of his age, June 27th, 1857."[7]

A MEMORABLE RIOT. During the Seymour and Blair campaign of 1868 a riot occurred on the public square at Asheville
in which one negro was killed and two others seriously wounded.
Trouble had been expected, and when a negro knocked a young
Mississippian down, twenty or more pistols were discharged

into the crowd of negroes, while from several store doors and second-story windows shotguns and rifles were discharged into the fleeing blacks. That night a drum was beaten in the woods where now is Aston park and a crowd of negroes assembled there, and reports spread that they would burn the town. Messengers were sent to surrounding towns, and by daylight three hundred armed white men from adjoining counties arrived. For two weeks the streets were patrolled at night. Oscar Eastman, in charge of the Freedman's Bureau, had an office in the Thomas building on the southwest corner of the square; but after the riot Eastman could not be found for several days, as it was thought he had incited the negroes to arm themselves with stout hickory sticks and shout for Grant and Colfax, the immediate casus belli. Giles McDowell, a large, bushy-headed negro and a Democrat, came up South Main street and shouted "Hurrah for Seymour and Blair," whereupon the other negroes made a rush for him, during which the young Mississippian was knocked down. Giles fled; but another darky by the name of Jim Greenlee fell on his face at the first shot, groaning and hollering. After the shooting was over it developed that Jim was unhurt, but had wisely pretended to be hurt in order to keep anyone from firing at him. In 1874, Eastman, who had made himself very obnoxious, was indicted in Buncombe Superior court twenty-five times for retailing whiskey and once for gambling. At the Spring Term of 1869 George H. Bell, William Blair, Erwin Hardy, Gaston McDowell, Ben. Young, Natt Atkinson, J. M. Alexander, J. W. Shartle, E. H. Merrimon, Henry Patton, Simon Henry, Robert Patton, John Lang and Armistead Dudley, pleaded guilty to the charge of riot, and were taxed with the costs.

A BACKWOODS ABELARD AND ELOISE. The tomb of the Priest Abelard and his sweetheart Eloise, in Paris, is visited by greater numbers than that of Napoleon. But the grave of poor, ignorant and deluded Delilah Baird near Valle Crucis is neglected and unknown. Yet she as truly as Eloise gave her life for love; for although she knew that John Holsclaw was a married man, she thought he was taking her to Kentucky when as a child of fifteen she followed him to the Big Bottoms of Elk in the spring of 1826, where she lived a life of faithfulness and devotion to her lover and their son and daughter, and died constant and true to her role as his widow in God's sight, if not in that of man's. Having sold her land the poor repressed, stinted creature indulged in gay dressing in her later years, which caused some of her relatives to fear that she was not competent to manage her money matters; but a commission of which Smith Coffey was a member, found that she was. (Deed Books R., p. 574, and A., p. 498.) In 1881-82 she wrote to a childhood friend, not a former sweetheart, Ben Dyer, at Grapevine, Texas, to come and protect her interests and she would give him a home. He came, but was not satisfied, and on May 26, 1882, sued her for his traveling expenses and the worth of his time; but recovered only $47.50, the price of a ticket to Texas. (Judgment Roll and Docket A., p. 172, Watauga county; See Chapter 13, "Lochinvar Redux.")

NIMROD S. JARRETT. In the early fall of 1873 Bayliss Henderson, a desperado from Tennessee, wandering about, heard that Col. N. S. Jarrett would leave his home at the Apple Tree place on the Nantahala river, six miles above Nantahala station on the Western North Carolina Railroad, and the same distance below Aquone, where his daughter, Mrs. Alexander P. Munday, and her husband lived. Henderson had been told that Jarrett would carry a large sum of money with him as he had to go to Franklin to settle as guardian for wards who had become of age. On a bright Sunday morning he was to start alone, as Henderson had been told, and on that morning he did start and alone. Half a mile below the home where Micajah Lunsford used to live he overtook Henderson, who was strolling idly along the road. Henderson walked a short distance by Jarrett's horse, but falling back a pace drew his pistol and shot the Colonel in the back of the head at the base of the brain. He took his watch and chain and the little money he had in his pocket, and hearing some one coming he waded across the Nantahala river and watched. The person he had heard was Mrs. Jarrett, the dead man's wife, a cripple, who had ridden rapidly in order to overtake her husband and ride with him to Aquone where she was to have stayed till he returned from Franklin. She went on and told Micajah Lunsford and a crowd soon gathered about the body. The footprints of a man near the body were measured, but before the body was removed Henderson came upon the scene. It was noticed that the heels of his shoes were missing, but that in other respects his shoes made a print exactly like those which had been there before his arrival. He was arrested and taken to Franklin. The trial was removed to Jackson county, where he was convicted and hanged, the Supreme court refusing a new trial. (68 N. C.) While Henderson was in Macon jail he sent a man named Holland to a certain tree near the scene of the murder, where he found the watch, chain and money. Later on Henderson escaped and went back to the place where he had lived before the murder, but was found hiding in a brush-heap soon afterwards and returned to prison. Col. Jarrett was 73 years old.

A FORGOTTEN CRIME. In the spring of 1855 the home of Col. Nimrod S. Jarrett at Aquone, Macon county, was burned in the day time, and one of his children, a little girl, perished in the flames, though her mother had gone into the burning dwelling in the effort to find and rescue her, and had been dragged out by force. About 1898 a man named Bill Dills died on the head of Wusser creek, and confessed that he had set fire to the house in order to prevent suspicion falling on him for having stolen several small sums of money, his idea being that their loss when discovered, would be attributed to the fire.

QUAKING BALD. "The most famous of the restless mountains of North Carolina is 'Shaking Bald.'" The first shock, which occurred February 10, 1874, was followed in quick succession by others and caused general alarm in the vicinity. This mountain for a time received national attention. Within six months more than one hundred shocks were felt.

The general facts of these terrestrial disturbances have never been disputed, but concerning their cause, there has been widely diversified speculation. Is there an upheaval or subsidence of the mountains gradually going on? Are they the effect of explosions caused by the chemical action of minerals under the influence of electric currents? Are they the effect of gases forced through fissures in the rocks from the center of the earth, seeking an outlet at the surface? These are questions on which scientists differ. Be the cause what it may, there is no occasion to fear the eruption of an active volcano.

"The famous Bald mountain forms the north wall of the valley. Its sterile face is distinctly visible from the porch of the Logan hotel. Caves similar to Bat cave are high on its front. In 1874 Bald mountain pushed itself into prominence by shaking its eastern end with an earthquake-like rumble, that rattled plates on pantry shelves in the cabins of the valleys, shook windows to pieces in their sashes, and even startled the quiet inhabitants of Rutherfordton, seventeen miles away. Since then rumblings have occasionally been heard, and some people say they have seen smoke rising in the atmosphere. There is an idea, wide-spread, that the mountain is an extinct volcano. As evidence of a crater, they point to a fissure about half a mile long, six feet wide in some places, and of unmeasured depth. This fissure, bordered with trees, extends across the eastern end of the peak. But the crater idea is effectually choked up by the fact that the crack is of recent appearance. The crack widens every year and, as it widens, stones are dislodged from the mountain steeps. Their thundering falls from the heights may explain the rumbling, and their clouds of dust account for what appears to be smoke. The widening of the crack is possibly due to the gradual upheaval of the mountain." [8]

TRIAL OF THOMAS W. STRANGE. On the 27th day of April, 1876, Thomas W. Strange was acquitted in Asheville for the murder on the 19th of August, 1875, of James A. Murray of Haywood county before Judge Samuel Watts and the following jurors: W. P. Bassett, J. L.Weaver, John H. Murphy, Owen Smith, W. W. McDowell, B. F. Young, John Chesbrough, G. W. Whitson, S. M. Banks, W. A. Weddin, and P. F. Patton. W. L. Tate of Waynesville was the solicitor. There was much feeling in Haywood and Buncombe counties because of this acquittal. During his confinement in jail Preston L. Bridgers, his friend, voluntarily stayed with Thomas Strange. The court was held in the chapel of the Asheville Female College, now the high school. Judge Watts was from the eastern part of the State and was nick-named "Greasy Sam."

"BIG TOM" WILSON. Thomas D. Wilson, commonly known as "Big Tom," on account of his great size, was born December 1, 1825, on Toe river, near the mouth of Crabtree creek, in the Deyton Bend. The "D" in his name was solely for euphony. He married Niagara Ray, daughter of Amos L. Ray, and settled at the Green Ponds, afterwards known as the Murchison boundary. The place was so called because of several pools or ponds in Cane river, on the rock bottom of which a green moss grows. He died at a great age a few years ago. He was a great woodsman, hunter and trapper—a typical frontiersman, picturesque in appearance and original in speech and manner. He is said to have killed over one hundred bears during his life. His knowledge of woodcraft enabled him to discover Prof. Mitchell's trail, resulting in the recovery of his body, when the scientist lost his life on Black mountain in the summer of 1857. [13]

LEWIS REDMOND, OUTLAW. He was part Indian, and was born and reared in Transylvania county, having "hawk-like eyes and raven-black hair." When fifteen years of age he was taken into the family of "Uncle Wash Galloway," a pioneer farmer of the county, and after he was grown and had left his home at Galloway's, he began "moonshining." Warrants were issued for his arrest, but the deputy United States marshals were afraid to arrest him. Marshal R. M. Douglass, however, deputized Alfred F. Duckworth a member of a large and influential family of Transylvania county. Redmond had sworn he would not be arrested, but young Duckworth went after him notwithstanding. Another deputy by the name of Lankford accompanied him. They came up with Redmond in the neighborhood of the East Fork, March 1, 1876. Redmond and his brother-in-law Ladd were driving a wagon. Duckworth told Redmond to stop, as he had a warrant for his arrest. Redmond stopped the wagon, and asked to hear the warrant read. Duckworth dismounted from his horse and began reading the warrant, but holding his pistol in one of his hands while he did so. Redmond said, "All right, put up your pistol, Alf, I will go along with you." While Duckworth was putting his pistol in his pocket, Ladd passed a pistol to Duckworth, and before "a man standing near by could speak," Redmond put the pistol to Duckworth's throat and fired. Then he and Ladd jumped from the wagon and ran. Duckworth followed them a dozen or more steps, firing his pistol as he ran; but fell in the road from the shock of his wound. He died soon after being taken to his home, and Redmond escaped. Redmond was caught later in South Carolina for some offence committed there, but escaped. [9] Later on he was captured in Swain county at or near Maple Springs, five miles above Almond. He was living in a house which commanded a view of the only approach to it, a canoe landing and trail leading from it. A posse crossed in the night and were in hiding near-by when daylight came. Redmond left the house and went in the upper part of the clearing with a gun to shoot a squirrel. One of the posse ordered him to surrender. Redmond whirled to shoot at him, when another of the posse fired on him from another quarter, filling his back with buckshot, disabling but not killing him. He was taken to Bryson City, and while recuperating from his wounds received a visit from his wife. She managed to give him a pistol secretly which Redmond concealed under his pillow. A girl living in the house found it out, and told Judge Jeter C. Pritchard, who was one of the men guarding him at that time. He told his companions, and it was agreed that he should disarm him. This was done, warning having first been given Redmond that if he moved he would be killed. "Redmond served a term in the United States prison at Albany N. Y., and after being released moved to South Carolina, where, I am informed, he killed another man, an officer, and was again sent to prison." [9] During the term of Gov. Wade Hampton a long petition, extensively signed by many ladies of South Carolina, was presented to the governor for his pardon. He called himself a "Major," and claimed to be dying of tuberculosis. The pardon was granted in 1878, and Redmond has given no trouble since. He was never tried for killing Duckworth. [10]

ESCAPE OF RAY AND ANDERSON. In the summer of 1885 several prisoners escaped from the county jail on Valley street in Asheville. They were J. P. Sluder, charged with the murder of L. C. Sluder; C. M. York, also charged with another murder; and E. W. Ray and W. A. Anderson of Mitchell county, who had been convicted in Caldwell county—Anderson of murder and Ray of manslaughter, for the killing of three men in a struggle for the possession of a mica mine in Mitchell county. The last two men were members of prominent families. On the night of July 3, 1885, these men with an ax broke a hole in the brick wall of the jail, and escaped. They had forced the sheriff, the late J. R. Rich, and J. D. Henderson, the jailor, into the cage in which the prisoners were confined, when they were tied and gagged. The military company was called out to recapture the prisoners, but with-

out result. Proceedings were instituted against Rich and
Henderson for suffering these escapes, but both were acquitted
in January, 1886.

PHENOMENA NOTED AND EXPLAINED. In his "Speeches
and Writings" (Raleigh, 1877), Gen. Thomas L. Clingman
has described and explained many phenomena, among which
was the meteor of 1860 (p. 53), which was originally published
in *Appleton's Journal*, January 7, 1871; the falling of several
destructive water-spouts in Macon and Jackson counties
(p. 68) on the 15th of June, 1876; and what he terms "low
volcanic action" in the mountains of Haywood, at the head
of Fines creek, which he visited in 1848 and 1851, and which
had caused "cracks in the solid granite . . . chasms,
none of them above four feet in width, generally extending
north and south" where large trees had been thrown down,
hillocks on which saplings grew obliquely to the horizon,
showing they had attained some size before the hillocks were
elevated. He again visited this place in 1867, when he saw
evidences of further disturbances, a large "oak tree of great
age and four or five feet in diameter having been split open
from root to top and thrown down so that the two halves lay
several feet apart" (p. 78 *et seq.*). This was first published
in the *National Intelligencer* of November 15, 1848.

A CRIME NECESSITATING LEGISLATION. It was on the Cherokee county boundary line that on the 11th day of July, 1892,
William Hall shot and killed Andrew Bryson. He stood on
the North Carolina side of the boundary line between the two
States and, shooting across that line, killed Bryson while he
was in Tennessee. William Hall and John Dickey were tried
with Hall as accessories before the fact, and all were convicted
of murder at the spring term of the Superior court of Cherokee
county in 1893. But the Supreme court granted a new trial
at the February term of 1894[11] on the ground that Hall could
not be guilty of homicide in Tennessee. This decision was
immediately followed by efforts on the part of the State of
Tennessee to extradite the defendants under the act of Congress, but the Supreme court of North Carolina held on habeas
corpus proceedings[12] that no one can be alleged to have fled
from the justice of a State in whose domain he has never been
corporeally present since the commission of the crime. The
prisoners were discharged and have never been tried again in

North Carolina. These decisions were followed by remedial legislation embodied in the Acts of 1895, Chapter 169, making similar homicides crimes in North Carolina as well as in Tennessee.

THE EMMA BURGLARY. Following are the facts of a sensational burglary which occurred in Buncombe county February 8, 1901, as taken from the case of the *State v. Foster*, 129 N. C. Reports, p. 704:

"Indictment against Ben Foster, R. S. Gates, Harry Mills and Frank Johnston, heard by Judge Frederick Moore and a jury, at June (Special) Term, 1901, of the Superior Court of Buncombe County. From a verdict of guilty and judgment thereon, the defendants appealed.

"The facts are substantially as follows :

"D. J. McClelland was the owner of a store at a place called 'Emma', a few miles from the city of Asheville, in the county of Buncombe. Samuel H. Alexander is his clerk, and had been for more than three years boarding in the family of McClelland and sleeping in the store. There was a room in said store building fitted up and furnished with a bed and other furniture as a sleeping apartment, in which said Alexander kept his trunk and other belongings, and slept there, and had done so regularly for three years or more. On the night of the 8th of February, 1901, he closed and fastened all the windows and outer doors of said store building, and between eight and nine o'clock he went into his bedroom, but, thinking some customer might come, and not being ready to retire, he left a lamp burning in the store-room. There was a partition wall between his sleeping-room and the store-room, in which there was a doorway and a shutter, but the shutter was rarely ever closed and was not closed that night. Soon after he went into his sleeping room, he heard a noise at one of the outer doors of the store building, and, thinking it was some one wanting to trade, he went to the door and asked who was there. Some one answered 'We want to come in; we want some coffee and flour.' He then took down the bar used in securing the door, unlocked the same, and when he had opened the door about twelve inches, still having the knob in his hand, two men forced the door open, rushed in the house, covered him with pistols, told him to hold up his hands, that they had come for business. With the pistols still drawn upon him, they marched him into his bed-room, where they searched him and the things he had in his room, taking his pistol and other things. They then carried him into the store-room and made an effort to break into the postoffice department, there being a postoffice kept there. But not succeeding readily in getting into this, they abandoned it for the present, saying they supposed there was nothing in it, except postage stamps, and they would attend to them later. They then turned their attention to an iron safe and compelled him to assist in opening it, one of them still holding his pistol on him. After the safe was open and one of them going through it, taking what money and other valuables he found, a cat made a noise in the back part of the store, and the man with the pistol bearing on him turned his attention to that; and, as he did so, Alexander seized his own pistol they had taken from his room and which the man who was robbing the safe had laid on the end of the counter, and shot the man robbing the safe, and also shot the other man, but, in the meantime, the man whose attention had been attracted by the cat shot Alexander. They were all badly shot, but none of them died."

This testimony was that of Alexander alone, neither prisoner going on the stand. Henry Mills and R. S. Gates, indicted as being present, aiding and abetting, were tried with Ben Foster and Frank Johnston, charged as principals. All were convicted of burglary in the first degree. The judgment was sustained and Ben Foster and Frank Johnston were hanged at Asheville, the governor having commuted the sentence of the two others to life imprisonment in the penitentiary.

NANCY HANKS TRADITION. For a hundred years a tradition has persisted in these mountains to the effect that between 1803 and 1808 Abraham Enloe came from Rutherford county and settled, first on Soco creek, and afterwards on Ocona Lufty, about seven miles from Whittier, in what is now Swain county; that he brought with his family a girl whose name was Nancy Hanks; that this girl lived in Enloe's family till after his daughter Nancy ran away with and married a man named Thompson, from Hardin county, Ky. An intimacy had grown up between Nancy Hanks and Abraham Enloe, and a son was born to her, which caused Enloe's wife, whose maiden name had been Edgerton, to suspect that her husband was the father of Nancy's child. Soon after the birth of this child, the tradition relates, Mrs. Nancy Thompson came to visit her parents and on her return to Kentucky or Tennessee took Nancy Hanks and her son with her, much to Mrs. Enloe's relief. Abraham Enloe is said to have been a large, tall, dark man, a horse and slave trader,[14] a justice of the peace and the leading man in his community. Thus far the tradition as given above is supported by such reputable citizens as the following, most of whom are now dead: Col. Allen T. Davidson, whose sister Celia married into the Enloe family, Captain James W. Terrell, the late Epp Everett of Bryson City, Phillip Dills of Dillsborough, Abraham Battle of Haywood, Wm. H. Conley of Haywood, Judge Gilmore of Fort Worth, Texas, H. J. Beck of Ocona Lufty, D. K.

Collins of Bryson City, Col. W. H. Thomas and the late John D. Mingus, son-in-law of Abraham Enloe.

ABRAHAM LINCOLN TELLS OF HIS PARENTAGE. That the child so born to Nancy Hanks on Ocona Lufty was Abraham Lincoln is supported by the alleged statements that in the fall of 1861 a young man named Davis, of Rutherford, had, during the fifties, settled near Springfield, Ill., where he became intimate with Abraham Lincoln and "in a private and confidential talk which he had with Mr. Lincoln, the latter told him that he was of Southern extraction; that his right name was, or ought to have been, Enloe, but that he had always gone by the name of his step-father."[14] After the Civil War a man representing himself as a son of Mrs. Nancy Thompson, a daughter of Abraham Enloe of Ocona Lufty, called on the late Col. Allen T. Davidson, a lawyer, in his office in Asheville, and told him that President Lincoln had appointed him Indian agent or to some other office in the Indian service "because he (Lincoln) was under some great obligation to Thompson's mother, and desired to aid her, and at her request he made her son Indian agent."[15] Col. Davidson as a lawyer had settled the Abraham Enloe estate, had heard of this tradition all his life and had no doubt as to its truth. There is another version to the effect that the child Abraham was not born till after his mother had reached Kentucky and also that Felix Walker, then congressman from the mountain district, aided Nancy Hanks in getting to Tennessee, where Thompson lived.

"TRUTH IS STRANGER THAN FICTION." The above facts or statements have been taken from a small book of the name given, by James H. Cathey, once a member of the North Carolina legislature, and a resident of Jackson county. It was published in 1899. The various statements upon which the tradition was based are set forth in detail, accompanied by short biographies of each person named. No one can read these accounts without being impressed with their air of truthfulness.

EVIDENCE SUSTAINING THE ENLOE PARENTAGE. The late Captain James W. Terrell refers to an article in *Bledsoe's Review* "in which the writer gives an account of a difficulty between Mr. Lincoln's reputed father and a man named Enloe" (p. 47) and states, as one of the reasons for sending

Nancy Hanks to Kentucky, the fact that at that time some of the Enloe kindred were living there (p. 49). On page 54, a Judge Gilmore, living then within three miles of Fort Worth, Texas, told Joseph A. Collins of Clyde, Haywood county, North Carolina, that he knew Nancy Hanks before she was married, and that she then had a child she called Abraham; that she afterwards married a man by the name of Lincoln, a whiskey distiller, and very poor, and that they lived in a small house.[16]   Col. T. G. C. Davis of St. Louis, Mo., a native of Kentucky, a cousin of President Jefferson Davis, a lawyer who once practiced law· with Mr. Lincoln in Illinois, is quoted as saying that he knew the mother of Lincoln; that he was raised in the same neighborhood; and that it was generally understood, without question, in that neighborhood, that Lincoln, the man that married the President's mother, was not the father of the President, but that his father's name was Enloe" (p. 78). The foregoing are the most important facts alleged; but there is one statement, on page 55, to the effect that a man named Wells visited the Enloe home while Nancy Hanks was there and witnessed a disagreement or coolness between Enloe and his wife on her account. This man said he had gone there while selling tinware and buying furs, teathers and ginseng for William Johnston of Waynesville. This could not have been true, as William Johnston did not emigrate from Ireland to Charleston till 1818. Soon after the appearance of this book the writer visited Wesley Enloe at his home on Ocona Lufty for the purpose of learning what he could of his connection with Abraham Lincoln; but, like the correspondent of the *Charlotte Observer* of September 17, 1893 (quoted on pages 63 *et seq.*), I did not observe any likeness between him and the pictures of Mr. Lincoln which I had seen, as Mr. Enloe was blue-eyed and florid. He also stated to me that he had never heard his father's name mentioned in his family in connection with Abraham Lincoln's, just as he stated to that correspondent, on page 70.

CLARK W. THOMPSON. Col. Davidson was a man of such unquestioned integrity that any statement from him is worthy of belief; and in the interest of truth a letter was written to the Commissioner of Indian Affairs, Washington, on March 8, 1913, asking "whether a man named Thompson was ever appointed by President Lincoln to some position in the Indian Service," and on the 25th of the same month, Hon. F. H. Abbott, acting commissioner, wrote as follows: ". . . You are advised that the records show that Clark W. Thompson, of Minnesota, was nominated by President Lincoln to be Superintendent of Indian Affairs for the northern superintendency on March 26, 1861, and his appointment was confirmed by the Senate on the following day. There is nothing in the record to show reasons influencing this appointment. . . ." Of course this does not prove that Clark W. Thompson was a son of Mrs. Nancy Enloe Thompson, and is merely given for what it may be worth. In "The Child That Toileth Not," Major Dawley, its author, says (p. 271): "Where Mingus creek joins Ocona Lufty, in a broad bottom, is an old, partially demolished log-house, used as a barn, in which tradition says that Nancy Hanks, the mother of Lincoln, served as a house girl," etc.

THE NANCY HANKS HISTORY. As opposed to this traditional evidence we have the voluminous history of Nickolay and Hay, Mr. Lincoln's secretaries, called "Abraham Lincoln," in which the fact that the immortal President's mother was married to Thomas Lincoln June 12, 1806, by Rev. Jesse Head, at Beechland, near Elizabethton, Washington county, Ky., and a copy of his marriage bond for fifty pounds, as was then required by the laws of Kentucky, is set forth in full, with Richard Barry as surety. In addition to this, there was published by Doubleday & McClure Co., New York, in 1899, by Carolina Hanks Hitchcock, "Nancy Hanks, the Story of Abraham Lincoln's Mother," giving in detail the facts of her birth in Virginia, her removal to Kentucky with her family, and her marriage to Thomas Lincoln on the date above given, and many other facts which, it would seem, place this date beyond all doubt. Col. Henry Watterson, in an address, presenting the Speed statue of Lincoln to the State of Kentucky and the Nation, November 8, 1911, said: "Let me speak with some particularity and the authority of fact, tardily but conclusively ascertained, touching the . . . maternity of Abraham Lincoln. Few passages of history have been so greatly misrepresented and misconceived. Some confusion was made by his own mistake as to the marriage of his father and mother, which had not been celebrated in Hardin county, but in Washington county, Kentucky, the absence of any marriage papers in the old court house at Elizabethton, the county seat of Hardin county, leading to the notion that there had never been any marriage at all. It is easy to conceive that such a discrepancy might give occasion for any amount and all sorts of partisan falsification, the distorted stories winning popular belief among the credulous and inflamed. Lincoln himself died without surely knowing that he was born in honest wedlock and came from an ancestry upon both sides of which he had no reason to be ashamed. For a long time a cloud hung over the name of Nancy Hanks, the mother of Abraham Lincoln. Persistent and intelligent research has brought about a vindication in every way complete. It has been clearly established that as the ward of a decent family she lived a happy and industrious girl until she was twenty-three years of age, when Thomas Lincoln, who had learned his carpenter's trade of one of her uncles, married her, June 12, 1806. The entire record is in existence and intact. The marriage bond to the amount of 50 pounds . . . was duly recorded seven days before the wedding, which was solemnized as became well-to-do folk in those days. The uncle and aunt gave an 'infare', to which the neighboring countryside was invited. Dr. Christopher Columbus Graham, one of the best known and most highly respected of Kentuckians, before his death in 1885, wrote at my request his remembrances of that festival and testified to this before a notary public in the ninety-sixth year of his age." (The affidavit is set forth in full.)[17]

WHY THE TRADITION PERSISTS. After reading the foregoing article, a feeling of indignation naturally arises that anyone should longer doubt or discuss the legitimacy of the Great Emancipator, and it was that feeling which led to an examination of the "authority of fact tardily but conclusively ascertained touching the maternity of Abraham Lincoln." Naturally, too, the story was ascribed to "partisan falsification." Nicolay and Hay's account seemed to fix the date of the marriage as in June, 1806, since the marriage bond is dated on June 10th; and Miss Tarbell has settled the exact date as of June 12th of that year. So far, so good. But Miss Tarbell states (Vol. I, 7) that Mrs. Caroline Hanks Hitchcock had compiled the genealogy of the Hanks family, which, "though not yet printed, has fortunately cleared up the mystery of her birth." This little book, now out of print, [18] was obtained after great trouble, and what was found? That instead of clearing up the mystery of Nancy Hanks' birth, Mrs. Hitchcock has only made confusion worse confounded. In fact, she shows that Thomas Lincoln married an altogether different Nancy Hanks from the one the President remembered, the one Dennis Hanks knew, and the one Herndon has so particularly described in his carefully prepared work on the origin of Abraham Lincoln. She also discredits every subsequent statement by trying to show that Thomas Lincoln was not "the shiftless character" he has been represented as being (p. 54). After that, one naturally looks with suspicion upon every statement of fact in the little volume.

THE LINEAGE OF LINCOLN'S REAL MOTHER. Almost immediately after the death of Mr. Lincoln his former law partner, Wm. H. Herndon, Esq., set out to interview every member of the Lincoln and Hanks families then living. He kept up this investigation for years. What did Abraham Lincoln himself have to say as to who his mother was? Herndon says (p. 3) that in 1850, while they were in a buggy together, going to Menard county court, Lincoln told him that his mother "was the daughter of Lucy Hanks and a well-bred but obscure Virginia farmer." Who that farmer was is not stated; but Lucy Hanks, after the birth of Nancy, married a man named Henry Sparrow, and Nicolay and Hay say that Nancy Hanks was sometimes called Nancy Sparrow (Vol. I, p. 7). Herndon also says with exactness (p. 10) that "Nancy Hanks, the mother of the President, at a very early age, was taken from her mother Lucy—afterwards married to Henry Sparrow— and sent to live with her aunt and uncle, Thomas and Betsy Sparrow. Under this same roof the irrepressible and cheerful waif, Dennis Hanks, . . . also found shelter." Now who was Dennis Hanks? He was the illegitimate son of Nancy Hanks and Friend. Which Nancy Hanks was this? The sister of Lucy Hanks (p. 10). Miss Tarbell calls him Dennis Friend (pp. 14 and 25) and says misfortune had made him an inmate of Thomas Lincoln's Indiana home.

THE LINEAGE OF MRS. HITCHCOCK'S NANCY HANKS. Her father was Joseph Hanks and her mother Nancy Shipley, and was born February 5, 1784, (p. 25) and came with her parents

from Virginia to Kentucky about 1789, and settled near Elizabethton in what is now Nelson county (p. 40). Her father died
January 9, 1793, and his will was probated May 14, 1793, by
which her brother Joseph got all her parents' land and she
herself got a pied heifer, although there were eight children—
Joseph Hanks, Sr.'s widow and his son William being executors
(pp. 43-45). Miss Tarbell adopts the same lineage for her
Nancy (p. 8), and they both place this Nancy in the home of
Lucy Shipley, wife of Richard Berry, when Nancy was nine
years old.

PHYSICAL CHARACTERISTICS OF LINCOLN'S REAL MOTHER.
Herndon says (p. 10) that "at the time of her marriage to
Thomas Lincoln, Nancy was in her 23d year. She was
above the ordinary height in stature, weighed about 130
pounds, was slenderly built, and had much the appearance
of one inclined to consumption. Her skin was dark; hair dark
brown; eyes gray and small; forehead prominent; face sharp
and angular, with a marked expression of melancholy which
fixed itself in the memory of everyone who ever saw or knew
her. . . . "

PHYSICAL FEATURES OF MRS. HITCHCOCK'S NANCY. "Bright,
scintillating, noted for her keen wit and repartee, she had
withal a loving heart," is Mrs. Hitchcock's (p. 51) notion
of Nancy Hanks' manner. "Traditions of Nancy Hanks'
appearance at this time [of her marriage] all agree in calling
her a beautiful girl. She is said to have been of medium
height, weighing about 130 pounds (p. 59), light hair, beautiful eyes, a sweet, sensitive mouth, and a kindly and gentle
manner." In another place (p. 73) she says that when Nancy
Hanks went to her cousins', Frank and Ned Berry, the legend
is that "her cheerful disposition and active habits were a
dower to those pioneers." Frank and Ned were sons of
Richard Berry.

HERNDON'S THOMAS LINCOLN. "Thomas was roving and
shiftless. . . . He was proverbially slow of movement,
mentally and physically; was careless, inert and dull. He
had a liking for jokes and stories. . . . At the time of his
marriage to Nancy Hanks he could neither read nor write
(p. 8). . . . He was a carpenter by trade, and essayed
farming, too; but in this, as in almost every other undertaking,
he was singularly unsuccessful. He was placed in possession

of several tracts of land at different times in his life, but was never able to pay for a single one of them" (p. 9). He hunted for game only when driven to do so by hunger (p. 29).

MRS. HITCHCOCK'S THOMAS LINCOLN. "Thomas Lincoln had been forced to shift for himself in a young and undeveloped country (p. 56). He had no bad habits, was temperate and a church-goer" (p. 54). She quotes an affidavit of Dr. C. C. Graham to the effect that he was present at the marriage of Thomas Lincoln, but he says nothing more of him, except that he had one feather bed, and when the doctor was there, Thomas and his wife slept on the floor. This same Dr. Graham is quoted as saying that it is untrue that Thomas kept his family in a doorless and windowless house. But Miss Tarbell (p. 19) and Herndon (p. 18) say that Thomas Lincoln kept his family in a "half-face camp" for a year, and that after the cabin was built it had but one room and a loft, with no window, door or floor; not even the traditional deer-skin hung before the exit; there was no oiled paper over the opening for light; there was no puncheon floor on the ground . . . and there were few families, even in that day who were forced to practice more make-shifts to get a living"; and that sometimes the only food on the table was potatoes (p. 20). And yet Mrs. Hitchcock says he was not shiftless!

ABRAHAM LINCOLN AND HIS PARENTS. Mr. Herndon says (p. 1) that if Mr. Lincoln ever mentioned the subject of his parents at all it was with great reluctance and with significant reserve. "There was something about his origin he never cared to dwell upon." To a Mr. Scripps of the *Chicago Tribune*, in 1860, Mr. Lincoln communicated some facts concerning his ancestry which he did not wish to have published then and which Scripps never revealed to anyone" (p. 2). In the record of his family which Mr. Lincoln gave to Jesse W. Fell, he does not even give his mother's maiden name; but says that she came "of a family of the name of Hanks." (Footnote on page 3). He gives but three lines to his mother and nearly a page to the Lincolns. And "Mr. Lincoln himself said to me in 1851 . . . that whatever might be said of his parents and however unpromising the early surroundings of his mother may have been, she was highly intellectual by nature, had a strong memory, acute judgment, and was cool and heroic" (p. 11). His school days he never alluded to; and Herndon says he slept in the loft of the Indiana cabin, which he reached by climbing on pegs driven in the wall, while Miss Tarbell says that "he slept on a heap of dry leaves in a corner of the loft" (p. 19), while his parents reclined on a bedstead made of poles resting between the logs and on a crotched stick, with skins for the chief covering." Although in the highest office in the land for four years before his death, Mr. Lincoln left his mother's grave unmarked, and when his father was dying he allowed sickness in his own family to deter him from paying him a last visit, writing instead a letter advising him to put his trust in God.

HERNDON'S ESTIMATE OF THE HANKSES. "As a family the Hankses were peculiar to the civilization of early Kentucky. Illiterate and superstitious, they corresponded to that nomadic class still to be met with throughout the South, and known as 'poor whites.' They are happily and vividly depicted in the description of a camp-meeting held at Elizabethton, Ky., in 1806, which was furnished me in August, 1865, by an eye-witness (J. B. Helm). 'The Hanks girls', narrates the latter, 'were great at Camp-meetings,'" and the scene is then described of a young man and young woman with their clothing arranged for what was to follow, who approached and embraced each other in front of the congregation: "When the altar was reached the two closed, with their arms around each other, the man singing and shouting at the top of his voice, 'I have my Jesus in my arms, sweet as honey, strong as baconham.' She was a Hanks, and the couple were to be married the next week; but whether she was Nancy Hanks or not my informant does not state; though, as she did marry that year, gives color to the belief that she was. But the performance described must have required a little more emotion and enthusiasm than the tardy and inert carpenter was in the habit of manifesting" (p. 12).

CONFIRMATION OF THE ENLOE TRADITION. One might suppose that the Enloe story has no other basis than that recorded in Mr. Cathey's book. But this is far from being the fact, though most of the biographers of Lincoln make no reference to the Enloes whatever. But Mr. Herndon, on page 27, remarks of Thomas Lincoln's second wife, Sarah

Bush, that her social status is fixed by the comparison of a
neighbor who contrasted the "life among the Hankses, the
Lincolns, and the Enloes with that among the Bushes, Sarah
having married Daniel Johnston, the jailer, as her first matri-
monial venture. Dr. C. C. Graham, in his hundredth year, made
a statement as to the Lincoln family, which is published in full
by McClure's in magazine form and called "The Early Life
of Abraham Lincoln," by Ida M. Tarbell. This is dated in
1896. Herndon and all the biographers agree that, although
so old, Dr. Graham was a competent witness as to Lincoln's
early life. Indeed, all of pages 227 to 232 of this little magazine book are devoted to testimonials establishing his credibility. But, although Tarbell's Life of Lincoln is an enlargement of this magazine story, and contains four large volumes,
very little of Dr. Graham's long statement, covering over
five closely printed pages, is preserved. And among the things
that have been suppressed is this: "Some said she (Nancy
Hanks, Thomas Lincoln's first wife) died of heart trouble,
from slanders about her and old Abe Enloe, called Inlow
while her Abe, named for the pioneer Abraham Linkhorn,
was still living." Neither Mrs. Hitchcock nor Miss Tarbell
seems to have attached the slightest importance to this statement. But that is not all. Herndon records the fact (p.
29) that when he interviewed Mrs. Sarah Bush Lincoln,
Thomas Lincoln's second wife, in September, 1865, "She declined to say much in answer to my questions about Nancy
Hanks, her predecessor in the Lincoln household, but spoke
feelingly of the latter's daughter and son."

Thus, it will be observed, that most of the testimony on
which the stories concerning Nancy Hanks are based do *not*
rest on the fabrications of his political enemies, but on the
statements and significant silence of himself, his friends, relatives and biographers.

THE CALHOUN TRADITION. If anywhere in the world
Lincoln had enemies, it was in South Carolina. If anywhere
in the world a motive could exist to ruin his political fortunes,
it was among the politicians of the Palmetto State. It is
true that for years there has been an intangible rumor about
John C. Calhoun and Nancy Hanks; but the world must
perforce bear witness that such rumors have met with little
or no encouragement from the people of that State. Yet, dur-

ing all the years that have flown since early in the last century,
many men and women knew of a story which connected the
name of the Great Nullifier with that of Nancy Hanks, the
mother of Abraham Lincoln.   It has lain untold all these
years; but in 1911, Mr. D. J. Knotts of Swansea, S. C., brought
it to the light of day.   The reason for this delay was due to the
respect that the custodians of the secret entertained for the
wishes of the Calhoun family.   For, even now, some of those
to whom the facts had been communicated by Judge Orr
and Gen. Burt, will not permit their names to be used in connection with the story.   But the main facts seem to be well
established by other testimony, and although these articles
have been before the public since 1910, no one has as yet
attempted their refutation.   Abbeville "District," as it was
called, in South Carolina, was the home of John C. Calhoun
and of Gen. Armistead Burt, who married Calhoun's niece.
They were fast friends and political supporters of State
Rights.   Judge James L. Orr was born in Craytonville, S. C.,
May 12, 1822, and was in Congress from 1849 to 1859,
having been speaker of the 35th Congress.   He thus began
his congressional career the year after Mr. Lincoln had completed his single term; but John C. Calhoun was serving then
as senator, dying March 31, 1850.   Judge Orr was probably
born in the very tavern which had previously been kept by
Ann Hanks at Craytonville, as Orr's father certainly kept the
same hostelry during his life.

THE STORY IS TOLD AT LAST.   During 1911 the Columbia
State published four articles on the "Parentage of Lincoln,"
by D. J. Knotts, of Swansea, S. C.   Briefly stated, his story
is to the effect that in 1807, John C. Calhoun began the practice of law in Abbeville county, where he lived till his removal
to Fort Hill in 1824.   Anderson county was not established
till 1828; but in 1789 Luke Hanks died and left a will, which
was probated in Abbeville county in October of that year, by
which his widow, Ann Hanks, a relative of Benjamin Harris of
Buncombe county, N. C., and John Haynie were made executors.   No deed can be found to land of Luke or Ann Hanks,
but there is a grant to 210 acres to her brother in 1797.   However, the appraisers of the property under Luke Hanks' will
valued these 210 acres at one dollar per acre, and the personal
property at $500.   Just how long after Luke's death it was

that his widow, Ann Hanks, took charge of a tavern at the cross roads, called Craytonville and Claytonville, was not stated; but it is alleged that she kept this tavern in 1807, and for several years thereafter. This cross-roads place is between Anderson, Abbeville and Pendleton—all flourishing towns at this time. At this tavern John C. Calhoun stopped in going to and from the courts, and became involved in a love affair with Ann Hanks' youngest child, Nancy. At this tavern also stopped Abraham Enloe on his way South from Ocona Lufty with negroes and stock for sale. With him came as a hireling Thomas Lincoln, the putative father of the President. Nancy Hanks began to be troublesome and Mr. Calhoun is said to have induced Thomas Lincoln to take her with him on his return with Abraham Enloe—paying him $500 to do so. Lincoln is said to have conducted Nancy to the home of Abraham Enloe, where she became a member of the family. This is a confirmation of the Enloe tradition, except that Nancy is said to have gone there from Rutherford county.

THE PETITION FOR PARTITION. Ann Hanks, who seems to have had a life estate in the 210 acres of land, must have died about 1838 or 1839, for we find that Luke Hanks' heirs tried to divide the property without the aid of a lawyer, making two efforts to that end, but failing in both. In 1842, however, an Anderson attorney straightened things out by bringing in Nancy Hanks as the twelfth child of Luke and Ann Hanks, and the property was divided into twelve equal shares, it having been alleged that Nancy Hanks had left the State and that her whereabouts were unknown. Col. John Martin became the purchaser of this land, which is in a neighborhood called Ebenezer, and is within three or four miles of the tavern at Craytonville.

LINCOLN IS TOLD OF A REMARKABLE RESEMBLANCE. In 1849, while John C. Calhoun and Gen. Burt were attending Congress, young James L. Orr, not yet a member, but wishing to see the workings of that body over which he was one day to preside, made a visit to Washington, D. C., and as he had grown up with the Hanks family near Craytonville, he was at once impressed with the remarkable resemblance between those Anderson county Hankses and a raw-boned member from the State of Illinois, by name Abraham Lincoln. He told Lincoln of the fact, and the latter replied that his mother's name was Nancy Hanks. Thereupon, it is stated, Orr wanted to go into particulars, but Lincoln at once became reticent and would not discuss the matter further. This aroused Orr's suspicions, and on his return to Anderson he mentioned it to the Hankses of Ebenezer, who having but recently heard the almost forgotten story of John C. Calhoun's connection with Nancy and her disappearance from the State early in the century (in the partition case) related it to Judge Orr in all its details. Gen. Burt also became possessed of the story, but guarded his secret jealously, his wife being Calhoun's niece. But, when Lincoln was assassinated Judge Orr, who was a brother in-law of Mrs. Fannie Marshall, a second cousin of John C. Calhoun, told her and her husband what he had learned from the Anderson Hankses; and in 1866 Gen. Armistead Burt, under the seal of an inviolable secrecy, told what he knew to a group of lawyers all of whom were his friends. So inviolably have they kept this secret that even to this day several of them refuse to allow their names to be mentioned in connection with it. But the Hankses also told their family physician, Dr. W. C. Brown, the story of their kinswoman and John C. Calhoun, and he mentioned it to others. John Hanks, also, is said to have told Dr. Harris that Nancy Hanks had gone to an uncle in Kentucky when her condition became known at the Enloe farm; for it seems that a Richard Berry has been located as buying land in Anderson county in 1803, and as disappearing entirely from the records of Anderson county thereafter.

Mr. Knotts introduced much other evidence, and has accumulated much additional testimony since, which he will soon publish in full, giving book and page of all records and full extracts from all documents.

MINOR MATTERS. Mr. Knotts also states that Dr. W. C. Brown was a brother of "Joe" Brown, the "War Governor" of Georgia; that Mr. Herndon's first life of Lincoln contained several statements which Lincoln had made as to his illegitimacy; but that friends of Lincoln "had tried to recall the volumes and failed to get a few of them in for destruction"; but that Mr. Knotts had secured a copy, from which he made (pp. 5 and 6) the following statement: "Mr. Herndon, says Mr. Weik, his co-laborer in the work, spent a large amount of time

and trouble hunting down this tradition in Kentucky, and finally
found a family in Bourbon county named Inlow, who stated
to him that an older relative, Abraham Inlow, a man of
wealth and influence, induced Thomas Lincoln to assume the
paternity of Abraham Lincoln, whose mother was a nice
looking woman of good family named Nancy Hanks, and that
after marriage he removed to Hardin or Washington county,
where this infant was born." Mr. Knotts also makes the point
that there could have been no contemporaneous record of
Lincoln's birth, and that he made the date himself in the
family Bible, years after he became a man; that in that record
he nowhere records the fact or the date of his father's marriage
to Nancy Hanks, although he is careful to record his father's
second marriage to Sarah Bush Johnston, and his own marriage to Mary Todd; also that he speaks of his sister Sarah,
when she married Aaron Grigsby, as the daughter of Thomas
Lincoln alone; and when she died, he again speaks of her as
the daughter of Thomas Lincoln and wife of Aaron Grigsby,
but never mentions her as the daughter of Nancy Lincoln.
No one has ever accounted for the mutilation of the family
record made by Abraham Lincoln himself in the family Bible.
In every instance in which discredit might fall on Nancy
Hanks, the dates have been carefully obliterated in some
vital point. Surely Lincoln's political enemies did not do
this thing, the doing of which has cast more suspicion on his
legitimacy than all things else combined.

THE RUTHERFORD COUNTY HANKSES. When this last
tradition was called to the writer's attention, it was
apparent that the only way to discredit it was to follow
the clue which stated that the Nancy Hanks of Abraham Enloe's household had gone there from Rutherford county.
Accordingly, diligent enquiries were instituted in the counties
of Rutherford, Lincoln and Gaston with the result that no
trace could be found of Nancy Hanks in either of them, or
elsewhere in the State. All persons who seemed to know
anything of the Hanks family referred to Mr. L. M. Hoffman
of Dallas, N. C., who wrote, June 2, 1913, to the effect that
for several years he had been working on a genealogical history
of all the families who first settled that section from whom
he is descended. Among these were a Hanks family; and
while he obtained 600 manuscript pages concerning all the

W. N. C.—21

other families from which he has descended "the want of time
and the difficulty of getting reliable information . . .
has caused me (him) to nearly close my (his) search. . . . "
Further correspondence resulted in discovering little more
than that there once existed a Bible of the Hanks family in
the possession of the Jenkins family; but Mr. Hoffman, who
examined and made extracts from it, found nothing of record
regarding Nancy Hanks. He then gave several discoveries
that he made, and adds: "This only illustrates how I failed
to get anything like a connected story of the Hanks family.
There are several of the Hanks family here still, but they
know almost nothing of their ancestors. . . . " When it
is remembered that there are several Hanks men in Anderson
county, S. C., who are said to resemble Abraham Lincoln in
a most striking way, it is evident that the probabilities are
largely that Nancy Hanks went to Abraham Enloe's from
South Carolina rather than from Rutherford county, N. C.

THE TENNESSEE TRADITION. On the farm of G. W. Wagner, formerly owned by Isaac Lincoln—a few miles from
Elizabethton and opposite the little station called Hunter—
is a tombstone on which is carved: "Sacred to the memory
of Isaac Lincoln, who departed this life June 10, 1816,
aged about 64 years." [19]   In McClure's Early Life of Lincoln,
Isaac Lincoln is mentioned as one of the brothers of Abraham
Lincoln, the grandfather of the President (p. 223). Tradition
says that to this farm came Thomas Lincoln after the
death of his father in 1788 had, according to Miss Tarbell
(p. 6), turned him " adrift to become a wandering
laboring boy before he had learned to read." Tradition
also says that a Nancy Hanks at one time lived in that neighborhood; but that Thomas was so shiftless that his Uncle
Isaac drove him away, when Nancy disappeared also. The
lady referred to on page 73 of J. H. Cathey's book by Col.
Davidson was his sister, Miss Elvira Davidson, who was a visitor in the home of Felix Walker, one of whose sons she afterwards married; and it was while there, according to her statement to her niece, that she had seen Abraham Enloe call Felix
Walker to the gate and talk earnestly with him, and that
when Walker came back he told Mrs. Walker Abraham Enloe
had arranged with him (Walker) to have Nancy Hanks taken
to Tennessee, instead of Kentucky, when Mrs. Walker re-

marked that Mrs. Enloe would "be happy again." Mrs.
Enloe and Mrs. Walker were great friends. Elvira Davidson was a young girl at this time. She first married Joseph
Walker and years afterwards was left a widow. Her second
husband was Thomas Gaston, whose descendants are in Buncombe today.

THE SOUTH CAROLINA RECORD. This record is in the
office of the Ordinary, corresponding to that of probate judge
in most States, its number is 964, and is entitled: "*Valentine
Davis and wife, applicant, v. Luke Hanie and others.*" The
summons in relief was filed before William McGee, Ordinary
of Anderson District, S. C., December 26, 1842; it relates to
the real estate of Ann Hanks, and is recorded in real estate
book, volume 1, p. 59. The summons is to the "legal heirs
and representatives of Ann Hanks, who died intestate," and
requires the parties named therein—among whom is Nancy
Hanks—to appear on the 3d day of April, 1843, and "show
cause why the real estate of Ann Hanks, deceased, situated
in said district on waters of Rocky river, bounding Brig. R.
Haney, John Martin and others, should not be divided or sold,
allotting the same as it proceeds among you." Valentine
Davis was appointed and consented to act as the guardian
ad litem of the minor heirs named in the summons; a large
number of heirs accepted legal service of the summons; while
the Ordinary notes that he "cited" several others to appear
in court, etc. A rule was also issued December 26, 1842,
to twenty-seven of the defendants "who reside without the
State," among whom is the name of Nancy Hanks, all of
whom are required to "appear and object to the sale or division
of the real estate of Hanks on or before the third day of April
next, or their consent to the same will be entered of record."
There is also in this record an assignment to Mary Hanks by
her son James R. Hanks, of Crittenden county, Kentucky, of
his interest "in the real estate of my grandmother Ann Hanks,
which came to me by right of my father, George Hanks, which
was sold by the Court of Ordinary in Anderson District,
South Carolina, in June, 1843, which claim or claims I re-
nounce to my said mother Mary during her natural life, from
me, my executors or assigns, so long as the said Mary Hanks
shall live, but at the said Mary's death to revert back me to
and my heirs," etc.

This assignment of interest is dated April 1, 1844, and was probated before James Cruce, justice of the peace of Crittenden county, Ky., by William Stinson and Reuben Bennett, subscribing witnesses, on the first of April, 1844.

The record fails to show any receipt from Nancy Hanks for her share in the proceeds of this real estate, which would seem to indicate that she was dead and that her heirs received no actual notice of this proceeding. The foregoing excerpts have been furnished by Thomas Allen, Esq., of the Anderson, S. C., bar.

REALITY OF ISAAC LINCOLN'S RESIDENCE. Of the residence of Isaac Lincoln and Mary (nee Ward) his wife, in what is now Carter county, Tenn., there can be no doubt, the deed books of that county showing many conveyances to and from Isaac Lincoln, one of which (B, p. 14) is indexed as from Isaac "Linkhorn" to John Carter, which bears the early date of March 4, 1777, and conveys 303 acres on the north side of Doe river known by the name of the "Flag Pond," for one hundred pounds. The deed, however, is signed "Isaac Lincoln," not "Linkhorn"; but it was not registered till July 22, 1806. Lincoln and Carter are both described as of "Watauga" simply. Other conveyances show that he owned several lots in what is now Elizabethton, the county seat of Carter county (B, 18). There is also a conveyance from Johnson Hampton, with whom Thomas Lincoln and Nancy Hanks are said (according to a letter from D. J. Knotts to J. D. Jenkins, 1913) to have gone from Abraham Enloe's to Thomas Lincoln's brother's home on Lynn mountain, five miles above Elizabethton, on Watauga river. But this conveyance is dated March 13, 1834, and is to Mordeca (sic) Lincoln and John Berry of the "county of Green and Carter," Tenn. (Book D, p. 373). The site of the cabin in which Isaac and Mary lived is still pointed out at the base of Lynn mountain.

ISAAC AND MARY LINCOLN SLAVEOWNERS. The will of Isaac Lincoln, dated April 22, 1816, is filed in the office of the clerk of the circuit court of Carter county, Tenn., and, though yellow with age, is in a good state of preservation. By it he leaves all his property to his wife Mary; and when her will (filed in the same office) is examined, it is found to bequeath at least 28 negroes, naming each one separately, and providing for the support of two of them during life. William Stover, who got the bulk of her estate, was the son of her sister and Daniel Stover; and Phoebe Crow, wife of Campbell Crow, to whom she left the "negro girl Margaret and her four children, to wit: Lucy, Mima, Martin and Mahala, was Phoebe Williams, a niece of Mary Lincoln. Campbell Crow was left "the lower plantation, it being the one on which he now lives, adjoining the land of Alfred M. Carter on the west and south and of John Carriger on the east." To Christian Carriger, Sr., she bequeathed seven negroes; to Mary Lincoln Carriger, wife of Christian Carriger Sr., she left two negro girls. Christian Carriger, Sr., had married a sister of Mary Lincoln. Daniel Stover—J. D. Jenkins' great-grandfather—married another sister of Mary Lincoln. Daniel Stover's son William had a son Daniel, who married Mary, a daughter of Andrew Johnson, the successor of Abraham Lincoln in the Presidency, and he (Johnson) died in her house, a few miles above Elizabethton, July 31, 1875. P. T. Brummit lives there now. It was not a part of the Lincoln farm. The house is still visible from the railroad, the log portion thereof having been torn away; but the room in which Andrew Johnson died, in the second story of the framed addition to the original house, still stands. W. Butler Stover, great-grandnephew of Mary Lincoln, of Jonesboro (R. F. D.), Tenn., still has Mary Lincoln's Bible; but he wrote (March 6, 1914) that "it gives no dates of births or deaths or marriages of any of the Lincolns." William Stover was Butler Stover's grandfather and inherited the farm on which Mary and Isaac Lincoln are buried, as their tombstones attest, Mary's stating that she died August 27, 1834, "aged about 76 years." It is said that Isaac and Mary Lincoln had but one child, a boy, who was drowned before reaching manhood. Mrs. H. M. Folsom of Elizabethton is related to Mordecai Lincoln, while Mrs. W. M. Vought of the same place was a Carriger. Dr. Natt Hyder, who died twenty-odd years ago, and whose widow still lives at Gap Creek, in the Sixth District, told James D. Jenkins that old people had told him—"Old Man" Lewis particularly—that Abraham Lincoln was born on the side of Lynn mountain, and was taken in his mother's arms to Kentucky, going by way of Stony Fork creek and Bristol. An anonymous writer—supposed to be B. Clay Middleton—in an article which was published in the *Carter County News*, February 13, 1914, says: "Tradition says that it was here, in the beautiful Watauga Valley, so rich in history, that the young Thomas Lincoln first met and wooed the gentle Nancy Hanks, whose name was destined to become immortal through the achievements of her illustrious son. Tradition further says that for a while before Thomas Lincoln and Nancy Hanks left for Kentucky they lived for a time together as common law husband and wife in a little cabin on Lynn mountain, which overlooks the Watauga valley. I have been informed that old people in that vicinity still recall the site of what was known as the Tom Lincoln cabin, and traces of the spot where the cabin stood still remain in the way of stone foundations, etc." He also cites as "a little singular that the life of Andrew Johnson in a way should be interwoven with the name of Lincoln, whom he succeeded as President of the United States. When he married Miss Eliza McCardle, at Greenville, Tenn., it was 'Squire Mordecai Lincoln who performed the ceremony. His daughter Mary married Col. Dan Stover, the great nephew of Isaac Lincoln.'"

NOTES.

[1] Statements made to J. P. A. in 1912.

[2] Letter from S. J. Silver to J. P. A., dated November 18, 1912.

[3] Zebulon settled near French Broad River in Buncombe county, 2½ miles below Asheville, where the National Casket Factory is now, and died there years ago.

[4] Bedent settled on Beaver Dam, two miles north of Asheville, at what is now the Way place, where he died in 1839. Letter of Dr. J. S. T. Baird to J. P. A., December 16, 1912. Dr. Baird died in April, 1913.

[5] Andrew, a brother of Zebulon and Bedent Baird, settled in Burke; but the Valle Crucis Baird did not claim descent from him   John Burton was really the founder of Asheville, as on July 7, 1794, he obtained a grant for 200 acres covering what is now the center of that city. Condensed from Asheville's Centenary. He afterwards moved to Ashe County and in April, 1799, he entered 200 acres near the Virginia line. Deed Book A., p. 339.

[6] Condensed and quoted from T. L. Clingman's "Speeches and Writings," pp. 138, *et seq.*

[7] University Magazine of 1888–89.

[8] Zeigler & Grosscup, p. 245.

[9] Letter of C. C. Duckworth to J. P. A., May 1, 1912.

[10] Letter from C. C. Duckworth to J. P. A., May 1, 1912; letter from D. K. Collins, June 7, 1912; statement of Hon. J. C. Pritchard, June, 1912. In "The Child That Toileth Not" (p. 448) Pickens county, S. C., is given as the one in which Redmond held forth twenty years ago, etc.

[11] *State v. Hall*, 114 N. C., p. 909.

[12] *State v. Hall*, 115 N. C., p. 811.

[13] For Hon. Z. B. Vance's account of the finding of Prof. Mitchell's body, see "Balsam Groves of the Grandfather Mountain," by S. M. Dugger (p. 261). In this account appears a list of those who assisted in the search. From this account it seems that what is now known as Mitchell's Peak was put down in Cook's Map as Mt. Clingman. and that Prof. Mitchell insisted that he had measured it in 1844, while Gen. Clingman claimed to have been the first to measure it.

[14] "Truth Is Stranger Than Fiction," pp. 130-137-139.

[14] Ibid., p. 86.

[15] Ibid., p. 74.

[16] According to Herndon, Thomas set up house-keeping in Indiana with the tools and liquor he had recovered from his capsized river boat, p. 17.

[17] From *Louisville Courier Journal*, of Thursday, Novmber 9, 1911.

[18] "The Story of Abraham Lincoln's Mother," by Carolina Hanks Hitchcock, 1889.

[19] Tradition as related by James D. Jenkins, Esq., recorder of Elizabethton, Tenn., who also stated that Isaac Lincoln's wife was Sarah Stover, of Pennsylvania. Also that President Andrew Johnson had died on the Isaac Lincoln farm.

CHAPTER XII

HUMOROUS AND ROMANTIC

A FAITHFUL PICTURE OF THE PAST. "Somewhere about 1830," writes Judge A. C. Avery, "my father had a summer house constructed of hewn logs, containing four rooms and a hall, with outhouses, at the place now called Plumtree. It remained till about 1909, when it was destroyed by fire. This was a mile below the 'Quarter,' where the overseer kept house and my father's sons, who successively managed the stock, stayed. There were a number of negro cabins around the Craborchard proper, which was located about half a mile from where Waightstill W. Avery now lives. My father had large meadows there, on which he raised a quantity of hay and wintered hundreds of heads of cattle that ranged on the mountains in summer. These mountains were the Roan and the Yellow, on whose bald summits grass grew luxuriantly.

HAYMAKING IN THE SUMMERTIME. "During August of every year, after laying by his crop in Burke county, my father took a number of negroes and several wagons and teams over to the Craborchard, and moved his family for a stay of two months or more to his summer house at Plumtree. He hired white men from all over Yancey county to help his negroes in saving the hay.

OPEN HOUSE AND GRAND FROLIC. "He kept open house at the summer place and large parties of ladies and gentlemen went out there from time to time and had a grand frolic. Many of the young people rode out on horseback, and some of the ladies in carriages. Parties were continually riding out to the Roan, the Yellow and to Linville Falls. The woods were full of deer, and all the streams were full of speckled trout that could be caught with redworm bait. So, the ladies and gentlemen fished in Toe river and its tributaries while others of the gentlemen hunted deer, often killing them near enough to the summer house for the shot to be heard."

WHERE THE BOYS WERE "HANGED." "The late James Gudger, who was brought in his early infancy to his father's residence on Swannanoa, just settled, and who, in 1830, and

1836, represented Buncombe county in the North Carolina Senate, told his grandson, Capt. J. M. Gudger, that when he was a very small boy it was the custom to send a number of boys with bags of grain to mill to be ground, and leave it there until a month later, when the boys would return with other grain and carry back the meal ground from the first. He further said that usually a man accompanied the party to put on the sacks when they should fall from the horses, but that on one occasion as he, then a very small boy, was returning from the mill, with his companions of about the same age, the man for some reason was not along, and one of the sacks fell off on the Battery Park hill over which they had to pass; that while endeavoring in vain to replace the sacks a party of Indians came upon them, and from pure mischief threatened and actually began to hang them; that the boys [1] were badly frightened, but finally the Indians left them unharmed, and they went on their way, and that the hill was afterwards known through the country as 'the hill where the boys were hung.' [1]

HANDLEN MOUNTAIN. "He still further said that the miller in charge of the mill, whose name was Handlen, undertook to cultivate a crop on the mountain on the western side of the French Broad, but as he did not return to the settlement for a long while his friends became frightened, and in a party went to the clearing, where they found him killed and scalped, and his crop destroyed, and that from this incident that mountain took its name of the Handlen mountain. [1]

"TALKING FOR BUNCOMBE." "Famous as Buncombe deservedly is, she has acquired some notoriety that no place less merits. Her name has become synonymous with empty talk, a *lucus a non lucendo*. In the sixteenth Congress of the United States the district of North Carolina which embraced Buncombe county was represented in the lower house by Felix Walker. The Missouri question was under discussion and the house, tired of speeches, wanted to come to a vote. At this time Mr. Walker secured the floor and was proceeding with his address, at best not very forceful or entertaining, when some impatient member whispered to him to sit down and let the vote be taken. This he refused to do, saying that he must 'make a speech for Buncombe,' that is, for his constituents; or, as others say, certain members rose and left the hall while he was speaking and, when he saw them going, he turned to those who remained and told them that they might go, too, if they wished, as he was 'only speaking for Buncombe.' The phrase was at once caught up and the vocabulary of the English language was enriched by the addition of a new term."[2]

ISOLATION OF MOUNTAIN NEIGHBORHOODS. So sequestered were many of these mountain coves which lay off the main lines of travel, that persons living within only short distances of each other were as though "oceans rolled between"; as the following incident abundantly proves:

MONT. RAY'S FLIGHT, RETURN AND TRIAL.[3] Soon after the Civil War Mont. Ray killed Jack Brown of Ivy, between Ivy and Burnsville, and went to Buck's tanyard, just west of Carver's gap under the Roan mountain, where he supported himself making and mending shoes till many of the most important witnesses against him had gotten beyond the juris-diction of the court—by death or removal—when he returned and stood his trial in Burnsville and was acquitted. He had never been forty miles away, had remained there twelve years; yet no one ever suspected that he was a fugitive from justice.

A FORGOTTEN BATTLE-FIELD. *The Star*, a newspaper pub-lished in Sparta, Alleghany county, in its issue of February 29, 1912, contained the following: "A few years ago, along New river, near the northern border of this county, was found what is believed to be indications of a battle of which no one now living has any knowledge, nor is there any tradition among our people concerning it. On the land of Squire John Gambill, near the bank of New river, after a severe rain-storm and wash-out, some white objects were noticed lying on the ground. On examination these were found to be human skulls and other parts of human skeletons. Further exami-nation revealed other marks of battle, such as leaden balls buried in old trees lying on the ground, etc. Squire Gambill's ancestors have resided in this section for one and a half cen-turies; yet, they have never heard of the occurrence, nor had they any tradition of it. Who fought this battle? Why was it fought? Was there a fort here? Was it fought between the whites and Indians?" (See ante, p. 108.)

ANDREW JACKSON LOSES A HORSE RACE.[4] In the late summer or early fall of 1788, Andrew Jackson and Robert

Love had a horse race in the Greasy Cove, just above what it now Ervin, Tenn. It seems that Jackson's jockey could not ride and "Old Hickory" was forced to ride his horse himself, while Love's jockey was on hand and rode Love's horse, winning the race. When the result was known "just for a moment there was a deep, ominous hush; then a pandemonium of noise and tumult that might have been heard in the two neighboring counties. Jackson was the chief actor in this riot of passion and frenzy. His brow was corrugated with wrath. His tall, sinewy form shook like an aspen leaf. His face was the livid color of the storm cloud—when it is hurling its bolts of thunder. His Irish blood was up to the boiling point, and his eyes flashed with the fire of war. He was an overflowing Vesuvius of rage, pouring the hot lava of denunciation on the Love family in general and his victorious rival in particular. Col. Love stood before this storm unblanched and unappalled—for he, too, had plenty of 'sand,' and as lightly esteemed the value of life—and answered burning invective with burning invective hissing with the same degree of heat and exasperation. Jackson denounced the Loves as a 'band of land pirates' because they held the ownership of nearly all the choice lands in that section. Love retorted by calling Jackson 'a damned, long, gangling, sorrel-topped soap stick.' The exasperating offensiveness of this retort may be better understood when it is explained that in those days women 'conjured' their soap by stirring it with a long sassafras stick. The dangerous character of both men was well known, and it was ended by the interference of mutual friends, who led the enraged rivals from the grounds in different directions." [4]

Two Old-Time Gentlemen. Major O. F. Neal was a lawyer and farmer who lived in Jefferson, and who died in 1894. He and his brother Ben were punctilious on all matters of politeness. On one occasion, after a long walk, they reached a spring. Ben insisted that, as the Major was a lawyer and lived in town, he should drink first; but the Major claimed that as Ben was the elder he must drink first. As neither would yield to the other, they politely and good-naturedly refused to drink at all, and returned home more thirsty than ever.

THE FIRST DEPARTMENT STORE. Two miles from Old
Field, Ashe county, was kept from about 1870 to about 1890
the first department store known. It was kept by that enterprising merchant Arthur D. Cole, and the large, but now
empty, buildings still standing there show the extent of his
business. He kept as many as twelve clerks employed, and
boasted that there were but two things he did not carry constantly in stock, one being the grace of God and the other
blue wool. A friend thought he had him "stumped" one
day when he called for goose yokes; but Cole quietly took him
up stairs and showed him a gross which he had had on hand
for years. He and his father did more to develop the root
and herb business in North Carolina than anyone else. He
failed in business, after nearly twenty years of success.

A MYSTERIOUS DISAPPEARANCE. Zachariah Sawyer, grandfather of George Washington Sawyer, now register of deeds of
Ashe county, came to Ashe from east of the Blue Ridge
eighty-odd years ago. He learned that he was entitled to a
share in a large estate in England and went there to collect
his interest. After he had been in that country a short time
he wrote home that he had succeeded in collecting his share
and would soon start home. He was never afterwards heard of.

WELBURN WATERS, HERMIT HUNTER OF WHITE TOP. In
a well written book, Mr. J. A. Testerman of Jefferson has
drawn a striking portrait of this old-time hunter and backwoodsman. The last edition is dated 1911. From it one
gathers that Waters was born on Reddy's river in Wilkes
county, November 20, 1812, the son of John P. Waters, a French
Huguenot, and a half-breed Catawba woman. His conversion
and his distraction at a conference held at Abingdon, Va., in
1859 because he was afraid some harm would come to a new
hat he had carried to church are amusingly told, while his
encounters with wild beasts and his solitary life on White
Top are graphically portrayed.

LOCHINVAR REDUX. "About the year 1816, John Holsclaw, a young and adventurous hunter, and a regular Lochinvar, as the sequel will show, built a bark 'shanty' on the
waters of Elk at the 'Big Bottoms,' where he lived for many
years. The romance of his life was that he went over to Valle
Crucis, a settlement only eight miles distant, and there by
sheer force of will, or love, I will not say which, carried away,

captive, a young daughter of Col. Bedent Baird, and took her over the mountains by a route so circuitous that, from what her conductor told her, she verily believed she was in Kentucky. She was kept in ignorance of where she actually did live for many years, and only by accident found out better. One day she heard a bell whose tinkle seemed strangely familiar. She went to the steer on which it was hung and found that it belonged to her father. This clue led to the discovery that, instead of being in Kentucky she was not eight miles as the crow flies from her old home at Valle Crucis. Of course, she thanked her husband for the deception, as all women do, and they lived happy ever afterwards.

"For many years after John Holsclaw settled on the 'Big Bottoms of Elk' with his youthful bride, they lived solitary and alone; and in after years she was wont to tell how she had frightened away the wolves which prowled around when her husband was away, by thrusting firebrands at them, when they would scamper off a distance and make night hideous with their howls. And how, in after years, when they built a rude log house with only one small window to admit the light, and had moved into it, Mr. Holsclaw killed a deer and dressed it, and had gone away, a panther, smelling the fresh venison, came to the house and tried to get in, screaming with all the ferocity of a beast brought almost to the point of starvation. There was no one in the house but the woman and one child, but she bravely held her own till her husband returned, when the fierce beast was frightened away. She lived to a great age, and only a few years ago died,[5] and lies buried on a beautiful hillock hard by the place of her nativity, on the land now owned by one of her nephews, Mr. W. B. Baird, one time sheriff of Watauga."

WHO WAS SELLER AND WHO WAS SOLD? Col. Carson Vance lived on Rose's creek, between Alta Pass and Spruce Pine before and during and after the Civil War. He was a bright, but eccentric man. He was admitted to the bar and practiced law to some extent. But he and a free negro named John Jackson made up a plot at the commencement of the Civil War whereby they were to go together to New Orleans, Vance as master and Jackson as slave. At New Orleans Jackson was to be sold for all the cash he would bring, after which Vance was to disappear. Then Jackson was to prove

that he was a "free person of color," regain his freedom and
rejoin Vance on the outskirts of New Orleans. It is said that
this scheme worked successfully and that Vance and Jackson
divided the proceeds of the sale.

LOVE FINDS A WAY. On the 21st of June, 1856, W. M.
Blalock, commonly called Keith Blalock, and Malinda Pritchard were married in Caldwell county, close to the Grandfather mountain. In 1862 the conscript law of the Confederacy went into operation, and Keith, though a Union man,
was clearly subject to conscription. There was no escape
from it except by volunteering. But to do that would be
to part with his wife. So they resolved to enlist together
and seek their first opportunity of deserting and getting over
into the Federal lines. They went to Kinston, N. C., and
joined the 26th N. C. regiment, then commanded by Col.
Zebulon B. Vance, soon afterwards to become governor. This
was on the 12th of April, 1862. She wore a regular private's
uniform and tented and messed with her husband. She enlisted and was known as Sam Blalock. She stood guard,
drilled and handled her musket like a man, and no one ever
suspected her sex. But they were too far from the Federal
lines, with little prospect of getting nearer. So Keith went
into a swamp and rubbed himself all over with poison oak.
They sent him to the hospital in Kinston, where the surgeons
disagreed as to his ailment, and he was returned to his own
regiment, where his surgeon recommended his discharge. It
was granted and he left the camp. Then his wife presented
herself to Col. Vance and said that as long as they had sent
her man home she wanted to go, too. An explanation followed with confirmation "strong as proof of holy writ." She
was discharged. Keith joined the Union army and drew
a pension. Mrs. Blalock died March 9, 1901. He was called
"Keith" because when a boy he was a great fighter, and could
"whip his weight in wild-cats," as the saying went. At that
time there was a fighter, full grown and of great renown, who
lived at Burnsville, by the name of Alfred Keith. The
boys Blalock played with, "double-teamed" on him sometimes, but always got thrashed. They then called him "Old
Keith." He died in September, 1913, at Montezuma.

THE WILD CAT. In February, 1848, when she was sixteen
years old, Mary Garland, afterwards the wife of Judge Jacob

W. Bowman, killed a wild cat which had followed some ducks
into her yard. She hemmed it in a fence corner and beat it
to death with a "battling stick"—a stout, paddle-like stick
used to beat clothes when they are being washed. This was
on Big Rock creek, Mitchell county. Her cousins, Jane and
Nancy Stanley, while tending the boiling of maple sugar sap
in a camp on the waters of Big Rock creek in the spring of
1842, when sixteen and thirteen years old respectively, killed
a black bear which had been attracted by the smell of sugar,
by driving it into a small tree and killing it with an ax.

A MOONSHINER'S HEAVEN. Forty years ago Lost Cove was
almost inaccessible, except by trails; but last year (1912) a wagon
road over three miles long was constructed to it over the
ridges from Poplar Station on the C. C. & O. Railroad. Such a
secluded place was a great temptation to moonshiners, and
when to its inaccessibility was added the fact that it was in
dispute between Tennessee and North Carolina, its fascina-
tions became irresistible. Accordingly John D. Tipton was
accused of having begun business by the light of the moon,
as was evidenced by sundry indictments in the United States
court at Asheville. His example was soon followed by others;
but, whenever it appeared to Judge R. P. Dick that the al-
ledged stills were in the disputed territory, he directed the
discharge of the defendants. However, a mighty change has
taken place in Lost Cove within the past few years, and not
only is there no moonshining there now, even when fair Luna
is at the full, but the good people will not suffer the "critter"
to be brought in from Tennessee. And better still, in 1910
they built a school house and a church, and voted a special
school tax, the first school having been taught in 1911.

PEGGY'S HOLE. Three-quarters of a mile above Elk Cross
Roads, now Todd, is a high bluff, covered with laurel, pines
and ivy. It is at a bend of New river. About 1815 Mrs.
Peggy Clauson was going to church on a bright Sunday morning. Dogs had run a bear off the bluff into a deep hole at
the base of a cliff, and Mrs. Clauson saw him swimming
around in the water. She waded in and, seizing the brute by
both ears, forced his head under the water and held it there
until Bruin had drowned. It has been called Peggy's Hole
ever since.

THE HERMIT OF BALD MOUNTAIN. [6] "In Yancey county, visible from the Roan, and forty-five miles from Asheville, is a peak known as Grier's Bald, named in memory of David Grier, a hermit, who lived upon it for thirty-two years. From posthumous papers of Silas McDowell, we learn the following facts of the hermit's singular history. A native of South Carolina, he came into the mountains in 1798, and made his home with Colonel David Vance, whose daughter he fell in love with. His suit was not encouraged; the young lady was married to another, and Grier, with mind evidently crazed, plunged into the wilderness. This was in 1802. On reaching the bald summit of the peak which bears his name, he determined to erect a permanent lodge in one of the coves. He built a log house and cleared a tract of nine acres, subsisting in the meantime by hunting and on a portion of the $250 paid him by Colonel Vance for his late services. He was twenty miles from a habitation. For years he lived undisturbed; then settlers began to encroach on his wild domains. In a quarrel about some of his real or imaginary landed rights, he killed a man named Holland Higgins. At the trial he was cleared on the ground of insanity, and returned home to meet death at the hands of one of Holland's friends. Grier was a man of strong mind and fair education. After killing Higgins, he published a pamphlet in justification of his act, and sold it on the streets. He left papers of interest, containing his life's record and views of life in general, showing that he was a deist, and a believer in the right of every man to take the executive power of the law into his own hands."

OLD CATALOOCHEE STORIES. Owing to the fact that the late Col. Allen T. Davidson spent much of his young manhood hunting and fishing in Cataloochee valley, much of its early history has been preserved. From him it was learned that years ago Zach White shot a deputy sheriff named Rayburn when Col. Davidson was a boy, and hid near a big rock in a little flat one half mile above the late Lafayette Palmer's home, where for years Neddy McFalls and Dick Clark fed him. He also stayed on Shanty branch near where Harrison Caldwell now lives. This branch got its name from a shanty or shed that Old Smart, a slave of Mitchell Davidson, built there while he tended cattle for his master years before any white people ever lived in that valley. The cattle ranged on the Bunk mountain and on Mount Sterling, and one day when Neddy McFalls was looking for them to salt them he could not find a trace of them anywhere. His nickname for Col. Davidson was Twitty. Now the Round Bunk mountain stands between the lefthand fork of the Little Cataloochee and Deep Gap, while the Long branch runs from the balsam on Mount Sterling and between the headwaters of Little Cataloochee and Indian creek. It was on the Long Branch that Col. Davidson and Neddy McFalls were standing when the latter put his hands to his mouth and cried out: "Low, Dudley, low!", Dudley being the name of the bull with the herd of cattle; and almost immediately they heard Dudley from the top of Mount Sterling give a long, loud low, and they knew that their cattle were found. Richard Clark is the one who gave the name to the Bunk mountain.[7] Neddy McFalls was a great believer in witchcraft. He carried a rifle that had been made by a man of the name of Gallaspie on the head of the French Broad river, while Col. Davidson's gun was known as the Aaron Price gun. Neddy missed a fair shot at a buck one day and nothing could persuade him from leaving Cataloochee and traveling miles to a female witch doctor who was to take the "spell" off his gun. Jim Price was found dead of milk sick west of the "Purchase," formerly the home of John L. Ferguson on top of Cataloochee mountain, on another branch, also known as the Long branch. A little dog, stayed with the body and attracted the searchers to it by getting on a foot-log and howling.

It was said that the Indians had killed Neddy McFall's father and that he had a grudge against all Indians in consequence. So one day Neddy and Sam McGaha were together and saw an Indian seated on a log. Neddy told McGaha that the triggers on his rifle were "set," that is locked, and asked him to take a good aim at the Indian just for fun. Not knowing that the triggers were really "sprung," and that the slightest touch on the "hair-trigger" would fire the rifle, McGaha did as he was asked, with the result that the Indian fell dead. It is said that Neddy had to run for his life to escape the wrath of McGaha.

PRIVATE WM. NICODEMUS. An Indian named Christie lived on the site of the present town of Murphy, and a ford crossing Valley river between the two bridges of the present day was for years called the Christie ford. The first house built by a white man in Cherokee county was a large two-story log house with several rooms, erected by A. R. S. Hunter, originally of Virginia, but who moved into North Carolina from Georgia. Its furniture was of mahogany and was brought by Indians on their shoulders from Walhalla, South Carolina, there being no wagon roads at that time. Mr. Hunter, in about 1838, built a better house. General Wool and General Winfield Scott were entertained by the Hunters during the time of the removal of the Cherokees. Several of the United States soldiers engaged in that heart-rending process died and were buried near this old residence; but these remains were removed in 1905 or 1906 to the National cemetery at Marietta, Georgia. On one of the old headstones a single name is yet decipherable —that of Wm. Nicodemus.

CUPID AND THE GENERAL'S SURGEON. Fort Butler was on a hill not far from the Hunter home. Mr. Hunter had one child, a daughter, who married Dr. Charles M. Hitchcock, a surgeon on Gen. Wool's staff during the "Removal" and the Mexican War. They afterwards moved to California, where they acquired many valuable lands and settled at San Francisco. They had one child, a daughter, Lily, who is now a Mrs. Coit, and spends much of her time in Paris, France. She still owns all the lands in Cherokee county which were acquired by her grandfather, Mr. Hunter. They embrace all the land between the Notla and the Hiwassee, the "Meadows," on the head of Tallulah creek in Graham county, and land in Murphy, where she owns a house near the west end of the bridge over the Hiwassee river.

A FRIGHTENED ENTRY-TAKER. The Entry-Taker's office was opened in Murphy on the last of March, 1842, when much excitement prevailed, as it was strictly a case of "first come, first served." It is said that so eager and demonstrative was the crowd that Drewry Weeks became alarmed and hid himself in one of the upstairs rooms of the old jail, and that, when he was finally discovered, the rush that was made upon him was really terrifying. They broke out the window lights with their fists and handed or threw their bundles of entries and surveys through these openings. One land-hungry citizen, Stephen Whitaker by name, used to tell how he climbed upon the shoulders of the dense crowd of men who were packed

in front of the window of the jail and scrambled and crawled
on hands and knees over the heads of those who were so
crowded together that they could not use their fists upon him,
or dislodge him by allowing him to drop by his own weight,
till he reached the window and so got a place near the head
of the list. It is said, however, that the execrations and
maledictions—commonly called curses—which were hurled
at him were enough to damn him eternally, if mere words
could accomplish that result.

A STRANGE DREAM. Dr. J. E. West was drowned March
19, 1881, while attempting to ford the Tuckaseegee river at
the Bear Ford, and remained in the water about two weeks,
when Rachel Grant, a poor woman whose son Dr. West had
been treating, dreamed that he came to her and on seeing
him she expressed surprise and told him she thought that he
was drowned. He told her that he was and wanted to tell
her where to direct the men, when they came to search, where
to find his body. He said to tell them to get into the canoe
and pole toward two maples on the opposite side and when
they got near the current that came around a rock to put
their pole down and they would find him. When she awoke
in the moring she dressed and walked up to the landing to see
if it looked like she had seen it while dreaming. She was so
impressed that she sat and waited till the searching party
came, to whom she told her story. Of course, some were
amused while a few had faith enough to follow her directions,
and when they did so found the body in the precise place she
had pointed out to them. Mrs. Grant is still living in this
county, as well as some of those who found the body. It had
floated about one-half mile.[8]

THE DELOSIA "MIND."[9] A man named Edward Delosia,
of Blount county, Tenn., claimed to have discovered a gold
mine in the Smoky mountains years before the Civil War;
and it is said that he left a "way bill" or chart telling where
it might be found. This chart located it at some point from
which the Little Tennessee river could be seen in three places
coming toward the observer and in three places going from
the observer. No such place has ever been discovered, though
there are points on the Gregory and Parsons Balds from which
the river can be seen in several places. It was said that Delosia claimed he had cut off solid "chunks" of gold with his

hatchet. Many have hunted for it, and many more will continue to seek it, but in vain. Many others had and still have what may very properly be termed the "Delosia Mind," or the belief that sooner or later they would or will discover minerals of untold value in these mountains.

A THRILLING BOAT RIDE. A large whale boat had been built at Robbinsville and hauled to a place on Snowbird creek just below Ab. Moody's, where it was put into the creek, and it was floated down that creek to Cheoah river and thence to Johnson's post-office, where Pat Jenkins then lived. It was hauled from there by wagon to Rocky Point, where, in April, 1893, Calvin Lord, Mike Crise and Sam McFalls, lumbermen working for the Belding Lumber Company, got into it and started down the Little Tennessee on a "tide" or freshet. No one ever expected to see them alive again. But they survived. By catching the overhanging branches when swept toward the northern bank at the mouth of the Cheoah river the crew managed to effect a landing, where they spent the night. They started again the next morning at daylight and got to Rabbit branch, where the men who had been sent to hunt them found them. They spent three days there till the tide subsided, then they went on to the Harden farm, which they reached just one week after leaving Rocky Point. No one has ever attempted this feat since, even when the water was not high. The boat was afterwards taken on to Lenoir City, Tenn.

A FAITHFUL DOG. Many incidents occurred in which our pioneer mothers showed grit equal to that of their intrepid husbands. But there is one of the intelligence and faithfulness of a dog that deserves to be recorded.

William Sawyer, one of the pioneers of that section, was living on Hazel creek, near where the famous Adams-Westfeldt copper lead was afterwards found. He left home one day in 1858, when there was what the natives call a "little blue snow" covering the landscape, taking with him his trusty rifle and his trustier dog. Together they went into the Bone Valley, on Bone creek, one of the head prongs of Hazel creek, and so called because a number of cattle had perished there from cold several years before, their bleaching bones remaining as a reminder of the blizzard that had locked everything in its icy fingers late in a preceding spring.

William Sawyer killed a large bear and proceeded to disembowel and skin him, after which he started home loaded down with bear meat.   But he did not get far before he fell dead in the trail.   The dog remained with him till after midnight, when, being satisfied that his master was dead, he left the cold body in the woods and proceeded back home.   Arriving there just before day, the faithful animal whined and scratched on the door till he was admitted.   Once inside the cabin, he kept up his whining and, catching the skirts of Mrs. Sawyer's dress in his mouth, tried to draw her to the door and outside the house.   Quickly divining the dog's purpose and concluding that he was trying to lead her to her husband, she summoned her neighbors and followed.   She soon discovered the body of her husband, cold and stiff.

AQUILLA ROSE.   This picturesque blockader lives at the head of Eagle creek in Swain county.   Soon after the Civil War he got into a row with a man named Rhodes a mile below Bryson City, and was shot through the body.   As Rose fell, however, he managed to cut his antagonist with a knife, wounding him mortally.   After this he went to Texas and stayed there some time, returning a few years later and settling with his faithful wife at his present home.   It is near the Tennessee line, and if anyone were searching for an inaccessible place at that time he could not have improved on Quil's choice.   He was never arrested for killing Rhodes, self-defence being too evident.   In 1912 he made a mistake about feeding some swill to his hogs and was "haled"—literally hauled —before Judge Boyd at Asheville on a charge of operating an illicit distillery near his peaceful home.   It was his violation of the eleventh commandment, to "never get ketched"; but Quil was getting old and probably needed a dram early in the morning, anyhow.   Judge Boyd was merciful, and it is safe to predict that Quil will keep that eleventh commandment hereafter.

THE GOLDEN CITY.   Wm. H. Herbert owned a large boundary of land in Clay which had been entered for Dr. David Christie of Cincinnati, Ohio, before the Civil War, say about 1857 or 1858, the warrants having been issued to M. L. Brittain and J. R. Dyche, who assigned them to Dr. Christie. He gave bonds to the State in 1859 ; but the Civil War came on and Dr. Christie returned to the North, and failed to pay for them.   On February 27, 1865, the North Carolina legislature passed an act authorizing any person to pay for these lands and take grants from the State for them. Wm. H. Herbert paid what was due on Christie's bonds and took grants for the lands.

He then sold three hundred acres (Grant No. 2989) to Peter Eckels, of Cincinnati, about 1870, and about 1874 Peter Eckels divided this tract into lots (on paper only) calling it The Golden City. But it was "Wild Land" on Tusquittee mountain at the head of Johnson creek, and was not very valuable. He sold several lots, however, to people in Cincinnati and years afterwards vain attempts were made to locate this Golden City.

A LARGE HEART. For several years after the Civil War and up to the time of his death the residence of the late John H. Johnson was the scene of much hospitality. The lawyers hurried through court duties at Murphy, Robbinsville and Hayesville in order to get to spend as much time as possible beneath his roof. It was at a certain hospitable house in Clay county that rose leaves were scattered between the mattresses and the sheets, and the table groaned with the good things provided by the owner, and which were deliciously served by his wife and five charming daughters. One love-sick "limb of the law" is said to have addressed four of them in quick succession one bright Sabbath day in the early seventies only to be rejected by each in turn. It seems that these sisters had told each other of the proposals received, and that the ardent lover had sworn that he loved each one to distraction. So, when he made this declaration to the fourth and youngest, she asked him if he had not made the same protestation of love and devotion to her three elder sisters. He promptly admitted that he had. When she asked him how it was possible for him to love four girls at once, he solemnly assured her that he had a heart as big as a horse collar.

BRUIN MEETS HIS FATE. It is a well authenticated fact that Mrs. Norton, then living in Cashier's Valley, was awakened one night while her husband was away from home, by hearing a great commotion and the squealing of hogs at the hog-pen near by. Her children were small and there was no "man pusson" about the place. The night was cold and she had no time to clothe herself, but, rushing from the cabin in her night dress and with bare feet, she snatched an axe from the wood-pile and hastening to the hog-pen, saw a large, black bear in the act of killing one of her pet "fattening hogs." She did not hesitate an instant, but went on and, aiming a well-directed blow at Bruin's cranium, split it from ears to chin and so had bear meat for breakfast instead of furnishing pork for the daring marauder.

NEDDY DAVIDSON AND "GRANNY" WEISS.[10]   Old Neddy Davidson, of Davidson river, was a mulatto who lived to be very old—some claiming that he was 116 years of age when he died. He was given his freedom by his master, Ben Davidson, and afterwards moved to Canada. But he returned to his old home on Davidson river before his death and about a year before that event Judge Shuford went to his house and spent half the day with him, listening to his stories of old times. He told of frequent fights at the Big Musters then common in this section, and of many other characters. Among the latter was a man named Johnson who used to live on Davidson river and "settled" what is now known as the Old Deaver (locally pronounced Devver) place. Something like one hundred years ago a cattle buyer named Carson stopped all night with Johnson and discovered the following morning that all his money, two or three hundred dollars, was missing. Having no reason to suspect Johnson or his family of the theft, he left for his home. Shortly after his departure Johnson was very seriously affected with gravel and sent for an old woman reputed to be a witch, known as "Granny" Weiss or Weice. She lived on the French Broad river, near the mouth of Davidson's river. On her way to attend the sick man she met his (Johnson's) wife carrying a lot of money. She explained to Granny Weiss that both she and her husband were convinced that his urinary affliction had been visited upon him because he had taken Carson's money and that it would not be relieved till the money had been thrown into the French Broad river.

A PRACTICAL "WITCH."[11]   Well, the story went, that if Granny was a witch, she was a wise and good one. For she immediately put her veto on throwing that money in the French Broad river. She admitted that its theft from Carson by Johnson was the real cause of the latter's sickness; but, insisted that instead of throwing the money into the French Broad the proper course would be to send for Carson, its true owner, and return it to him. This was done. Carson did not prosecute Johnson, but the true story got out and Johnson had to sell his place and move away.

A PATHETIC STORY. Mr. John Lyon of Great Britain was an assiduous collector of our plants, and was probably in these mountains prior to 1802. "He, however, spent several years there at a subsequent period, and died at Asheville in September, 1814, aged forty-nine years." In Riverside cemetery, Asheville, is a small tombstone bearing the following inscription: "In Memory of John Lyon, who departed this life Sept. 14, 1814, aged 49 years." From a letter written by the late Silas McDowell of Macon county, N. C., to Dr. M. A. Curtis, author of "Woody Plants of North Carolina," and dated October, 1877, we learn that Lyon had been "a low, thick-set, small man of fine countenance," and had come from Black Mountain in the early autumn of 1814, sick; that he took a room in the Eagle hotel. Also that for two summers prior to that time he had been seen in Asheville by Mr. McDowell. Lyon and James Johnston, a blacksmith from Kentucky, and a man of great size, had become friends. So, when Lyon took to his bed, Johnston had a bed placed in the same room for his own use, and attended the botanist at night. The boy, Silas McDowell, had also become attached to Mr. Lyon, and on the day of his death had gone to his room earlier than usual. "This day throughout had been one of those clear autumnal days," continues this letter, "when the blue heavens look so transcendantly pure! but now the day was drawing fast to a close, the sun was about sinking behind the distant blue mountains, its rays gleaming through a light haze of fleecy cloud that lay motionless upon the western horizon, and which the sun's rays were changing to that bright golden tint that we can look on and feel, but can't describe. The dying man caught a glimpse of the beautiful scene and observed: 'Friend Johnston, we are having a beautiful sunset—the last I shall ever behold—will you be so kind as to take me to the window and let me look out?' Johnston carried him to the window, took a seat and held the dying man in a position so that his eyes might take in the beautiful scene before him. With seraphic look he gazed intently, uttering the while a low prayer—or rather the soul's outburst of rapturous adoration and praise. After the sun sank out of sight, and the beautiful scene faded out, he exclaimed: 'Beautiful world, farewell! Friend Johnston, lay me down upon my bed—I feel as if I can sleep—I may not awake—kiss me Johnston—now farewell.' He fell asleep in a short time and soon all was still. All of John Lyon that was mortal was dead."

The kind-hearted blacksmith left Asheville soon afterward, but soon met and married a lady of property in Alabama, and had two sons. [12]

Soon after the death of John Lyon friends in Edinburgh, Scotland, sent the tombstone that now marks his grave. His grave had been in the graveyard of the First Presbyterian church, but was removed to Riverside in 1878, the late Col. Allen T. Davidson and Mr. W. S. Cornell, the keeper of the cemetery, bearing the expense.

THE JUDGE, THE WHISTLERS, AND THE GEESE. Judge J. M. Cloud of Salem rode the mountain circuit in 1871 and in 1872. He was a fearless and honest man whose knowledge of law consisted mainly in his knowledge of human nature, and in his own good sense. He was very eccentric and, apparently, the fiercest and sternest of jurists; but he was really a tender hearted gentleman. He was a bachelor and affected to hate whistling and the noise of geese and chickens; but he himself could shake a log house with his snoring. He was very fond of boiled sweet corn. On one occasion one of the lawyers who arrived at a certain noted hostelry at Valley Town in advance of the Judge told the landlady that his Honor had sent word by him to be sure to save him for supper twelve ears of corn and three bundles of fodder, the usual "feed" for a horse! Judge Cloud never forgave this joke. When he got to Asheville, several of the most mischievious young men serenaded him with sweet music at first and then with cat-mewing, tin pans and cow bells. One of their number, Mr. Samuel G. Weldon, made the others believe that the Judge had issued a bench warrant for their arrest for contempt of court, and two of them left town precipitately.

When the Judge got to Bakersville he was annoyed by a gang of geese which prowled the streets around the court house and hissed—hissed—hissed. Judge Cloud called the sheriff and ordered him to kill the geese. The sheriff told Stokes Penland, now living at Pinola, to shut the geese up in a barn till the judge left town. Stokes, a mere boy then, did so. When court "broke," as final adjournment is called, the sheriff presented his bill for $12. "What is this for?" fiercely demanded the judge. "For the twelve geese you ordered me to kill," answered the sheriff. "Show me their dead bodies," returned the Judge "or I'll not pay one cent." The sheriff called up Stokes, thinking he would carry out the joke and pretend that he had actually killed the geese. But he had failed to tell the boy what was expected of him. So he asked him: "What did you do with those twelve geese the judge told me to have killed?" "I shut them up in the barn, and they are there yet," was the surprising but truthful answer. At another court, however, that at Marshall, the geese had really been killed and the judge was forced to pay for them, willy nilly.

AN ASHEVILLE POO BAH. In a municipal campaign in 1874, while the late Albert T. Summey was mayor, he was opposed for re-election by the late Col. John A. Fagg, who declared in a speech that "Squire Summey held a separate office for each day in the week, being mayor on Monday, United States commissioner on Tuesday, justice of the peace on Wednesday, county commissioner on Thursday, chairman of the board of education on Friday, commissioner in bankruptcy on Saturday, and, in Prince Albert coat and silk hat, elder of the Presbyterian church on Sunday. 'Myself and my wife, my son George and his wife, us four and no more.' " .

MURDER OF DANIEL STERNBERGH. In 1874 G. W. Cunningham was arrested, tried and convicted for having killed and robbed Sternbergh of Kansas 6th June, 1874, near Stepp's on the North Fork of the Swannanoa. The case was tried in Madison, and the defendant executed after the Supreme Court had confirmed his conviction. (72 N. C., 469.)

WILL HARRIS, DESPERADO. At midnight, November 13, 1906, policemen Page and C. R. Blackstock were summoned to a house on Eagle street, and when Blackstock opened the rear door he was shot fatally by a mulatto man supposed to have been Will Harris or ———— Abernathy of Mecklenburg. Harris also shot Page in the arm as he went to headquarters to summon help. Harris started up Eagle street and on the way killed Jocko Corpening, a negro, and Ben Addington, also colored. As he turned into South Main Harris shot a hole in the clothes of a negro named George Jackson, and then started towards the square. . Policeman J. W. Bailey started to meet Harris, and placed himself behind a large telegraph post on the northeast corner of the square and South Main; but Harris, with a Savage rifle with steel-jacketed balls, dropped on one knee and fired at the post, the ball passing through it and through Policeman Bailey as well, killing him. Harris turned back down South Main, firing at three white men as he went, and at Kelsey Bell in a second-story window. There was snow that day, but the next Harris was shot to death about eleven o'clock in the forenoon near Fletcher's by a posse in pursuit.

THE LAST "BIG MUSTER." At the last Big Muster in Boone, which occurred on the second Saturday of October, 1861, the militia had a somewhat hilarious time; and after it was over Col. J. B. Todd, then clerk of the court, stood valiantly at the court house door, and vainly waved his sword in a frantic effort to prevent the sheriff and others from riding their horses into the court room, and pawing the big bass drum which some one had placed behind the bar for safe-keeping.

"FREEZING OUT OF JAIL." Joseph T. Wilson, nick-named "Lucky Joe," obtained a change of venue from Watauga to Ashe Superior court at the November term, 1883.[13] He had been indicted for stealing horses from Alloway and Henry Maines of the North Fork; but before he was removed from the Boone jail, a blizzard came on, and one morning Lucky Joe was found in his cell frozen stiff. A doctor pronounced him dead or beyond recovery; but he was taken to the Brick Row, an annex of the old Coffey hotel, and thawed out. Still protesting that he was stiff and frozen he was allowed to remain in that building a day or two, under guard. But one evening at dark the guard locked the door and went out for more fuel. When he returned Lucky Joe was absent. He was tracked through the snow three miles to the Jones place on Rich mountain; but he could not be overtaken. The following spring Alexander Perry, of Burke, captured him in one of the western States and returned him to Ashe, where he was convicted and sentenced to ten years in the penitentiary. There he became superintendent of the prison Sunday School, and had earned an early discharge; but when his baggage came to be examined it was discovered that he had stolen several articles from the penitentiary itself, and he was made to serve

his full term. Upon his return to Watauga he studied law
and tried to be "good" for several years; but at the June Term,
1904, [14] he was convicted under one and pleaded guilty to three
indictments and was sentenced to five years on the Iredell county
roads, where he died soon afterwards. The stories of his
career in Kentucky would fill a volume. He was born in 1846
or 1847, and was a Civil War pensioner.

A LONG-DISTANCE QUARREL. Long before the invention
of telephones two farmers of Beaver Dams, Watauga county,
established the fact that they at least had no need for wires
and electricity, by indulging in the first wireless telegraphy
on record. Elijah Dotson and Alfred Hilliard each owned
a hill-side farm three miles apart. One morning Alf saw
Elijah resting in his field, and jokingly told him to go to work;
whereupon Elijah told Alf to go to a region devoid of snow
and ice. This was the commencement of an oral duel that
lasted half the day, and until the dinner horn summoned
both to the midday meal. The success of this feat was due
to strong lungs rather than to any peculiar carrying power of the
atmosphere of Watauga, though it is the clearest and purest
in the State.

A ROMANCE OF SLAVERY DAYS. On October 16, 1849,
Silas Baker, a slave belonging to Miss Elizabeth Baker,
loved a negro woman named Mill or Millie, the property of William Mast of Valle Crucis. About this time Jacob
Mast, William's uncle, returned from Texas, and the servants
discovered that he would soon marry Elizabeth Baker, and
return with her to Texas. That she would take Silas with
her was most probable; and, unless Jacob Mast should buy
Millie and take her also, these dusky lovers would be separated forever. It is likely that they satisfied themselves that
Jacob would not buy Millie; but probably reasoned that, if
William Mast and his wife were dead, there would be a sale
of his slaves to settle the estate, at which they hoped that
Jacob would buy Millie. So, it is supposed, for there was
never any tangible proof against either, that these two ignorant and infatuated lovers poisoned William Mast and his wife
by putting wild or poison parsnips into their coffee. But the
scheme miscarried; for, though William and his wife died that
day (October 16), Jacob Mast took Silas to Texas with
him, while John Whittington bought Millie and sold her to

people in Tennessee, which effectually parted them forever. Elbert Dinkins of Caldwell county was then teaching school in the neighborhood, and was boarding at William Mast's; and he told Dr. J. B. Phillips of Cove creek the above facts.

ANOTHER VERSION. Will Shull, a respected colored man, who was born March 10, 1832, claims that Millie's motive was revenge for a severe chastisement which she had received at the hands of her master, William Mast, as punishment for having stolen a twenty-dollar gold-piece from his own young master and playmate, Andrew Mast, a son of David and Polly Mast, when she had been at this home washing clothes. Millie had given this money to Charles, another negro, who belonged to John Mast of Sugar Grove, to have changed for her; but Charles took the money to the store of Henry Taylor at that place, and as he and Andrew Mast were courting Emeline and Caroline, the two daughters of John Mast, Taylor asked Andrew if he could change the money for him. When Andrew saw it he recognized it as his own, as he had previously marked it. Charles, of course, laid the blame on Millie, who in turn tried to hold the colored boy Will Shull responsible. When Will heard of Millie's false charge, he loaded a small shotgun which had but recently been given him and started to shoot Millie, but was stopped by Mrs. Polly Mast, who told him Millie had confessed. Millie did not wish to poison Mrs. Mira Mast, who did not usually drink coffee; but on that fatal morning she had partaken with her husband, William Mast, of the potion Millie had prepared for him alone. William Mast was then at work on the bridge over the Watauga, a mile below Shull's Mills, when he was taken sick and got medicine from Philip Shull that morning. Will acquits Sile.

SILAS BAKER AND HIS BUGLE. Rev. L. W. Farthing, however, who remembers Sile well, says that the public sentiment of that day held Sile guilty as the prime mover and instigator of the plot. He says that Sile was a large, impudent black man, between thirty and forty years old, and blew a long tin horn on his way to and from his work—a bugle. This was probably a stage horn; for soon after the opening of the new turnpike down the Watauga river stage coaches ran on it from Abingdon via Mountain City (then Taylorsville), Trade, Sugar Grove, Shulls Mills, Blowing

Rock, and Lenoir, to Lincolnton. They were drawn by four horses and driven by colored drivers, a Mr. Dunn of Abingdon having been the owner of the line. One of the stands or stopping places, where the horses were changed, was at John Mast's at Sugar Grove; another was at Joseph Shull's (where James M. Shull now resides) and one was at the Coffey gap of the Blue Ridge, where Jones Coffey now lives. These stages ran for several years prior to 1861, when they were withdrawn.

JIM SPEER'S FATE. About ten or twelve years prior to the Civil War, four white men of Watauga county, went with James Speer of Beaver Dams to South Carolina. Their names are still remembered by a few of the older citizens. Speer was not considered "right bright," as the expression goes, meaning that while he was not utterly imbecile, he was yet stupid or dense intellectually. He agreed to be blacked and sold as a negro, with the understanding that he was to "wash up" after they had returned home, "escape" from bondage, and share in the proceeds of the sale. All these things were done except the division of the spoils. At the next Big Muster following Jim's return, a quarrel was overheard between him and his confederates in the swindle, during which it is supposed Jim demanded his share and threatened "to let the cat out of the bag" if it was not forthcoming. He returned to his home on Beaver Dams and shortly afterwards disappeared forever. It was supposed that he had been done away with. About 1893 John K. Perry, Esq., found a human skeleton in the cliffs in the rear of his dwelling on Beaver Dams, and still has the skull in his possession. These are supposed to be the remains of Jim Speer. [15]

JOSHUA PENNELL. In 1859 or 1860, Joshua Pennell of Wilkes left a will setting all his slaves free, and providing for their removal to a Free State, and their support there until they could raise a crop. Pennell was a bachelor. Joshua Winkler was made executor, and old citizens of Boone remember seeing him and the negroes pass through that town one bright Sabbath morning on their way to Kansas. Henry C. Pearson, Winkler's brother-in-law, accompanied them also. [16]

"A WANDERING MINSTREL HE." During the seventies, William Murphy of Greenville, S. C., wandered through these mountains making music every day. He, like Stephen

Foster, was regarded as a half-vagabond, but he was tolerated for the pleasure his enchanted violin gave whenever he drew his magic bow across its strings. There can be little doubt that men of his genius feel the indifference and neglect of their contemporaries; and it may be that, from their Calvaries of poverty, they, too, realize that we know not what we do. For to them the making of music is their sole mission here upon earth, and come poverty, obscurity or death, ay, come even disgrace and obliquy, they, like Martin Luther at Worms, "can do no otherwise, God helping them." Indeed, it is the highest form of worship, and David's Psalms still live while all the Ptolemies of the past have been forgotten. Foster's songs are linking earth to heaven more and more as time goes on, and will be sung for eons and for eons. There can be no higher destiny than that a man should pour out his full soul in strains of haunting melody; and though Stephen Foster be dead and "the lark become a sightless song," the legacy he has left behind him is more priceless and more bountiful than those of the builders of the pyramids or the conquests of Napoleon and Alexander.

Murphy, too, is dead, but while he lived, like the grasshopper "beating his tiny cymbals in the sun," he poured forth those matchless orisons that none who ever heard them can soon forget. For, while he was not a creator, he was the slave and seneschal of the masters who have left their melodies behind them for the ravishment of a money-mad and sordid world. And when he drew his magic bow across his violin's sentient strings, his genius thence evoked sweet strains informed with soul to all who had the heart to comprehend their message and their meaning.

Was it a jig or waltz or stately minuet? one's feet moved rythmically to the "sweet melodic phrase." Was it dirge, lament or lovelorn lilt? one saw again the hearse-plumes nod, sobbed out his heart with pallid Jeane, or caught the note of bonny bird blythe fluting by the Doon. Was it martial air or battle-hymn? then, once again, came forth the bagpipe's skirl, the pibroch's wail, "what time the plaided clans came down to battle with Montrose." Again, with change of air, there dawned once more that "reddest day in history, when Pickett's legions, undismayed, leapt forth to ruin's red embrace."

But best, ah, far, far best of all, was that wonder-woven race his fine dramatic instinct had translated into song, in which the section-riven days of 'Sixty-one were conjured back again from out their graves and ghostly crements, and masqueraded full of life and hate and jealousy. For then we saw, as if by magic, the mighty racer, Black Hawk, typifying the North, and his unconquerable rival, Gray Eagle, the steel-sinewed champion of the South, start once again on that matchless contest on the turf at Louisville. We heard again the wild, divided concourse cheer its favorite steed along the track, and saw the straining stallions, foam-flecked with sweat—now neck and neck, then one ahead, but soon overtaken, and both flying side by side again, their flame-shot nostrils dripping blood—till Gray Hawk, spent, but in the lead, dropped dead an inch without the goal, his great heart broken, as the South's was doomed to be a few years thence, when

"Men saw a gray, gigantic ghost
Receding through the battle-cloud ;
And heard across the tempest loud
The death-cry of a nation lost!"

THE VALLEY OF COUSINS. Valle Crucis is also called the Valley of Cousins because of the kinship between most of its inhabitants. Ex-Sheriff David F. Baird, a descendant of Bedent, says that all of Valle Crucis between the ford of the river on the road to Cove creek up to the ford at Shipley's home was sold by the original Hix who came to this section, for a shot-gun, a pair of leggins and a hound dog. A man named Hix was drowned in a "hole" of water in Watauga river below D. F. Baird's farm, and the place is called the "Hix Hole" yet. This original Samuel Hix was the first settler of this valley, but Bedent Baird was not long behind him. Bedent's son Franklin was the father of David F. Baird, who was born June 10, 1835, and was sheriff from 1882 till 1886, and from 1890 till 1894. He went with his uncle Joel Moody to carry the body of Rev. Wm. Thurston from its place of temporary burial at Valle Crucis to Pittsboro, N. C., in 1856. Another prominent family of this section, which has inter-married with the Baird family, is that of the Shulls. Frederick Shull and his wife came from Germany about the year 1750. He was a weaver and paid for their voyage by weaving while his wife worked in the field. Her name was Charity.

Simon Shull was a son of this marriage, and the father of
seven children by his wife, Mary Sheifler, a daughter of
Phillip and Mary Ormatenfer Sheifler. She was born in
Loudon county, Va., May 5, 1772. Simon Shull was born
in Lincoln county, October 24, 1767. Simon Shull's children
were Mary, Sarah, Phillip, John, Joseph, Temperance and
Elizabeth, born between March 19, 1793, and April 10, 1808.
Joseph was the father of James M. Shull, and Phillip of
Joseph C. Shull. Simon Shull was married on Upper creek,
Burke county, by Rev. William Penland, March 25, 1790,
and died February 12, 1813.

OTHER CLOSELY RELATED FAMILIES. Reuben Mast first
lived where David F. Baird now lives, but the place had been
settled before Mast went there. Reuben Mast sold it to John
Gragg about 1849, and moved to Texas, where he died.
Gragg lived there till 1867 and sold to David Wagner, and
moved to Tennessee. David Wagner divided the place
among his three sons, and David F. Baird bought the shares
of John and Daniel Wagner on the east side of the river,
about 1874. He had married a sister of these two Wagners
in 1870. Joel Mast lived below the road at the place where
T. Hardee Taylor lives. David Mast lived where Finley
Mast now lives. John Mast lived at Sugar Grove, while
Noah Mast lived on Watauga river where Wm. Winkler now
lives. These were brothers. Henry Taylor came to Sugar
Grove from Davidson county about 1849 and went into mer-
chandising there. He married Emaline, daughter of John
Mast, buying the Joel Mast farm at public auction. Taylor
then moved to Valle Crucis, and bought the place where
his son, T. Hardee Taylor, now lives from Joel Mast about
1850 or 1851. He made his money by selling to those who
earned wages by the building of the turnpike. He was born
August 20, 1819. His wife was born January 5, 1826. They
had six children. After her death, September 21, 1880, he
married Rachel Gray, by whom he had four children. He
died March 6, 1899, and his last wife died March 3 of the
same year. He bought the Ives land from Robert Miller
before the Civil War. Into the valley of Cove creek in 1791
came Cutliff Harmon, from Randolph county, and bought
522 acres from James Gwyn, to whom it had been granted
May 18, 1791, his deed from Gwyn bearing date August 6,

1791. Cutliff married Susan Fouts, and was about ninety years of age when he died in 1838, his wife having died several years before, and he having married Elizabeth Parker, a widow. He had ten children by his first marriage, none by his second. Among his children were Mary, who married Bedent Baird; Andrew, who married Sabra Hix; Eli, who married the widow Rhoda Dyer (born Dugger); Mathias, who married and moved to Indiana; Catherine, who married Benjamin Ward, and went west; Rebecca, who married Frank Adams and moved to Indiana; Rachel, who married Holden Davis; Sarah, who married John Mast; Nancy, who married Thomas Curtis, and Rev. D. C. Harmon, born April 17, 1826, and died December 23, 1904. Among those who came about the time Cutliff did were the Eggers, Smith, Councill, Horton, Dugger, Mast and Hix families. The farm Cutliff bought is now owned by M. C., D. F. and D. C. Harmon. "Patch farming" was the rule, the settlers going to the Globe on Johns river for corn, as they raised only rye, buckwheat, Irish potatoes, cabbages, onions and pumpkins on the new and cold land of Watauga river. A common diet was milk and mush for breakfast and soup and cider for dinner and supper, according to Malden C. Harmon in the *Watauga Democrat* of April, 1891. The intermarriage of these families has brought about a neighborhood of closely related citizens, and Cove Creek and Valle Crucis are spoken of as the Valley of Cousins, Sugar Grove being also a part of Valle Crucis. Just down Watauga river from Valle Crucis is another settlement called Watauga Falls. Among the first to settle there was Benjamin Ward, who had seven sons, Duke, Daniel, Benjamin, Nicodemus, McCaleb, Jesse and James. He also had three daughters, one of whom was named Celia. Benjamin Ward, Sr., was a most enterprising and worthy man, and his widow lived to be 105 years of age, while their son Ben lived to be 110. Duke married Sabra, widow of Andrew Harmon, and moved to Illinois. Ben. Jr., went to Cumberland gap, and his son Duke came back and married Lucy Tester; while Amos, son of Duke, Sr., came back from Illinois and married Sally, sister of Lucy Tester. They had two sons, L. D. and John, the latter having been killed before Richmond in 1863.

W. N. C.—23

SAMUEL HIX, LOYALIST.   According to Rev. L. W. Farthing, who was born April 18, 1838, and has lived in Beaver
Dam township and at Watauga Falls postoffice all his long
life, Samuel was the name of the first Hix who came to what
is now Watauga county.   He got possession of all of what
is now known as Valle Crucis, including the Sheriff Baird
farm, either by grant from the Crown or from the State, and
was there during the Revolutionary War.   Being a Loyalist
he kept himself concealed by retiring to a shanty near Valle
Crucis, still pointed out as his "Improvement."   He sold the
Valle Crucis land for a rifle, dog and sheepskin to Benjamin
Ward, the latter later selling it to Reuben Mast.   Hix then
got possession of the land at the mouth of Cove creek, but
Ward got this also and sold it to a family named Summers.
This family, consisting of man and wife and five children,
were all drowned in their cabin at night during a freshet in
the Watauga river, and their dog swam about the cabin and
would allow no one to enter till it had been killed.   This is
still spoken of as the "Summers Fresh"— the highest anyone
now remembers.   The bodies of the family were recovered
and are buried on the opposite side of the river from the
mouth of Cove creek.   Samuel Hix in 1816 obtained a grant
to 126 acres, on part of which Rev. L. W. Farthing now lives,
and his grave-stone still stands three miles below St. Judes
postoffice, and a quarter of a mile below Antioch Baptist
church.   Benjamin Howard took the oath of allegiance to
the American government in 1778 (Col. Rec., Vol. 22, page
172), but Samuel Hix seems never to have become reconciled.   Even after the war he hid out, coming home at dark
for his supplies.   His five boys were mischievous, and they
manufactured a pistol out of a buck's horn, which they fired
by applying a live coal to the touch-hole, when their father
returned from the house carrying his rations, thus fright-
ening him so much that he would drop them and return to
his concealed camp in the mountains.   The children of Samuel Hix were Golder, David, Samuel, Harmon and William;
Sally, who married Barney Oaks; Sabra, who married Andrew
Harmon, who was killed by a falling tree on L. W. Farthing's
present farm, and Fanny who never married.   Samuel Hix
cared more about hunting than anything else, and it was
said he knew where there was a lead mine in the mountains

out of which he ran his own bullets. James Hix and James (?) Tester, were drowned in what is still known as the Hix "Hole" in Watauga river below Sheriff Baird's farm, and Sam Tester rode his bull into the water in order to recover the two bodies, about 1835. Samuel Hix had a negro slave named Jeff, and two apple trees planted soon after his removal to the L. W. Farthing place, one at Samuel's cabin and the other at Jeff's, lived till within recent years.

NOTES.

[1]"Asheville's Centenary."
[2]Ibid.
[3]Stokes Penland's statement, October, 1912, at Pinola.
[4]Chapter seven of "Dropped Stitches."
[5]Account by T. L. Lowe, Esq.
[6]From "The Heart of the Alleghanies," p. 271.
[7]So called from its fancied resemblance to a bunk.
[8]Letter of Col. D. K. Collins to J. P. A., June 7, 1912.
[9]Frequently called "mind" for mine.
[10]Related by Judge G. A. Shuford.
[11]Ibid.
[12]From same letter.
[13]Minute Docket B, p. 202, Watauga.
[14]Ibid., E, p. 352.
[15]Statements of J. K. Perry and W. L. Bryan, May, 1913.
[16]Statement of W. L. Bryan, July, 1913.

CHAPTER XIV

DUELS

THE LAW OF DUELING. From the beginning of the nineteenth century the practice of dueling had been common
throughout America, the North, even, not being exempt, as
witness the fatal encounter between Aaron Burr and Alexander Hamilton. North Carolina had, in 1802, (Rev. Stat.,
Ch. 34, sec. 3) made it a crime to send a challenge or fight a
duel or to aid or abet in doing either; but, according to the
strict letter of the law, it would be no crime to send a challenge from without the State or to fight a duel on the soil of
another State, and in all the duels fought in this section great
care was taken to go across the State line into either South
Carolina or Tennessee. No effort, apparently, was ever
made to punish those who as principals, seconds or surgeons
had participated in such encounters, it having been considered
that the law of North Carolina had not been violated unless
the duel had actually been fought on its soil. No duel was
fought within the State; but in the Erwin-Baxter and the
Hilliard-Hyman duels, the challenges had most probably been
sent and accepted in Buncombe county. However, as such
matters were of a secret and confidential nature, it is likely
that no evidence of such challenges was ever presented to a
grand jury of that county, as, if it had been, true bills would
doubtless have been returned against those charged with
having sent or accepted the challenges. For dueling was
never approved by the common people of this section, and
its practice was confined strictly to a small class of profes-
sional men and politicians. The quarrels of farmers, merchants and others were settled in the good old fist and skull,
or rough and tumble, style, in which knives and pistols were
never used. Section two of Article XIV of the Constitution
of North Carolina of 1868 gave dueling its death blow forever; for, while there is nothing more sacred than a politician's
honor, prior to 1868 nothing had been found that could prevent him from fighting duels for its preservation; whereas,
the moment he discovered that unless he found some other
means of protecting it he would have to forego the honor of

A. C. AVERY.

holding office in North Carolina, he immediately and forth-with discovered a way!

THE JACKSON-AVERY DUEL. At some time prior to the admission of Tennessee into the Union Andrew Jackson and Waightstill Avery, lawyers, fought a duel on "the hill on the south side of Jonesboro, Tenn. It seems to have been arranged that neither party desired to injure the other, and both fired into the air, pistols being the weapons used. John Adair was Avery's second, Jackson's being unknown.

"There are two versions as to the cause of the duel, the first being that Jackson had ridiculed Avery's pet authority—Bacon's Abridgment—and Avery, in his retort, had grown, as he afterwards admitted, too sarcastic, intimating that Jackson had much to learn before he would be competent to criticise any law book whatever. Jackson sprang to his feet and cried: 'I may not know as much law as there is in Ba-con's Abridgment, but I know enough not to take illegal fees.' Avery at once demanded whether he meant to charge him with taking illegal fees, and Jackson answered 'I do, sir,' meaning to add that he had done so because of his ignor-ance of the latest law fixing a schedule of fees. But Avery had not waited for him to finish his sentence and hissed in Jackson's teeth 'It's as false as hell.' Then Jackson had challenged Avery and Avery had accepted the challenge. When they had arrived on the ground and exchanged shots, they shook hands; after which Jackson took from under his arm a package which he presented to Avery, saying that he knew that if he had hit Avery and had not killed him the greatest comfort he could have would be Bacon's Abridg-ment.' When the parcel was opened it contained, cut to the exact size of a law book, a piece of well cured bacon.

"The other version is that Avery promised to produce Bacon's Abridgment in court the following morning and that Jackson had gone to Avery's room and removing the book had sub-stituted a piece of bacon in its stead in Avery's green bag. When Avery opened this bag in court the next day and the bacon fell out, he was so incensed that he challenged Jackson at once. The challenge had been accepted and shots ex-changed, whereupon each had expressed himself as satisfied and the matter ended." [1]

COL. F. A. OLDS' ACCOUNT.   In *Harper's Weekly* for December 31, 1904, is an account of this duel which had and still has the approval of Hon. Alfonzo C. Avery, oldest descendant then living of Hon. Waightstill Avery.   It contains the challenge, which follows:

August 12, 1788.

Sir :

When a man's feelings & character are injured he ought to seek a speedy redress; you recd a few lines from me yesterday & undoubtedly you understand me.   My character you have Injured; and further you have insulted me in the presence of a court and a large audience.   I therefore call upon you as a gentleman to give me satisfaction for the same.   I further call upon you to give me an answer immediately without Equivocation and I hope you can do without dinner until the business is done; for it is consistent with the character of a gentleman when he Injures a man to make speedy reparation; therefore I hope you will not fail in meeting me this day from yr Hbl. St.

Col. Avery.   Yrs. ANDW. JACKSON.

"P. S.—This Evening after court is adjourned."

THE FACTS OF THE CASE.   These were told to Judge A. C. Avery by his father Col. Isaac T. Avery, who was the only son of Waightstill Avery. "When the latter practiced law in Mecklenburg, N. C., he and young Jackson were well acquainted.   Avery was elected in 1777 the first attorney general of North Carolina.   He afterwards married a lady who lived near Newberne, in Jones county, and soon after this marriage resigned and settled in Jones, becoming colonel of that county's regiment of militia.   His command was not in active service during the Revolution, except in some occasional troubles with the Tories, until it was called out when Lord Cornwallis invaded North Carolina. . . .   He secured the passage of a bill creating the county of Washington, which embraced the whole State of Tennessee, and then became the leading member of the bar at Jonesboro, which was the county seat.   At the close of the Revolutionary War Andrew Jackson went to Burke county and applied to Waightstill Avery to take him as a boarder at his country home and instruct him as a law student.   Col. Avery told him he had just moved to the place, and had built nothing but cabins, and could not grant his request.   Jackson went to Salisbury, studied law there [under Judge Spruce McCay], and settled at Jonesboro, until the new county of Davidson (with Nashville as the county seat) was established. . . .   Just before the challenge to fight was sent by Jackson, Avery appeared in some lawsuit at Jonesboro as opposing counsel to Jackson, and ridiculed the position taken by Jackson, who had preceded him in argument. Jackson considered the argument insulting and sent him the challenge. Col. Avery was raised a Puritan. He graduated at Princeton with the highest honors in 1766, and remained there a year as a tutor, under the celebrated Jonathan Edwards and the famous Dr. Witherspoon, who signed the Declaration of Independence as a representative of New Jersey. Avery was a Presbyterian and opposed on principle to dueling, but he so far yielded to the imperious custom of the time as to accept the challenge and go to the field, with Colonel, afterwards Governor, Adair of Kentucky as his second. After the usual preliminaries he allowed Jackson to shoot at him, but did not return the fire. Thereupon, having shown that he was not afraid to be shot at, Avery walked up to young Jackson and delivered a lecture to him, very much in the style a father would use in lecturing a son. Avery was very calm, and his talk to the brave young man who had fired at him was full of good sense, dispassionate and high in tone, and was heard with great attention by the seconds of both parties, who agreed that the trouble must go no further, but should end at this point, and so then and there a reconciliation was effected between these two brave spirits. Col. Avery took the challenge home and filed it, as he was accustomed to file all his letters and papers, endorsing it 'Challenge from Andrew Jackson.'"

THE VANCE–CARSON DUEL. To the late Silas McDowell of Macon county we are indebted for many facts concerning the duel between Dr. Robert Brank Vance of Buncombe and Hon. Samuel P. Carson of Burke. Mr. McDowell was the friend of both these gentlemen; and, although he waited forty-nine years after the duel had been fought, and he himself was in his eighty-first year before committing his recollection of that lamentable event to paper, it must be accepted as the most authentic, because the only, account now available of that affair. Hon. A. C. Avery of Morganton, in an article published in the *North Carolina Review* (Raleigh) for March, 1913, has supplemented this statement with many important facts bearing on the principals and seconds concerned; and from these two statements the following facts have been carefully compiled:

SAMUEL P. CARSON. He was the son of Col. John Carson and of his wife, who, before her marriage to him, had been the widow of the late Gen. Joseph McDowell of Pleasant Gardens, N. C. He, like his father, was a Democrat, and was young, handsome, eloquent, magnetic, blessed with a charming voice, delighting in all the pleasures and opportunities of a healthful, vigorous physique. He was educated at the "Old Field Schools" of the neighborhood till he reached his nineteenth year, when he was taken into the family of his half brother, Joseph M. Carson, where he was taught grammar and directed in a course of reading with an eye to political advancement; and before he was 22 years of age he represented the county of Burke in the legislature, defeating his kinsman James R. McDowell for that place. He was born about the year 1797, and was about four years younger than Dr. Vance. Even when a boy he was a great favorite not only with people of his own walk in life, but was worshipped by the negroes on his father's plantation. His mother was a Methodist and young Samuel was a great favorite at camp meetings where his deep-toned and harmonious voice led in their congregational singing. He was also popular with ladies.

GEN. ALNEY BURGIN. He was Carson's second, and was a social and political leader of Burke county, having several times been elected to the legislature. He preserved the challenge which Mr. Carson sent by him to Dr. Vance. This challenge had been written by Carson at Pleasant Gardens and was dated September 12, 1827, taken to Jonesboro, Tenn., and sent from there in order to avoid a violation of the law of North Carolina regarding dueling; for he states in the challenge: "I will do no act in violation of the laws of my State; but as you have boasted that you had *flung* the *gauntlet* before me, which in point of fact is not true; for, in the language of chivalry, to fling the gauntlet is to *challenge*—to throw down the iron glove; . . . but, if you are serious, *make good* your boast; throw the gauntlet upon *neutral ground*; then, if not accepted, boast your victory." He notified Dr. Vance that he would pass through Asheville to meet friends in East Tennessee, where he would spend a week at Jonesboro, and expected to receive an answer by way of Old Fort, near which place Gen. Burgin lived. His son,

Joseph McD. Burgin, was the father of Mrs. Locke Craig, the wife of the present governor.

HON. WARREN DAVIS. This gentleman was a South Carolinian, a cousin of John C. Calhoun, a member of Congress, a man of decided ability, and "thoroughly conversant with the intricate rules of the Code Duello." He was called in by Mr. Carson as an additional second because Gen. Burgin was not well versed in the punctillio of the duello, and Davis "was expected in the arrangements for the encounter and any correspondence that might ensue, to protect Carson."

ROBERT BRANK VANCE. He was born in Burke county about 1793, and was the son of David Vance, who, after serving as an ensign under Washington, married the daughter of Peter Brank, who lived about a mile from Morganton, and fought as captain of a company in McDowell's regiment at Ramseur's Mill, Cowpens and Kings Mountain, while his uncle, Robert Brank, for whom Dr. Vance was named, had the reputation of being one of the most daring soldiers in his company. Young Vance was a fine scholar as a school boy; but, owing to an affliction which had settled in his left leg, that member had been shortened about six inches and so retarded his physical development that when fully grown he was only five feet and five inches in height. His face, however, was handsome, and his "mind was of no common order." His family were Presbyterians and he attended the Newton academy near Asheville, afterwards graduating from an unnamed medical school and commencing the practice of medicine in Asheville in 1818. But, having drawn a five-thousand-dollar prize in a lottery, and his father having willed him a large portion of his estate, Dr. Vance purchased a fine library and retired from practice three years after opening his office. He was encouraged by his friends, and especially by young Samuel P. Carson, then in the legislature from Burke, to oppose Felix Walker, whose popularity then "was in the descending node," for Congress, but declined to do so till 1823, when he ran for Congress and was elected by a majority of one vote. It was said that when he appeared in Congress John Randolph of Roanoke, struck by his diminutive size and physical deformity, remarked, "Surely that little man has come to apply for a pension." But Vance soon convinced the strong men of the house "that Aesop's mind could be hid,

but not long, under an Aesop's form, and at the close of the term
he had the respect of every distinguished man in the house."
The most important measure before the session was an appropriation of $250,000—"and many townships of land" for
Gen. Lafayette; and for this measure Vance voted.

FRIENDS BECOME POLITICAL RIVALS.   In 1825 Samuel P.
Carson and Dr. Vance were opposing candidates for Congress,
and Carson was elected; but in 1827 Dr. Vance invited some
of his friends to meet at Asheville, and announced that he
would oppose Carson's re-election, and would insist on his defeat because he had voted for an appropriation of $25,000 to
the citizens of Alexandria, Virginia, which had been recently destroyed by fire. To this meeting Silas McDowell was invited, but
his opposition to Vance's idea that Carson could be defeated
because of this vote displeased all of Vance's friends, but
not Vance himself. Vance and Carson accordingly were
opposing candidates in 1827, and at the first meeting at Asheville Carson spoke first; but, in reviewing his course in Congress,
he omitted to refer to his vote for the appropriation for the citizens of Alexandria.   When Dr. Vance spoke he called attention to the fact that Carson had not referred to that vote,
whereupon Carson answered that the city had been destroyed
by fire and its citizens left homeless and destitute; and that
Vance himself, if he had been in Carson's place, would have
voted likewise, because "I think he has a heart." Vance
retorted that if those who had applauded Carson's statement
"could admire, as some seem to do, the heart promptings
that send a man's benevolent hand into some other man's
pocket than his own, all I have to say about it is—I can't."
Upon this Carson answered that "until Vance should withdraw the charge that he had put his hand into another's
pocket to save his own," they could be friends no longer;
and proceeded to charge Vance with inconsistency as he
himself had voted when in congress for the larger donation
to Lafayette.   Thereupon Vance charged Carson with being
a demagogue, and when Carson replied that but for Vance's
diminutive size he would hold him to account for his "vile
utterances," Vance retorted: "You are a coward and fear
to do it." This closed the debate.

THE CASUS BELLI.   According to Mr. McDowell, Carson's failure to challenge Vance, after having been publicly

called a coward, confirmed Vance in his belief that he would not
fight; this idea of Carson's cowardice having been suggested
in the first instance by Carson's refusal to accept a challenge
from Hugh M. Stokes, a lawyer, and a son of Gen. Mumford
Stokes of Wilkes, on the alleged ground that young Stokes
had forfeited his right to recognition as a gentleman because
of his intemperate indulgence in strong drink. A second
meeting of Vance's friends was soon held at Asheville, but
from it Silas McDowell was excluded. There it was determined that Vance should attack the character of Carson's
father "on a floating tradition that, after the defeat of our
army at Camden, Carson, with many other hitherto patriotic
citizens of North Carolina, had applied to Cornwallis, while
near Charlotte, to protect their property. The tradition went
so far as to include many of the patriotic men of Mecklenburg
county. Up to this day that tradition is an historic doubt."
But Judge Avery points out that Col. John Carson had been
elected by the people of Burke to attend the convention held
at Fayetteville for the Constitution of 1787 of the United
States, as a sufficient refutation of the charge as applied to
him. But, at the next joint debate, which was at Morganton,
Vance used these words: "The Bible tells us that 'because
the fathers have eaten sour grapes, their sons' teeth have
been set on edge.' . . . My father never ate sour grapes
and my competitor's father did. . . . In the time of the
Revolutionary War my father, Col. Vance, stood up to fight,
while my competitor's father, Col. Carson, skulked, and took
British protection."

THE INSULT IS RESENTED. All of Samuel P. Carson's
brothers were present when this statement was made "and
made a move as though they would attack Vance, when
prominent citizens interfered and the excitement calmed
down." The election resulted in Vance's defeat, three to
one, Vance getting only 2,419 votes. Afterwards, "Col.
Carson wrote Vance an ill-natured and abusive letter, to which
Vance sent the brief reply. . . . 'I can have no alterca-
tion with a man of your age; and, if I have aggrieved you,
you certainly have some of your chivalrous sons that will
protect you from insult.' A few days thereafter Gen. Alney
Burgin came to Asheville . . . to enquire which one
of Colonel Carson's sons Vance alluded to in his lines to his

father," and Vance replied "Sam knows well enough I meant him." Then the challenge was delivered and accepted.

THE DUEL. It was agreed that three weeks should elapse before the duel, which was to be fought at Saluda Gap, on the line between North and South Carolina, on the Greenville turnpike. Gen. Franklin Patton was Vance's second and Dr. George Phillips his surgeon, while Dr. Shuflin was Carson's surgeon. "A few special friends attended as spectators, and, though invited by both gentlemen," Mr. McDowell did not go. Davy Crockett, who, according to Dr. Sondley, in "Asheville's Centenary," had married a Miss Patton, of Swannanoa, is said to have been present as a friend of Carson's. The distance was ten paces and the firing was to be done between the words "Fire, One, Two, Three," with rising or falling pistols. Vance chose the rising and Carson the falling mode; and at the word "Fire," Carson sent a ball entirely through Vance's body, entering one and a half inches above the point of the hip and lodging in the skin on the opposite side. It does not appear that Vance fired at all. Vance died the next day, thirty-two hours after having received his wound, at a hotel on the road, probably Davis's.

CONTRITION. When he saw that Vance had been wounded Carson expressed a wish to speak to him, but was led away; and before his death Vance expressed regret that Carson had not been permitted to speak with him, and stated that he had "not the first unkind feeling for him." Vance also told Gen. Burgin that he had fallen where he had always wished to die—"on the field of honor." He was buried at the family grave-yard on Reems creek.

CARSON'S SUBSEQUENT CAREER. Mr. Carson went on to Congress after the duel, was elected a delegate to the State convention of 1835, moved to Texas and became Secretary of State in David G. Burnett's cabinet, never returning to North Carolina. The result of this duel is said to have embittered his life. Mr. McDowell hints at an attachment for Miss Donaldson, the pretty niece of Andrew Jackson; but Carson died unmarried.

PREMONITION. It is quite evident that Vance expected to be killed; for he made his will (dated November 3, 1827) in which he referred to the approaching duel, and after his death it was admitted to probate, though, when the court house was destroyed in the spring of 1865, the record book containing it was destroyed. Fortunately, however, a certified copy had been obtained prior to the fire, which copy is still in existence. [2] Judge Avery also states that Dr. Vance stopped at his father's house on his way to the dueling ground "and though almost everyone knew what was about to occur, no allusion was made to it by the family in conversation with their guest. The impression was made on some of the family that Vance seemed sad. Though recklessly fearless, it was natural that he should seem depressed in view of the prospect that he or Carson, or both, would probably be killed."

VANCE'S MOTIVE. Although Mr. McDowell had been "excluded" from the second conference between Vance and his friends at Asheville, he and Dr. Vance lodged at the same house at Morganton, and he said: "When Vance returned to our room . . . I remarked to him, 'Doctor, you have this day sounded the death knell over yours or Carson's grave—perhaps both.' To this Vance answered: 'There is no fight in Carson. I wish he would fight and kill me. Do you wish to know why? I will tell you: My life has no future prospect. All before me is deep, dark gloom, my way to Congress being closed forever, and to fall back upon my profession or former resources of enjoyment makes me shudder to think of. Understand me, McDowell, I have no wish to kill or injure Carson; but I do wish for him to kill me, as, perhaps, it would save me from self-slaughter.'" Would such a statement have been made except to a trusted friend and under the sacred seal of friendship?

COL. JOHN CARSON'S IMPLACABILITY. Judge Avery tells us that, after the Morganton insult, Col. Carson agreed to forego his privilege of challenging Vance only upon the promise of his six sons that if "Samuel Carson should first challenge Vance, and, if he should fall, then the oldest son, Joseph McDowell Carson, should challenge him, and if every one of the six should fall in separate encounters with Vance, then the old Colonel should be at liberty to wipe out the insult to the family by meeting Vance on the field of honor." He adds: "Vance was not only mistaken in expecting a back down, but in fact he was provoking a difficulty with six cool and courageous men, everyone of whom was a crack marksman." But that was not all. Judge Avery further states that Warren Davis, Carson's second, refused to "act as his second unless he would promise to do his best or use his utmost skill to hit Vance." Dr. Vance must have known who Davis was and why he had been brought from South Carolina, as well as of the marksmanship of the six Carsons; and that he had deliberately offered a deadly insult to the venerable head of an old and distinguished family because he believed that Samuel P. Carson would not fight is almost incredible. That Dr. Vance should wish to be killed by his boyhood's friend is even more unbelievable. But, whatever his motive, criticism of his conduct was silenced above his open grave; for he went to his death with a courage that was sublime; and for more than three quarters of a century censure has remained dumb, "with a finger on her lips and a meaning in her eyes."

JUDGE AVERY'S ACCOUNT. In his "Historic Homes of North Carolina" (in the N. C. Booklet, Vol. IV, No. 3) the late Hon. A. C. Avery recorded the fact that on the night after the debate between Vance and Carson at Morganton, Samuel P. Carson, his six brothers and his father agreed that if the father would not challenge Vance Samuel would do so, and if he fell each son in succession should challenge Vance till he should be killed. In the event that all the seven Carson sons should fall, then, Col. Carson, the father would send a challenge. It is also stated that Carson went to Tennessee to send the challenge in order not to violate the law of this state; and that David Crockett was one of Carson's friends at the duel. Just before taking his position on the field Carson told Warren Davis that he (Carson) could hit Vance wherever he chose, but preferred not to inflict a mortal wound. Thereupon, Davis said: "Vance will try to kill you, and if he receives only a flesh wound, he will demand another shot, which will mean another chance to kill you. I will not act for you unless you promise to do your best to kill him." Carson promised, and Vance fell mortally wounded, Carson lamenting that the demands of an imperious custom had forced him to wreck his own peace of mind in order to save the honor of his family. In 1835 Carson was elected to the Constitutional Convention of that year. He emigrated to Texas in 1836, was a member of the Constitutional Convention of 1836 in that State, and Sam Houston made him secretary of State. Carson was active in securing the annexation of Texas. The Biographical Congressional Directory, 1911, says that Carson "after his retirement from Congress moved to Arkansas; died

in Hot Springs, Ark., in November, 1840" (p. 532).   The
same work (p. 1076) says that Vance "moved to Nashville,
Nash county, where he held several local positions." All
of which is wrong.   It does not give the date of his birth or
of his death

THE CLINGMAN–YANCEY DUEL.[3] "Although kind, social
and friendly in his private intercourse, Gen. Thomas L. Clingman's character is not of that negative kind so concisely
described by Dr. Johnson of one 'who never had generosity
enough to acquire a friend, or spirit enough to provoke an
enemy.'   Whenever the rights of his State and his personal
honor were infringed, he was prompt and ready to repel the
assailant.   He has followed the advice of Polonius to his son:

> ' Beware of entrance
> Into a quarrel; but being in,
> So bear thyself that thy opposer
> Will beware of thee.'

"In 1845, Hon. William Yancey, of Alabama, well known
in his day as 'a rabid fire eater,' attempted some liberty with
General Clingman.   A challenge ensued.   Huger, of South
Carolina, was Yancey's friend; and Charles Lee Jones, of
Washington City, was the friend of Clingman.   They fought
at Bladenburg.

"Mr. Jones, the second of General Clingman, in his graphic
description of this duel, published in the *Capital*, states:

" 'After the principles had been posted, Mr Huger, who had won the
giving of the word, asked, "Are you ready?   FIRE !"'
" 'Mr Clingman, who had remained perfectly cool, fired, missing his
adversary, but drawing his fire, in the ground, considerably out of line,
the bullet scattering dust and gravel upon the person of Mr. Clingman.
After this fire the difficulty was adjusted.'

"Hon. Kenneth Rayner, the colleague of Mr. Clingman
in Congress, who was on the ground, states that 'he had never
seen more composure and firmness in danger than was manifested by Mr. Clingman on this occasion.'   On seeing his friend
covered by the dust and gravel, and standing at his post
unmoved he thought he was mortally wounded.   He rushed
to him and asked him if he was hurt.   'He has thrown some
dirt on my new coat,' he replied.   . . .   On other occasions,
as with Hon. Edward Stanley and others, Gen. Clingman
has evidenced a proper regard for his own honor by repelling
the insults of others. "

ERWIN-BAXTER DUEL. At some time between 1851 and 1857 the late Major Marcus Erwin and the late Judge John Baxter fought a duel with pistols at Saluda Gap on the Greenville, South Carolina, turnpike. Judge Baxter was shot in the knuckle of the right hand, the ball ranging up and along the right arm to the shoulder. It was not a serious wound, but disabled its recipient for a second shot. It was claimed by Baxter's friends that he was opposed to dueling, and had not fired to hit Erwin. Erwin's friends retorted that if his right arm had not been pointing toward Erwin when Erwin's bullet struck Baxter's knuckle, the ball would not have ranged up it to his shoulder. [4] The late Dr. Edward Jones of Hendersonville was Erwin's second and the late Dr. W. L. Hilliard was Erwin's surgeon. Terrill W. Taylor was Baxter's second and Dr. W. D. Whitted his surgeon. [5]

RESULT OF A POLITICAL QUARREL. It is agreed that the cause of this duel was politics pure and simple; but the special offence alleged has been forgotten. Judge A. C. Avery writes:

"My recollection is—in fact, I know—that the duel was fought just south of our State line at Saluda gap. According to my best recollection it occurred in 1852, soon after Gen. Clingman and others had followed Calhoun in opposing the compromise measure of 1851 and had been put beyond the pale of the Whig party, on that account. Marcus Erwin was editing a Democratic paper established shortly before that time in Asheville. My impression is that the name of the paper was the *News*. I know it was sent to me at the Bingham School. My impression is that Erwin had written some very strong articles or editorials advocating the doctrine of State's Rights. Mr. Baxter, who then lived in Hendersonville, wrote a communication to the Whig paper in which he criticised Mr. Erwin, calling him the 'Fire-eating Editor of the *News*' (if that was the name of the paper); and in answer to him Mr. Erwin wrote a very caustic criticism of Mr Baxter, in which he. said, enclosing the article, in substance, that Mr. Baxter had called him a fire-eater; but that, while he did not devour that element, Mr. Baxter would find him ready and willing to face it. This editorial, as I recollect it, called forth a challenge from Baxter, which was accepted and Mr. Erwin selected Saluda as the place for the duel. Judge Avery thinks Dr. Jones was Erwin's second and Dr. Whitted of Hendersonville was Baxter's surgeon, but could not recall Baxter's second." [6]

"But Dr. J. S. T. Baird, who remembers seeing Judge Baxter at court while the Doctor was its clerk, between 1853 and 1857, with his hand bandaged from the effects of the wound, scouts the idea that Baxter sent the challenge. Elias Gibbs, who now (1912) lives near Hendersonville, was sitting talking to Mr. Baxter when the challenge came. Col.

Baxter read the challenge, showed it to him, then tore it into minute scraps and threw them on the floor. He accepted, and with his second, Terrell Taylor, father of Mrs. Joseph Bryson, went on horse-back to the South Carolina line, fearing the law in his own state. His (Baxter's) wife's suspicions became aroused after he left, so, she with a number of slaves gathered the torn fragments together and read them, discovering her husband's whereabouts. Col. Baxter was tinged with Quakerism, was a very conscientious and honorable man. When it came to fighting the duel, a large crowd of citizens had learned of it, and were present. Col. Baxter did not wish to show the white feather by not standing up, but without any intention of injuring his opponent, shot at his feet."[7]

Major Erwin was, by many, considered the "brainiest" man in the State; while Mr. Baxter afterwards moved to Tennessee where he was made United States circuit judge, and served with distinction till his death.

THE HYMAN–HILLIARD DUEL. In the Summer of 1855 John D. Hyman, editor of the *Spectator* said in his paper that the mail service was not as efficiently conducted as when it had been under the management of the Whigs. Dr. W. L. Hilliard, now deceased, was then the postmaster, and a partner of the late Dr. J. F. E. Hardy.[8] Besides this, both were Democrats. Dr. Hilliard sent Dr. Hardy to Col. Hyman with a polite request for a retraction and apology, which were refused. Thereupon a challenge to mortal combat followed, which was promptly accepted, rifles designated as the weapons, and Paint Rock on the Tennessee line agreed on as the place of meeting.

Dr. Hilliard had married the year before Miss Margaret Love, a daughter of Col. J. R. Love, and was living over the drug store of Dr. Thomas C. Lester in a brick building, then on the site now occupied by the Falk Music Store. Between this and what is now Aston street, then a mere lane, lived Mr. James Patton. In the rear of Dr. Hilliard's apartments were his barn and stable, with a single exit, that on South Main street. The postoffice was just above his house and on that street. Capt. James P. Sawyer, or Captain Frank M. Miller, was the clerk in charge.

Now, Col. Hyman and his party had left the day before the duel was to be fought; but Drs. Hilliard and Hardy and Col. David Coleman, Dr. Hilliard's second, knew that the authorities had been informed of the contemplated duel and that they would be arrested if they should openly attempt to

leave town. So they waited till nightfall, when they had the
plank from the rear wall of the stable removed and slipped
their horses out into the lane that is now Aston street.   They
were afraid also that if they followed the most direct route
to Paint Rock, that down the eastern bank of the French Broad,
they might be arrested.   Consequently, they crossed the
French Broad at Smith's Bridge and went down the left-hand
side of the river.   But it is forty miles to Paint Rock, and
ride as hard as they could through the dark night, dawn was
breaking when they reached the bridge at Warm Springs.
As the duel was fixed for sunrise the Hyman party began to
fear that the doctor had been arrested, but Col. John A. Fagg,
who lived at Paint Rock, said that he knew Hilliard and
that they need have no apprehensions.

According to the recollection of Francis Marion Wells, now
91 (1912) years old, and living on Grass creek, Madison county,
within less than one mile from where the duel was fought, the
Hyman party arrived at Paint Rock the day before that on
which the duel was to be fought.   People living in the neighborhood began to suspect the truth, and the authorities of
Cocke county, Tennessee, were notified, So that when the
Hilliard party reached the scene early on the morning of the
day set for the duel, from forty to fifty men had assembled
to see what might occur. Among these were peace officers
of North Carolina. The belligerants, realizing that a duel in
the circumstances would most likely be interfered with by
the authorities of North Carolina or Tennessee, announced
publicly that the effort to have the encounter take place had
been abandoned and all parties started on their return to
Asheville. This seemed to have accomplished its purpose,
for no one followed. But when Hot Springs was reached the
parties merely crossed to the left or western bank of the French
Broad, not for the purpose of ascending the river to Asheville, but of descending it to the Tennessee line by a road leading to the mouth of Wolf creek. As they passed Mr. Wells'
house he noted particularly the men who were present: They
were John D. Hyman and John Baxter, his second, and Dr.
Charles Candler, his surgeon. With Dr. W. L. Hilliard was
his second, Marcus Erwin, [9] and Dr. J. F. E. Hardy, his surgeon. Col. John A. Fagg was along to show the way. The
duel was fought with rifles at fifty paces just about 100 yards

over the North Carolina line. Dr. Candler told Wells that he weighed the powder and lead that went into each rifle. The road on which the duel was fought is partly grown up now, coming into the new road in a slightly oblique direction from the gap of the little ridge. The spot is about one and a half miles west of the French Broad river. As the party returned Col. John Baxter shouted to Squire Wells as he passed: "Nobody hurt," which proved to be true. Only one shot was exchanged, a second shot not having been demanded. There is a tradition that but for the fact that Col. Fagg cried "Halt!" as the commands to fire were being given, Hyman would probably have killed Hilliard, as the latter fired first, his ball striking the ground near Hyman's feet. Also that Hyman's bullet clipped a button from Hilliard's coat.

A ONE-SIDED DUEL ACROSS THE STATE LINE. All unconsciously two men of Cherokee county imitated famous duelists of former years by standing in one State and killing a man in another:

On the 11th day of July, 1892, William Hall and John Dockery were on the "State Ridge," which is the boundary line between North Carolina and Tennessee. They had a warrant for the arrest of Andrew Bryson whom they soon descried coming up the ridge in front of them. They hid behind a large oak tree until Bryson came within gunshot range, when Hall told him to surrender. Bryson was then just over the line and in Tennessee, whereas Hall and Dockery were in North Carolina. Instead of surrendering, Bryson started to draw his gun, when he was shot and killed. The case was tried and the defendants found guilty at the spring term, 1893, of the Superior court of Cherokee county.[10] A new trial was granted by the Supreme court at the February term of 1894, on the ground that at common law there could be no conviction unless the men who were killed were within the jurisdiction of the court at the time the shot was fired.[11] The defendants were re-tried and acquitted. The legislature at its next session passed a statute making such an act murder.[12]

NOTES.

[1]From "Dropped Stitches," Ch. VIII.
[2]It was probated in January, 1828, and the certified copy was made March 11, 1848.
[3]Hon. J. H. Wheeler's "Reminiscences."
[4]Hon. A. C. Avery to J. P. A., Dec. 12, 1912.
[5]Dr. T. A. Allen of Hendersonville writes, November 12, 1912, that Dr. W. D. Whitted was Baxter's surgeon and T. W. Taylor may have been his second. But Col. Wm. M.

Davies, a distinguished teacher of law at Asheville, was a boy in Hendersonville at the time, and insists that John D. Hyman was Baxter's second. It is difficult to state positively who the second was.

⁶Letter from Judge Avery to J. P. A.

⁷Mrs. Mattie S. Candler's "History of Henderson County," 1912. As Judge Avery heard of it while he was at Bingham's school and graduated there in 1857. it is clear that the duel was not prior to that date.

⁸Dr. Hilliard was born in Georgia in 1823. He practiced medicine in Asheville nearly forty years, and stood in the front rank. He was a surgeon in the Confederate army from May, 1861, to August, 1863, when he took charge of a hospital in Asheville. After the war he resumed practice, and died in 1890. From Dr. G. S. Tennent's "Medicine in Buncombe," 1906.

⁹Dr. W. D. Hilliard, Dr. W. L. Hilliard's son, and Theo. F. Davidson, however, agree in saying that Col. David Coleman was Dr. W. L. Hilliard's second.

¹⁰114 N. C. Reports, p. 909.

¹¹115 N. C. Reports, p. 811.

¹²Chapter 169, Laws of 1895.

A. S. Memminger

CHAPTER XV

BENCH AND BAR[1]

FIRST JUDICIARY ACT.[2] In 1777 (Ch. 115, p. 281) the State was divided into six districts, viz. : Wilmington, New Bern, Halifax, Hillsborough and Salisbury, in each of which places a Superior court for the trial of civil and criminal causes should be held, to consist of three judges who were to hold office during good behavior, the jurisdiction and terms being prescribed. It is sometimes thought that the Superior court was not established till 1806; but that is a mistake; the act of 1806 having simply prescribed two terms in each county after having changed the districts into so many circuits (Ch. 693, Laws 1806, p. 1050) but with the same jurisdiction.

COUNTY COURTS OF PLEAS AND QUARTER SESSIONS.[3] These courts were provided for in the same chapter, and their jurisdiction and terms prescribed. (P. 297, *et seq.*)

APPEALS. Provision was made in the act of 1777 (Ch. 115) for appeals from the County courts of Pleas and Quarter Sessions to the Superior courts, but none from the decisions of the Superior courts, till 1799. In that year was established (Ch. 520)[4]

A CONFERENCE COURT, consisting of all the Superior court judges, who were to meet at Raleigh on the 10th day of June and December of each year, appoint a clerk and decide all "questions of law and equity which had arisen upon the circuit before any of the judges of the Superior courts, which the judge sitting may be unwilling to determine, and shall be desirous of further consideration thereon, . . . [by] a conference with the other judges; or where any questions of law or equity have already arisen on the circuit, and have remained undecided by reason of a disagreement of the judges on the circuit." (See 2nd Murphy's Reports.)

NAME CHANGED TO SUPREME COURT. In 1805 (Ch. 674, p. 1039) "the name and style of the court of conference shall hereafter be that of the Supreme court of North Carolina," and it was made the duty of the sheriff of Wake county to attend its sessions. It was not, however, till 1818 (Ch. 962) that the Supreme court, composed of judges elected for the

purpose of hearing appeals, etc., alone, was provided for. The
court was to consist of three judges to be elected by the legislature and to hold office during good behavior. Terms were
to be held in Raleigh May and November 20th of each year. [3]

TENNESSEE SUPERIOR COURT. [4] "The act of the general
assembly of North Carolina, providing for or establishing a
Superior court of Law and Equity for the counties of Davidson, Sumner and Tennessee, was not passed till November,
1778. . . . The first volume of the original record of
the minutes of the Superior Court . . . for the District
of Washington—then the 'Western District'—at Jonesboro,
shows that David Campbell alone held that court from the
February term, 1788 (which was the first term), until the
February term, 1789, at which latter term the record shows
that Judge McNairy appeared and sat with Judge Campbell."

JUDGE SPRUCE McCAY. This judge held the second term
of the Superior court of Ashe county, in September, 1907.
He had married a daughter of Gen. Griffith Rutherford, and
lived at Salisbury. [5] It was he who had held the August,
1782, term of the "Court of Oyer and Terminer & Gaol Delivery," in Jonesborough, in what was then Washington District, now in Tennessee. "He had the court opened by proclamation, and with all the formality and solemnity charac-
terizing the opening of the English courts. On the first day
of the term, John Vann was found guilty, by a jury, of horse-
stealing, the punishment for which, at that time, was death.
On the same day the record contains an entry to the effect
that 'the Jury who passed upon the Tryal of Vann beg Leave
to Recommend him to the Court for Mercy'; but no mercy
was shown him by 'the Honl. Spruce McCay, Esqr.' . . .
During the week two more unfortunates—Isaac Chote and
William White—were found guilty of horse-stealing; and, on
the last day of the term (August 20), Judge McCay disposed
of all three of these criminals in one order, as follows : 'Ord.
that John Vann, Isaac Chote & Wm. White, now Under Sentence of Death, be executed on the tenth day of September
next.' This is the whole of the entry." [6] The author, John
Allison, now a chancellor of Tennessee, says : "It is not
probable that a parallel proceeding can be found in judicial
history." He adds that "tradition in that country gave
Judge McCay the character of a heartless tyrant." But the

juries of that day and section of North Carolina seem to have
been equal to the occasion; for at the same term of court the
following incident is mentioned : "The juries could not be
driven or intimidated into giving verdicts contrary to their
convictions; and whenever they differed with the judge—and
they always knew his views—in a case of weight or serious
results, they would deliberately disperse, go to their homes,
and not return any more during that term of court. In a
case styled 'State v. Taylor,' the record shows that the jury
was sworn and the defendant put on 'Tryal.' Nothing more
appears except the following significant entry : 'State v.
Taylor. The jury having failed to come back into court, it
is therefore a mistrial.'" [7]

"LEWIS AND ELIAS PYBOURN." At the May Term, 1783, at
Jonesborough, an order was made allowing these men "who
is at this time Lying out" to return home upon giving bond
for good behavior, which, probably was done. But whether
it was done or not, seven years later, at the August term of
the same court, 1790, Elias Pybourn was convicted of horse-
stealing, and was sentenced to "the public pillory one hour.
That he have both his ears nailed to the pillory and severed
from his head; that he receive at the public whipping post
thirty-nine lashes well laid on; and be branded on the right
cheek with the letter H, and on his left cheek with the letter
T. . . ."

JOSEPH CULTON'S RIGHT EAR. At the November Term,
1788, at Jonesborough, Joseph Culton proved by the oath of
Alexander Moffit that he had lost his left ear in a fight with
a certain Charles Young, and prayed that the same be
entered on record, and it was so ordered.

WITHOUT PASS OR RECOMMENDATION. When a stranger
came into the Watauga settlement he was asked to account
for his being there, and if his explanation proved to be unsatisfactory, he was required to give bond for his good behavior or to leave. Wm. Clatry was a "trancient person" and was
required to give security for his behavior, and return to his
family "within five months," he having confessed that he had
left home and taken up with another woman.

However, it is not to Judge Spruce McCay to whom we
are indebted for the following.

A GRUESOME RECORD. At the March Term, 1809, of the
Superior court of Ashe, Judge Francis Locke presiding, the

case of the *State v. Carter Whittington*, indicted for perjury
was tried, the following names appearing as those of the
jurors : James Dixon, Charles Sherrer, Daniel Moxley, Josiah Connolly, Young Edwards, Alex. Latham, Wm. Powers,
Andrew Sherrer, Chris Crider, Thomas Tirey (Tire?), Charles
Francis, Jesse Reeves. The jury found the defendant Carter
Whittington "guilty in manner and form as charged in the bill
of indictment." David and Elijah Estep, sureties, thereupon
delivered up Carter Whittington, and he was ordered into the
custody of the sheriff. "Reasons in arrest of judgement in
the case of Carter Whittington were filed by Mr. McGimsey, [8]
his attorney—after solemn argument, the reasons are overruled by the court."

" JUDGMENT.

"Fined £10, and the said Carter Whittington stand in the pillory for
one hour, at the expiration of which time, both his ears to be cut off and
entirely severed from his head, and that his ears so cut off be nailed to
the pillory by the officers and there remain till the setting of the sun,
and that the sheriff of this county carry this judgment immediately into
execution, and that the said Carter Whittington be confined until the fine
and fees are paid. . . . Solicitor's fees of £1-6-8 paid by deft."

THE UNWRITTEN LAW IN 1811. [9] At the March term, 1811,
of the Superior court of Ashe, Samuel Lowery, judge presiding, an order was made for the removal to Wilkes court, to be
held on the third Monday of March, of the case of the *State
v. William Tolliver*, indicted for the murder of a man named
Reeves; and the sheriff of Ashe was required to "procure a
sufficient guard of eight men from the proper officers of the
militia to convey safely the said William Tolliver to the
Superior court of Wilkes county," thus indicating either
that there was danger of a lynching or a rescue. Tradition
says that Tolliver was acquitted at Wilkesboro on the ground
that Reeves had attempted liberties with Tolliver's wife.
Robert Henry of Buncombe defended him.

HANGING OF DAVID MASON. When Dr. W. A. Askew was
about fifteen years old he stayed all night with the late James
Gudger, the ancestor of most of the Gudgers of this section,
in what is now Madison county. Young Askew was then on
his way from his home on Spring creek to see the "hanging"
of a man named David Mason who had been convicted of
the murder of his wife by cutting her throat in Haywood county.
Askew rode to "town" (Asheville) with Dr. Montraville W.

Gudger, a son of "Old Jimmie." The evidence upon which
Morgan had been convicted indicated that he had slipped up on
his wife while she was carding in her cabin home and killed her.
Pierce Roberts was the sheriff of Buncombe then, and the
execution took place in the woods below and behind Col.
Lusk's residence on College Street, or where J. D. Henderson's
residence now stands—there being two accounts as to its
location. This must have been between 1847 and 1850. When
asked on the gallows if he had anything to say Morgan called
up Aaron Fullbright and another man whose name Dr. Askew
has forgotten and pointing his finger at them said : "You
have sworn my life away."

Twenty-five years ago (1887), according to Dr. Askew, a
woman in Sevier county, Tennessee, confessed on her death-
bed that she had killed David Mason's wife.

COL. DAVIDSON'S RECOLLECTIONS OF THE BAR. The late
Col. Allen T. Davidson, in the *Lyceum* for May, 1891, says:

"I entered the profession of the law January 1, 1845, with Gen. R.
M. Henry and J. A. B. Fitzgerald as my classmates. We were the stu-
dents of Michael Francis of Waynesville. . . . The gentlemen then
in full practice were Joshua Roberts, Geo. W. Candler, Felix Axley, John
Rolen, Michael Francis, N. W. Woodfin, John Baxter, George Baxter,
Col. B. S. Gaither, Wm. Shipp, Gen. R. M. Henry and J. A. B. Fitz-
gerald. These constituted the bar and rode the circuit, as we did then,
until about 1855, when Judge A. S. Merrimon, Senator Z. B. Vance,
Maj. Marcus Erwin, Gen. B. M. Edney, P. W. Roberts, and Col. David
Coleman were added to the list. . . . Several distinguished lawyers left the profession just as I entered, Gen. John G. Bynum and Gen.
T. L. Clingman, who, added to the list, made an array of talent and
sound ability rarely met with. . . . The court usually began in
Cherokee (where I then lived) in March and September, and we all
joined and made the circuit from thence eastward to Asheville, where I
usually stopped. We traveled together on horseback, stopped at the
same hotels in the towns, and at the same wayside inns in the country;
and it was not unusual to have ten or fifteen of us together at one of
these country stopping places, where the wit and humor of the profession broke loose in all its force, and good humor ruled the house. It is
a fact that nearly all of those mentioned were gentlemen of fine humor,
and but few given to strong drink, so that the jest and humor were of
the best character, without boistering or noise. Mr. N. W. Woodfin was
remarkable for his humor, clear-cut and original. Mr. Candler excelled
in his country stories . . . and when he took the floor he usually
held it in silence till the climax, when there were uprorious bursts of
applause. Mr. J. W. Woodfin was the sunshine of the circle, was always
in a good humor, and told a story well. . . . I recall many of the
stopping places, the first going from Asheville being James Patton's be-

yond the Pigeon. Here we would meet a good-humored fine old gentleman as landlord, with his big country fire-places, and roaring hickory wood fires, a table groaning with all that was desirable to eat, good beds and plenty of cheer, supper, lodging and breakfast, horse well fed and groomed, bill fifty cents, and this was uniform for twenty years. So at Daniel Bryson's on Scott's creek, same fare and same bill. At Wm. Walker's at Valleytown, one of the best houses in Western North Carolina, the bill for man and horse was fifty cents. A great staying place was N. S. Jarrett's on the Nantahala, at a place called Aquone. Here we met, here we chased the deer, here we beguiled the trout in that crystal stream with the fly, here we whiled away many a pleasant summer afternoon in these attractive sports. Good, dear old friends! I can see you all now[10] in fancy; but this vanishes and I remember that you are no more. . . . I must be allowed to close with a general resume intended to embrace the years between 1845 and 1861 : the profession was able, studious, painstaking and thorough. I have been an honest and careful observer of many deliberative assemblies; have watched with much care and interest the application and power of the human mind so as to learn from careful observation how great men, so-called, look at subjects and reach conclusions . . . but after all I am bound to say that the trial of cases in the mountain circuit has impressed me more than the proceedings of any other body of men I have ever met for its sincerity, force and logic. Here we were, in a large and extensive district of country, the courts distantly situated, without books, at each town finding only the Revised Statutes and perhaps a digest; yet with these we tried our cases ably and well, and our contentions have been well sustained by adjudged cases. In court the common law pleading prevailed, beginning with the writ, thus bringing the defendant into court. Upon the appearance of the defendant the issues were joined and the case was ready for trial without circumlocution or clerical talent. The fight was an old-field, drawn out set-to. As Judge Read says : "We drew the sword and threw away the scabbard; or, in less classical words, "The Devil take the hindmost." It is a fact, however, that with all the spirit with which the case was tried, often with the manifestation of temper, no unkind or angry feeling ever went outside the court house, and we all closed the circuit to enter our homes as friends."

JUDGE v. JUDGE. When the county seat was at Jewel Hill Dr. J. S. T. Baird was clerk. A church was used for this purpose and having a window the sash of which was made to open by sliding along horizontally instead of being raised, as is usual, the presiding judge, needing air, tried to raise this sash, and failing kicked a hole in the glass. For this the late Col. John A. Fagg, then Chairman of the County Court of Pleas and Quarter Sessions of Madison county, fined his Honor, the presiding Judge, ten dollars and his Honor paid it!

CERTIFICATE AS TO WHY RIGHT EAR WAS MISSING. From the minutes of the County court of Buncombe, October, 1793, it appears that it was "Ordered by court that Thomas Hopper, upon his own motion, have a certificate from the clerk, certifying that his right ear was bit off by Philip Williams in a fight between said Hopper and Williams. Certificate issued." This was necessary in order that the loss of a part of his ear might not cause those ignorant of the facts to conclude that the missing part had been removed as a punishment for perjury or forgery.

WHERE THE SOW–SKIN LAY. As far back as 1840, probably, James Gwynn of Wilkes county was solicitor of this circuit, which embraced all the mountain counties except Ashe. James Gwynn of the East Fork of Pigeon river, Haywood county, is a near relative and bears his honored name. He married a Miss Lenoir of Fort Defiance, and was a man of very decided ability, though of little education. His spelling was execrable, but his power over a jury was great. Judge J. L. Bailey and Gen. Clingman knew and appreciated his ability, and through them two anecdotes survive. When Nathan asked David for an opinion of the man who took the ewe-lamb of another, and David had expressed himself thereon, then "Nathan said unto David, Thou art the man."[11] When attempting to quote this to a jury Mr. Gwynn got the names of the principal actors confounded with two other Biblical characters, and after detailing the circumstances of a hog-stealing case, pointed with his finger at the defendant and exclaimed: "As Abraham said unto Isaac, Thou art the man." The other story was also of a hog stealing case; but had reference specifically to a sow. The sow had been stolen and her flesh eaten. But the sow's skin had been discovered, and it was upon it and the place of its concealment near the defendant's home, that the solicitor relied for a conviction. "Where, gentlemen of the jury," he asked impressively, "was the sow skin?" He raised himself on his toes and shouted the answer: "Far up under the shadder of the Big Yaller, where the rocks are rough, and the waters run deep, and the laurels wave *high* (crescendo) the sow skin lay!"

SAD ENDING OF A PRISON SENTENCE.[11] About the year 1856 or 1857 a talented and highly respected physician of Hendersonville by the name of Edward R. Jones took umbrage at something a tailor by the name of A. J. Fain had said or done, both being politicians to some extent. Jones probably considered Fain his social inferior. At any rate, instead of appealing to the code of honor, as was the custom of that day, Dr. Jones entered Fain's tailor shop and literally carved him to death. He was indicted and the case removed to Rutherfordton, where the late Colonels N. W. and John W. Woodfin defended, while the late John Baxter prosecuted. Jones was convicted of manslaughter and sentenced to a term of imprisonment in the Rutherford jail. While serving that sentence he, in a fit of despondency, cut his throat and died.

ASHEVILLE'S FIRST ATTORNEYS. "At its first session in April, 1792, the county court elected Reuben Wood, Esq., 'attorney for the state.' He is the first lawyer who appears as practicing in Buncombe county. Waightstill Avery, the first attorney general of North Carolina, attended at the next session of the court and made therein his first motion, which "was overruled by the court." At this term Wallace Alexander also became a member of the Buncombe bar. Joseph McDowell appeared at October term, 1793, presented his license, took "the oath of an attorney, and was admitted to the bar in said county." On the next day James Holland "came into court, made it appear (by) Mr. Avery and Mr. Wood, that he has a license to practice as an attorney—but had forgot them." He too was admitted as an attorney of the court. At January court, 1794, Joseph Spencer proved to the court that he had license to practice, and was likewise admitted as an attorney of the court, and at April term, 1795, upon the resignation of Reuben Wood, he was elected solicitor of the county. The next attorney admitted was Bennett Smith. Upon motion of Wallace Alexander in April, 1802, Robert Williamson was admitted to the practice.

ROBERT HENRY.[12] "Then, in July, 1802, on motion of Joseph Spencer, and the production of his county court license, Robert Henry, Esq., became an attorney of the court. This singular, versatile and able man has left his impress upon Buncombe county and Western North Carolina. Born in Tryon (afterward Lincoln) county, North Carolina, on February 10, 1765, in a rail pen, he was the son of Thomas Henry, an emigrant from the north of Ireland.[13] When Robert was a schoolboy he fought on the American side of Kings

Mountain, and was badly wounded in the hand by a bayonet thrust. Later he was in the heat of the fight at Cowan's Ford, and was very near Gen. William Davidson when the latter was killed. After the war he removed to Buncombe county and on the Swannanoa taught the first school ever held in that county. He then became a surveyor, and after a long and extensive experience, in which he surveyed many of the large grants in all the counties of western North Carolina and even in middle Tennessee, and participated in 1799, as such, in locating and marking the line between the State of North Carolina and the State of Tennessee, he turned his attention to the study of law. In January, 1806, he was made solicitor of Buncombe county. He it was who opened up and for years conducted as a public resort the Sulphur Springs near Asheville, later known as Deaver's Springs and still more recently as Carrier's Springs. On January 6, 1863, he died in Clay county, N. C., at the age of 98 years, and was 'undoubtedly the last of the heroes of Kings Mountain. . . . ' To him we are indebted for the preservation and, in part, authorship of the most graphic and detailed accounts of the fights at Kings Mountain and Cowan's ford which now exist. He was the first resident lawyer of Buncombe county."

COLONEL DAVIDSON'S RECOLLECTIONS OF ROBERT HENRY.

"I must not omit . . . to mention Robert Henry, who lived, owned and settled the Sulphur Springs. He was an old man when I first knew him, say fifty years ago [that was in 1891]; he had then retired from the profession of the law which he had practiced many years. This was before I knew him well. He was tedious and slow in conversation, but always interesting to the student. He had been a fine lawyer, and remarkable in criminal cases.[14] He could recite his experiences of cases in most minute detail. He insisted that, underlying all, there was invariably a principle which settled every rule of evidence and point of law. I chanced to get some of his old criminal law books, such as Foster's Crown Law, Hale's Pleas of the Crown, etc., and I found them well annotated with accurate marginal notes, showing great industry and thought in their perusal. He had a grand history in our struggle for independence; was at Charlotte when the Declaration of Independence was made;[15] but, being a boy at this time, he did not understand the character of the resolutions; but said he heard the crowd shout and declared themselves freed from the British government. He afterwards fought at the battle of Kings Mountain and was severely wounded in the hand and thigh, by a bayonet in the charge of Ferguson's men."[16]

MICHAEL FRANCIS. Col. Allen T. Davidson, in the same paper, has left this record concerning this man, once known as "the Great Westerner":

"Michael Francis was a Scotchman, educated in Edinburgh, a thorough scholar, was one of those warm hearted, florid Scotchmen so characteristic of Bonnie Scotland. He weighed three hundred and thirty pounds, was one of the most forcible and clear logicians at the bar, was remarkable for his study and observation of the human mind. He was always a complete master of the facts of his cases, and was able to deduce from them the true intent of the mind of the witness, and had a happy and forcible way of illustrating the methods by which the ordinary intellect reaches conclusions. He had studied human nature so closely that he could divine the secret intents of the heart. As a consequence, he was a power invincible before a jury. Added to this, he was a thorough lawyer, able to cope with the best, and remarkable for his power of condensation and forcible expression. He was a pioneer in the settlement of many new points of law in this circuit, as many cases argued by him before the Supreme court will attest. . . . He was a great platform speaker and a leader in the formation of political sentiment. He was a member of the house and senate and discharged every public duty with honor and credit. . . . He was my good preceptor whom I have closely studied and tried to follow."

ISRAEL PICKENS AND OTHERS. [17] The next lawyers admitted in that county were, in the order in which their names are given: Thomas Barren, Israel Pickens, Joseph Wilson, Joseph Carson, Robert H. Burton, Henry Harrison, Saunders Donoho, John C. Elliott, Henry Y. Webb, Tench Cox, Jr., A. R. Ruffin, and John Paxton. These were admitted between January, 1804, and October, 1812, from time to time. Probably the most distinguished of them were Israel Pickens, representative of the Buncombe District in the lower house of the Congress of the United States from 1811 to 1817, inclusive, and afterwards governor of Alabama and United States senator from that State; Joseph Wilson, afterwards famous as a solicitor in convicting Abe Collins, Sr., and the other counterfeiters who carried on in Rutherford county in the first quarter of this century extensive operations in the manufacture and circulation of counterfeit money; and Robert H. Burton and John Paxton, who became judges of the Superior courts of North Carolina in 1818.

DAVID L. SWAIN. [17] The first lawyer of Buncombe county who was a native thereof was the late Gov. D. L. Swain. Born, as has been already stated, at the head of Beaverdam, on January 4, 1801, he was educated under the Rev. George Newton and the Rev. Mr. Porter at Newton Academy, where he had for classmates B. F. Perry, afterward governor of South Carolina, Waddy Thompson, of South Carolina, distinguished as congressman and minister to Mexico, and M. Patton, R. B. Vance and James W. Patton of Buncombe county. In 1821 he was for a short while at the University of North Carolina. In December, 1822, he was of the Edenton Circuit, and in 1832 became, and for five years continued to be, a representative of Buncombe county in the House of Commons of the State, in 1829 was elected solicitor, admitted to practice law in 1824, became governor of the State. After the expiration of three successive terms as governor, he became president of the University of North Carolina in 1835, and continued in that place until August 27, 1868, the time of his death. He was largely instrumental in securing the passage of the act incorporating the Buncombe Turnpike Company, and to him more than to any other man North Carolina is indebted for the preservation of her history and the defence of her fame. His early practice as a lawyer was begun in Asheville. For further details than are given here in regard to the life of this truly great man, the reader is referred to Wheeler's History of North Carolina, and his Reminiscences, and to the more accurate lecture of the late Governor Z. B. Vance on the Life and Character of Hon. David L. Swain.

"OLD WARPING BARS."[18] Governor Swain was tall and ungainly in figure and awkward in manner. When he was elected judge the candidate of the opposing party was Judge Seawell, a very popular man, whom up to that time, his opponents, after repeated efforts with different aspirants, had found it impossible to defeat. "Then," said a member of the legislature from Iredell county, "we took up Old Warping Bars from Buncombe and warped him out." From this remark Mr. Swain acquired the nickname of "Old Warping Bars," a not inapt appellation, which stuck to him until he became president of the University when the students bestowed upon him the name of "Old Bunk." He continued to be Old Bunk all the rest of his life. While he was practicing at the bar the lawyers rode the circuits. Beginning at the first term of the court in which they practiced, they followed the courts through all the counties of that circuit. Among Swain's fellow lawyers on the Western Circuit were James R. Dodge (afterwards clerk of the Supreme court of the State and a nephew of Washington Irving), Samuel Hillman and Thomas Dews.

DODGE, HILLMAN, SWAIN AND DEWS.[19] On one occasion these were all present at a court in one of the western counties and Dodge was making a speech to the jury. Swain had somewhere seen a punning epitaph on a man whose name was Dodge. This he wrote off on a piece of paper and passed it around among the lawyers, creating much merriment at Dodge's expense. After the latter took his seat some one handed it to him. It read :

"EPITAPH ON JAMES R. DODGE, ATTORNEY AT LAW.

"Here lies a Dodge, who dodged all good,
    And dodged a lot of evil;
But, after dodging all he could
    He could not dodge the devil."

"Mr Dodge perceived immediately that it was Swain's writing, and supposed that Hillman and Dews had had something to do with it. He at once wrote this impromptu reply :

"ANOTHER EPITAPH ON THREE ATTORNEYS.

" Here lies a Hillman and a Swain—
    Their lot let no man choose.
They lived in sin and died in pain,
    And the devil got his Dews."[20]

THEIR LIVES A PART OF THE STATE'S HISTORY. "Of the late Thomas L. Clingman, who was for many years a member of the Asheville bar, the late Gov. Z. B. Vance, who was born in Buncombe county, and began life as a lawyer in Asheville, and to whose memory a granite monument upon her public square is now in process of erection,[21] and the late A. S. Merrimon, chief justice of North Carolina, who studied law at Asheville and continued his practice here till about 1867, it is unnecessary to speak here. Their careers have recently closed and are known to all who care for Asheville or her affairs."[22]

COL. NICHOLAS W. WOODFIN. "Soon after Gov. Swain began the practice, Nicholas W. Woodfin became a lawyer, and served as the connecting link between the old times and the

modern bar for many years. He was born in Buncombe
county on the upper French Broad river, and began life under
the most unfavorable circumstances, and for awhile labored
under the greatest disadvantages. He became, however, one
of North Carolina's most famous and astute lawyers. But
few men have ever met with such distinguished success at
the bar as he. He was Buncombe's representative in the
State senate in 1844, 1846, 1848, 1850, 1852. In the course of his
career he acquired a large fortune, and owned great quantities of land in Asheville and its neighborhood. With the
practice of law he carried on an extensive business as a farmer,
in which he was famous for the introduction of many useful
improvements in agriculture. He it was who first introduced
orchard grass in Buncombe county, and turned the attention
of her farmers to the raising of cattle on a large scale and the
cultivation of sorghum." [23]

He was born in old Buncombe, now Henderson, county,
January 29, 1810, and was married to Miss Eliza Grace
McDowell at Quaker Meadows, near Morganton, the 16th of
June, 1840, afterwards residing on North Main street, Asheville, N. C., now a girls' school, till his death, May 23, 1875,
she surviving him less than one year. He was always identified with any movement for the uplift and progress of his
State, and especially of Buncombe county. Much has been
written of his success as a lawyer, his humanitarianism, his
devotion to his family and his care of his aged parents.

COLONEL JOHN W. WOODFIN. He was born in what is now
Henderson county in 1818, married Miss Maria McDowell
at Quaker Meadows, and lived in Asheville. He was a brilliant lawyer, a brave soldier, and formed one of the first companies in Buncombe county, saying he had enlisted for the
war. He was killed by Kirk's men at Hot Springs in the
fall of 1863.

THE FIRST TRIAL. [24] The first case tried in Buncombe
county was that of the *State v. Richard Yardly*, in July, 1792.
He was indicted for petit larceny, was convicted, and appealed
to Morgan [Burke] Superior court. The first civil suit was that of
W. Avery v. William Fletcher, which was tried by order of the
court on the premises on the third Monday in April, 1795,
by a jury summoned for that purpose. The first pauper provided for by the court was Susannah Baker with her child.

The first processioning was in April, 1776, when William Whitson the processioner thereof returned into court "the processioning of a tract of two hundred acres of land, on the east side of French Broad river about one mile and a quarter from Morristown, the place whereon James Henderson now lives," dated April 20, 1796. This embraces the property lying on Park avenue and in that vicinity. Its eastern boundary line is formed in part by the Lining Branch, the small branch immediately eastward of, and for some distance parallel with, Depot street. The first will admitted to probate therein was that of Jonas Gooch in July, 1792.[25] The first dower assigned was to Demey Gash, widow of Joseph Gash, April, 1805."

To SUPPRESS VICE AND IMMORALITY.[26] Mr. Sondley mentions also that at the October term, 1800, the Rev. George Newton, the first Presbyterian preacher in Buncombe, presented to the court a petition from the Presbytery of Concord which "humbly sheweth" many gross immoralities as abounding among our citizens all of which were in violation of laws already enacted. Wherefore, they asked that those laws be "carried into vigorous execution." At the January term, 1801, the court resolved to exert itself to suppress "such enormous practices."

JUDICIAL SANCTION OF A LOTTERY.[27] In January, 1810, the court ordered that the managers of the Newton Academy lottery "come into court and enter into bond for the discharge of office and took the oath of office." This lottery was probably for educational purposes.

"TWENTY-FIVE LASHES ON HIS BARE BACK, WELL LAID ON."[27] Such was the order of the court in 1799, when the jury had found Edward Williams guilty of petty larceny. This was to be inflicted at the public whipping post; but an appeal was "prayed," and it may be that Edward Williams got off.

ADJUDGED FIT "TO BE SET FREE."[27] At this term the court adjudged that Jerry Smith, a slave belonging to Thomas Foster, was a fit person to be set free and emancipated, and the clerk was ordered to issue a license or certificate to the said Jerry Smith for his freedom "during his, the said Jerry's, natural life."

BUNCOMBE'S FIRST FAIRS.[27] At the July term, 1799, the court ordered two fairs to be established in Buncombe to commence the first Thursday and Friday in November following and the first Thursday and Friday in June following, and continue on said days annually, "without said court should find it more convenient to make other alterations."

FIRST CASE OF MOTHER-IN-LAW.[27] At the July term, 1802, it was ordered that the deposition of Caty Troxell, to the effect that her daughter Judith had married John Morrice on the *nineteenth and twentienth* of May, 1796, and that for two years they had lived together "for the space of two years in all possible connuptial (*sic*) love and friendship," after which, "without cause assigned or any application for a divorce," he had "absconded and has never been heard of by his said wife or any other person." In the description which followed he is described as having been at that time "upwards of twenty large odd years of age . . . with his speech rather on the shrill key."

POWER OF COUNTY COURTS.[27] "All the elections to county offices at this time from sheriff and clerk, register of deeds, coroner, entry taker, surveyor and treasurer, down to treasurer of public buildings and standard keeper, were made by the county court.

SUPERIOR COURTS.[27] "It will be remembered, too, that at the beginning the Superior courts were held at Morganton. In 1806, the legislature of the State, after reciting that 'the delays and expenses inseparable from the constitution of the courts of this State do often amount to a denial of justice, the ruin of suitors, and render a change in the same indispensibly necessary,' enacted 'that a Superior court shall be held at the court house in each county in the State twice in every year,' and divided the State into six circuits, of whicht he last comprised the counties of Surry, Wilkes, Ashe, Buncombe, Rutherford, Burke, Lincoln, Iredell, Cabarrus and Mecklenburg, and directed the courts to be held in Buncombe the first Monday after the fourth Monday in March and September."

RANDALL DELK'S CONVICTION.[27] "Thus in 1807 was held Buncombe's first Superior court, in the spring of that year. The first trial for a capital offence in Buncombe county was that of Randall Delk. This trial occurred in 1807 or 1808.

Delk had fled after the commission of the offence to the Indian nation, but he was followed, brought back, tried, condemned and hung. This was the first execution in Buncombe county, and took place just south of Patton avenue opposite to the postoffice. It is said that soon after a negro was executed in the county, but the third capital execution in Buncombe is the most celebrated in her annals.

JUDICIAL MURDER.[27] "Subsequent to the execution of Delk and between the years 1832 and 1835, inclusive, Sneed and Henry, two Tennesseeans, were charged with highway robbery committed upon one Holcombe at the Maple Spring, about one-half mile east of the [former] city water works, on the road until recently traveled up Swannanoa. This was then a capital offence. They strenuously insisted that they had won from Holcombe in gambling the horse and other articles of which he claimed that they had robbed him. They were convicted, however, and hanged in the immediate vicintiy of the crossing of East and Seney streets. The field here was until recently known as the Gallows Field. The trial created intense public excitement, and it has always been the popular opinion that it was a judicial murder. It is said that after their conviction they sent for Holcombe, who shrank from facing them, and that the subsequent life of this man was one of continued misfortune and suffering."

COL. A. T. DAVIDSON'S RECOLLECTION OF THIS EXECUTION.[28] "The first time I ever was in Asheville was in 1835 . . . when I was sixteen years of age. It was on the occasion of the hanging of Sneed and Henry. The town was then small; to me, however, it seemed very large. I remember distinctly Wiley Jones, sheriff, and Col. Enoch Cunningham, captain of the guard. The religious services at the scaffold were conducted by Thomas Stradley and Joseph Haskew. What a surging, rushing, mad, excited crowd! This was my introduction to the county."

DR. J. S. T. BAIRD'S REMINISCENCES. About the year 1855 Know-Nothingism was rampant even in Buncombe, and Dr. J. S. T. Baird was temporarily won by its wiles; but he soon deserted. From 1853 to 1857 Dr. Baird was clerk of Buncombe county court, and was called to attend a term at Jewel Hill, Madison county. Neely Tweed was the clerk and Ransom P. Merrill sheriff; the latter was killed by the former at Marshall in a political quarrel after the Civil War. Sheriff Merrill made a return on a *fi. fa.* as follows : "Trew Sarch made. No goods, chattles, lands or tenements to be found in my county. The defendant is dead and in hell, or in Texas, I don't know which." For this facetiousness Judge Caldwell summoned the sheriff to the bar and gave him a reprimand. Dr. Baird defeated Philetus W. Roberts, incumbent, in 1853, J. M. Israel in 1855, and Silas Dougherty for clerk of court in 1857.

The following recollections of incidents and members of the bar are taken from Dr. J. S. T. Baird's sparkling "Reminiscences" [about 1840] published in the Asheville *Saturday Register* in 1905.

Court House.

"The court house was a brick building two stories high and about thirty-six by twenty-four feet in dimensions. The upper room was used for court purposes and was reached by a flight of stone steps about eight feet wide, and on the front outside of the building, commencing at the corners at the ground and rising gradually till they formed a wide landing in front of and on a level with the door of the court room. The judge's bench or pulpit, as some called it, was a sort of box open at the top and one side, with plank in front for the judge to lay his 'specks' on. He entered it from the open space in the rear and sat on an old stool-bottom chair, which raised his head parely above the 'spectacle board.' There was room enough in this little box for such slim men as Judge J. L. Bailey, David Caldwell, David Settle and others of their build, but when such men as Judge Romulus M. Saunders came along he filled it plumb 'up.' Most of the lower story was without floors or door shutters and furnished comfortable quarters for Mr. James M. Smith's hogs and occasionally a few straggling cattle that could not find shelter elsewhere.

In Terror of the Whipping-Post.

"It will be remembered that in those days the great terror set up before rogues was the whipping-post where the fellow convicted of larceny got thirty-nine lashes well laid on his bare back with long keen switches in the hands of the sheriff. This writer never had the heart to witness but one of these performances. A fellow by the name of Tom G. had been convicted of stealing a dozen bundles of oats and ordered by the court to be whipped. The sheriff, Pierce Roberts, took this writer and some other boys, and went to Battery Park hill, which was then a dense chinquapin thicket, and there cut eight of the nicest and keenest switches to be found and, returning, took Mr. G. from the jail, placed his feet and hands in the stocks, and stripping him 'stark naked' from neck to hips, laid upon his bare back thirty-nine distinct stripes from some of which the blood oozed out and ran down his back. Five strokes were given with each switch save the last, and with it four. The sheriff was merciful and made his strokes as light as possible, yet he gave him a blooming back to carry out of the state with him, for he went instanter.

"M" FOR MANSLAUGHTER.

"In that day the penalty for manslaughter was branding in the palm of the right hand with a red hot iron shaped to the letter M. I saw one fellow taken through this barbarous process and this was enough for me. He was convicted and ordered to be branded. The sheriff went to the tinner's shop and procured a little hand stove filled with good live coals and brought it into the court room and, putting his branding iron into it, soon had it to a white heat. In the meantime the prisoner's hand and arm were securely strapped to the railing of the bar, and then all things were ready. During the branding the prisoner was required to repeat three times the words : 'God save the state,' and the duration of the branding was limited by the time in which he could repeat those words. In this case the prisoner's counsel, General B. M. Edney, who was a rapid talker, had gotten the consent of the judge, inasmuch as the prisoner was much agitated and slow spoken anyway, for him to repeat the words for his client. When the hot iron was applied, for some reason, the general got tangled and his mouth did not go off well, but the iron was doing its work and the fellow was writhing and groaning all the same. At this juncture the general sprang forward, and knocking the iron aside, said : 'Mr Sheriff, you have burnt him enough.' The judge then taking his hands from over his face, heaved a sigh of relief and ordered the prisoner turned loose. A story was told of a fellow who, a few years before this, was branded by the sheriff whose name was David Tate. The prisoner was a man of wonderful nerve. He felt very resentful toward the sheriff whom he considered responsible for all his suffering. When the iron was applied he repeated the required words three times in a firm voice. Saying : 'God save the State, God save the State, God save the State,' and then raising his voice to a high pitch he yelled out : '——— d—n old Dave Tate'! This last is tradition. I will not vouch for the truth of it. Yet grotesque scenes often characterized the courts of that day.

OLD LAWYERS.

"The bar of Asheville in 1840 was not large in numbers but was exceedingly strong in all the qualities that go to make up a grand and noble profession. General Thomas L. Clingman early turned aside from his profession and gave his life to politics, in which field he maintained through a long career and to the day of his death the purity of his escutcheon. Although not as magnetic in his personality as some men, yet a wiser statesman or braver soldier or truer, grander man and patriot North Carolina has never produced. The people especially of Western North Carolina owe to his memory a lasting monument.

"Ezekiel McClure, was a man of good attainments in the law, but being enamored of rural life, gave up his profession at an early day and spent his life quietly in the country.

Not a "Skelper."

"William Williams went from the mercantile counter to the bar but failed to reach 'the top.' I will not class him with the 'skelpers'; but then he was what Capt. Jim Gudger would term 'shifty.' The word 'skelper' in fox hunter's parlance when applied to a dog means one that for want of bottom, cannot come down to 'dead packing' and follow the game tlrough all its windings and doublings, but short cuts and skims the high ridges and jumps high to see and catch the game unawares.

Gen. Bayles M. Edney, Wit.

"General Bayles M. Edney was a man of fine physique, who always kept his whiskers trimmed 'a la mode'. He was of commanding appearance and possessed of sparkling wit and infinite and pleasing humor. He was a stormer before a jury."

THE NOMINAL FINE AND THE REAL COW.[29] One of his clients in Yancey county, having been convicted, was called up for sentence. Col. Edney urged in mitigation that he was a poor man and a good citizen, and the Court said he would impose a nominal fine of twenty dollars. Whereupon, Bayles retorted that it would take not a nominal but a real cow to pay that nominal fine.

JOSHUA ROBERTS, OLD-TIME GENTLEMAN.[30] "Mr. Roberts, about the time of which I [Dr. Baird] write (1840), established a most pleasant and delightful home on the French Broad, about where the Southern depot now stands, and there he spent his life and raised a large family. To bear testimony to the high character and noble, sterling qualities of such a man as Joshua Roberts is a privilege of which I am glad to avail myself. He was truly a model old-time gentleman; a lawyer by profession, though not engaging largely in practice at the bar. It was said of him, by those who were capable of judging, that he had no superior as far as knowledge of the law was concerned. He was especially held in high esteem by the boys and young men toward whom his manner was always kindly and gracious. He took great interest and pride in the institution of Free Masonry and was the first and, for many years, the Worshipful Master of Mt. Hermon Lodge. He loved to bring men into the order for he believed in and practiced its principles.

ANOTHER CHARMING FAMILY.[30] "His family consisted of four sons and four daughters. The sons were Philetus W., John M., William and Martin; the daughters were Miss Aurelia, who married a Methodist minister, Rev. Mr. Wells; Miss Sarah, who married Mr. John H. Christie; Miss Harriett, who married Rev. William M. Kerr, well known to many citizens of Asheville and father of Mr. J. P. Kerr; Miss Jane, who married Dr. George W. Whitson, who is also well known to our people.

PHILETUS W. ROBERTS. [30]   "Philetus W. Roberts was an able young lawyer and was just entering upon a career which promised great usefulness and success when the Civil War came up, in which he sacrificed his life for his country. This writer succeeded him as clerk of the Superior court of Buncombe in 1853 . . . and I have never known a more scrupulously honest and conscientious man in all my life."

OTIUM "CUM" DIGNITATE. [30]   General Robert M. Henry, who came to the bar some later, was a fine lawyer, but a great lover of "rest and ease."   He loved to hear and tell good jokes and laugh in his deep sepulchral tones.   From 1868 to 1876 he was solicitor of the Western circuit.

JUDGE RILEY H. CANNON. [30]   Riley H. Cannon, who came in about this time, was a modest and even-timed man.   He was not prominent until after the war when he was made a judge of the Superior courts of the State.

COL. JOHN W. WOODFIN. [30]   Maj. John W. Woodfin came to the bar, I think, about 1845.   He was a man of splendid qualities all round.   He was a magnetic man, a genial, sunny man.   While not possessing the "heft" of his brother Nicholas as a lawyer, he was nevertheless a fine lawyer and succeeded well in his profession.   In his forensic efforts he often found occasion to deal in bitter sarcasm and keen and withering invective, which he could do to perfection for he was a master of both.   He was a handsome, dashing and brave man, and gave his life for his country's cause.

> "How sleep the brave who sink to rest
> By all their country's wishes blest.
> There honor comes a pilgrim gray,
> To bless the turf that wraps their clay."

COL. N. W. WOODFIN'S CHARMING FAMILY. [30]   Mr. Woodfin married Miss Eliza McDowell, daughter of Col. Charles McDowell of Burke County.   She was a queenly woman and most gracious and lovable in her disposition.   The family, consisting of three daughters, who are all now [1905] living in Asheville, are as follows: Miss Anna, so well beloved by all the people of Asheville; Mrs. Lillie Jones, widow of Mr. Benson Jones, who died many years ago, and Mrs. Mira Holland.

GEORGE W. CANDLER.[30] Almost the exact counterpart of Mr. N. W. Woodfin was George W. Candler. Here was a sturdy, stalwart, rugged man of the people, with brawn and brain to match, a powerful frame encasing a big, warm heart, and all presided over by a masterly intellect. When he began to planth imself for a legal battle on the "Serug" style, it was like a mighty giant placing his feet and clothing his neck and gathering his strength to upturn everything that came in his way, and he generally did so. He, too, was a close student of human nature and knew where to feel for a responsive chord. This and his exceeding plain manner made him a "power" before a jury. He generally won his cases. He was fond of rural life and loved much more to wade in the creeks and fish than to "bother with courts." We shall see few, if any, more like him. He was my valued friend and I cherish with affection his memory.

NON-RESIDENT LAWYERS.[30] Those who attended the courts of Buncombe from other counties were: Col. John Gray Bynum, Col. Burgess S. Gaither, Col. Waightstill W. Avery, Col. John Baxter, George Baxter, Esq., Samuel Fleming, Michael Francis and William Bryson, with occasionally some others. These were all exceedingly strong lawyers and when they were all present with our local bar and with such judges to preside as Romulus M. Saunders or David R. Caldwell or John L. Bailey or David Settle, John M. Dick or Mathias Manly, it was "court right and commanded universal respect."

STICKLERS FOR FASHION AS WELL AS FORM.[30] The lawyers of that day almost universally dressed in regulation style and not as they do now. A coat of the finest French broadcloth of swallow-tail or cutaway style with fine doe-skin cassimer pants, silk or satin vest, "nine biler" silk hat, ruffled and fluted bosom shirt and French calf-skin boots and a handsome necktie, made up the lawyer's suit.

YOUNG MEN OF ABILITY.[30] "From about 1849 to 1852, there came to the bar of Asheville half a dozen young men who, for brilliancy and real ability, have never been equaled at any bar in the State, coming as they did so nearly at the same time.   There were Philetus W. Roberts, Marcus Erwin, Newton Coleman, David Coleman, Zebulon B. Vance, James L. Henry, and Augustus S. Merrimon.   All these were men of the first order of ability and those of them who lived to maturer manhood all made their mark, not only in their profession, but in the councils of the State and nation as well and some have left their names emblazoned high on the roll of fame, but of all of those of whom I have written, there is no one left to greet me today.   They have all passed to the 'other shore' and are resting with the great silent host. May we see them all again in that 'great bright morning.'"

JOSEPH W. TODD, ESQ., was born in Jefferson September 3, 1834, was admitted to the bar after the Civil War, in which he had served gallantly.   He is said to have been the only lawyer who ever told a joke (successfully) to the State Supreme court. He was never a very ardent student, but his wit, humor and resourcefulness, at the bar and on the hustings, were marked. He died June 28, 1909.   His contest with the Rev. Christian Moretz for the legislature in the seventies is still remembered for the vigor and energy displayed by both candidates.   He gave the name of "red-legged grass-hoppers" to the internal revenue agents, who, soon after the Civil War, were the first to wear leather leggins in their peregrinations through the mountains in search of blockade stills.   Those who remember the famous joint canvass of Gov. Vance and Judge Thomas Settle in the summer of 1876 for the office of governor will recall that Vance made much capital of the red-legged grass-hoppers, a name he applied to all in the service of the general government, until Settle showed that two of Vance's sons were in the service of the United States, one in the naval academy and the other at West Point.   Mr. Todd's daughter still preserves a caricature of this canvass.   He married Sallie Waugh of Shouns, Tenn.

"TWENTY-DOLLAR LAWYERS."   Under the act of 1868-69, (ch. 46) any male twenty-one years of age could, by proving a good character, and paying a license tax of twenty dollars— that was the main thing in the eyes of the carpet-bag legislators of that time—get a license to practice law in North Carolina without undergoing any examination as to academic or legal knowledge whatever.   Under it several lawyers began practice of this "learned profession."   This act, however, was repealed in 1872.

MARCUS ERWIN. He was the son of Leander Erwin and a grandson of Wm. Willoughby Erwin and a great grandson of Arthur Erwin. His father removed from Burke county to New Orleans, from which place Marcus was sent to Center College in Kentucky, where he was a college-mate of Gen. John C. Breckenridge. After graduation Marcus Erwin was studying law in New Orleans when the Mexican War began, in which he served six months. After this war he came to Asheville and became editor of the *News*, a Democratic paper, after having changed from Whig politics on account of the acquisition of new territory. His connection with this paper led to a duel with the late John Baxter. Later he became a prominent laywer and Democratic leader, and was elected solicitor of the large district extending from Cleveland to Cherokee. He was a member of the legislature in 1850, 1856 and 1860. "He was a powerful prosecutor, and maintained as high a reputation as B. S. Gaither and Joseph Wilson had established."[31] He was a Secessionist, and in the discussion between himself and Governor John M. Morehead in the State senate in 1860-61 made an especially powerful and memorable speech. He joined the Confederate Army and became a major in a battalion of which O. Jennings Wise, a son of Henry A. Wise of Virginia, was lieutenant-colonel. This battalion was captured in the fall of 1861 at Roanoke Island. Major Erwin "rendered volunteer service subsequently in the southwest. He ran as a candidate for the Confederate Congress, but was defeated. In 1868 he cast in his lot with the Republican party, and afterwards became assistant district attorney of the United States, where he displayed great ability." He was a man of varied attainments and versatile talents, and spoke a number of modern languages. He was familiar with the best literature and was one of the most effective and eloquent of political speakers. Governor Vance is said to have dreaded meeting Major Erwin on the stump more than any other. Their debates may be likened to the storied duel between the battle-ax of Richard and the cimeter of Saladin.

CALVIN MONROE McCLOUD. He was born at Franklin, Macon county, N. C., February 9, 1840, where he obtained only a common school education. He volunteered in the Confederate Army, where he served till the close of the War. In 1865-66 he studied law in Asheville under the late Judge J. L. Bailey. On the 5th of July, 1866, he married Miss Ella Pulliam, daughter of the late R. W. Pulliam. He formed a partnership with the late N. W. Woodfin for the practice of law. He died June 20, 1891. He was a public spirited citizen and did much to promote the welfare of Asheville and the community, having been among 'the first to agitate a street railway, gas, telegraph, and other enterprises.

JUDGE EDWARD J. ASTON. He was born in November, 1826, in Rogersville, Tenn. He married Miss Cordelia Gilliland in November, 1852, moving to Asheville in 1853, where he engaged in the drug, stationery and bookstore business. He was three times mayor of Asheville and a director of the first railroad. He was among the first to see Asheville's great future as a health and pleasure resort. He not only donated books but supplied the first room for the Asheville public library. In 1865 he added real estate to his business, and later on insurance, soon becoming head of the firm of Aston, Rawls & Co. He is credited with having originated the idea of making Asheville the sanatorium of the nation. He devoted much time and large means to the distribution of circulars and literature setting forth the advantages of this climate. In 1871 he interested the Gatchel brothers in establishing the first sanatorium at Forest Hill. Then he got Dr. Gleitzman of Germany to open another in Asheville. It was largely through his influence that the Rev. L. M. Pease established his school for girls here. He also had much to do with getting the late G. W. Pack to build a home in Asheville. Judge Aston was so called because he had studied law, but had abandoned the practice. He died in 1893.

POST-BELLUM LAWYERS. Space can be given to only a few of the more prominent attorneys who came to the bar after the Civil War and have passed beyond the *nisi prius* courts. William Henry Malone wrote several valuable law books, his "Real Property Trials" being indispensable; Melvin E. Carter for years was one of the most prominent and able of the Asheville bar, enjoying an extensive practice, and being a sound lawyer; T. H. Cobb was one of the clearest and most forceful of attorneys; Kope Elias of Franklin enjoyed an extensive practice in Cherokee, Macon, Clay, Graham and Jackson counties. For a sketch of Gen. James G. Martin, who came to the bar late in life, after the Civil War, see chapter 27. He was one of the commissioners in the investigation of the Swepson and Littlefield frauds.

JUDGE JOHN BAXTER. He was the son of William Baxter and Catherine Lee, and was born at Rutherfordton, N. C., March 19, 1819. He was admitted to the bar in 1840. He married Orra Alexander, daughter of James M. Alexander of Buncombe, June 26, 1842. He was a member of the legislature from Rutherford county in 1842. He lived for several years in Hendersonville, but afterwards removed to Asheville. About 1852 he fought a duel with the late Marcus Erwin, Esq., and was wounded in the hand. He moved to Knoxville, Tennessee, in May, 1857. He was a strong Union man during and before the Civil War. He was appointed United States Circuit Judge by President Hayes in December, 1877, for the sixth circuit — Tennessee, Kentucky, Ohio and Michigan. Some of his decisions are said to stand high with the English courts. He died at Hot Springs, Arkansas, April 2, 1886, and was buried in Gray cemetery, Knoxville, Tennessee.

JUDGE J. C. L. GUDGER. He was born in Buncombe county, July 4, 1837. His father was Samuel Bell Gudger and his mother Elizabeth Siler Lowery, a daughter of James Lowery who held a captain's commission in the war of 1812. He was educated at Sand Hill academy and Reems Creek high school, now known as Weaverville college. He was admitted to the bar in August, 1860. He enlisted in the 25th N. C. Infantry July 22, 1861, and served till the close of the war. He moved to Waynesville December, 1865. He was married to Miss Mary Goodwin Willis of Buncombe county August 28, 1861. He was elected judge of the Superior court in August 1878, and served eight years. He held a position in the United States Treasury for years. He died January 29, 1913.

JUDGE WILLIAM L. NORWOOD. He was born in Franklin county, N. C., July 1, 1841. His father was James H. Norwood, a native of Hillsborough and a graduate of the State University. In 1846 James H. Norwood moved with his family to Haywood county and engaged in the practice of the law, and for several years conducted a classical school. In 1852 he was murdered at Sargents Bluff on the Missouri river, while serving as agent of the Sioux Indians. W. L.

Norwood was graduated from Bingham's School in 1856, after which he attended the school of Leonidas F. Siler in Macon county. He taught school in Haywood county till 1861, when he enlisted in Arkansas and served throughout the war. He was admitted to the bar in 1866, and was elected judge of the Superior court in November, 1894, from which position he resigned in 1899. On March 4, 1872, Judge Norwood married Miss Anna Duckworth of Brevard. He died about 1909.

JUDGE EUGENE DOUGLAS CARTER. He was the eldest son of Thomas D. and Sarah A. E. Carter, and was born May 18, 1856, in North Cove, McDowell county, was educated at Col. Lee's school in Chunn's cove, at Wafford College, at Weaverville College, and at the University of North Carolina. He married Miss Sallie M. Crisp in June, 1877, at Fayetteville, and began the practice of law at that place, but soon removed to Asheville, where he was several times elected solicitor of the Criminal court of Buncombe county, making an excellent prosecutor. He was appointed by Gov. Russell in the summer of 1898 to fill the vacancy caused by the supposed resignation of Judge W. L. Norwood as judge of the Superior court. But Judge Norwood denied that he had legally resigned, and began *quo warranto* proceedings to recover the office, which abated by Judge Carter's death, October 10, 1898. Judge Carter evinced throughout his life a high order of literary and oratorical talent. As an advocate he had no superior at this bar.

JUDGE JOHN LANCASTER BAILEY. He was born August 13, 1795, in eastern North Carolina; was married June 21, 1821, to Miss Priscilla E. Brownrigg; was admitted to the bar at some date prior to 1821; was representative from Pasquotank county in House of Commons in 1824 and a senator in 1828 and 1832; was a delegate to the State Convention of 1835; was elected judge of the Superior court January 11, 1837, and resigned therefrom November 29, 1863, after a service of over twenty-six years; practiced law at Elizabeth City, and also taught law there, probably up to the time of his election as judge. It was about the time of his election as judge or a few years afterward that he removed to Hillsboro, and with Judge Nash taught school there. In 1859 he moved to Black Mountain, near what is now the intake of the Asheville water system and Mrs. J. K. Connally's summer home, where he taught a law school from 1859 to 1861. He moved to Asheville in 1865 and taught a law school there until about 1876. He also practiced law in Asheville in copartnership with the late Gen. J. G. Martin. He died June 20, 1877. Judge Bailey was loved and honored by all as an able and upright lawyer and a worthy and useful citizen. (For fuller sketch see "Biographical History of North Carolina, Vol. IV, p. 52, and Vol. VI, p. 6.)

JUDGE FRED MOORE was born in Buncombe county on the 10th day September, 1869. He was the son of Daniel K. Moore, and the grandson of Charles Moore and the great-grandson of William Moore, one of the pioneers who helped to drive back the Indians and establish peace in this section. He attended school at Sand Hill near his home, and was admitted to the bar at the September term, 1892, of the Supreme court. He spent part of his youth in Macon and Clay counties, and began the practice of the law at Webster, Jackson county as a partner of his cousin, Hon. Walter E. Moore. In 1893 he removed to Asheville and formed a copartnership with another cousin, Hon. Charles A. Moore. In 1898 he was elected judge of the Superior court of this judicial district. He died in August, 1908. Judge Moore's mother was a Miss Dickey of Cherokee, and his wife a Miss Enloe of Webster. He tried many important cases, and his rulings and decisions were fair and sound. His life was as nearly blameless as it is possible for human lives to be. When first made a judge he was probably the youngest who ever served on the Superior court.

JUDGE GEORGE A. JONES. He was born in Buncombe county February 15, 1849, a son of Andrew and Margaret Jones. He attended Sandhill Academy on Hominy creek while it was open during the Civil War, and early in the seventies removed to Franklin, Macon county, where he became an assistant in the high school and later principal. He was admitted to the bar in 1878, having married in December, 1875, Miss Lily Lyle, daughter of Dr. J. M. Lyle and Mrs. Laura Siler Lyle, his wife. There were six children by the union, and after the death of his first wife, he married, January 31, 1895, Miss Hattie B. Sloan, by whom he had four children. She was a daughter of Mr. and Mrs. W. M. Sloan. In 1889 Judge Jones represented Macon county in the legislature. In 1891 he was elected solicitor of the twelfth judicial district, and was re-elected in 1895, serving two full terms. In 1901 he was appointed by Gov. Aycock judge of Superior court of the newly created sixteenth judicial district and served about two years, when he resumed the practice of law at Franklin, where he died August 13, 1906.

JUDGE ROBERT P. DICK. Judge Dick was for many years U. S. district judge for the district of western North Carolina, having been appointed soon after the close of the Civil War, and serving continuously till July, 1898, when President McKinley appointed Hamilton G. Ewart of Hendersonville to that position; but as the senate failed to act upon this appointment the President sent his name to three successive sessions of the senate. But as that body persisted in its refusal either to reject or confirm this appointment, Judge Ewart's name was withdrawn and that of Hon. James E. Boyd sent in instead. This appointment was confirmed in 1900, Judge Ewart having served since July 13, 1898. Judge Dick had a great deal to do with the trial and sentencing of those who had violated the internal revenue laws, and was always considerate and merciful in imposing punishment on the poor people who were found guilty in this court, "thirty days in jail and a hundred dollars fine" being the almost universal sentence.

JUDGE LEONIDAS L. GREENE. He was born in Watauga county, in November, 1845, and was elected Superior Court Judge in 1896, and served as such till his death, November 2, 1898.

HON. CHARLES H. SIMONTON. Judge Simonton of Charleston, N. C., was Circuit judge of the United States for a number of years, succeeding the late Judge Hugh Bond of Baltimore of KuKluxfame. Upon his death in May, 1904, President Roosevelt appointed Hon. Jeter C. Pritchard judge of this circuit, and he was confirmed by the senate without reference to the judiciary committee. He qualified June 1st, 1904, having remained in Washington as judge of the District court there to try an important case by special request of President Roosevelt.

COLONEL ALLEN TURNER DAVIDSON. He was born on Jonathan's creek, Haywood county, May 9, 1819. His father was William Mitchell Davidson and his mother Elizabeth Vance

A. S. Davidson

of Burke county, a daughter of Captain David Vance of Revolutionary fame. William Davidson, first senator from Buncombe county and a soldier of the Revolutionary War, was the father of William Mitchell Davidson, and a cousin of Gen. William Davidson who was killed at Cowan's Ford. Col. Allen T. Davidson attended the country schools of his day, and at twenty years of age he was employed in his father's store at Waynesville, and in 1842 married Miss Elizabeth A. Howell. He began the study of law, and in 1843 became clerk and master in equity of Haywood county, being admitted to the bar in 1845. In 1846 he removed to Murphy, Cherokee county, then a remote backwoods place. He at once took a leading place at the bar of the western circuit, and during his sixteen years residence there served as solicitor of Cherokee county, and became one of the leading lawyers of this section. In April, 1860, he became president of the Merchants and Miners Bank. The secession convention of 1861 chose him one of the delegates from Macon county to the provisional congress of the Southern Confederacy. He served out the provisional term and was elected in 1862 a member of the permanent congress, serving till the spring of 1864, being succeeded by the late Judge G. W. Logan of Rutherford county. In 1864-65 he served as a member of the council of Governor Vance, and at the same time acted as agent of the commissary department of the State in supplying the families of Confederate soldiers in this section. In the fall of 1865 he settled in Franklin, Macon county, and in 1869 he came to Asheville to live, buying and occupying the Morrison house, which stood where the present county court house stands. He soon became leader of the Asheville bar, and continued in active practice till 1885, when he retired. He died at Asheville, January 24, 1905.

Following is an editorial which appeared in the Asheville *Gazette-News* on that date:

"The last survivor of the Confederate Congress is no more. After a long and eventful life he has now been introduced to the mystery of the Infinite. He has read the riddle of life in the darkness of death. He knows it all now. The veil has been lifted and the contracted vision of earth has been expanded into the measureless profundity of eternity. Born, lived and died—behold the great epitome of man.

"The announcement of the passing of this historic figure from the familiar scenes of life will awaken sorrow in many hearts from the Blue

Ridge to the Unakas and the Great Smokies, for it was upon this elevated stage that his active life was spent. It was here that he began, a strong-limbed herder of cattle upon the verdant slopes and ghostly balds of the Cataloochee mountains, that career of activity that led him by successive stages to the bar, to the Confederate Congress, to the chancel-rail of the church, and to a warm place in the hearts of many of the best people of the State.

"Twelve years ago (1893) he stood on the Bunk mountain in Haywood county with a boyhood companion (Lafayette Palmer) and pointed out the place of the lick-logs where he had been wont to repair at intervals to tend the cattle pastured there; and, looking fondly around at the once familiar scene, said, as great tears streamed down the age-furrowed face, 'Good-bye, world!' That was his last visit to that sacred spot, and he said then that he would never look upon that scene again. Probably there was no tie that he had to break as age grew upon him that caused him a sharper pang than the parting from his beloved mountains. Certainly no man will be more missed by the people who live in these mountains than this man who bade them farewell so many years ago.

"Col. Davidson was a strong and rugged character. He had strong passions, strong muscles, strong intellect. He wore his heart upon his sleeve. He was open and above-board in his likes and dislikes. He was a true and faithful friend and a bold and unconcealed enemy. Meeting in mid-life the stormy discords of civil strife in a community rent asunder over the question of union or disunion, it was inevitable that he should have awakened animosities.

"But no man had any reason to doubt where Allen Davidson stood' on personal, public or other questions. He spoke his mind freely and fearlessly. He hated shams and pretenses with holy hatred.

"From 1865 until 1885 he was admittedly the leader of the bar of what was then known as the Western Circuit, extending to Cherokee in the west and to Yancey and Mitchell in the north. There was no large case tried in this section between the years named in which he did not take a conspicuous and important part. Bold, aggressive and persistent, he stormed the defences of his opponents with all the dash and elan of a Prentiss or a Pinckney.

"Like a true poet he was 'dowered with the hate of hate, the scorn of scorn, the love of love.' His sense of humor was acute and never failing. No adversity could quench it. Some of his remarks will live as long as the traditions of the old bar survive. He knew the life and habits of the mountain people better, perhaps, than any other man at the bar, and his speeches always pointed a moral and adorned a tale. Juries and judges were swayed by his intense earnestness, for he always made his client's cause his own.

"Even in his old age he 'was yet in love with life and raptured with the world.' He rejoiced in his youth as, with halting foot-step he went downward to the grave; but for him the evil days came not nor did the years draw nigh in which he said : 'I have no pleasure in them.' Strong, vigorous and healthy in mind and body, he enjoyed to the utmost the good things of life and made no hypocritical pretense of despising them. With splendid physical development he towered among his fellows like a giant, and to him fear was an alien and a stranger.

"He was a kind-hearted and charitable man, loving to give of whatever he had of worldly goods, sympathy or kindly deeds. He was a faithful and affectionate husband, father, friend. A commanding and picturesque figure has passed from our midst."

His widow still survives him, and of his children the following still emulate his name and example most worthily: Hon. Theo. F. Davidson, late attorney general of the State; Mrs. Theodore S. Morrison, Mrs. W. B. Williamson, Mrs. William S. Child, Robert Vance Davidson, for several terms attorney general of Texas, Wilber S. Davidson, president of the First National Bank of Beaumont, Texas

JUDGE JAMES L. HENRY. He was born in Buncombe county, in 1838, and received only such education as the schools of the county afforded. He was a son of Robert Henry and Dorcas Bell Love, his wife. He was elected Superior court judge of the eighth judicial district in 1868, and served till 1878, having previously acted as solicitor for that district. [3][2] He was editor at the age of nineteen of the *Asheville Spectator*, served in the Civil War as adjutant of the 1st North Carolina Cavalry, and on Hampton's and Stewart's staffs, and as colonel of a cavalry battalion stationed at Asheville. He died in 1885.

COL. DAVID COLEMAN. He was born in Buncombe county February 5, 1824, and died at Asheville March 5, 1883. His father was William Coleman and his mother Miss Cynthia Swain, a sister of Governor D. L. Swain. He attended Newton Academy and entered the State University, and just prior to graduation entered the Naval Academy at Annapolis, graduated, and served in the navy till he resigned in 1850, returning to Asheville and entering upon the practice of law. In 1854 he was the Democratic candidate for State senator, defeating Col. N. W. Woodfin, and was reelected in 1856, defeating Zebulon Baird Vance, the only defeat by the people Vance ever sustained. In 1858 Coleman and Vance were rivals for Congress, but Vance won. Coleman was one of the few men of this section who were secessionists, and was appointed to the command of a ship, but the delays in its fitting out tried his spirit beyond endurance and he entered the army, and was assigned to a battalion which afterwards became the

39th North Carolina regiment, of which he was colonel. He resumed the practice of the law after the War, and was eminent as a lawyer. He was solicitor for a time and represented Buncombe county with Gen. Clingman in the State convention of 1875. He was a highly cultivated gentleman, a brave soldier and a lawyer above all chicanery. He never married. Gov. Swain was the first boy to enter the State University from the west, David Coleman was the second, and James Alfred Patton, a son of James W. Patton, the third. [33]

JUDGE RILEY H. CANNON. The following extract is taken from his obituary, written by the Hon. Robert D. Gilmer, late attorney general of North Carolina: "He was born in Buncombe county March 26, 1822, went to school at Sandhill Academy, was graduated from Emory and Henry College, Virginia; married Ann Sorrels October 18, 1850, to whom four children were born, namely, George W., once postmaster at Asheville, Eva, Lula A., and Laura. He was admitted to the bar in 1851, was appointed judge of the Superior court in 1868, and wore the judicial ermine during a troubled period in our State history. It was said, even by his political opponents, that he never allowed it to trail in the dust of party rancor or become soiled by the stains of partial rulings. He was a member of the Methodist Church for thirty years. He died in that faith February 15, 1886. He was an honest man."

JACOB W. BOWMAN was born in what is now Mitchell county July 31, 1831, and died at Bakersville, June 9, 1905. He married Miss Mary Garland in 1850. He was admitted to the bar before the Civil War, and was appointed United States assessor of internal revenue by Gen. Grant April, 1869. Governor Russell appointed him Superior court judge in November, 1898, to fill an unexpired term. He received the nomination of the Republicans for the full term, but was defeated by Judge Councill, Democrat.

JUDGE GEORGE W. LOGAN. He was born in Rutherford county. He lived near the Pools at Hickory Nut Falls, where he kept a tavern. He was elected to the Confederate Congress and qualified in May, 1864. He was a Superior Court judge from 1868 till his death in 1874.

JUDGE JOSEPH SHEPARD ADAMS. He was born at Strawberry Plains, Tennessee, October 12, 1850, and died at War-

renton, N. C., April 2, 1911. His father was Rev. Stephen
B. Adams and his mother Miss Cordelia Shepard. His father
established a school at Burnsville, Yancey county, before the
Civil War, which was known as Burnsville Academy. Joseph
Adams was a pupil at this academy, and afterwards attended
the school of Col. Stephen Lee in Chunn's Cove. He was
graduated with honor from Emory and Henry College, Virginia, in 1872. He studied law at Asheville under the late
Judge J. L. Bailey, and was soon afterwards admitted to
practice, opening an office at Bakersville. He was elected
solicitor of the Eighth district soon after beginning practice
and served in that capacity eight years. In 1877 he married
Miss Sallie Sneed Green of Greensboro, N. C. She died
November 16, 1901, leaving six children surviving. In 1885
he moved from Statesville to Asheville and began the practice of law, which he continued till his election to fill out the
unexpired term of the late Judge Fred Moore in 1908. He
was elected for a full term in 1910.

ALFONZO CALHOUN AVERY. He was the son of Isaac T.
and the grandson of Waightstill Avery, and was born at Swan
Ponds near Morganton, Burke county, September 11, 1835.
He died at Morganton, June 13, 1913. He attended Bingham
School in Orange county and graduated from the State University as A. B. in 1857, first in his class. He was admitted
to practice before the county courts in June, 1860, and before
the Superior courts in 1866. He was an officer in the Sixth
North Carolina regiment, and later became major and adjutant general of Gen. D. H. Hill's division. Later he was on
the staffs of Generals Breckenridge, Hood and Hindman.
In 1864 he was made colonel of a battalion in western North
Carolina, was captured near Salisbury by Stoneman's army,
and confined at Camp Chase till August, 1865. In 1861 he
married at Charlotte Miss Susan W. Morrison, a sister
of Mrs. "Stonewall" Jackson, and after her death he
married Miss Sarah Love Thomas in 1889. She was a
daughter of the late Col. W. H. Thomas of Jackson
county. In 1866 he was elected State senator from the Burke
district, and aided in building the Western North Carolina
Railroad to Asheville and in locating the State hospital for the
insane at Morganton. He was presidential elector in 1876,
and in 1878 he was elected judge of the Superior court. In

1889 he was elected associate justice of the Supreme court, and resumed the practice of his profession in 1897, at Morganton, and was active till his death. In 1889 the State University conferred upon him the degree of doctor of laws, and for more than twenty-five years he was a ruling elder of the Morganton Presbyterian church.

NOTES.

[1]A sketch of the judges of this State to 1865 will be found in the fourth volume of Battle's Digest, by W. H. Battle, Esq., and in Vol. II, Rev. St. N. C., p. 527 *et seq.*, is a "Sketch of the Judicial History of North Carolina," with a list of the judges and attorney generals since the adoption of the constitution. It also contains a sketch of the judicial procedure under the proprietary government. 103 N. C. Rep. has history of Supreme court.

[2]Potter's Revisal, p. 281 and p. 1050.

[3]Ibid., p. 297.

[4]Ibid., p. 887.

[3]Chief Justice Pearson is said to have pronounced Judges Leonard Henderson and John Hall the most profound jurists ever in North Carolina.

[4]Dropped Stitches.

[3]Potter's Revisal, p. 1039.

[5]Battle's Digest.

[6]Dropped Stitches, pp. 51-52.

[7]Ibid., pp. 52-53.

[8]Mr. McGimpsey was one of the ancestors of Judge Jeter C. Pritchard of Asheville.

[9]Ashe county record—not paged.

[10]Soon after the formation of one of the newer counties Judge Boykin gave a defendant his choice between thirty days in jail and one week at the only hotel in town. The defendant chose the jail. This was since the war, however.

[11]Recollection of Hon. J. H. Merrimon and Dr. T. A. Allen, Sr.

[12]Asheville's Centenary.

[13]Thomas Henry also was a soldier of the Revolution, and although he died soon thereafter, his name appears as a pensioner. Col. Rec., Vol. XVII, p. 217, where it appears that, he was paid through A. Lytle £60, 15s, 8d, according to the "Abstracts of the N. C. Line" settled by commissioners at Halifax from September 1, 1784, to February 1, 1785. He fought at Eutaw Springs.

[14]"I have myself heard my grandfather Michael Shenck, of Lincolnton, N. C., speak of Mr. Henry as 'a great land lawyer'." D. Schenck, Sr., March 28, 1891, in note to "Narrative of the Battle of Cowan's Ford," published by D. Schenck, Sr.

[15]He said he asked his father what the shouting was about, and he answered that "They are declaring for Liberty." W. L. Henry's affidavit filed with Mecklenburg Declaration Committee in 1897.

[16]Col. A. T. Davidson in Lyceum, p. 24, April, 1891.

[17]Asheville's Centenary.

[18]Ibid.

[19]Ibid.

[20]According to Judge James H. Merrimon, Hillman and Dews lived at Rutherfordton. He does not know the given name of Mr. Hillman, but states that Mr. Dew's was Thomas, and that in crossing the Green river he was drowned while yet a very young man, not much if any over twenty-five years of age. He says that the late Mr. N. W. Woodfin considered Dews the ablest man in the State of his age.

[21]The reference is to 1898, the monument having been completed in that year

[22]The same is true of Governor Swain, Generals Sevier, Waightstill Avery, the two McDowells, Rutherford, Shelby, Pickens, and others of Revolutionary fame, and little or no space can be spared in this volume in re-recording what has been already written and preserved of them.

[23]Asheville's Centenary.

[24]Ibid.

[25]Ibid.

[26]Ibid.

[27]Ibid.

[28]The Lyceum, April, 1891, p. 23.

[29]Related by Judge Geo. A. Shuford.

[30]From Reminiscences of Dr. J. S. T. Baird, published in 1905.

[31]From Mrs. Mattie S. Candler's History of "Henderson County."

[32]J. H. Wheeler's "Reminiscences."

[33]Miss Fanny L. Patton in the "Woman's Edition of the Asheville Citizen," November 28, 1895.

CHAPTER XVI

NOTABLE CASES AND DECISIONS

NOT ESPECIALLY CONTENTIOUS. Considering our ancestry and former isolation, we are not more contentious or litigious than others of our kind; but it must be admitted that we sometimes indulge in a lot of unnecessary litigation. Some of us are accused even of taking delight therein. Mr. J. H. Martin tells of an old Covenanter who announced with glee that all his children were married off, all his own debts paid, and that he had nothing else to do now but "to spend the balance of his life a-lawin'." Owing to the legislation regarding land grants and the registration of deeds, etc., much litigation has arisen, notably the large case of *Gilbert v. Hopkins*, involving many thousands of acres of land in Graham and Cherokee counties. That case was tried before Judge Connor in the U. S. Court at Asheville in 1910, but the jury disagreed. It was tried again before Judge Boyd at the same place, and he decided it in favor of defendants, plaintiffs appealing. A new trial was granted. But as no final decision has been reached in it, no results can be stated here. In it are involved almost every point of real estate law possible to arise. Pains have been taken to refer in this work only to the most notable cases that have been heard and decided. Each was of interest at the time it was tried.

LITIGATION AND LEGISLATION. James McConnell Smith was the first white child born west of the Blue Ridge, in Buncombe county, but he will be remembered longer than many because of his will. He died December 11, 1853, leaving a will by which he devised to his daughter, Elizabeth A., wife of J. H. Gudger, certain real estate in Asheville, "to her sole and separate use and benefit for and during her natural life, with remainder to such children as she may leave surviving her, and those representing the interest of any that may die leaving children." [1] A petition was filed in the Superior court asking for an order to sell this property, and such an order was made and several lots were sold with partial payments made of the purchase money, when a question was raised as to the power of the court to order the sale of the property so devised. In

Miller, *ex parte* (90 N. C. Reports, p. 625), the Supreme court held that land so devised could "not be sold for partition during the continuance of the estate of the life tenant; for, until the death of the life tenant, those in remainder cannot be ascertained." The sales so made, were, therefore, void.

But years passed and some of the property became quite valuable, while another part of it, being unimproved, was nonproductive, and a charge upon the productive portion. But there seemed to be no remedy till the city of Asheville condemned a portion of the productive part for the widening of College Street. The question then arose as to how the money paid by the city for the land so appropriated to public use should be applied. On this question the Supreme court decided in *Miller v. Asheville* (112 N. C. Reports, 759), that the money so paid by way of damages should be substituted for the realty, and upon the happening of the contingency—the death of the life tenant—be divided among the parties entitled in the same manner as the realty would have been if left intact.

Upon this hint, on the petition of the life tenant and the remaindermen, a special act was passed by the legislature (Private Laws of N. C., 1897, Ch. 152, p. 286) appointing C. H. Miller a commissioner of the General Assembly to sell the land, the proceeds to become a trust fund to be applied as the will directs.

This was done; but the Supreme court (*Miller v. Alexander,* 122 N. C., 718) held this was in effect an attempted judicial act and therefore unconstitutional. The legislature afterwards passed a general act, which is embodied in section 1590 of the Revisal, for the sale of estates similarly situated, and under this authority some of the land was sold and the proceeds were applied to the construction of a hotel on another part. The proceeds, however, proved insufficient to complete the hotel, and in an action brought to sell still more of this land for the purpose of completing the hotel, the Supreme court held in *Smith v. Miller* (151 N. C., p. 620), that, while the purchasers of the land already sold had received valid title to the same, still as the hotel, when completed, would not be a desirable investment, the decree for the sale of the other land, in order to provide funds for its completion, was void because it did not meet the statutory requirements that the interests involved be properly safeguarded.

A Long Legal Battle. In July, 1897, the First National
Bank of Asheville failed, and indictments were found in
in Greensboro against W. E. Breese, president, W. H. Penland, cashier, and J. E. Dickerson, a director, for violating
the United States banking laws. [2] In 1909 Breese and Dickerson were tried on a new indictment at Asheville before Judge
Purnell, Judge of the United States District court of the
Eastern District of North Carolina, assigned to hold the court
for this trial. The defendants were convicted, but took an
appeal and a new trial was granted. In 1902 Breese alone
was tried at Asheville before Judge Jackson of Virginia, and
there was a mistrial. In the same year the case was sent to
Charlotte and there was another mistrial. He was tried there
again and convicted, and sentenced to seven years in the penitentiary; but the court of appeals quashed the indictment
because two members of the grand jury who found the true
bill had not paid their poll taxes. This apparently ended
these cases, as the offences by this time had been barred by
the statute of limitations. But District Attorney Holton
resurrected the indictment found first at Greensboro in 1907, and
Breese and Dickerson were tried at Asheville upon that before
Judge Newman of Atlanta, in the summer of 1909, and convicted.
They were sentenced to two years and to a fine of $2,500
each, but appealed. The court of appeals were unable to
agree and, in November, 1911, certified the case to the Supreme court of the United States. In the spring of 1912 a
motion was made before that court to advance the case upon
the docket. It was granted and the appeal decided adversely
to the defendants in October, 1912.

THE SOLICITORSHIP. In the controversies over the Solicitorship in this section, between Ewart and Jones, [3] McCall and
Webb, [4] McCall and Zachery, [5] and McCall and Gardner, the
impression has gone out that, in one or the other of these
cases, the Supreme court reversed its holding in *Hoke v. Henderson*, [6] to the effect that an office to which a salary was
attached was property, and that the legislature could not de-
prive one elected to such an office of his rights by abolishing
the position. This, however, is wrong, as that case was not
overruled until August, 1903, in *Mile v. Ellington* (134 N. C.
Reports, 131).

MANY LEGAL POINTS SETTLED. The Western Carolina

Bank was chartered in 1887 (Ch. 48) and began business in
January, 1889. It failed, however, October 12, 1897, and
its officers executed a deed of assignment to Lewis Maddux,
its president, and L. P. McCloud, its cashier; but the Battery Park Bank and other creditors commenced an action
against the bank for the purpose of setting this deed of assignment aside; in consequence of which Judge H. G. Ewart,
judge of the Circuit Criminal court, undertook to appoint
receivers of the property. A few days later Judge W. L.
Norwood, holding Superior court in Clay county, appointed
the same parties receivers, there being doubt as to Judge
Ewart's jurisdiction.[8] George H. Smathers alone, however,
acted as receiver, the others having declined or resigned.
There was a class of creditors which filed a general creditors'
bill between the date of the appointment of receivers by
Judge Ewart and the date of the appointment by Judge Norwood, who thus sought to secure priority over the assets not
affected by the lien of creditors who had obtained judgments
before justices of the peace, as many had done; but the Supreme court refused priority to those thus seeking to secure
it.[7]

There were many other questions settled in the ensuing
litigation, for Receiver Smathers was removed and W. W.
Jones, Esq., appointed in his place in May, 1902; and he
immediately began to collect the assets of the bank, and to
compel Madison county to pay certain of its bonds which he
held among the assets of the defunct bank. The Supreme
court decided that each stockholder was liable to the extent
of double the amount of his stock.[9] It at first denied the
mandamus asked for to compel the commissioners of Madison county to levy a tax to pay its bonds[10] but on a rehearing
granted the mandamus. (137 N. C., 579.)

The question as to whether a married woman could escape
her liability as a stockholder was also settled adversely to
such claim.[11] In pursuit of the stockholders it became necessary for the receiver to get the legislature to pass an act
authorizing him to sue outside the State.[12]

LINVILLE LITIGATION. S. T. Kelsey and C. C. Hutchinson
had started Highlands; but Mr. Hutchinson, who was to
have provided the r   ͏y, found himself unable to do so,
and Mr. Henry Ste   ͏ditor of the agricultural depart-

ment of a New York newspaper, bought, through Kelsey, all the land Hutchinson was to have paid for. Then Stewart broke with Kelsey and the latter turned his attention to the development of the Linville country. Mr. S. P. Ravenal, Sr., advanced $500 for preliminary investigations, which resulted in the formation, about 1890, of the Linville Improvement Company with Messrs. Ravenal and Kelsey and the late Mr. Donald MacRae of Wilmington, N. C., as the principal stockholders. Neither Ravenal nor MacRae held a majority of the stock, thus giving Kelsey the balance of power.

There were three distinct lines of policy advocated by each of these gentlemen. Mr. MacRae wanted to bond the property for the construction of a railroad from Cranberry; Mr. Kelsey wished to establish an industrial center at Linville City; and Mr. Ravenal opposed both, but wanted to establish a health and pleasure resort at Linville City, sell lots and hold the 15,000 acres of timber land the company had acquired for future development. After a while Mr. Thomas F. Parker succeeded Mr. Ravenal and Mr. Hugh MacRae succeeded his father, Mr. Donald MacRae. These two could not agree and Mr. Kelsey, siding with the McRaes, a receiver was applied for and appointed between September 1, 1893, and September 1, 1894.

These disagreements among the stockholders of the Linville Improvement Company in relation to the general policy to be pursued by the officers in control, and especially in respect to the method of liquidating the outstanding indebtedness and encumbering the property of the company, were involved in an action brought against that company by T. B. Lenoir, executor of W. W. Lenoir, and decided by the Supreme court. (See 117 N. C. Reports, p. 471.) Thomas F. Parker had been president from September 1, 1893, to September 1, 1894, and Harlan P. Kelsey secretary for the same time. A special master had rejected the claims of these two officers for pay for services during this time, and the court held that they should have been allowed to prove that they had a contract for employment with the company for the entire year and not only up to the time of the appointment of a receiver.

After a while Mr. MacRae offered to sell his interest or buy that of Mr. Ravenal at a certain price. Mr. Ravenal sold.

A railroad was finally built to Pinola and Montezuma, two miles from Linville City. But the golden opportunity had passed. For, while the company was constructing the Yonahlossie turnpike from Linville City around the base of the Grandfather mountain to Blowing Rock, erecting a fine hotel and constructing a large dam for a lake at Linville City, the press was ringing with praises of the beauty of the scenery, the healthfulness of the surroundings and the general attractiveness of the place. Visitors came in numbers from various parts of the country and wished to invest in lots and build cottages. But, as the property was in litigation, titles could not be made to the lots, and the boom subsided. Blowing Rock, however, which before had been a mere hamlet, suddenly developed rapidly and substantially, and is today one of the finest and most attractive health and pleasure resorts in the mountains.

COLOR OF TITLE. In all countries one who enters upon land and holds possession under any paper writing of record that proclaims to the world that he is there by some real or pretended authority will secure title by adverse occupancy sooner than will he who "squats" upon land without any pretence that he has any right to be there other than his bare possession. In the early days of North Carolina the State granted large tracts of land to William Cochran and William Tate in July, 1795; and in July, 1796, just one year later, William Cathcart secured grants which were found to lap on those lands already granted to Tate and Cochran. It was impossible for Tate and Cochran to put settlers on their lands at that time, and having the senior grant they rested on their rights. But Cathcart was unwilling to lose any portion of the land he had paid the State ten cents an acre for, even though part of it was already the property of Tate and Cochran. So, in September, 1838, he leased all this disputed land to Abram Johnson, put him in possession of a part of it, and told him to exercise rights of ownership over as much as he did not actually occupy as he could. In order to do this Johnson built a forge near the Old Fields of Toe, and cut timber and burnt charcoal at many other places on the land. More than one hundred years after all these grants had been taken out the Supreme court decided that Cathcart's lease to Johnson was color of title to the lands described therein,

and that his title had ripened in seven years after the date
of the lease and Johnson's entry and occupancy, the lease
having been duly recorded in Morganton. Thus a junior
grant had held over its senior, because of this color of title.
(*Cochran v. Improvement Co.*, 127 N. C., 387.)

ADAMS V. WESTFELDT. As early as 1850 or 1851, the late
Stephen Munday entered land on Little Fork ridge, the Foster ridge, south and southeast of Haw Gap, and south of
Thunderhead mountain, because he believed that copper was
in the land; but positive indications of its existence were not
found until about 1858. The war coming on and interest
dying out, nothing further was done about investigating the
indications until about 1899.

In 1869 George Westfeldt of New Orleans bought, at the
bankrupt sale of E. H. Cunningham, four tracts of land on
the waters of Hazel creek which had been granted to the
latter. In 1877 Westfeldt, through his agent, Tennent, tried
to locate these tracts, but had to call in Wm. R. McDowell,
who lived near Franklin, to assist. He located them several
miles from where Tennent thought they lay. About 1888
copper was discovered on one of these tracts and men named
Cook, Hall, Mark Bryson and others attempted to find what
grant covered the copper deposit. They discovered that Epp.
Everett of Bryson City had several grants which he had not
succeeded in locating satisfactorily, but which he appeared to
think were several miles from the Westfeldt lands. It was
charged that, in attempting to locate one of these grants on
the copper vein, Adam Wilson had hacked a tree and then
smoked the hacks with pine splinters in order to give the
marks the appearance of age. On the other hand, Adams'
side claimed that persons in the interest of Westfeldt had
chopped the marks entirely out of a corner tree and had carried the marks off in the block of wood which had been removed. From this smoked tree it was claimed the line had
been run in 1890; but it was not satisfactory, and was abandoned, until in 1899, when W. S. Adams, of Massachusetts,
bought up the Everett grants and took possession of the copper lands. An old man living in Tennessee by the name of
Proctor, who had carried the chain when the Everett grants
were originally located, was brought to the land to help
establish Adams' contention as to the location. Westfeldt

had warned Adams not to trespass on this land and, in 1901, he sued Adams in Swain county and won the suit. But a new trial was granted by the Supreme court on the ground of the admission of incompetent evidence. The case was, by consent, removed to Haywood county, where the North Carolina Mining Company was made an additional defendant, and it set up a claim to the land in dispute, under the act of 1893, for determining adverse claims to real estate. Westfeldt won again, but the Supreme court granted still another new trial, because the trial judge had failed to call proper attention to the difference between substantive evidence and evidence that went merely to the credibility of a witness. Then the North Carolina Mining Company brought its bill in equity in the United States court for the Western District of North Carolina, to clear the title of the cloud placed upon it by Westfeldt's claim to the land. Judge Pritchard decided that he had jurisdiction, notwithstanding the pendency of the action between substantially the same parties in the State court. He heard the testimony, sitting as a chancellor, and without a jury to enlighten the court upon the disputed facts; and a short time before the case was to have been tried in Haywood, he filed his decree holding against Westfeldt.

After several years of effort the Supreme court of the United States decided that Judge Pritchard had not had jurisdiction when he took the case from the Superior court of Haywood county, and in 1910 the cause was tried at Waynesville, the plaintiff winning. The Supreme court of North Carolina in 1912 set the verdict aside, however, and the case will have to be tried again.[13] Both Westfeldt and Adams have since died.

AN ERRONEOUS IMPRESSION. It is sometimes said that the Supreme court of North Carolina has decided that a municipality may legally freeze a prisoner to death. This is wrong, the decision in *Moffit v. Asheville* having held quite to the contrary (103 N. C., p. 237). It was decided that when towns are "exercising the judicial, discretionary or legislative authority conferred by their directors, or are discharging a duty imposed solely for the public benefit, they are not liable for the negligence of their officers, unless some statute subjects them to liability for such negligence." Consequently, they held that the city was not liable for a severe cold and illness caused to Moffit by confinement, January 5, 1887, in a cell in a room from which window lights had been broken, the city having provided fuel and a stove and police officers to keep the room comfortable.

CRANBERRY MAGNETIC IRON MINES. From Hon. A. C. Avery of Morganton it has been learned that about 1780 Reuben White took out a grant for the 100 acres supposed to cover the iron deposit at these mines, and that Hon. Waightstill Avery took out four small grants surrounding the Reuben White grant.[14] In addition, he took out hundreds of 640-acre grants, covering almost all of the North Toe valley from its source to Toecane, except that here and there along the valley some older grants intervened. He also took grants to lands along Squirrel, Roaring, Henson and Three - Mile creeks, and the lower valley of South Toe and Linville rivers. In 1795 William Cathcart took out two large grants, one known as the "99,000-Acre Tract" and the other as the "59,000-Acre Tract," which two grants covered practically all of what is now Mitchell and Avery counties, except some tracts along the Blue Ridge, and embrace all the tracts along the streams theretofore granted to Waightstill Avery. He devised all these lands to his son, Isaac T. Avery. A controversy arose between the father of John Evans Brown, agent for the claimants under the Cathcart grants, which resulted in the execution of compromise deeds in 1852, by which I. T. Avery got a quit claim to about 50,000 acres of land, so as to include most of the land described, including the Cranberry Mines. The Reuben White tract had in the meantime passed by a succession of conveyances to William Dugger, who sold his interest to Hoke, Hutchinson and Sumner; Dugger, Avery and Brown having entered into a written agreement under which Avery and Brown were to hold one-half of one-fourth each of the mineral interest in all the Dugger land outside of the Reuben White tract. . . . But, before Dugger conveyed to Hoke, Hutchinson and Sumner, he had contracted to sell to John Harding, Miller and another, and had put Harding in possession, so that the Hoke purchase was from Harding and associates, taking the legal title from Dugger. Judge A. C. Avery, as executor of his father's (I. T. Avery) estate, gave notice to Hoke and company of the equitable claim of Brown and Avery in three thousand acres, embracing the Cranberry ore bank, before they bought from Dugger, and in the ensuing litigation compelled Hoke and Company to pay between fifteen and twenty thousand dollars for the Brown and Avery interests in the Cranberry ore bank.

BEFORE THE LITIGATION BEGAN. Exactly when the Cranberry Iron mine was first operated cannot be determined now. Joshua Perkins and a man named Asher built what was afterwards known as the Dugger mine, on the right bank of the Watauga in what is now Johnson county, Tenn., and four miles above Butler. Remains of the old forge are still visible there, just above the present iron bridge, the forge itself having been washed away in the freshet of 1886 or 1887. Tradition says that Perkins and Asher sold this forge to William, Abe and John Dugger, and then went to Cranberry and built the forge there. These Dugger brothers were the sons of Julius Dugger who owned a farm on the right bank of the Watauga, opposite Fish Springs; and soon took charge of the forge Perkins had built at Cranberry. But when either forge was built "no man knoweth." Only one fact could be secured, and that was that in November, 1886, Joshua Perkins bought a bill of goods at Curtis and Farthing's store at Butler. All agree that he was then over eighty years of age, and that he died soon afterwards. Assuming, then, that he was eighty-six years of age in 1886, and that he was at least twenty-one when he built the Dugger forge four miles above Butler, the Cranberry forge most probably was built not earlier than 1821 to 1825. Benjamin Dugger was also concerned in this Cranberry forge, but afterwards went to Ducktown, Tenn. Upon his death John Hardin went into possession of the mine, either by his own right or as guardian of Able's heirs. It was sold by John Hardin or his son Councill Hardin, to Gen. R. F. Hoke for $10,000 and he sold to the company now owning it. Shep. M. Dugger, in his "Balsam Groves of the Grandfather Mountain" (p. 15), says: "In the year 1850 the now famous Cranberry Iron mines were in their infantile state of development. The Dugger family had been the first to build forges and hammer iron in Tennessee, and the writer's grandfather and great uncle had now crossed the line, and purchased the mines and tilt-hammer forge at Cranberry."

THE CARTER AND HOKE LITIGATION. Thomas D. Carter had an equitable contract for the sale of a part of the interest held under bond for title by John Hardin, Miller and another, and this led to the litigation which culminated in the case of *Thomas D. Carter v. Robert F. Hoke and others* (64 N. C. Rep., p. 348). It appears that, in May, 1867, the plaintiff agreed to convey his interest in the Cranberry Iron mines to Gen. Hoke and others for $44,000, and when he tendered a deed therefor he was given a sight draft on a New York bank for the amount of the purchase money, which draft was protested and never paid; but that the reason it had not been paid was because it had been well understood by the parties to the transaction that, although it was a sight draft, the funds to meet it were to have been provided by the proceeds of a sale of the same property by Hoke and associates to another purchaser, which contemplated sale Carter had defeated. Upon this state of facts a receiver was appointed and the sale of the property was enjoined. At the Spring term, 1869, of the Superior court of Madison county, Hoke moved to dissolve the injunction and end the receivership. Upon the hearing of that motion it appeared that Hoke and associates had effected another sale of the property to the Russells and associates, for $50,000, and they claimed to have been innocent purchasers without notice. Judge Henry granted the motion; but on appeal the Supreme court continued the injunction against a sale of the property till Carter had been paid and the question as to whether the Russells were innocent purchasers had been tried. Hoke and company soon afterwards compromised with Carter and the title to the property was thus settled so far as Carter was concerned.

A FURTHER STORY OF THE LITIGATION. The interests of the original purchasers of the White and Avery Ore-Bank tracts, as well as the interests of the claimants of adjacent lands under a forge bounty grant (junior to the 59,000-acre grant of 1796), were sold for partition under a decree of the Supreme court at its session at Morganton before the Civil War, and was bought by William Dugger. He subsequently paid the purchase money and got a decree that James R. Dodge, clerk of the Supreme court at Morganton, should make title to him. Before getting his title, however, but after he had paid the purchase money, William Dugger en-

tered into an agreement with Isaac T. Avery and J. Evans
Brown that the three should hold an equal one-third interest
in all the mineral outside of the original White Ore-Bank
tract.   But this agreement seems not to have been registered;
and, the Civil War coming on, the sessions of the Supreme court
at Morganton were abolished.   Then Col. Dodge, the clerk, died
without having made title to William Dugger.   Meantime,
Judge A. C. Avery secured through Hon. B. F. Moore an
ordinance of the Convention of 1866 authorizing Mr. Freeman, who was then clerk of the Supreme court at Raleigh,
to make the title to William Dugger which Col. Dodge should
have made.   Clerk Freeman made this title to Dugger, but
failed to include in it any reference to the equitable agreement which had been made between William Dugger, Isaac
T. Avery and J. Evans Brown to the effect that each should
have a one-third interest in the property outside of the original White Ore-Bank tract.   William Dugger, too, had sold
his interest in the property without excepting the two-thirds
interest equitably owned by Avery and Brown, and executed
a deed therefor.   These purchasers were proposing to sell
under their deed from Dugger without notice to Avery and
Brown; whereupon Judge A. C. Avery, as executor of Isaac
T. Avery, who had died, and J. Evans Brown gave notice of
their equity to the proposed purchasers, and thereby compelled the purchasers from Dugger to buy their interest in
the property.   This covered all interests in the property.[15]

THE NANTAHALA TALC CASE.   About 1895 or 1896 there
was considerable litigation over the rich and valuable talc
and marble mine or quarry at Hewitts in Swain county.
Thomas and others had bought from the late Alexander P.
Munday, as executor of the late Nimrod S. Jarrett.   The
Nantahala Marble and Talc Company of Atlanta had also
bought land adjoining from the same party.   On a question
of the location of a boundary line between these properties
the case was tried at Asheville before the late Judge Paul,
United States district judge of Virginia, who had been transferred to this jurisdiction for the purpose of hearing this case.
He decided it in favor of Thomas and his co-plaintiffs; and
it was appealed to the circuit court of appeals, where in February, 1901, this decision was sustained. (106 Fed. Rep.,
p. 379, and 76 Fed. Rep., p. 59.)

NOTES.

[1]Mrs. Elizabeth Smith died in October, 1912.
[2]W. H. Penland, having agreed to furnish valuable information to the government, was not tried.
[3]116 N. C., 570.
[4]126 N. C., 760.
[5]4 Dev., p. 1.
[6]Dev., p. 1.
[7]*Fisher v. Bank*, 132 N. C., 769.
[8]*Bank v. Bank*, 127 N. C. Rep., 432.
[9]*Smathers v. Bank*, 135 N. C., 410.
[10]*Jones v. Com.*, 135 N. C. Rep., p. 215.
[11]*Bank v. Maddux*, 156 N. C.
[12]Pub. Laws 1903, Ch. 283.
[13]In this decision it was held that lands in the vacant and unsurveyed class as shown on the maps required to be made by the act of 1836 and deposited in register of deeds office at Franklin were subject to entry, Justice Walker discussing the matter fully.
[14]*Cochrans v. Improvement Co.*, 127 N. C., 387, and *Dugger v. Robbins*, 100 N. C., 1.
[15]Letter of Hon. A. C. Avery to J. P. A., February 7, 1913.

CHAPTER XVII

SCHOOLS AND COLLEGES

A LAGGARD IN EDUCATION. North Carolina has little reason to be proud of her early history in the cause of education. For years there was greater illiteracy in this State than in any other, and the improvement of late years has not been any greater than it should have been. In 1816 the legislature appointed a committee with Archibald D. Murphey at its head to suggest a plan for State education. The plan suggested in 1817 provided for primary schools in each county and for ten academies in different parts of the State, with the State University at the head. A school for deaf, dumb and blind was provided for and the children of the poor were to be supported while at school. But this benevolent scheme to provide for the children of the poor defeated the entire plan. [1]

THE LITERARY FUND. In 1825 the legislature created a literary fund which was to come from the sale of swamp lands and other sources. In 1837 part of a large sum derived from the United States was added, making the entire fund about $2,000,000. [2]

PUBLIC SCHOOLS BEGIN. With the income from this and a tax voted by most of the counties public schools were begun in 1840. In 1852 Calvin H. Wiley was elected superintendent of public instruction, which office he held till 1865. The schools grew from 777 in 1840 to 4,369 in 1860. The number of all students in colleges, academies and primary schools increased from 18,681 in 1840 to 177,400 in 1860. This applies to the entire State.

LOSS OF THE LITERARY FUND. The State kept the literary fund intact during the entire period of the Civil War, keeping the schools open and conducting them with such books as could be provided. It needed the literary fund for the soldiers in the field, but it would not touch a penny except to educate its children. But this fund was held by the banks of the State, and when the Reconstruction legislature voted not to pay the Confederate debt, the banks were ruined, for the State owed them large sums. Thus one million dollars of the fund was lost.

THE EDUCATIONAL GOVERNOR. Gov. Aycock did much for education during his term from 1900 to 1904. Rural libraries were started and a loan fund provided.

PIONEER TEACHERS AND PREACHERS. In 1778 or 1779 Samuel Doak, who was educated at Princeton College, N. J., came to Washington county and soon after his arrival opened a good school in a log cabin on his own farm. This is said to have been the first real institution of learning in the Mississippi valley. In 1788 Doak's school was incorporated by North Carolina as Martin Academy. In 1795 the territorial legislature incorporated Martin Academy as Washington College, located at Salem, and Doak was made its president. [3] In 1785 the legislature of North Carolina incorporated Davidson Academy, near Nashville.

THE FIRST SCHOOLMASTER OF BUNCOMBE. Soon after the Swannanoa settlement was established in 1782, a school was started in accordance with the principles of the Presbyterians. " Robert Henry taught the first school in North Carolina west of the Blue Ridge." [4]

OLD-FIELD SCHOOLS. Col. J. M. Ray gives the following description of these antiquated methods of teaching the young idea how not to shoot : In lieu of kindergarten, graded and normal schools "was the Old-Field school, of which there were generally only one or two in a county, and they were in session only when it was not 'crop-time.' They were attended by little and big, old and young, sometimes by as many as a hundred, and all jammed into one room—a log-cabin with a fire-place at each end—puncheon floor, slab benches, and no windows, except an opening made in the wall by cutting out a section of one of the logs, here and there. The pedagogue in charge (and no matter how large the school there was but one) prided himself upon his knowledge of and efficiency in teaching the 'three R's'—readin', 'ritin' and 'rithmetic—and upon his ability to use effectively the rod, of which a good supply was always kept in stock. He must know, too, how to make a quill pen from the wing-feather of goose or turkey, steel and gold pens not having come into general use. The ink used was made from 'ink-balls'— sometimes from poke-berries—and was kept in little slim vials partly filled with cotton. These vials not having base enough to stand alone, were suspended on nails near the writer. The schools

were paid for from a public fund, the teacher boarding with
the scholars.   The common plan was for all to study aloud,
and this was universally so when getting the spelling lesson,
which was the concluding exercise and most exciting part of
the inside program.   Two of the good spellers of the school
were appointed by the teacher as captains, and they made
selections alternately from the scholars for their respective
sides in the spelling match.   The first choice was determined
by spitting on a chip and tossing it up, the captain tossing it
asking the other 'Wet or dry?' and the other stating his choice.
If the chip fell with the side up as designated, he had 'first
pick' of the spellers, and of course selected the one thought
best.   If he lost, his opponent had first pick.   Another plan
was 'Cross or pile?' when a knife was used the same way, the
side of the handle with the ornament being the cross.   Some
of these old pedagogues were very rigid in discipline—almost
tyrants—a day without several floggings being unusual.   They
sometimes resorted to queer plans to catch up with mischievous scholars; one I distinctly remember—it is not necessary to
say why I so distinctly remember it—was to put the school
on its behavior and leave the building, cut around to some
crack or opening and watch inside movements.   This watching generally resulted in something.

OLD SCHOOL GAMES.   "The outside sports made bearable
all inside oppression, however.   'Base,' 'cat,' 'bull-pen,' and
'marbles,' were the leading popular games, and were entered
into with a zest and enthusiasm unknown in these times.   The
sensational occurrence of the session was, however, the chase
given some party who, in passing, should holler 'school butter!'   But such party always took the precaution to be at a
safe distance and to have a good start, and stood not upon
the order of his going, but went for all that was in him; for
to be taken was to be roughly handled—soused in some creek,
pond or mud-hole.   The pursuers were eager and determined,
sometimes following for miles and miles, and having but small
fear of being punished for neglect of studies.   On the contrary, the offence was of so high an order (and I never understood just why) that sometimes the teacher would join in the
race."[5]

A PRIMITIVE SPELLING BOOK.   Col. Allen T. Davidson
gives this picture of a time earlier than any Col. Ray can

remember: " The first schoolmaster I remember (on Jonathan's creek) was an old man by the name of Hayes. He was a good old man, and had a nice family, and had come to that back-country to 'learn' the young idea how to shoot. I was about six years old (1825). We could not then get spelling-books readily. I had none, and was more inclined to fun than study. The old man or his daughters dressed a board as broad as a shingle, printed the alphabet on it, bored a hole through the top, put a string in it, tied it around my neck and told me to get my lesson. I did not make much progress; but was greatly indulged by the old man, and 'went out' without the 'stick,' which was the passport for the others. The old man wore a pair of black steel-rim spectacles, with the largest eyes I ever saw, and was a great smoker. There were no matches in those days, and no way to get fire except by punk and steel; hence, he had to keep fire covered up in the ashes in the fire-place to light his pipe. . . . When I would bring in the sticks with which to replenish the fire, I would usually bring in two or three buckeyes, which I slipped into the ashes as I covered the wood. The wood would smolder to a coal and the buckeyes would get hot, but they would not explode until the air reached them, when they would explode like the report of a musket, scattering the hulls, ashes and embers all over the house, in the old man's face and against his spectacles. This always happened whenever he uncovered the coals to light his pipe. The good old man never did discover the cause of the explosions. He has long since gone to his reward, and I remember him with tenderest affection." [6]

THE BLAB SCHOOL. At the earliest period of the most isolated schools, there were but few books, and spelling was usually taught and learned by a sort of chant or singsong, in which all, teacher and scholars, joined. Young and old joined in this exercise, and children often learned to spell who did not readily distinguish the letters of the alphabet. These were often chalked or written with charcoal on boards against the walls.

NEWTON ACADEMY. From 1797 to 1814 the Rev. George Newton taught a classical school at this place [Newton Academy] which was famous throughout several States. [7] Mr. Newton was a Presbyterian minister, reported to the Synod

at Bethel church, South Carolina, October 18, 1798, as having been received by ordination by the Presbytery of Concord (Foote's Sketches on North Carolina, 297). He lived
on Swannanoa until 1814, when he removed to Bedford county,
Tennessee. There for many years he was principal of Dickson Academy and pastor of the Presbyterian church in Shel-
byville, and there he died about 1841.[7] "At that time there
was a building which had been used for church and school
purposes, known as Union Hill Academy. The house, which
was a log one, was removed and in 1809 a brick house took
its place. In the same year its name was changed to that of
Newton Academy."[8] Here for many years the people
resorted to preaching and sent their children to school, and
buried their dead. In 1857 or 1858 the brick building between
the present academy and the grave yard was removed and the
brick academy now there was erected. (See *Clayton v. Trustees*, 95 N. C., 298.)

DR. ERASTUS ROWLEY. "The old Newton Academy was
the only institution in the county which, up to 1840, had
ever been dignified with as big a name as that of Academy.
This was a very old structure when I first entered it in 1844.
Dr. Erastus Rowley taught here that year. The house was
a very long one and rather wide—one story, divided into two
rooms—one very long room and one small one. It was built
of brick and stood on the top of the knoll some distance above
where the present one stands. Many of the older men of
this section received their education at this widely known
institution and its fame has always been almost co-extensive
with that of Asheville."[9]

DR. SAMUEL DICKSON. "In 1835 Dr. Samuel Dickson,
a Presbyterian minister, established here a seminary for
young ladies, which was most successfully carried on for many
years. It was a school which even in this day of improved
educational methods would stand in the highest rank. Miss
Marguerite Smith of Rhode Island also taught in this building at
the same time. At it were educated all the girls in this section of the country. Dr. Dickson lived and carried on this
school in the first brick house put up in Asheville. It was a
handsome colonial residence, known afterwards as the 'Pulliam place,' on South Main street. The first woman who
ever became a regular practitioner of medicine in America
was a member of this school, Dr. Elizabeth Blackwell."[10]

COLONEL STEPHEN LEE, SOLDIER AND SCHOOLMASTER.
"Dr. Erastus Rowley also taught the male school at the old
Newton Academy for quite a while.   He was a 'Yankee'
but a most excellent teacher, as well as a fine preacher.   Col.
Stephen Lee, about this time, established a school for boys
on the Swannanoa four miles from Asheville, which had a
wide reputation and he did good in all this mountain section.
It may be said without intended disparagement to others
that Col. Lee's equal as a teacher has scarcely been found
in this country; his memory lingers with and is blessed by
many of the 'old boys' of today.
    "Col. Lee's school for boys was far famed and many of the
best citizens of this country and South Carolina remembered
with gratitude, not only the drilling in Latin and Greek received from this most successful educator, but also the lessons in high toned honor and manhood imparted by this
knight 'without fear and without reproach.'   Col. Lee came
from South Carolina and opened his school first in a large
brick house built by himself on Swannanoa, known as 'The
Lodge'— afterwards famous as the hospitable summer residence of Mr. William Patton.   Colonel Lee afterwards moved
to Chunn's Cove, where he taught until, at the call of his
country, he and his sons and his pupils enlisted in the cause
which they believed to be right.   He was a graduate of West
Point and distantly related to Gen. R. E. Lee." [11]
    Col. Stephen Lee, son of Judge Thomas Lee of Charleston,
S. C., was born in Charleston, June 7, 1801, was educated at
West Point and for some years after taught in the Charleston College.   In September, 1825, he was married to his
cousin, Caroline Lee, also of Charleston; they had fifteen children, nine boys and six girls.   Some years after he was married
he moved to Spartanburg, S. C., where he lived only a few
years, moving with his family to Buncombe county, N. C.
In Chunn's Cove he started his school for boys, which he
kept up as long as he lived, except for two or three years in
the sixties, a part of which time he was in command of the
16th N. C. Regiment, serving his country in West Virginia
and the rest of the time drilling new recruits and preparing them
for service.   Besides serving himself, he sent eight boys into
the Confederate army, four of whom gave their lives to the
cause.   At the close of the war he returned to his school du-

ties and prepared many young men for their life work. He died in 1879, and is buried in the Asheville cemetery.

MRS. MORRISON AND MISS COUSINS' SCHOOL. Another school now long passed away, and existing only in the tender memories of its pupils, was taught for girls by Mrs. Morrison and Miss Cousins, on Haywood street, the present residence of Dr. H. H. Briggs.

SAND HILL SCHOOL. Captain Charles Moore, son of Captain Wm. Moore, was a man of ability and learning, a strict Presbyterian and a most useful citizen, who early realized the importance of education to a people so isolated as were the men of his time. Consequently, early in the nineteenth century he erected a small frame building on his farm, since famous as Sand Hill School. It was a school house and church for ministers sent out by the Mecklenburg Presbytery, and later became the most useful institution of learning west of the Blue Ridge, to which boys from all the surrounding counties came as long as Captain Moore lived. Among them were the late James L. Henry, Superior court judge; J. C. L. Gudger, Superior court judge; the late Riley H. Cannon, Superior court judge, and Judge George A. Jones of Macon, who held the position of judge by appointment for nearly two years. Among those living, are Captain James M. Gudger, Sr., solicitor; J. M. Gudger, Jr., member of Congress; H. A. Gudger, chief justice of the Panama Canal Zone; Superior Court Judge Geo. A. Shuford, Judge Charles A. Moore, the late Hirschel S. Harkins, former internal revenue collector for this district; the late Fred Moore, Superior court judge; the late James Cooper, a prominent lawyer of Murphy; Hon. W. G. Candler, member of the legislature; Thomas J. Candler, Dr. James Candler, and Dr. David M. Gudger. Captain Charles Moore is said to have been largely instrumental in erecting the first Presbyterian church in Asheville. He insisted on employing only the most competent teachers for Sand Hill School, among them being Prof. Hood and W. H. Graves, both highly educated teachers. He died about the close of the Civil War. Professor S. F. Venable, a graduate of the University of Virginia, also taught at Sand Hill.

ANOTHER EARLY SCHOOL. Bishop Asbury records the fact that in September, 1806, he and Moses Lawrence lost their way in Buncombe county when within a mile of Killion's on Beaverdam creek, and spent the night in a school house, without a fire. The floor of this school room was of dirt, on which Moses slept, while the Bishop had a "bed wherever I could find a bench." This was not Newton Academy, for he had already recorded the fact that he knew the Rev. George Newton in November, 1800. Besides, Newton Academy was more than three miles from Killion's. Just where this school house was seems to have escaped the knowledge of all our local historians.

SILAS MCDOWELL. He was born in York District, S. C., in 1795, and for three sessions was a student at Newton Academy, near Asheville. He was apprenticed to learn the tailor's trade at Charleston, S. C., and worked as such at Morganton and Asheville. He married a niece of Governor Swain, and moved to Macon county in 1830, where for sixteen years he was clerk of Superior court. He was a practical mineralogist and geologist, botanist and a scientist of original views. His descriptions of mountain peaks attracted much attention; but his "Theory of the Thermal Zone" gave him great reputation and was published in the Agricultural Reports of the United States. He died in Macon county, July 14, 1879.

A BENEVOLENT "SQUEERS."[12] A most unique character among the teachers of that day was Robert Woods or "Uncle Baldy," as he was generally called, for his head was bald as a door knob with the exception of a light fringe at the base of his cranium. Although a finished classical scholar and perfect in mathematics as well as all the higher branches taught in that day, he would not teach in the higher schools, but preferred to labor in what was then known as the "old field," where there was seldom anything taught but the elementary branches—such as spelling, reading, writing "ciphering." Occasionally he would have a boy who wanted to take a little Latin or Greek, or the higher mathematics, which he was thoroughly competent to teach. He was singular and very economical in his notions of dress. He made one suit last him for many years. I can see him now in imagination, with a long tail blue jeans coat that came down to his knees and which had seen service so long that the threads of white filling were showing plainly. The collar was large and when turned up came nearly to the top of his head. His pants were of heavy "linsey woolsey" of deep brown color and very baggy. His vest was of the same material and buttoned up to his chin, with a good flap at the top, his shirts were of heavy red or purple flannel, his shoes were of a style of heavy home made comfortable brogan that were very generally worn in that day. This was his dress and the only one I ever saw him wear. When he was not hearing recitations he constantly walked the floor of the school room from end to end with a swinging walk with his hands crossed upon his back and in one of them a six foot birch "tidivator," and when he would catch a boy with his eyes wandering or at meanness he would give him a keen rap across the shoulders and say in a savage tone, "mind your book." In the summer time when the flies were bad he would tie a large red bandanna handkerchief over his head which he could arrange something after the fashion of a woman's sunbonnet and thus he could save fighting the flies, but with all his queer ways and habits he was a most excellent, useful and successful teacher and a good old gentleman. For many years he taught acceptably in various parts of this county.

FIRST SCHOOL HOUSE IN ASHE. The first school house in Jefferson was of logs and stood on a branch in the eastern end of Jefferson in a lot owned by Felix Barr, just left of the blacksmith shop. He removed it in 1873 or 1874. A fine spring is near the former site.

BURNSVILLE ACADEMY. In 1851 Rev. Stephen B. Adams, now deceased, of the Methodist Church, established the Burnsville Academy and taught there several years. He was the father of Judge Joseph S. Adams, also now deceased. Out of this grew

MARS HILL COLLEGE, which was established by the most prominent members of the Baptist denomination in 1857, after realizing the necessity for such a college. Thomas Ray, John Radford, E. D. Carter, Daniel Carter, Stephen Ammons, Shepard Deaver, Rev. J. W. Anderson and Rev. Humphrey Deweese were prominent in establishing this institution. During part of the Civil War the buildings were used by the soldiers, but after the close of that struggle the buildings were repaired and others added. It has done and still is doing great good.

WEAVERVILLE COLLEGE was established by the Methodist Church, South, about the year 1856. It is situated on land where formerly camp meetings were held. It has been greatly enlarged and improved of late years. It is co-educational. It has done excellent work in the past and continues to do the same now.

ASHEVILLE MALE ACADEMY. In 1847-48 the citizens of Asheville erected a brick building on the north side of what is now College street about a hundred yards east of Oak. It stood till August, 1912, when it was removed. In it Prof. James H. Norwood taught till about 1850, when he removed to Waynesville, where he remained till shortly before the Civil War, when, having been appointed Indian agent in the Northwest, he removed there and was afterwards killed by the Indians. During part of the time he taught at this academy Col. Stephen Lee also taught there, but soon removed to Chunn's cove.

ASHEVILLE FEMALE COLLEGE. About 1850 or 1851 this college was established on the land now bounded on the north by Woodfin, on the east by Locust, on the south by College and on the west by Oak streets. Part of it is used as a hotel and the remainder is now the high school's property. At first it was Holston Conference Female College, but was afterwards known as the Asheville Female College, and subsequently as the Asheville College for Women. It prospered and had a large patronage from the start under the presidency of Dr. John M. Carlisle, Dr. Anson W. Cummings, Dr. James S. Kennedy, Dr. R. N. Price, Dr. James Atkins, Mr. Archibald Jones.

ASHEVILLE SCHOOL FOR GIRLS. This was begun in 1911, with Miss Ford as principal, assisted by several competent teachers. It occupies the handsome and commodious residence built by Col. N. W. Woodfin at the corner of North Main and Woodfin streets, Asheville, and enlarged by the late Dr. J. H. Burroughs.

SULPHUR SPRINGS SCHOOL. William Hawkins taught in the school house on the hill above Sulphur Springs from 1838 till long after 1845. A school had been maintained at that place by Robert Henry's influence and largely at his expense since 1836. The grave yard still there is just back of the place where the old school house stood. The late Riley Cannon, the Jones, Hawkins and Moore children attended school there in the old days.

Mrs. Hutsell's Girls' School. Mrs. Hutsell, the wife of the Rev. Mr. Hutsell, a Methodist preacher, taught a school for girls about four miles west of Sulphur Springs from 1840 to 1853, and took some of the scholars to board at her house. Her husband and Francis Marion Wells of Grassy Creek, Madison county, were brothers-in-law.

"Order of the Holy Cross" at Valle Crucis. [13] In 1840 a gentleman from New York, in search of rare wild flowers, wandered into Valle Crucis. He called this beautiful vale to the attention of Bishop Levi S. Ives of the Protestant Episcopal Church, who, on July 20, 1842, held services there and promised to send a missionary. In December, 1842, Rev. Henry H. Prout arrived and began work in the Lower Settlement, near the Tennessee line. In August, 1843, Bishop Ives returned and purchased 125 acres of land which was subsequently increased to 2,000 acres. His first intention was to "make this valley an important center of work for the entire diocese, to include a missionary station, a training school for the ministry, and a classical and agricultural school for boys." The necessary buildings having been constructed in 1844, school was opened early in 1845, with thirty boys which number increased to fifty during that summer. Rev. Mr. Thurston was at the head of the mission and of the school. There were seven candidates for the ministry, several of whom were assistant teachers. Upon the death of Mr. Thurston the Rev. Jarvis Buxton, then a candidate for holy orders, took charge of the school and Mr. Prout carried on the missionary work. But Dr. Buxton removed to Asheville in 1847, where he became rector of Trinity church, resigning that position in March, 1890. This withdrawal from Valle Crucis was in consequence of the introduction into the mission of Valle Crucis by Bishop Ives, in June 1847, of the "Order of the Holy Cross," planned by himself and which he intended, it was said, to develop into a monastic institution. The Bishop was the General of the Order, the members of which were divided into three classes: those in the abbey at Valle Crucis only taking the mediæval vows of chastity, poverty and obedience; others taking lighter vows; and some taking lighter vows still.

Both the clergy and laity might belong to either class. The Rev. Mr. French was appointed Superior, Mr. Buxton having declined the appointment. Many divinity students became connected with the order, but none of them abandoned the church. The chapel having been destroyed by fire, the little band rebuilt it by themselves, locating it in a little grove at the foot of a hill. Instead of bells a bugle was used to summon them to worship, and to work. Rev. William West Skyles of Hertford county, had joined the mission in 1844 as a farmer, and was ordained a deacon in August, 1847. He was now called "Brother William," while the Rev. Mr. French was addressed as "Father William." All were required to work the farm two hours every day. But reports of the new order had spread through the diocese, funds had failed to arrive, but the committee on the State of the church at the convention held at Wilmington in 1848, favored the mission, saying that its importance "is immense as the nursery of a future ministry because of its retirement, . . . its hardy and useful discipline and great economy." At the convention held at Salisbury in May, 1849, Bishop Ives gave assurance that "at this religious house no doctrine will be taught or practice allowed" not in accord with the principles and usages of the church, "the property of the establishment having been secured to the church for the use of the mission on the specified conditions." At a later day the Bishop declared that from the date of the convention at Salisbury the order had been dissolved. Its regular existence, therefore, scarcely covered two years. The committee on the state of the church having reported in 1849 that they had assurances on which they could rely that "no society whose character, rules and practices are at variance with the spirit if not with the laws of this church is at present in existence in this diocese," the convention ordered 1,000 copies of the report distributed throughout the diocese. In July, 1849, Bishop Ives visited Valle Crucis, however, and addressed a pastoral letter to the diocese which was considered a defiance and a partial retraction of the assurances he had given the convention during the previous May. Consequently, funds for the mission almost entirely ceased, and some of the students sought work elsewhere. Mr. French left the mission in the winter of 1850 and Bishop Ives appointed the Rev. George Wetmore to take charge of Valle Crucis. At the convention of 1850, held at Elizabeth City in May, Bishop Ives alluded to his assurances of 1849, in which he had denied private confession, absolution and Christ's real presence in the Eucharist, etc., and still claimed that there had been no heresy or schism. A committee in 1851 investigated Valle Crucis and reported that the Bishop's explanation was satisfactory.

Bishop Ives visited Valle Crucis in the summer of 1852 and consecrated Easter chapel above Shull's Mills. In September, 1852, he asked for $1,000 and six months' leave of absence. He sailed for Europe and on the 22d of December, 1852, he resigned as bishop and declared his "intention to make his submission to the church of Rome." He had been bishop over twenty years. Dr. Thomas Atkinson, who had been rector of Grace church, Baltimore, was elected to succeed him May 22, 1853. The title of the Valle Crucis property was never in the Episcopal church. It was sold by Dr. Ives' legal representatives to Robert Miller who worked the mission grounds as a farm.

The little chapel which Rev. Mr. Skiles had succeeded in having built on Lower Watauga at a cost of $700, was consecrated by Bishop Atkinson August 22, 1862. Mr. Skiles, who had done many deeds of charity and love, died at the home of Col. J. B. Palmer near what is now Altamont, in Avery county, December 8, 1862. His remains were interred in the churchyard of St. John the Baptist, December 18, 1862. This chapel was removed in 1882 to a spot higher up the Watauga river, near St. Jude postoffice, and in 1889 Mr. Skiles' remains were re-interred in the new churchyard under the direction of Rev. George Bell of Asheville.

The Episcopal church has purchased a large part of the original mission property and now maintains a flourishing school for girls there. The buildings are large, handsome and modern, the orchards and farms are well cultivated and the work accomplished is uplifting and enduring. The principal credit for this work is due Right Reverend Junius M. Horner, Bishop of Asheville, who since his consecration in 1900 has been untiring in building up at this favored spot a useful and elevating school for girls. An investigation of this work and the success which is already evident will convince the most skeptical of its value and importance.

VALLE CRUCIS SCHOOL FOR GIRLS. "The school property consists of a farm of 500 acres, woodlands, apple orchards, dairy farm, vegetable garden and poultry yard. It is in Watauga county. There are two fine buildings, Auxiliary Hall and Auchmuty Hall. Auxiliary Hall was built with that portion of money given the Bishop of Asheville, Rt. Rev. Junius M. Horner, from the united offerings of 1901, added to other smaller gifts. It is a frame building of handsome proportions, and contains the assembly hall for the school and six class rooms on the first floor; the dining room and kitchen on the second floor; and a dormitory for two teachers and twelve girls, on the third floor, with linen closets and bath rooms adjoining.

"Auchmuty Hall is the regular dormitory building for the school. It is built of concrete blocks, and has thirty rooms with capacity for six teachers and sixty girls. The ground floor has office for the principal, a living room, and a prayer room, where daily morning and evening prayers are said. This building was put up at a cost of $15,000, the gift of friends personally interested in the school and missionary work. These buildings are well designed for school purposes and those in authority are diligent in carrying out the deliberately planned policy of the school, viz.: that of making this a model school industry, that shall be sufficiently economic to be self-supporting after the equipment of $50,000 is completed and an endowment of $50,000 is added to insure the salaries of the necessary teachers in the school. It is the policy of the Bishop of Asheville to have here an industrial school which will educate women, home makers, so that the growing generation of men and women from the Appalachian mountains shall be the type known as 'faithful unto death.'

"Half a century ago a school for boys was opened at Valle Crucis by Bishop Ives who named the place because of the natural formation of the valleys, Valle Crucis, or the Vale of the Cross.

"The property of the school, however, was lost to the church until a few years ago when sufficient interest in the mountain region was awakened to enable the church to buy back the best portions of the old school farm and commence the erection of the present industrial school."

SKYLAND INSTITUTE at Blowing Rock was established about twenty-five years ago (1891) by Miss E. C. Prudden, and is supported by the American Missionary Association. It is a girls' school with industrial training.

W. N. C.—28

MAST SEMINARY. This is at Mast postoffice on Cove creek, Watauga, and is the gift of Mr. N. L. Mast to the Presbyterian Church. It is only a little over two years old, but will flourish. Both sexes taught.

WATAUGA ACADEMY. This was established in the summer of 1899 by Messers D. D. and B. B. Daugherty at Boone, their childhood home. They are brothers. [14] The Dougherty family, both men and women, not only in Ashe and Watauga, but in Johnson county, Tenn., also, have for years been zealous in the work of education, religion and the uplift of their States. This was the beginning of the Appalachian Training School.

COVE CREEK ACADEMY. Twenty years ago (1893) this useful and successful school in the western part of Watauga county, was presided over by Mr. Julius C. Martin, now a distinguished lawyer of Asheville. It flourished under his management as principal, and has continued on the road to success.

ASHEVILLE FREE KINDERGARTEN. Miss Sara Garrison was a teacher in 1889 in a kindergarten school in the factory district. In the same year an association was formed and two kindergartens established and placed in charge of Miss Garrison and Miss Slack of Baltimore. They were so successful that a training school was established for fitting women to teach such schools, and Mrs. Orpha Quale of Indianapolis taught a class of eight young ladies. Four kindergartens were in operation. Mr. George W. Pack having donated a school building necessitated the incorporation of the association in 1892. He met most of the expenses of one of the teachers who worked at half rates rather than have the school suspend. In 1894 only two kindergartens were in operation and Mr. George W. Vanderbilt opened another for colored children in the Young Men's Institute at his own expense. A New England lady secured $200 from friends in Boston and the Asheville board of aldermen gave $150 for a kindergarten to be re-established in the factory district. The public kindergartens were suspended for want of funds in the year 1912, but arrangements have been made to re-open them.

BURNSVILLE BAPTIST COLLEGE. About the time the Presbyterians established their college at Burnsville the Baptists erected a large and handsome set of college buildings, which have done a great work ever since.

BINGHAM SCHOOL was founded in 1793, at Mebaneville, N. C., by Rev. Wm. Bingham, who was succeeded by the late W. J. Bingham, and he by the late Col. Wm. Bingham. After the death of the last named, in 1873, Major Robert Bingham became superintendent. The military feature, introduced during the Civil War, has been retained. This school was removed to Asheville under Col. Robert Bingham's superintendence in the fall of 1891; though the original Bingham School, as it is claimed, continues to flourish at Mebaneville. Both schools are doing well.

RURAL LIBRARIES. Small but carefully chosen libraries have been placed in our country schools. This means that six hundred thousand country children have such opportunities of enriching their lives by reading as were never before offered to the young people of North Carolina.

ALLEGHANY SCHOOLS. Sparta has had a high school almost from the beginning of the town, Prof. Brown having located there in 1870, and with the exception of short intervals, has had charge of it ever since. There are also a good many academy buildings at Whitehead, Laurel Springs, Scottville, Piney Creek, Elk Creek and Turkey Knob. In 1909 the Orange Presbytery established a high school at Glade Valley, there being four buildings, all steam-heated and modernly equipped.

BAPTIST MOUNTAIN MISSIONS AND SCHOOLS. Mr. A. E. Brown has furnished a list of schools which are maintained by the Home Mission Board of the Southern Baptist Church. A tract gives the following information:

" Some Mountain Mission School work in this region is being done by Northern Methodists, the Congregationalists, the Disciples and the Southern Presbyterians. Aside from the work done by Southern Baptists, however, the Northern Presbyterians are doing the largest Mountain Mission School work in the South. Here and there in the mountain region Baptists have tried to operate schools all along during the past, but not until the Home Mission Board put the denomination behind the educational efforts in the mountains was there any permanency in the work. The people have responded nobly to the leadership and backing furnished by the Home Board. Southern Baptists are probably better equipped for this work than any other denomination. This is ground on which to base a deepened sense of responsibility and not ground for any unworthy pride.

"To sum up : There are more white people per square mile in the mountains than in any region of equal size in the South. The isolation of the mountains is for lack of means for inter-communication, and not for lack of people.

"There are more native born American whites ready to be trained and to profit by training in this district than in any other."

The schools in the mountains of North Carolina follow:

"Mars Hill College, Mars Hill. Five buildings, nine teachers, 360 students; territory, Madison county and part of Buncombe; draws students from every section of the South.

"Yancey Institute, Burnsville. Four buildings, five teachers, 261 students; territory, Yancey county.

"Mitchell Institute, Bakersville. Two buildings (with the third to be erected in the near future), four teachers, 140 students; territory, Mitchell and Avery counties.

"Fruitland Institute, Hendersonville. Four buildings, seven teachers, 221 students; territory, Hendersonville, Transylvania and Polk counties.

"Round Hill Academy, Union Mills. Three buildings, six teachers, 169 students; territory, Rutherford and McDowell counties.

"Haywood Institute, Clyde, N. C. Two buildings, four teachers, 80 students; territory, Haywood county.

"Sylva Institute, Sylva. Four buildings, three teachers, 87 students; territory, Jackson and Macon counties.

"Murphy Institute, Murphy. Three buildings, three teachers, 96 students; territory, Cherokee and Clay counties, N. C., and Polk county, Tennessee."

JOHN O. HICKS, PEDAGOGUE.[15] John O. Hicks, originally from Tennessee, built a school at Hayesville just at the close of the Civil War that has been a noted high-school ever since. Hicks, after some thirty years of successful teaching, turned the school over to N. A. Fessenden of Boston, Mass., and went to Walhalla, South Carolina, and after a few years teaching at that place moved to Texas, where he died in 1910.

The same school that John O. Hicks organized and built up at Hayesville is still in operation with an enrollment of over two hundred. The influence that has gone out from this school has permeated the whole county until the public schools of the county are unsurpassed. From this school have gone out hundreds of men and women who are prominent over the United States. Among them are the Revs. Ferd. McConnell, Geo. W. Truett and T. F. Marr; the Doctors W. S., M. H., and W. E. Sanderson of Texas and Oklahoma; lawyers, O. L. Anderson, J. H. and Luther Truett and the lamented Judge Fred Moore.

APPALACHIAN TRAINING SCHOOL was incorporated in 1903, succeeding the private school of Professors B. B. and

D. D. Dougherty, at Boone. It began in 1899 when $1,500 was appropriated on condition that an equal sum should be provided from private sources. In addition, $2,000 per annum was appropriated for maintenance. With the first $3,000 appropriated the present brick administration building was started. Other appropriations followed and other buildings were erected until in 1911 the maintenance fund was increased to $10,000 per annum for all succeeding years. There have been contributions from people in every State east of the Mississippi river except from New England. There are now 500 acres of valuable land, six large buildings, farm houses and barns, two dormitories and a mess hall. There are three sessions annually of four and a half months in the fall and spring, and two and a half months in summer. Average attendance is 200, while over 400 were taught in 1911. There is a full faculty. Board for women is $6.50 and for boys $7.50 per month. In 1913 the legislature appropriated $15,000 to erect a brick dormitory for girls capable of holding 200 students. It is in course of erection.

A CAMP SCHOOL. There is a summer camp which comes to Bryson City every summer, and is situated on the left bank of the Tuckaseegee river about half a mile below the town. It is composed of boys from various colleges who thus pursue their studies through the summer. They live in tents, but the kitchen and mess hall are of wood. The professors have their families with them and live in the same camps.

SOLITUDE, OR ASHLAND. Toward the close of the nineteenth century Professor F. M. Wautenpaugh of Omaha, Neb., succeeded in having a large and convenient building erected on a high hill overlooking Solitude, and for four or five years conducted a business college and high school most satisfactorily. But the stockholders grew impatient for a dividend on the money they had invested in the enterprise and the school closed. It is now owned by a religious society popularly known as the Holiness People. A religious paper, called *The Sword of the Lord*, is published monthly at Solitude by Rev. E. L. Stewart. There is also a public school house, neat and attractive, which is attended by about 140 children.

BAPTIST HIGH SCHOOL, MURPHY. The Baptist high school occupying the site of the former residence of the late Ben Posey, Esq., a distinguished lawyer, was built in 1906-7, and

afterwards enlarged. There are dormitories and other buildings. It is in the southern part of town, about half a mile
from the court house.

THE MURPHY GRADED SCHOOL. The Murphy graded
school cost $30,000 and stands on Valley River avenue
in the eastern part of the town, midway between Murphy and
East Murphy. It is built after the colonial style and overlooks
Valley river from its site on a splendid elevation. It has
twelve class rooms, a library, an auditorium, a principal's
office, closets, electric lights and water. It was built in 1909
and is a credit to the community.

CULLOWHEE NORMAL AND INDUSTRIAL SCHOOL. " In
1888, a number. of the leading citizens of Cullowhee, desirous
of a better school than the ordinary public school of that day,
organized themselves into a board of trustees for the establishment of what was to be known as the Cullowhee High
School. They procured the services of Prof. Robert L. Madison as principal, and under his leadership and supervision
the school began to flourish and make rapid progress. In 1893,
the institution was recognized by the State, and through the
efforts of Hon. Walter E. Moore, representative from Jackson, an appropriation was secured for the purpose of establishing a Normal department of the school for the training of
teachers. At the session of the General Assembly, in 1905,
through the efforts of Hon. Felix E. Alley, representative
from Jackson, the appropriations were still further increased
and the name of the school was changed to Cullowhee Normal
and Industrial School, the institution then becoming a State
school for the training of teachers.

"The State has recently erected a large and commodious
home for young ladies. The building was designed by a competent architect, is well furnished, and is equipped with water
works, steam heat and electric lights. The administration
building is furnished with patent desks and chairs, is lighted
by electricity and heated by steam. The handsome auditorium is seated with opera chairs and will accommodate six
hundred persons. The institution has a newly installed
sewerage system and is supplied with an abundance of pure
water from distant mountain springs. The electric light and
steam heating plants are both located on the school grounds
and owned and operated by the institution.

"The supreme purpose of the school is the development and training of teachers. It proposes not only to give the student training in the fundamental and cultural branches of study, but so to train him or her as to prepare them to teach."

MISSION WORK OF NORTHERN PRESBYTERIANS. In the summer of 1884 Dr. Thomas Lawrence was a guest of Rev. L. M. Pease, originally of New York city, who, with his wife, had founded the famous Five Points mission in New York city, but who had removed to Asheville in the seventies, and had started and was then conducting a school for girls. On a drive into the country Dr. Lawrence was impressed with the fine looks and intelligence of some boys he saw at a school, and Mr. Pease offered to devote all his landed property near Asheville for a training school for girls of the vicinage. At that time the Home Mission Board was seeking a location for some such training school. The result of this conversation was the transfer of this property to the Home Mission Board. The late Mrs. D. Stuart Dodge was active and influential in effecting this. The terms were satisfactory to all concerned, and a life annuity from the private purse of the Rev. D. Stuart Dodge, D. D., of New York, having been secured to Mr. and Mrs. Pease, the Home Industrial school was soon thereafter organized, in 1887, with Mr. Pease as superintendent and Miss Florence Stephenson as principal, a position she still holds. The success of this school encouraged the evangelization of the mountain region and the Normal and Collegiate Institute was opened in September, 1892, with Dr. Lawrence as president and Mrs. Lawrence as principal, with a faculty of fourteen expert teachers and officers, on part of the Pease property. Dr. Lawrence retired when he reached seventy-five years of age in 1907, and Prof. E. P. Childs succeeded him. Thereafter five other boarding schools have been established in this section, it being the policy of the Presbyterian Church to hand these flourishing schools to their respective communities just as soon as they are able to assume the expense and responsibility of their support and management. Of the twenty-two elementary day schools planted during the last quarter of a century in the more sequestered and needy communities seven have been successfully transferred to local public school authorities. The remaining fifteen are still doing good work; while in four other centers additional social, kindergarten and Sabbath school work is being done under the management of the board. Miss Florence Stephenson, Miss Mary Johns, Miss Julia Phillips, Miss Frances Goodrich, Dr. J. P. Roger, a Christian physician, have done a great work for our people and their names are household words in many a mountain cabin. Dr. G. S. Baskerville made a success of the farm school on the Swannanoa river, after the school had been organized by Prof. Samuel Jeffries, a graduate of the agricultural department of Cornell University, in 1893. Dr. J. P. Roger is in charge of the farm school now.

The following is a list of the schools and churches established in Western North Carolina, exclusive of those established elsewhere in the South:

Normal and Collegiate Institute, 1902. Prof. E. P. Childs, president. Miss Mary F. Hickok, principal. Fifteen teachers and officers. Average enrollment, 304.

Home Industrial School (preparatory to the Normal and Collegiate Institue), 1887. Miss Florence Stephenson, principal. Teachers and officers, ten. Average enrollment, 140.

Pease Home (for little girls), 1908. Miss Edith P. Thorpe, matron. Adjunct to Home Industrial School, and furnishing school of practice for Normal and Collegiate Institute.

These three boarding schools for girls occupy, with the chapel, manse, and superintendent's home, the beautiful suburb of Asheville, ceded by Mr. Pease. The whole plant is valued at $200,000.

Farm School, nine miles from Asheville, on the Swannanoa river, 1895, J. P. Rogers, superintendent. Sixteen teachers and officers. Spacious school and farm buildings and 650 acres of fertile land.

These four flourishing boarding schools form the Asheville group. Their success has been largely possible through the wise counsel and constant beneficence of Dr. D. Stuart Dodge, New York City, who inherits a name which has, for three generations, been synonymous with philanthropy.

Bell Institute, Walnut, Madison county, 1908. Miss Margaret E. Griffith, principal. Five teachers and officers. Average attendance, 284; 65 boarders. Value of school property, $12,000.

Dorland Institute, Hot Springs, Madison county, 1887.

Established by the late Dr. Luke Dorland, in his old age, after a long life of eminent usefulness in other fields. Miss Julia E. Phillips, principal. Eleven teachers and officers. The plant is valued at $40,000, and provides school room and dormitory accommodations for 70 girls, farm and home for 30 boys, having, in addition, an attendance of 60 day pupils.

Stanly McCormick Academy, Burnsville, Yancey county. Prof. Lowrie Corry, principal. Seven teachers and officers. Six buildings, including school building, principal's home, separate dormitories for boys and girls. Average attendance, 206; 50 boarders. Building and grounds valued at $46,000. This prosperous academy has a magnificent patron in Miss Nettie McCormick, Chicago, Ill.

Besides the schools of higher grade, above mentioned, a successful academy was maintained more than ten years at Marshall, which prepared for and subsequently gave place to the excellent graded school now being maintained by the public authorities.

In addition to these boarding schools, 21 elementary day schools were meanwhile being planted in the remotest and most inaccessible regions, under carefully trained Christian teachers—fourteen in Madison, four in Buncombe, and three in Yancey county, with an average attendance of 1,200 pupils, under 41 teachers. The moneys invested in school buildings and teachers' homes, the people contributing as they were able, would aggregate $30,000.

In accordance with their policy, as already remarked, the board, in the more recent years, has been gradually retiring from these fields as the local authorities became able and willing to take over the work. The value of properties in buildings and lands, held for educational purposes, including the seven boarding and 21 day schools, aggregates $400,000, not to make mention of the salaries of, on an average, more than 100 efficiently trained teachers necessarily employed.

Col. Robert Bingham, one of the most experienced and eminent educators of the commonwealth, in an article published in the *North American Review*, refers to the prudence and wisdom which has characterized the administration of this mission school work, and says, in substance: "Of all the moneys donated by northern philanthropists for the betterment of education in the South, those contributed by the

Northern Presbyterian Church has been most judiciously and wisely expended."

The list of the organized churches is as follows: Oakland Heights, Asheville, Buncombe county; College Hill, Riceville, Buncombe county; Reems Creek, Reems Creek, Buncombe county; Brittain's Cove, Brittain's Cove, Buncombe county; Jupiter, Jupiter, Buncombe county; Cooper's Memorial, Marshall, Madison county; Barnard, Barnard, Madison county; Allanstand, Allanstand, Madison county; Big Laurel, Big Laurel, Madison county; Dorland Memorial, Hot Springs, Madison county; Burnsville, Burnsville, Yancey county.

SOUTHERN PRESBYTERIAN CHURCH SCHOOLS.[16]   Glade Valley School, near Sparta; organized 1910; boarding and day school for boys and girls; buildings and furnishings worth $20,000. Five teachers in regular service; 130 students; full academic course; board and tuition per month, $10.

Lees-McRae Institute, at Banner Elk; established 1901; boarding and day school for girls; industrial, there being no servants. Buildings, furnishings and farm worth $25,000. Eight teachers; 165 students; usual academic course with manual training. Tuition and board per month, $8.

Lees-McRae Institute at Plumtree; organized 1902; boarding and day school for boys; industrial, large farm connected with school; buildings, farm, furnishings, stock, etc., worth $22,000. Five teachers and about 110 students. Course prepares for freshman class in good college. Board and tuition, $8, many of the students making as much by their own labor.

Mission Industrial School, near Franklin; organized 1911; boarding and day school for girls; industrial, no servants. Buildings and furnishings worth $10,000. Five teachers and 75 students. Course same as that of best high schools. Board and tuition, $8 per month.

The Maxwell Home and School, near Franklin; organized 1911, for homeless boys who are destitute. Manual training, chiefly, the farm containing 500 acres. Buildings, furnishings and farm, worth $15,000. Three teachers, capacity for 30 boys at present. With $50 to get a start, a boy can make his own way here.

Mountain Orphanage. At Balfour, established in 1905 by Home Mission Committee of Asheville Presbytery. Mr.

and Mrs. A. H. Temple have charge of 40 children. Property worth $5,000.

COLORED PEOPLE'S SCHOOLS. [17] "Very soon after the war the importance of the education of the colored people, now citizens and voters, was impressed upon the minds of the thinking people of this section. The first effort in this direction was the parochial school of the Protestant Episcopal Church, which was opened in 1870, and was taught by Miss A. L. Chapman of Rochester, N. Y. After two years she was succeeded by Rev. Mr. Berry, who was both pastor and teacher. This double office has been filled without interruption by educated and influential colored men up to the present time, and many heads of families look back with gratitude to the little room on South Main street, and the parochial school building on Valley street, where the rudiments of an education were obtained, and foundations of character laid, which have been a blessing to them and their households.

"In 1885 Rev. L. M. Pease, recognizing the importance of hand, as well as head and heart training, erected a building for an Industrial school on College street, and opened it the same autumn with three thoroughly educated colored teachers. At the close of the school year, being financially unable to continue it, he deeded the property to the Woman's Board of Home Missions of the Methodist Episcopal Church, which continued the work under the superintendence of Rev. Newell Albright, whose health was such as to require a residence in this climate. When Mr. Albright resigned after one year, the school was thoroughly organized and established and has continued to do excellent work under the superintendence of Miss A. B. Dole, who, by her judicious management of the race question, and devotion to the interests of the colored people, has made many friends among both races.

"Rev. C. E. Dusenberry of the Presbyterian Church has a parochial school on Eagle street, under the auspices of the Holston Presbytery, where industrial work is taught to some extent, and a kitchen garden conducted. The purpose of this is to teach correct methods of housekeeping, such as making fires, washing dishes, setting and waiting on tables, laundry and chamber work.

"In the Victoria suburb a combined chapel and school house

was erected five years ago by a donation from Mr. Taylor of Cleveland, O., where a flourishing day school has greatly benefited the population. Mrs. W. J. Erdman was the projector and manager of this school till her removal to Philadelphia one year ago. The teacher's salary is paid by the Freedman's Board of the Presbyterian Church, by which they are also appointed.

"In 1892, Mr. Stevens, the principal of the public school for colored pupils, was greatly impressed with the necessity of an institution for colored young men on the plan of the Y. M. C. A. He set about devising plans for the erection of a building for this purpose, and made a journey during vacation to Bar Harbor, Me., for the purpose of soliciting aid from Mr. George Vanderbilt. In this he was successful, and Mr. Charles McNamee was commissioned to erect a structure, suitable for the purpose contemplated, on the corner of Eagle and Market streets. It is a fine, substantial building with a tiled roof. There are stores and offices on the first floor and a large lecture hall. On the second floor is a library and reading room, a parlor and school room and the office of the superintendent. This was occupied by Mr. Stevens for one year, and the following one by Mr. John Love, an Asheville boy, who was graduated at Oberlin, O., and resigned one year ago to take work in Washington, D. C. The present incumbent is B. H. Baker, a graduate of Howard University.

"The lecture hall has been in demand for lectures, concerts, exhibitions and entertainments, and on Sunday afternoons for a song service with a large attendance. There is a religious service one night in the week, a night school for boys and a kindergarten eight months in the year."

CHARLES McNAMEE, ESQ., for many years the attorney and adviser of Mr. George W. Vanderbilt, who erected the Young Men's Institute at the corner of Eagle and Spruce streets, Asheville, for the use of colored people, about the year 1893, in a letter dated October 24, 1895, says that he is the trustee of the property and that "It was the original intention that the income of the building over and above the running expenses should be devoted to paying Mr. Vanderbilt back the principal and interest of the cost of the building and ground." The foregoing references are to times prior to November, 1895.

MRS. HETTY MARTIN. This good lady was the wife of the

late General James Green Martin. They came to Asheville during the Civil War, after which they faced poverty with brave hearts. Mrs. Martin was the daughter of the ate Charles King, president of Columbia College, New York, granddaughter of Rufus King, first American minister to the Court of St. James, and a sister of General Rufus King of the United States army. Notwithstanding her northern birth and ancestry, Mrs. Martin's fidelity to the South was unquestioned. Recognizing the fact that if left to their own resources the newly enfranchised negro race of the South must necessarily retrograde, Mrs. Martin soon after the Civil War exerted herself to advance their educational and religious training. It was through her influence that St. Mathias Episcopal church was organized and for years supported by the aid of white people. She also assisted in the erection and furnishing of the fine new church that crowns one of the hill-tops in the eastern part of Asheville, and in which so many reputable and self-respecting colored men, women and children have received spiritual guidance. Her influence for good in this community is incalculable.

MISS ANNA WOODFIN. This good woman is a daughter of Col. N. W. Woodfin, and although a confirmed invalid for many years, she has, nevertheless, exerted a wonderful influence for good in this community. In 1884 she was largely instrumental in organizing the Flower Mission, of which she is still an honored member. This was intended to be "an auxiliary to the State branch of that department of the National Woman's Christian Temperance Union, with the object of carrying flowers to the homes of the sick and destitute, to prison cells, to hospitals and almshouses." Bible texts and songs and readings often went with the flowers. Its work revealed the need of a hospital and, as the society was interdenominational, the cooperation of all the churches was secured, and soon the Mission Hospital was opened in 1885. The Associated Charities is also an outgrowth of this grand scheme.

DONATION OF A LIBRARY. About 1905 Professor Charles Hallet Wing, of Brighton, Mass., donated to the county of Mitchell on certain conditions a large and well-arranged library building and 15,000 selected and valuable books, a book-bindery, etc., all situated at Ledger, on the road from

Marion to Bakersville, where Professor Wing lived several years and gave the people in the neighborhood the free use of his library, besides binding without charge any pamphlets or books in need of such treatment.

PROFESSOR CHARLES HALLET WING. Of this public-spirited gentleman we read (Carolina Mountains, p. 326) that "after many years of notable service as professor of chemistry in the Boston Institute of Technology" he came to Ledger, Mitchell county, N. C., "before there had been any change in the customs of the country, to escape the turmoil of the outer world. Professor Wing vehemently disclaimed any share in changing — he would not call it 'improving'— the life of the people, but he made his charming log house, his barn and outbuildings, also his fences with their help." He also built a school house and library building, provided two teachers, and himself "conducted a manual training department." There were 250 applicants for admission to his school the first year it was opened, ranging from six to forty years in age. This school was successfully conducted "without the infliction of any sort of punishment." Fifteen thousand books were sent there by friends of Prof. Wing, and the library was kept by a native youth who was taught to rebind books, "as some of the most used books were those that had been discarded by the Boston Public Library." Small traveling libraries of seventy-five volumes each were sent around the country and loaned. "The library was free, with rules, but no fines, and it is illustrative of the quality of the people that the rules were not broken and that at the end of the first year not a book was missing, none had been kept out overtime, while less than six per cent of those taken out had been fiction" (p. 327).

GEORGE W. PACK. Elsewhere has been mentioned the donation by this gentleman of a valuable library building to the city of Asheville, and his aid to the free kindergartens of that city.

BREVARD INSTITUTE. This school for training girls and boys in the practical things of life is situated near Brevard, and was started in 1895. "Besides the ordinary academic subjects and special religious training the pupils are taught 'a dread of debt, promptness in attending to business obligations of every sort, a love for thoroughness and accuracy in doing work of every sort, self-control in the expenditure of money, and a knowledge of simple business transactions.'" There is also a business course, a department of music and one of domestic art. (Carolina Mountains, pp. 225-226.)

ALLENSTAND COTTAGE INDUSTRIES. This is a form of settlement work which began, "long before the present wave of prosperity had drawn near the mountains," in the north-western portion of Buncombe county "away up on Little Laurel, near the Tennessee line . . . and close under the wild Bald mountains." It was "formerly a stopping place or 'stand' for drovers who stopped over night with their cattle, sheep, horses and swine" on their way from Tennessee to South Carolina. Here old-fashioned spinning, weaving and dyeing were revived and are being taught. (Carolina Mountains, pp. 226-228.)

BILTMORE INDUSTRIES. From the same work (p. 231) we read that wood-carving is taught and practiced at Biltmore, as well as old-fashioned spinning, weaving and dyeing, and also embroidery, some of the graduates in wood-carving carving chairs for the great establishment of Tiffany of New York, and more than one hundred of the pupils are earning a livelihood by the wood-carving craft.

SCOTCH BLOOD ANSWERS FIRST CRY TO BATTLE. From the Carolina Mountains (p. 149) we learn that although the men of these mountains had remained for years without an ideal and were without opportunity to display their natural ability and trustworthiness of character, nevertheless, when George W. Vanderbilt began his operations at Biltmore he employed these very men and kept them under an almost iron discipline. He found "the Scotch blood at the first call to battle ready," and now "all the directors of the great estate, excepting a few of the highest officials, are drawn from the ranks of the people, who proved themselves so trustworthy and capable that in all these years only three or four of Biltmore's mountaineer employees have had to be discharged for inefficiency or bad conduct."

NOTES.

[1]Hill, p. 375.
[2]Ibid., 376.
[3]G. R. McGee's, p. 110.
[4]From "Alexander-Davidson Reunion," 1911, by F. A. Sondley, Esq., p. 24.
[5]Col. J. M. Ray in Lyceum, p. 19, December, 1890.
[6]Col. Allen T. Davidson in Lyceum, p. 6, January, 1891
[7]Asheville Centenary.
NOTE: Newton Academy is on the east side of South Main Street, Asheville, and nearly opposite the Normal and Collegiate Institute.

[8]From Judge J. C. Pritchard's address before Normal and Collegiate Institute, 1907.
[9]"Reminiscences" of Dr. J. S. T. Baird, 1905.
[10]Ibid.
[11]Ibid.
[12]Ibid.
[13]Condensed from William West Skiles' "A Sketch of Missionary Life," 1842-1862. Edited by Susan Fenimore Cooper, N. Y., J. P. Pott & Co., Publishers.
[14]From facts furnished by Prof. D. D. Dougherty.
[15]By G. H. Haigler, Hayesville. N. C.
[16]Information furnished by Rev. R. P. Smith. superintendent and treasurer.
[17]Woman's Edition, Asheville Citizen. The references are prior to November, 1895.

CHAPTER XVIII

NEWSPAPERS

HIGHLAND MESSENGER. At some time prior to 1842 the late Joshua Roberts and Rev. David R. McAnally founded the first newspaper ever printed in Asheville, the *Highland Messenger*. John H. Christy, a practical printer, was associated with them in its publication. He married Miss Ann Aurelia Roberts August 23, 1842, which must have been after the paper had been started, she having been a daughter of Joshua Roberts. J. H. Christy subsequently moved to Athens, Ga., where he published for many years the weekly *Southern Watchman*, and during Reconstruction was elected member of Congress from the Athens district, but was not allowed to take his seat on account of political disabilities. His son is now one of the publishers of the *Andrews Sun*. Dr. David R. McAnally was a Methodist preacher and moved to St. Louis, Mo., where he edited the *Christian Advocate*. He was sometimes mentioned in connection with the bishopric in the Southern Methodist Church.

James M. Edney obtained control of the *Highland Messenger* and it afterwards became the *Spectator*. It was edited by John D. Hyman, who moved to Asheville about 1853, and Z. B. Vance. In it, in 1857, Gov. Vance published an account of the finding of Prof. Elisha Mitchell's body. [1] Thomas Atkin, of Knoxville, established the *Asheville News* about 1848 or 1850 and it ran a long time under that name. The late Major Marcus Erwin as editor wrote brilliantly for it. This paper, although nominally independent, supported Major W. W. Rollins for the State senate in 1866. On the day the election returns had to be made, Lee Gash, of Henderson county, was 27 votes ahead of Major Rollins, at sundown, with the votes of Mitchell county still not in. At ten o'clock that night the Rev. Stephen Collis arrived with them, having been delayed by high water. There were 770 votes for W. W. Rollins and only one vote for Mr. Gash; but they had arrived a few hours too late. [2]

THE ASHEVILLE CITIZEN. This paper, at first a weekly, was established by Randolph Shotwell, who came to Asheville from Rutherford in 1869. About 1870 Col. V. S. Lusk sent a bill to the grand jury, while he was solicitor, against certain men for Ku-Kluxing some negroes, and the grand jury threw it out. There then ensued some newspaper controversy, and the next Col. Lusk knew of it was a blow, dealt by Shotwell, knocking him to his knees. While in this position Lusk fired upward and wounded Shotwell in both legs. Shotwell gave Lusk a Masonic sign and Lusk fired no more. This happened on the public square about 1870 or 1871. Shotwell sold the *Citizen* to Natt Atkinson and went to Rutherford, after having been convicted of assault upon Lusk, sentence having been suspended at Lusk's request. Shotwell was soon afterwards convicted of Ku-Kluxing and sent to the Albany penitentiary, but was pardoned by Gen. Grant upon application of Col. Lusk, who had then been appointed United States district attorney.

JOHN P. KERR'S RECOLLECTIONS. In a letter dated June 11, 1912, Col. John P. Kerr, a veteran newspaper man, and now private secretary to Gov. Craig, wrote as follows:

"The first newspaper published in Asheville within my recollection was the *News and Farmer*. I am sure that this was the successor of the *News*, which had been printed by Rev. Thomas (?) Atkins, a Methodist preacher, subsequent to and perhaps during the war. R. M. Stokes was the editor of the *News and Farmer*, as I recollect, in 1868-1869. The printing office was in the building now known as the 'Hub,' N. W. Pack Square and N. Main street. It was up stairs. Stokes subsequently moved his paper to Union, S. C. The *Pioneer*, a weekly Republican paper, was also being published in Asheville in 1868-1869. I began my apprenticeship as a printer on this paper. It was at this time edited by A. H. Dowell, with C. W. Eve as local editor. This paper was founded, I think, by A. H. Jones who represented this district in Congress at this time. The office was on the third story of the Patton Building, corner S. Main and S. E. Pack Square. Capt. Atkinson printed a paper in the rear room on the second story of the same building that the *News and Farmer* occupied, and I set type for him as a printer. About 1869 or 1870 the *News and Farmer* was purchased by Randolph Shotwell, who changed its name to the *Asheville Citizen*. Between 1870 and 1874 R. M. Furman took hold of the *Citizen*. His office was in the basement of the same building, the 'Hub.' [3] Randolph A. Shotwell was either associated with Furman or else he ran another paper for a short time in Asheville during the period above mentioned. Thomas D. Carter started during this same period the *Expositor*; which also had its office in this same building when it began, but it was subsequently moved to the Legal Building, which covered the site now occupied by the big Oates building, and I think became the property of Gen. R. B. Vance, then a member of Congress, and was edited by his brother-in-law, Maj. W. H. Malone. During this period Jordan Stone became associated with Furman in the *Citizen*, as did also Col. J. D. Cameron. I feel sure that the *Citizen* was a daily when I returned to Asheville in 1887. After an absence of several years Jordan Stone sold his interest in the paper about 1888, and went to California. Subsequently, perhaps about a year later, R. M. Furman sold his interest, and Col. J. D. Cameron ran the *Citizen* for a few weeks or months alone. The paper was then sold to Capt. T. W. Patton and J. G. Martin. Mr. Martin soon sold his interest and in either 1889 or 1890 a company was formed composed of T. W. Patton, W. F. Randolph, A. E. Robinson and John P. Kerr, who took charge of the paper. This was continued for only one year, after which Randolph Robinson and Kerr ran the paper until 1889, with F. E. Robinson as editor. In 1889 J. P. Kerr sold his interest to Dr. W. G. Eggleston, who became the editor. Dr. Eggleston remained with the paper for less than a year. After this there were a number of changes in the ownership of the paper which can be more accurately ascertained by the files of the paper itself. In 1887 Theodore Hobgood was running a daily paper in Asheville called the *Advance*. Its offices were in the basement of the old Legal Building. The present *Gazette-News* was the outgrowth of the *Advance*.

" I have no definite recollection as to the various steps in the life of the *Gazette-News*. After the sale or discontinuance of the *Advance*, Theodore Hobgood and ———— Fitzgerald began the publication of a morning newspaper in the Barnard Building, or the building which preceded it. This ran only a short time when they sold it to W. F. Randolph and John P. Kerr, who ran it only a few weeks. This was about 1888. The *Asheville Register* was the name of a Republican weekly paper published for a number of years, and founded, I believe, by R. M. Deaver. R. B. Roberts was its editor for some years."

THE ASHEVILLE CITIZEN PUBLISHING COMPANY was incorporated April 1, 1890, A. H. Fuller, T. W. Patton, J. G. Martin and T. A. Jones being named as incorporators. It was the influence of this paper largely which secured the election of the late Capt. T. W. Patton as mayor on an independent ticket, in May, 1893.

THE ASHEVILLE DAILY GAZETTE was established in March, 1896. It was incorporated as the Gazette Publishing Company April 2, 1897, Fred A. Johnson, J. M. Johnson and James E. Norton being named as incorporators. Mr. Norton, who had had fifteen years experience in reportorial and editorial positions on the New York *Tribune*, *Times*, *Commercial Advertiser* and *Brooklyn Eagle*, continued in active management of the editorial and business affairs of the paper, except for a short interval in the fall of 1898 (?) when the late Robert M. Furman had control of the editorials, till 1903-04, when the paper was sold to the *Evening News* Publishing Company. It was then converted into an afternoon paper, the *Citizen*, which before that had been an evening paper, having taken the field as a morning journal. The *Gazette* was a Republican paper during the last three years of its existence. Geo. L. Hackney had the two papers combined as the *Gazette-News*, under which name it has continued to flourish.

WATAUGA DEMOCRAT. It was started by Joseph Spainhour and the Democratic party prior to June 13, 1888. R. C. Rivers, its present owner, and D. D. Dougherty took charge July 4, 1889. Mr. Rivers has been with it since.

WATAUGA ENTERPRISE AND NEWS. The former ran in Boone in 1888, L. L. Green and Thomas Bingham conducting it. The *News* was begun in January, 1913, [4] by Don. H. Phillips.

JEFFERSON OBSERVER. This paper is a weekly Democratic paper, published at Jefferson, Ashe county, and was established about 1901 by Talbott W. Adams, formerly of Edgefield county, S. C. He is still in control of it. A Republican paper was started in 1909 but failed. It was called the *Jefferson Watchman*, and ran only three or four months. In 1910 an effort was made to revive it under the name of the Industrial-Republican Publishing Company of Jefferson, N. C., but it failed.

GENERAL ERASTUS ROWLEY HAMPTON. For several years, during 1890 and thereafter, Gen. Hampton published a weekly paper in Jackson county.

FRANKLIN PRESS. This Democratic weekly was conducted by the late W. A. Curtis at Franklin, Macon county, for a number of years prior to his death in 1900. It is still flourishing.

THE CAROLINA BAPTIST was the first newspaper printed in Hendersonville. In 1855 Rev. James Blythe, W. C. Berin and J. M. Bryan, as editors, started this paper, but later Prof. W. A. G. Brown became its editor. A copy was recently shown dated June 22, 1859.

HENDERSONVILLE HUSTLER. This newspaper was started in Hendersonville ten or a dozen years ago and is still flourishing. Now M. L. Shipman, Commissioner of Labor and Printing, is its editor and proprietor.

FROM THE REPORT OF THE COMMISSIONER OF LABOR AND
PRINTING.

WEEKLY NEWSPAPERS.

COUNTY	Town	Name of Paper	Editor	Proprietor
Mitchell	Bakersville	Mitchell County Kronicle.	T. M. Gosorn	T. H. Gosorn
Swain	Bryson City	Bryson City Times	H. W. Carter	H. W. Carter
Transylvania	Brevard	Sylvan Valley News	O. L. Jones R. B. Wilson	Jones & Wilson
Watauga	Boone	Watauga Democrat	R. C. Rivers	R. C. Rivers
Yancey	Burnsville	Eagle	J. M. Lyon	Eagle Pub. Co.
Ashe	Jefferson	Recorder	W. T. Adams	W. T. Adams

CAPTAIN NATT ATKINSON was born November 15, 1832, in
McMinn county, Tenn., near Charleston. He was a graduate
of Hiwassee College and of Col. Wilson's private school in
Alamance county, N. C. He married Harriet Newell Baird,
daughter of Mary and Israel Baird, of Buncombe county, N. C.,
February 2, 1858. There were twelve children. He was
admitted to the Asheville bar in 1868, and practiced law till
1873. He purchased the *Asheville Citizen* in 1870, and edited
the same for three years following, when he sold that paper
and moved to a farm on Swannanoa river, where he remained
till 1882, when he returned to Asheville and entered the real
estate business, which he continued till his death, August 25,
1894, at Salisbury, N. C. He was one of the most useful and
enterprising of Asheville's citizens, encouraging every enterprise of merit, and forgetting his own interest in that of the
community. He was the president of the Atlanta, Asheville and Baltimore Railroad Company, and began the actual
construction of the first street railway in Asheville under
what is known as the Farinholt charter, which he sold to E.
D. Davidson and associates, thus defeating an attempt that
was making to build and operate a steam railway through
the streets of Asheville and insuring the present electric
system. He was also interested in the construction of other
railways, and was really the father of the graded schools of
Asheville. He was elected to the legislature of 1879 and by
legislation secured largely through his efforts saved the State
what he estimated to be $175,000. He was a captain in Gen.
M. Vaughan's brigade of the Confederate Army, and was
one of the personal escort of Hon. Jefferson Davis on his flight
southward from Richmond via Charlotte in April, 1865.

THE LYCEUM. This monthly was published in Asheville from May, 1890, until some time in 1892. Tilman R. Gaines of South Carolina was its editor and proprietor. In it were published many papers of value, among which should be mentioned "Reminiscenses of Western North Carolina," by Col. Allen T. Davidson; "Poets of the South," by L. M. Hatch; "Persecution of the Jews," by W. H. Malone; "Protection of Birds," by J. D. Cameron; "State Landlordism and Liberty," by Judge C. E. Fenner; "Two Days with Gen. Lee at Charleston," by Col. L. M. Hatch; "Reminiscenses of Forty Years Ago," by Col. J. M. Ray; "Should Women Vote?" by H. B. Stevens, and an address by Col. Charles W. Woolsey on "The Asheville Art Club."

THE ASHEVILLE EVENING JOURNAL. About September, 1889, this paper started on its career, Messers. Clegg & Donohue being its editors and proprietors. Its advertisement in the *Lyceum* of September, 1890, (p. 22) mentions that it "is now in its second year."

THE ASHEVILLE NEWS AND HOTEL REPORTER. This was a weekly paper which began publication in January, 1895, at Asheville with the late Natt Rogers as editor and the late Richard M. Furman as manager and publisher. It was intended as an advertising medium for hotels principally, but soon reached a wider sphere of usefulness, and until the health of Mr. Rogers became too much impaired it enjoyed a period of popularity and considerable prosperity. Its life was about sixteen months.

ROBERT McKNIGHT FURMAN. He was born September 21, 1846, at Louisburg, N. C., and enlisted in the Confederate army in the spring of 1862, and served till the close of the Civil War. He moved to Asheville in the spring of 1870, and in 1873 he was married at Tarboro to Miss Mary Mathewson. He edited the *Asheville Citizen* from 1873 till Messers J. D. Cameron and Jordan Stone joined him, after which the three conducted that paper till about 1880. He moved to Raleigh in 1898 and became editor of the *Morning Post*, which flourished under his management till after his death at Beaufort, N. C., May 12, 1904.

THOMAS WALTON PATTON. He was for several years editor of the *Asheville Citizen*, during which time its columns were open to all public spirited causes. He was born at Asheville, May 8, 1841, his father, James W. Patton, having been a son of James Patton, one of the pioneers of Asheville. His mother was Miss Clara Walton of Burke, and his grandmother on his father's side was a daughter of Francis Reynolds of Wilkes county. His mother's father was Andrew Kerr of Kelso, Scotland. He was educated by Col. Stephen Lee, from whose school he was graduated in 1860, after which he went to Charleston, S. C., and entered the office of his uncle, Thomas Kerr, a cotton factor. He enlisted in the Buncombe Rifles in April, 1861, and at the expiration of the six months' enlistment, he reenlisted, becoming captain of company "C" of the Sixtieth North Carolina Infantry, in which he served till the surrender of Johnston's army. In 1862 he married at Greensboro, Ala., Miss Annabella Beaty Pearson. In 1866 he removed to Alabama, where his wife and child soon afterwards died. He returned to Asheville and went into co-partnership with the late Albert T. Summey, in the mercantile business, for a short time. In 1871 he married Miss Martha Bell Turner, a daughter of James Calder Turner, a civil engineer who aided in the laying out and construction of the Western North Carolina railroad to Asheville. He and his sister, Miss Frances L. Patton, soon became active in all charitable and philanthropic work. He was elected a county commissioner in 1878, when he made it his first business "to visit the county paupers, whom he found 'farmed out' to the lowest bidder and living in huts far from the public road or any possibility of public inspection," which system he immediately abolished. He also visited the jails regularly, keeping up the practice of visiting prisoners and paupers till his death. "When, in 1893, he considered that the city administration was extravagant, if not actually corrupt, he did not hesitate one instant, but declared himself an independent candidate for mayor," and was overwhelmingly elected. His two terms as mayor, for $25 a month as a salary, resulted in much "economy, honesty, progressiveness and efficiency" which reduced "expenses one-half without in the least diminishing the efficiency of the public service." In April, 1898, he enlisted in the First North Carolina regiment, and served in Cuba, as adjutant. His object was to influence the younger men for good, and the survivors of that war have named the local camp in his honor. He did much, with his sister, Miss F. L. Patton, to establish and operate the Mission Hospital, the Children's Home, and other works of benevolence. He died at Philadelphia, November 6, 1907, and was buried at Asheville with every mark of respect.

THOMAS DEWEESE CARTER. He was born on Little Ivy in what is now Yancey county, February 14, 1834, and died July 29, 1894. He married Miss Sarah A. E. Brown of McDowell county, August 14, 1855. He owned a large interest in the Cranberry iron mine in Mitchell, now Avery, county, and during the Civil War manufactured tools there for the Confederate government. About 1870 he wrote a series of spirited articles on the political situation for the *Raleigh Sentinel* and the *Asheville Citizen*. This was the commencement of a long and active experience as a militant newspaper editor, for his power as a writer of virile English was pronounced. In the spring of 1872 he came to Asheville and began a series of articles concerning the Swepson and Littlefield frauds, publishing his communications in the *Citizen*, till Captain Natt Atkinson, its editor and owner, sold that paper to Robert M. Furman, which necessitated the launching of a new weekly known as the *Western Expositor*, by Col. Carter. This paper immediately attracted attention not only throughout the State, but the *New York Herald* paid editorial tribute to the vigor of the *Expositor's* well written and vigorous editorials. Just about 1876 Col. Carter sold the *Expositor* to the late W. H. Malone, retaining only control of the editorials till after the great campaign of 1876, when the Democrats again gained control of the political affairs of North Carolina.

NOTES.

[1] A copy of this article can be found in ''The Balsam Groves of Grandfather Mountain,'' by S. M. Dugger, p. 261.
[2] W. W. Rollins to J. P. A., May 31, 1912.
[3] In July, 1871, the late Captain Natt Atkinson was running the *Weekly Citizen*, and continued to do so till 1873, when the late Robert M. Furman took charge of it.
[4] *The Watauga Journal* was the first paper ever published in Boone. but was soon succeeded by the *Enterprise*, both being Republican. *The Journal* was started by a Mr. McLauchlin of Mooresville, N. C., but he afterwards removed to Johnson City, Tenn. The *Watauga News* suspended publication in 1914.

Nicholas W. Woodfin.

CHAPTER XIX

SWEPSON AND LITTLEFIELD

That the "evil that men do lives after them while the good is oft interred with their bones" seems to be untrue in the case of the frauds of Swepson and Littlefield. The former was a native of North Carolina and Littlefield of Maine. Together, they managed to sell about $4,000,000 of the bonds of the Western North Carolina railroad, which had been endorsed by the State, and appropriated the proceeds to their own use. This delayed the building of that road from 1869 to 1880. But most of the younger people have never even heard of this gigantic theft. The true story as told to the Shipp Fraud Investigating Commission follows in condensed form, and every statement in this chapter not otherwise noted was taken from that report between pages 220 and 498.

Soon after the Reconstruction election of 1868 there was a special session of the legislature which, by an act ratified August 19, 1868, divided the Western North Carolina railroad into the Eastern Division—to extend from Salisbury to Asheville—and the Western Division—to extend in two lines, one to Paint Rock and the other to Ducktown, in Tennessee. The State also agreed to take two-thirds of the stock of the Western Division, which was authorized to issue its stock, not exceeding $12,000,000, for the completion of these two lines. Under this act, subscriptions were invited, and 3,080 shares of stock subscribed. Of this stock Milton S. Littlefield, a carpet-bag adventurer, subscribed to 2,000 shares and Hugh Reynolds, of Statesville, to 1,000 shares. But only five per cent of eighty shares subscribed by citizens along the line of this proposed road was paid in cash, Littlefield and Reynolds giving their drafts for five per cent of their subscriptions, payable to the order of Geo. W. Simpson, who was elected president at the meeting to organize the Western Division, which was held in Morganton October 15, 1868. Four directors, representing the private stockholders, and eight, representing the State, were also elected at that meeting. As, however, the whole of the Western Division was required to be under contract for its construction before the State could be called on for its subscription, the directors made a contract with M. S. Littlefield for this work; but it was understood that it was a mere nominal contract, for the purpose of complying with the terms of the charter, the actual work to be let afterwards to bona fide contractors. But, as no provision had been made for a special tax levy to pay the interest on the bonds, the act did not accomplish its purpose.

Mr. Swepson went to Raleigh in the fall of 1868 and urged the passage of another bill through the legislature to cure this defect; but was told by Littlefield and a man named John T. Deweese, who were lobby lawyers, that he would get no bills through the legislature unless he paid the same percentage that all the other railroad presidents had agreed to pay — viz., "ten per cent in kind of the amount of the appropriations." Swepson agreed to this and claimed that he afterwards "paid Littlefield $240,000 in money and some bonds for his services in procuring the passage" of the necessary legislation (Ch. 7 and 20, Laws 1868-9). Swepson had certified to the Executive of the State on October 19, 1868, "that the entire road had been let to contract"; and at some subsequent date he received from the State treasurer $6,367,000 of special tax bonds of the State, and began hypothecating or selling them in New York.

But in the spring of 1869 the case of the *University Railroad v. Holden* (63 N. C., p. 410) came before the Supreme court on the question of the constitutionality of the special tax bonds authorized to be levied for the railroad; and Chief Justice Pearson, believing that his associates on that bench would be compelled to agree with his reasoning, wrote an opinion declaring those bonds unconstitutional, meaning to submit it to his brethren for their approval or rejection. So confident was he that they would agree with his conclusions, that he told Col. Wm. Johnson, a lawyer and an intimate friend, that the court had decided the University Railroad bonds to be unconstitutional. He then read his opinion to Col. Johnson, and Johnson told Swepson on Thursday, July 1, 1869, that "he had just seen the opinion in Judge Pearson's room" and that it "made the whole of the special tax bonds unconstitutional."[1] But, before the decision of the court was announced, a motion was made by Judge Fowle for a further hearing. The motion was granted and the majority of the judges concurred in holding the University railroad act to be constitutional, thus over-ruling the chief justice, who, however, filed a dissenting opinion. Mr. T. H. Porter, representing Soutter and Company, stock brokers of New York City, came to Raleigh and arranged with the lawyers for the rehearing.

There was much discussion in the State as to this decision. According to the testimony of James C. Turner, as given before the Shipp Fraud Commission (p. 307), G. W. Swepson told him in New York "on more than one occasion that he had in his pocket a decision adverse to the one given and published by the court, and that it had cost a large amount to obtain the published opinion." Indeed, Mr. Swepson himself swore (p. 207) that his proportion, as president of the Western Division of the Western North Carolina railroad was "60 State bonds, charged as paid attorneys, and the following cash charges: Paid attorneys in Raleigh $2,000. Attorneys, establishing validity of bonds, $21,250." When it is remembered that there were ten railroads to which bonds aggregating $25,250,000 were authorized to be issued at the same session as the University railroad bonds had been authorized, Swepson's proportion of expenses in securing a favorable decision would indicate the expenditure of an enormous sum of money.

But the Shipp Fraud Commission examined Judges R. M. Pearson, E. G. Reade, W. B. Rodman and R. P. Dick, four of the Supreme court judges, upon the question of obtaining this decision, and found that none of these judges knew of any improper or corrupt means or practice concerning it. The only thing that could be construed as of a doubtful character was Judge Rodman's statement, to the effect that, in August 1869, after the decision had been rendered, G. W. Swepson voluntarily offered his personal guarantee to a brokerage firm in New York for the margin on $100,000 of special tax bonds for ten days; but claimed that, as the bonds had not been sold till after the expiration of ten days, Swepson's liability had ended and the loss had been charged to the judge. As this is the only instance in the history of the State in which our Supreme court was even suspected of having been corruptly influenced, it is pleasant to be able to record the fact that the men who paid out the money and the men who received it have left their testimony on record completely exonerating the members of the court. Yet ———!

T. H. Porter, in a letter of May 31, 1870, states that Badger, Fowle, Col. E. G. Haywood, and Judge S. J. Person, attorneys, agreed to undertake the case for $15,000, and if they won, they were to receive an addition in State bonds.   Judge Daniel G. Fowle testified before the Shipp Fraud Commission (p. 463) that he and his associates had received the cash and bonds agreed upon, the suit having been won.

It appears that the only roads which Mr. Porter represented in this suit were the two divisions of the Western North Carolina, the Wilmington, Charlotte and Rutherford, and the Western railroad companies. [2]   Twenty-five of the bonds received by the attorneys were those of the Wilmington, Charlotte and Rutherford railroad and fifty of the Western Division of the Western North Carolina railroad—the Western railroad seemingly not having contributed any.   (This was not the Western North Carolina Railroad, however.)   As Swepson's share was $60,000 in bonds and $21,250 in cash, and as the attorneys got $75,000 in bonds and $15,000 in money, nearly $100,000 in bonds, and $6,250 in cash remain unaccounted for.   It may be that Soutter & Co., the New York brokers represented by Mr. Porter, got this difference.

But, as indicative of the methods then in vogue, John T. Deweese, represented by Swepson as Littlefield's partner, had difficulty in settling with the Atlantic, Tennessee & Ohio railroad for services in getting the legislature to authorize that road to issue its bonds (ratified February 3, 1869) in exchange for a like amount of State bonds, and gave Mr. R. C. Kahoe $4,000 of these bonds to act as nominal plaintiff in an action to restrain the State treasurer, D. A. Jenkins, from issuing $2,000,000 of these bonds.   John T. Deweese, the real party in interest not having been a tax payer, sued out the injunction in June, 1869; and R. Y. McAden, Swepson's nephew, settled this suit by handing over more than $100,000 of these bonds.   Of these bonds, Judge Watts got $5,000, "in accordance with the contract between Deweese and himself, as stated in the report of the Bragg committee."   Fowle and Badger, lawyers associated with E. G. Haywood, Esq., received $16,000 of these bonds for their services in this case, but returned them to the railroad company upon becoming satisfied that it was really a blackmailing scheme.   As, by the time the bonds were issued, they had fallen in price to less than 30 cents on the dollar, the Atlantic, Tennessee & Ohio railroad returned to the State treasurer all except such as had been used in compromising the injunction suit.

According to the testimony of Col. N. W. Woodfin before the Shipp Fraud Commission (p. 291) Swepson and Littlefield intended to build the Western Division, but to do it upon mortgage bonds, and otherwise so leave it in debt as to enable themselves to buy it in when sold for the debt. In the meantime, the money for which the special tax bonds might be sold was to be used by them "in speculation and otherwise, in order to strengthen themselves to buy it."

But, long before this time, people of the mountain section were clamoring that work should begin on the railroad, while Swepson was trying to sell as many of the bonds of the Western Division as possible before the price declined in consequence of the sudden flooding of the market with the special tax bonds to which the other nine railroads were also entitled. On various pretexts he postponed the signing of actual contracts for actual work until he could obtain better prices for his bonds, and caused the State treasurer, D. A. Jenkins, to issue some of the bonds for the Western Division prior to all others, and to decline to furnish bonds to the other railroads entitled to them on the ground that the plate from which they were to be printed had been broken. A question had arisen in New York as to Swepson's right to sell the bonds of the Western Division, and at a called meeting of the directors, held in Asheville, July 2, 1869, the president of the company was "*authorized to sell any securities of the company, or to pledge them for loans when in his judgment the interests of the company required it; and in case such securities be sold to invest the proceeds in such way as he may deem best.*" A certified copy of the above resolution was sent to him in New York.

SWEPSON AND DIRECTORS. At this time no one in North Carolina stood higher in public respect than George W. Swepson, while the directors were of the best people in this section. They did not, and had no reason to, suspect him of duplicity. They had had no experience either in the building of railroads or the management of corporations. He told them that unless he could sell the bonds he could not build the railroad, and that he could not sell them unless they gave him full authority not only to sell but to apply the proceeds as he saw fit. They gave it unsuspectingly and in full confidence in him. No breath of suspicion ever fell upon any of them in consequence, or that they shared any of Swepson's ill-gotten gains. They had done in good faith what they believed right in order to secure the speedy building of the railroad.

On the 13th of October, 1869, at a meeting of the stockholders at Asheville, M. S. Littlefield was elected president in place of G. W. Swepson, who refused to serve any longer on the ground that "his management had been a good deal censured and he was suspected of improper conduct . . . by the Western people. . . ." Gen. Clingman, Col. Davidson and Col. Woodfin opposed the election of Littlefield to office.

So outspoken had become the criticism of the management of this railroad and the sale of all the special tax bonds that the legislature, by an act which was ratified March 24, 1870, appointed J. L. Henry, N. W. Woodfin, W. P. Welch, W. G. Candler and W. W. Rollins commissioners to "examine fully into the affairs of the Western Division and to make a full and final settlement of all accounts and liabilities of Geo. W. Swepson, and to collect all assets" and apply the same to "the construction of the railroad." It had full power and was authorized to sit in New York or elsewhere.

But by the time this commission was appointed both Swepson and Littlefield had left the State, the latter never to return. The commissioners, however, immediately took up their work, going to Washington and New York, and effected a settlement with Swepson before the act appointing them was repealed, which was done at the session of 1873-74. (Ch. 119.)

The grand jury of Buncombe county returned a true bill against Swepson and Littlefield (Minute Docket E., No. 32) for conspiracy to defraud the State; and by a joint resolution of January 25, 1871, the governor was requested to offer a reward of $5,000 for the delivery of Milton S. Littlefield to the sheriff of Buncombe county. But Littlefield was in Florida, Holland or England, and the governor of Florida refused to grant an order for his extradition from that State.

The settlement which the commission had effected with Swepson was dated the 16th day of April, 1870, at Washington, D. C., and was probably the best possible in the circumstances, as Swepson made it appear that he had already so encumbered all his tangible property that if a suit were brought "it was almost certain that nothing would be realized." Swepson was frightened and penitent, and Littlefield was not present to inspire him with courage.

Now, as the directors had authorized Swepson to sell and pledge these securities and invest their proceeds as he saw fit, and as they had not advertised that the contracts would go to the lowest bidders, and as, in the contracts themselves, no time limit was made the "essence of the contract," it was plain that Swepson and Littlefield were not alone to blame for the condition into which the affairs of the Western Division had fallen. In his testimony before the Shipp Fraud Commission Judge J. H. Merrimon said (p. 277): "It appeared to me, from what I saw at the meetings of the board of directors, which I attended, that they were a useless body of men; did nothing, and if they had any power or authority to do anything, they seemed never to exercise it, except when they were told by Swepson."

By this compromise Swepson paid $50,000 cash and gave his drafts on Littlefield as president of the Jacksonville, Pensacola and Mobile railroad and endorsed by M. S. Littlefield and G. W. Swepson as president of the Florida Central railroad, aggregating $264,000, payable four and twelve months after date, $164,000 of which was secured by a mortgage on certain lands of Swepson's in North Carolina, the said lands to be discharged upon payment on each tract as follows:

Eagle hotel in Asheville upon payment of	$ 5,000
Gid Morris place of 1,600 acres upon payment of	12,000
David Hennessee lands in Cherokee upon payment of	7,500
Charles Moore place of 600 acres upon payment of	6,500
The Sharp place of about 300 acres upon payment of	3,000
The Woodfin place in Macon county upon pament of	2,000
The Jarrett place on Nantahala river upon payment of	5,000
The Horshaw lands on Valley river upon payment of	5,500
The Fain lands in Cherokee county upon payment of	5,000
	$51,500

In addition to the above, upon which no amount was fixed for their redemption, the mortgage was to cover the marble and lime lands in Catawba county, owned in co-partnership with Dr. A. M. Powell, "about 90,000 acres in Macon, Cherokee and Clay counties, known as the Olmstead lands, and a lot of about 50,000 acres held by Joseph Keener in trust for Geo. W. Swepson."

It was further agreed that the draft for $164,000 might be paid in railroad iron delivered at Portsmouth, Virginia; and that if an umpire, to be appointed by N. W. Woodfin and M. W. Ransom, in case they could not agree, should decide that Swepson had not been authorized by his board of directors to invest the proceeds of the sales of these bonds in these Florida railroads, then Swepson was to guarantee that $880,-000 of the amount of $1,287,436.03 transferred in Florida railroad securities should be paid or made fully secure; and that, otherwise, there should be no such obligation on Swepson's part.

In addition to the above the agreement provided that an interest in the above named railroad, amounting to $1,287,-466.03, should be transferred and conveyed to the Western Division of the Western North Carolina Railroad Company.

It developed soon afterwards that, although Swepson claimed to have turned over these securities in the Florida railroads to Littlefield, yet, when the latter became president of the Western Division, in October, 1869, he then stated that they were the property of the Western Division, having been purchased with the proceeds of the sale of the special tax bonds of said railroad, but had been pledged with Edward Houston, of Georgia to secure the payment of a large indebtedness of Littlefield to said Houston, and were about to be sold. Thereupon the Western Division obtained an injunction in the Supreme court of the State of New York in October, 1870, restraining Littlefield and Houston from making the sale. But, before the order could be served, Houston "fled with the said stock and bonds from New York to New Jersey, and from there to Georgia, in order to avoid the law and keep fraudulent possession" of the securities, which rightfully belonged to the Western Division. This stock consisted "of about 4,370 shares (being nearly the entire capital stock)" of the Florida Central Railroad Company, "which company had then no mortgage debt upon its line of railroad, which was sixty miles long, completed and in good running order." The bonds of the Pensacola and Georgia railroad and of the Tallahassee railroad amounted to $1,000,000, and cost Swepson $720,000 of the proceeds of the special tax bonds of the Western Division, including "some stock in said company and paying expenses incident to such purchases." These railroads had been sold in March, 1869, under foreclosure, and brought in by the trustees of the Internal Improvement Fund of the State of Florida for $1,400,000, "the amount of the whole mortgage indebtedness of both of the railroads." Thus, the Western Division had secured legal title to a majority of the stock of an unencumbered railroad 60 miles in length and owned ten-fourteenths of two other Florida railroads absolutely unencumbered. If, therefore, the settlement effected at Washington had stood intact, there is little doubt but that the courts would have confirmed the interest of the Western Division in these three Florida railroads, as its money had been invested in them.

But Col. Woodfin was soon called to London, England, where a supplemental settlement was made on the 10th of November, 1870, with Littlefield, representing the Florida railroads, by which he agreed to take for the interest of the Western Division in those Florida railroads 800 eight per cent bonds of the State of Florida, of $1,000 each, and enough rails, etc., to lay 53 miles of railroad down the French Broad river to Paint Rock, including sidings, etc. This iron was to be delivered duty free at Norfolk, Va., in three lots, aggregating 1,800 tons, and the rest at New York, the last shipment to be completed by September 1, 1871. An additional shipment was to be made of 1,000 tons to New York, with the necessary chairs and spikes to lay the same, by September 1, 1871, "the shipping of which the said S. W. Hopkins & Co. are to guarantee." But, to get this settlement, Mr. Woodfin had to agree in writing that he would pay a claim of $20,000 held by Henry Clews & Co., of New York, against Geo. W. Swepson, and to leave the 800 Florida bonds with Hopkins & Co. for sale at such price as Mr. Woodfin should direct. Mr. Woodfin also receipted for two hundred pounds sterling, paid him at that time. With the lights before him, this was a most excellent settlement. He did not know of the complications existing in Florida.

This iron was shipped according to agreement but was diverted by Hopkins & Co., to Detroit, Mich., for the purpose of completing the Rock Fish Railroad, a branch of the Michigan Central. Major Rollins discovered this before the iron was actually laid down, and attached it. Mr. Woodfin arrived soon afterwards from New York with a warrant for the arrest and a requisition for the return to New York of S. W. Hop-

kins, the contractor, with whom Major Rollins had thought
he was about to effect a satisfactory settlement. The officer
from New York would not wait till this settlement could be
effected and hurried his prisoner, Hopkins, back to New York
City. By the time the case was to be heard on the question of
ownership of the iron the clerk who had identified it for Major
Rollins had disappeared and the iron and $10,000 in cash
which had been deposited to indemnify the real owner of the
iron was lost to the State. The clerk had been "seen."

But that was not to be the end of the bunco game by any
means; for in May of the very year of which in April he had
signed the Washington agreement, Geo. W. Swepson, while
president of the Florida Central railroad had, without any
authority of the board of directors of that road, issued $1,000-
000 of bonds, which he signed as president in Washington,
D. C., and caused one H. H. Thompson, who was not the
treasurer of that road, to sign as such treasurer, F. H.
Flagg being then the lawful treasurer. But Swepson and
Littlefield gave Houston, to whom Littlefield was indebted, Littlefield's note for $163,000 secured by 4,370
shares of stock and 103 Pensacola and Georgia railroad bonds, and the $1,000,000 of Florida Central railroad
bonds, which were to be fraudulently issued by them. Thus,
the value of the interest in the Florida railroads had been sur-
reptitiously reduced very materially if not altogether destroyed;
for in January, 1871, Littlefield paid his $163,000 note and ob-
tained from Houston the surrender of the collateral which had
been given to secure its payment. Then, one Thomas E. Codrington appeared on the scene and got possession of the fraudulent $1,000,000 of Florida Central bonds, which, under acts
of the Florida legislature of June 24, 1869, and January 28,
1870, he surrendered to the State of Florida, and obtained in
their stead a like number of Florida State bonds. But, strange
to relate, Codrington got, instead of Florida State bonds,
$1,000,000 of bonds of the Jacksonville, Pensacola and Mobile
Railroad Company, which had been authorized by act of the
Florida legislature of June 24, 1869, but of which only $3,000,000
of an authorized issue of $4,000,000 had been issued by the gov-
ernor of Florida. Thus, apparently, had been cured the ille-
gality of the same amount of bonds which Swepson had issued
in Washington for the benefit of the Florida Central Railroad

Company, to which the signature of H. H. Thompson, the fictitious treasurer, had been attached.

For this transaction, in January, 1872, Governor Harrison Reed of Florida was impeached and removed, and after the carpet-bag regime was entirely overthrown in 1876, and Hon. Thomas Settle of North Carolina had been appointed judge of the district court of the northern district of Florida, a hope was entertained that a court of equity would place the Western Division of the Western North Carolina Railroad in at least as good a position as it had occupied when its money had been originally invested in the three Florida railroads, and would not allow it to suffer by the illegal and fraudulent acts of those who had ceased to be its agents when those acts had been committed.

Now, Major Rollins had been elected president of the Western Division of the Western North Carolina railroad upon the disappearance of M. S. Littlefield and, subsequently, to the presidency of the Eastern Division, and, followed the railroad's interest into Florida, and the control of the Florida railroads. Accordingly, in February, 1877, he instituted a suit in equity in the circuit court of the United States for the Northern district of Florida, in which the Western Division of the Western North Carolina railroad sought to have the bonds of the Florida Central railroads, which had been exchanged for Florida State bonds, declared unlawful; but Judge Joseph P. Bradley, one of the justices of the Supreme Court of the United States, in an opinion filed May 31, 1879, dismissed the bill with costs, on the ground that the Western Division of the Western North Carolina railroad, by agreements made at Washington and in London, had "acquiesced in the issue of the bonds and only claimed to share in the proceeds thereof." The Supreme Court of the United States afterwards affirmed this decision in a case entitled *Florida Central Railroad Company v. Schutte and others*, upon the ground that, in the language of Chief Justice Waite: "There can be no doubt that the governor of Florida was active in promoting the sale, as was also the chairman of the commission appointed by the General Assembly of North Carolina. The bonds were taken at once to London and from there put on the market in Holland where most or all of these sales appear to have been made. The bonds were undoubtedly steeped in fraud at their inception, but they·were nevertheless State bonds on the market in a foreign country, etc.'' The court held in effect that as the Western Division had adopted the property purchased by an embezzler with its money, its rights were subordinate to those of innocent purchasers of the same class of securities, and were charged with all the liens Swepson had put upon them. [3]

North Carolina afterwards repudiated all of these special tax bonds along with others which had been issued by the carpet-bag government of 1868-70.

NOTES.

[1]In *Galloway v. Jenkins* (63 N. C., p. 147) the Supreme Court had held only a short time before that the State could not contract a debt to build a new railroad except by an affirmative vote of the people, because to do so before the bonds of the State had reached par would violate Art. 5, Sec. 5, of the State Constitution; although it is true that in this case Judges Reade and Settle had dissented.

[2]Hon. Samuel W. Watts was the Superior court judge who had issued the injunction in June, 1869. Shipp's Fraud Com. Rep., p. 447

[3]103 U. S. Rep., 327 (13 Otto—118-145).

WILLIAM H. THOMAS,
"Father of Western North Carolina Railroad."

CHAPTER XX

RAILROADS

THE FIRST RAILROAD PROJECT.[1] "When, about the year 1836, a railroad from Cincinnati to Charleston, which should pass through Asheville, was projected, Robert Y. Hayne, the great South Carolinian who had vanquished Daniel Webster in debate, was made its president. At a meeting of this company, held in Asheville in 1839, Mr. Hayne, who had continued to be its president, became dangerously ill, and died here September 24, 1839, in the old Eagle Hotel building."

The railroads which had been built prior to 1845 "were all in the eastern portion of the State. The need of a road toward the mountains was strikingly shown by the failure of the crops in the western counties.[2] Owing to this failure, even the necessaries of life became dear in that section. Corn rose from fifty cents to a dollar and a half a bushel; and yet, at the same time, corn in the eastern counties was rotting in the fields for lack of a market, and fish were being used to enrich the ground. The condition of the [wagon] roads in 1848 was, however, such as to discourage further expense."

A CROP FAILURE STARTED RAILROAD INTEREST. This general failure of crops in the mountain regions called attention to the want of communication between the two sections of the State; and in 1850-51 $12,000 was appropriated by the legislature to survey a route for a railroad from Salisbury to the Tennessee line where the French Broad river passes into Tennessee.

THE WESTERN NORTH CAROLINA RAILROAD. Although it is generally supposed that the Western North Carolina railroad had its genesis in 1855, the North Carolina and Western railroad, to run from Salisbury to the Tennessee line, was chartered as early as 1852 (Ch. 136). Its authorized capital stock was $3,000,000. Nothing of consequence, however, was accomplished under this charter.

LEGISLATIVE HISTORY. "In 1854 the State of North Carolina was completeing the construction of her great work, the North Carolina railroad, and emboldened by this success and having in view a connection of her then existing system

of railroads with the proposed Blue Ridge railroad, and so with
the Great West, there was passed an act entitled: 'An Act
to incorporate the Western North Carolina Railroad Com
pany,' ratified February 15, 1855 (Laws of North Carolina 1854-55, ch. 228, p. 257), which, after reciting the purpose 'of constructing a railroad to effect a communication
between the North Carolina railroad and the Valley of the
Mississippi,' provided for the organization of a corporation
under the style of Western North Carolina Railroad Company,
with power 'to construct a railroad, with one or more tracks,
from the town of Salisbury on the North Carolina railroad,
passing by or as near as practicable to Statesville, in the county
of Iredell, to some point on the French Broad river, beyond
the Blue Ridge, and if the legislature shall hereafter determine,
to such point as it shall designate, at a future session.'   Four
years later, when the line had been located from Salisbury
to the French Broad river at Asheville, the general assembly
supplemented this original charter and definitely fixed the
route of the proposed line in an act entitled: 'An Act to
amend an Act entitled: "An Act to incorporate the Western
North Carolina Railroad Company" passed at the session
of 1854-55, and also an act amendatory thereof passed at the
session of 1856-57' (Ratified February 15, 1859.   Private
Laws of North Carolina 1858-59, ch. 170, p. 217). [3]   This
directed that the survey be continued 'from the point near
Asheville to which the survey has already been made, extending west through the valley of the Pigeon and Tuckaseegee
rivers, to a point on the line of the Blue Ridge railroad on the
Tennessee river, or to the Tennessee line at or near Ducktown,
in the county of Cherokee,' and thereby located a line which
would connect the North Carolina railroad with the Blue Ridge
railroad, an extension which has since been realized, without
the Blue Ridge railroad connection, in the existing Murphy
branch.

"As the legislature was intent, however, on effecting some
western connection for the North Carolina system of railroads, the Western North Carolina was not limited to an
alliance with the Blue Ridge railroad, but it was provided
that the extension from Asheville might be 'down the French
Broad river, through Madison county, to the line of the State
of Tennessee at or near Paint Rock,' which might 'connect

with any company that has been formed or may be formed to complete the railroad connection with the East Tennessee and Virginia railroad.' " [4]

Surveys were accordingly made for both of these proposed lines, and these surveys were duly approved by the legislature at its next session in an act ratified February 18, 1861. (Private Laws of North Carolina 1860-61, ch. 138, p. 154).

"The alternative, or Paint Rock line so authorized, being that of Louisville, Cincinnati, and Charleston, which had been pronounced in the reports of the engineer read at the Knoxville convention in 1836 to be extraordinarily feasible for a railroad, would no doubt have been originally adopted by the Western North Carolina but for the fact that in 1859 the Blue Ridge railroad was still considered certain of construction, while the Cincinnati, Cumberland Gap and Charleston Railroad Company, which held the Tennessee franchise to carry on the old Louisville, Cincinnati and Charleston line from Paint Rock to a connection with the East Tennessee and Virginia railroad at Morristown, was financially weak.

"As the securing of a through trunk line was the principal object for which the construction of the Western North Carolina was undertaken, the proposed Blue Ridge connection accordingly dictated the adoption of the line from Asheville toward Murphy as the main line of the Western North Carolina and it was so considered as late as 1868 when the Constitutional convention, then in session, passed an ordinance entitled: 'An ordinance for the completion of the Western North Carolina Railroad,' ratified March 14, 1868 (Ordinances of 1868, ch. 50, p. 100), which provided that no part of the subscription of the State to the Western North Carolina should be used in the construction of branch lines, except the line to Paint Rock, until 'the main trunk line of said railroad shall have been completed to Copper Mine, at or near Ducktown' and furthermore that the General Assembly 'is hereby authorized and directed to make such further appropriation or subscription to the capital stock of said railroad company as will insure the completion of said road at the earliest practicable day.'

" The Paint Rock line, thus relegated to the status of a branch, was not, however, abandoned, but it was considered that the

Tennessee enterprise of the Cincinnati, Cumberland Gap and Charleston was primarily interested therein, as is evidenced by the act entitled: 'An Act to amend the Charter of the Western North Carolina Railroad' ratified March 4, 1867, (Public Laws of N. C. 1866-67, ch. 94, p. 152), which authorized the Western North Carolina to construct its line from Asheville to Paint Rock upon the 'Tennessee Gauge,' and to so maintain it until the entire line was completed, and the gauge of the North Carolina railroad could be established thereon uniformly. 'It was the realization of the Paint Rock line in 1881, however, that opened the only railroad which has ever been built through the southern ranges of the Appalachian Mountains." [4]

ROUTE AND CONNECTIONS. It will be seen from the above how the route was changed from that originally contemplated. [5] It was never purposed to build this railroad by way of Franklin; as that town was on the proposed Blue Ridge line from Walhalla, S. C., and it was the intention to connect with that line; but this connection was contemplated at some point west of Franklin, Ducktown, Tennessee, having been considered at one time as the point of junction, due to ignorance of the topography of the western part of the State, as the connection must necessarily have been somewhere on the Little Tennessee, that stream rising in Raburn gap, Ga.

RAPID PROGRESS. The Western North Carolina railroad was chartered by an act which was ratified February 15, 1855, and work was begun and the railroad completed and put into operation to within a few miles east of Morganton by the summer of 1861. A contract had been given to Crockford, Malone & Co., in September, 1860, when Dr. A. M. Powell was president of the railroad company, for the completion of the road from a point near Old Fort to the western portal of the Swannanoa tunnel, for a specified sum, plus 20 per cent for contingencies. These contractors stopped work in the spring of 1861 on account of the war, having done about $27,-000 worth of work. Soon after the close of the Civil War, while Mr. ———— Caldwell was president and Capt. Samuel Kirkland was chief engineer, the road was completed to Morganton by paying 50 per cent increase on estimates made previous to the war, the increase being due to depreciation of currency. Colonel W. A. Eliason was elected chief engineer in 1868 and continued as such till April, 1871. Previous to 1868 Col. Eliason had been assistant engineer. The line had been changed in the winter of 1860-61 for a considerable distance on sections 6, 7, 8, 9 and 10 and this reduced the estimates by $171,293.

LOCATION ON THE BLUE RIDGE CHANGED. The route up the eastern slope of the Blue Ridge was changed after the war to one with longer, safer and lighter grades than those of the original survey. [6]

ENGINEERS AND MOUNTAIN WORK. While Col. J. W. Wilson was chief engineer Col. S. W. McD. Tate became president, and in October, 1866, the board of directors ordered the resumption of work west of Morganton, and the precedent of paying 50 per cent advance was followed. In January, 1868, the contract for the work from Old Fort to the western portal of the Swannanoa tunnel was let to John Malone & Co., diminished by the work which had been done by Crockford, Malone & Co., plus 50 per cent to the original estimates.

A PROPOSITION was afterwards made to Col. Wilson that, if he would turn over $200,000 of first mortgage bonds of the road, the chief engineer would make out estimates for $701,000 in addition to what he had received, which would be a majority of the $1,400,000 bonds authorized by the act of December 19, 1866. This proposition was made at the Boyden House in Salisbury in December, 1870, and the object was claimed to be to get control of the majority of the bonds and thus prevent a forced foreclosure of the railroad:

" Some time in the fall of 1869 I had conversation with Col. Tate in relation to the condition of the road. [7] . . . In one of those conversations in Morganton it was suggested that the sale of the road could not be forced unless a majority of the bonds got into the hands of one person. I suggested to Col. Tate that probably the contract with John Malone & Co. could be made useful in preventing the sale; that they claimed compensation for their work according to the old estimates and contract with Crockford and Malone. I thought they were bound by the estimates on the line as changed by me, but that I would sign the estimates according to the old notes, with the understanding that 600 of the bonds were to be delivered to Maj. Wilson, and 200 were to be placed in my hands ; for the whole was to be held so that they would not be put on the market and get into the hands of the New York speculators, and thereby endanger the sale of the road. The 800 were to be divided between Maj. Wilson and myself, so that no one was to have a majority of the bonds. 'Col. Wilson declined this proposition,' as it was 'much more than was due me, and I regarded the transaction as corrupt.' " [8]

A CHANGE OF OFFICERS. Dr. J. J. Mott succeeded Col. Tate as president of this division of the road, Col. Tate becoming financial agent when he secured the State bonds issued on account of the company. The office of financial agent was abolished in 1869. Col. Tate accounted for all these bonds before the Bragg committee, which found his official conduct correct.

JOHN MALONE & CO. The firm of John Malone & Co., was composed of John Malone, J. W. Wilson and Mr. Goldsborough of Maryland.   J. W. Wilson had been the chief engineer and superintendent of the road from the summer of 1864 until the provisional governor was appointed in 1865. He was afterwards reappointed by the directors named by Gov. Worth and held the position until the spring of 1867, when he resigned in order to go into business. Up to September, 1871, John Malone & Co., had been paid for their work about $600,-000, the estimate of the whole contract having been $1,959,-000, two-thirds of which was to be paid in cash and one-third in stock, leaving $220,000 still due to the contractors. The Swepson and Littlefield frauds brought all work to a stop in 1870. (See Chapter XIX.)

WESTERN DIVISION ABOLISHED. At its session of 1873-74 the legislature repealed the act appointing the Woodfin commission and required the commissioners to turn over all the books and property of the Western Division to the directors of the Western North Carolina railroad, upon whom devolved the former duties of the commissioners; and the legislature of 1876-77 required the president of the railroad to report what property he had acquired from Swepson and Littlefield in his settlement with them. This Western Division consisted of the Murphy and Paint Rock lines. The Eastern Division was the line from Salisbury to Asheville.

EARLY LITIGATION. The Western North Carolina railroad got into trouble with its creditors, and, in 1874-75, we find a joint resolution to ascertain what the claims against the road

could be bought for, and another joint resolution to appeal
to the Supreme Court of the United States from the decision of the United States court at Greensboro in the case of
*Henry Clews, Hiram Sibley and others v. the Western Division
of the Western North Carolina railroad,* and, finally (Ch. 150)
an act to authorize the purchase of the road under the decree
for its sale at not more than $850,000, with authority to
issue seven per cent bonds to that amount, secured by a mortgage of the property; and to complete the road to Paint Rock
and Murphy, the State to have three-fourths of the stock
and the private stockholders the other third.

"By an act ratified March 13, 1875 (laws of North Carolina
1874-75, ch. 150, p. 172), the Governor, Curtis H. Brogden,
the president of the senate, R. F. Armfield, and the Speaker
of the House, James L. Robinson, were constituted a commission with power to purchase the Western North Carolina
railroad at the forthcoming sale in the Sibley suit for not
exceeding $850,000, the amount which had been adjudged
due on the outstanding first mortgage bonds issued by the
Eastern Division. In order to force through the negotiations
for the purchase of the outstanding claims, this commission
was later authorized to prosecute an appeal in the Sibley suit
to the Supreme Court of the United States, by resolution adopted
March 20, 1875. (Laws of North Carolina 1874-75, p. 405.
See also a resolution concerning the expenses of this commission, ratified January 11, 1877, Laws of North Carolina 1876-77,
p. 582.)

"This finally resulted in the execution of an agreement
under date of April 17, 1875, whereby all the parties in interest,
including the East Tennessee, Virginia and Georgia, the North
Carolina Railroad Company and McAden, assigned all their
claims to the State commission consisting of Messrs. Brogden, Armfield and Robinson, in consideration of their agreement to purchase and reorganize the Western North Carolina, and to issue new first mortgage bonds for $850,000 to be
ratably distributed among the parties in interest. This
agreement was thereupon carried out, and reorganization
by the State followed; the new corporation, hereinafter styled
Western North Carolina Railroad Company No. 2, taking
possession of the property on October 1, 1875." [9]

ORGANIZATION. By chapter 105 of the laws of 1876-77 the

Western North Carolina railroad was organized with a capital stock of $850,000, three-fourths of which belonged to the State and one-fourth to the private stockholders to be appointed according to their several interests. The State also undertook to furnish 500 convicts to work on the road and the governor was authorized to buy iron to lay the track from the then terminus near Old Fort. It was also provided that when the road should have been completed to Asheville the convicts were to be divided equally, one-half to work on the Paint Rock line and the other half on the Murphy division, and that after the line should have been completed to Paint Rock, all the convicts were to be employed on the line to Murphy. Apparently, however, the State became uncertain as to the securities of the Richmond & Danville railroad for its lease of the Western North Carolina Railroad, for on the 23d of January, 1877, a joint resolution was adopted to enquire into the sufficiency of those securities. In 1879 the Western Division was abolished and consolidated with the Eastern Division under the name of the Western North Carolina Railroad Company.

W. J. BEST & Co.   A special session of the legislature was called and by an act of March 29, 1880, (Ch. 26) the State agreed to sell the Western North Carolina railroad to Wm. J. Best, Wm. R. Grace, James D. Fish and J. Nelson Tappan subject to the mortgage of 1875 for $850,000, on which the purchasers were to pay the interest, etc.

The agreement of April 27, 1880, between Wm. J. Best *et al.* and the State of North Carolina, among other things, recited:

" The Act of March 29, 1880, and provides in consideration of the delivery of a deed by the Commissioners named in said act to the United Trust Company, to be held in escrow, that the purchasers will :

" 1.   Complete the line to Paint Rock on or before July 1, 1881, and to Murphy on or before January 1, 1885.

" 2.   Repay to the State all moneys expended on the road after March 29, 1880.

" 3.   Pay to the State $125 per annum rent for each of five hundred able-bodied convicts.

" 4.   That no bonds will be issued except as provided in the act.

" 5.   That they will deliver $520,000 of their first mortgage bonds, when issued and $30,000 cash, to make up the aggregate of $550,000, invested by the State in the property, to the State Treasurer.

"6. That they will pay the interest on the outstanding $850,000 of W. N. C. No. 2 bonds."[10]

CLYDE, LOGAN AND BUFORD. "Clyde, Logan and Buford, in 1880, loaned W. J. Best money and he failed to pay same back and forfeited the road, he assigning all his interest to Messrs. Clyde, Logan and Buford on May 28, 1880."[10] These men controlled both the Richmond and Danville Railroad Company and the Richmond and West Point Terminal Company.[11]

THE RICHMOND AND DANVILLE. The Richmond and Danville Railroad Company at one time owned the Richmond and West Point Terminal Company, and afterwards the Richmond and West Point Terminal Company bought the Richmond and Danville. Under the assignment from Best the Richmond Terminal Company came into control of the Western North Carolina and immediately proceeded with the work, issuing two mortgages for this purpose.[13]

"The Richmond Terminal Company acquired the Western North Carolina in the interest of the expanding R. &. D system to extend its line from a connection at Salisbury with the North Carolina Railroad, which the R. & D. was operating in 1880 under lease.

"For the next five years while the construction of the Western North Carolina was being completed the operation was carried on in the name of Western North Carolina No. 3 as is evidenced by an act entitled :

" 'An Act empowering the Western North Carolina Railroad Company to construct telegraph and telephone lines on its right of way.'

"Ratified March 6, 1885.

"Laws of North Carolina 1885, ch. 294, p. 542, which authorized the company to do a general telegraph business, but in 1886, when the R. & D. was assuming the operation of most of the Richmond Terminal lines in its own name, the following lease was executed :

" 'Western North Carolina Railroad Co., to Richmond and Danville Railroad Company, lease dated April 30, 1886 : Term Ninety-nine years. Rental : Net earnings above fixed charges. (Abrogated May 5, 1894.)' "[12]

RICHMOND TERMINAL. "From this it will be seen that the property was operated as the Western North Carolina but was held by the Richmond Terminal Company up to April 30, 1886, from which time to May 5, 1894, when the Southern Railway purchased the property, it was operated by the Richmond & Danville under lease."[12]

THE STATE SELLS THE RAILROAD. By an act of 1883 (ch. 241) the State agreed to sell the road to Clyde, Logan and

Buford, assignees of W. J. Best and associates, provided they should complete it to the mouth of the Nantahala river by September 1, 1884, and should keep at work beyond that point 75 convicts. They were also required to purchase of the State treasurer $520,000 of the coupon bonds of the Western North Carolina railroad which they had deposited with the State treasurer under sections 12 and 24 of the act of March 29, 1880. The road was finished into Andrews in the summer of 1889 and to Murphy in 1891. Soon thereafter, to wit, on June 15, 1892, the old Richmond & Danville Railroad went into the hands of receivers, Fred W. Hidekoper, Reuben Foster, and, later on, Samuel Spencer, and emerged therefrom as the Southern Railway Company, August 22, 1894, when the order was made confirming the sale of the road which had been made by Charles Price, special master, on August 21 at Salisbury, for $500,000.

COMPLETION OF THE RAILROAD. From 1869 and thereafter for several years, passengers were taken from Old Fort, the terminus of the railroad, to Asheville in stage coaches operated by the late Ed. T. Clemmons, contractor. Jack Pence "drove the mountain," as the end of the line nearest Old Fort was called, handling "the ribbons" over six beautiful white horses. The part of the trip down the mountains was always made at night, but there was never an accident. After several years the road was completed to a station called Henry's, where it remained till 1879, when it had been finished to Azalia, 130 miles west of Salisbury. The formidable Blue Ridge had been successfully surmounted at last.

THE ANDREWS GEYSER. A hotel and geyser-like fountain were maintained at Round Knob from about 1885 to about the close of the last century, when the hotel was burned. The fountain had ceased some time before that; but in 1911 George F. Baker of New York, as a testimonial to the services Col. A. B. Andrews had rendered in the development of Western North Carolina, restored the fountain at his own expense. It throws a stream of water 250 feet into the air.

ARRIVAL AT VARIOUS POINTS. [14] The railroad was completed to Biltmore on Sunday, October 3, 1880; to Alexanders, 10 miles below Asheville on the French Broad, on the 4th day of July, 1881, and to Paint Rock January 25, 1882. The bridge at Marshall was finished June 15, 1882. The Murphy branch was completed to Pigeon river, now Canton, January 28, 1882, reaching Waynesville later in the same year.

PROGRESS WEST OF WAYNESVILLE. If the original plan to have a tunnel through the Balsam mountain had been adhered to the terminus of the road must have remained at Waynesville many years; but the road was built over the mountain by a difficult and dangerous grade, and the work which had been done on the tunnel in 1869 and 1870 was abandoned. This Balsam gap is the highest railroad pass east of the Rocky mountains, being about 3,100 feet above sea level. . . . The road was completed to Dillsboro in 1883 and to Bryson city in 1884. It reached Jarrett's station, or Nantahala, at the mouth of the Red Marble creek, November 23, 1884. Here it stayed a long time, due to the fact that a tunnel had been contemplated through the Red Marble gap of the Valley River Mountain; but after the grading had been completed nearly to the gap it was discovered that the soil would not support the roof and sides of a tunnel, and the whole work had to be done over again and the roadbed placed on a much higher grade. This serious error cost many thousands of dollars and long delay. The road was finished to Andrews in the summer of 1889, and its entrance into Murphy was celebrated in 1891, on the same day the cornerstone of the fine new court house was laid. The original survey required the road to go by old Valley Town, but it was changed. Several of the convicts who helped to build this road settled in Murphy when their terms expired and are making good citizens

SPARTANBURG AND ASHEVILLE RAILROAD. This road was completed to Saluda, twelve miles east of Hendersonville in 1879, and to Hendersonville about 1882. It was necessary that Buncombe county should contribute to the building of this railroad.

BUNCOMBE'S SUBSCRIPTION. On the 5th of August, 1875, there were 1,944 votes for subscription to $100,000 of the stock of the Spartanburg and Asheville railroad, and only 242 votes against subscription, and the bonds were issued, bearing six per cent interest and due in twenty years. But they were issued only as the grading was completed and amounted at the end to only $98,000 in all. These bonds were refunded at par by new bonds dated July 1, 1895, due in twenty years, under Chapter 172, Public Laws 1893. But at the meeting of the Republican board of county commissioners on December 27, 1897, they ratified a contract which had been made by the board and Hon. A. C. Avery, Mark W. Brown and Moore & Moore, attorneys, to contest the validity of the bonds in a case entitled the *County Commissioners v. W. R. Payne, County Treasurer.* This attempted repudiation was used by the Democrats to defeat the Republicans in November, 1898. But the Democrats themselves afterwards employed counsel to carry out the repudiation of these bonds on the ground that the bill had not been read on three separate days in each house. However, certain holders of these bonds soon brought an action in the District court of the United States, which held that the bonds were valid.

RICHMOND PEARSON'S BILL. Having secured the $100,000 subscription from Buncombe county, the officers of this road seemed satisfied to keep its terminal at Hendersonville indefinitely. Consequently, in 1885, Hon. Richmond Pearson, of Buncombe, introduced a bill in the legislature to declare forfeited the charter of the Spartanburg and Asheville Railroad Company, but before it could be read a second time, the railroad company began work and in 1886 completed the road to Asheville. During the time the road's terminus remained at Hendersonville Buncombe county was paying interest on the $98,000 of bonds which had been issued.

THE SOUTH AND WESTERN RAILROAD. The South and Western railroad was completed from Johnson City, Tennessee, to Huntdale, Yancey county, North Carolina, in 1900. It was afterwards built to Spruce Pine in 1904.

THE SOUTHERN RAILWAY IN THE MANGER. From the decision of the Supreme court in the case of the Johnson City Southern Railway against the South and Western Railroad Company[15] it is clear that the Southern Railway Company in 1907 attempted to defeat the building of this incomparable railroad now crossing the mountains from Marion, North Carolina, to Johnson City, Tennessee, by alleging that it (the Southern) was seeking to condemn land along the North Toe river in Yancey county for the purpose of constructing a railway from the coal fields to tidewater, when in point of fact it "did not in good faith intend to construct a railroad over the line

in controversy," but had caused the Johnson City railroad
to be "incorporated for the purpose of hindering, delaying
and obstructing the building of a railroad along the North
Toe by the South and Western Railway Company which
was in good faith constructing a railroad from Johnson City
. . . to Spruce Pine in North Carolina, and was operating the same."[15]

THE SOUTHERN'S PLAN. The plan of the Southern Railway had been to pretend that it meant to build a railroad
along this river, although it was well aware that the South
and Western had already built such a road along the stream
from Johnson City to Spruce Pine; and, by appealing to the
courts, to prevent the real road from changing its track from
the east to the west bank of the river in order to obtain a better grade, which it had commenced to do in November, 1905,
while the dummy corporation the Southern railway was using
for this purpose had not been incorporated till December
of the following year. Upon this the court said:

COURTS NOT TO BE USED TO PREVENT PROGRESS. "It is
not of so much interest to the public which of two corporations
build the road as it is that, by using the courts in the way
suggested, they prevent either from doing so. If the course
proposed by the 'Southern Railway' be permitted, the State
has granted her franchise, with its sovereign power, to her
own hindrance. If in creating two corporations she has
conferred power upon both by which, through the instrumentality of her own courts, the building of railroads may
be retarded, if not ultimately defeated, and her mountain
fastnesses remain locked in their primitive isolation, the
legislature may well consider whether some restriction should
not be put upon corporations enjoying such power. If the
course proposed by the 'Southern Railway' be permitted,
railroad building may be 'tied up' indefinitely by repeatedly
renewed condemnation proceedings, contested until the end
has been reached, and then withdrawn, only to be repeated
in another form."[15]

THE CAROLINA, CLINCHFIELD AND OHIO RAILROAD. The
South and Western, also known as the "Three C's," but now the
Carolina, Clinchfield and Ohio, was completed to Marion,
in 1908. It is the best constructed railroad in the mountains,
the grades and curvatures being far less than those of the
Southern from Old Fort to Morristown.

ALLEGED PEONAGE. During the time the heavy work on the eastern slope of the Blue Ridge was being done, construction companies were given contracts for the building of certain sections of the line. Among these contractors was the Carolina Construction Company. Labor was hard to get, and in order to secure laborers this Construction Company paid the expenses of certain men to their camp. They worked half a day and slipped off, were followed, captured, returned to camp and imprisoned till nightfall, when they were taken out and severely whipped. The facts appear in *Buckner v. South & Western Railway Co.*, 159 N. C., going up on appeal from Buncombe county. This was known as the "peonage case."

THE SNOW BIRD VALLEY RAILROAD. The Kanawha Hardwood Company, with that progressive and public spirited Virginian, J. Q. Barker, at its head, came in 1902 and constructed the Snow Bird Valley logging railroad for a distance of fifteen miles from Andrews over the Snow Bird mountains to the head of Snow Bird creek in 1907-08. The Cherokee Tanning and Extract Company began business in 1903, and the Andrews Lumber Company, under the management of Mr. H. R. Campbell, came in the spring of 1911, and have since completed fifteen miles of logging railroad of standard gauge into heavily timbered lands in Macon county on Chogah creek. This company has also built a saw mill near Andrews with a capacity of 80,000 feet a day.

EAST TENNESSEE AND WESTERN NORTH CAROLINA RAILROAD. This road was completed from Johnson City, Tenn., via Elizabethton to the Cranberry iron mines in 1882. It is a narrow gauge road. In 1900 or thereabout it was extended to Pinola or Saginaw, in what is now Avery county. This extension was paid for in coffee for a long time, funds being short, and was called the Arbuckle line. Its real name, however, is

LINVILLE RIVER RAILROAD COMPANY, and was built by E. B. Camp, who owned a considerable body of timber near Saginaw, the company operating the road and saw mills being the Pinola Lumber and Trading Company. Both companies went into the hands of a receiver, however, and were bought in by Isaac T. Mann of Bramley, W. Va. He got the W. M. Ritter Lumber Company interested in it and both properties finally went to that company, including a very good inn, called the Pinola Inn. A majority of its stock was transferred to the Cranberry Iron and Coal Company in April, 1913 by the W. M. Ritter Lumber Company.

HENDERSONVILLE AND BREVARD RAILROAD. This road was built in 1894 by the late Tam C. McNeeley. Thos. S. Boswell was the engineer, and after it went into the hands of a receiver in 1897 he operated it as superintendent, when it was bought by J. F. Hays and associates, who afterwards organized

THE TRANSYLVANIA RAILROAD COMPANY, and in 1900 extended the road to Rosman, N. C., a point ten miles southwest of Brevard. From there it was to have been constructed to Seneca, S. C., which would have given a shorter route south from Asheville by 35 miles; but the Southern Railway leased it and that put an end to that scheme. In 1903 this road, as the Transylvania railroad, was extended to Lake Toxaway, nine miles beyond Rosman, and it was in this year that the Toxaway Inn was built, the lake having been dammed in the same year, Thos. S. Boswell having been the engineer.

"The building of the Transylvania road and its extension, resulted in the construction of the plant of the Toxaway Tanning Company at Rosman, N. C., in about 1901, as I recall. This has also resulted in the development of the Gloucester Lumber Company at that place; this concern is operating 20,000 acres on the western end of the Pisgah Forest tract of the Vanderbilt estate and have their mills located at Rosman, and carry on quite a large operation, with probably 20 miles of railroad. Also, at Rosman is located the plant of the Shaffer Lumber Company, and they have a line of railroad running to the south from Rosman and have quite a large operation with their mills located on their line of road. Also, the building of the Transylvania resulted in the location of the plant of the Brevard Tanning Company at Pisgah Forest, two miles northeast of Brevard, which has had a very successful operation."[16]

THE ELKIN AND ALLEGHANY RAILROAD. The great drawback to Alleghany county has been the lack of a railroad. The legislature of 1907 authorized the State to furnish not less than 50 convicts for the purpose of constructing a railroad from Elkin to Sparta. The State took stock in this road to the amount of the work done by the convicts, and the work of grading was begun in the fall of 1907. In the early part of the year 1911 the directors, John T. Miles, Capt. Roth, H. G. Chatham, R. A. Doughton, A. H. Eller, C. C. Smoot, Henry Fries and others, succeeded in interesting John A. Mills in this enterprise, and he helped to procure the financial aid. And now the railroad has every appearance of being rapidly pushed to completion. The train is now running to the foot of the mountain, nearly halfway to Sparta.

THE PIGEON RIVER RAILROAD. This was one of the first enterprises planned by the Champion Fiber Company; but it decided that a flume from Sunburst to Canton would be cheaper and answer its purposes as well as a railroad. This proved impracticable, on account of difficulties in securing rights of way; and a railroad was commenced a few years ago, of standard gauge, and it is now completed.

GEORGIA AND NORTH CAROLINA RAILROAD. The Georgia and North Carolina railroad, from Marietta, Georgia, to Murphy (ch. 167, Laws of 1870-71) was the first railroad to run into Cherokee, and the late Mercer Fain was its first president and was the most active in its construction. It reached Murphy in 1888, and at first was a narrow gauge. It was afterwards absorbed by the Marietta and North Georgia railroad, which extended it from Blue Ridge, Georgia, to Knoxville, leaving the Murphy end a mere branch. It was originally intended that this road should go down the Hiwassee and Tennessee rivers to Chattanooga, but others had already obtained a charter for a road by that route which they refused to surrender or assign except upon prohibitive terms. Hence the route via Blue Ridge was adopted. The dog-in-the-manger policy has thus prevented a road down the Hiwassee river and has not produced any benefit to those who not only would not build themselves but would not allow others to do so.

THE APPALACHIAN RAILROAD. There is also a short railroad which leaves the Murphy branch about five miles east of Bryson City and runs a short distance up Ocona Lufty creek.

TALLULAH FALLS AND FRANKLIN RAILROAD. This road was completed from Cornelia, in Georgia, via Tallulah Falls and Rabun Gap to Franklin, in 1908. It affords an outlet for a large section of this region, and practically makes the whole of Macon county tributary to Georgia. If the Southern

Railway would complete the link between Franklin and Almond, and down the Little Tennessee river from Bushnel to Maryville, Tenn., Franklin would have two other outlets, one into our own State via Asheville, and into Tennessee via Bushnel and Murphy. [17] This is more of the dog-in-the-manger spirit.

THE DAMASCUS LUMBER COMPANY RAILROAD. In 1902 the Hemlock Extract Company, D. K. Stouffer, manager, was built, and several years afterwards the Damascus Lumber Company built a narrow gauge railroad from Laurel Bloomery in Tennessee, on the Laurel Railway Company's line, over the Cut Laurel gap. It is operated exclusively as a logging road, but the grade, generally, is good enough for a standard road, and there is no reason why it should not be electrified and operated as it is for freight and passengers. Its terminus at Hemlock is only 19 miles from Jefferson, the county seat of Ashe county, the grade down Laurel creek to the North Fork of the New river is good, and the road should be extended to Jefferson at least, the principal barrier to mountain roads having been overcome in the passage of the Cut Laurel gap.

THE TENNESSEE AND NORTH CAROLINA RAILROAD was completed to the mouth of Big creek on the Pigeon river about 1897, and then extended two miles up to Mount Sterling post office, where there has been a large saw mill plant since about 1900. The design is to complete this line up the Pigeon to Canton at least; and ultimately up the Pigeon to Sunburst, and thence into Transylvania county. Should it get as far as the mouth of Cataloochee creek it will have tapped the finest body of virgin hardwood timber left in the mountains.

ASHEVILLE AND CRAGGY MOUNTAIN RAILWAY. On March 29, 1901, the city of Asheville authorized the Craggy Mountain Railway Company to transfer its rights over Charlotte street to the reorganized Asheville Street Railroad Company. Mr. R. S. Howland operated this road to Overlook Park, on Sunset Mountain, several summers; but, by September, 1904, he had demonstrated to his own satisfaction that it could not be made to pay. In that month it was torn up and the rails and ties used to build a track from the Golf Club to Grace and thence to the French Broad river at Craggy Station on the Southern Railway, and the Weaver Power Company plant and dam, then but recently erected, and to the factory of the

William Whittam Textile Company, which had been incorporated February 1, 1902. He also built a trestle across the French Broad river to the opposite bank, where the Southern Railway established a station called Craggy.

QUARRY. Meantime, however, not losing sight of the objective point of the Craggy Railway Company, Mr. Howland graded a roadbed and laid a track for a steam railroad from the new Music Hall at Overlook Park, to Locust Gap, a distance of about two miles, and opened a new quarry about a quarter of a mile from the Music Hall, with a track extending down to it. He also leased a part of the old James M. Smith property, in rear of the present Langren Hotel, where he established bins, and from which he sold all sorts of stone, bringing it down the mountain by a steam dummy engine, and hauling it through the streets of Asheville with a large electric motor engine. The ties and rails on the track to Locust Gap and to the new quarry were also taken up and placed on the railroad leading to Grace and Craggy Station. He also graded a traction road from near Locust Gap through the lands of J. W. Shartle, C. A. Webb and others to Craven Gap at the head of Beaver Dam creek, and thence to within half a mile of Bull Gap at the head of Ox creek on the North and Bull creek on the south. This road is to form a part of the projected automobile road from Asheville via Mitchell's Peak, and thence along the crest of the Blue Ridge to Blowing Rock. During this time Mr. Howland experimented with steam traction engines; but they were not satisfactory for the mountain roads.

ASHEVILLE LOOP LINE RAILWAY. Mr. Howland operated the railroad down to Craggy Station and to the Elk Mountain Cotton Mill till April, 1906, when he sold that portion of the railroad between New Bridge on the Burnsville road and Craggy Station to the Southern Railway, but continued to run cars from the Golf Club to New Bridge. The sale of the lower portion of this railroad also carried with it the corporate rights, etc., of the Asheville and Craggy Mountain Railroad Company, and it then became necessary to organize the Asheville Loop Line Railway to operate what was left of the Craggy Mountain Railway. This company, during the summer of 1906, leased from the Southern Railway that portion of the railway between New Bridge and Craggy Station and operated the en-

tire line from the Golf Club to the river. The water im-
pounded by the Weaver Power Company dam was called
Lake Tahkeeostee, and proved quite an attraction to summer
visitors who were in Asheville in great numbers during the
season. The railroad paid a slight profit.

ASHEVILLE RAPID TRANSIT RAILROAD. During the fall of 1906
Messrs. Culver and Whittlesey, attorneys, and Mr. R. H. Ting-
ley, civil engineer, of New York City, got control of the Loop
Line railroad and determined to rebuild the track to the
Music Hall on Sunset mountain. To do this they formed
a new corporation called the Asheville Rapid Transit Company, December 18, 1906, and in March of 1907 obtained a
franchise to build an electric railway from the corner of Water
street and Patton avenue across North Main street, and
thence along Merrimon avenue to a point near the Manor,
and thence over private property to the Golf Club. In order
to secure this concession from the city they deposited $1,000,
to be forfeited in case they did not commence to build the railway into town by the following September and complete it
within a few months thereafter.

MERRIMON AVENUE LINE. These gentlemen secured
enough money to reconstruct the track up the mountain to
the Music Hall, which was in full operation by July 4, 1907,
on which day two thousand passengers were transported over
the new road. They continued to operate the road during
the summer and opened a restaurant and moving picture
show at Overlook Park. But the money they had expected
to borrow for the completion of the railway into the city via
Merrimon avenue could not be obtained, and they abandoned
the enterprise, turning the property back to Mr. R. S. Howland in the spring of 1908. As there were several local debts
due by the company the board of aldermen very consider-
ately returned the $1,000 which had been deposited as a
forfeit, upon the abandonment and release by the company
of all rights on the streets, on condition that it should
be so applied. In June, 1908, Mr. R. S. Howland took
charge of the company again; but the company, not having paid the Asheville Electric Company for the power
which had been furnished for some time previous, the latter
company refused to supply electric current for the operation
of cars to Sunset mountain. An arrangement, however, was

soon afterwards made for power to operate the cars from the
Golf Club to New Bridge and this continued to be done till
August 27, when the Rapid Transit Company was placed in
the hands of a receiver. It was sold in December, 1908, to
R. S. Howland and associates for $25,000. By an arrange-
ment between Messrs. LaBarbe, Moale & Chiles and R. S.
Howland the latter was to have the roadbed from the Golf
Club to New Bridge and certain other property, and the
former the track up the mountain and ten acres around Music
Hall. This led to some litigation between these parties, which,
however, was adjusted in 1911.

EAST TENNESSEE AND NORTH CAROLINA RAILROAD. During
1909 R. S. Howland built a trolley railroad from New Bridge
to Weaverville, thus giving a continuous line from Grace
to Weaverville. By a subsequent agreement with the Asheville Electric Company and the Asheville and East Tennessee
Railroad Company, as this Weaverville railway company is
called, under its charter, the latter has the right to operate
its cars over the track of the former from Grace to Pack Square.
This line passes over Merrimon avenue under a franchise
granted the Asheville Electric Company by the city soon after
its rights over that avenue had been abandoned by the Rapid
Transit Company. Both the Merrimon Avenue line in the
city and the railway from Grace to Weaversville have proven
great conveniences to the public.

SUNSET MOUNTAIN RAILWAY COMPANY. Under this name
LaBarbe, Moale and Chiles operated the road up Sunset mountain to Music Hall during the summer of 1910, but soon sold it
to the E. W. Grove Park Company, who also bought about
300 acres on Sunset mountain from the Howlands. The
track has been removed and the roadbed converted into an
automobile road.

THE HIWASSEE VALLEY RAILROAD. In 1913 Clay and Cherokee counties each voted $75,000 for the construction of a rail-
road from Andrews via Marble down the Hiwassee river
to Hayesville, crossing Peach Tree and Hiwassee at the Clay
county line. It will be 35 miles long, standard gauge, etc.,
and will be operated by electricity from a power plant to be
erected on Hiwassee river. A question has arisen as to the
legality of the vote, and the company is now enjoined from
proceeding further in securing aid from either county. J.

Q. Barker is president, and Samuel Cover, treasurer, and D. S. Russell, secretary.

BETTER THAN RAISING CORN AND COTTON. If Ashe, Clay, Graham, and Watauga counties; four of the richest counties in the mountains naturally, had railroads the enhanced value of their property would give the State a larger and more constant revenue from taxation than she now derives from the raising of uncertain crops of cotton and corn on the State farms by working her convicts in that malarious section of the State. If these convicts were taken to the healthful and invigorating climate of the mountains and put to work grading railroads, for their support in provisions alone, it would not be long before every county west of the Blue Ridge would be adequately served with an outlet for their crops, lumber and minerals, while new health and pleasure resorts would be opened up for summer tourists and health seekers.

Ashe is less known than any mountain county, but it is the finest of them all, agriculturally and in minerals and water power. Yet in the decade between 1900 and 1910 its population decreased from 19,581 to 19,074. Clay's population fell from 4,532 in 1900 to 3,909. Yet the lands of Clay are rich and productive and its jail is empty nine-tenths of the time. Watauga, which in many respects is unsurpassed, gained only a little over one hundred inhabitants in the same period. These three fine counties are really retrograding for want of railroads. If the increase in population and wealth of Buncombe in 1880, before railroads reached its borders, compared with its population and wealth in 1913, is an index of what railroads accomplish for communities, it will be evident that the convicts could be more advantageously employed in the mountains building wagon- and railroads than in raising precarious crops of cotton and corn near Weldon.

The territory that in 1911 was erected into the county of Avery is more mountainous and was formerly more inaccessible than any other part of the mountains. Yet, having a railroad, it gained nearly 2,000 in population in the last ten years.

OTHER RAILROADS. In November, 1912, the county of Watauga by a large majority voted $100,000 toward the construction of a railroad through Cook's Gap, Boone and down the Watauga river, and the State has since provided thirty convicts for work thereon. Work has already begun. The Virginia - Carolina Railway obtained from the Legislature of North Carolina in 1911, authority to construct a railroad from its line in Grayson and Washington counties, Virginia, into the counties of Ashe and Watauga, and in June, 1913, let the entire line to the Callahan Construction Company, from Konarok, Va., via Jefferson to Todd, or Elk Cross Roads; all grading to be completed by July, 1914. That the link between Canton and the mouth of Big creek, near Mount Sterling post office, will be built shortly seems probable, as the line has only to follow the Pigeon river to complete this link, thus opening up a large boundary of timber and acid wood and bark in the Cataloochee valley. There is also hope that a railroad will be built from Saginaw (Pinola) to Mortimer or Collettsville. A lumber road from Black Mountain station to Mitchell's peak is being constructed rapidly.

THE BLATHERSKITE RAILROAD. This road has been building (in the newspapers) for ten years or more, but never hauls any freight or passengers. It is quiescent until there is talk of a bona fide railroad, and then it develops a state of activity and construction (still in the newspapers) wherever it is proposed to locate such new railway.

NOTES.

[1]From Asheville's Centenary.
[2]Hill's, p. 259.
[3]Col. Wm. H. Thomas was more active in securing this amendment than anyone else.
[4]Harrison's Legal History of the Lines of the Southern Railway.
[5]Under the act incorporating the Western North Carolina R. R., commissioners were appointed to take subscriptions to the capital stock in Salisbury, Lincolnton, Newton, Statesville, Hendersonville, Lenoir, Boone, Taylorsville, Morganton, Marion, Rutherfordton, Shelby, Mocksville, and Asheville. The act provided for the construction of a railroad to effect a communication between the North Carolina R. R. and the Valley of the Mississippi, no route being specified.
[6]Shipp Fraud Com. Rep., pp. 250 and 307.
[7]Wm. A. Eliason Testimony, Shipp Fraud Com., p. 357.
[8]J. W. Wilson before Shipp Fraud Commission, p. 365.
[9]Harrison's ''Legal History of the Lines of the Southern Railway.''
[10]Fairfax Harrison's ''Legal History of the Lines of the Southern Railway.''
[11]Letter from Col. A. B. Andrews to J. P. A., July, 1912.
[12]Fairfax Harrison's ''Legal History of the Lines of the Southern Railway.''
[13]Letter from Col. A. B. Andrews to J. P. A., July, 1912.
[14]These dates are from letters from Col. A. B. Andrews to J. P. A., dated July 19 and 21, 1913.
[15]148 N. C. Reports, p. 59.
[16]Letter of J. F. Hays to J. P. A., 1912.
[17]The Southern's line has been extended from Bushnel to Eagle creek, on the Little Tennessee, sixteen miles; but it is used principally for hauling lumber. The scenery is unsurpassed.

CHAPTER XXI

NOTABLE RESORTS AND IMPROVEMENTS

THE BUCK HOTEL. This ancient hostelry was built by the late James M. Smith and stood where the new Langren hotel now stands. It was the first hotel west of the Blue Ridge, but when it was built is not stated in Asheville's Centenary (1898), the best authority we have on local ancient history. He was the son of Col. Daniel Smith of New Jersey, who died May 17, 1824, aged 67. James M. was born January 7, 1794, near the present Asheville passenger depot. His mother was Mary, a daughter of William Davidson, a cousin of Gen. William Davidson, who was killed at Cowan's Ford.[1] It was Gen. Davidson's brother Samuel who was killed by the Indians at the head of Swannanoa in 1781-82. James M. Smith married Polly Patton, a daughter of Col. John Patton, who was a merchant, hotel keeper, manufacturer, farmer, tanner, large landowner, and very wealthy. The Buck hotel stood till about 1907, when it was removed.

THE EAGLE HOTEL.[2] This was built by the late James Patton, father of the late James W. Patton, and grandfather of the late Thomas W. Patton. He was born in Ireland February 13, 1756, and came to America in 1783. He was a weaver, but soon became a merchant. In 1791 he met Andrew Erwin, who married his sister and became his partner in business. In 1807 they moved to the Swannanoa at what is known as the Murphy place, where they remained till 1814, when they moved to Asheville, Mr. Patton opening a store and the Eagle Hotel—the central or wooden part. In 1831 he bought and improved the Warm Springs, and died at Asheville September 9, 1846.[3] James W. Patton was born February 13, 1803, and died in December, 1861. His life was full of good deeds. His son, Thomas W. Patton, was foremost in all good works, and in 1894 came to the rescue of Asheville in a crisis of her affairs as mayor on an independent ticket.

THE HOT SPRINGS. "The Warm Springs on the French Broad had been discovered in 1778 by Henry Reynolds and Thomas Morgan, two men kept out in advance of the settlement to watch the movements of the Indians. They followed some stolen horses to the point opposite, and leaving their own horses on the north bank, waded across the river. On the southern shore, in passing through a little branch, they were surprised to find the water warm." "The next year," says Ramsey, "the Warm Springs were resorted to by invalids." Soon after his graduation at Washington College, Tenn., young Z. B. Vance was a clerk at this hotel. [4]

Grant No. 668, dated July 11, 1788, and signed at Fairfield, by Samuel Johnston, governor, conveyed to Gaser Dagg, or Dagy, or Dager, 200 acres of land on the south side of the French Broad river in Green county, including the Warm Springs. [5] This land was then supposed to be in Green county, in what is now Tennessee. William Neilson then acquired an interest in the Springs for on April 27, 1829, Philip Hale Neilson, who appears to have inherited an undivided one-half interest to this property, conveyed it to Green K. Cessna, [6] who with Joseph L. Chunn and wife conveyed the entire property to James W. and John E. Patton, by deed dated December 6, 1831, for $20,662. [7] William Mathias appears to have kept the Hot Springs before John E. Patton took charge in 1832. He owned it till 1862, when J. H. Rumbough bought it. He has owned it since.

OLD WARM SPRINGS. [8] The old Patton hotel at Warm Springs faced the river and was on the left bank, a bridge crossing the French Broad at that point. [9] The thirteen large white pillars in front were very imposing looking, and represented the original States. The Lover's Leap rock was on the right bank of the river, and little less than half a mile above the hotel. It was a sheer precipice thirty or forty feet in height. What is now called Lover's Leap, on the left bank and a mile below, is much higher, but was not so precipitous in former days, the passage of the railroad necessitating the blasting away of the lower portion of the cliff. Old Man Peters is said to have fallen from it years before the Civil War while coon-hunting, but recovered. The Hale Neilson property was at Paint Rock, and what is still called the Old Love road leaves the river about six miles below Hot Springs and joins the present road up Paint creek twelve miles east of Greenville, Tenn. It appears to be very little traveled these days, and is probably the one Bishop Asbury first used, crossing the French Broad at what is still put down on the United States contour maps as Love's Ferry. Thaddeus Weaver lived at the mouth of Paint creek, and the old Allen House, at the mouth of Wolfe creek, is still standing. The old Neilson hotel at Warm Springs was burned between 1821 and 1840. The present hotel faces the railroad, and has its back to the river.

FLAT ROCK. From that storehouse of information, "Asheville's Centenary" (1898), we learn that in 1828 the turnpike from Saluda gap via Asheville was completed to Warm Springs, and that "brought a stream of travel through western North Carolina." Among these were visitors from Charleston, S. C., some of whom were attracted by the charming scenery and surroundings of Flat Rock. Charles B. Baring bought land and built there, his deed bearing date September 13, 1830.[10] Judge Mitchell King also bought land, his deed being dated October 28, 1829.[11] There was a small hotel there kept by Williams Brittain, in which they probably stayed till they could build homes of their own. What is now the Major Barker place was the Mollineaux home. Following is from the history of Henderson (town and county) by Mrs. Mattie S. Chandler, written expressly for this work:

The home of Judge Mitchell King (who afterward donated the land upon which Hendersonville stands) was one of the very first built at Flat Rock, and numbers of his descendants continue to come there, maintaining handsome homes of their own. This place later passed into the ownership of Col. C. G. Memminger, and is now owned by the Smythes.

Count de Choiseul, one of the most famous of these old residents, modeled his dwelling there after the magnificent old French country homes. He lived there many years, until after the death of one of his sons in the War between the States. He then returned to France that his remaining son might inherit his titles as well as his immense property there.

The old Urqhardt home, one time residence of Cora Urqhardt, now Mrs. James Potter Brown, is practically unchanged. It belongs to the Misses Norton of Louisville, Ky., who spend the summers there.

Charles Baring came to Flat Rock from Charleston in 1820, and built in 1828 what is now the summer home of George J. Baldwin (prominent business man of Savannah). There are a

number of the descendants of the Barings who have lived
for many years in this county, and they tell many interesting
stories of this family.   Charles Baring, member of the Banking
firm of Baring Bros., London, came first to Charleston to
negotiate a match between Lord Ashburton and a beautiful
English widow then in Charleston, a Mrs. Heyward, sister
of Lady Barclay.   It proved to be a case of John Alden and
Priscilla, he "asked her himself."   They were married and
early in their married life came to Flat Rock.

Mrs. Baring was brilliant, clever, well known in these early
days in Charleston as a dramatic writer, and amateur actress.
She entertained extensively and brilliantly at Flat Rock, her
birthday balls having been quite famous.   On this occasion
she is said to have invariably worn a remarkable costume
of purple velvet, with headpiece of purple plumes, and many
diamonds.   Judging from a very handsome portrait of her,
now in the possession of a Hendersonville lady of her kin,
she must have been very beautiful.   Miss Sue Farmer of
Hendersonville, daughter of Henry Tudor Farmer, and grand-
niece of this lady, has in her possession many of Mrs. Baring's belongings, among which are a quaint old jewel casket
with glass handles, with many compartments and little
secret drawers and pockets.   In the Baldwin home, in what
was Mrs. Baring's bedroom, there still remains the curious
old wall paper with its designs of the Crusaders.

She it was who built the far-famed St. John-in-the-Wilderness, the Episcopal church at Flat Rock, said to be the
oldest of its denomination in the State.   Both she and her
husband are buried under the floor of this church, and the
tablets erected to their memory are in the church.

At the age of seventy, Charles Baring was married a second
time to a young lady, Miss Constance Dent, daughter of Commodore Dent of Charleston.   He then built another home,
which was known for many years as the Rhett place, and on
which spot now stands the beautiful new Highland Lake
Club, with its numerous cottages and buildings, and which
on summer evenings presents such a brilliant scene, where
hundreds of wealthy visitors come to spend the summer.

The well-known old Farmer Hotel was built by Charles
Baring, and kept by his nephew and ward, Henry Farmer,
for many years.   It was perhaps better known as the Flat

Rock Inn and gained quite a reputation for the old Southern hospitality dispensed there. It was built in 1850, and stands practically unchanged; through having fallen into disuse in late years, it has grown rather dilapidated. After Mr. Farmer's death it was sold to a company of the Charlestonian residents and used as a country club.

Henry Tudor Farmer, father of the one named above, was born in England, and though he never lived in Flat Rock for any time he is said to have written some of his later verse there. In "The Nineteenth Century," by Wm. Gilmore Simms, state historian of Southern History, under date of 1869, a very detailed account of his works is given, extracts as follows: "He lived in New York for some time before coming to Charleston. There he made the acquaintance of all the wits about town. He was intimate with Francis, the most famous of reminiscents. He has jested at the Cafe with Halleck and Drake of the firm of the 'Croakers.' He knew Bryant and Sands Hillhouse and Percival at their beginnings, and himself published a volume of poems both in New York and London. His work is highly complimented for its skill and dainty imagery, as well as the easy-flowing rhythm."

As Seen Through Northern Eyes. In the "Carolina Mountains," we read (p. 112): "Long before the train had surmounted the barrier of Blue Ridge, the beauty and salubrity of the high mountains had called up from the eastern lowlands people of wealth and refinement to make here and there their summer homes. The first and most important of these patrician settlements was at Flat Rock, the people coming from Charleston, the center of civilization in the far South, and choosing Flat Rock because of its accessibility, and because the level nature of the country offered opportunity for the development of beautiful estates and the making of pleasure roads through the primeval forests that in those days had not been disturbed. Into this great, sweet wilderness, now quite safe from Indians, these children of fortune brought their servants and their laborers, and selecting the finest sites whence were extensive views of the not too distant mountains, surrounded by the charming growths of the region, in a land emblazoned and carpeted with flowers, built their homes of refuge from the burning heat and equally burning mosquitoes of the coastland. . . .   These people drove

in their own carriages, accompanied by a retinue of servants
and provision wagons. . . .   This procession up the mountains had fewer trappings on the horses and less gayly attired
escort than did those of the olden time; but we may be sure
that the carriages of the gentlefolk of the eighteenth century
were pleasanter conveyances than the mule-litters of the Middle
Ages, and we may also be sure that no lovelier faces looked
out from the gorgeous retinue on its way across the hills of
the past than could be seen in the carriages where sat the
ladies of the New World, with their patrician beauty and
their gracious manners.   And, although the escort of the
New World travelers did not number one thousand gayly
dressed cavaliers, it consisted of a retinue of those ebony children of the sun, who loved the pleasant journey, and loved
their gentle lords and ladies—for all this happened in those
halcyon days 'before the War' when . . .   the real
'quality' cherished their slaves and were greatly loved by
them."

DISTINGUISHED PIONEERS.   This writer continues: "The
Lodge" was built by one of the English Barings, Charles, of banking fame, on which place was a 'tumble-down stile,' like
the one near Stratford-on-Avon."   "Coming somewhat later,
as friends of Mr. Baring," were Mr. Molyneux, British consul at Savannah, and Count de Choiseuil, French consul a
the same place.   "Perhaps the most cherished name of this
mountain settlement was that of the Rev. John G. Drayton,
for many years rector of St. John-in-the-Wilderness, and to
whom the dignified and noble estate of Ravenswood at Flat
Rock owes its origin, as well as the wonderful Magnolia Gardens on the Ashley river, near Charleston—gardens where
one wanders away into a dreamland of flowers unlike any
other dreamland in the world. . . .   And always when
talking to anyone of the old residents of Flat Rock, comes
forth the name of Dr. Mitchell C. King, who, for more than
half a century, was the greatly beloved physician of the community, and who, while a student at the University of Got-
tingen, formed so warm a friendship with a fellow student,
known as Otto von Bismarck, that, for many years after, a
regular correspondence was carried on 'between them' these
letters being carefully preserved by the descendants of the
doctor."   She also mentions the Memmingers, the Rutledges

the Lowndeses, the Elliotts, the Pinckneys, the Middletons and many others.

THE MAN WHO BROUGHT US TO THE SPRINGS.[12] Colonel V. Ripley, father of Mrs. Lila Ripley Barnwell, was one of the early settlers in Hendersonville. He was of English descent, his immediate branch of the family having come to New England in 1636. Colonel Ripley was a native of Virginia, from which state he came to North Carolina when quite a young man. He was a man of wide experience and fine business ability. In 1835 the business of mail contracts, extending from Florida when the state was a territory to the upper part of South Carolina, was almost entirely in his hands. This business was continued until June, 1855.

HIS WIFE AN AUTHORESS.[12] Mr. Ripley's first wife was the daughter of James M. Smith of Buncombe, who was the first white child to be born west of the Blue Ridge in Buncombe county, he having been born on Swannanoa.[13] During the War between the States, Col. Ripley was married to Mrs. Mary A. Ewart of Columbia, S. C., a lady of great culture, refinement and strong intellectuality. In her early years, Mrs. Ripley was an author of considerable distinction, and was a regular contributor to many of the leading magazines and periodicals of her day. Perhaps her most valuable production was "Ellen Campbell, of Kings Mountain," a prize story which was contested for by many of the well known writers of the South. The description of the battle of Kings Mountain in this story is one of the most graphic ever given of that famous engagement. It increased enormously the circulation of the paper in which it was published. She was the author of "Edith Egerton," "Avalona" and several other novelettes, as also of many beautiful poems.[14] Mrs. Lila Ripley Barnwell, her daughter, has been inseparably identified with the later development of Hendersonville; she is well known in western North Carolina as a writer, and a broadly public-spirited woman, as well as a friend to all who need a friend—and this is saying much.

CASHIERS VALLEY.[15] About 1818 a man named Millsaps settled in the upper end of Cashiers Valley. Soon after that date James McKinney came to the valley and bought the lands then owned by Millsaps. A short time after, John Zachary and sons, Jefferson, Mordecai, Alfred, Jonathan, and

Alexander, came to the valley and settled in the lower end thereof. All the Zacharys seem to have been artizans. Alexander was a brick mason and also a brickmaker. He evidently burned the first bricks in the south end of Jackson county. Alfred was a hatter and made both fur and wool hats. It was customary in those days to take coon-skins or lambs-wool to his "shop" to be made up on shares. A good home-made wool or fur hat cost seventy-five cents. Mordecai Zachary was a carpenter and built a fine house for those days. The Zacharys built the first saw-mill in the valley.

Cashiers Valley is a mountain plateau of the Blue Ridge 3,400 feet in altitude, from four to five miles long, and a mile and a half wide. Attracted by its climate, freedom from dampness, its utter isolation from the populated haunts of man, the rugged character of its scenery and deer and bear infested wildwoods, years since, wealthy planters of South Carolina drifted in there with each recurring summer. Now a few homes of these people are scattered along the highland roads. One residence, the pleasant summer home of Gen. Wade Hampton, governor of South Carolina in 1876, the earliest settler from the Palmetto State, is situated, as it appears from the road, in the gap between Chimney Top and Brown mountain, through which, twenty miles away, can be seen a range of purple mountains. A grove of pines surrounds the house. Governor Hampton formerly spent the summers here, engaged, among other pastimes, in fishing for trout along the head streams of the Chatooga, which have been stocked with this fish by the Hampton family, and in hunting deer. Chief Justice A. J. Willard of Columbia, S. C., afterwards had a residence nearby.

WHITESIDE COVE.[15] The first settler in Whiteside Cove was Barak Norton. He came from South Carolina and settled in the Cove about 1820. Barak Norton and others took up State grant No. 307 on the 24th day of December, 1838. Barak Norton in his own name took up State grant No. 322 on the 27th of December of the same year. His oldest daughter, Mira Norton, took up State grant No. 320 on same date of same year. He lived to the advanced age of 99 or 100 and died at James Wright's, about three miles north of Highlands, near Short Off, in 1868 or

1870.   His wife, Mary Norton, nee Nicholson, also lived to an advanced age of nearly 100 years.   Barak Norton and his wife Mary were strong adherents to the Universalist belief and died strong in the faith.

HORSE COVE.[15]   Soon after the settlement of Whiteside Cove and Cashiers Valley, Horse Cove was settled by George and William Barnes, Mark Burrill and Evan Talley.   The Barnes families seem to have been the first to settle there. Gold was discovered about 1840.

DULA SPRINGS.   These springs were opened to the public about 1900, and are the property of the Chambers family. There are several houses which afford accommodations for from thirty to fifty people on most reasonable terms.   They are about two miles north of Weaverville, which is reached by an electric line from Asheville.

HIGHLANDS, MACON COUNTY.[15]   Early in 1875 S. T. Kelsey and C. C. Hutchinson, of Kansas, bought 800 acres of J. W. Dobson, to which land Kelsey moved his family in February, 1875.   T. Baxter White of Marblehead, Mass., followed in April.   In May Hutchinson and family came, and White became postmaster, and for two years carried the mail in his coat pocket to Horse Cove and back.   About 1877 Dr. George Kibbee came from Oregon, and, having been successful in treating yellow fever in Knoxville by using rubber beds and cold water baths, he went to New Orleans in 1879 when yellow fever was epidemic there.   He contracted the disease there and died.   Joseph Halleck of Minnesota, a brother of Gen. W. H. Halleck of the Civil War, kept the first hotel. In 1888-89 the Davis house was opened and was popular till 1909, when Miss Davis, who had kept it admirably, died. John Norton built a store in 1879, and Charles O. Smith of Indiana bought the Polly Norton farm and lived there till his death.   Captain S. P. Ravenel of Charleston, S. C., came in 1879 and built a beautiful residence on the crest of the Blue Ridge, commanding a fine view, hauling all the lumber, except that for the frame, from Walhalla, S. C.   By the aid of his family a Presbyterian church was built and dedicated by the Rev. Dr. Miller of Charlotte, N. C., in September, 1885.   It need not be said that this little community has had excellent schools from the first.   A debating society every Friday night used to keep things lively and brought the community together.   Mr. Kelsey was a practical disciple of good roads, going out and building them himself.   Highlands is a fine town.

LINVILLE CITY.   This beautiful little town was built and is owned largely by the Linville Improvement Company, which in 1890 was composed principally of S. T. Kelsey, S. P. Ravenel and Donald MacRae.   They built the Yonahlossee turnpike from this town to Blowing Rock, about twenty miles distant, at a cost of about $18,000, less than $1,000 per mile. It is the most beautiful and best constructed mountain road in the State.   But, at the time it was completed and the Linville River Railroad had reached Pinola and Montezuma, less than two miles distant, there were such serious dissensions among the directors of the company that a lawsuit resulted.   Until it had been settled it was impossible to give clear title to any of the lots which had been largely advertised for sale.   When the trouble was finally adjusted the golden moment had passed. [16]   But Blowing Rock had benefited by the construction of the turnpike.   There is a nice little inn and a fine lake filled with trout at Linville City.   It is within the shadow of the Grandfather mountain and about 4,000 feet above sea level.

BLOWING ROCK.   In 1875 William Morris lived at Blowing Rock and took a few summer boarders.   The fame of his culinary art, or that of his wife, spread and brought his place to the attention of the late Senator M. W. Ransom.   He bought and built a summer home there.   Others followed. The Green Park Hotel, the Watauga Hotel and other fine hostelries were built, and when the Yonahlossee turnpike was completed Blowing Rock was quite popular.   There is no finer scenery anywhere, the water is pure and hotels and private boarding houses numerous.   The following have fine homes at this charming place: Col. W. W. Stringfellow; Miss Esther Ransom, of Weldon; Mr. E. H. Hughes, of Charleston, S. C.; Prof. W. J. Martin, of Davidson College; Rev. C. G. Vardell, of Red Springs; Mrs. Moses H. Cone, Mr. A. W. Washburn, of Charlotte; Mr. Elliott Dangerfield, of New York; Rev. J. S. Vance, of Nashville, Tenn.; Mr. D. A. Tompkins, of Charlotte; Mr. E. H. Williamson, of Fayetteville; Judge G. W. Gage, of Chester, S. C.; Mrs. W. G. Randall, of Greensboro, N. C.; Rev. D. E.

Snapp, of Baltimore, Md.; Mr. J. Lamb Perry, of Charleston, S. C.; Mrs. W. G. Randall, and many others.

ROARING GAP HOTEL. Within the last few years Roaring Gap, on the crest of the Blue Ridge and at the head of Roaring river, has become a popular summer resort, with a large and well-arranged hotel, commanding fine views. There are also a number of nice cottages. It is nearly 3,500 feet above sea level.

THOMPSON'S BROMINE ARSENIC SPRINGS. Nine miles from Jefferson is a mineral spring, hotel and outbuildings, situated 3,000 feet above sea level, that is almost a specific for eczema, all forms of skin troubles and all kidney and bladder affections. It can be reached from Troutdale, Va., (leaving Norfolk & Western train at Marion, Va., for Troutdale) or from Wilkesboro, N. C., on Southern Railway, from which it is distant forty miles. It opens May 15. H. M. Wiley is the proprietor and the postoffice is Crumpler, Ashe county, N. C.

MOSES H. CONE. He was born at Jonesborough, Tenn., June 27, 1857, and died at Baltimore, Md., December 8, 1908. In September, 1897, he began the acquisition of the 3,500 acres of land which make up what is now Flat Top Manor. [17] He died childless and intestate; but his widow, Mrs. Bertha Lindau Cone, and his brothers, and sisters, Ceasar Cone and wife, Jeannette Cone, L. N. Cone, Julius W. Cone, Bernard M. Cone and wife of Guilford county; Frederick W. Cone, Moses D. Long and his wife, Carrie Cone Long, of Buncombe; Sydney M. Cone and wife, and C. and E. Cone of Baltimore, Md., in May, 1911, in recognition of "the deep love and lasting affection" for the people of Watauga of Moses H. Cone, conveyed to the Cone Memorial Hospital, a corporation of Guilford county, the whole of the Flat Top Manor and three smaller tracts which had been acquired by Mrs. Cone since her husband's death—the entire propety, aggregating 3,517 acres—to be called the "Moses H. Cone Memorial Park," to be used as "a park and pleasure ground for the public in perpetuity," in order "to make an everlasting memorial" to the said Moses H. Cone. A life estate in this property is, however, reserved to Mrs. Cone, and a plat of ground 400 feet square in which Moses H. Cone is buried. [18] There are scores of poor people in Watauga county who will never forget the goodness of Moses H. Cone.

THE LINDSAY PATTERSON FARMS. This gentleman, with his Revolutionary War ancestry, and his estimable wife, not content with trying to preserve the history of this section, has purchased two fine farms in Watauga, one on Meat Camp creek, five miles north of Boone, containing 350 acres, and the other, eight miles further north, containing 2,000 acres, and lying in Watauga and Ashe counties. This latter is called the Bald Mountain farm, because the mountain on which it lies is largely bare of forests. Grain, hay, potatoes, and vegetables are produced in abundance on the Meat Camp farm; while horses, mules, cattle, ponies, sheep, hogs, turkeys, geese, ducks and chickens, flourish and grow fat on the other.

ASHEVILLE SULPHUR SPRINGS. On the last day of February, 1827, Robert Henry and his slave Sam discovered this spring, five miles west of Asheville, and about the year 1830 his son-in-law, Col. Reuben Deaver, built a wooden hotel on the hill above and began taking summer boarders. Such was the patronage that an addition had to be made to the hotel every year. As many as five hundred are said to have been there at one time, and the neighborhood was ransacked for beds, bedding, chairs, and provisions. Most of the visitors came from South Carolina, among whom were the Pinckneys, Elmores, Butlers, Pickenses, Prestons, Alstons, Kerrisons, and others. Mr. John Keitt was the first person buried on Sulphur Springs hill, August 27, 1836.[19] The fact that the Pinckneys were almost constant visitors accounts for the prevalence of the given name Pink in the neighborhood of Asheville. The Alstons reserved the corner rooms on the second floor from May till frost every season. Besides the hotel, an L-shaped building, there were cabins on the grounds. There were bowling alleys, billiard tables, shuffle-boards and other games. A large ball-room and a string band, composed of free negroes from Charleston and Columbia, provided the music for dancing. One of these negroes was named Randall, who had been presented with a purse of $5,000 by the white people of South Carolina for having given information about a contemplated negro insurrection at Charleston;[20] and another of these musicians was named Lapitude, who owned a plantation near Charleston and forty slaves. He was a man of some education, and the manner of a Chesterfield.[21] From its opening till 1860 there were more summer visitors at

Deaver's Springs than in Asheville. Col. James M. Ray gives us this picture of Asheville sixty years ago: "Well, what of Asheville in these long past years? It was about like Leicester or Marshall—a very small village on the 'turnpike,' midway between the two Greenvilles. The two 'hotels', Eagle and Buck, even many years later, not doing near the business of many of the country inns or stock stands on the Warm Springs road. For anyone to stop at either of these two hotels longer than for dinner or for the night was not thought of; though a few summer visitors would sometimes make a short stop in passing through to Deaver's Springs or to Warm Springs, Wade Hampton and others with fast teams driving from Asheville to Warm Springs for dinner."[22] The old hotel was burned in December, 1862, was rebuilt by E. G. Carrier—of brick this time—in 1887, and known, first as Carrier's Springs and then as The Belmont. It was again burned in September, 1891, while under the management of Dr. Carl Von Ruck. From 1889 till 1894 an electric railway ran from Asheville to the spring, but it was abandoned.

CLOUDLAND HOTEL. In 1878 Gen. J. H. Wilder of Knoxville built a hotel on the top of the Roan mountain and opened it for guests, having previously constructed a wagon road from Roan Mountain Station on what is now the East Tennessee and Western North Carolina Railroad. Later he built a much larger hotel, which met a public want admirably, as it afforded sufferers from hay-fever immediate relief. It is built across the State line between Tennessee and North Carolina, and guests frequently sleep with one part of their bodies in one state and the rest in the other. It was very popular till a few years ago, when it was closed, but will soon be reopened.

EAGLE'S NEST, near Waynesville, has divided this patronage with the Cloudland since 1900. In the year 1900 Mr. S. C. Satterthwait of Waynesville built a hotel on top of one of the highest of the Balsams, calling the range the Junaluskas. It is five miles from Waynesville and is reached by a good wagon road. It is 5,050 feet above sea-level, and is one of the hay-fever resorts in this section, Cloudland hotel on the Roan, 6,000 feet, being the only other. Tents supplement the rooming accommodations when desired. Accommodations for about 100 guests. The magnificent Plott Balsam mountain is in full view.

BALSAM INN. Soon after the completion of the railroad to Balsam gap, seven miles west of Waynesville, Christie Brothers of Athens, Ga., opened a railroad eating house at that point, and furnished venison, wild turkey and mountain trout and the best cuisine in the State. They had only rough and small houses, and did not seek any patronage except from railroad passengers. But about 1905 a large and commodious hotel was erected there, with accommodations for many guests. Baths, acetylene lights, music and other attractions keep the hotel filled during the summer season.

OUR FIRST LANDSCAPE ARCHITECT. Our first settlers sought house sites near springs, caring little for views or being viewed. Knolls and commanding eminences were too far from water, as a rule, and required a climb up-hill to reach. In 1821 the late Dr. J. F. E. Hardy came to Asheville from Newberry District, S. C., where he had been born in 1802. His first residence was on the southwest corner of Eagle and South Main streets, at one time the finest residence in Asheville, where he resided for fifteen years after his marriage to Miss Jane Patton in 1824. In 1840 he married Miss Erwin of Morganton, and soon afterwards moved to Swannanoa Hill at the corner of Biltmore road or South Main street and the Swannanoa river. This is on a hill, and the roads and approaches, lined with white pines, cedars and other trees and shrubbery, still make this one of the prettiest places in this section. But when he first improved it, it was far in advance of anything theretofore seen in these parts. It commands a fine view. Here he lived till 1860, when he bought Belleview on the eastern side of South Main street, another commanding hill with a splendid view. The winding roadway, bordered by pines and cedars, which led from the road to the house, is still intact except at the lower end, where the former road, now street, has been dug down far below its former level, leaving the entrance to the approach road high in the air. Mrs. Bucannon now owns this property. Soon after the Civil War Dr. Hardy built the brick house on the west side of the Hendersonville road beyond Biltmore, which commanded another fine view. Here he died at the age of eighty. He was one of the most eminent physicians of his day. He was of commanding presence, with the manner of a lord. At his home was dispensed much of the hospitality for which this section was noted, distinguished strangers finding there entertainment and intelligence at least equal to that of larger places. His son, Dr. J. Geddings Hardy, succeeded to his practice, and no call ever went unanswered by him.

BILTMORE. Soon after the opening of the Battery Park Hotel Mr. George W. Vanderbilt of New York visited Asheville and was at once struck with its possibilities. He tried at first to secure Fernihurst, owned by Mrs. J. K. Connally, but failing, turned his attention to the land south of the Swannanoa and east of the French Broad. Charles McNamee, Esq., a lawyer of New York, and a kinsman, first took options and deeds in his own name; but it soon became noised about that he was buying for Mr. Vanderbilt and prices began to soar. The first deed recorded is from J. G. Martin, trustee and commissioner, to the Williams property, and is dated September, 1889, followed by many others till the 16th of June, 1890, when Henry Allen White conveyed 134 acres directly to Mr. Vanderbilt, after which there was no attempt to disguise the fact that this gentleman, "having all the world before him where to choose," had chosen Buncombe as the site of his future home. The influence of this choice on the outside world was immense. These purchases of small tracts have resulted in the accumulation of about 12,500 acres in what is called Biltmore House tract, and about 100,000 acres in Buncombe, Transylvania and Henderson counties in. what is known as Pisgah Forest. The services of Frederick Law Olmstead, the distinguished landscape architect of New York, were secured, and he planned the roads, bridges, forests, lakes, waterfalls, etc., on the Biltmore House tract. Those roads are unsurpassed by even the drives in Central Park, New York, being kept in perfect condition at all times. Biltmore house was begun in 1891 and completed in 1896. This house was modeled after Chateau Blois, France; and the Rampe Douce, or gentle slope, immediately in front of the house but beyond the lawn known as the Esplanade, is a close imitation of a like construction at Vaux le Vicomte, France. The garden to the right of the front of the house and on a lower level than the esplanade is called the "walled garden," and the stone images or sphinxes on the four gate posts at the entrances were brought from Egypt, and are the busts of women on the bodies of lions couchant. They are said to be of great age. Fine tapestries, paintings, statuary and other objects of art, with a large library of rare books, have been gathered into the house. Fountains, conservatories, dairies, vegetable gardens, model farms, and other attractions add to the beauty and charm of the place, probably the finest private residence in America. Birds and wild animals are protected on this estate, and on the lakes wild ducks are seen in winter when they cannot be found on the rivers nearby. Pisgah Forest was bought for its forests, and Hon. Gifford Pinchot was placed in charge as forester.

PISGAH FOREST. Mr. Vanderbilt was the first to see the paramount necessity for forest conservation. Pisgah Forest prospered under the expert guidance of Mr. Pinchot till he was succeeded by Mr. Schenck, who for years conducted a school of forestry. Biltmore village, at the end of South Main street of Asheville, is planned after English villages, with the ivied church, the hedges and the "simple village green." But it is not probable that any English village is as spick and span as Biltmore is every day, where streets, lawns, hedges, sidewalks, drains and shrubbery are constantly on dress parade—an object lesson in municipal government without politics.

The National Park Commission and Mr. Vanderbilt could not agree on a price for Pisgah Forest in June, 1913, but after Mr. Vanderbilt's death, March 5, 1914, his widow sold the entire tract.

"THE BEAUTIFUL SAPPHIRE COUNTRY." The completion of the railroad to Lake Toxaway in 1900 led to the following developments, and were due largely to the energy and enterprise of Mr. J. F. Hays: The Toxaway property as a whole was made up of property purchased from the receivers of the Sapphire Valley Company, and other smaller properties. The Fairfield Inn, on Lake Fairfield, was built, together with the dam for the lake, in 1896. The Franklin Hotel at Brevard, which was a part of this same operation, was built in the year of 1900. Later the Franklin was sold to a Mr. Robinson and associates, of Charlotte, N. C., and they are at present owners of that property. The Toxaway property was sold in 1911 under foreclosure, and is now held as the property of Mr. E. H. Jennings of Pittsburgh, Pa. Toxaway Inn, as well as Fairfield Inn, and The Franklin, had their greatest success in the years 1904-1907.

WAYNESVILLE WHITE SULPHUR SPRING.   This spring was
discovered by "Uncle" Jerry, a slave of the late James R.
Love, in 1845 or 1846. Col. Love soon after built a large
residence there, which he occupied till his death in 1864. It
was burned in August, 1885. Col. W. W. Stringfield, who
had married his daughter Maria, built a brick hotel on the
site of this residence after it had been burned, about 1886. [23]
It is now owned by Ben Johnston Sloan. It is less than one
mile from Waynesville.

EPP'S SPRING.   This was the property of the late Epp
Everett of Bryson City, and is about five miles from that
town on the right bank of the Tuckaseegee river, at the
mouth of Cane Brake branch. It is a chalybeate spring,
and there are one or two cabins there.

OLD VALLEY TOWN TAVERN.   This famous hostelry was
kept by the late Mrs. Margaret Walker for a number of
years after the Civil War, and was popular with lawyers and
their clients. Although there was no court house there, the
lawyers would hurry through Graham, Cherokee and Clay
county courts in order to get to spend as much time at this
hotel as possible.

THE LANGREN HOTEL.   This fine structure of reinforced
concrete was finished and thrown open July 4, 1912. It is
near the Pack Square, Asheville, and stands on the much
litigated Smith property on the corner of North Main and
College streets, where formerly stood the old Buck hotel. It
is a commercial and tourist hotel, and popular.

KENILWORTH INN.   This handsome hotel was opened about
1890. It stood on the eminence above the junction of South
Main street and the Swannanoa river road, and from it Craggy
and the Blacks were visible. It was popular until its destruction by fire at 3 a. m., April 14th, 1909, J. M. Gazzam
of Philadelphia, chief owner, escaping at the risk of his life
and the expense of great injuries from which he afterwards recovered. It was insured for $70,000.

OAKLAND HEIGHTS.   This hotel was built by the late Alexander Garrett and his son, Robert U. Garrett, in 1889. It
afterwards became a girls' school, and then a hotel, having
passed into the hands of the Presbyterian Board of Home
Missions. It then became Victoria Inn, and during 1911
was purchased by the Catholic Church and is now St. Gene-
vieve's College, a most excellent school for girls.

THE GRAND CENTRAL HOTEL. This was built by the late
S. H. Chedester. It was afterwards operated as the Hotel
Berkeley, but in 1911 was converted into a department store
by Solomon Lipinsky.

MARGO TERRACE. This home-like hotel was built by Miss
Gano in 1889. In 1904 it became the property of Pat Branch,
who in 1912 doubled its capacity and greatly improved its
outward appearance.

VANCE'S MONUMENT. This handsome granite column was
erected on the Public Square at Asheville in 1897, George W.
Pack, after whom the Square was soon named, having contributed $2,000—and the public, $1,300—for its erection to
the memory of Zebulon Baird Vance, Buncombe's most distinguished and honored citizen and great "War Governor."

GEORGE W. PACK MEMORIAL LIBRARY. This was established in 1879, and had many homes before the late George
W. Pack donated the fine building on Pack Square in 1899.

BATTERY PARK HOTEL. Having a railroad did not by
any means complete Asheville's happiness; for it had no hotel
accommodations at all commensurate with the tide of travel
which immediately set in. At this juncture came the late
Col. Frank Coxe, who built the present Battery Park Hotel.
It was opened July 12, 1886, with Col. C. H. Southwick
manager. It has remained the principal hotel of Asheville
ever since. It has been twice enlarged and frequently improved. For several years it was managed by the late E. P.
McKissick. It is a credit to this community, and has become
an indispensable asset.

THE TELEGRAPH LINE. The first telegraph line reached
Asheville July 28, 1877, with Samuel C. Weldon as operator.
Through the efforts of the late Capt. C. M. McLoud, the line
was soon afterwards extended to Hendersonville. Then
Mr. Weldon became the owner and operator thereof till the
railroad company took it off his hands.

OTHER ENTERPRISES. The Asheville Cemetery Company was
incorporated August 4, 1885; the Telephone Company, October
1, 1885; the Western North Carolina Fair, January 30, 1884; the
Gas and Light Company, May 25, 1886. In 1887 Alex. and R.
U. Garrett built the Oakland Heights Hotel. The Swannanoa
Hotel was completed in 1879 and opened for business in the
summer of 1880.

ASHEVILLE STREET RAILWAY. This most necessary common carrier was built by Dr. S. Westray Battle, James G. Martin, W. T. Penniman, and E. D. Davidson, the latter of New York, and began to run in January, 1889. It failed in 1893 and was sold out in 1894, and bid in by White Brothers of New York. It finally went into the Asheville Electric Company's properties, and is now part of the Asheville Power and Light Company.

"THE DRUMMER'S HOME." This hotel at Murphy, presided over by Mrs. Dickey for years, has made a name for itself that will endure. It was for years the most popular house west of Asheville.

WEST ASHEVILLE. In 1885 Mr. Edwin G. Carrier and family moved to Asheville from Michigan. He soon afterwards bought several hundred acres of land west of the French Broad river, including the Sulphur Springs and the J. P. Gaston tracts of land. In 1887 he built a large brick hotel on the site of the wooden structure that was burned during the Civil War, and soon thereafter, 1891, constructed an electric railway from Asheville to Sulphur Springs, crossing the French Broad river near the mouth of the Swannanoa on a fine steel bridge. This railway first ran only to the passenger station; but, on October 13, 1891, it was granted a franchise by the city to extend its line through Depot street, Bartlett street and French Broad avenue to the corner of West College and North Main streets. It stopped, however, at what is now the corner of Haywood street and Battery Park Place, then called Government street. It was called the West Asheville and Sulphur Springs Railway Company.

A race track was established just south of Strawberry Hill and between the Sulphur Springs railway and French Broad river. A grand-stand was erected and a high fence built around the race track. There were several exciting races, all of which were well attended.

SUNSET MOUNTAIN. During the summer of 1889, Capt. R. P. Foster and the late Walter B. Gwyn, Esq., completed a railway from Charlotte street to a point on Sunset mountain, known as the "Old Quarry," near which is a fine spring, and from which can be had one of the finest views in this section. This road was operated by a small steam engine, called a "dummy," and was chartered as the "Asheville & Craggy

Mountain Railway Company," its objective being the top of Craggy mountain. On November 28, 1890, the city granted this company a charter to build its track and operate its cars along Charlotte street northward to the city limits in that direction. This line was quite popular.

RICHARD S. HOWLAND. In 1904 Lewis Maddux, as receiver of the Asheville Street Railway Company, strung a trolley wire from Chestnut street along Charlotte street to what used to be known as the "Golf Club" and operated cars to that point by an arrangement with Mr. Gwyn. In 1901 Richard S. Howland, Esq., came from Providence, R. I., and bought property near the foot of Sunset mountain and erected a fine residence there. He acquired control of the Craggy Mountain Railway and completed it to the top of the mountain, where he erected a music and dance hall. He also obtained the right to operate his cars to the public square. The terminus of the railroad was called Overlook Park.

COGGINS SPRINGS. These springs are near Bull creek, and are chalybeate and sulphur water. There are no hotels or boarding places, except farm houses, near. They are about eight miles east of Asheville.

THE GROVE PARK HOTEL. This unique and costly series of grottoes, built of rough mountain rock, was completed in 1913 (July), in the E. W. Grove park, near Asheville. It is said to have cost one million dollars.

ASHEVILLE'S GRAVITY LINE. During Mayor Miller's administration Charles T. Rawls was chairman of the finance committee, and was most active and energetic. He visited Atlanta and studied the system of municipal government of that city and succeeded in getting its best features adopted by Asheville, especially the manner of keeping the books and accounts. At his instance, and largely through his influence, the city voted $200,000 of four per cent bonds for the adoption of a gravity water works system, by which the water of the North Fork of the Swannanoa river is conveyed through a sixteen-inch pipe to the city. The contract for constructing this line was awarded to M. H. Kelly in August, 1903. The city acquired about 9,500 acres of land above the intake on which there is no human habitation. Certain patriots did what they could to force the city to pay them an exorbitant price for land claimed or controlled by them, and litigation followed.

The city finally got this land at a reasonable price. The returns from this water system, after all expenses have been paid, are sufficient to pay the interest on the city's entire bonded debt of about one million dollars. Mr. Rawls was elected mayor, but his health temporarily broke down before his time expired. He got the legislature to authorize the aldermen to tax the cost of building sewers on the abutting property instead of paying for them out of the general fund.[24] The result has been the most complete and satisfactory sewer system in the South.

COL. JAMES G. MARTIN. He was a son of Gen. James G. Martin, and from 1885 to 1893, when he removed to New York City, was the leader in most of the public enterprises in Asheville and Western North Carolina. He died in 1912, aged about 59 years. He was a most useful citizen.

GEORGE WILLIS PACK, of Cleveland, Ohio, was a most generous friend to Asheville, having donated 11 acres of land for Aston Park, about four acres for a court house, a kindergarten school, a library building, and most of the money for the Vance Monument.

NOTES.

[1]Asheville's Centenary.
[2]Ibid.
[3]Ibid.
[4]J. H. Wheeler's "Reminiscenses."
[5]Buncombe County Deed Book A, p. 491.
[6]Ibid, Deed Book No. 16, p. 74.
[7]Ibid, p. 413.
[8]Statements of Captain B. F. Patton, March 25, 1913. He spent his boyhood at Old Warm Springs. Mrs. M. A. Chambers of Columbia, S. C., now in her ninetieth year, remembers visiting this hotel, Hickory Nut Falls, and Flat Rock, when a girl, about 1833.
[9]Charles Dudley Warner ("On Horsehack," p. 135), in 1884, called this hotel "a palatial hovel."
[10]Buncombe County Deed Book No. 16, p. 375.
[11]Ibid, p. 193.
[12]From Mrs. Mattie Smathers Chandler's history of Henderson county.
[13]As Ashe county was settled in 1755, according to Wheeler's History (p. 27), many white children were born in that county years before James M. Smith was born in Buncombe county.
[14]Mrs. Ripley was the mother, by a former marriage, of Hon. Hamilton Glover Ewart, member of Congress from 1887 to 1889, and appointed U. S. District Judge in 1898.
[15]Information furnished by T. Baxter White, J. Pierson and others.
[16]Information furnished by S. P. Ravenel, Esq., of Asheville.
[17]Watauga County Deed Book R, p. 131.
[18]Ibid, No. 11, p. 517.
[19]Robert Henry's diary, now in possession of his daughter-in-law, Mrs. C. C. Henry, of Acton, N. C.
[20]"South Carolina Women in the Confederacy," p. 249.
[21]Statements of Mrs. Eugenia E. Hopson, daughter of Col. Reuben Deaver, and of Mrs. Martha A. Arthur, daughter of Robert Henry.
[22]Col. James M. Ray in The Lyceum, p. 19, December, 1890.
[23]Letter of Col. W. W. Stringfield to J. P. A., January 27, 1912.
[24]In *Justice v. Asheville*, decided at the December Term (1912) of the Supreme Court, this act was sustained.

CHAPTER XXII

FLORA AND FAUNA

PRIMEVAL CONDITIONS. Exactly what the forests were like in the days of the earliest settlers and what were the kinds and habits of its wild denizens can be known only by the accounts that have come down from our ancestors. Whether the country was more open than now or whether the wild animals were tamer than we now find them, are matters that cannot be absolutely determined by any mathematical process. Some claim that the Indians kept the undergrowth thinned out by annually setting the fallen leaves afire in order that they might see the game the better, while others suppose that there were thickets and saplings beneath the giant forest trees as there are at this time. Following are some thoughts upon this question:

"It is also doubtless true that 150 or 200 years ago the forests were not nearly so well grown up as at present, and that would in a measure account for the presence of such animals as the moose or even elk. Old hunters have told me that when they could first recollect there was scarcely any laurel, with only now and then a small bunch, and that the woods were open and no underbrush at all; that they could see through the forest ever so far, and that the growth of the hemlock was nothing like it is at present. Now and then a giant monarch of the forest and all around for a considerable distance would be small hemlocks. At the writer's own home at Banners Elk, I had occasion a year or so ago to make a practical demonstration of that fact. There was evidence of one of those giant hemlocks that had fallen down perhaps a hundred years ago. It was all decayed but the knots, of which I piled up more than 125. The tree itself must have been 120 feet high when standing. All around, the hemlocks grew thick from two to two and one-half feet in diameter. That the forests have become more thicketty in the last thirty years is the observation of every thoughtful man." [1]

A MYSTERIOUS FLORAL SISTERHOOD. In the "Carolina Mountains" (ch. VI) we are told that in the Himalayas and the mountains of the Far East are found the flame-colored azalea, the silver-bell tree, the fringe bush, the wisteria, and ginseng, which are found nowhere else except in our own Appalachians. What bond, the author asks, tore these tender flowers asunder, separating them by continents and vast seas? We are also told that the Rhododendron Vaseyii, which, unlike the other rhododendrons, sheds its leaves in the fall, was supposed to have become extinct (p. 59) but that it is still found on the north side of the Grandfather mountain. We learn also that Shortia was named for Prof. Short of Kentucky, and was rediscovered on the Horse Shoe Pasture river a few miles south of Lake Toxaway, "literally coloring acres of the earth with its charming flowers" (p. 275).

BOTANY AND BOTANISTS. The abundance, variety and beauty of the wild flowers, bushes and shrubs attracted the attention of botanists at an early date. William Bertram of Philadelphia was in the Cherokee country in 1776. [2] Andrew Michaux was sent to this country by the French government to collect seeds, shrubs and trees for the royal gardens in 1785, and, on the 30th of August, 1794, reached the summit of the Grandfather, "the highest in all North America," he declared; "and with my companion and guide sang the hymn of the Marseillaise." [3] The following year Michaux explored the mountains of Burke and Yancey, carrying away in the fall 2,500 specimens of trees, shrubs and plants. In 1794 he visited the Linville, Black, Yellow, Roan, Grandfather and Table mountains. The late Col. Davenport of Yadkin Valley was his guide. His "Flora Boreali-Americana" is yet a classic. Mr. Fraser, a Scotchman, made botanical collections in these mountains in 1787 and 1789; and, under the patronage of the Russian government, he explored them again in 1799, accompanied by his eldest son, when he found the laurel or Rhododendron Catawbiense. They came again in 1807, and in 1811 the son returned, spending several years, and annually sending large consignments of plants and seed to Great Britain. F. A. Michaux, son of Andre, was here in 1802, and published his "Forest Trees of North America" in 1857. Thomas Nuttall, an Englishman, examined a portion of our mountains, and wrote "Genera of North American Plants." He died in 1859. Prof. Asa Gray of the University of Cambridge and John Carey of New York were in the mountains of Ashe and Yancey in 1841; and in 1843 Prof. Gray, with Mr. Sullivan of Ohio, came into our mountains from Virginia. S. B. Buckley came by the Hiwassee in 1842, and in the same year Mr. Rugel, a German collector, was here. In 1844 Mr. Dow, a young botanist, traversed the entire length of our mountain range. In 1840 Prof. Gray found the Lilium Canadense, but Dr. Sereno Watson discovered that it possessed traits peculiar to itself alone, "set it aside as a distinct species and honored it with its discoverer's name." In 1839 Dr. Gray observed in Paris an unnamed specimen brought there by the elder Michaux from "les hautes montagnes de Carolinie"; but on his return failed to find it till in 1877 G. M. Hymes, then a boy, accidentally discovered it on the bank of the Catawba near Marion. Dr. Gray had already named it Shortia in honor of Dr. C. W. Short. In September, 1886, Professor Sargent discovered that the Hogback mountain above Lake Toxaway is the original habitat of the Shortia, just 98 years after Michaux had first found it and probably near the same spot.

PIONEERS IN FORESTRY. Before the railroad got to Asheville, and afterwards, shrewd men went through these mountains buying standing timber and paying for it with a song, if with that. Thousands of the finest black walnut trees were branded as the property of the purchasers and left to grow on the land of the seller. Later on the finest poplars and cherries were also purchased and left to grow, while the railroads were ever drawing nearer. The walnut trees were first cut and their trunks hauled for miles to the head of the railroad. Later still the poplars and cherries followed. Then followed a demand for the stumps of the walnuts, and these also found a ready market, and brought more than the trees which had been cut from them, for by this time we had grown in knowledge and knew somewhat of the value of our timber. We had not known it before the Civil War, having used black walnut and cherry and poplar rails for the building of fences.

SCOTTISH LAND AND TIMBER COMPANY. In the eighties this company, managed by Alexander A. Arthur from Scotland, bought up ten square miles of the finest timber on Big Pigeon, between Cataloochee and Big creeks, and tried to float the logs down the Pigeon; but it was soon discovered that it did not pay at that time. Later on the Bushnells of Ohio, one of whom was afterward governor of Ohio, came and set up extensive mills at the junction of Little Tennessee and Tuckaseegee rivers, where they established booms; but the first flood swept booms and logs away. The place was called Bushnell and still retains the name. The Ritters, Whitings and others have followed.

Mills to the Timber. During this time many small
concerns were taking small steam engines to the timber and
cutting it near where it stood.   Even this did not pay in many
cases, and it became a saying that if you had a grudge against
a man, just give him a steam saw-mill and his ruin would
soon follow. The business has since thriven in some cases
and proven disastrous in others.

Wealth in Forests. It is in her forests, however, especially of late years, that this section has found its greatest
wealth. There are at least a dozen well recognized species of
oak, while most of the hardwoods and the coniferous and de-
ciduous growths common to this latitude can be found in
great abundance. Already saw mills, pulp mills, acid mills,
and other mills for the utilization of these forests have been
established and thousands of men are employed where only
a few found employment before. The railroads are taxed to
supply cars in which to haul the products of the forest to
market. With the adoption of intelligent forestry methods
promised by the United States Government, which is now
acquiring many of these forested areas, the future seems to
hold out the hope that these forests will continue to be a
source of revenue for all time to come.

Forest Fires. From the report of J. S. Holmes (State
Forester) of 1911, it appears that the forest fires in the various mountain counties in 1910 have wrought considerable
damage; table four of that report giving the facts in detail.
From the same paper can be gathered the steps that have
been taken to prevent these fires, including the State and
National legislation on the subject. In 1909 the legislature
of this State passed a law to declare any wooded land above
2,000 feet elevation a "State Forest," and the appointment
of wardens as the owner of the land may request; but advantage has not been generally taken of its provisions, because it
requires the owner to pay one-half a cent an acre additional
tax for the benefit of the school fund, while he has also to
pay the wardens for their services.

From Advance Sheet of Forest Service of the United
States, 1912. Estimated amount of standing timber in
thousand feet board measure, trees 10 inches and over in
diameter breast high, in western North Carolina, by counties :

Counties	Total Area (Acres)	Area Forested (Acres)	Per Cent of Forest Land	Average Stand Per Acre (Board Feet)	Total (Thousand Feet)
Cherokee........	288,640	228,473	76	1,635	373,690
Clay.............	118,400	99,650	84	3,804	379,027
Graham..........	193,280	173,763	90	6,255	1,086,937
Swain...........	358,400	336,850	94	4,747	1,598,927
Macon...........	339,840	288,234	85	2,980	858,795
Jackson.........	316,160	284,105	90	2,765	785,449
Haywood.........	346,240	287,592	83	4,960	1,426,498
Transylvania......	237,440	208,573	88	1,712	357,064
Henderson........	231,680	140,299	61	1,862	261,182
Buncombe........	399,360	198,807	50	1,673	332,539
Madison..........	275,840	196,763	71	2,908	572,222
Yancey...........	193,280	159,660	83	4,625	738,504
Mitchell..........	231,680	178,479	77	3,596	641,750
Watauga.........	211,200	147,901	70	4,534	670,555
Ashe.............	255,360	145,741	57	3,594	523,848
Alleghany........	142,720	53,071	77	2,030	107,728
Total........	4,139,520	3,127,961	76	3,425	10,714,715

EASTERN FOREST RESERVES. In 1900 Dr. C. P. Ambler, George S. Powell, Hon. Locke Craig and Hon. Josephus Daniels inaugurated the Appalachian National Park movement at Asheville, which culminated in March, 1910, in the passage by Congress of the Weeks act, under which $10,000,-000 were appropriated for the purchase of wild lands in the mountains at the heads of the navigable rivers of the eastern States. But as only $2,000,000 could be expended in any year, and as the act could not be put into force between March and June 30, 1910, the expiration of the fiscal year, only $8,000,000 were available. The operation of this act expires in 1915. At the expiration of 1913 the following purchases had been made :

SOUTHERN APPALACHIANS :

State	Tracts	Acres	Price	Value
Georgia	148	77,235	$6.75	$507,311.70
North Carolina........	146	108,518	7.88	855,605.25
South Carolina........	68	23,286	5.50	128,157.25
Tennessee	19	164,605	4.88	798,624.00
Virginia	77	208,134	3.31	689,245.66
West Virginia.........	25	63,786	2.67	170,296.20
Total............	483	645,564		$3,149,240.06
WHITE MOUNTAINS :				
New Hampshire.......	22	100,437	$7.01	704,112.50
Grand total......	505	746,001	$5.17	$3,853,352.56

As indicative of the rapid advance in the price of timber-
land in the mountains, the Murchison boundary in Yancey
county may be cited. It was sold at Sheriff's sale about
1879 to the Murchisons for $2,200, who held it intact as a
timber and game preserve until December, 1909, when they
sold it for $225,000 to Carr and Keys, These held it about
a year and sold it to ———— Brown for $300,000. The
late R. B. Johnston, who owned 5,000 acres on Cat Tail creek,
adjoining the Murchison tract, vainly offered it to Big Tom
Wilson for $750 in 1879 as a goat farm. In January, 1911, John-
ston's heirs sold the timber on this tract to the Carolina Spruce
Company for $110,000. In October, 1912, G. W. Vanderbilt sold
to Lewis Carr of Virginia, the timber, wood and bark, standing and down, on 69,326 acres of mountain land in Transylvania, Henderson and Buncombe counties for $12 per acre,
payable in installments in twenty years. He had bought this
land twenty years before for less than $3 per acre. (Deed
Book, Buncombe, No. 161, p. 518.)

ELK AND BUFFALO. The native fauna, alas! has largely disappeared. But when Daniel Boone and his contemporaries
first crossed the Blue Ridge they found black bear and red
deer in the greatest numbers; while, in the neighborhood of
Banner Elk have, even in recent years, been discovered the
bones of elk and caribou. Elk mountain and Bull Gap in
Buncombe county take their names from the elk. There is
reason to believe that buffalo used to pasture along the lonely
streams of this elevated plateau, while smaller game, such as
the opossum, the raccoon, mink and otter, have not entirely
disappeared to this day. The beaver, however, has long been
extinct, leaving its name to innumerable streams. (See *ante*
pp. 42, 65, 251, 252 and 253.)

DOGS FOR FOOD? In that storehouse of information con-
cerning this section of country, the Nineteenth Annual Re-
port of the Bureau of American Ethnology,[4] page 26, it ap-
pears that when DeSoto arrived at Guaxule, which the author,
James Moody, identifies as "the great Nacoochee mound, in
White county, Ga., a few miles northwest of the present
Clarksville," and near Franklin, N. C., the Cherokees "gave
the Spaniards 300 dogs for food, although, according to the
Elvas narrative, the Indians themselves did not eat them."
In a foot note it is stated that "Elvas, Biedma, and Ranjel

all make special reference to the dogs given them at this place; they seem to have been of the same small breed ('perrillos') which Ranjel says the Indians used for food." Mention is also made of the "delicious service berry of the southern mountains." [6]

FIRST BUFFALOES. From the same work, page 26, it is learned that when DeSoto was resting at Chiha, near the present Columbus, Ga., he met with "a chief who confirmed what the Spaniards had heard before concerning mines in the province of Chisca," saying that there was "a melting of copper and of another metal of about the same color, but softer, and therefore not so much used," and that DeSoto sent two soldiers on foot with the Indian guides to find Chisca, [5] which was "northward from Chiaha, somewhere in upper Georgia or the adjacent part of Alabama or Tennessee." When these soldiers returned to DeSoto they reported that they had been taken "through a country so poor in corn, so rough, and over so high mountains that it would be impossible for the army to follow"; but they had "brought back with them a dressed buffalo skin which the Indians there had given them, the first ever obtained by white men, and described in the quaint old chronicle as "an ox hide as thin as a calf's skin, and the hair like a soft wool between the coarse and fine wool of sheep." This must have been in the mountains of North Carolina.

FRUIT CULTURE. As to the adaptability of the soil and climate of the mountains to fruit culture, the State Agricultural Department has this to say in a pamphlet entitled "Orchard Lands," and dated at Raleigh, N. C., October 7, 1910 :

"The Appalachian mountain region attains in North Carolina its maximum development, for here it reaches the greatest height east of the Rockies. This gives it a cool climate, like that of the northern states and Canada. In addition to its altitude, it has, on account of its southern latitude, a longer growing season and a more abundant and brighter sunlight. This makes it ideal for the commercial production of hardy fruits. The apples grown in this region are of very high color and of fine quality. The rainfall is heavy in summer, giving a rapid growth and making fruit of large size. The fall weather is dry, cool, and bright, thus giving the most favorable conditions for fruit harvesting and marketing. The soils of the mountains are rich and fertile and produce a good growth both of tree and fruit. Healthy old trees are growing in many parts which have been bearing heavily for upwards of a century.

In the deep, rich, alluvial soil of mountain coves the famous Albemarle Pippin finds the soil that brings it to its greatest perfection. On the mountainsides, in many places, are found the thermal zones that are so rarely visited by frost that total failures of fruit are practically unknown. It is destined to be the most noted apple-growing section in the whole country. Apples from the mountain country have twice carried off the first prize at the Madison Square Garden in New York City in competition with the whole United States. Peaches attain a color and quality there which they do not reach in the lower country. They grow as handsome as the California peaches, and as to quality the California product is hardly to be named in comparison with them."

LIVE STOCK. Of the raising of live stock, the same excellent authority, in a pamphlet entitled "North Carolina : A Land of Opportunity In Fruit Growing, Farming and Trucking," has this to say, in a chapter called "Climates" (p. 36):

"It is a region of fertile valleys and elevated plateaus, with a climate very similar to that of the northern middle states. The summers are cool and pleasant and the whole region is an attractive one to the summer visitor and is becoming a great summer resort. The winters are cold, but shorter than those of the middle states north. In most mountain regions the mountainsides are rocky and sterile, but in the mountains of North Carolina, as a rule, the mountain slopes are covered with fertile soil and in some parts of the mountain country the treeless 'balds' have their slopes to their lofty tops covered with fertile soil and rich grasses, on which great herds of cattle are grazed in summer. The valleys in the southern section of the mountain country are less elevated and the climate is mild and pleasant, while the snowfall is very light. The clear streams of water that flow everywhere and the natural growth of fine grasses mark this region for cattle and the dairy, while on the uplands fruit of all kinds flourishes as it seldom does elsewhere."

GRAINS RICH IN PROTEIDS. Agriculturally the soil of this section is hospitable to the growth of all the fruits, vegetables and cereals of the temperate zone.[7] Some of the lands are too high and cold for maize or Indian corn, but rye and buckwheat can be grown there in great abundance. The soil is generally too thin to produce a large yield of corn or wheat to the acre, but the corn grown, being small and hard and maturing quickly, is richer in the proteids and all nutritive qualities than the larger and softer kernels which grow in such abundance from the black soil of the prairie states in the corn belt proper. It more than makes up in quality what it lacks in abundance. Corn grown on Tuskeegee creek in Swain county, in 1893, by John M. Sawyer, took the prize at the Columbian Exposition for being richer in the proteids

than any other corn grown in the United States.   Col. W. L.
Bryan of Boone was awarded a diploma and bronze medal by
the same exposition for buckwheat grown in Watauga county
in 1893.

THE HOME OF THE APPLE.   But, while most fruits and
melons thrive in this soil, it is the apple which does best and
brings most credit and notoriety to this section.   Apples
from this country took the prize at the Philadelphia Centennial in 1876 over all apples grown in America, while prizes
have been awarded to this fruit at the Chicago and St. Louis
fairs. [8]   It is a crop that rarely fails.   There is a black soil
in different localities of this section peculiarly adapted to the
growth of apples, but they do well in any soil and require
very little attention.   The United States Geological Survey
publishes maps showing the different variety of soils in the
mountain region of North Carolina.

GRASSES AND STOCK.   In the counties of Ashe, Alleghany,
and Watauga grasses flourish so abundantly that little corn
is planted, as it pays better to raise stock on the rich grass
and hay and to buy such corn as is needed for work stock
and human consumption than to plough up the grass and
raise this cereal.   In all the mountain region in these counties
the land is not so steep but that it can be broken up and planted
in grass, the result being that, with the exception of a fringe
of trees upon the crest of the ridges, almost the entire country
is given up to grass.   Very little timber is left hereabout.   On
all the mountains, after the timber has been removed and
the surface ground exposed to sunlight, grasses grow abundantly.

STOCK "RANGING."   In other counties, where grass does
not thrive so well, owing to the shade of the thick timber,
and where the land is too steep to plough, cattle, mules,
horses and hogs are "ranged" in the mountains from May
until November and are then driven in, fat and sleek.

BEAR, DEER AND TURKEY.   While, as has been said, most
of the big game has been killed, there are still a few black
bear left in the more remote and inaccessible mountains, in
the pursuit of which much sport can be had.   There are
also a few red deer scattered here and there, and a few tame
herds maintained in private parks.   Gray squirrels, pheas-
ants, quail, wild turkey, the red and gray fox and an occasional
wolf can still be found in the more remote sections.

Mountain and Rainbow Trout. The introduction of
the California or Rainbow trout into the clear and cold mountain creeks and rivers, and black bass in the larger streams,
has proven a great success; and, while the mountain or speckled
trout proper are being consumed by their rainbow brothers,
the latter still afford great sport for the anglers who visit
these mountains every spring and summer in increasing
numbers. But for the reprehensible and unlawful practice
of dynamiting the bass streams by irresponsible people, this
gamest of all game fish would soon multiply so rapidly as to afford
sport for all who might care to take them. There are no
finer streams anywhere for bass than the Cheowah, Tennessee, Tuckaseegee, lower Nantahala, upper French Broad,
Hiwassee, Nollechucky or Toe, Watauga and New rivers.

Where and When it was too Cold to Raise Corn.
From Col. W. L. Bryan's "Primitive History of the Mountain Region," we learn that when Ashe and Watauga were
first settled "the seasons would not mature corn and the
pioneer settlers had to get their corn from the valley of the
Yadkin river, carrying the same on their backs, for few had
horses at that time.   .   .   .   There being no roads save the
trails which had been made by the Indians and the great
pioneer, Boone, those who had horses would place two and
a half bushels of corn in a strong homespun and woven tow
sack, throw it on their horse's back and fasten it by the use
of a surcingle, turn the horse in the path and walk behind."

Pea Vine. From the same authority we learn that "in
the earlier days of our country there was a growth called
pea-vine, which was a very rich food for stock, and had an
almost limitless range throughout the entire almost boundless forest."

Some Famous Hunters of the Olden Day. "Near
the headwaters of the Watauga is the Linville gap separating
the Grandfather from Hanging Rock mountain and the waters
of the Main fork of Watauga from the head prong of the Linville river. Near this gap used to live James Aldrich, a noted
hunter, when bear, deer, elk, wolves and panther abounded.
Harrison Aldrich, James' son, also lived there, and was a great
hunter, having killed over one hundred bear." An encounter
between Aldrich and a bear in a cave, while George Dugger,
"another pioneer hunter and one of the very best of men,"

waited on the outside, is related by Col. Bryan; and another in which Aldrich shot a sleeping bear in a cave, striking him in the burr of the ear and killing "him so dead he never waked up." Of like courage and skill was Big Tom Wilson of Yancey, and Welborn Waters of Whitetop. Near the branch where James Winkler now lives, near Boone, and when Jordan Councill, Jr., was living there, a dog treed an unknown animal. Thinking it was a coon Jordan Councill went up the tree and followed the unknown "varmint" out on a limb. When it dragged its tail in Mr. Councill's face he knew it was a panther. He hastened down, got a torch, "shined" the eyes of the great cat and shot it.

FIRE-HUNTING. According to Col. Bryan, this sport was conducted by hunters during a certain season when the stones in creeks and rivers are covered with a peculiar moss of which deer and elk are very fond. The hunter would take a canoe or other small boat, place a torch in the front end and himself remain in the stern. The boat was poled or paddled by another. The boat would be silently floated up to deer standing belly-deep in the water and plunging their muzzles into the river to get the moss upon the rocks. Blinded by the light the deer would stand still till their eyes reflecting the light of the torch afforded a perfect target. Then the leaden missile would speed upon its fatal way. Cows also like this moss, and sometimes hunters would kill their own stock.

RAVENS. The ravens which fed Elijah the Tishbite by the brook Cherith (1 Kings, xvii, 6) did not thereby secure veneration for their descendants of our mountains after their settlement by the whites; for, when spring opened, they came down from the cliffs and crags and preyed upon the young pigs and lambs of the settlers, first plucking out their eyes and then clipping off their ears and finally killing and eating them. At the report of a gun in the remote mountains seventy-five years ago all the ravens within hearing flocked to the hunter, in the hope of preying upon whatever he might have killed or wounded. Fresh raw meat was, when hidden in tree-tops, kept from their beaks only by the wad of tow which had been used to clean the foul barrels of the guns.

WOLVES. On the 6th of June, 1794, Gideon Lewis entered 68 acres "under the Three Tops mountain," at what is now Creston. (Deed Book A, Ashe coutny, p. 38.) Gideon and

his family were great hunters; but his sons, Gideon and
Nathan, were for years the great wolf hunters of Ashe county.
They would follow the gaunt female to her den, and while one
waited outside, the other brother crawled in and secured the
pups, from six to ten in each litter, but allowing the mother to
escape.   The young were then skalped, the skalp of a young
wolf being paid for the same as that of the mature animal.
For each skalp the county paid $2.50.   When asked why he
never killed grown wolves, Gideon Lewis answered: "Would
you expect a man to kill his milch-cow?"   Wolves had greatly
increased during the Civil War, and soon after its close the
late Thomas Sutherland of Ashe county, with other cattle
herders, hired the late Welborn Waters to kill all the wolves
from the White Top to the Roan mountain.   He would con-
ceal himself in the wildest parts of the mountains and howl in
imitation of a wolf.   When the wolves which had heard him
came, he shot them from his place of concealment.   This soon
exterminated the breed along the Tennessee line.

GINSENG. David Miller, Col. Bryan's grandfather, dug
"a root of ginseng that weighed one pound, avoirdupois, and
would frequently dig two bushels and a half of this root in a
day.   The price then was only ten cents per pound."

This is usually called "sang" by our people.   Its value,
use and how to prepare it for the market of China were first
taught us by Andre Michaux on his first visit to the Blue
Ridge in August, 1794.[9]   It is called Gentian by some.[10]

COLONEL BYRD'S RHAPSODY.   In his "Writings" Col. Byrd
of Westover (pp. 211-212) thus sings the praises of this indig-
enous herb : When near the Dan river on his famous survey of the dividing line between Virginia and North Carolina, he chewed a root of ginseng, which "kept up my spirits,
and made me trip away as nimbly in my half Jack-Boots as
younger men could in their shoes.   This plant is now in high
esteem in China where it sells for its Weight in Silver.   (The
capitals are all Col Byrd's).   Indeed it does not grow there,
but in the Mountains of Tartary, to which place the Emperor
of China Sends 10,000 Men every Year on purpose to gather
it.   .   .   .   Indeed, it is a vegetable of so many vertues
(sic), that Providence has planted it very thin in every Country that has the hapiness to Produce it.   .   .   .   This noble
Plant grows likewise at the Cape of Good Hope, where it is

called Kanna, and is in wonderful Esteem among the Hottentots. It grows also on the northern Continent of America, near the Mountains, but as sparingly as Truth and Public Spirit. . . . Its vertues are, that it gives an uncommon warmth to the Blood, and frisks the spirits, beyond any other Cordial. It cheers the heart even of a Man that has a bad Wife, and makes him look down with great Composure on the crosses of the world. It promotes insensible Perspiration, dissolves all Phlegmatic and Viscous Humors that are apt to obstruct the Narrow Channels of the Nerves. It helps the Memory and would quicken even Helvetian [Shades of Julius Cæsar!] dullness. 'Tis friendly to the Lungs, much more than Scolding itself. It comforts the Stomach, and Strengthens the Bowels, preventing all Colicks and Fluxes. In one word, it will make a man live a great while, and very well while he does live. And what is more, it will make Old Age amiable, by rendering it lively, cheerful and good-humored.''

The Associated Press dispatches on August 6, 1913, said that 150,000 pounds of ginseng was shipped to China from the United States for the past year, valued at $1,500,000—or ten dollars a pound, whereas it used to be sold for 12½ cents in the mountains. Also that 155,000 pounds of the same herb had been exported the year before, valued at $7 per pound. It was also stated that before the wild forest supply diminished largely it brought only 40 cents per pound; and that its cultivation began in 1898.

FINE FOR DOGS BUT FINER FOR SHEEP IF— In a country so ideally situated for sheep-raising as these mountains, it is difficult to explain why that industry has not been more successful than it has been, unless the destructiveness of dogs is the reason. These faithful canine friends were indispensable to the pioneer, but their possession is now no longer necessary, and the farmers are getting rid of all that are not required for dairy purposes. This eliminates many hounds and worthless mongrels and substitutes for them the intelligent Scotch collie and shepherd. All efforts to tax useless dogs out of existence have thus far failed to eliminate the superfluity of our canine friends.

WILD PIGEONS. These birds used to come in flocks which literally darkened the heavens. At night their roosts were visited by men and boys bearing torches who wantonly killed thousands of these light-blinded birds. They come no longer. Pigeon river in Haywood county and Pigeon Roost creek in Mitchell have been named for these migrants.

THERMAL BELTS. In the pamphlet of the N. C. Agricultural Department, called "North Carolina : A Land of Opportunity in Fruit Growing, Farming and Trucking" (Raleigh), is a most admirable article on thermal belts written by the late Silas McDowell, of Macon county, in 1858, for the U. S. Patent Office Report, from observations made near Franklin; and in the same paper are excerpts from a report made by the late Professor John LeConte on the thermal belts or "frostless zones of the flanks of the mountain spurs adjacent to the valleys of the Blue Ridge." His observations were made at Flat Rock, Henderson county, fifty miles east of Franklin. "These facts point out this region as the best place to be found for the cultivation of celery, cauliflower, tomatoes and other vegetables for canning; raspberries and strawberries, for shipment and preserving; for peaches, pears, fine apples, cherries, quinces and currants; also for the finer table and wine grapes."

MILK SICK. In former years, before the country had been cleared of its forests, far more than at the present time, though the malady still exists in certain localities, there was prevalent a disease popularly known as "milk sick," socalled because it was supposed to be caused by the drinking of the milk of cows which had been pastured on "milk sick" land. The cows themselves do not at first disclose the fact that they were suffering any ill effects from having pastured there, as, if they did, it would be easy for people to avoid the disease by refraining from the use of milk of such cattle. On the contrary, such cows seem to be normal. This sickness is usually fatal to the victim unless properly treated. There were, and still are, for that matter, men and women peculiarly skilled and successful in the treatment of this obscure disease, who were called "milk sick" doctors. Sometimes they were not doctors or physicians at all, and did not pretend to practice medicine generally, seeming to know how to treat nothing except "milk sick." Whiskey or brandy with honey is the usual remedy; but in the doses and proportionate parts of each ingredient and when to administer it consisted the skill of the physician. When the "patch" of land supposed to contain milk sick had been located it was fenced off and all cattle kept from grazing there.

SYMPTOMS. In his "Medicine in Buncombe County Down to 1885 : Historical and Biographical Sketches," 1906, Dr. Galliard S. Tennent, M. D., says :

"The symptoms, those of severe gastro-enteritis with some variations, were said to follow the ingestion of milk or butter from an infected cow. The origin was variously ascribed to some plant or fungus growth, or to some mineral poison occurring in certain spots."

DISEASE CANNOT BE ACCOUNTED FOR. Here is what the United States Department of Agriculture says on the subject :[11]

"In reply I beg to advise you that many efforts have been made to elucidate the question regarding the nature and cause of milk sickness, but although many theories have been discussed none of them have so far been generally accepted. Some investigators hold that the disease is of micro-organismal origin, some that it is due to an autointoxication, while others think it is caused by vegetable or mineral poisons. All seem, however, to agree that the disease is limited to low swampy uncultivated land, and that the area of the places where it occurs is often restricted to one of a few acres. Furthermore, that when such land or pastures have been cultivated and drained the disease disappears completely.

"The discovery of a new focus of this disease in the Pecos Valley of New Mexico in November, 1907, gave Jordan and Harris the opportunity of studying this peculiar affection by modern bacteriological methods. As a result they have succeeded in isolating in pure cultures from the blood and organs of animals dead of this disease a spore-forming bacillus which they name *Bacillus lactimorbi*. With this bacillus they have reproduced in experiment animals the symptoms and lesions peculiar to milk sickness or trembles, and from these animals the same organism has been recovered in purity. It therefore appears to have been demonstrated that the bacillus in question is the actual cause of the disease. As Jordan and Harris have already indicated, more comprehensive studies, based on a larger supply of material, are desirable in order that the many obscure and mystifying features connected with the etiology of this rapidly disappearing disease may be elucidated.

"The proper means of preventing losses from this disease is by excluding access to such pastures where the disease is known to occur. This has been done with good results in many places by the use of barb wire fences.

"The affected animals should be kept as quiet as possible and a dose of one pound of Epsom salts dissolved in water administered as a drench. If the symptoms become alarming a competent veterinarian should be employed."

HONEY DEW OR PLANT LICE. There is a sugary formation often observable on the leaves of certain trees and saplings—usually of chestnut, oak and hickory—which looks like a coating of honey which has dried upon the upper surface of such leaves. It has a sweetish taste, which has given it the name of honey-dew. Many persons really believe it is a sweet dew which settles on the upper surface of the leaves; but when the question as to the cause of this deposit was asked, the United States Department of Agriculture thus explained it :[1][2]

"The honey-dew, in question, is secreted by plant lice, scale insects, or leaf-hoppers, and more especially by plant lice, which appear early in the season and become frequently very numerous and gradually disappear as the summer advances. The honey-dew is exuded by them from the anal end of the body and accumulates on the leaves below them."

NOTES.

[1]T. L. Lowe's "History of Watauga County."

[2]The facts stated herein are from "Southern Wild Flowers," by Alice Loundesberry, and P. M. Hale's "Woods and Timbers of North Carolina."

[3]Michaux's journal and facts about his life are set out in Dugger's book, pp. 251-259, and were taken from a memoir prepared by Mr. Charles S. Sargent for the American Philosophical Society of Philadelphia.

[4]J. W. Powell, director, 1897-'98.

[5]Ibid., p. 27.

[6]These berries grow wild, and it is surprising that no effort has been made to cultivate them.

[7]See "North Carolina, A Land of Opportunity in Fruit Growing, Farming and Trucking," issued by the Department of Agriculture, Raleigh, N. C.

[8]See Bulletin of "North Carolina Fruit Land for Sale," issued by Department of Agriculture, Raleigh, 1910.

[9]Balsam Groves, 248.

[10]McClure, 233.

[11]Letter of A. D. Melvin to Hon. J. C. Pritchard, February 7, 1912. Nancy Hanks, Abraham Lincoln's mother, died of milk-sick.

[12]L. O. Howard to Hon. J. C. Pritchard, February 9, 1912.

CHAPTER XXIII

PHYSICAL PECULIARITIES

AN IMPOSSIBLE TASK. To give a full and detailed account or description of all the peculiar physical features of this Land of the Sky would be impossible in the allotted space. Doubtless there are many that are unknown to the writer. The facts given, however, may be relied on as an under—rather than as an over—statement.

WAS IT EVER "LAKE TAHKEEOSTEE?" "Whether or not the valley of the French Broad near Asheville was ever, as has been supposed, the head of a mountain lake, whose lower or deepest part was above Mountain Island and Hot Springs, is an unsettled question for the geologists. [1] Certain it is that the French Broad has cut its way through the mountains at Mountain Island, as is apparent to the most casual observer of the mountains at that place, not only in the obvious signs that still remain to indicate the exact spot where it cut through, but also in the unquestionable beds of that river in the days gone by now on the tops of the mountain ridges which lie along its western banks, probably 200 feet higher than its present bed, and only a short distance above the Mountain Island. These old beds cross the channel of the present stream below the Palisades at Stackhouse's and above the Mountain Island. They contain many stones worn smooth and rounded by the abrasions to which their position in the river subjected them." This is also true of the stones on Battery Park hill. Dr. Sondley suggests that this may have been the famous lake mentioned by Lederer in his account of exploration into North Carolina in 1669-70, as it "fits the description and lies near the place," describing his visit to the Sara Indians who were subject to "a neighbor king residing upon the bank of a great lake called the Ushery, environed on all sides with mountains and Wisacky marsh." The water of this lake was a little brackish, due to mineral waters flowing into it, and was about ten leagues broad. He cites Hawk's History of North Carolina, p. 49.

MINOR ODDITIES. On the waters of Meat Camp, Watauga, is a field formerly belonging to David Miller who represented

Ashe in the House of Commons in 1810, 1811 and 1813, still known as the "Sinking Spring Field," because its water sinks shortly after appearing on the surface of the ground. In this field was also the largest white oak of which people still speak, said to have been 32½ feet in circumference and from 50 to 60 feet to the first limbs. There are several immense springs which gush out of the earth in what is still known as The Meadows, mentioned in the will of Robert Henry as having belonged to him at the time of his death, but which is now owned by the heirs of Dr. Hitchcock of Murphy. On a ridge on the bank of Little Santeetla, near where John Denton used to live, is the largest single spring in the mountains, the stream from it being almost a creek. On the same ridge at the point known as Howard's Knob, near Boone, and probably half a mile to the northeast, is a place about ten feet in diameter on which it is said no snow was ever known to lie, and a piece of the ore taken from it melted into lead. There is also still some talk of a Swift and Munday mine, now long lost, but supposed to be somewhere in Ashe. What metal it was supposed to contain is not now known.

CHEOAH AND NANTAHALA RIVERS ORIGINALLY ONE. In the description of the Nantahala quadrangle (1907) the United States Geological survey says of the Nantahala and Cheoah rivers:

"Nantahala river has by far the greatest descent, falling from 4,100 feet on the Blue Ridge to a little less than 1,600 feet at the point where it joins the Little Tennessee, an average grade of about 65 feet per mile, the greater part of it coming in the upper 25 miles. A similarly rapid fall characterizes the lower portion of Cheoah river. Originally the Nantahala flowed in a direct course down the Cheoah valley. It was diverted about midway in its course by a branch of Little Tennessee river, working back along the soluble Murphy marble. Its old elevation of 2,800 feet is marked by pebble deposits on summits one and one-half miles nearly west and three miles nearly southeast of Nantahala. On the upper reaches of both these streams small plateaus and terraces, rarely over a mile in width, accompany the watercourses. Below Aquone, on the Nantahala, and Buffalo creek, on the Cheoah, the channels of the rivers descend in narrow and rapidly deepening canyons. Similar plateaus, from two to four miles wide, border the upper parts of the Little Tennessee and Tuckaseegee. The river channels have cut their way 200 to 500 feet below the surface of these plateaus. Not far beyond the junction of these two rivers the valley is hemmed in by steep mountains and becomes a narrow and rocky gorge. The descent of 4,000 feet from Hangover to the mouth of Cheoah river is accomplished in a trifle over four miles."

W. N. C.—34

THE BALDS. There are no balds on the Blue Ridge; but from Whitetop at the Virginia line to the Stratton and Hooper balds in Graham county, the Great Smoky mountain summits, abound in bald spots. They are usually above the 5,000-foot mark, and contain no trees whatever. Instead, they are carpeted with rich wild grass, and tradition says that before white men turned their cattle on them to graze, this grass was "saddle-high." Some of the transverse ranges have these balds also, notably the Nantahalas and the Balsams. There must be a thousand acres of almost level and perfectly bald lands on the Roan and Yellow mountains, and a large acreage on the Tusquittee and Nantahala. From Thunderhead in Swain to the Little Tennessee river there is a succession of bald summits, and the Andrews bald just north of Clingman's Dome covers a considerable area. There are invariably small springs flowing from the edges of these bald spots, where cattle slake their thirst in midsummer. From a distance these green patches seem to be yellow, hence the name of the Yellow mountain just north of the Roan. Surrounding these balds are usually forests of balsam trees in primeval state. The Blacks and Clingman's Dome are covered with them, also the Balsam mountains, in Haywood county. The soil is black and deep.

STRATTON AND HOOPER BALDS. At the head of Santeetla and Buffalo creeks in Graham county, near its junction with Cherokee, are the Hooper and Stratton Balds, named for first settlers by those names. Near them are the Haw Knob and Laurel Top; and to the north Hangover, Hayo and Fodder Stack mountains. Just below the Hangover is the residence of Dave Orr, one of the pioneers of that section and still a famous bear hunter. In 1897 a bear caught his bell-wether, and the next day Dave belled a cowardly young hound and left him to gnaw upon the carcass of the dead sheep, and waited. Soon the pup came running, with bruin at his heels. Dave had a "mess of bar meat for dinner that day."

TUSQUITTEE BALDS. The view from the balds of Tusquittee is unsurpassed in the mountains. There are several bald prominences on this mountain, one of which is known as the Medlock Bald and another the Pot Rock Bald, from a depression in the rock almost the exact size and depth of an ordinary pot. It is at least two miles along the top of this mountain, which forms an elbow in its course.

To the north of this range and scarcely three miles distant
is the parallel range, known as Valley River mountains, and
they are separated by Fires creek. They come together at
a point called Nigger Head. This is at the head of Tunah
and Chogah creeks, and there is a high, narrow ridge running
from it to the Weatherman Bald, across which deer and bear
used to have to pass when driven by the hunters from the
head of Chogah creek or Fires creek. It was along this sharp
ridge, scarcely wide enough for a narrow footpath, that
"Standers" used to be placed in order to get a shot at the
fleeing game. The late Alex. P. Munday of Aquone used to
be a famous bear hunter, and his old dog, "Nig," and his
gray stallion, "Buck," knew better where to go than he did
himself in order to get the best stand for a shot. It is near
here that one finds the Juckers and Weatherman "roughs,"
or rocky places, grown up in vines, laurel and spruce pines.
"Roughs" is sufficiently descriptive of them. On the Valley
River mountains the principal peaks are Beal's Knob, White
Oak Knob, the Big Stamp Knob and the Peachtree Knob.

MITCHELL'S PEAK. This highest point east of the Rocky
mountains is about thirty miles from Asheville. The road
used to go via what is now Black Mountain Station and the
old Patton house, near what is the intake of the city water
works and Gombroon, up the North Fork of the Swannanoa
river almost to the Estatoe gap, where it took to the left, and
passing the Half Way house, built by the late William Patton of Charleston, S. C., zig-zagged up to the top. There is
now a road via Montreat and Graybeard. Another trail
is from Pensacola, in Yancey, in trying to follow which, Prof.
Mitchell lost his life, and another from South Toe river. It
is also possible to go along the ridge from Celo at the head
of Cattail. In 1905 Mr. R. S. Howland constructed a road
from what is now the E. W. Grove park to the top of Sunset mountain, thence to Locust gap, thence to Craven's gap,
and thence to within half a mile of Bull gap, the grade being
about one per cent from Overlook Park, and costing over
$50,000. Later on Dr. C. P. Ambler constructed a road from
this terminus to his house on a slope of Craggy, and known
as Rattlesnake Lodge. From there on, in 1911, a riding way
was built via Craggy to Mitchell's Peak; but it was never
finished. This is the road that will be converted into "The

Crest of the Blue Ridge" highway, and will pass Mitchell's
Peak and go on via Altamont to Linville gap, over the Yonahlossie road to Blowing Rock. Work was done on this road
near Altamont in the Summer of 1912. The view from
Mitchell's Peak is somewhat obstructed by the balsam growth
surrounding it, and as clouds hover over it almost constantly,
disappointment often attends a visit to this lofty point. In
1877 there was a hut made of balsam logs and covered with
boughs, that afforded shelter to visitors, in addition to that
under the shelving ledge of rock, beneath which hundreds of
visitors have shivered and lain awake for hours. About 1885
the U. S. Weather Bureau established a station there, when
more comfortable quarters were constructed for the observers.
They had to "pack" their supplies up late in the fall, and
were practically isolated till spring. That house, however,
like the first spoken of, was afterwards burned by vandals.
Other vandals, later on have shot holes through the monument to Prof. Mitchell, and one fiend sank his axe-blade clean
through one of its sides. There is a good spring near the
peak. In 1912 a lumber company erected another shelter on
top, and quarters can be secured for a night's lodging under
certain conditions. Mr. William Patton of Charleston built
the first trail to the top in 1857-58.

THE GRANDFATHER. From Linville city in Avery county,
from Banner Elk, and from Blowing Rock good trails run
to the top of the highest of the five peaks of the Grandfather.
Pinola and Montezuma on the Linville river railroad are the
nearest railroad points. The view is splendid—unsurpassed,
in fact. Near the top is a spring which is said to be the coldest in the mountains, being 45° in all seasons. Alexander
McRae's and the Grandfather Inn are the nearest stopping
places. McRea was born in Glenelg, Inverness county, Scotland,
and came over to America in 1885, and has furnished music on
the bagpipes to visitors to the Grandfather ever since. [2]

THE ROAN MOUNTAIN. This can be reached from Roan
Mountain station on the East Tennessee and Western North
Carolina Railroad or from Bakersville, three miles from
Toecane on the Cincinnati, Clinchfield and Ohio Railroad.
It is much patronized by hay-fever patients. There is a
fine hotel there. The view is better than any other. It is
over 6,000 feet above the sea.

NANTAHALA BALDS. The Wayah, Wine Spring, Rocky, Jarrett's and Little balds are the principal peaks. They can be reached from Franklin or from Aquone, both in Macon county. The view is splendid.

THUNDERHEAD. Just above what is still known as the Anderson Road, an abandoned wagon road from Tennessee to the Spence cabin in Swain, stands Thunderhead, one of the lofty peaks of the Great Smokies. From it Miss Mary N. Murfree saw the picture her pen painted in one of her stories of this region :

A PEN PICTURE. "On a certain steep and savage slope of the Great Smoky Mountains the primeval wilderness for many miles is unbroken save one meagre clearing. The presence of humanity upon the earth is further attested only by a log cabin, high on the rugged slant. At night, the stars seem hardly more aloof than the valley below. By day, the mountains assert their solemn vicinage, an austere company. The clouds that silently commune with the great peaks, the sinister and scathing deeds of the lightnings, the passionate rhetoric of the thunders, the triumphant pageantry of the sunset tides, and the wistful yearnings of the dawn aspiring to the day—these might seem only incidents of this lonely and exalted life. So august is this mountain scheme that it fills all the world with its massive multitudinous presence: still stretching out into the dim blue distances an infinite perspective of peak and range and lateral spur, till one may hardly believe that the fancy does not juggle with the fact."[3]

HELLS. There are many tangles and thicketty places in the coves of these mountains, and others where the laurel and ivy and small spruce pines so cover the banks of the streams as to render locomotion along them impossible. Axes are necessary to hew a way in many places, and woe to that man who ventures too far into their depths by crawling or creeping between their rigid branches. At the head of Tellico creek in Tennessee and in the Rainbow country of North Carolina, where the State line is now in dispute, is what is called Jeffries Hell. It is said that many years ago a man named Jeffries got bewildered in that place and spent nine days there without food before he managed to effect his escape. There are other hells in the mountains, but Jeffries' is the largest and most famous.

THE CHIMNEYS. At the head of one of the Pigeons, and just west of Collins gap, visible from the Ocona Lufty road, are three sharp, pyramidal shaped pinnacles called the Chimneys. They are covered with small spruce pines and rocks, but how any soil manages to cling to such steep mountain sides is a mystery. They are green in winter because of the spruce pines covering them, and present a striking contrast to other peaks around them.

GRAPHIC PEN PICTURES. In "The Heart of the Alleghanies" we have glowing descriptions of the view from Clingman's Dome, the culminating point of the Great Smoky range, and which Gen. Clingman measured in 1857; of the Great Balsam Divide, the Plott Balsams, and of the mysterious Juda-Culla Old Field, just south of the Old Bald gap between Richland creek and Caney Fork river; which always "presents a weird and unnatural appearance. . . . Its only growth presents a peculiar yellowish look, and the fact that no tree or sapling has ever grown within its limits has not been accounted for scientifically." Here, the legend says, the giant Tsulkalu made a clearing for his farm. Here flint arrow-heads and broken pottery have been found, showing "almost conclusively that some of the Cherokees themselves . . . occupied it as an abiding place for years." This book also tells of the "fire-scalds," and of the Devil's Court House in the Balsams, which, however, is not his Supreme court house, the latter being on Whiteside mountain. Gen. Clingman, in his "Speeches and Writings," describes Shining Rock in the Balsams most strikingly; and says of the Devil's Old Field on the Balsams that it was the Devil's chosen resting place. He also accounts for the balds by saying the Indians supposed they were made by the devil's footsteps as he walked over the tops of the mountains. A fine description of the Tuckaseegee falls above Webster is given in the "Heart of the Alleghanies."

OTHER NOTED ROCKS. Buzzards' Rocks and the Dogs' Ears, near Shull's Mills, Watauga county; Black Rock, above Horse Cove; Satula (pronounced Stooly), near Highlands; Samson's Chimney, near Howard's Knob at Boone; Hawk's Bill and Table Rock, between Morganton and Linville mountain; Riddle's and Howard's Knobs, near Boone; Nigger Head, near Jefferson, and scores of others are objects of local

interest in various localities.   Hanging Rock, above Banner
Elk, and the North Pinnacle, on the Beech mountain, in the
same locality, are noted rocks, from the last of which a fine
view can be had after an easy climb from a good road.

TRACK ROCKS. "Some distance further to the west (from
Juda-Culla Old Field) on the north bank of Caney Fork, about
one mile above Moses' creek and perhaps ten miles above
Webster, is the Juda-Culla Rock, a large soap-stone slab covered with rude carvings, which, according to .   .   .   tradition, are scratches made by the giant in jumping from his
farm on the mountain to the creek below." [4]   Tracks of elk,
wolves, etc., are said to be visible in a rock at the head of
Devil's creek in Mitchell county.

"THE ROCKS." What are locally known as "The Rocks"
are two immense masses of stone standing detached in a pasture field on the road from Plumtree to Bakersville.   They
are a landmark.   Bynum's Bluff is also noted.

SMALL NATURAL BRIDGE. Just over the ridge from the
Caney Fork of the Tuckaseegee river, in what is called Canada, and where it has been suspected that one or more blockade stills have existed in time past, present and (will) to come,
is Tennessee creek.   It flows under a small natural rock bridge
when it is normal, and over it when it is "full."

THE TRIANGLE TREE. Almost one mile above Fairfax
post office on the Little Tennessee river, in Swain county,
stood, until a great freshet came and washed it away eight
or ten years ago, one of the most unusual and remarkable
freaks in the shape of tree growth in America.   But so isolated
had it become by reason of the practical abandonment of late
years of the wagon road from Bushnel to Rocky Point that
few strangers ever saw it, while to the few natives of that
region, who had seen it for years and years, it called for no
marked attention.

It was a large spruce pine at least three feet in diameter
five feet above the ground where a limb or branch of a
diameter of at least eighteen inches left the main trunk at an
angle of about forty-five degrees and extended out toward
the river, while three feet above its point of departure from the
main trunk a second limb or branch, twelve inches in diameter,
shot out in the same direction as the first, but at an angle of
seventy-five or eighty degrees and joined itself to the first limb

six or seven feet from its base so perfectly that it grew into and had become a part thereof, thus forming with the main trunk a perfect triangle of living wood. It was easy to climb into this triangle and by sitting astride the first or lower limb to hold the body erect against the trunk of the tree immediately under the second limb. It is a pity it was never photographed, but the dimensions given above are accurate, since they were carefully measured and noted while the tree was still standing in all its glory.

THE HIGH ROCKS. Just below the mouth of Eagle creek are what are locally called the "High Rocks." They are a tumbled mass of solid rocks, some of them larger than a two-roomed house, resting one upon the other above the riverside and extending almost to the top of the mountain. They are apparently now just where they found themselves when eons and eons ago some cataclysm of nature tumbled these mountains about as though they had been pebbles and grains of sand.

THE CHIMNEYS. On the road from Montezuma to Banner Elk and just before reaching the Sugar Gap, are two other large masses of rock projecting out of the side of the mountain like two enormous and discolored incisor teeth. One of them is said to be eighty feet in height and the other and further one from the road, nearly as high. There is no photograph of these immense rock heaps, but fortunately there is no danger of their destruction by a freshet or other cause. They are called "The Chimneys."

THE DEVIL'S CAP. Eight miles from Altamont and about three from the Cold Spring hotel in Burke county, on Ginger Cake mountain, and just east of Linville river, below Linville Falls, is what is called the Devil's Cap. It is a perpendicular mass of rock sixty or seventy feet high and about twenty feet in diameter, surmounted by a large flat stone so placed on its pedestal as to look as if it must surely soon slide off and fall to the ground. It is in a little swag or gap in this ridge, and is best seen from the top of a precipice near by, from which can also be had, through a rift in the dense foliage, a magnificent view of the wild and romantic Linville Gorge, the wildest and most inaccessible in the mountains, with the possible exception of that of the Nantahala, between the "Apple Tree" place and Jarrett's Station on the Murphy branch of the Western North

Carolina Railroad. This freak of nature, the Devil's Cap, however, has been photographed.

DUTCH CREEK FALLS. Within half a mile of Valle Crucis school, Watauga, are the Dutch creek falls, which are about eighty feet in height. The little stream spreads itself evenly over the surface of the precipice down which it slides rather than falls, forming a fine picture as seen from the gloomy gorge below. It is more easy of access than falls generally are, and is well worth a visit.

LINVILLE FALLS are at Linville, a postoffice and village in what is now Avery county. The falls had in 1876 two distinct falls, each about 35 feet in height, the upper falls pouring into a small basin and then plunging over another precipice into the black pool below. But, of late years, the lower ledge of rock has given way from some cause, and much of the water passes under and around the boulders into which it has been broken, instead of falling smoothly over a straight line of rock, as formerly. It is the most accessible of all falls now.

ELK FALLS. Three miles from Cranberry are the Falls of Elk, and they are about as high as the Dutch creek falls, but carrying more water in the descent. The cascades or rapids of the same creek a few miles above, at Banner's Elk, are also worth a visit.

WATAUGA FALLS are a few hundred feet west of the North Carolina and Tennessee line. They are hardly falls, but rapids, pouring an immense volume of water through a narrow gorge, and requiring several hundred feet at that place to gain comparative smoothness. The scenery around the falls is wild and imposing, the rocks left bare by the current being immense. It is only about a quarter of a mile from the Butler-Valle Crucis turnpike.

THE "DRY" FALLS. The Dry, or Pitcher falls, of the Cullasaga river, four miles from Highlands, are so called because the stream leaps from the precipice above and leaves a clear dry space beneath, behind and under which one can pass to the further side dry-shod. It is about seventy-five feet in height and the water pours over the rock ledge from which it leaps much as does a stream poured from the mouth of a pitcher.

HICKORY-NUT FALLS. The Hickory Nut Falls are just east of the Hickory Nut gap of the Blue Ridge. This appears to be a mere ribbon of water hung from the top of the precipice, but in reality it is a creek of such size as to have power to turn a grist mill before leaping to the gorge nine hundred feet below.

CHIMNEY ROCK. Between this loftiest waterfall in the Appalachians and the Hickory Nut gap road is the Chimney Rock, an enormous rock mass on the eastern slope of the Blue Ridge, eighty or ninety feet in height. The large trees growing around it reveal by contrast its immense size and height. Though, till within the last twenty years, no man had ever scaled its height to let the plummet down, a ladder-like stairway now reaches its summit and a wooden railing extends all the way around it.

THE POOLS. The Pools, just above the old Logan hotel or tavern in the same picturesque locality, are three circular holes from eight to fifteen feet in diameter, in the rock bed of the creek, all of which are said to be bottomless. It is evident that they were made by the revolution of small stones on the softer surface of the creek bed, kept in constant motion by the continual flow of the creek; but they are not bottomless, nor is there any danger of suction, as swimmers disport themselves in their cool depths every summer.

ESMERALDA'S CABIN. Just across the road is the detached rock mass locally known as Esmeralda's cabin, because of the delightful romance located in that region by the gifted Mrs. Frances Hodgson Burnett, called "Esmeralda," and which was popular twenty-five years ago. Indeed, the novel was dramatized and successfully played at that time in New York and all over the country.

SHAKING BALD. Here, too, is Esmeralda Inn, long kept by Col. Thomas Turner, a veteran of the Federal Army, and now by his son, while not far away is Bat Cave, a gloomy cavern in the face of the mountain above one prong of the Broad river; and Shaking Bald, a mountain top which, in the seventies, caused considerable newspaper comment because of the noises said to have been heard in that locality. Earthquake shocks and volcanoes even were predicted for several years, but nothing ever came of the stories. This locality, one of the most charming and picturesque in the mountains, is adequately described in Christian Reid's "Land of the Sky," the novel which gave its name to this entire region. It was

published in 1875 [5] and was one of the means of drawing public attention to the beautiful scenery of the mountain region
of North Carolina and its unsurpassed summer climate. The
Hickory Nut region is in what is called the Thermal Belt.

HOT SPRINGS. Paint Rock and Hot Springs, on the French
Broad river, about forty miles northwest from Asheville, are
two other remarkable places in this mountain region worthy
of mention, which the same gifted author described with her
facile pen in the same charming story. Hot Springs was discovered in 1887 by some soldiers from the Watauga settlement when in pursuit of a band of Cherokee Indians, and has
been a noted health resort ever since. Although its waters
are strongly impregnated with mineral and have medicinal
properties, they are as clear as crystal. They are very bene-
ficial for gouty and rheumatic troubles. There is a large and
well appointed hotel which is very popular every season of
the year.

PAINT ROCK. "The Painted Rock" of old Cherokee days,
or "Paint Rock" of our times, is a rock cliff over a hundred
feet in height which has a red stain on its outer surface
caused by the oxidation of the iron in its composition. Whatever figures of men or animals ever existed upon
its face have long since disappeared. There is the usual romantic story of one or two lovers throwing himself or herself,
or themselves, from the top of this rock and from the top of
another rock nearly as high in the neighborhood of Hot
Springs, called Lover's Leap, but there is no tangible evidence that any local lovers ever were so foolish.

THE SMOKING MOUNTAIN. Twenty years ago there were a
series of newspaper stories of a smoking mountain above Bee
Tree creek in Buncombe county, and many citizens visited
the locality in question only to be disappointed, while none
save those living constantly in the neighborhood ever saw the
smoke, and by the time others were called from a distance
it had disappeared. What it was, if anything more than
autumn haze or imagination, was never established. It,
however, "had nothing to do with anything regarding volcanic action." [6]

THE WALKS. A short distance below Flat Shoals of
Watauga river, and near the Tennessee line, are a series of im-
movable natural stepping stones, regularly placed across the

bed of the river, and over which one may walk dry-shod even when the stream is considerably swolen.   Hence the name— The Walks.

"Thus Far."   Almost from the Virginia line to the Little Tennessee river there is a fringe of balsam or white spruce crowning the crest of the western escarpment known as the Smoky mountains, except where the dense blue fringe of trees is broken by the "balds."   But, remarkable as it may seem, there is not a single tree or sapling of the balsam growth south of the Little Tennessee, although the Gregory Bald, only a few miles to the northeast, is fringed by a dense growth of balsams which extend to both the Big and Little Parson balds.   The soil and climate and, indeed, the altitude of the range south of the Little Tennessee, are almost identical with those to the north, but neither bird nor breeze has ever carried the balsam seed across the river and imbedded it in the soil beyond in a manner that has resulted in its growth across the dead line of that rapid stream.

Hell's Half-Acre. [7]   "The bear-hunters are the only men familiar with these head-waters of the Richland creek.   At the foot of the steep, funereal wall lies one spot known as Hell's Half-Acre.   Did you ever notice, in places along the bank of a wide woodland river, after a spring flood, the great piles of huge drift-logs, sometimes covering an entire field, and heaped as high as a house?   Hell's Half-Acre is like one of these fields.   It is wind and time, however, which bring the trees, loosened from their hold on the dizzy heights and craggy slopes, thundering down into this pit.

"The Chimbleys and Shinies." [7]   The "Chimbleys and Shinies," as called by the mountaineers, form another feature of the region of the Gulfs.   The former are walls of rock, either bare or overgrown with wild vines and ivy.   They take their name from their resemblance to chimneys as the fogs curl up their faces and away from their tops.   The Shinies are sloping ledges of rock, bare like the Chimneys, or covered with great thick plaits of shrubs, like the poisonous hemlock, the rhododendron, and kalmia.   Water usually trickles over their faces.   In winter it freezes, making surfaces that, seen from a distance, dazzle the eye.

"Herrycanes."   The effects of a hurricane in the Balsam mountains are described thus in "The Heart of the Alleghanies":

"For two miles, along this sharp ridge, nearly every other tree had been whirled by the storm from its footing. They not only covered the path with their trunks bristling with straight branches; but, instead of being cut off short, the wind had torn them up by the roots, lifting thereby all the soil from the black rocks, and leaving great holes for us to descend into, cross and then ascend. It was a continuous crawl and climb for this distance."

Violent windstorms are rare in these mountains, owing to the fact that they are broken up as they approach from the lowlands east, west and south; but there are two other places called "herrycanes," one being on a branch at the head of Tusquittee creek in Clay county, and the other on Indian creek just above its junction with Ugly creek, thus forming Cataloochee creek in Haywood county. The Clay hurricane occurred soon after the Civil War or during it, and the Haywood hurricane about 1896. The fallen timber in Clay is still visible, while a whole mountain side in front of Jesse Palmer's residence is covered with the rent fragments of giant trees which have been uprooted or twisted from their trunks bodily.

LOOKING-GLASS FALLS. These are in Transylvania county and are on G. W. Vanderbilt's "Pisgah Forest tract." In the sale of his timber in 1812, he reserved twenty acres around these falls. [8]

NOTES.

[1]From "Asheville's Centenary."
[2]Balsam Groves, 231-232.
[3]From "The Despot of Broomsedge Cove," by Miss Mary N. Murfree.
[4]Nineteenth Eth. Rep., p. 407.
[5]D. Appleton & Co., publishers, but now out of print.
[6]Joseph Hyde Pratt, State Geologist, to J. P. A., April 5, 1912.
[7]Zeigler and Grosscup, p. 64.
[8]Buncombe Deed Book, No. 161, p. 518.

CHAPTER XXIV

MINERALOGY AND GEOLOGY

"The State publications tell us, with well founded pride, that North Carolina was the first government in America to order a geological survey. Can she, on that account, afford to be the last state to publish a full exposition of her geological structure and mineral resources?"—"Heart of the Alleghanies," page 198.

WHERE TO GET THE FACTS AND FIGURES. North Carolina no longer deserves this reproach, as Bulletin No. 18 of the North Carolina Geological and Economic Survey, published in 1909, is a bibliography of North Carolina geology, mineralogy and geography, with a list of maps. It contains, with an admirable index, 428 pages, and is devoted exclusively to an alphabetical arrangement of the names of authors, their writings on geology and mineralogy, mining and other matters connected with minerals, etc., of this region. It was prepared by Dr. Francis Baker Laney, Ph.D., assistant curator of geology of the U. S. National Museum, and Katharine Hill Wood. It is thorough and exhaustive.

In addition thereto Professor Joseph Hyde Pratt, State Geologist, and Professor Joseph Volney Lewis, formerly of the Survey, but now of Rutgers College, N. J., are the authors of Volume I of the Reports of the North Carolina Geological Survey, which contains a description of the corundum and the periodite deposits of Western North Carolina. It also was published in 1905, and contains maps, drawings, pictures and designs illustrative of the subjects treated. It contains, with the index, 464 pages, and either or both of the above volumes will be sent on application, if accompanied with the postage.

There are also several others of great value, among which are Economic Paper No. 22, on forest fires and their prevention; Economic Paper No. 3, on talc and pyrophyllite deposits in North Carolina; Economic Paper No. 1, on the maple sugar industry; Economic Paper No. 20, on the wood using industries of North Carolina; Economic Paper No. 23, on the mining industry in North Carolina during 1908, 1909 and 1910, and No. 15 on mineral waters.

AVAILABLE SCIENTIFIC AND POPULAR DESCRIPTIONS. A scientific explanation of the formation of the Asheville quadrangle will be found in the Asheville Folio, No. 116, U. S. Geological Survey; and an interesting dissertation on the geological formation and age of the Grandfather mountain is contained in "The Heart of the Alleghanies"; and in the same volume is a reference to Mr. King, the artist, who made a journey through these mountains in 1874, and gave a description of their mineral possibilities in *Scribner's* for that year. September 15, 1864, Prof. Charles Upham Shepard of Yale gave his views as to what minerals and metals might be discovered here, among which are gold and diamonds, and he is quoted in Gen. Clingman's "Speeches and Writings."

GEOLOGICAL HISTORY OF WESTERN NORTH CAROLINA

BY JOSEPH HYDE PRATT

The State of North Carolina is divided into three physiographic divisions, which have been designated as the Coastal Plain, the Piedmont Plateau, and Mountain Region. That part of the State lying to the west of the Blue Ridge is in the Mountain region. This includes the Blue Ridge and the Great Smokies and the country between, which is cut across by numerous cross ranges separated by narrow valleys and deep gorges. The average elevation of this region is about 2,700 feet above the sea level, but the summits of a great many ridges and peaks are over 5,000 feet, while a considerable number of peaks have a height of over 6,000, the highest of which is Mount Mitchell with an elevation of 6,711 feet. Over the larger part of this region are to be found the older crystalline rocks, gneisses, granites, schists, and diarite that are of pre-Cambrian age, which are greatly folded and turned on their edges. On the western and eastern borders of this mountain region, approximately along the line of the Blue Ridge and Great Smokies, there are two narrow belts of younger sedimentary rocks, consisting of limestone, shales, and conglomerates, and their metamorphosed equivalents, marbles, quartzites, and slates of Cambrian age.

The sedimentary rocks have been formed from sand, gravel, and mud which have been deposited as the result of alteration and erosion of the older rocks.

By the present position of the rocks we are able to obtain records regarding the order in which the rocks of western North Carolina were formed, and thus obtain a geological history of the Mountain section. All the rocks of western North Carolina are amongst the oldest geologic formations, although there is considerable variation in the time at which the various rocks encountered were formed. The oldest rock formation is known as the Carolina gneiss, which consists of large areas of mica, and garnet schists; and mica, garnet and cyanite gneisses. The exact origin of this rock has not been definitely determined : it may have resulted from the metamorphism of a granite rock. Mount Mitchell and the other mountain peaks of the Black mountains are of Carolina gneiss, as are also Gray Beard, the Craggies, Sunset Mountain, Pisgah, Great Hogback (Toxaway), and Standing Indian (Clay county).

The next oldest rock formation of Western North Carolina is known as the Roan gneiss, which is not as extensive as the Carolina gneiss, but forms much smaller areas and, as a rule, forms long narrow bands cutting the Carolina gneiss. They are also much less altered and are undoubtedly younger. Roan, High Knob, Big Yellow Mountain, Cocks Knob, the eastern slope of Craggy Dome and Bull Head Mountain, Nofat mountain, and part of Cæsar's Head, are all of Roan gneiss. These mountains are, therefore, younger formations than those mountains composed of Carolina gneiss.

Another granite formation has been intruded into the Carolina and Roan gneisses, forming rather small areas in the northwestern portions of the mountains. These granites, known as the Cranberry and Beech granites, are observed in the vicinity of Blowing Rock, Beech mountain, Rich mountains, and part of Pumpkin Patch mountain. A similar granite, known as the Henderson granite and of approximately the same age, is found over a considerable area of southeastern portions of Transylvania and Henderson counties and southwestern portions of Buncombe county.

All these rocks referred to above are of deep-seated origin and the lapse of time between the formation of the different ones was undoubtedly very great. They formed mountain ranges that were much higher than now observed, but these have been subject to erosion which has brought them to their present outline.

The next formation was the lava rocks, which were poured forth upon the surface of the Archean rocks. These lava flows are of considerably later period than the granites and gneisses and are older than the overlying Cambrian sedimentary rocks, and they may belong to the Algonkian age. Some of these rocks were undoubtedly of volcanic nature, the intrusions coming to the surface as flows of lava and spreading out over the Carolina and Roan gneisses and the Cranberry and Beech granites. There was a very long interval between the formation of the last of the Archean rocks before the volcanic activity; and during this period these old Plutonic rocks were subject to very excessive erosion. This volcanic activity probably extended into the Cambrian time, and many of the lava flows were probably at the surface when the Cambrian strata were laid down. The indication of this is the finding of sheets of basalt conglomerate interstratified with the lower strata of the Cambrian. Rocks of this period include metadiabase, found just north of Linville and to the east in Grandmother gap and crossing the Yonahlossee road at several places; blue and green epidotic schists, which have probably been altered from basalt, such as are to be seen in the vicinity of Pinola and Montezuma, Avery county, and Hanging Rock, Caldwell county; a gray and black schist probably formed by the alteration of an andicitic rock, which is to be observed on Flat Top mountain and Pine Ridge, Watauga county; and metarhyolite, such as is found on the slopes of Dugger mountain, Sampson mountain and in Cook's gap, Watauga county.

These Archean rocks, with the volcanic formations, were then subjected to a long period of erosion, and the sea at the same time encroached upon large areas of the dry land. The sediments deposited formed the rocks which are known as the Cambrian. Portions of the Archean rocks were submerged and at times uplifted, and there was not a continuous series of these sedimentary deposits.

These sedimentary rocks, formed from the erosion of the Archean and Algonkian rocks and from salicious and calcareous material deposited from animal life found in the sea, consist of conglomerates, sandstones, shale, limestone, and their metamorphic equivalents, quartzite, slate, and marble. These are observed very extensively over considerable areas of western North Carolina, but principally, as stated above, near the western and eastern sections of the mountain region. Grandfather mountain is composed of one of these conglomerates of the Cambrian age, as is also Grandmother mountain, a large part of the area around Linville, and just to the east of Pinola. A narrow strip of these rocks is to be found extending across the extreme western part of Buncombe county, across Henderson and Transylvania counties. Brevard is situated in an area of these rocks, as is also Boylston, Mills River, and Fletcher, Henderson county. Practically all of Cherokee and Graham counties is composed of Cambrian rocks and the western parts of Clay, Macon, and Haywood counties. Swain county is composed largely of these Cambrian rocks, with the exception of an area of Archean rocks that is exposed around Bryson and for some distance to the northeast. West of Asheville these Cambrian rocks are observed in the vicinity of Stackhouse, Hot Springs, and Paint Rock. They include all the limestones, such as are being mined at Fletchers, Mills River, and other places in Henderson and Transylvania counties; the limestones of Madison county; and the marbles of Cherokee, Graham, and Swain counties.

From the above it will be seen that the larger part of the area of western North Carolina is composed of the Archean rocks, representing the oldest geologic formations.

Associated with the rocks described above are various minerals of economic importance, the history of which may be of interest in connection with the geologic history of western North Carolina. The precious metals occur very sparingly in nearly all the counties of this section of the state, but in only a very few places has any attempt been made to systematically produce them, and this has been largely by placer mining. Both the rocks of the Archean and Cambrian ages apparently contain minute quantities of gold, but in none of these have deposits been found of sufficient richness to be profitably mined. In the early history of western North Carolina it was customary for many of the inhabitants to pan the various streams for gold and to pay their taxes in native gold. Just how much gold has been taken from western North Carolina in this way is not known; but it evidently was several hundred thousand dollars.

Iron was discovered in western North Carolina almost as soon as the country began to be settled, and the manufacture of iron dates back before the Revolutionary War. These early iron works consisted of the primitive Catalan forge blown by the water trompe. Such forges were in operation in Ashe, Mitchell, and Cherokee counties, and as late as 1893 one of these, the Pasley forge on Helton creek in Ashe county, was in operation. These early forges supplied iron for all local uses and the forges in Cherokee county shipped a good deal into Tennessee. The most celebrated iron mine of western North Carolina is the Cranberry, and this iron was worked in Catalan forges as early as 1820. The following forges made iron from the Cranberry ore:[1]

"Cranberry Bloomery Forge, on Cranberry creek; built in 1820; rebuilt in 1856; two fires and one hammer; made 17 tons of bars in 1857.

"Toe river Bloomery Forge, situated five miles south of Cranberry forge; built in 1843; two fires and one hammer; made about four tons of bars in 1856.

"Johnson's Bloomery Forge, six miles east of south from Cranberry; built in 1841; had two fires and one hammer; made one and one-half tons of bars in 1856."

This ore made an excellent quality of iron and soon became known and attracted a great deal of attention throughout the United States. Since 1882 the mine has been worked almost continuously, and the ore was treated in a modern blast furnace

Similar grades of iron ore are found in Ashe county, and the following is a summary of the history of the Catalan forges that were operated on these Ashe county magnetic ores:

"The Pasley forge was built by John Ballou at the mouth of Helton creek in 1859; in 1871 it was rebuilt by the present owner, W. J. Pasley, and is now sadly in need of repairs.

"Helton Bloomery Forge, on Helton creek, 12 miles N. N. W. of Jefferson; built in 1829; two fires and one hammer; made in 1856 about 15 tons of bars. Washed away in 1858. Another forge was built one and one-fourth miles lower down the creek in 1902, but did not stand long.

"Harbard's Bloomery Forge was situated near the mouth of Helton creek; built in 1807 and washed away in 1817.

"Ballou's Bloomery Forge was situated 12 miles N. E. of Jefferson, at the falls of North Fork of New river; built in 1817; washed away in 1832 by an ice freshet.

"North Fork Bloomery Forge was situated on North Fork of New river, 8 miles N. W. of Jefferson; built in 1825; abandoned in 1829; washed away in 1840.

"Laurel Bloomery Forge, on Laurel creek, 15 miles west of Jefferson; built in 1847; abandoned in 1853. [1]

"New River Forge, on South Fork of New river, one-half mile above its junction with North Fork; built in 1871; washed away in 1878."

The brown hematite ores of Cherokee county which occur in the Cambrian rocks were worked in forges as early as 1840, supplying the surrounding country with bar iron. We have record of the following forges:

"Lovinggood Bloomery Forge, situated on Hanging Dog creek, two miles above Fain forge; built from 1845 to 1853; two fires and one hammer; made in 1856 about 13 tons of bars.

"Lower Hanging Dog Bloomery Forge, on Hanging Dog Creek, five miles northwest from Murphy; built in 1840; two fires and one hammer; made in 1856 about four tons of bars. [1]

"Killian Bloomery Forge, situated one-half mile below the Lower Hanging Dog Forge; built in 1843; abandoned in 1849.

"Fain Bloomery Forge, on Owl creek, two miles below the Lovinggood forge; built in 1854; two fires and one hammer; made in 1856 about 24 tons of bars.

"Persimmon Creek Bloomery Forge, situated on Persimmon creek, 12 miles southwest from Murphy; built in 1848; two fires and one hammer; made in 1855 about 45 tons of bars.

"Shoal Creek Bloomery Forge, situated on Shoal creek, five miles west of the Persimmon Creek Forge; built about 1854; one fire and one hammer; made in 1854 about one-half ton of bars."

With the exception of the blast furnace at Cranberry which uses the magnetic iron ore from the Cranberry mine, no other furnace has been erected in western North Carolina for the treatment of iron ores; and when the Pasley forge on Helton creek went out of commission, there was no other point in western North Carolina, except Cranberry, where iron was being made. A small amount of ore has been shipped from time to time from various localities.

Copper mining at one time was a prominent industry of western North Carolina; and while I have no definite data as to when copper mines were first operated in western North Carolina, we do know that copper properties were worked before the Civil War, principally in Ashe and Alleghany counties. The most noted mine was the Ore Knob, which is in the southeast corner of Ashe county near the top of the Blue Ridge and about two miles from New river. This mine was first opened sometime before the War, but it was not until some years after the war that it was developed to any great extent. The ore deposit was worked to a depth of 400 feet by means of numerous shafts and drifts. The mine was equipped with a smelter for producing a high grade of copper. The amount of copper produced and shipped from January 1879 to April 1880, which was the time the mine was fully operated, was something over 1,640 tons. The cost to produce and market this copper was ten and thirty-nine one-hundredth cents a pound. The mine has not been worked since about 1882. Other copper properties that were worked were the Copper Knob or Gap Creek mine in the southeast part of Ashe county; the Peach Bottom mine on Elk creek, Alleghany county; the Cullowhee mine on Cullowhee mountain, and Savannah mine on Savannah creek, Jackson county.

Another mineral for which western North Carolina is noted is corundum. In 1870, Mr. Hiram Crisp found the first corundum that attracted attention to the present mining region of North Carolina, at what is now the Corundum Hill mine. A specimen was sent to Prof. Kerr, then state geologist, for identification, and considerable interest was aroused when it was discovered that it was corundum. In the same year Mr. J. H. Adams found corundum in a similar occurrence at Pelham, Massachusetts.

In 1870-71 much activity was displayed in the search for corundum in the periodite regions of the southwestern counties of North Carolina, and new localities were soon brought to light in Macon, Jackson, Buncombe, and Yancey counties. About this time Mr. Crisp and Dr. C. D. Smith began active work on the Corundum Hill property, and obtained about a thousand pounds of corundum, part of which was sold to collectors for cabinet specimens. Some of the masses that were found weighed as much as 40 pounds.

Systematic mining for corundum did not begin until the fall of 1871, when the Corundum Hill property was purchased by Col. Chas. W. Jenks, of St. Louis, Missouri, and Mr. E. B. Ward, of Detroit, Michigan, and work was soon begun under the superintendence of Col. Jenks. This was the first systematic mining of common corundum, as distinguished from emery and the gem varieties, ever undertaken, while the first mining of the emery variety of corundum in America was at Chester, Massachusetts. The Corundum Hill mine produced corundum almost continuously from 1872 to 1901. Other mines that have produced corundum are the Buck

Creek mine in Clay county; the Ellijay mine in Macon county; the Carter mine in Madison county; and the Higden mine and Behr mine in Clay county.

Mica mining in North Carolina began about 1870, and for the first five years practically all the mica mined was handled by Heap and Clapp, and was obtained from the mines of Mitchell and Yancey counties. Mica has continued to be mined almost constantly since that time not only in Yancy and Mitchell counties, but in Ashe, Buncombe, Haywood, Jackson, and Macon counties. There are a great many old workings on these mica deposits, and before they had been investigated and the mica discovered they were supposed to be old workings of the Spaniards who were hunting for silver. It is now supposed that these old workings were made by the Indians for these sheets of mica; and it is known that mica has been found in Indian mounds and was used by the Indians who inhabited what is now Ohio in the manufacture of their beads. North Carolina mica is still known as standard mica, as it was reckoned from the beginning.

Several other minerals should be mentioned in connection with the descriptions given above, as they were first identified in North Carolina. The mineral that stands out most strikingly is the rhodolite, a gem mineral which was discovered in Macon county about 1894 and was given its name from the resemblance of its color to that of certain rhododendrons.

MITCHELLITE, a variety of chromite, was discovered near Webster, Jackson county, in 1892, and was named in honor of the late Prof. Elisha Mitchell of North Carolina.

WELLSITE, one of the minerals of the zeolite group, was discovered in 1892 at the Buck Creek mine, Clay county, and was named in honor of Prof. H. L. Wells of Yale University.

The following, belonging to the vermiculite group of minerals, have been found associated with corundum, and were described by Doctor Genth; they were all discovered about the same time in 1872 or 1873 : Culsageeite, a variety of Jefferisite, found at the Corundum Hill mine and named for a postoffice near that place; Kerrite, found at Corundum Hill mine, and named in honor of Mr. W. C. Kerr, former State Geologist of North Carolina; Maconite, found at the Corundum Hill mine and named after Macon county; Lucasite, found at the Corundum Hill mine and named after Dr. H. S.

Lucas, who owned the Corundum Hill mine; Willcoxite, found at the Buck creek (Cullakeene) mine, Clay county, and named after Joseph Willcox of Philadelphia; Aurelite, found at the Freeman mine, Green river, Henderson county, about 1888— it is a thorium mineral, and was named for Dr. Carl Auer von Welsbach; Hatchettolite, a tantalium-uranium, was found at the Wiseman Mica mine, Mitchell county, about 1877, and was named after the English chemist, Charles Hatchett; phosphuranylite, a uranium mineral, found at the Flat Rock mine,. Mitchell county, about 1879, and named from the chemical composition of the mineral; and Rogersite, a niobium mineral, found at the Wiseman Mica mine, Mitchell county, about 1877, named after Prof. W. B. Rogers."

NOTES.

[1]From "The Iron Manufacturer's Guide," 1859, by J. P. Lesley.
NOTE : The United States Geological Survey has ready for distribution, upon the receipt of 25 cents each, the following geologic folios each of which contains descriptive text, topographic map, areal geology map, economic geology map, structure section sheet and columnar section sheet.   All information as to the geology and mineralogy of the quadrangles treated can be found in these folios:
Cranberry Folio, No. 90, issued 1903.
Asheville Folio, No. 116, issued 1904.
Mount Mitchell Folio, No. 124, issued 1905.
Nantahala Folio, No. 143, issued 1907.
Pisgah Folio, No. 147, issued 1907.
Roan Mountain Folio, No. 151, issued 1907.

CHAPTER XXV

MINES AND MINING

PREHISTORIC WORKINGS. Evidences of the early working of mines in this mountain region are so frequent and unmistakable as to leave no doubt that in several places mining was carried on at least three hundred years ago. But by whom is the problem.

The *Andrews Sun* of January 4, 1912, having stated that Tristan de Velazquez carried on mining in Cherokee county, the matter was submitted to the Librarian of Congress with the following result:

NOT TRISTAN DE VELASQUEZ. "We have been unable to find any mention of Tristan de Velazquez in the histories of early Spanish explorations in the southeastern states. It seems probable that the article quoted has confused the names of Don Luis de Velasco and Don Tristan de Luna y Arellano. Velasco, as viceroy of New Spain, sent out an expedition in 1559 under command of Luna y Arellano to establish a colony in Florida. One of the latter's lieutenants appears to have led an expedition into northeastern Alabama in 1560. According to Charles C. Jones, in his 'Hernando de Soto,' 1880, Luna's expedition penetrated into the Valley river valley in Georgia and there mined for gold, but this statement is questioned by Woodbury Lowery in his 'Spanish settlements within the present limits of the United States,' New York, 1901, p. 367. There appears to be no authority for the statement that this expedition entered the present limits of North Carolina. A Spanish account of this expedition will be found in Garcilasco de la Vega's 'La Florida del Inca,' Lisbon, 1605." [1]

A brief history of early gold mining in the Southern states may be found in George F. Becker's "Gold fields of the Southern Appalachians," in 16th annual report of the United States Geological Survey, 1894-95. Some historical notes of interest are given in Nitze and Wilkins' "Gold Mining in North Carolina," Raleigh, 1897. (North Carolina Geological Survey Bulletin, No. 10.) [2]

"THE SPECIMEN" STATE. There are a great many kinds of minerals in North Carolina, especially in the mountain region. But, with few exceptions, the veins or deposits are in small quantities—so small in fact as to have given the State the title of the "Specimen State." Iron, copper, mica, talc, kaolin, barytes, corundum, garnet, and lime, however, have been found in paying quantities.

ANCIENT DIGGINGS. In his "Speeches and Writings" (p. 130) Gen. Clingman gives an account of his work at the Sink Hole mines in Mitchell county in 1867. He thought there was silver ore there and exhibited some of it to several western miners in New York City, who declared it would assay three hundred dollars to a ton; but it produced only about three dollars. Gen. Clingman, however, had caused a shaft to be sunk and two tunnels to be carried entirely below the old excavations, but found nothing but mica. In the same chapter he speaks of a tradition among the Indians that long ago white men came on mules from the South during the summer and carried off a white metal with them, and thinks the remains of old works in Cherokee give countenance to the report.

SINK HOLE MINES. These are about seven miles southwest from Bakersville and two miles from Galax. From present appearances it would seem that a large number of men had been at work there for years. The mines are on a ridge in front of D. Pinkney Chandler's home, and are from sixty to eighty feet in diameter at the top. They extend along a ridge for one-third of a mile. They seem to have been a series of concentric holes, all of which have long since filled up from the debris which had been removed from them. But, standing with their roots on some of this waste originally taken from these holes are several large trees nearly three feet in diameter. "Timber," says Gen. Clingman, "which I examined, that had grown on the earth thrown out, had been growing as long as three hundred years." He speaks also of "a slab of stone near one of these workings that had evidently been marked by blows of a metalic tool." But Mr. Chandler, who has lived there and worked in the mines, thinks the miners carried the waste from these holes on their heads or shoulders, and dug downward only so long as the inclined, cone-like sides would bear a narrow, spiral track used to remove the earth. The walls are not perpendicular, but sloping, making a hole in the shape of an inverted cone. The marks of tools are still visible on these sloping sides when the dirt that has fallen back is thrown out; for this earth that once had been removed is still loose, and one can tell the moment he gets outside the original excavation by the increased hardness of the ground. Stone tools five or six inches in length, flattened, and two or three inches broad are still there, and some have been found at the bottom of these holes. Mr. Charles D. Stewart of Pinola dug out one of the highest of these sink holes in 1872 to a depth of 42 feet, removing therefrom a tree that had grown in the hole, with three hundred rings in its trunk. He also got stone tools out of this hole. While Gen. Clingman was at work there a tinner named Heap happened in, and taking a block of the mica, which had been thrown out as worthless, to Knoxville found that there was a market for it, and returned with a partner named Clapp, and these worked the mine profitably several years. William Silver, about this time, ran a tunnel under this ridge seventeen hundred feet to drain the mine on his land, which was about halfway the length of the ridge. J. K. Irby and D. K. Young also worked there. Others are working there now, but getting only small returns. At the bottom of these mines the ground is too hard for stone tools. Gen. Clingman also mined for silver on Clingman's branch of Beech creek in 1871. (Watauga County Deed Book No. 3, page 595.)

THE GARRETT RAY MINES. These are near Bakersville, and when a boy Mr. Ray observed a line of stone posts about fifteen feet apart on a mountain slope of his father's farm, and years afterward found that they marked a valuable mica mine, whose limits did not extend beyond them. They had never been worked, though there were a series of round basin-like holes in the soil of the slope.

ANCIENT MINING IN CLAY COUNTY. On a ridge on the left bank of Toonah creek, in Clay county, are many evidences of early mining, the surface of the earth having been left in many small but distinct ridges. Gold in small quantities is found in the creek bed, and the character of the white quartz rock and pebbles still tempts searchers after gold to pan and wash the sand and gravel from the nearby hills. It has never paid, however.

Mica Mines in Ashe. Of the mica mines in Ashe county the Director of the United States Geological Survey says (1909):

"Hamilton Mine is on the west slope of a mountain two miles northwest of Beaver creek. It was reopened by the Johnson-Hardin Company in 1907. Two tunnels were run into the hillside along the vein." The character and quality of the mica are stated.

The North Hardin mine is on a ridge about one and a half miles west of Beaver creek and has been worked on a large scale. It was operated by two open cuts and other pits, etc., which have proved the continuity of the pigmatite for over 100 yards and shown the thickness to vary from three to eight feet. "The mica has a beautiful rum color and is of the best grade."

The South Hardin mine is near the top of a small mountain or hill about one and one-half miles southwest of Beaver creek. "The color of the mica obtained was a clear rum color and the quality the best." The quartz streaks along the foot wall of the pigmatite contained beryl crystals from less than an inch to six to eight inches in diameter.

Other Noted Mica Mines. There are other noted mica mines in what was formerly Mitchell county, among them being Clarissa, the Seeb Miller mine near Flat Rock, where Ray and Anderson killed two men in a fight over the property in 1884, and the Deake mine, near Spruce Pine. There are several mica mines in Yancey and Macon, from one of the latter, the Iotla Bridge kaolin and mica mine, a block of mica was taken "in 1907, which measured about 29 by 36 inches across and was about four feet thick."[3] There are numerous other mica mines, in Jackson, Madison and Transylvania. In 1910 there were over 150 producers.

Uses for Mica. Mica is used in sheet and ground form—sheet mica for stoves and lamps and for glazing, and it is also punched into disks and washers or cut by shears for use in stoves and electrical apparatus. Ground mica is used as an insulating material in electrical machinery, wall paper, etc. The value of the production of mica in North Carolina in 1910 was $230,460,[4] as compared with $148,424 in 1909. The average price of sheet mica in the United States in 1910 was 11.5 cents per pound, as compared with 12.9 in 1909; but the average price of sheet mica in North Carolina was 42.5 per pound, by far the highest price paid.

"Among the many varieties of mica only two are considered of economic importance because of their physical properties; *i. e.*, muscovite and phlogopite. Of these two varieties muscovite alone is found in quantities of commercial importance in North Carolina. Small quantities of biotite mica (black mica) have been used for commercial purposes within the last few years, however, and another variety, the lepidolite, has been used as a source of lithium salts. Chemically, muscovite is a silicate of aluminum and potash with a small amount of water; phlogophite is a silicate of magnesium, aluminum and potassium; and piotite is a silicate of magnesium, iron, aluminum, and potassium. The three micas are very similar in physical properties except color."

CORUNDUM AND EMERY. These minerals are found in Clay, Macon, Swain, Jackson, Transylvania, Buncombe, Madison, Yancey and Mitchell counties. The following facts are from Vol. I of the N. C. Geological Survey, 1905, on Corundum and the Periodites. It contains 464 pages and is devoted entirely to this subject. It can be had by paying the postage. It covers the ground fully.

Corundum was first discovered in Madison county in 1847, about three miles below Marshall, at the mouth of Little Pine creek. The late Dr. C. D. Smith of Franklin, discovered corundum on both sides of Buck creek in Clay county prior to 1875, and Major Bryson did some prospecting there in that year, followed two years later by Frank Meminger, who worked six months and removed about 30 tons. In 1887 a Mr. Ernst did some work at Buck creek, but from then till about 1891 the mine lay idle. About this time, however, Mr. Gregory Hart of Detroit, Mich., worked it on a larger scale for about eighteen months. About 1893 the Hamden Emery and Corundum Company purchased the mine and worked it to some extent, sending the mined product to the Corundum Hill works to be cleaned. It is now owned by the International Emery and Corundum Company of New York. There is every indication of an almost inexhaustible amount of corundum at this mine. It is said to be too far from the nearest railroad point to justify its operation. The completion of a short logging road from Andrews to Chogah gap will considerably lessen this distance. Just across the mountain, on the head of Shooting creek is the Isbel mine and factory, where considerable work was done about 1897-1898. It is now idle.

CORUNDUM HILL. Corundum Hill mine, seven miles from Franklin on Cullasaja creek, was worked as early as 1871 by the late Col. C. W. Jenks. From 1878 to 1900 from 200 to 300 tons of corundum were cleaned up there every year, since which time only a small amount has been mined. It is owned by the International Emery and Corundum Company of New York. The late Dr. H. S. Lucas was active in mining these minerals in Macon county for several years, and is credited with having made money in the business. The Buck creek and Corundum Hill mines are the most important as they have been the most productive mines in the State.

CRANBERRY ORE BANK. "The Cranberry Ore Bank in Mitchell [now Avery] is pronounced by Professor Kerr 'one of the most remarkable iron deposits in America.' Its location is on the western slope of Iron mountain, in the northwest part of the county, about three miles from the Tennessee line. It takes the name Cranberry from the creek which flows near the outcrop at the foot of the mountain. The surrounding and associated rocks are gneisses and gneissoids, hornblende, slate and syenite. The ore is a pure, massive and coarse granular magnetite. The steep slope of the mountain and ridges, which the bed occupies, are covered with blocks of ore, some weighing hundreds of pounds, and at places bare, vertical walls of massive ore, 10 to 15 feet thick, are exposed, and over several acres the solid ore is found everywhere near the surface. The length of the outcrop is 1,500 feet, and the width 200 to 800 feet" (State Geological Report). It was worked in 1820[5] by the Dugger family. (See Chapter XVI, "Notable Cases and Decisions," section headed "Carter v. Hoke.")

CRANBERRY'S ANTECEDENTS. Dayton Hunter, Esq., a lawyer of Elizabethton, Tenn., owns the land on which stood the first iron works of Tennessee, a deed now in Jonesboro, Tenn., calling in 1778 for Landon Carter's Forge Race. This forge stood about 700 feet east of the present court house of Carter county. This Landon Carter was the father of S. P. Carter, who was both an admiral in the navy and a lieutenant general in the army of the United States. Dayton Hunter married a daughter of Rev. W. B. Carter, a Presbyterian minister and a noted Greek and Latin scholar. Whether Charles Asher had anything to do with this forge is not known, but on the 18th of December, 1795, he and his wife Molly

conveyed to Julius Dugger for seventy pounds, "current money
of Virginia," (Deed Book A, p. 178), 88¾ acres on the south
side of Watauga river, being part of a grant from North Carolina to said Charles Asher; and in May, 1802, John Asher conveyed to the same Dugger 45 additional acres on the same
side of the same river (Deed Book C, p. 421). On the 20th of
November, 1822, John Asher (a son of Charles and Molly) conveyed to William Dugger (Deed Book C, p. 577) one-fourth
of all the land on Watauga river, "including the Forge,"
beginning on a mulberry tree on the north side of the Forge
dam, and containing three acres and 54 poles, "which bar-
gained land and one-fourth of the same, including the iron
works, with all appurtenances thereunto belonging, or in
anywise appertaining, with free privilege of roads for the
use of said iron works, together with the building or repair-
ing timber for the use of said Forge, and free course for water
to said Iron Works," is the first reference on the records to
the old Dugger Forge, four miles above Butler, Tenn., on
the north side of Watauga river. This would also indicate,
what tradition preserves, that Asher was the original iron
master, and that he took the Duggers in with him. Joshua
Perkins, who is said to have built the Cranberry forge for
the Duggers, was a son of Jacob Perkins to whom on the 18th
of September, 1811, Richard White, of Washington county,
Va., conveyed, for $1,500, 250 acres on the north side of
Watauga river opposite the mouth of Elk creek, reserving to
himself a right of way over the land conveyed, "up the hollow,"
in order to avoid the jutting rock-cliff which formerly blocked
the passage of the road on the right bank. This is the time
that Richard White left for Missouri, according to the tradition of that locality. So it would seem that Landon Carter
was the forefather of Cranberry Forge, that he was succeeded
by Charles and John Asher, and the Duggers, while Joshua
Perkins was the real builder of Cranberry Forge in 1820.

MAGNETIC CITY. Soon after the Civil War John L. Wilder
and associates started a forge on Big Rock creek, and a town,
which received the name of Magnetic City. But it was too
far at that time from a railroad, and the forge was abandoned.
The white houses around Magnetic City and the little valley
in which they are situated afford a pleasant surprise to the
traveler when he first catches a glimpse of them.

THE DAVIDSON RIVER IRON WORKS. Charles Moore, grandfather of Judge Charles A. Moore of Asheville, James W. Patton and Thomas Miller of Henderson county, many years before the Civil War, made a contract with George Shuford, a millwright, father of Judge George A. Shuford, to build a forge or furnace and a mill on Davidson River, some of the iron ore being hauled from Boylston creek, although some was brought only three or four miles from a mine on the Boylston road. The hammer used in connection with this iron forge or furnace was operated by water. These owners afterwards became incorporated as the Davidson River Iron Works. It was in operation until after the commencement of the Civil War, when the Confederate Government took charge of it and operated it till its collapse. After the war it was reopened and Judge Shuford remembers seeing from fifty to sixty hands at work there as late as 1866. [6]

THE SUTTON FORGE. There was also another iron forge or furnace on Mills river, known as the Sutton forge, because it was owned by a man named Sutton. This, however, was not on so large a scale as that on Davidson river.

MEREDITH BALLOU, PIONEER MINER. From Mr. V. E. Ballou of Grassy creek we learn that there are valuable iron mines from eight to twelve miles from Jefferson and about fifteen miles from Troutdale, Va., the nearest railroad station. [7] They were first discovered by Meredith Ballou, the great-grandfather of V. E. Ballou who came to Ashe from Virginia among the first settlers. These iron properties are still owned principally by natives of Ashe county, among whom are J. U. Ballou, Dr. Thos. J. Jones, the Gentry heirs, B. Sturgill and J. U. Ballou. Napoleon B. Ballou was the son of Meredith and the father of J. U. Ballou "who built the first bloomery forge and made the first iron in the State, which industry was carried on till about the year 1890 or 1891. Since that time there has been expended in Ashe county some $275,000 or $300,000 in the way of purchase money and development work. This work has proven that there are large, well defined veins of ore of a superior quality in this section of the State, but only one of these properties has been transferred to any large capitalist." (See J. H. Pratt's "Geological History of Western North Carolina," in Chapter XXIV of this history.)

IRON PRODUCTION. [8] The Cranberry Iron mine has produced almost all the iron that has been produced in North Carolina for years. It produces a pig iron of exceptional quality, commanding a high price. It is magnetic, and the crude ore is shipped to Knoxville for reduction. It has been a constant producer for twenty-five years. Nearly one hundred years ago iron was made there by the old Bloomery methods, and no better iron has since been made by any method.

AUTHENTIC INFORMATION. From "The Iron Manufacturer's Guide" (1859, by J. P. Lesley), quoted by Prof. Joseph Hyde Pratt in his "Geological History of Western North Carolina," in the chapter preceding this in this history, we get what is otherwise a matter of conjecture and doubt as to the date and names of the different "bloomeries" and iron works of this region. There is also a mass of valuable information concerning other mines and mining by Prof. Pratt in that article, to which reference is particularly invited.

ORE KNOB COPPER MINE OF ASHE COUNTY. (Information by Messrs. John Dent and H. D. Baker.) About nine miles east of Jefferson, is the Ore Knob Copper mine in Ashe county, which was first opened and worked for iron by Meredith Ballou, a Frenchman, many years ago. He mined the ore and hauled it to his forge at the mouth of Helton creek, and made wrought iron of it; but it was found to contain too much copper and sulphur, coating up the tools with copper, and was not so good as that from the North fork of the New river. About four years before the Civil War a Virginia corporation, known as the Buckhannon Company, operated Ore Knob for copper, and hauled the richest ore to Wytheville, Va., sixty miles away, by wagons, drawn by shod oxen. These men had bought it from Jesse Reeves, and after working the mine a year or more, sold it to George S. Miller and associates, who, after the Civil War, sold it to the Clayton Co., of Baltimore, Md. This company, under the management of John Dent, now a resident of Jefferson, developed the mine scientifically, had the best of machinery installed, and established a smelter at the mine. They began work about 1873 and continued it till about 1877, when the price of copper declined. They shipped the manufactured sheet copper to Baltimore, via Marion, Va., and worked from 300 to 600 hands. Work seems to have continued in a smaller way till 1880, when it stopped altogether, Mr. Dent leaving there in December, 1883. This is the first place in North Carolina where copper was made from the ore and refined up to the Lake Superior grade. The ore was piled on burning wood heaps and burned from five to to seven weeks, by which time most of the sulphur would have been driven off, after which the roasted ore was smelted with charcoal in shaft furnaces and refined down to 99½ per cent pure copper. The vein's general direction is northeast and southwest, with nearly a vertical dip. Among the principal stockholders of the company were James E. and S. S. Clayton and J. S. and Herman Williams.[9] The land in which the mine lay had belonged to John W. Martin, who conveyed his interest therein to the Clayton Company, the mineral rights therein having been sold under execution at the court house door and bought in by the same company. Work was commenced on the 17th day of March, 1873. Some suppose that this was a mere pocket; but its distance from a railroad was probably the true reason of its abandonment. There is an undeveloped copper mine on Gap creek, near the line between Ashe and Watauga.

ELK KNOB COPPER COMPANY.[10] In 1899 this company entered into a contract with J. A. Zinns and Joseph Bock of Minnesota for the operation of a copper mine on Elk Knob, and bought the engine of Vassas Brothers, who had failed at making pipes out of laurel roots in Boone, which business they had started in 1897 in a building in the rear of Blackburn's hotel.[11] The copper mine was abandoned in a few years, and litigation ensued between Zinns and Bock.

CULLOWHEE COPPER MINE. This is in Jackson county, where some copper was produced in 1909 and 1910; but it is almost too far from a railroad to pay. It has a shaft 177 feet deep and a tunnel 4,000 feet in length.

ADAMS-WESTFELDT COPPER MINE. This is on Hazel creek in Swain county; but the property has been in litigation since 1900. It is on the lead from Ducktown, and is said to be rich. (See this case in Chapter XVI.)

GRAPHITE. The Connally mine at Graphiteville, between Round Knob and the Swannanoa tunnel is in McDowell county. It was operated a few years prior to 1907, but, owing to the difficulty of extracting the ore economically, it was abandoned. There is said to be an inexhaustible quantity on the land.

KAOLIN. Is obtained principally from Jackson, Mitchell and Swain counties. Over $100,000 of this mineral has been produced in this State in a year.

AMETHYST has been found in Macon, especially on Tessentee creek. The Connally mine on this creek has been worked by the American Gem and Pearl Company of New York, and the Rhodes mine by the Passmore Gem Company of Boston.

TALC AND PYROPHYLITE DEPOSITS. There are talc deposits in Swain and Cherokee counties. A. A. Campbell of Cherokee was the pioneer in this mining, having shipped it by wagons before the days of railroads to Cleveland, Tennessee. It was then $80 per ton, however. It was used as early as 1859 to line the copper furnaces at Ducktown, Tenn. The principal talc mines are the North Carolina Talc and Mining Company at Hewitts, Swain county; the Alba Mineral Company near Kinsey, Cherokee county; the American Talc Company, and the Glendon Mining and Manufacturing Company, at Glendon, Moore county. Hewitts mine is the largest and best. Water interfered with the operation some years ago, but that has since been remedied. There is also a talc mine in Mitchell county, near Spruce Pine.

BARYTES. Crude barytes has been produced in the vicinity of Marshall, Stackhouse, Sandy Bottom and Hot Springs in Madison county. This substance has been produced in this county since 1884. The value of the product in 1910 was $145,315. Owing to its weight, it is called "heavy spar." There was a mill for crushing barytes at Warm Springs (now Hot Springs) in August, 1884. ("On Horseback," page 139.)

THULITE was mined in North Carolina, in the Flat Rock mine, in 1908. It furnishes attractive gems when cut *en cabochon* with the enclosing feldspar.

ZIRCON was produced in 1909 from the Jones mine near Zirconia, Henderson county, when operated by M. C. and C. F. Toms. Two thousand pounds in 1909 was valued at $250.

PRECIOUS STONES. During 1908, 1909 and 1910 there was little systematic mining for gems in this region.

MARBLE AND LIMESTONE. The main marble outcropping begins on the Nantahala river below Hewitts and extends

southward down to Valley river, a distance of over 25 miles.
A shorter and parallel band extends from the head of Peach-
tree creek nearly ten miles southwestward and up Little
Brasstown creek. The North Carolina Mining and Talc
Company are developing their marble deposits at Hewitts.
High freight rates prevent the development of this property.

THE CASPERIS MARBLE COMPANY. The Casperis Marble
Company is now operating marble quarries at Regal, a few
miles east of Murphy, and is supplying stone to several railroads. Mr. S. Casperis of Columbus, Ohio, is one of the
largest stone operators in the United States. An extensive
finishing plant employing about 50 men is operated in connection with the quarry. The quality of what this company
calls the "Regal Blue," now being quarried, is said to be
unexceled in the United States. The possibilities of marble
production near Andrews and Brasstown appear to be almost
limitless.

CHASING PETROLEUM RAINBOWS. Notwithstanding the
opinion of scientists that "there is no petroleum to be found
in the area west of the Blue Ridge in North Carolina, as the
rocks were formed long before the period of time at which
those carrying petroleum were formed," in the year of grace
1902, in the county of Buncombe, and within two miles of
Asheville, W. A. Baird and wife and many others on Beaverdam creek in Buncombe county, gave W. T. Sidell and E.
E. Stewart of West Virginia, leases to mine oil and gas for
one-eighth part of the oil and $200 a year for the use of all
the gas that might be discovered or produced. (Deed Book,
124, p. 73.)

OIL EXCITEMENT ON COVE CREEK. Soon after the Big
Freshet of May, 1901, indications of oil appeared near N. L.
Mast's store on Cove creek, Watauga county; and A. J.
McBride, a reputable citizen, collected the oily film on top of
a pool of water by absorbing it with blotting paper. This
burned brilliantly; and in July, 1902, W. R. Lovill, Esq., a
lawyer of Boone, obtained options on the lands of J. T. Combs
and members of his family, B. F. Bingham, T. B. Fletcher and
others, for one year. Mr. Lovill interested Gen. J. S. Carr of
Durham in the matter, and the latter sent Major Hamlet of
Roanoke to investigate. The flat formation of the rock strata
indicates unmistakably the presence of oil, but the ancient

character of the rocks contradicted these indications, they being gneiss of the oldest character. But, during the year 1907, the Carolina Valley Oil and Gas Company, composed of men from New York and Pennsylvania, put down a hole near N. L. Mast's store 800 feet deep, and then abandoned the work, claiming that the drill had begun to take a slanting course. This company had a map prepared which indicated that there is oil in many places in Watauga and Avery counties. It is certain that the formation of the rock strata along the lower part of Cove creek and below its entrance into Watauga river is as nearly flat as it is possible to be. Oil leases were also taken on lands around Sutherland, Ashe county.

AGE OF OUR ROCK FORMATION. From Professor Pratt's Geological History of Western North Carolina, Chapter XXIV, in this work, it is clear that "all the rocks of Western North Carolina are amongst the oldest geologic formations," from which we may conclude that we are occupying land that is more ancient than that of the Euphrates, the Nile, or the Jordan, so long associated in our minds with the Garden of Eden, the Ptolemys and Old Testament stories.

HIGH HONOR FOR OUR NATIVE GEMS. In the "Carolina Mountains" we learn that the finest specimens of emerald green crystalized corundum in the world, measuring 4½x2x 1½ inches, is now in the Morgan-Bemet collection in New York. It was taken from Corundum Hill, near Franklin, in 1871. From Cowee creek comes the new gem Rhodolite, "remarkable for its transparency and great brilliancy (p. 268)," large sea-blue aquamarines, and beryls, both sea-green and yellow, tourmalines, purple amethyst, discovered on Tessentee creek by a landslide, and "smoky and citron-green quartz crystals in the Black mountains, . . . from which have been cut many beautiful objects by the Tiffany lapidaries of New York" (p. 272). Salmon-pink chalcedony, agates, green chrysoprase and red and yellow jasper, also are mentioned. North Carolina minerals "are treasured in the greatest collections in the world, in this country very fine ones being on exhibition in the Metropolitan Museum of Art and the American Museum of Natural History (N. Y.), in the U. S. National Museum at Washington, D. C., in the Field Columbian Museum, Chicago, as well as many smaller museums."

VALUE OF MINERAL PRODUCTION IN FOLLOWING COUNTIES.[12]

County	1909	1910
Alleghany	$ 400	$ 500
Ashe	155	500
Buncombe	82,844	64,505
Cherokee	31,283	22,325
Clay	......	......
Graham	......	......
Haywood	1,550	7,075
Henderson	99,480	60,882
Jackson	51,599	53,804
Macon	45,732	50,300
Madison	21,785	20,224
Mitchell	191,777	259,127
Swain	99,564	80,983
Transylvania	7,337	6,771
Watauga and Wayne	46,338	59,810
Yancey	32,660	59,284

NOTES.

[1]H. H. B. Meyer, Chief Bibliographer Congressional Library, to J. P. A., January 16, 1912.

[2]Ibid.

[3]Economic Paper No. 23, N. C. Geo. and Econ. Survey, 1911.

[4]Ibid.

[5]From "The Iron Manufacturer's Guide," 1859, by J. P. Lesley.

[6]Not mentioned in "The Iron Manufacturer's Guide," 1859, by J. P. Lesley.

[7]Harbard's Bloomery Forge at the mouth of Holton creek was built in 1807, and washed away in 1817; "Iron Manufacturer's Guide," 1859.

[8]Economic Paper No. 23, N. C. G. and E. Survey, 1911, p. 30.

[9]The Ore Knob Mining Co. was incorporated by Ch. 29, Pr. Laws of N. C., 1881, John S. Williams, Washington Booth, James E. Tyson and others of Baltimore and James E. Clayton and others of Ashe incorporators.

[10]Deed Book V, Watauga, p. 238.

[11]Ibid, T, p. 472.

[12]From 25th Annual Report of the Department of Labor, 1911.

CHAPTER XXVI

THE CHEROKEES

THE ORIGIN OF THE INDIANS. William Penn saw a striking likeness between the Jews of London and the American Indians. Some claim that the stories of the Old Testament are legends in some Indian tribes. In the Jewish Encyclopedia it is said that the Hebrews, after the captivity, separated themselves from the heathen in order to observe their peculiar laws; and Manasseh Ben Israel claims that America and India were once joined, at Bering strait, by a peninsula, over which these Hebrews came to America. All Indian legends affirm that they came from the northwest. When first visited by Europeans, Indians were very religious, worshiping one Great Spirit, but never bowing down to idols. Their name for the deity was Ale, the old Hebrew name for God. In their dances they said "Hallelujah" distinctly. They had annual festivals, performed morning and evening sacrifices, offered their first fruits to God, practiced circumcision, and there were "cities of refuge," to which offenders might fly and be safe; they reckoned time as did the Hebrews, similar superstitions mark their burial places "and the same creeds were the rule of their lives, both as to the present and the future." They had chief-ruled tribes, and forms of government almost identical with those of the Hebrews. Each tribe had a totem, usually some animal, as had the Israelites, and this explains why, in the blessing of Jacob upon his sons, Judah is surnamed a lion, Dan a serpent, Benjamin a wolf, and Joseph a bough. [1] There are also resemblances in their language to the Latin and Greek tongues, Chickamauga meaning the field of death, and Aquone the sound of water.

THE CHEROKEES A SUPERIOR TRIBE. [2] They have been known as one of the largest and most noteworthy of the aboriginal tribes, and formed an important factor in both English and Spanish pioneering. Those who dwelt in the mountains were known as the Otari or Overhill Cherokees, while those dwelling in the lowlands were called the Erati [3] or Lowland Cherokees. They had their own national government, and numbered from 20,000 to 25,000 persons. They are "well advanced along the white man's road." What is now known as the Eastern band, in the heart of the Carolina mountains, outnumbers today such well-known Western tribes as the Omaha, Pawnee, Comanche and Kiowas, and it is among these, "the old conservative Kituhwa element, that the ancient things have been preserved." In the forests of Nantahala and Oconaluftee, "the Cherokee priest still treasures the legends and repeats the mystic rituals" of his ancestors. The original boundary embraced about 40,000 square miles, from the head streams of the Kanawha to Atlanta, and from the Blue Ridge to the Cumberland range, with Itsati, or Echota, on the south bank of the Little Tennessee river, a few miles above the mouth of Tellico creek, in Tennessee, as its capital. This was called the "City of Refuge." They call themselves the Yunwiga, or real people, and on ceremonial occasions speak of themselves as Ani-Kituhwagi, or people of Kituhwa, an ancient settlement on the Tuckaseegee river, and apparently the original nucleus of the tribe. The name by which they are now known—Cherokee—has no meaning in their language, and the form among them is Tsalagi or Tsargi. It first appears as Chalaque in the Portugese narrative of DeSoto's expedition, while Cheraqui appears in a French document in 1699. It got its present form in 1708, thus having an authentic history at this time (1913) of 275 years. They admit that they built the mounds on Grave creek in Ohio, and the mounds near Charlottesville, Va. They had also lived at the Peaks of Otter, Va. But they disclaim all knowledge of the mounds and petroglyphs in North Carolina, Tennessee and Georgia.

TRADITIONS OF WHITE AND LILLIPUTIAN RACES. There is a dim but persistent tradition of a white race having preceded the Cherokees; and of a tribe of Lilliputians or very small people, who once lived on the site of the ancient mound on the northern side of Hiwassee river, at the mouth of Peachtree creek, and afterwards went west. This was long before the normal sized whites came. Miss Murphrey has preserved this tradition in her "In the Stranger Peoples' Country."

INTRODUCTION OF SMALL ARMS AND SMALLPOX. About 1700 the first guns were introduced among the Cherokees, and in 1738 or 1739 smallpox nearly exterminated the tribe within a single year. It had been brought to Charleston, S. C., on a slave ship.

OTHER EARLY INCIDENTS. About 1740 a trading path from Augusta to the Cherokee towns at the head of the Savannah, and thence to the west was marked out by this tribe, and in that year the Cherokees took part under their war chief, "The Raven," in Oglethorpe's expedition against the Spaniards at St. Augustine. In 1736 Christian Priber, a Jesuit, acting in French interest, became influential among them. He was a most worthy member of that illustrious order whose scholarship, devotion and courage have been exemplified from the days of Jogues and Marquette down to DeSmet and Mengarini. In 1756 Fort Prince George was built at the head of the Savannah, and Fort Loudon near the junction of Tellico creek and the Little Tennessee river, beyond the mountains. Disagreements between the Cherokees and the South Carolina colonists finally resulted in the seizure of Oconostota, a young war chief, and his retention at Fort Prince George as a hostage. This led to war, and the Cherokees besieged Fort Loudon. In June, 1760, Col. Montgomery, with 1,600 men, crossed the Indian frontier and drove the Cherokees from about Fort Prince George, and then destroyed every one of the Lower Cherokee towns, killing more than a hundred Indians and driving the whole population into the mountains. He then crossed the mountains without opposition till he came near Echoe, a few miles above the sacred town of Kikwasi, now Franklin, N. C., where he met their full force, which compelled Montgomery to retire in a battle fought June 27, 1760. He retreated to Fort Prince George after losing 100 men in killed and wounded.

MASSACRE AT FORT LOUDON. This retreat sealed the fate of the garrison at Fort Loudon, which had been reduced to the necessity of eating horses and dogs, though Indian women, who had found sweethearts among the soldiers, brought them what food they could. On August 8, Capt. Demere surrendered his garrison of about 200 to Oconostota upon promise that they should be allowed to retire with sufficient arms and ammunition for the march. The garrison made a day's march up Tellico creek and camped, while the Cherokees plundered the fort. It was then that they discovered ten bags of powder and a large quantity of ball that the garrison had secretly buried in the fort before surrendering. Cannon and small arms also had been thrown into the river, which was a breach of the terms of the capitulation. Enraged at this duplicity the Indians attacked the retiring garrison at sunrise the next morning, killing Demere and 25 others at the first fire, and taking the rest prisoners, to be ransomed some time later on. Capt. Stuart, second in command, was claimed by Ata-kullakulla, a Cherokee chief, who managed to conduct him, after nine days' march, to his friends in Virginia. A treaty was concluded at Augusta, November 10, 1763, by which the Cherokees lost all north of the present Tennessee line and east of the Blue Ridge and Savannah. A royal proclamation was issued this year barring the whites from occupying Indian lands west of the Blue Ridge; while in 1768 a treaty fixed the northern limit as downward along the New and Kanawha rivers from the North Carolina line. This treaty was made at Hard Labor, S. C.; while on March 17, 1775, a treaty cut off the Cherokees from the Ohio and their rich Kentucky hunting grounds.

THREE STATES COMBINE AGAINST THE CHEROKEES. But the constant encroachments of the whites upon the Indian territory resulted, in 1776, in an agreement between Virginia, North and South Carolina by which each sent a punitive expedition into the Cherokee country, and laid it waste for miles, killing men and even women, and driving many into the mountains for refuge. In August Gen. Griffith Rutherford, with 2,400 men, crossed Swannanoa gap, and after following the present line of railroad to the French Broad, out Hominy creek and following up the Richland, struck the first Indian town at Stecoee, the present site of Whittier, on the Tuckaseegee. This he burned, and then destroyed all towns on Oconaluftee, Tuckaseegee and the upper part of Little Tennessee; also those on the Hiwassee below the junction of Valley river, making 36 towns in all. He also destroyed all crops. The chaplain of this expedition was Rev. James Hall, D. D., a Presbyterian. At Sugartown (Kuletsiyi), east of the present Franklin, a detachment sent to destroy it was surprised by the Cherokees and escaped only through the aid of another force sent to its rescue. Rutherford himself encountered a force in Wayah gap of the Nantahalas, between Franklin and Aquone, where he lost forty killed and wounded, but finally repulsing the Indians. [4] An Indian killed in this fight proved to have been a woman dressed as a man. An

account of the route followed by Rutherford, with many other
facts, can be found in the North Carolina Booklet, Vol. IV, No.
8, for December, 1904; from which it appears that Williamson of South Carolina was to have joined Rutherford at Cowee,
but as he did not appear, Rutherford, without a proper guide,
crossed the Nantahalas at an unusual place, thus missing
the Wayah gap, where 500 braves had assembled to oppose
him and that two days later Williamson, hurrying up Car-
toogachaye creek, crossed at the usual place, and fell into
the ambush which had been prepared for Rutherford; and that
Rutherford lost but three men in the entire expedition. This
latter account is probably the true one. Williamson joined
Rutherford on the Hiwassee. It was considered unnecessary
to await the arrival of Col. Christian from Virginia, who was
coming via the Holston river, as all the Cherokee towns had
been destroyed. Col. Andrew Williamson's force of South
Carolinians was 1,860 strong, including a number of Catawbas,
and came through Rabun gap of the Blue Ridge.[5] It was
near Murphy that Rutherford and Williamson's forces joined
September 26, 1776. Among Christian's men was a regiment
from Surry county, N. C., under Colonels Joseph Williams and
Love, and Major Winston. They had assembled on the Holston and pressed cautiously along the great warpath to the
crossing of the French Broad in Tennessee, and thence advanced
without opposition to the Little Tennessee, where, early in November, Christian was proceeding to destroy their towns, when
the Indians sought peace. Col. Christian, hoping to draw
trade from the South Carolina Indians, accepted the promise
of the Cherokees to "surrender all their prisoners and to
cede all the disputed territory . . . in the Tennessee
settlements," suspended hostilities and withdrew, but not
till he had burned the town of Tuckaseegee because its inhabitants had been concerned in the burning of a white boy,
named Moore, who had been captured with a Mrs. Bean;
but he spared the peace town of Echota. But Col. Williams
of Surry was not pleased with Christian's leniency, and on the
22d of November, 1776, wrote to the North Carolina Congress from Surry, enclosing documents which he claimed
proved conclusively "that some of the Virginia gentlemen
are desirious of having the Cherokees under their protection,"
which Williams did not think right as most of the territory

was within North Carolina and should be under her protection. In this warfare every Indian was scalped and even
women were shot down and afterwards "helped to their end."
Prisoners were "taken and put up at auction as slaves, when
not killed on the spot."

HOLSTON AND HOPEWELL TREATIES. At Long Island of
the Holston a treaty was concluded July 20, 1777, by which
the Middle and Upper Cherokees ceded everything east of
the Blue Ridge, and all disputed territory on the Watauga,
Nollechucky, upper Holston and New rivers. This ended
the treaties with the separate States. The first treaty made
with the United States was at Hopewell, S. C., November
28, 1785, by which the whole country east of the Blue Ridge,
with the Watauga and Cumberland settlements, was given
to the whites, but leaving the whole of western North Carolina
to the Cherokees.

TREATIES OF WHITE'S FORT AND TELLICO. In the summer
of 1791 the Cherokees made a treaty at White's Fort, now
Knoxville, by which they ceded a "triangular section of Tennessee and North Carolina extending from the Clinch river
almost to the Blue Ridge, and including nearly the whole
of the French Broad and lower Holston and the sites of the
present Knoxville, and Greeneville, Tenn., and Asheville, N. C.,
most of which territory was already occupied by the whites.
Permission was also given for a road from the eastern settlements to those of the Cumberland, with free navigation
of the Tennessee river." This treaty was signed by 41 principal chiefs and was concluded July 2, 1791, and probably
gave legal title to the whites to as far west of the Blue Ridge
as the Pigeon river in Haywood county. There were four
treaties of Tellico, the first having been signed October 2, 1798,
by 39 chiefs, by which were ceded a tract between the Clinch river
and the Cumberland ridge, another along the northern bank
of the Little Tennessee, extending up to the Chilhowie mountains, and a third in North Carolina on the head of the French
Broad and Pigeon rivers, and including what are now Waynesville and Hendersonville; thus making the Balsam mountains
the western boundary. In 1804 and 1805, three additional
treaties were concluded at Tellico by Return J. Meigs, by
which the Cherokees were shorn of 8,000 square miles, not
affecting the limits of North Carolina; but it was then that

Meigs originated what he termed a "silent consideration," by which a smaller amount was named in the public treaty, to-wit: $2,000—while he had agreed that "one thousand dollars and some rifles" in addition should be given to some of the chiefs who signed it. This treaty however was concluded at Washington, D. C., January 7, 1806. In 1813 the Cherokees agreed that a company should lay off and build a free public road from the Tennessee river to the head of navigation of the Tuggaloo branch of the Savannah; and this road was completed within the next three years, and became the great highway from the coast to the Tennessee settlements. The road began where Toccoa creek enters the Savannah, and passed through Clarksville and Hiwassee in Georgia, and Hayesville and Murphy, N. C., though those towns had not been established by the whites at that time. From Murphy it passed over the Unaka or White mountains into Tennessee to Echota, the capital town of the Cherokees. It was officially styled the Unicoi Turnpike, but was commonly known in North Carolina as the Wachese or Watsisa trail, because it passed near the home of a noted Indian who lived near the place at which it crossed Beaverdam creek—his name having been Watsisa—and because this portion of the road followed the old trail which already bore that name.

NANAKATAHKE AND JUNALUSKA. The former was a sister of Yonaguska, and the mother-in-law of Gid. F. Morris, a South Carolinian who came to Cherokee county about the same time that Betty Bly or Blythe, came there, according to the statement of the late Col. A. T. Davidson, who said that Nanakatahke told him that she was the mother of Wachesa, or Grass-hopper. Junaluska, spelled Tsunulahunski in Cherokee, is the best remembered of the Cherokee chiefs, of whom a full account will be found in Chapter XII, pp. 292-293.

THE REMOVAL TREATIES. On the 8th of July, 1817, at the Cherokee agency (now Calhoun, Tenn.), a treaty was made by which, in return for land in Georgia and Tennessee, the Cherokees were to receive a tract within the present limits of Arkansas, and payment for any substantial improvements they had made on the ceded lands they would abandon by going to Arkansas. Each warrior who left no improvements behind was to be given for his abandoned field and hut a rifle, ammunition, a blanket, a kettle or a beaver trap. Boats and provisions for the journey were also to be furnished the Indians who might go. It was also provided that those who chose to remain might do so and become citizens, the amount of land occupied by such to be deducted from the total cession. But the majority of the Cherokees opposed removal bitterly, and only 31 of the principal men of the eastern band and 15 of the western signed for the tribe. A protest signed by 67 chiefs and headsmen was presented to the commissioners for the government; but it was ignored and the treaty ratified. In fact, the authorities for the United States did not even wait for the ratification, but at once took steps for the removal of all who desired to go west, and before 1819, six thousand had been removed, according to the estimate. This, however, did not effect North Carolina territory; but on February 27, 1819, a treaty was made at Washington by which the Indians ceded to the United States, among other tracts in Alabama, Tennessee and Georgia, "nearly everything remaining to them" in North Carolina east of the Nantahala mountains; though individual reservations one mile square within the ceded area were allowed a number of families, who preferred to remain and become citizens. In order to conform to the laws of civilization, those who were to remain adopted a regular republican form of government modeled after that of the United States, with New Echota, a few miles above the present Calhoun, Ga., as the capital. John Ross was the first Cherokee president. They passed laws for the collection of taxes, and debts, for repairs of roads, for the support of schools and for the regulation of the liquor traffic; to punish horse stealing and theft, and to compel all marriages between white men and Indian women to be celebrated according to regular legal or church form, and to discourage polygamy. By a special decree the right of Blood Revenge, or capital punishment, was taken from the seven clans and vested in the authorities of the Indian nation. Death was the punishment to individual Indians who might sell lands to the whites without the consent of the Indian authorities. White men were not allowed to vote or hold office in the nation.

YONAGUSKA, THE BLOOD AVENGER. The late Col. Allen T. Davidson told the writer that John Welch, a half-breed Frenchman, killed Leech, a full-blooded Cherokee, near old

Valleytown in Cherokee county, and as Yonaguska was Leech's next of kin, he was therefore his blood avenger, and not only entitled to kill Welch, but the custom of the tribe made it his duty to do so. He, therefore, followed Welch first to the Smoky mountains, and then to Paint Rock; thence to the New Found range west of Asheville, and to Pickens, S. C., where Welch stopped and rested. Here it was, though, that Welch became infatuated with a white girl named Betty Bly, and told Betty that he feared that Yonaguska, whom he had seen loitering near, was seeking a chance to kill him. She then sought out Yonaguska and persuaded him to let Welch off.

THE BAPTISTS ESTABLISH THE FIRST CHEROKEE MISSION. In 1820 the Baptists founded five principal missions, one of which was in Cherokee county, on the site of the old Nachez town on the north side of Hiwassee river, just above the mouth of Peachtree creek. It was established at the instance of Currahee Dick, a prominent mixed - blood chief, and was placed in charge of the Rev. Evan Jones, known as the translator of the New Testament into the Cherokee language, with James D. Wafford, a mixed-blood pupil, who compiled a spelling book in the same language, as his assistant. The late Rev. Humphrey Posey afterwards became principal of this mission, and did a wonderful amount of work for the improvement and education of the Cherokees. The place is still known as "The Mission Farm," and is one of the most productive and desirable in the mountains. Worcester and Boudinot's translation of Matthew, first published at New Echota, Ga., in 1829, was introduced to the Kituwas Cherokees, and in the absence of missionaries, was read from house to house, after which Rev. Ulrich Keener, a Methodist, began to preach at irregular intervals, and was soon followed by Baptists.

SEQUOYA AND HIS SYLLABARY. About this time (1821) Sikwayi (Sequoya) a half or quarter breed Cherokee, known among the whites as George Gist or Guest or Guess, invented the Cherokee syllabary or alphabet, which was "soon recognized as an invaluable invention for the elevation of the tribe, and within a few months thousands of hitherto illiterate Cherokees were able to read and write their own language, teaching each other in the cabins and along the roadside.

. . . It had an immediate and wonderful effect on Cherokee development, and on account of the remarkable adaptation
of the syllabary to the language, it was only necessary to learn
the characters to be able to read at once. . . . In the
fall of 1824 Atsi or John Arch, a young native convert, made
a manuscript translation of a portion of St. John's gospel, in
the syllabary, this being the first Bible translation ever given
to the Cherokee." On the 21st of February, 1828, "the
first number of the newspaper *Taslagi Tsulehisanun*, the
Cherokee Phoenix, 'printed' in English and Cherokee, was published at New Echota from type cast for that purpose in Boston under the supervision of the noted missionary, Worcester. Sequoya was born, probably about 1760 at Luck-a-See-
gee town in Tennessee, just outside of old Fort Loudon, near
where old Choto had stood." Here his mind dwelt also on
the old tradition of a lost band of Cherokee living somewhere
toward the western mountains. In 1841 and 1842, with a
few Cherokee companions and with his provisions and papers
loaded in an ox cart, he made several journeys into the west, and
was received everywhere with kindness by even the wildest tribes.
Disappointed in his philologic results, he started out in 1843
in quest of the lost Cherokees, who were believed to be somewhere in northern Mexico, but, being now an old man and
worn out by hardship, he sank under the effort and died alone
and unattended, it is said, near the village of San Fernando,
Mexico, in August of that year. The Cherokees had voted
him a pension of three hundred dollars which was continued
to his widow, "the only literary pension in the United States."
The great trees of California (*Sequoia gigantea*) were named in
his honor and preserve his memory.

OUTRAGES FOLLOW DAHLONEGA GOLD DISCOVERY. The
discovery of gold in the Dahlonega district caused the Georgia
legislature on the 20th of December, 1828, to annex that part
of the Cherokee country to Georgia and to annul all Cherokee
laws and customs therein. This act was to take effect June
1, 1830, the land was mapped into counties and divided into
"land lots" of 160 acres and "gold lots" of 40 acres, which
were to be distributed among the white citizens of Georgia by
public lottery. Provision was made for the settlement of
contested lottery claims among the white citizens, but no
Indian could bring a suit or testify in court. "About the

same time the Cherokees were forbidden to hold councils, or to assemble for any public purpose or to dig for gold upon their own lands." The outrages which followed are disgraceful to the white men of that section and time.

TREATY OF REMOVAL OF 1835. On the 29th of December, 1835, by the treaty of New Echota, "the Cherokee nation ceded to the United States its whole remaining territory east of the Mississippi for the sum of $5,000,000 and a common joint interest in the territory already occupied by the western Cherokees in what is now the Indian Territory, with an additional smaller tract on the northeast in what is now Kansas. Improvements were to be paid for, and the Indians were to be removed at the expense of the United States, and subsisted for one year after their arrival in the new country. The removal was to take place within two years. . . ." It was also distinctly agreed that a limited number of Cherokees might remain behind and become citizens after they had been adjudged "qualified or calculated to become useful citizens," together with a few who held individual reservations under former treaties. But this provision was struck out by President Jackson, who insisted that the "whole Cherokee people should remove together." The treaty was ratified by the senate May 23, 1836, the official census of 1835 having fixed the number of Cherokees in North Carolina at 3,644.

THE PATHETIC STORY OF THE REMOVAL. This story exceeds in weight of grief and pathos any in American history; for notwithstanding that nearly 16,000 out of a total of 16,-542 Indians in North Carolina, Tennessee, Georgia and Alabama, had signed a protest against the treaty, Gen. Wool was sent to carry the treaty into effect; but so fixed was the determination of the Cherokees to remain that Gen. Winfield Scott was sent to remove them by force. He took command, his forces amounting to 7,000 men—regulars, militia and volunteers, with New Echota as his headquarters, May 10, 1838, only 2,000 Cherokees having gone voluntarily. Old people tell of the harrowing scenes which accompanied the hunting down and removal of these brave people who clung to their homes with all the passion of the Swiss.

REMOVAL FORTS. The following forts or stockades were built for the collection of the unwilling Cherokees: Fort Lindsay, on the south side of the Little Tennessee at the junction of the Nantahala; Fort Scott, at Aquone, twenty miles further up the Nantahala; Fort Montgomery, at what is now Robbinsville; Fort Hembrie, at what is now Hayesville; Fort Delaney, at Old Valleytown, and Fort Butler, at Murphy.

WHY SOME WERE ALLOWED TO REMAIN. Old man Tsali, or Charley, with his wife, his brother and his three sons and their families, was seized and taken to a stockade near the junction of the Tuckaseegee and the Little Tennessee rivers, where they spent the night, during which their squaws concealed knives and tomahawks about their clothing. When this band, escorted by soldiers, reached the mouth of what is now called Paine's branch, opposite Tuskeegee creek, in the Little Tennessee, the squaws passed the knives and hatchets to the men, and they fell upon the soldiers and killed two of them upon the spot, and so mortally wounded a third, Geddings by name, that he died at Calhoun, Tenn. Still another soldier was struck on the back of his head with a tomahawk, and so hurt that although he retained his seat upon his horse, he died three miles below at what is now called Fairfax, on the right bank of the Little Tennessee. Two stones still mark his grave, while the two who were killed at Paine's branch were buried there. If the skirts of the coat of the lieutenant in charge had not torn away when he was seized on each side by an Indian, it is likely that he would have been dragged from his horse and killed, too. But he escaped, and the Indians went immediately to the Great Smoky mountains scarcely ten miles away, and their recapture by the heavy dragoons sent after them within a short time was impossible. These soldiers camped just below where Burton Welch used to live, one and a half miles below Bushnel, and a mountain peak nearby on which they stationed sentinels, is still called Watch Mountain. In fact, these escaping Indians had spent the night at the house of Burton Welch's father when their squaws hid the weapons in their skirts. It is said that the late Col. W. H. Thomas had accompanied this party as far as the mouth of Noland's creek, where he left them for the purpose of getting another small party to join them the next day; and that if he had continued with Old Charley's party it is probable that no attempt would have been made to

escape, such was his influence over them. The names of
the male Indians who escaped were Charley, Alonzo, Jake,
George and a boy named Washington, but pronounced by
the Cherokees Wasituna. Old Charley's squaw was named
Nancy.

TERMS OF COMPROMISE. Mr. James Mooney's account
in the Nineteenth Ethnological report states that after Gen.
Scott became convinced that his soldiers could not recapture
Old Charley and his band, he made an agreement with Col.
Thomas to the effect that if he would cause the arrest of Old
Charley and his adult sons he would use his influence at Washington to get permission that all who had not yet been removed
should remain. Also, that Col. Thomas went to the leader
of those who had not been captured, Utsala or "Lichen," by
name, who had made his headquarters at the head of Oconaluftee, and told him that if he assisted in bringing in Charley
and his band, Utsali and his followers, 1,000 in number,
would be allowed to remain. Utsali consented and Thomas
returned and reported to Gen. Scott, who offered to furnish
an escort for Thomas on a proposed visit to Charley, who
was hiding in a cave of the Great Smoky mountains. But
Thomas declined the escort and went alone to the cave and
got Charley to consent to surrender voluntarily, which he
did shortly afterwards, thus making a vicarious sacrifice for
the rest of his people.

AN EYE WITNESSES' ACCOUNT. But Mr. and Mrs. Burton
Welch used to tell an altogether different story. They were
living there at the time, and presumably knew much more
than those who got their information at second hand sixty
years later. Their account is that Utsali and his followers
ran Old Charley and his sons down and brought them to Gen.
Scott's soldiers; but insisted on killing them themselves instead
of having them shot by the soldiers. But they had not been
captured together, Alonzo, Jake and George having been
caught first at the head of Forney's creek, and shot at a point
on the right bank of the Little Tennessee nearly opposite
the mouth of Panther creek, and just below Burton Welch's
home, where Jake gave a soldier ten cents to give to his squaw,
that being all he had on earth to leave her. The three trees
to which they were tied are now dead, but Burton Welch,
who when a boy witnessed the execution, used to declare that

these trees never grew any larger after having been made to serve as stakes for the shedding of human blood. These three Indians are buried in one grave near by, but there is now nothing to mark the spot.

OLD CHARLEY IS KILLED AND HIS SQUAW MOURNS. It was some time afterwards that Old Charley was caught in the Smokies, brought to within a short distance below what is now Bryson City and shot by Indians. Mrs. Welch, who was a first cousin of Captain James P. Sawyer of Asheville, saw Old Charley killed. This was before her marriage to Burton Welch, and she remembers that Charley had a white cloth tied around his forehead, and that she saw it stain red before she heard the report of the guns of the firing squad. The fugitive squaws were never punished. But Charley's squaw came to Mrs. Welch's father's house, where she was shown Old Charley's grave. She sat down beside it and piled up the sand with her hands until she made a mound, and then rocked herself to and fro and cried. Mrs. Welch went shortly afterwards to Old Charley's former home, one mile from the mouth of the Nantahala river. She spoke of the deserted look of the place, the little cabin with its open door, and old Nancy's spinning-wheel, her loom and warping bars, while outside, in the chimney corner, was Old Charley's plough-stock and harness, the traces of which had been made of hickory bark.

DID THE GOVERNMENT WINK AT THIS COMPROMISE? As it seemed exceedingly improbable that the government would deliberately violate the terms of a treaty that had been solemnly made with the Cherokees without the approval of the Senate, and allow a thousand Cherokees to remain behind, especially after General Jackson had emphatically refused to allow any of them to remain on any terms, the Commissioner of Indian Affairs was asked for any official information that might be on file in his office concerning this matter, with this result: "It is true that by supplemental articles of agreement pre-emption rights and reservations provided for the Cherokees who remained east of the Mississippi were relinquished and declared void. (See 7 Stat. L, 488) However, many of the Indians did remain east of the Mississippi and the Act of July 29, 1848, (9 Stat. L., 264) provided for the setting aside of a fund for these Indians, the interest of which was to be paid them annually until their removal west of the

Mississippi, when the principal was to be paid them." This
letter is dated January 29, 1913, and was supplemental to
another of January 21, 1913, in which this language is used:
"You are advised that nothing has been found in the files
of this office regarding the alleged agreement of General Scott
to allow part of the Cherokees to remain in North Carolina
on condition that they surrender Old Charlie and his sons."
Again, on February 27, 1913, he wrote: "I have of course
no objection to your quoting all or any part of office letters
to you on this subject. As to your following these letters
with the quotation given in your letter, I would rather not
express an opinion, since I had a search of the records made
and found nothing about the alleged agreement to allow
certain of the Cherokees to remain east of the Mississippi.
I would not be warranted in saying that such an agreement
was not made, since there were many things happening in the
Indian country about that period of which this office has no
record."

RECOGNITION OF THE RIGHTS OF THE EASTERN BAND. On
August 6, 1846, a treaty was concluded at Washington by
which the rights of the Eastern Cherokees to a participation
in the benefits of the New Echota treaty of 1835 were distinctly recognized, and provision made for the final adjustment of all unpaid and pending claims due under that treaty;
the government having insisted before that time that those
rights were conditional upon their removal to the West. Col.
W. H. Thomas then took charge of the Eastern Band. [6]

WILLIAM HOLLAND THOMAS. He was born in 1805 in
Haywood county. His father was of a Welch family,
fought at Kings Mountain under Col. Campbell, and was
related to Zachary Taylor. His mother was descended from
a Maryland family of Revolutionary stock. He was an only
and posthumous child, his father having been accidentally
drowned a short time before he was born. When twelve
years old he was engaged to tend an Indian trading store on
Soco creek by Felix Walker, son of the congressman who made
a national reputation by "talking for Buncombe." Here
he studied law, and was duly admitted to practice. He was
adopted by Yonaguska, the Cherokee chief, and was called
Will-Usdi, or "Little Will." He learned the spoken and written language, acquiring the Sequoya syllabary shortly after its

invention. Soon after the removal of the Cherokees Thomas bought a fine farm near Whittier, and built a home which he called Stekoa, after the Indian town on the same site which had been destroyed by Rutherford in 1776. At the time of the removal he owned five trading stores, viz: at Quallatown, at Murphy, at Charleston, Tenn., at Robbinsville and at Webster. As agent for the Cherokees he bought the five towns for them at Bird-town, Paint-town, Wolf-town, Yellow-hill, and Big Cove. He drew up a simple form of government for them, which was executed by Yonaguska till his death and afterwards by Thomas. In 1848 he entered the State Senate, and inaugurated a system of road improvement and was the father of the Western North Carolina railroad. He voted for secession in 1861, and in 1862 organized the Thomas Legion, composed of Cherokees and white citizens. After the war his health failed. His conduct of Cherokee affairs was settled by arbitrators, and it was found that the Indians had lost nothing, and had gained largely under his leadership. Col. Thomas, with 300 Indians and Col. James R. Love with 300 white soldiers, confronted Col. Bartlett of New York in April, 1865, near Waynesville. At sight of the Indians and after hearing their yells Bartlett agreed to surrender, and Col. Thomas paroled his men, allowing them to retain their side arms.[7] Col. Thomas died May 12, 1893.

THE LATE CAPTAIN JAMES W. TERRELL. "In 1852 (Capt.) James W. Terrell was engaged by (Col. W. H.) Thomas, then in the State Senate, to take charge of his store at Qualla, and remained associated with him and in close contact with the Indians from then until after the close of the war, assisting, as special United States Agent, in the disbursement of the interest payments, and afterward as a Confederate officer in the organization of the Indian companies, holding a commission as captain of Company A, Sixty-ninth North Carolina Confederate infantry. Being of an investigating bent, Captain Terrell was led to give attention to the customs and mythology of the Cherokee, and to accumulate a fund of information on the subject seldom possessed by a white man."

NORTH CAROLINA GIVES PERMISSION. "In 1855 Congress directed the per capita payment to the East Cherokees of the removal fund established for them in 1848, provided that North Carolina should first give assurance that they would be allowed to remain permanently in that State. This assurance, however, was not given until 1866, and the money was therefore not distributed, but remained in the treasury until 1875, when it was made applicable to the purchase of lands and the quieting of titles for the benefit of the Indians."

LANMAN, DANIEL WEBSTER'S SECRETARY. In the spring of 1848 the author, Lanman, visited the East Cherokees and has left an interesting account of their condition at the time, together with a description of their ball-plays, dances, and customs generally, having been the guest of Colonel Thomas, of whom he speaks as the guide, counselor, and friend of the Indians, as well as their business agent and chief, so that the connection was like that existing between a father and his children. He puts the number of Indians at about 800 Cherokee and 100 Catawba on the "Quallatown" reservation— the name being in use thus early—with 200 more Indians residing in the more westerly portion of the State. Of their general condition he says :

CONDITION OF INDIANS IN 1848. "About three-fourths of the entire population can read in their own language, and, though the majority of them understand English, a very few can speak the language. They practice, to a considerable extent, the science of agriculture, and have acquired such a knowledge of the mechanic arts as answers them for all ordinary purposes, for they manufacture their own clothing, their own ploughs, and other farming utensils, their own axes, and even their own guns. Their women are no longer treated as slaves, but as equals; the men labor in the fields and their wives are devoted entirely to household employments. They keep the same domestic animals that are kept by their white neighbors, and cultivate all the common grains of the country. They are probably as temperate as any other class of people on the face of the earth, honest in their business intercourse, moral in their thoughts, words, and deeds, and distinguished for their faithfulness in performing the duties of religion. They are chiefly Methodists and Baptists, and have regularly ordained ministers, who preach to them on every Sabbath, and they have also abandoned many of their more senseless superstitions. They have their own court and try their criminals by a regular jury. Their judges and lawyers are chosen from among themselves. They keep in order the public roads leading through their settlement. By a law of the State they have a right to vote, but seldom exercise that right, as they do not like the idea of being identified with any of the political parties. Excepting on festive days, they dress after the manner of the white man, but far more picturesquely. They live in small log houses of their own construction, and have everything they need or desire in the way of food. They are, in fact, the happiest community that I have yet met with in this southern country."

SALALI. Among the other notables Lanman speaks thus of Salili, "Squirrel," a born mechanic of the band, who died only a few years since :

"He is quite a young man and has a remarkably thoughtful face He is the blacksmith of his nation, and with some assistance supplies the whole of Qualla town with all their axes and plows; but what is more, he has manufactured a number of very superior rifles and pistols, including stock, barrel, and lock, and he is also the builder of grist mills, which grind all the corn which his people eat. A specimen of his workmanship in the way of a rifle may be seen at the Patent Office in Washington, where it was deposited by Mr. Thomas; and I believe Salali is the first Indian who ever manufactured an entire gun. But when it is remembered that he never received a particle of education in any of the mechanic arts, but is entirely self-taught, his attainments must be considered truly remarkable."

COLONEL THOMAS THWARTS GENERAL KIRBY SMITH. "From 1855 until after the Civil War we find no official notice of the East Cherokees, and our information must be obtained from other sources. It was, however, a most momentous period in their history. At the outbreak of the war Thomas was serving his seventh consecutive term in the State Senate. Being an ardent Confederate sympathizer, he was elected a delegate to the convention which passed the secession ordinance, and immediately after voting in favor of that measure resigned from the Senate in order to work for the Southern cause. As he was already well advanced in years it is doubtful if his effort would have gone beyond the raising of funds and other supplies but for the fact that at this juncture an effort was made by the Confederate General Kirby Smith to enlist the East Cherokees for active service.

KIRBY SMITH'S EMISSARY. "The agent sent for this purpose was Washington Morgan, known to the Indians as Aganstata, son of that Colonel Gideon Morgan who had commanded the Cherokee at the Horseshoe Bend. By virtue of his Indian blood and historic ancestry he was deemed the most fitting emissary for the purpose. Early in 1862 he arrived among the Cherokee, and by appealing to old-time memories so aroused the war spirit among them that a large number declared themselves ready to follow wherever he led. Conceiving the question at issue in the war to be one that did not concern the Indians, Thomas had discouraged their participation in it and advised them to remain at home in quiet neutrality. Now, however, knowing Morgan's reputation for reckless daring, he became alarmed at the possible result to them of such leadership. Forced either to see them go from his own protection or to lead them himself, he chose the latter alternative and proposed to them to enlist in the Confederate legion which he was about to organize. His object, as he himself has stated, was to keep them out of danger so far as possible by utilizing them as scouts and home guards through the mountains, away from the path of the large armies. Nothing of this was said to the Indains, who might not have been satisfied with such an arrangement. Morgan went back alone and the Cherokee enrolled under the command of their white chief.

FORMATION OF THOMAS'S LEGION. "The 'Thomas Legion,' recruited in 1862 by William H. Thomas for the Confederate service and commanded by him as colonel, consisted originally of one infantry regiment of ten companies (Sixty-ninth North Carolina Infantry), one infantry battalion of six companies, one cavalry battalion of eight companies (First North Carolina Cavalry Battalion), one field battery (Light Battery) of 103 officers and men, and one company of engineers; in all about 2,800 men. The infantry battalion was recruited toward the close of the war to a full regiment of ten companies . . . and two other companies of the infantry regiment recruited later were composed almost entirely of East Cherokee Indians, most of the commissioned officers being white men. The whole number of Cherokee thus enlisted was nearly four hundred, or about every able-bodied man in the tribe."

ONE SECRET OF COL. THOMAS'S SUCCESS. Many have wondered how Col. Thomas could so soon have obtained complete control of all the affairs of the Eastern Band of Cherokees, and how he could have obtained from the Confederate government its consent for the organization of these Indians into an independent legion, subject almost entirely to his control, and required to operate only in the restricted territory immediately surrounding their reservation at Quallytown. But when it is remembered that his mother was Temperance Calvert, and that he himself was closely related to Zachary Taylor, President of the United States, whose daughter became the wife of Jefferson Davis, President of the Southern Confederacy, much that was incomprehensible becomes plain. Indeed, all the so called Colvards of Ashe, Graham and Haywood counties claim that their real name was originally Calvert; that they are descendants of the Calverts of Maryland; and the late Captain James W. Terrell always insisted that Temperance Calvert was a grand-niece of Lord Baltimore himself. Col. Thomas was also first cousin to John Strother, whose family was one of influence and standing in Virginia in former days. (See N. C. University Magazine for May, 1899, pp. 291 to 295.)

CHEROKEE SCOUTS AND HOME GUARDS. "In accordance with Thomas's plan the Indians were employed chiefly as scouts and home guards in the mountain region along the Tennessee-Carolina border, where, according to the testimony of Colonel Stringfield, they did good work and service for the South. The most important engagement in which they were concerned occurred at Baptist gap, Tennessee, September 15, 1862, where Lieutenant Astugataga, a splendid specimen of Indian manhood, was killed in a charge. The Indians were furious at his death, and before they could be restrained they scalped one or two of the Federal dead. For this action ample apologies were afterwards given by their superior officers. The war, in fact, brought out all the latent Indian in their nature. Before starting to the front every man consulted an oracle stone to learn whether or not he might hope to return in safety. The start was celebrated with a grand old-time war-dance at the townhouse on Soco, . . . the Indians being painted and feathered in good old style, Thomas himself frequently assisting as master of ceremonies. The ball-play, too, was not forgotten, and on one occasion a detachment of Cherokees, left to guard a bridge, became so engrossed in the excitement of the game as to narrowly escape capture by a

sudden dash of the Federals. Owing to Thomas's care for
their welfare, they suffered but slightly in actual battle,
although a number died of hardship and disease. When the
Confederates evacuated eastern Tennessee, in the winter of
1863-64, some of the white troops of the legion, with one or
two of the Cherokee companies, were shifted to western Virginia, and by assignment to other regiments a few of the
Cherokee were present at the final siege and surrender of
Richmond. The main body of the Indians, with the rest
of the Thomas Legion, crossed over into North Carolina and
did service protecting the western border until the close of
the war, when they surrendered on parole at Waynesville,
North Carolina, in May 1865, all those of the command being
allowed to keep their guns. It is claimed by their officers
that they were the last of the Confederate forces to surrender.
About fifty of the Cherokee veterans still survive (in 1899), nearly
half of whom, under conduct of Colonel Stringfield, attended
the Confederate reunion at Louisville, Kentucky, in 1900,
where they attracted much attention.

CONFEDERATE CONGRESS PROVIDES FUNDS. "In 1863,
by resolution of February 12, the Confederate House of Representatives called for information as to the number and
condition of the East Cherokee, and their pending relations
with the Federal government at the beginning of the war,
with a view to continuing these relations under Confederate
auspices. In response to this inquiry a report was submitted
by the Confederate Commissioner of Indian Affairs, S. S. Scott,
based on information furnished by Colonel Thomas and Captain
James W. Terrell, their former disbursing agent, showing
that interest upon the 'removal and subsistence fund' established in 1848 had been paid annually up to and including
the year 1859, at the rate of $3.20 per capita, or an aggregate,
exclusive of disbursing agent's commission, of $4,838.40 an-
nually, based upon the original Mullay enumeration of 1,517.

"Upon receipt of this report it was enacted by the Con-
federate Congress that the sum of $19,352.36 be paid the
East Cherokee to cover the interest period of four years from
May 23, 1860 to May 23, 1864.

CAPTURED CHEROKEES DESERT CONFEDERACY. "In a
skirmish near Bryson City (then Charleston), Swain county,
North Carolina, about a year after enlistment, a small party

of Cherokees—perhaps a dozen in number—were captured by a detachment of Union troops and carried to Knoxville, where, having become dissatisfied with their experience in the Confederate service, they were easily persuaded to go over to the Union side. Through the influence of their principal man, Diganeski, several others were induced to desert to the Union army, making about thirty in all. As a part of the Third North Carolina Mounted Volunteer Infantry, they served with the Union forces in the same region until the close of the war, when they returned to their homes to find their tribesmen so bitterly incensed against them that for some time their lives were in danger. Eight of these were still alive in 1900.

AFTER CIVIL WAR. "Shortly after this event Colonel Thomas was compelled by physical and mental infirmity to retire from further active participation in the affairs of the East Cherokee, after more than half a century spent in intimate connection with them, during the greater portion of which time he had been their most trusted friend and adviser. Their affairs at once became the prey of confusion and factional strife, which continued until the United States stepped in as arbiter.

CHEROKEES ADOPT NEW GOVERNMENT, 1870. "On December 9, 1868, a general council of the East Cherokee assembled at Cheowa, in Graham county, North Carolina, took preliminary steps toward the adoption of a regular form of tribal government under a constitution. N. J. Smith, afterward principal chief, was clerk of the council. The new government was formally inaugurated on December 1, 1870.

STATUS OF INDIAN LANDS. "The status of the lands held by the Indians had now become a matter of serious concern. As has been stated, the deeds had been made out by Thomas in his own name, as the State laws at that time forbade Indian ownership of real estate. In consequence of his losses during the war and his subsequent disability, the Thomas properties, of which the Cherokee lands were technically a part, had become involved, so that the entire estate had passed into the hands of creditors, the most important of whom, William Johnston, had obtained sheriff's deeds in 1869 for all of these Indian lands under three several judgments against Thomas, aggregating $33,887.11. To adjust the matter so as to secure title and possession to the Indians, Congress in 1870 authorized suit to be brought in their name for the recovery of their interest. This suit was begun in May, 1873, in the United States Circuit Court for western North Carolina. A year later the matters in dispute were submitted by agreement to a board of arbitrators, whose award was confirmed by the court in November, 1874.

LAND STATUS SETTLED BY ARBITRATION. "The award finds that Thomas had purchased with Indian funds a tract estimated to contain 50,000 acres on Oconaluftee river and Soco creek, and known as the Qualla boundary, together with a number of individual tracts outside the boundary; that the Indians were still indebted to Thomas toward the purchase of the Qualla boundary lands for the sum of $18,250, from which should be deducted $6,500 paid by them to Johnston to release titles, with interest to date of award, making an aggregate of $8,486, together with a further sum of $2,478, which had been intrusted to Terrell, the business clerk and assistant of Thomas, and by him turned over to Thomas, as creditor of the Indians, under power of attorney, this latter sum, with interest to date of award, aggregating $2,697.89; thus leaving a balance due from the Indians to Thomas or his legal creditor, Johnston, of $7,066.11. The award declares that Johnston should be allowed to hold the lands bought by him only as security for the balance due him until paid, and that on the payment of the said balance of $7,066.11, with interest at six per cent from the date of the award, the Indians should be entitled to a clear conveyance from him of the legal title to all the lands embraced within the Qualla boundary.

PART OF SUBSISTENCE FUND USED TO CLEAR TITLE. "To enable the Indians to clear off this lien on their lands and for other purposes, Congress in 1875 directed that as much as remained of the 'removal and subsistence fund' set apart for their benefit in 1848 should be used 'in perfecting the titles to the lands awarded to them, and to pay the costs, expenses, and liabilities attending their recent litigations, also to purchase and extinguish the titles of any white persons to lands within the general boundaries alotted to them by the court, and for the education, improvement, and civilization of their people.' In accordance with this authority the unpaid balance and interest due Johnston, amounting to $7,242.76, was paid him in the same year, and shortly afterward there was purchased on behalf of the Indians some fifteen thousand acres additional, the Commissioner of Indian Affairs being constituted trustee for the Indians.   For the better protection of the Indians the lands were made inalienable except by assent of the council and upon approval of the President of the United States.

DEPARTMENT OF INDIAN AFFAIRS ASSUMES CONTROL.   "The titles and boundaries having been adjusted, the Indian Office assumed regular supervision of East Cherokee affairs, and in June, 1875, the first agent since the retirement of Thomas was sent out in the person of W. C. McCarthy. He found the Indians, according to his report, destitute and discouraged, almost without stock or farming tools.   There were no schools, and very few full-bloods could speak English, although to their credit nearly all could read and write their own language, the parents teaching the children. Under his authority a distribution was made of stock animals, seed wheat, and farming tools, and several schools were started. In the next year, however, the agency was discontinued and the educational interests of the band turned over to the State School Superintendent.

THE OLD INDIAN FRIENDS, THE QUAKERS. "The neglected condition of the East Cherokee having been brought to the attention of those old time friends of the Indian, the Quakers, through an appeal made in their behalf by members of that society residing in North Carolina, the Western Yearly Meeting, of Indiana, volunteered to undertake the work of civilization and education. On May 31, 1881, representatives of the Friends entered into a contract with the Indians, subject to approval by the Government, to establish and continue among them for ten years an industrial school and other common schools, to be supported in part from the annual interest of the trust fund held by the Government to the credit of the East Cherokee and in part by funds furnished by the Friends themselves. Through the efforts of Barnabas C. Hobbs, of the Western Yearly Meeting, a yearly contract to the same effect was entered into with the Commissioner of Indian Affairs later in the same year, and was renewed by successive commissioners to cover the period of ten years ending June 30, 1892, when the contract system was terminated and the Government assumed direct control. Under the joint arrangement, with some aid at the outset from the North Carolina Meeting, work was begun in 1881 by Thomas Brown with several teachers sent out by the Indiana Friends, who established a small training school at the agency headquarters at Cherokee, and several day schools in the outlying settlements. He was succeeded three years later by H. W. Spray, an experienced educator, who, with a corps of efficient assistants and greatly enlarged facilities, continued to do good work for the elevation of the Indians until the close of the contract system eight years later. After an interregnum, during which the schools suffered from frequent changes, he was reappointed as government agent and superintendent in 1898, a position which he still holds in 1901. To the work conducted under his auspices the East Cherokee owe much of what they have today of civilization and enlightenment.

EASTERN BAND SUES IN COURT OF CLAIMS. "The East Cherokee had never ceased to contend for a participation in the rights and privileges accruing to the western nation under treaties with the government. In 1882 a special agent had been appointed to investigate their claims and in the following year, under authority of Congress, the eastern band of Cherokee brought suit in the Court of Claims against the United States and the Cherokee Indians. . . . The case was decided adversely to the eastern band, first by the Court of Claims in 1885, and finally, on appeal, by the Supreme Court on March 1, 1886, that court holding in its decision that the Cherokee in North Carolina had dissolved their connection with the Cherokee nation and ceased to be a part of it when they refused to accompany the main body at the Removal, and that if Indians in North Carolina or in any state east of the Mississippi wished to enjoy the benefits of the common property of the Cherokee Nation in any form whatever they must be readmitted to citizenship in the Cherokee Nation and comply with its constitution and laws.

EASTERN BAND INCORPORATED. "In order to acquire a more definite legal status, the Cherokee residing in North Carolina—being practically all those of the eastern band having genuine Indian interests—became a corporate body under the laws of the state in 1889. In 1894 the long-standing litigation between the East Cherokee and a number of creditors and claimants to Indian lands within and adjoining the Qualla boundary was finally settled by a compromise by which the several white tenants and claimants within the boundary agreed to execute a quitclaim and vacate on payment to them by the Indians of sums aggregating $24,552, while for another disputed adjoining tract of 33,000 acres the United States agreed to pay, for the Indians, at the rate of $1.25 per acre. The necessary government approval having been obtained, Congress appropriated a sufficient amount for carrying into effect the agreement, thus at last completing a perfect and unencumbered title to all the lands claimed by the Indians, with the exception of a few outlying tracts of comparative unimportance.

EXACT LEGAL STATUS STILL IN DISPUTE. "The exact legal status of the East Cherokee is still a matter of dispute, they being at once wards of the government, citizens of the United States, and (in North Carolina) a corporate body under state laws. They pay real estate taxes and road service, exercise the voting privilege and are amenable to local courts, but do not pay poll tax or receive any pauper assistance from the counties; neither can they make free contracts or alienate their lands. Under their tribal constitution they are governed by a principal and an assistant chief, elected for a term of four years, with an executive council appointed by the chief, and sixteen councilors elected by the various settlements for a term of two years. The annual council is held in October at Cherokee, on the reservation, the proceedings being in the Cherokee language and recorded by their clerk in the Cherokee alphabet, as well as in English.

PRESENT MATERIAL CONDITIONS. "The majority are fairly comfortable, far above the condition of most Indian tribes, and but little, if any, behind their white neighbors. In literary ability they may even be said to surpass them, as in addition to the result of nearly twenty years of school work among the younger people, nearly all the men and some of the women can read and write their own language. All wear civilized costumes, though an occasional pair of moccasins is seen, while the women find means to gratify the racial love of color in the wearing of red bandanna kerchiefs in place of bonnets. The older people still cling to their ancient rites and sacred traditions, but the dance and the ballplay wither and the Indian day is nearly spent."

EASTERN BAND TRY TO SELL TIMBER. Since Mr. Moody's concluding words were written the courts have managed still more to confuse the legal status of the Cherokees, for in September, 1893, the Eastern Band of Cherokee Indians, acting as a corporation of the State of North Carolina, by virtue of Chapter 211, Private Laws of 1889, sold and conveyed to David L. Boyd certain timber on the Cathcart tract of the Qualla boundary, containing about 30,000 acres. In January, 1894, David L. Boyd sold said trees to H. M. Dickson and William T. Mason, who afterwards conveyed them to the Dickson-Mason Lumber Company. Before beginning to cut these trees the Dickson-Mason Company was apprised of the fact that the Department of the Interior of the United States had not sanctioned the sale of this timber, and refused to ratify the contract. This company, on the other hand, had been advised that the band of Indians were citizens of North Carolina and not tribal Indians, and, therefore, had the right to convey the trees; and desiring to have the question tested by the courts, put a few men to work cutting the timber, at the same time notifying the agents of the Government and the United States District Attorney of the fact. The government instituted a suit in which it asked a perpetual injunction against the Dickson-Mason Company; but at the next term of the United States Court at Asheville, in November, 1894, the government voluntarily took a nonsuit in the cause, the Attorney General holding that "the legal status of the Indians in question is that of citizens of North Carolina; that they have been in all respects citizens since the date of or soon after the treaty with the Cherokees of 1885 [1835?], and this with the consent of the United States expressed in that treaty, by the election of the Indians and the consent of North Carolina. They have voted at all elections for half a century, and are citizens of the United States. It seems clear that Congress could not, by the Act of July 27, 1868, or otherwise (if such was the intention) make of them an Indian tribe or place them under the control of the United States as Indians, any more effectually than if they had been white citizens of Massachusetts or Georgia (Eastern Band *Cherokee Indians v. the United States and Cherokee Nation,*

117 U. S. 228). Neither could such citizens of North Carolina make themselves a tribe of Indians within that State."

INTERIOR DEPARTMENT INTERVENES. Accordingly, the Dickson-Mason Company began making large and expensive preparations for cutting the timber on the Cathcart boundary. But, it turned out later, that the Interior Department was not satisfied with this disposition of the matter and commenced another action based on the same facts, but alleging fraud in obtaining the Boyd contract from the Indians. Judge C. H. Simonton (in *U. S. v. Boyd*, 68 Fed. Rep., 587) held that the Eastern Band of Cherokees were not tribal Indians, but wards of the Government which, like any other guardian, had the right to see that any contract made by them was for their benefit and not to their detriment. In an opinion filed by him he held that "the case of the Cherokee trust fund (117 U. S., 288) does not conflict with these views. That case decides that this Eastern Band of Cherokee Indians is not a part of the nation of Cherokees with which this Government treats, and that they have no recognized separate political existence. But, at the same time, their distinct unity is recognized, and the fostering care of the Government over them as such distinct unit. This being so, the United States have the right in their own Courts to bring such suits as may be necessary to protect these Indians."

GOVERNMENT APPEALS FROM DECISION. The case was then referred to Hon. R. M. Douglas, Standing Master, who, in November, 1895, found that the price paid for the timber ($15,000) was fair and that there was no fraud in making the contract. This report was confirmed, but the Government appealed to the Circuit Court of Appeals from so much of the decree as held that the Court had the power to permit the parties to carry out the contract without the sanction of the Interior Department, upon the ground that "these Indians were tribal Indians and embraced within the terms of congressional enactments for the protection of tribal Indians." This contention was sustained on appeal (see *U. S. v. Boyd and others*, 83 Fed. Rep., 547), though "no reference is made by the Court to the decision of the United States Supreme Court in the case of the *Eastern Band of the Cherokee Indians v. United States and Cherokee Nation* (117 U. S. Rep., 288) where the whole subject is discussed, and where, on page 309, the Court says : '. . . . they have never been recognized by the United States; no treaty has been made with them; they can pass no laws; they are citizens of that State [North Carolina] and bound by its laws.'"

LUMBER COMPANY APPEALS. From this decision the Dickson‑Mason Company appealed to the United States Supreme Court in May, 1888, but before its perfection the Interior Department re-investigated the contract of sale of the timber, and fully ratified the same. The appeal, therefore, was abandoned; and the anomaly remains that the Cherokees are citizens of North Carolina, according to the United States Supreme Court, while they are still tribal Indains whose contracts are void without the approval of the Department of the Interior, according to the decision of an inferior tribunal, that of the U. S. Court of Appeals. (For a full report of these cases see Private Calender No. 725, 61st Congress, 3d Session, House Rep. Report No. 1926, January 17, 1911.) Thus each party to this proceeding obtained what was sought by it; the Dickson-Mason company the right to cut and remove the timber, and the Interior Department a decision which gives it a right to review every contract made by the Eastern Band of Cherokees. And it is well that this is so, for while there was no fraud in this particular contract, nevertheless, there may be in contracts yet to be made.

UNITED STATES VACILLATES, STATE STANDS FIRM. The above is the work of the United States authorities. So far as North Carolina is concerned, her courts have finally and forever settled the status of the Cherokee Indians in her borders as citizens of this State, as will fully appear by reference to *Frazier v. Cherokee Indians*, 146 N. C., 477, and *State v. Wolfe*, 145 N. C., 440.

FINAL DISTRIBUTION. "In 1910 was distributed to the Eastern Band of Cherokees about $133 *per capita*.[8] This is the final payment on their claims against the Government for a balance due them under the New Echota treaty of 1835-1836, under which the Government had promised to pay the Eastern Band of Cherokees (before the removal) $5,000,000 for a release to all of their lands east of the Mississippi river, part of which was to be paid in cash and the balance invested in bonds and held for their benefit. But there is another provision under which each Indian was to be paid for transportation to the Indian Territory and for one year's subsistence after arriving there. There was a question as to whether this money was to be in addition to the $5,000,000 to be paid for the lands or was to be deducted from that fund. In a subsequent settlement with the Government (1852) the Indians gave a receipt which was in full of all claims and demands, although at that time the question of this transportation and subsistence payment had not been discussed. [9] It was afterwards raised, however, but the United States claimed that the Cherokees were estopped by their receipt above referred to. Thus matters stood when Hon. Hoke Smith, Secretary of the Interior under President Cleveland, sought to purchase of the Western Band the Cherokee Strip of the Indian Territory (25 Stat., 1005 of 1889). The Cherokees then refused to consider any proposition to sell until the Government agreed to allow them to prove any claim they might still have against the Government under the New Echota treaty. This the Government agreed to December 19, 1891, and the Cherokee Strip was sold. The Interior Department investigated their claims and reported that there was due the Indians $1,111,284.71 which, at five per cent from 12th June, 1838, amounted to about $4,500,000. But the Department of Justice decided against the admission of the Department of the Interior, the Attorney General holding that the receipt of 1852 estopped the Indians from setting up any further claims, March 2, 1893. Whereupon, Congress passed an act authorizing the Indians to set up their contentions before the Court of Claims, which decided in favor of the Indians. But the United States appealed to the Supreme Court, which sustained the Court of Claims, with some slight modifications. An effort was made to pay out this money *per stirpes*, but that was found to be impracticable and the payment had to be made *per capita*, owing to intermarriages between the Indians and the whites. According to the roll of 1851 the Eastern Band composed about one-ninth of the Cherokee Nation, but in the final payment they were found to be only about one-eighteenth of the whole. See *Eastern Cherokees v. United States*, No. 23214 Court of Claims, decided March 7, 1910."

WESTERN CHEROKEE NATION DISSOLVED. In 1887 Congress abandoned the reservation plan, and enacted the Land

Allotment Law, by which the land was divided into individual holdings to be held in trust by the government till each individual owner was considered competent to hold it in fee. This has now been done, the task of converting the Cherokees from a tribe into a body of individual owners of land having been commenced in 1902. Prior to that date, in 1898, Congress had passed the Curtis act providing for the valuation and allotment of the lands of the Five Civilized Tribes. In 1906 the legislative, and judicial departments of the Cherokees ceased; but the executive branch was kept in existence under Principal Chief W. C. Rogers. When Oklahoma became a state in 1907 all members of the tribe became citizens of the new state. By July 1, 1914, all community property had been converted into cash, amounting to about $600,000, or about $15 *per capita*, to 41,798 members, including about 2,000 full-blooded whites and 3,000 full-blooded negroes, descendants of slaves freed in 1865. The four other nations, Creek, Chickasaw, Seminole and Chocktaw, will soon pass into full citizenship also. The Cherokees were admittedly the most advanced native American race since the Spanish exterminated the Incas and Aztecs. Ethnologically the Cherokees are said to have been a branch of the Iroquois family, though never allied with them politically. It is claimed that they were driven from their original home in the Appomattox basin, Virginia, into Georgia, the Carolinas and Tennessee. When the Supreme Court of the United States sustained the Cherokee treaties, Andrew Jackson remarked: "Now let John Marshall enforce his decision."

POPULATION. There are at this time in Swain, Jackson, Cherokee and Graham counties, North Carolina, a considerable number of Cherokee Indians. "The total population of the Cherokees, as given by the superintendent in charge for 1911, is 2,015. The enrollment in the different schools is as follows:

Cherokee Indian School (Boarding)...................... 175
Birdtown Day School................................. 45
Snow Bird Gap (Day School)......................... 34
Little Snow Bird..................................... 20

"A considerable number attend public schools where the degree of Indian blood is small. The non-reservation boarding schools provided by the Federal Government also have a number of pupils from this reservation."

INDIAN WEAPONS. From the Handbook of American Indians (Bulletin 30 of the Bureau of American Ethnology, Smithsonian Institution, 90-94) can be obtained a full description of the arrowheads, arrows, bows and quivers, etc., of the American Indians; with pictures of arrowshaft straighteners, stone arrowshaft rubber, and the various methods of arrow release. It is generally supposed that the process by which the Indians manufactured the arrow- and spear-heads out of flint is among the lost arts; but Dr. W. H. Holmes, head curator of the department of anthropology of the Smithsonian Institution, wrote me, August 29, 1913, that "the processes referred to are well known and have been observed in practice among a number of western tribes, and the art has been acquired by numerous students of the subject, among others myself. In preparing a work for publication in the near future, I have described twenty processes practiced by different primitive peoples. The flint is usually quarried from pits at Flint Ridge, Ohio, and in many parts of Georgia and the Carolinas. It is broken into fragments and the thin favorable ones are chosen and the shape is roughed out by means of small hammerstones. These hammerstones are found in great numbers in flint bearing regions and are globular in shape or discoidal. Sometimes they have pits in opposite sides to accommodate the thumb and fingers while in use. When the shape is roughed out by strokes of the hammer, and the edges are in approximate shape, a piece of hard bone or antler is taken and the flakes are struck off on the edges by means of quick, hard pressure with the bone point. Sometimes the implement being shaped is held in the hand, the hand being protected by a pad of buckskin. Again, the implement being shaped is laid upon a solid surface of wood or stone beneath which is a pad of buckskin and the flakes are broken off by downward pressure of the instrument."

CHEROKEE MYTHS.
(Condensed from the 19th Annual Report of the Bureau of Ethnology.)

ORIGIN OF THE MOUNDS. Were built for town-houses from which to witness dances and games, and be above freshets.

CHEOWA MAXIMA. A bald mountain at head of Cheowa river, was the place of hornets, from a monster hornet which nested there.

JOANNA BALD. A bald mountain between Graham and Cherokee, called "lizard place," from a great lizard with shining throat.

JUDACULLA OLD FIELD. On slope of Tennessee bald, where a giant of that name had had his residence and field.

JUDACULLA ROCK. On the north bank of Caney fork, a mile above Moses' creek, being a large soapstone slab covered with rude carvings.

NANTAHALA. A river in Macon, being a corruption of Nundayeli, or middle sun, because between the river banks the sun can be seen only at noonday. Others say it means a maiden's bosom.

NUGATSANI. A ridge below Yellow Hill, said to be the resort of fairies. The word denotes a gradual or gentle slope.

QUALLA. A name given a locality where there was a trading post because a woman named Polly lived there, the Indians pronouncing it Qually, being unable to articulate the letter *p*.

SOCO GAP. At the head of Soco creek, and means an ambush or where they were ambushed, from which point they watched for enemies approaching from the north. It was there they ambushed an invading party of Shawano. Hence the name.

STANDING INDIAN. A high peak at the head of Nantahala river, meaning "where the man stood" (Yunwitsulenunyi), from a rock that used to jut out from the summit, but is now broken off.

STEKOA. The W. H. Thomas farm above Whittier, the true meaning of which is lost. It does not mean "little fat," as some suppose.

SWANNANOA. It does not mean "beautiful," but is a corruption of Suwali-nunna (hi), Suwali trail, the Cherokee name, not of the stream, but of the trail crossing the gap to the country of the Ani-Suwali or Cheraw.

TUSQUITTEE BALD. A mountain in Clay, meaning "where the water-dogs laughed"; because a hunter thought he heard dogs laugh there, but found that their pond had dried up, and they were on their way to Nantahala river, saying their gills had dried up.

VENGEANCE CREEK. A south branch of Valley river, because of the cross looks of an Indian woman who lived there.

WAYAH GAP. In Nantahala mountains on road from Aquone to Franklin, and is Cherokee for wolf. A fight occurred here in 1776. Some call it Warrior gap.

WEBSTER. Used to be called Unadantiyi, or "Where they conjured," though the name properly belongs to a gap three miles east of Webster on trail up Scott's creek.

McNAIR'S GRAVE. Just inside the Tennessee line is a stone-walled grave, with a slab on which is an epitaph telling of the Removal heartbreak, having this inscription: "Sacred to the memory of David and Delilah A. McNair, who departed this life, the former on the 15th August, 1836, and the latter on the 30th November, 1838. Their children being members of the Cherokee nation and having to go with their people to the West, do leave this monument, not only to show their regard for their parents, but to guard their sacred ashes against the unhallowed intrusion of the white man."

NOTES.

[1]Condensed from Literary Digest, p. 472, September 21, 1912.
[2]Unless otherwise noted all in this chapter is based on the Nineteenth Annual Report of the Bureau of Ethnology, 1897, Part I.
[3]Roosevelt, Vol. I, p. 74.
[4]In the Lyceum for April, 1891. pp. 22-23, the late Col. A. T. Davidson gives an account of the burial of two brass field pieces by Rutherford's men in a swamp below the residence of the late Elam Slagle, and near the mouth of Warrior creek, so called because of the battle there.
[5]N. C. Booklet, for December, 1904.
[6]In Wheeler, Vol. II (pp. 205-6) is a letter from Col. Thomas to Hon. James Graham, dated October 15, 1838, in which he gives a brief account of the Eastern Band and why they were allowed to remain.
[7]Condensed from 19th An. Rep. Bureau Am. Ethnology, and N. C. Booklet, Vol. III, No. 2. These notes were from the Nineteenth Report, and I have already sufficiently stated that everything not otherwise noted (Note 2) is taken from that authority.
[8]Statement of Hon. Geo. H. Smathers, attorney for the Eastern Band, to J. P. A., May 28, 1912.
[9]See 9 Stat. L. 544-556-570-572; 40 Court of Claims, 281-252; 202 U. S. Rep., 101-130.

CHAPTER XXVII

THE CIVIL WAR PERIOD

INTRODUCTORY REMARKS. That there were many outrages committed on and near the Tennessee line during the Civil War is too well known to admit of doubt. That all the blame does not rest on one side alone is equally certain. These mountains were full of "outliers," as they were called, and they had to live somehow. They did not belong especially to either side; they simply wanted to keep out of the war. It was a great temptation to cold and hungry men on foot to steal horses, food, bedding and clothing, and many of them yielded to the desire. Raiding parties went into Tennessee from North Carolina and raiding parties from Tennessee came into the North Carolina mountains. The trails and wagon roads through these mountains were usually guarded by Confederate troops. When they could not capture those who were riding or driving horses and mules from one side to the other they shot them down. Toward the close of the war lawless men robbed those they thought had money or other valuables. That the names of those who figured in this unfortunate period as oppressors or oppressed should be preserved, as far as possible, is evident to all who appreciate the duties of impartial history. Therefore, not to keep alive unpleasant memories, but to preserve names, dates and events, some of these occurrences are here related. Some of them were attended with unnecessary cruelty, but no mention is made thereof. That some of the women at home had as hard a time as the men in the field is shown by Mrs. Margaret Walker's story. The facts given in this chapter are meant merely to supplement those given in "The North Carolina Regiments," published by the State in 1901.

NORTH CAROLINA IN THE CIVIL WAR. [1] From the address at Raleigh, May 10, 1904, by Hon. Theo. F. Davidson, the following is taken : "She [North Carolina] was next to the last state to secede from the Union, and in February, 1861, she voted against secession by 30,000 majority; yet, with a military population of 115,365, the State of North Carolina furnished to the Confederate army 125,000 men. . . . Of

(600)

the ten regiments on either side which sustained the heaviest loss in any one engagement during the war, Georgia, Alabama, Tennessee, Illinois, New York, Pennsylvania and New Jersey furnished one each, and North Carolina furnished three. North Carolina furnished from first to last one-fifth of the entire Confederate army, and at the surrender at Appomattox, one-half of the muskets stacked were from North Carolina. The last charge of the Army of Northern Virginia under Lee was made by North Carolina troops, and the last gun fired was by Flanner's battery from Wilmington, N. C. The men of North Carolina were found dead farthest up the blood-stained slopes of Gettysburg. 40,275 soldiers from North Carolina gave their lives to the Confederacy—more than one third of her entire military population, and a loss of more than double in percentage that sustained by the soldiers from any other state. Of this number 19,678 were killed upon the field of battle or died of wounds; and it is now a historical fact, questioned by none, that the greatest loss sustained by any regiment on either side during the war was that of the twenty-sixth North Carolina regiment at Gettysburg. [3] It carried into action 800 men and came out with eighty, who, with torn ranks and tattered flag, were still eager for the fray. The charge of the fifth North Carolina regiment at Williamsburg ranks in military history with that of the Light Brigade at Balaclava. That charge gave the regiment and its brave and illustrious commander, Col. D. K. McRae, to immortality." [2]

Carved on the Confederate monument at Raleigh are these words :

"FIRST AT BETHEL, FARTHEST AT GETTYSBURG AND CHICKA-
MAUGA, AND LAST AT APPOMATTOX."

These claims are amply sustained in Vol. I, "Literary and Historical Activities in North Carolina, 1900-1905," as follows: First at Bethel, by E. J. Hale (p. 427); Farthest to the Front at Gettysburg, by W. A. Montgomery (p. 432); Longstreet's Assault at Gettysburg, by W. R. Bond (p. 446); Farthest to the Front at Chickamauga, by A. C. Avery (p. 459); The Last at Appomattox, by Henry A. London (p. 471); The Last Capture of Guns, by E. J. Holt (p. 481), and Number of Losses of North Carolina Troops (p. 484).

ASHEVILLE A MILITARY CENTER. "During the War Between the States, Asheville became in a small way a military
center.[3] Confederate troops were from time to time encamped
at Camp Patton, at Camp Clingman on French Broad Avenue and Phillip street, on Battery Porter Hill (now called
Battery Park), at Camp Jeter (northeast and northwest corners of Cherry and Flint streets), and in the vicinity of Lookout Park. Fortifications were erected on Beaucatcher, Battery Porter, Woodfin street opposite the Oaks Hotel, Montford avenue near the residence of J. E. Rumbough, on the
hill near the end of Riverside drive north of T. S. Morrison's,
and on the ridge immediately east of the place where North
Main street last crosses Glenn's creek, now [1898] owned by the
children of the late N. W. Woodfin. At this last place, on
April 11th, 1865, a battle was fought between the Confederate troops at Asheville and a detachment of United States
troops, who came up the French Broad river. The latter was
defeated and compelled to return into Tennessee. This was
the Battle of Asheville.

WAR-TIME LOCATIONS IN ASHEVILLE. "The Confederate
postoffice was in the old Buck Hotel building on North Main
street.. The Confederate commissary was on the east side of
North Main street between the public square and College
street. This old building was afterwards removed to Patton
avenue, whence it was removed again to give way to a brick
building. The Confederate hospital stood on the grounds
afterwards occupied by the Legal building, where is now the
Citizen office.[4] The chief armories of the Confederate states
were at Richmond, Va., and Fayetteville, N. C., but there
were two smaller establishments, one at Asheville, N. C.,
and the other at Tallahassee, Ala. (1 Davis's Rise and Fall
of the Confederate Government, 480.)

CONFEDERATE ARMORY. "The armory at Asheville was in
charge of an Englishman by the name of Riley as chief ma-
chinist. It stood on the branch immediately east of where
Valley street crosses it. Here, when North Carolina was one
of the Confederate States of America, the Confederate flag
from a high flag-pole was constantly displayed. There it
floated in the breeze, and rested in the sunlight, the emblem—

>   Of liberty born of a patriot's dream,
>   Of a storm-cradled nation that fell.

"These buildings were burned by the United States troops when they entered the town in the latter part of April, 1865."

THE FLAG OF BETHEL. The flag of Bethel was made and presented to the Buncombe Riflemen by Misses Anna and Lillie Woodfin, Fanny and Annie Patton, Mary Gains and Kate Smith. It was made of their silk dresses. Miss Anna Woodfin made the presentation speech and after the war embroidered upon it "Bethel." It was carried by the First North Carolina regiment at the battle of Bethel Church, the first battle of the Civil War.

A HERO OF THE MERRIMAC. Riley Powers of Buncombe was a member of the crew of the "Merrimac" when she fought the "Monitor" in Hampton Roads. He saw her launched and witnessed her blowing up.

LIEUTENANT-COLONEL J. A. KEITH. In the spring of 1863 Lieutenant-Colonel J. A. Keith of Marshall, with part of the 64th Regiment, went to the Shelton Laurel country in Madison county to punish those of that section who had taken part in the looting of Marshall, which had taken place only a short time before. At this looting men and boys from Shelton Laurel had broken into stores and removed salt and other property. Col. Keith captured thirteen old men and youths. He made them sit on a log, and without having given them even the pretense of a trial had them shot. . . . Some of these were mere boys. The trench in which they were buried is still shown to the curious. This section was filled with deserters from both armies and those seeking to escape conscription in Tennessee and North Carolina. They carried on a sort of guerrilla warfare, and fought from rocks and crags. But this wholesale execution instantly aroused the indignation of the entire mountain section. Governor Vance demanded Keith's resignation, and he was dismissed from office in disgrace. [5] He was arrested after the Civil War and placed in jail at Asheville; but before he could be tried in the Circuit Court of the United States for the Western District of North Carolina, President Johnson's proclamation of amnesty was issued and he escaped trial altogether. In the account of the 64th Regiment by Capt. B. T. Morris, in "North Carolina Regiments," this act is characterized as being too cruel. [6]

EARLY SIGNS OF DISAFFECTION IN THE MOUNTAINS. On the 7th of July, 1863, the General Assembly of the State pro-

vided for the organization of the Guard for Home Defence,
commonly called the Home Guard, which was to consist of all
males from 18 to 50 not in the Confederate Army, and John
W. McElroy was appointed brigadier general and placed in
command, with headquarters at Burnsville.[7] On the 12th
of April, 1864, he wrote to Gov. Vance from Mars Hill College,
where he then had his headquarters, that on the Sunday night
before a band of tories, headed by Montrevail Ray, numbering
about 75 men, had surprised the small guard he had left at Burnsville, and broken open the magazine and removed all the arms
and ammunition. They had also broken open Brayley's
[Bailey?] store, and carried off the contents; had attacked
Captain Lyons, the local enrolling officer, in his room, wounding him slightly, but allowing him to escape. They had
broken all the guns they could not carry off, taking about
100 State guns; also some bacon. On the day before, being
Saturday the 9th of April, a band of about fifty white women
of the county assembled together and marched in a body to
a store-house near David Proffitt's, where they "pressed"—
appropriated — about sixty bushels of government wheat,
which they carried off. He adds: "The county is gone up.
It has got to be impossible to get any man out there unless he is
dragged out, with but very few exceptions. There was but
a small guard there, and the citizens all ran on the first approach
of the tories. I have 100 men at this place to guard against
Kirk, of Laurel, and cannot reduce the force; and to call out
any more home guards at this time is only certain destruction
to the country eventually. In fact, it seems to me, that
there is a determination of the people in the country generally
to do no more service in the cause. Swarms of men liable to
conscription are gone to the tories or to the Yankees—some
men that you have no idea of—while many others are fleeing
east of the Blue Ridge for refuge. John S. McElroy and all
the cavalry, J. W. Anderson and many others, are gone to
Burke for refuge. This discourages those who are left behind, and on the back of that, conscription [is] now going on
and a very tyrannical course pursued by the officers charged
with the business, and men [are] conscripted and cleaned
out as [if] raked with a fine-toothed comb; and if any are
left, if they are called upon to do a little home-guard service,
they at once apply for a writ of *habeas corpus* and get off.

Some three or four cases have been tried by Judge Read the last two weeks, and the men released. . . . If something is not done immediately for this county we will all be ruined, for the home-guards now will not do to depend on."[8] Thus North Carolina, the only Southern State which did not suspend the writ of *habeas corpus* during the Civil War, was paying the penalty.

COL. KIRK'S CAMP VANCE RAID. On the 13th of June, 1864, Colonel Kirk, with about 130 men, left Morristown, Tenn., and marched via Bull's Gap, Greenville and Crab Orchard, Tenn., to Camp Vance in North Carolina, six miles below Morganton, "where he routed the enemy with loss to them of one commissioned officer, and ten men killed—number of wounded unknown. His own losses were one man killed, one mortally wounded, and five slightly wounded, including himself. He destroyed one locomotive in good condition, three cars, the depot and commissary buildings, 1200 small arms, with amunition, and 3,000 bushels of grain. He captured 279 prisoners, who surrendered with the camp. Of these he brought 132 to Knoxville, with 32 negroes and 48 horses and mules. He obtained forty recruits for his regiment; but did not, however, accomplish his principal object: the destruction of the railroad bridge over the Yadkin river. He made arrangements to have it done secretly after he had gone, but they miscarried. On July 21, 1864, Gen. Stoneman from Atlanta thanked and complimented Col. Kirk upon this raid; but instructed Gen. Scofield at Knoxville to encourage Col. Kirk to organize the enemies of Jeff Davis in Western North Carolina rather than undertake such hazardous expeditions."[9]

DETAILS OF THE EXPEDITION FROM THE GUIDE. They were afoot, carrying their rations, blankets, arms and ammunition on their shoulders.[10] They had no wagons or pack animals while going there. They reached what is now Carter county, Tenn., on the 25th, where they were joined by Joseph V. Franklin, who now lives at Drexel, Burke county, N. C., who acted as guide. They went from Crab Orchard on Doe river—the same place that Sevier and his men had passed on their way to Kings Mountain— crossing the Big Hump mountain and fording the Toe river about six miles south of Cranberry forge, where they camped near David Ellis's. He was a Union man and cooked rations

for them.   On the 26th they scouted through the mountains
till they came to Linville river, which they crossed about
one mile below what is now Pinola, and camped.   They met
John Franklin and made him go back a few miles with them,
when they released him.   The next day they passed through
a long "stretch of mountains"[11] and it was evening when they
got down on the eastern side; but, instead of camping then,
they pushed on, and crossing Upper creek came to the public
road leading to Morganton just at dark.   This was twelve
miles from Morganton, but they marched all night, and at
daybreak got to "the conscript camp at Berry's Mill Pond,
just above what was then the terminus of the Western North
Carolina railroad.   Here they formed a line of battle and sent
in a flag of truce, demanding surrender of the camp in ten
minutes, at the end of which time it capitulated without resistance."   Accounts differ as to the number of conscripts in the
camp, Kirk's men claiming 300 and[12] Judge Avery giving
their number as "over one hundred of the Junior Reserves
who had been gathered there to be organized into a battalion."

Kirk "then took a few men and went down to the head of
the railroad and captured a train and the depot.   We had
aimed to go to Salisbury, but the news got ahead of us, and we
gave it out . . .   We had an engineer along for the purpose of running the locomotive and a car or two to carry us
to Salisbury, where we intended to release the Federal prisoners confined there, arm them, and bring them back with us;
but the news of our coming had gone on ahead of us, and we
gave it out."[13]   "While the militia and citizens who did
not belong to the Home Guards were gathering on the day
of the capture, 28th June, one of Kirk's scouts[14] was shot at
Hunting creek about half a mile from Morganton by R. C.
Pearson, a leading citizen of the town."[15]   Kirk then turned
back, crossed the Catawba river and camped for the night.
The next morning they resumed the march, crossing Johns
river, and came into the road leading from Morganton to
Piedmont Springs.   Following this road they crossed Brown's
mountain, where they were fired into by the pursuing Confederates.   This was fourteen miles from Morganton and one
mile from the home of Col. George Anderson Loven, who was
one of the party of sixty-five men and boys who attacked
Kirk at Brown's mountain.   This was about 3:00 or 3:30
p. m.

"Kirk formed a line of battle, putting fifteen or twenty prisoners taken from Camp Vance in front. About fifty of our men fired on Kirk's men, killing one prisoner, B. A. Bowles, a drummer boy of Camp Vance, who was about thirty years of age, and wounding also a boy of seventeen years of age from Alleghany county, another one of Kirk's prisoners. Dr. Robert C. Pearson was seriously wounded in the knee by Kirk's men. We then retreated, but Kirk retained his position for ten minutes after we had gone. When we fired on them I heard Kirk shout: 'Look at the damned fools, shooting their own men,' referring to the Camp Vance prisoners whom he had so placed as to receive our fire. Kirk's men had about sixty horses and mules loaded down with all the best wearing apparel they could gather up through the country, and all the bedding they could find, all of which they had packed into bed ticks from which the feathers and straw had been emptied. After our militia had withdrawn, Kirk's men remounted, the horsemen going around the fence, and the infantry, three hundred or more, going up through Israel Beck's field for a near cut to the road above."[16] According to J. V. Franklin, he, Col. Kirk and several others were wounded at Beck's farm near Brown mountain.

"We then crossed Upper creek," continues Franklin's account, "and came to the foot of Ripshin mountain and went up the Winding Stairs road, where we took up camp for the night." This position is near what is now called the Bark House and only two miles from Loven's Cold Spring tavern. They camped behind a low ridge, which commands the only road by which the Confederates could approach, but down which they could be enfiladed. This was twenty-one miles from Morganton. At daybreak Kirk's pickets reported that the Confederates were approaching, "when Col. Kirk took twenty-five men and went back and had a fight with the pursuing Confederates. It was here that Col. Waightstill Avery was wounded and several others. . . ."[17] According to Joseph V. Franklin's letter, "there were twelve Cherokees and thirteen white men who fought Col. Avery's pursuing party.

"The fog was dense as the militia came up the road. Col. Thomas George Walton was in command of the militia. Kirk's men formed on a ridge and behind trees, from which position

they could enfilade the column, which had to approach by a
narrow road.   Kirk's men fired on the advance files before
the main body had come up.   Col. W. W. Avery, Alexander
Perry, seventeen years of age, and N. B. Beck were in front.
They fired on Kirk.   Avery was mortally wounded and an
old gentleman named Philip Chandler, from Morganton,
also was mortally wounded.   Col. Calvin Houck was shot
through the wrist, and Powell Benfield through the thigh,
neither wound being serious. ﹒ Col. Avery died the third day
after having received the wound.   There were said to have
been twelve hundred men in the militia under Col. Walton;
but only a few were in the advance when they came upon
Kirk's camp, as they were scattered for a mile or more along
the road down the mountain; and having no room in which
to form except the narrow cart-way that was enfiladed by
the enemy, they retired.   Kirk went across Jonas's Ridge
unmolested, burning the residence of the late Col. John B.
Palmer as they passed about ten o'clock that morning.
Two conscripts named Jones and Andrew McAlpin had been detailed by the Confederate government, under the late Thomas
D. Carter, to dam Linville river just above the Falls for the
purpose of making a forge for the manufacture of iron
which was to have been hauled from Cranberry mines;
and when they heard that Kirk had passed down,
they went down Linville mountain by a trail, and sent two
teams and wagons loaded with property from the dam above
Linville Falls to follow, only they were to go by the Winding
Stairs road, the only one practicable at that time. [3]   These
wagoners had gone into camp at the top of the Winding Stairs
road when Kirk and his men arrived after their fight at Beck's
farm.   Of course, they were promptly captured and turned
back." [18]   The buildings at Camp Vance were burned. [19]
" There were bacon and crackers there which Kirk's men packed
on mules which they captured, and took away with them. [20]
George Barringer was another man they met on Jonas's Ridge
and forced to go a part of the way with them, but he escaped.
The yarn thread found at Camp Vance was given to the neighborhood women before the camp was burned. [20]   They got
back to Knoxville, having lost but one man (Hack Norton)
and sent their prisoners to Camp Chace in Ohio.   No recruits
joined them going or returning.   The distance traveled was
about two hundred miles."

W. H. THOMAS AND THE UNION MEN OF EAST TENNESSEE.
Col. Thomas was not a Secessionist, but claimed that any people, when denied their constitutional rights, if oppressed, always
had the right of self-defense, or revolution.   It was his desire
to keep the Southern people united that induced him to enter
the Confederate army, coupled with a desire to keep the Cherokee Indians from joining the Federal army, as some of them
had done at the commencement of the Civil War.[21]   He
wanted to keep them out of danger and to guard the mountain barriers from the incursions of Federal raiding parties
from the Tennessee side; for he never doubted that the Mississippi valley would, sooner or later, be in the possession of
the United States troops.   So, he got an order from General
Kirby Smith in the spring of 1862 to raise a battalion of sappers and miners, and enlisted over five hundred of the people
of East Tennessee, where the Union sentiment was predomi-
nant, and put them to making roads, notably a road from
Sevier county, Tennessee, to Jackson county, N. C.   This
road followed the old Indian Trail over the Collins gap, down
the Ocona Lufty river to near what is now Whittier, N. C.
He was conciliating the East Tennesseans who had joined his
sappers and miners when General Kirby Smith was transferred to another field of activity. The first order of Smith's successor in command required these Union men of East Tennessee to lay down their picks and shovels and join the Confederate army.   In 24 hours there were 500 desertions.   Then
followed the attempt to enforce the Confederate conscript
law, which drove these East Tennesseans to join the army of
General Burnside.   This army soon forced Col. Thomas and
his Indians back from Strawberry Plains into the mountains
of North Carolina, and the white wing of his Legion to Bristol, Virginia.

COSBY CREEK.   After the Confederates lost possession of
East Tennessee it was the policy of the Confederate government at Richmond to guard all the passes on the Tennessee
boundary so as to keep free and clear their line of communication from Richmond through Danville, Greensboro, Salisbury and Charlotte to Columbia and the South.   In order to do
so this section of the country was made into the Military District of Western North Carolina and Brigadier General R. B.
Vance was placed in command.   He had a brigade under

his command.   They succeeded in keeping the Federals under General Burnside penned up in Knoxville, but never did dislodge them from that city.   After Chickamauga, General Longstreet came from Virginia and drove the Federals back into Knoxville and besieged that place.   But the exigencies of General Lee's army were such that Longstreet was ordered to return with his army to Virginia.   No sooner had Longstreet started with his army for Richmond than Burnside followed him, harrassing his men, and it was to draw Burnside off that General Vance was ordered to make a demonstration by going through Quallytown, up Ocona Lufty and through the Collins Gap down into Tennessee.   It was during a cold snap in January, 1864, and fortunately Vance had but two or three wagons; but he managed to take them up the mountain successfully.   Still, when the artillery got to the top, following the rough road Col. Thomas had constructed, it had a hard time getting down the other side.   The cannon were dismounted and dragged over the bare rocks to the bottom, while the wheels and axles of the carriages were taken apart, divided among the men and so carried to the foot of the mountain, when they were reassembled.   The guns were not tied to hollow logs, as in Napoleon's passage of the Alps, but were dragged naked as they were down the steep mountain side.   Capt. Theo. F. Davidson had this done.

GENERAL VANCE DIVIDED HIS FORCE.   After reaching the foot of Smoky mountain on the western side, General Vance sent Col. Thomas and his Indians and Col. J. L. Henry with his mounted battalion to Gatlinsburg, Tennessee, and taking with him from three to five hundred men went on toward Seviersville.   Much to his surprise, he captured an unguarded wagon train of about eighty loaded wagons and their teams and drivers, and immediately started back with them.   When he reached Cosby creek Meeting House he stopped his command to eat dinner, but failed to put out pickets to notify him of the approach of the enemy.   It was while engaged in eating dinner that a pursuing body of Federal cavalry dashed upon the resting Confederates and captured many of them, including the General himself, who was taken to Camp Chace and kept there till the close of the war.   Captain Theo. F. Davidson, who was acting adjutant general, and Dr. I. A. Harris, escaped by going to Big Creek and through Mount

Sterling gap into Haywood county, and thence to Asheville. Others also escaped. Colonels Thomas and Henry, learning of the fate of the rest of the expedition, returned into North Carolina by the route they had come, and Col. Thomas' Indians resumed their places near Ocona Lufty.

A SPARTAN MOTHER.[22] During the last year of the war deserters from both armies, who generally were thieves and murderers, banded themselves together, and were called bushwhackers. About this time three men were murdered twelve miles from Valleytown, near Andrews, and this band of lawless men swore revenge on the best five men in this valley. Mr. William Walker was warned of his danger, but said he was an innocent man, and had fed out nearly everything he had, and he would not desert his family. He was sick at the time, and friends pleaded in vain. "On October 6, 1864, there came to my house at 11 A. M., twenty-seven drunken men.[23] They had stopped at a still house and were nearly swearing drunk. Dinner was just set on the table, but they did not eat, as they were afraid they would be poisoned, but they broke dishes from the table, and went to my cupboards, and smashed my china and glassware. At the time Mr. Walker was warned, I took his papers and hid them, but he was so sure he would not be molested, that he made me put them back in his desk, but they were all taken." In spite of her tears and his pleadings he was taken from her. She followed with her sister the next day on horseback for fifteen miles, beyond which her sister was afraid to go; but Mrs. Walker went on six miles further, alone, where friends persuaded her to return home, which she did after one of them had gone to Long Ridge to ascertain if there were any tidings from her husband there. Nothing was found, however, and she has never had any satisfactory word of him since. She had searches made by the government, the Masons, the war department and others, but discovered nothing. When she got back home she found that these thieves and thugs had stolen nearly all her bedding, and had even taken her dead baby's clothing, leaving not even a pin, needle or knitting needle, and tramping her fifteen feather beds full of mud. Still, neighbors contributed to her assistance; but it was three years after the war closed before she could buy even a calico dress for herself. Coley Campbell, a Methodist preacher and a tailor, taught her to cut and make men's clothing and by dint of hard work and strict economy and fine business management she reared five boys into splendid men. She also kept boarders and won the reputation of being the finest housekeeper in the mountains. But she suffered : "I wept for three years," she says in her narrative, "and two pillows were so stiffened by salt tears that they crumbled to pieces. My husband told a woman, Mrs. McDaniel, where he stayed all night after his capture, that he only worried that I might not live to raise the boys; but that if I did, he knew they would be raised right." How nobly she carried out that prediction is attested in the lives and characters of these sons themselves. She died December 9, 1899.

WILLIAM JOHNSTONE. "During the last years of the war the mountains became infested with deserters from both armies, desperadoes, who lived in caves and dens and issued forth for plunder and robbery.[24] Among the number of murders committed by these we recall three of peculiar atrocity. The house of Mr. Wm. Johnstone, a wealthy South Carolinian, was entered by six men who demanded dinner; the old gentleman set before them all that his house afforded; after partaking of his dinner and without a word of dispute they shot him dead in the presence of his wife and young children.

OTHER OUTRAGES. "Gen. B. M. Edney, a brave man, was shot down in his own room after making a desperate resistance. Capt. Allen, son-in-law of Mr. Alexander Robinson, a man of wealth and high social position, and a gallant soldier, after the armies had surrendered, while working at a mill near his home trying to earn bread for his wife and child, was murdered in cold blood, and his body stripped of coat and boots and left on the roadside."

"AN OLD MAN, MY LORD." In the fall of 1864 Levi Guy, an old and inoffensive white man who had allowed his sons to shelter at his home when being hunted for their robberies in the neighborhood of Watauga Falls, was hanged by Confederates from a chestnut tree which grew between the present dwelling of David Reece and his barn across the State road. The tree has disappeared. Guy lived near Watauga Falls, just inside North Carolina. The names of those who committed this act are still known, and all those who have not died violent deaths have never prospered.

MURDERED BY MISTAKE.[25] "Old Billy Devver," as William Deaver was locally known, was killed at the old Deaver place in Transylvania towards the close of the Civil War. It occurred through a mistake. He had a son, James, who was a captain in the Confederate Army and among whose duties was that of the arrest of deserters and outliers from the Confederate Army. He thus had incurred the enmity of men of that class, who were called in that country by the plain and unmistakable word "robbers." One night one of these robbers called at the Deaver home, expecting to find the Confederate Captain within. It seems, however, that he was not at home, but that his father, William Deaver, was. Therefore, when this robber called at the house and Old Man Billy came to the door, the robber asked him if he was Captain Deaver. He said he was, and believing that he was the Confederate Captain for whom he was seeking, the robber shot him dead at his own door.

SHOT THEIR HOST AFTER DINNER.[26] Philip Sitton, near the Henderson and Transylvania line, was shot down by a party of these robbers as soon as they had finished eating a dinner they had ordered and which Sitton had furnished. They left him lying in his blood, believing his wound was mortal, but he recovered.

DEATH OF ROBERT THOMAS.[26] Robert Thomas, who lived on Willow creek in Transylvania county, was killed by these robbers in 1864.

JESSE LEVERETT A PENITENT. "In the time of the war there was a very notorious character at large in this part of the State," says Mrs. Mattie S. Candler in her history of Henderson county, "Jesse Leverett. He was known and feared by both sides, as he made a practice of piloting deserters through the Federal lines to Kentucky, taking them through here (Hendersonville) by way of Bat Cave and thence to the Tennessee lines. He was an outlaw and a desperado with such bold working methods that he continued this practice throughout the war, and was not even injured. Later he went to Illinois, discovered the error of his ways, and ended his career as a very earnest preacher."

"A HARD ROAD TO TRAVEL OUT OF DIXIE." Such was the title of an article in the *Century* for October, 1890, giving a very readable description of the escape and vicissitudes of a party of Federal prisoners who had escaped from prison in Columbia, S. C., and made their way to these mountains. They passed through Transylvania county, crossed Chunky Gal mountain between Macon and Clay and came down on Shooting creek where they had a fright at the house of a Mr. Kitchin. He had taken them in and was allowing them to sit before his fire when the Confederate Home Guard appeared on the scene, the prisoners escaping through a window. Another story in a later *Century* told of another party and their adventures on Tuckaseegee river in Jackson county. Col. Geo. W. Kirk began his military career in the Union Army by piloting Union men from these mountains into the Federal lines in Tennessee.

An Underground Mountain Railroad. Just as the Abolitionists before the Civil War had what were called "underground" railroads from Mason's and Dixon's line and the Ohio river to Canada, the Union element of these mountains had their underground railway to Kentucky and East Tennessee from the prisons of the South in which captured Federal soldiers were confined. T. L. Lowe, Esq., in his history of Watauga county, prepared for this work, gives some account of the assistance given by the late Lewis B. Banner, of Banners Elk:

"He was a strong Union man and his home was the home of the oppressed and struggling Union sympathizer trying to get through the Federal lines in Kentucky, and many a time through great personal sacrifice and danger did he pilot men through the mountains so as to avoid the vigilance of the Home-guard. On one occasion he rendered valuable services to a brave Massachusetts soldier, which services were remembered by the recipient for many years. The soldier's name was Major Lawrence N. Duchesney. He had been for 13 months a prisoner in the Libby prison, 73 days in the dungeon; was sent to Salisbury, N. C., and from there was being transferred to Danville, Virginia, and while *en route* jumped from the train and made his way across the country, and finally, foot-sore and weary, he reached the home of Mr. Banner where he was tenderly cared for until he was able to travel, and then Mr. Banner, or 'Uncle Lewis' as we all are ever wont to affectionately call him, took him on a horse at night through hidden paths through the mountains to a place of safety. Major Duchesny some few years ago paid the family of his deliverer a visit, but his old friend had been dead many years. Major Duchesney had a home at Skyland, N. C., where he and his wife lie buried."

Alleghany During the War Between the States.[27] Alleghany furnished several companies during the war; one, company F, 22d North Carolina regiment, with Jesse Reeves as the first captain, and Company I, 61st North Carolina regiment, with Dr. A. B. Cox as the first captain. J. H. Doughton, later in the war, organized another company, but when he arrived on the field of service, he found these two companies in such a depleted condition that he disorganized his company for the purpose of recruiting them. Alleghany furnished a great many more soldiers beside these companies, who served in various commands; some in Virginia, some in Tennessee, but mostly in the 37th Virginia battalion. Companies F and I were constantly recruited, but when the war was ended, there were not more than 50 or 60 men in both companies. But Alleghany's greatest trials were caused by deserters and bushwhackers. These men would hide in the mountains in order to evade active service on the battlefield. At first they seemed to have stolen only necessary food and raiment, but later took to robbing and murdering. With the able-bodied men in the army, the women and children were left at their mercy. The few old men and others unable for active service constituted a home guard, but were powerless to cope with these desperate outlaws. Alleghany appealed to Surry county in 1863 for aid—Surry county sent about 100 men to aid the Alleghany home guard; these men crossed the Blue Ridge at Thompson's gap and camped at what is known as the "Cabins." They sent four of their number to Duncan's Mills, about five miles distant for a supply of meal. These four men had passed Little River Church and it was almost dark, when the robbers snatched one of their men (Jeff Galyen) from his horse and hurried him off through the woods. The other men turned their horses and hurried back to the main body. Next morning early the whole force started in search of Galyen and the robbers. They found neither; and, after hanging Levi Fender (the stump of the old sapling on which he was hung can still be pointed out about one and one-half miles east of Sparta), they returned home. Within a few days Galyen was found in a few hundred yards of the place where the robbers had disappeared with him, on his knees by a tree, shot dead. One of the robbers, Tom Pollard, afterwards acknowledged to the killing, and said, he did it while Galyen was on his knees begging for his life. It was decided by the officers to send General Pierce with his soldiers into this section. These soldiers scoured the country, captured a number of the robbers and carried them to Laurel Springs, where a number of them were hung. Among those hung, were Lewis Wolfe and Morgan Phipps. Later Hoke's cavalry was sent into the county, but still robbery, murder and lawlessness continued.

In October, 1864, the fight at "Killen's Branch" took place. This is about one mile Northwest of Sparta, on the main road leading from Sparta to Mouth of Wilson, Virginia. Here the Home Guard was ambushed by a band of bushwhackers under Henry Taylor. The bushwhackers were concealed in a dense ivy thicket by the roadside and fired upon the Home Guard as they were passing. The Home Guard promptly returned the fire. The fighting continued for some time, when both sides withdrew. Of the Home Guard, Felix Reeves was killed and Wiley Maxwell, Jesse Reeves and Martin Crouse were mortally wounded. This was the last fight of any importance between the outlaws and the Home Guard.

A CIVIL WAR JOAN OF ARC. It was in this fight that Mrs. Cynthia Parks, wife of Col. James H. Parks, then living in Sparta, who, when she heard the firing and saw the horses, of the wounded men running loose through the streets of the town, mounted her horse and rode to the scene of the combat, in order that she might render what aid she could to the wounded Home Guard. Later on the same day she brought the mail into Sparta. The mail carrier had been fired upon and had deserted his mail. She went to the place where the mail had been left and brought it to the postoffice.

During Reconstruction, Alleghany did not suffer from carpet-bag misrule as did some of the other counties of the State, owing, probably, to the small number of negroes in the county, and to the fact that most of the outlaws had fled. But still, we find instances where such men as Captain J. H. Doughton and Jesse Bledsoe, the first sheriff of the county, were dragged before the court. Feudalism must not have existed to such a great extent as elsewhere in the South, for J. C. Jones, who was sheriff of the county during the war, continued to be sheriff under the provisional government.

IN HAYWOOD COUNTY. Owing to the remoteness of Cataloochee creek in Haywood county, raiding parties from both armies figured extensively hereabouts during the Civil War, and several soldiers were killed along the roadsides, among them being Manson Wells of Buncombe, while Lewis Williams, who was with him, escaped. Two men named Groomes and Mitchell Caldwell were killed just above the point where the Mount Sterling and Little Cataloochee roads join. Henry Barnes was killed one mile east of Big creek. Levi Shelton and Ellsworth Caldwell were killed in 1863 on Caldwell Fork, between the McGee house and the gap of the mountain behind Harrison Caldwell's. Solomon Groomes killed a man named Townshend on Big Creek in 1861 or 1862 with an ax, on account of his daughter's relations with Townshend, and although he pleaded insanity, he was hanged just west of the bridge across Richland creek, and near the present passenger depot at Waynesville, in 1862.

WATAUGA'S EXPERIENCES. When, on March 28, 1865, Stoneman came into Boone he was fired on from the upper story of the house now occupied by Mr. J. D. Councill, opposite the present Blair Hotel, and his men then killed the following: Ephraim Morris, J. Warren Greene, J. M. Councill, and wounded Sheriff McBride, Thomas Holder, Calvin Greene, W. W. Gragg and John Brown. Two days later Kirk's men came into Boone and fortified the court house, which then stood where Frank A. Linney, Esq., now resides, by cutting loop-holes in the walls, and erecting a stockade made of timbers from a partly finished building which then stood where the Blair Hotel now stands and a house which then stood near the present Blackburn Hotel. He remained in Boone till Stoneman returned, when he, too, left. He also fortified Cook's gap and Blowing Rock, cutting the trees away from the road leading up the mountain. He also arranged to signal from mountain-top to mountain-top from Butler, Tenn., to Blowing Rock. Fort Hill at Butler is still visible, and was one of his fortified posts. When Stoneman's men got to Patterson, Clem Osborne of North Fork was there after thread, and the Federals chased him to the top of the factory, firing on him as he ran. Just as he was about to be overtaken he gave a sign which was recognized by a Mason among his pursuers, and his life was not only spared but he was sent back home with his team and wagon and all that properly belonged to him. The people of Beaver Dams had a particularly trying time with the outliers, and many are the harrowing experiences they were forced to undergo for nearly three years. When salt got scarce during the war men cut small hickory saplings from one to two inches in diameter and bound them into bundles and took them by wagon to the Salt Works in Virginia and traded them for salt, the hickories being split and made into hoops for barrels. After the close of the war Union people sued the more prosperous of their neighbors on the border of Watauga and Tennessee for damages for killing, wounding and arresting Union marauders, and in most cases lost, though the expenses of the litigation were ruinous to the Southern men who won. Among those sued were Commodore Perry, father of J. K. Perry of Beaver Dams, and Thomas Dougherty of Dry Run, Johnson county, Tenn.

BUSHWHACKER KIRKLAND. Between Yellow creek and the Little Tennessee in Graham county as it now exists used to live two men by the name of Kirkland, one of whom came to be called before the end of the Civil War, "Bushwhacker" Kirkland, and the other "Turkey-Trot" John Kirkland. They joined the Confederate Army at the commencement of the Civil War, but soon afterwards found themselves members of an independent command which was frequently accused of committing certain depredations upon the property of certain Union-loving citizens living in East Tennessee and in the neighborhood of the Great Smoky mountains. According to John Denton of Santeetla, who had been in their company when they were in the regular Confederate Army, they were brave men physically.

CAPTAIN LYON'S RAID. During the expiring days of the Civil War Captain Lyon of the United States Army came from Tennessee through what is now known as the Belding Trail to Robbinsville, Graham county. That trail was then known as the Hudson trail from the name of the man who first lived where David Orr now lives on Slick Rock creek; but the trail itself had been used by the Cherokees for years when the first white people came to that section. Lyon's men killed Jesse Kirkland, a kinsman of "Bushwhacker" and "Turkey-Trot John," and two other men, one of whom was named Mashburn and the other Hamilton; and probably two or three others. This was done on Isaac Carringer's creek, about half a mile from its mouth. They killed an Indian in Robbinsville, which was then or had recently been the home of Junaluska, the Indian chieftain; and then went up Santeetla, where they spent the night, returning the next day to the Unaka mountains and camping that night on the Bob Stratton Meadow.

COL. KIRBY DRIVEN BACK. From "The Last Ninety Days of the War," chapter XVI, by Mrs. Cornelia Phillips Spencer, we learn that during the second week of April, 1865, a brigade of infantry under Col. Kirby was moved by the Federals from Greenville, Tenn., on Asheville, but were met near Camp Woodfin—now Doubleday—by a part of Gen. J. G. Martin's command, and so successfully repulsed that they turned about at once and returned to Greenville.

GENERALS MARTIN AND GILLAM AGREE. "When it was found that General Gillam intended to take Asheville Gen. Martin ordered his whole command, consisting of the 62d, 64th and 69th North Carolina, and a South Carolina battery (Porter's) and Love's regiment of Thomas's Legion, to the vicinity of Swannanoa gap. . . . Love's regiment reached the gap before Gillam did," fortified it and repulsed him. After vainly trying to effect a passage here Gen. Gillam moved to Hickory Nut gap. Palmer's brigade was ordered to meet them there; but Gen. Martin, giving an account of this affair, adds, "I regret to say the men refused to go." They had heard rumors of Lee's surrender. Porter's battery having been ordered to Greenville, S. C., was captured on the road there by Gen. Gillam. On Saturday April 22, Gen. Martin received news of Gen. Johnston's armistice with Gen. Sherman, and sent two flags of truce to Gen. Gillam, one of which met him on the Hendersonville road, six miles south of Asheville, on Sunday. At an interview between Generals Gillam and Martin, Monday, it was agreed that the former should proceed with his command to Tennessee and that he should be furnished with three days' rations. Gen. Gillam reached Asheville on the 25th and with his staff dined with Gen. Martin. The 9,000 rations were furnished him, and that night his command camped a few miles below Asheville, afterwards going on to Tennessee. Col. Kirk and staff had dashed into town while it was in possession of Gen. Gillam's troops, but perfect order was preserved while they were there, and they "were compelled to leave in advance of General Gillam." The People of Asheville had the mortification of

seeing the guns of Porter's battery, that had guarded the
crest of what is now Battery Park hill, just captured, driven
through by negroes. Following the Federal army was an
immense train of plunder, animals of all sorts, household
goods and treasures.

"Tuesday night passed quietly. The town was guarded
only by Captain Teague's company. A small party of Federals, under flag of truce, passed through during the 26th,
carrying dispatches to General Palmer, then approaching
from Morganton via Hickory Nut gap. At sunset on the
26th, Gen. Brown, in command of a portion of the same troops
that had just passed through with Gillam, suddenly reentered
the place, capturing all the officers and soldiers, and giving up the
town to plunder. The men captured were paroled to go home,
the officers to report to Gen. Stoneman at Knoxville." This
was within 24 hours after General Gillam had assured Gen.
Martin that he would give him the forty-eight hours' notice
provided for in the Johnston-Sherman truce before renewing
hostilities. The residences of Gen. Martin, Mrs. James W.
Patton, Judge Bailey, Dr. Chapman, a Presbyterian minister,
and others were pillaged. The author adds: "The Tenth
and Eleventh Michigan regiments certainly won for themselves
in Asheville that night a reputation that should damn them
to everlasting fame. . . . On Thursday, parties scoured
the country in all directions, carrying on the work of plunder
and destruction. On Friday they left, having destroyed all
the arms and ammunition they could find and burned the
armory. On Friday afternoon, they sent off the officers
they had captured under a guard," but Gen. Brown refused
to leave a guard behind for the protection of the town from
marauders. On the 28th Gen. Palmer sent a dispatch from
some point on the Hickory Nut gap road releasing Gen. Martin, his officers and men who had been captured by Gen.
Brown, because Brown had not given the promised notice of
the termination of the armistice. General Palmer also prevented two negro regiments in Yancey from entering Asheville.

GENERAL PALMER'S DISPATCH. Following is the dispatch
referred to:

HEADQUARTERS EAST TENNESSEE CAVALRY DIVISION,
HICKORY NUT GAP ROAD,
April 28, 1865.

General :—I could not learn any of the particulars of your capture
and that of Colonel Palmer and other officers and men at Asheville on

the 26th, and as my troops at that point were obliged to leave immediately, there was no time to make the necessary investigation. I therefore ordered your release on a parole of honor to report to General Stoneman. On further reflection I have come to the conclusion that our men should have given you, under all the circumstances, notice of the termination of the armistice, and that in honor we cannot profit by any failure to give this notice. You will therefore please inform all the officers and soldiers paroled by General Brown last evening and this morning, under the circumstances above referred to, that the parole they have given (which was by my order) is not binding, and that they may consider that it was never given. Regretting that your brother officers and yourself should have been placed in this delicate situation, I am, general, very respectfully your obedient servant,

                                        WM. J PALMER,
                                Brevet Brig. Gen. Commanding.
To Brig. Gen. J. G. Martin, Asheville.

PERRY GASTON BRINGS FIRST NEWS. J. P. Gaston of Hominy walked all the way from Appomattox and showed his parole. This was nearly three weeks after Lee's surrender. Stoneman was besieging Asheville on the South and Kirk's regiment on the north. Gen. Martin went out under a flag of truce and made an agreement to furnish three days' rations to the Federal troops—and furnished them—on condition that they should not disturb private or public property.

GENERAL JAMES GREEN MARTIN. He was the son of Dr. William Martin and Sophia Dange, and was born at Elizabeth City, N. C., February 14, 1819. He entered West Point in July, 1836, was graduated in July, 1840, and was commissioned a second lieutenant of the First regiment U. S. Artillery. In 1842 he served on the frontier of Canada in the Aroostock War, or "War of the Maps," and married at Newport, Rhode Island, July 12, 1844, Miss Mary Ann Murray Reed, a great granddaughter of George Reed, a signer of the Declaration of Independence, and also of Gen. William Thompson, a brigadier general of the Revolutionary army. During the three days' assault on Monterey, Mexico, September 21, 22, 23, 1846, he was still a second lieutenant, but he was in command of his battery, with "Stonewall" Jackson as his second in command. At Cherubusco, August 20, 1847, his right arm was shot off. He turned over his command to Jackson, and taking his sleeve in his teeth, rode off the field. He was brevetted major for "gallant and meritorious conduct" at the battles of Contreras and Cherubusco, and presented with a sword of honor

by the citizens of Pasquotank county, on which were engraved the battles in which he had taken part. He was then
transferred to the staff and appointed assistant quartermaster
and stationed at Fortress Monroe, Philadelphia and Governor's Island for several years, when he was ordered to Fort
Snelling, Minnesota, where Mrs. Martin died. February 8,
1858, he was married to Miss Hetty King, a sister of Gen. Rufus
King of the U. S. Army, and eldest daughter of Charles King,
president of Columbia College, New York, and the grand-
daughter of Rufus King, the first American minister to the
court of St. James. He was a member of the Utah expedition with Gen. Albert Sydney Johnston, and was at Fort Riley,
Kansas territory, when the Civil War began. He resigned
when North Carolina seceded, and served in this State and
in Virginia till the close of hostilities. Penniless after the
close of the war he read law and commenced its practice in
Asheville in copartnership with the late Judge J. L. Bailey.
He died and was buried at Asheville, October 4, 1879.

LEWIS M. HATCH. This distinguished citizen and soldier
served in South Carolina during part of the Civil War, and,
hence, is not mentioned in the records of "North Carolina
Regiments." He was born November 28, 1815, at Salem,
N. H., but went to Charleston, S. C., in 1833. He joined the
Washington Light Infantry, April 15, 1835, and served with
that company in 1837 in the Seminole War. He was promoted to the captaincy of that company in 1855, and in 1856
he marched his company to Cowpens, which trip resulted in
1876 in the erection of the Daniel Morgan monument at Spartanburg. He was an expert swordsman, an athlete, and walked
from Charleston to New York, when a young man, in thirty
days, averaging 30 miles a day. On the last day he walked
60 miles. Gov. Pickens appointed him quartermaster general in 1860, and the fine service from then till 1865 was due
to him. In 1861-62 he commanded the 21st South Carolina
Infantry. To him was largely due the victory at Secession-
ville in June, 1862. He served subsequently in Virginia. In
March, 1866, he moved to Asheville, where he died January
12, 1897. While living in Charleston he was in the commission business.

COLONEL JAMES THOMAS WEAVER. He was the youngest
son of Jacob Weaver and Elizabeth Siler Weaver. He was

born near Weaverville, Buncombe county, North Carolina, on November 30th, 1828. He received such education as the schools of that section would then afford. Later he attended the Burnsville Academy in Yancey county and prepared himself for civil engineering. May 24, 1855, he married Hester Ann Trotter, a daughter of William Trotter of Person county, N. C., but prior to the marriage of Hester Ann, William Trotter with his family moved to Macon county in the year 1846. During the seven years after his marriage, and prior to his enlistment in the army of the Confederacy, James Thomas Weaver was actively engaged in farming and as a surveyor of lands. During this interval he acquired a comfortable competency, consisting of lands, etc., and was considered a thrifty and progressive man in his community. He enlisted in the army early in 1862 as captain of Company A, which he organized, and this company was assigned to the Sixtieth North Carolina regiment. In 1864 he was made lieutenant colonel of this regiment. He served in the Army of Tennessee throughout the war, or until his death. He was in command of the Sixtieth regiment in the second battle near Murfreesboro, Tennessee, occurring between the armies of Hood and Thomas. He was killed in this engagement on December 7th, 1864.

COLONEL EDWARD F. LOVILL. He was born in Surry county, February 10, 1842, married Miss Josephine Marion of the same county February 15, 1866, and moved to Boone in 1874. He was admitted to the bar in February 1885, and was commissioner to the Chippewa Indians from 1893 to 1897. He was captain of Company A of the 28th North Carolina Infantry, and on the second day of Chancellorsville commanded that regiment in the absence of Col. Samuel D. Low. Of this incident Col. Lowe reported: "While absent, Gen. Stuart again commanded the line forward, and my regiment charged through the same terrible artillery firing the third time, led by Captain (Edward F.) Lovill of Company A, to the support of our batteries which I had just got into position on the hill from which those of the enemy had been driven."[29] Captain Lovill had commanded the same regiment during the midnight attack of the night before. Upon the death of Col. Asbury Speer at Reems Station and the resignation of Major Samuel Stowe, Captain Lovill was senior officer of the 28th till the surrender at Appomattox; and commanded the regiment at the battle of Jones' farm near Petersburg in the fall of 1864, where he was severely wounded. He returned to duty in March, 1865, and was recommended for promotion to the colonelcy of his regiment at the time that James Lineberger was recommended for the lieutenant - colonelcy and George McCauley for the majority, but the end came before these appointments were published. He was wounded in the right arm at Gettysburg. At Fredericksburg "Captain Lovill, of Company A, the right company of the regiment, stood on the railroad track all the time, waving his hat and cheering his men; and neither he nor Martin (who had just shot down the Federal color bearer) was struck."[29] Soon after the battle of Jericho Ford, in September, 1864, Natt Nixon, a seventeen-year-old boy of Mitchell's river, Surry, was desperately wounded, and at night Captain Lovill and Private M. H. Freeman, a cobbler of Dobson, went to get him, as he had been left within the enemy's lines. They called him and he answered, saying the Federals were between him and them, but had been to him and given him water. Freeman put down his gun and accoutrements and shouting in a loud voice "Natt, I'm coming after you. I am coming unarmed, and any man who shoots me is a damned coward," started. It was night, but no one fired at him, and he brought his stricken comrade back to Captain Lovill; but the poor boy died near a farm house to which he had been borne before daylight. Colonel Lovill is a director of the Oxford Orphanage, having been appointed by Gov. Aycock. He is chairman of board of trustees of the Appalachian Training School and a lawyer of ability.

MAJOR HARVEY BINGHAM. In the winter of 1864-65, the Home Guard battalion of Watauga was camped on Cove creek near what is now Sugar Grove, the name of their camp having been Camp Mast. Harvey Bingham was the major, and Geo. McGuire, who had been absent from the county for a long while before his return and election, was captain of Company A. Jordan Cook was captain of Company B, of which Col. W. L. Bryan of Boone was first lieutenant. Major Bingham and his adjutant, J. P. Mathewson, left camp to go to Ashe to confer with Captain McMillan, who commanded a cavalry company there, about cooperating with his battalion in a raid he then contemplated. During his absence

Company B, under command of Lieut. Bryan, was camped at Boone; and Captain McGuire sent him word about dark that he expected an attack on Camp Mast that night. Lieut. Bryan, however, did not start for that place till the following morning, and when he got near it, discovered the cabins in smoking ruins and all of Company A absent. McGuire had surrendered them to Col. Champion of the Federal Army the night before. They were taken to Camp Chace and kept till the close of the war. It is said, however, that McGuire was not treated as a prisoner, but was allowed a horse and rode away with the officers to whom he had surrendered his men. It was thought at the time that McGuire had betrayed his men to the enemy, and he certainly had surrendered them under the protest of many of his subordinate officers; one of whom, Paul Farthing, told him that if the company was surrendered Farthing's life would be surrendered, meaning that he would not survive captivity. He, and a nephew who was surrendered with him, shortly afterwards died in Camp Chace. After the war Major Bingham was a candidate for the State senate before a democratic convention held at Lenoir, and the late W. B. Farthing stated that Bingham was suspected of complicity with McGuire in the surrender of the troops at Camp Mast, and that if he was nominated the people of Watauga would not support him. This led to his defeat and there was talk of a duel between these two; but both decided it was best to leave the issue to the future rather than to two leaden bullets, and the matter was dropped. But feeling still ran high against Major Bingham, and he and his wife, a daughter of John B. Miller of Wilkes, left Watauga together and rode on horseback to one of the western counties, where they taught school till a better feeling pervaded their home county, when they returned. He soon removed to Statesville, where he studied law and practiced law. He died there, a respected citizen and able lawyer, and time has fully vindicated his memory of the unjust suspicion that once drove him from his home; and no one now doubts his entire loyalty to the cause of the Southern Confederacy.

POST-BELLUM TROUBLES. Soon after the surrender deserters from both armies committed depredations in and near Jefferson. The citizens of Jefferson sent a delegation to Salisbury for protection, and returned soon afterward with

Captain Wills of New York, who organized a home guard in every voting precinct. Union and Confederate soldiers who had served honorably were admitted, but their ranks were closed to deserters from each army. Jonathan Osborne was made captain of the North Fork company. Order was soon restored but not before 40 or 50 of these deserters had started into Jefferson, the leader of whom carried a United States flag. They came up Helton street, but when opposite the jail they were met by Joshua Baker, who had been sheriff. Single-handed and alone, he seized the flag, and and swore that no such gang of horse-thieves should disgrace it by carrying it. His brother, Zack Baker, stood near and told him to hold on to the flag. These two intrepid men cowed the band of outlaws and the flag was yielded up and given into the keeping of a Union man. Zach Baker was equally brave, and no deserter ever entered his dwelling near Creston till negro soldiers belonging to the regular United States army came at the close of hostilities and did some pilfering. Mr. Baker had sent word to these white marauders that he was waiting for them with a welcome they would not soon forget. They tried to take some of his horses once, but he defied them to do so; and on another occasion, after they had secretly stolen a few horses, he followed them to Tennessee, identified the horses as his property, and took them back with him in spite of the threats of the robbers to kill him.

NOTES.

[1]See Vol. I, "Literary and Historical Activities in N. C., 1900-1905," pp. 427 to 484.
[2]From *The Morning Post*, Raleigh, May 11, 1904.
[3]Co. A of this regiment went from Ashe county, and the "Wilkes Volunteers" from Wilkes. Z. B. Vance was its first colonel, but was soon elected governor of the State.
[3]From "Asheville's Centenary."
[4]The New Legal Building, the finest office building in the city, stands there now.
[5]See Governor Vance's Correspondence, 1863.
[6]Statements of Gen. James M. Ray and Judge J. C. Pritchard.
[7]Literary and Historical Activities in N. C., Vol. I, p. 485.
[8]Series 1, Vol. LIII, p. 326, Rebellion Records.
[9]Condensed from Rebellion Records, Series 1, Vol. XXXIX, p. 232. The guide, J. V. Franklin, says Kirk had only 130 men; but J. C. Chappell, who was with Kirk also, says he had 300 whites and 26 Indians. Wm. Blalock, who saw them at Strawberry Plains, says Kirk had 200 men. The official report says the number was 130. It was supposed by the people of Burke that Kirk intended to take an engine and car and go to Morganton and release and arm the Federal prisoners there.
[10]According to Wm. Blalock, Kirk's men passed through Crab Orchard, and went up Chucky river, passing through Limestone cove, and crossing the mountain at Miller's gap, two miles from Montezuma, then called Bull Scrape. They then got to the Clark settlement, two and one-half miles from Montezuma, and camped there in a pine thicket. Next day they passed through the Barrier Settlement on Jonas's Ridge.
[11]Letter of J. V. Franklin to J. P. A., March 2, 1912.
[12]From Judge A. C. Avery's account in Vol. IV, N. C. Regiments.
[13]J. V. Franklin's letter before quoted.
[14]Hack Norton of Madison county, N. C., was his name, according to same letter.
[15]Judge Avery's account, before quoted.
[16]Statement of Col. George Anderson Loven to J. P. A. at Cold Spring tavern, near Jonas's Ridge postoffice, N. C., June, 1910.
[17]J. V. Franklin's letter before quoted.

[18]Col. G. A. Loven's statement before quoted.
[19]Col. George W. Kirk was born in Greene county, Tenn., June 25, 1837. and died at Gilroy, Calif., February 15, 1905.
[20]J. V. Franklin's letter before quoted.
[21]Captain James W. Terrell in *The Commonwealth*, Asheville, June 1, 1893.
[22]From an account written by Mrs. Margaret Jane Walker, wife of Wm. Walker. She was born March 15, 1826. Married October 15, 1844.
[23]Ibid.
[24]From the "Woman's Edition" of the *Asheville Citizen*, Nov. 28, 1895, by Miss Fanny L. Patton.
[25]Related by Judge G. A. Shuford.
[26]Ibid.
[27]By S. F. Thompson, clerk of the court, Sparta, N. C.
[28]Series I, Vol. XXV, Part 1, Rebellion Records.
[29]Vol. II, N. C. Regiments, 1861-65, p. 475.

CHAPTER XXVIII

POLITICAL

IN THE DAYS OF GOOD "QUEEN BESS." On the 16th day of July, 1584, Sir Walter Raleigh's colony landed on Roanoke Island, and took formal possession of the country in the name of the Queen. No day more prophetic of the love of individual liberty, and no more gallant leader could have been found for the beginning of a people who afterwards fought at Alamance, drafted the Mecklenburg "Resolves," and "framed the first written compact that, west of the mountains, was writ for the guidance of liberty's feet." [1] The first colony was lost; but others followed, and on the 18th day of August, 1585, Virginia Dare became the first of that sweet and gentle galaxy of beautiful and exemplary women who have made North Carolina what it is today. In 1663, by a grant from King Charles II, all the country lying between the Pacific and Atlantic oceans, and included within the 31st and 36th parallels of north latitude, was given to certain men, and William Drummond was appointed governor of the colony of Carolina. North Carolina, the State, was modest, therefore, when, after the Revolutionary War, she claimed all territory west of the mountains to the Mississippi only. "In 1690 that portion of the province lying north of the Santee river was styled North Carolina, and the four southern counties were called South Carolina. From this period began that long series of oppressions and grievances which finally culminated in the overthrow of the British and the establishment of the independence of the colony.

CLARENDON. "In 1729 this territory would have been embraced in the county of Clarendon. [2] At this time the county of New Hanover, with indefinite western boundaries which seem to have extended to the Pacific Ocean, then called the South Seas, was formed, and the name of Clarendon as a county disappears. From New Hanover county in 1738 was cut off and erected the county of Bladen, whose western limits were left undefined. Again from the county of Bladen was formed in 1749 the county of Anson, still with undefined western limits. Here Buncombe's genealogy divides into two

branches, to be united again in her own creation. That portion of her territory which was taken from Burke may be traced from this point as follows. In 1758 Rowan county was formed from a part of Anson county, and up to the beginning of the Revolutionary War continued in its entirety. In 1777 was formed from its western portion a new county called Burke.

BUNCOMBE'S ANCESTRY. "That portion of Buncombe county which was taken from Rutherford may be traced as follows : In 1762 was formed from the western part of the county of Anson a new county called in honor of the new queen of England, Princess Charlotte of Mecklenburg, by the name of Macklenburg county. In 1768 the western part of Mecklenburg county was erected into a new county, and named in honor of North Carolina's notorious Colonial governor, Tryon county, but during the struggle for independence the North Carolinians were but little disposed to honor the name of their former oppressor, and when in 1779 this county had become inconveniently large, it was formed into two new counties, and the name of Tryon dropped, and the eastern part called Lincoln, while the western portion received the name of Rutherford county, in honor of Gen. Griffith Rutherford."

LOCKE'S CONSTITUTION. It is frequently forgotten that for several years the colony of Carolina was governed by Locke's "grand model" constitution; and but a few lawyers know that it is set forth in full in the second volume of the revised Statutes (1837) North Carolina, where can also be found that much vaunted but little known "palladium" of our liberties, "Magna Carta." Locke's plan provided that these backwoodsmen were to have "two kinds of nobles put over them : greater nobles, who were called landgraves; and lesser nobles, who were named casiques. The head of the nobles was to be called Palatine." [3]

THE EDENTON TEA PARTY. In Edenton on October 25, 1774, fifty-one ladies crowded into the home of Mrs. Elizabeth King and signed an agreement to do all in their power to carry out the wishes of the New Bern convention, and declined to allow any more English tea to be served on their tables. [4]

THE REVOLUTION. In 1773, John Harvey, Speaker, laid before the House of Commons appeals from several other

colonies for its concurrence in the appointment of a committee
to enquire into the wrongs imposed by England on the colonists. In August, 1774, the Assembly or Congress met at
New Bern, in defiance of the proclamation and denunciation of
royal authority. It endorsed the plan for a general congress
in Philadelphia in September following. In February, 1775,
John Harvey issued a call for the Assembly to meet at New
Bern on the 4th of the following April, and a notice to the
people to send delegates to a convention to be held at the
same time and place. On the 20th of May, 1775, the people
of Mecklenburg adopted a declaration of independence, a copy
of which was sent to the Continental Congress at Philadelphia.
Governor Martin, the royal governor, fled and the provisional congress met at Hillsboro on the 20th of August, 1775,
and adopted measures for offensive and defensive warfare. On
the 4th of April, 1776, the provincial congress met at Halifax,
and on the 12th of that month expressed the readiness of the
people to declare their independence of the Crown, appointing a committee of safety, with Cornelius Harnett as chairman. On the 12th of November, 1776, a convention of the
people adopted a constitution, which provided for a legislature, judiciary, etc., and the election of the governor by the
Legislature." [5]

SEEDS OF SECTIONALISM. Most of the population was in
the east and this constitution provided that each county
should have two members of the House of Commons, as the
popular branch was called, and one Senator. But, with the
rapid settlement of the western part of the State, dissatisfaction arose, and as early as 1790 efforts were made to remedy this uneven representation. By 1818 the feeling had
grown so intense that there was talk of a separation into two
States. [6] The western members wanted the members from
each county to correspond to the number of inhabitants, and
demanded that the governor be elected by the people direct.
Largely through the efforts of David L. Swain, then governor,
the question of calling a State convention was left to a vote
of the people and adopted by 5,856 majority. [6]

EARLY LEGISLATION. In the "Laws of North Carolina," as
revised by Henry Potter, J. L. Taylor and Bart. Yancey, Esqs.,
in two volumes, published in 1821, is found provision for
entry takers and surveyors, establishing courts (1777) and

regulating proceedings therein, directing methods of electing members of the legislature, to encourage the building of public mills (ch. 122); making parts of Surry county and of "the District of Washington, now a part of Tennessee, into Wilkes county (ch. 127); while chapter 154, laws of 1779, prohibits hunting deer in night time with guns and fire-light;[7] chapter 212, laws of 1784, prohibits killing deer in woods on the east side of the Appalachians between the 20th of February and 15th of August, but permitting the slaughter to continue to the west. Chapter 227, laws of 1784, empowers the county courts of pleas and quarter sessions to order the laying out of public roads. Chapter 201 of the laws of 1784 describes the lands granted to General Nathanael Greene (acts of 1782) to be laid off by Absalom Tatum, Isaac Shelby and Anthony Bledsoe, beginning on the south bank of the Duck river. That is now a part of Maury county, Tenn. Chapter 123, laws of 1777, provides a penalty for burning or setting fire to woods. Haywood's Manual, p. 377, provides for the enrollment (with certain excepted classes) of all males between 18 and 45 years of age, fixes penalties for failing to attend musters, gives such members of the militia free passage over all ferries, and exempts them from working roads on muster days. The confiscation of lands belonging to all who took up arms against the United States is provided for (ch. 17, laws of 1777), while chapter 2, laws of 1779, gives a list of those whose lands have been forfeited (Haywood's Manual, p. 123). Military land warrants were provided for in ch. 18, laws of 1741 (Haywood's Manual, p. 448), and on page 450 is found the requirement that prisons shall contain a criminals' room, a debtors' room, a female prisoners' room and a negroes' room.

PRISONS IN TOWNS AND COUNTRY. But in the year of our Lord, one thousand nine hundred and twelve there appeared in an Asheville daily newspaper the following:[8]

"'I have been visiting these places for five years,' said Mr. Crabtree. 'I have been urging that North Carolina do away with the chains and establish the merit system. The convicts need help. The work needs evangelists, chaplains. The prisoners have no encouragement.'

"One of the Buncombe road camps, that in lower Hominy, was visited. The officials were found to be kindly and courteous. The objectionable double bunk system is used. White and negro prisoners are kept together, 22 men packed in a 30 by eight feet iron cage. Sanitary conditions are very poor as to bed clothing."

There are also laws concerning runaways, slaves, free negroes and mulattoes.

CONFISCATION.   The act of 1779 (ch. 153, p. 384, Potter's Revisal) refers to an act of 1777 for the confiscation of the property of all persons inimical to "this or the United States," and provides methods for carrying that act into effect.   A list of those whose property is declared forfeited, comprising almost an entire page, is given.

FINANCIAL LEGISLATION.   In 1783 (ch. 185, p. 435) the legislature declared that "the opening of the land office and the granting of lands within the State would not only redeem the specie and other certificates due from (doubtless meaning 'to') the public, but greatly enhance the credit thereof (sic)." In 1783 (ch. 187) a table was given showing the scale by which to determine the value of the depreciation of paper currency, estimated in specie; and a "table of coins," giving the value in North Carolina currency of a guinea, a half-guinea, a French guinea, a moidore, a four pistole piece, a pistole, a double Johann'es, French and English crowns, a dollar, a pistareen and a shilling.

WASHINGTON DISTRICT AND COUNTY.   In 1777 (ch. 126, p. 349) the State recognized the "late district of Washington," the old Watauga Settlements, by erecting it into a new and distinct county by the name of Washington county.   It was to begin at the most northwesterly part of Wilkes, on the Virginia line, and run south 36 miles; then west to the ridge of the Great Iron mountains; thence southwestwardly to the Unicoy mountain where the trading path crosses, and then south to the South Carolina line, and then due west to the "great river Mississippi, then up the river to a point due west from the beginning."   Thus, Washington county embraced what is now Tennessee.

FOR THE RELIEF OF MORAVIANS, QUAKERS, MENNONITES AND DUNKARDS.   In 1780 (ch. 166, p. 406) an act was passed which recited that as an act had been already passed which required all persons to take an oath of allegiance to the State or be sent out of it, and deprived of civil rights therein, which oath certain persons "pretended" the Mennonites, Quakers, etc., etc., had not taken, and had, under this pretext, entered upon and were then claiming the lands of those sects, it was enacted that all such entries and proceedings thereon should be null and void.

FORMATION OF FIRST COUNTIES. In 1791 Buncombe was formed from Burke and Rutherford counties; in 1799 (Laws of N. C., p. 98) Ashe was formed, and it is the shortest act of the kind on record: "all that part of the county of Wilkes lying west of the extreme height of the Appalachian mountains shall be, and the same is hereby erected into a separate and distinct county by the name of Ashe." In 1808 Haywood was formed out of the western part of Buncombe, and it extended to the Tennessee line. The formation of these three counties required an interval of about ten years between each. Then followed the dead-lock of twenty years, extending to 1828, when Macon was allowed to become a county, it having been taken from Haywood. Yancey was formed in 1833, out of Burke and Buncombe. It had thus taken forty-two years to get five counties west of the Blue Ridge. But the leaven of discontent was working, and the convention of 1835 was called by a vote of the entire people of the State.

CONVENTION OF 1835. The convention met at Raleigh in January, 1835, and the demands of the west for the election of representatives and governor by the direct vote of the people were granted; the right of suffrage which hitherto had been enjoyed by certain "free persons of color"[9] was abrogated. Catholics were relieved of political disability, the governor's term was extended to two years, and biennial, instead of annual sessions of the legislature provided for. But something had been held back, and that was

"FREE AND EQUAL SUFFRAGE." The first Democratic governor chosen by the people was David S. Reid, in 1850, who favored what was called "free and equal suffrage." To understand this phrase it will be necessary to understand that, under the constitution of 1835, white males, 21 years old, who had paid their taxes could vote for members of the house of commons; but they could not vote for senators unless they owned fifty acres of land. "Free Suffrage" meant to allow any free white man to vote for a senator, whether the voter owned land or not.[10]

THE FLY STILL IN THE OINTMENT. Thus, the new constitution still left something to be desired: the senate was to consist of fifty. senators, the number from each senatorial district being determined, not by population, but by the amount of taxes paid. That did not suit the white men of the west at all.

PREVALENCE OF EASTERN NAMES. With the exception of Swain, no county west of the Blue Ridge is named for a citizen of this section; and, except Bakersville and Bryson city, no county seat is named for a son of the west. These honors had to be bartered away to get the legislature to consent to the formation of every other county west of the Blue Ridge. For even eastern men admit that we obtained our just dues only by barter and trade.

SECTIONALISM RAMPANT. Of this period Chief Justice Clark [11] says :

"During the time Capt. Burns was in the legislature [1821 to 1834] the east had a disproportionately large representation. The west had increased very greatly in population and demanded an increase in representation, either by the creation of new counties in the west or by calling a constitutional convention. These measures were voted down in the general assembly, or if a new county was created in the west a new one was created in the east—just as in congress before the war, if a non-slave-holding state was admitted into the Union, a slaveholding state was admitted to balance it. Capt. Burns, though he was from Carteret county, on the very borders of the ocean, his was the odd vote that created Macon county in 1827. In 1822 he voted for Davidson county. He voted for the creation of Yancey county in 1827, the vote being a tie. The speaker voted 'aye', but the bill was lost in the senate. In 1828 he voted for Cherokee, though the measure then failed, the county not being created till eleven years later, in 1839. In 1833 Capt. Burns was in the senate and again voted for the creation of Yancey county, which measure then passed. The grateful west promptly named the county seat of the new county 'Burnsville.'

"We of this day can hardly realize the bitter feeling that then existed between the east and west in our State until the inequality of representation was remedied by the constitutional convention of 1835."

As the Cherokees agreed to go west in 1835 we should have here a—

RECAPITULATION OF INDIAN TREATIES, the principal of which, concerning the mountains of Western North Carolina, may be briefly summed up as follows :

Treaty of 1761, by which the Blue Ridge was made the boundary;

Treaty of 1772 and purchase of 1773, by which the ridge between the Nollechucky and the Watauga rivers, from their sources in the Blue Ridge westward, and from the Blue Ridge to the Virginia line, was made the boundary line;

Treaty of Hopewell, 1785, by which the line was moved westward to a line running just east of Marshall, Asheville and Hendersonville;

Treaty of Holston, 1791, establishing Meigs & Freeman's line;

Treaty of 1819 by which the line was moved west to the Nantahala river;

Treaty of New Echota, or 1835, by which the Cherokees surrendered all lands east of the Mississippi, and agreed to remove.

FROM 1833 TO 1849.   Notwithstanding the changes wrought in the constitution by the convention of 1835, the west made but little progress politically, as during those sixteen years only one additional county was permitted to organize, and that was Henderson, taken from the southern part of Buncombe in 1838.   But, although the Senate was to continue to represent the landed interests till 1857, when the constitution was amended by the Legislature so as to distribute senators according to population,[12] between 1848 and 1862 seven new counties were established west of the Blue Ridge, viz.: Watauga, 1849; Jackson, 1851; Madison, 1851; Alleghany, 1859; Mitchell, 1861; Transylvania, 1861; and Clay, 1861.

A NATURAL DIPLOMAT.[13]   "In 1848 William H. Thomas entered the Senate from Macon county, and remained there till 1862.   In those twelve years he accomplished more for western North Carolina than any other man who ever lived. In addition to securing the creation of the seven new counties above referred to, he had the Western Turnpike from Salisbury to Murphy constructed and paid for out of the sale of Cherokee lands; he secured a charter for the Western North Carolina Railroad and saw it finished to within a few miles of Morganton at the foot of the Blue Ridge, and had the charter so altered that after the road should reach Asheville it should go west toward Murphy as rapidly as it proceeded northwest toward Paint Rock.   In addition to this he caused turnpike roads to be built all through the mountains, and helped to organize the companies which constructed them, by giving barbecues and holding public meetings at which he taught the people the importance of making good roads.   And, in the meantime, he was using his powers of persuasion to induce South Carolina to endorse four million dollars of the bonds of the Blue Ridge Railroad that was to enter our State at Rabun gap and proceed down the Little Tennessee to Cincinnati. He was also engaged at this time in looking after the affairs of the Eastern Band of Cherokees, by whom he had been adopted when a youth. He lived to see the railroad completed to Murphy." A monument of bronze is due to his memory from the people of Western North Carolina.

SECESSION. On the 30th day of January, 1861, the Legislature submitted to the people the question of holding a convention to consider secession; but it was voted down. But when, in April, 1861, President Lincoln issued a proclamation calling on North Carolina, with the other states still in the Union, to contribute her quota of troops to be used in coercing those states which had withdrawn to return to the Union, the Legislature voted for a convention, and on the 20th day of May it unanimously adopted the ordinance of secession.

NORTH CAROLINA DID NOT FIGHT FOR SLAVERY.[14] "One of the most significant proofs of the fact that the status of the negro was not, at the South, regarded as the issue, was the ardor with which the non-slaveholding portions of the population flew to arms at the call of their respective states, and the fidelity they exhibited for the cause through four years of struggle, self-denial, suffering, death and social destruction.

FEW SLAVE-HOLDERS IN THE MOUNTAINS. "Especially was this true of the North Carolina mountaineer. In the greater portion of that section of the State extending from the eastern foot-hills of the Blue Ridge to the western boundaries of Clay and Cherokee, the slave-owners in 1861 were so rare that the institution of slavery may be said, practically, to have had no existence; and yet that region sent more than fifteen thousand fighting men—volunteers—into the field.[15]

REGIMENTS. "The Sixteenth, Twenty-fifth, Twenty-ninth, Thirty-ninth, Fifty-eighth, Sixtieth, Sixty-second, Sixty-fourth, Sixty-fifth and Sixty-ninth regiments were composed exclusively of mountain men; and in addition they were numerously represented in the "Bethel," Ninth, Eleventh, Fourteenth, the "Immortal Twenty-sixth," the Nineteenth regiments, and other organizations. This estimate does not include a large number of men from the same territory, who during the progress of the war were embodied in independent commands, and did gallant service in the campaigns in Virginia, in the southwest and in the immediate locality of their homes. These mountaineers were the descendants of the sturdy, hard-fighting Scotch-Irish, who, to a man, were Whigs in the Revolution, and by their stubborn resistance of the British aggressions, contributed so much to the establishment of the independence of their country. Nor does it include thousands who joined the Federal army.

NOT REBELS, BUT SONS OF REVOLUTIONARY SIRES. "The men of Western Carolina, whose sublime devotion and courage, with that of their comrades from other portions of the South, have made the heights of Gettysburg and Fredericksburg and Sharpsburg, the plains of Manassas and Chickahominy, the wilderness of Chancellorsville and Chickamauga, the valleys of Virginia, Georgia and Tennessee, immortal, had in their veins the blood of the patriots who fought at Brandywine, Germantown, Monmouth, Yorktown, Savannah, Guilford, Eutaw Springs and Kings Mountain—and, let it never be forgotten, they fought, and fighting died, for the same great divine right—the right of a people to ordain and control their own government."[14]

OUR "WAR GOVERNOR'S" RIGHT HAND.[16] Governor Vance was the colonel of the 26th North Carolina regiment when he was elected to the high office of governing his people in the most momentous and troublous time in their history; but notwithstanding that fact, he realized that he was not a trained and educated soldier. He therefore, summoned to his side at the outset of his term that accomplished officer and gentleman, General James Green Martin, who had graduated from West Point in time to lose an arm in the Mexican War and to be brevetted for gallantry on the field of Cherubusco. He was, therefore, continued as adjutant general, to which position Gov. Clark had appointed him in 1861, and the legislature wisely gave him great power and put money freely at his command, in preparing our troops for battle. Without factories and without markets, forty thousand armed and well-drilled men had been turned over to the Confederacy within seven months; while in less than one year after North Carolina left the Union the State had nearly sixty thousand men in camp. He did not stop then, but as rapidly as possible Gen. Martin added regiment after regiment until seventy-two regular regiments had been formed. Later in the war three regiments of boys too young for regular duty were organized.   In addition to these, in the days of sore need, five regiments of old men were pressed into the service of the Confederacy.   Then came the Home Guard, the whole aggregating 125,000 soldiers.

ARMA VIRUMQUE.   And not only did he make soldiers, but he also went actively into the manufacture of arms.   He hired two Frenchmen to make swords and bayonets at the armory at Wilmington, while workmen in Guilford made 300 rifles a month.   The State took charge of the old United States arsenal at Fayetteville and made excellent rifles.   One powder mill near Raleigh made weekly 4,000 pounds of powder.   Pistols, swords, cartridge-boxes, gun-caps, bayonets, cartridges, powder, lead, etc., to the value of $1,673,308 were furnished the soldiers before April, 1864.

QUARTERMASTER; ALSO COMMISSARY.   The Legislature in 1861 directed Gen. Martin to clothe the soldiers as best he could, and he started a clothing factory at Raleigh, and required all the mills in the State to send him every yard of cloth they made.   Officers were sent into the far South to buy all the shoes and cloth they could find, while women at home furnished blankets, quilts and comforts, even cutting up their carpets and lining them with cotton to be used for blankets.   In 1862 Gen. Martin asked Gov. Clark to buy a ship to run the blockade and bring in supplies from foreign ports; but as the Governor's term was nearly out, he asked Gen. Martin to submit his plan to Governor Vance.   He did so, and the Governor approved it; and Gen. Martin sent John White to England, where he bought the Ad-Vance, named in honor of the Governor.   This ship brought in many cargoes of goods before it was captured.   The State bought cotton and rosin and in foreign ports exchanged these for such supplies as were most in demand.   Other ships ran the blockade also, bringing in 250,000 pairs of shoes and cloth for 250,000 suits, 2,000 fine rifles, 60,000 pairs of cotton cards, 500 sacks of coffee for the sick, medicine to the value of $50,-000 and other articles.   For these supplies the State spent $26,363,663.   From these stores North Carolina contributed largely to the Confederate government, and during the last months of the war we were feeding one-half of General Lee's army.

GENERAL MARTIN TAKES COMMAND AT ASHEVILLE. His work of organizing and supplying the troops having ended, Gen. Martin took command of the troops in and around Asheville in 1864. He spent the rest of his life here, and died a "mountain man" just as "Zeb" Vance had always been, though his residence had been in Charlotte for years, and we are proud of their records.

MANY WELCOME PEACE. The sentiment for the Old Union did not wholly die in Western North Carolina even during the heat of the armed conflict which followed secession; and after having in vain asserted by nearly four years' warfare its conscientious contention that the general government had no right to force any state to furnish troops to coerce any other state to remain in the Union, many of the best and most influential citizens of these mountains, after the defeat of Hood at Franklin, Tennessee, and the evacuation of Savannah by the Confederates, considered further resistance as not only futile but a needless waste of blood and treasure, and that such people at home should make known their sentiments to the commanders of the Union forces in the South. Their hope was thus to avert further bloodshed and the destruction of property; and, as Sherman had not then started on his barbarous march through South Carolina, it is interesting to consider how much of suffering and loss might have been spared to the women and children of that State and elsewhere if their counsel had been followed.

PEACEFUL OVERTURES. In pursuance of this sentiment there is the best authority for making public the following facts: In January, 1865, there met in one of the rooms of the Old Buck Hotel at Asheville the following men: A. S. Merrimon, Weston Holmes, Alfred M. Alexander, J. E. Reid, J. L. Henry, Adolphus E. Baird, G. M. Roberts, I. A. Harris, and Adolphus M. Gudger. A paper declaring that the people were tired of further warfare and desired peace and the restoration of the Union was prepared by Judge A. S. Merrimon and signed by each of the above-named citizens. Adolphus M. Gudger undertook to have it delivered to Judge John Baxter at Knoxville. He did so, and it was put into the hands of the military commander then in charge of that city. Major W. W. Rollins, now postmaster at Asheville, saw and read it in January, 1865. It doubtless did much good in the

saving of property when the Union forces invaded this territory in April and May following. Of these men A. M. Alexander, J. L. Henry and I. A. Harris were officers of the Confederate Army at the time they signed that paper. All are
now dead except Dr. I. A. Harris, who lives at Jupiter, Buncombe county. This paper is said to be in existence, and its
exact wording would be a matter of great interest at this time
when there is so universal a sentiment in favor of the Union. [17]

AFTER THE WAR. During the Civil War which followed
secession, the writ of habeas corpus was not suspended in
North Carolina or New York; but after peace had been declared
Governor W. W. Holden, provisional governor, suspended
it, and appointed Col. George W. Kirk, who had raided the
mountain section during the war, to enforce martial law.
North Carolina sent more troops into the Confederate army
than any other Southern State; and while there were many
desertions from the soldiers who had joined the Confederacy
from the West, the mountain section was by no means a laggard in defence of the cause of the Confederacy.

RECONSTRUCTION. Gov. Holden called a convention which
met in Raleigh October 2, 1865, but its work was rejected by
the people by a vote of 19,570 for and 21,552 against, many of
the whites being then disfranchised. Gen. E. R. Canby, commanding the Second Military District, ordered a constitutional
convention which met January 14, 1868. The office of lieutenant
governor was created, and that of superintendent of public
works; all voters were made eligible to office; the number of
the Supreme and Superior courts was increased and provision was made for their election and that of magistrates by
the people; the County Court system was abolished and
county government by a board of commissioners substituted.
The sessions of the Legislature were changed back to one
each year; provision was made to establish a penitentiary;
negroes were given equal rights before the law with all whites,
and a census of the State was ordered every ten years. A
homestead of $1,000 in real estate and $500 in personal property was exempted from execution; Gov. W. W. Holden was
impeached and removed from office in 1871; and Lieutenant
Governor Tod R. Caldwell succeeded him.

THE EXHAUSTION OF THE JUDICIARY. One of the charges
against Gov. Holden had been the suspension of the writ of

habeas corpus in Alamance and Caswell counties, during what was called Kirk's War, and the existence of the Ku-Klux Klan in 1869 and 1870, when, Col. Kirk, having refused to recognize the writs of the Supreme Court, Chief Justice Pearson had declared that "the judiciary was exhausted." Judge George W. Brooks, of the United States District Court for the eastern district, however, pitted the strong arm of the United States against this defiance of judicial authority, and Kirk and Holden yielded. [18]

CONVENTION OF 1875. There was a Constitutional Convention, against the calling of which the eastern counties had voted solidly, held in Raleigh, September 6, 1875, which provided that separate schools should be provided for white and colored; that there should be criminal and inferior courts; that there should be a department of agriculture; limiting the per diem of members of the Legislature to four dollars a day during a session of sixty days; providing for the election of magistrates by the Legislature; reducing the number of judges, and disfranchising persons who had been convicted of infamous crimes. Sessions of the Legislature were again made biennial. In 1900 an amendment was adopted requiring a quasi-educational qualification for voters after 1908, except for the descendants of those who could vote prior to 1860. The period during which that exception was operative passed in 1908; but the fact that certain "free persons of color" had enjoyed the right to vote prior to the constitution of 1835, [19] saved the exception, commonly called the "grandfather clause," from discriminating against anyone "on account of race, color or previous condition of servitude."

REGULATING PASSENGER RATES. In 1908 the Legislature passed an act limiting passenger rates on railroads to two cents per mile; and the railroads, after some litigation, finally compromised by agreeing to charge not over two and one-half cents per mile.

STATE-WIDE PROHIBITION. In 1908 the Legislature submitted to the people the question of prohibiting the manufacture and sale of malt and spiritous liquors anywhere in the State, and the measure was adopted by a large majority.

THE "NO-FENCE" LAW. In 1885, pursuant to an act of the Legislature passed at the request of Hon. Richmond Pearson, member of the House from Buncombe county, the voters of that county voted to eliminate fences in most of the townships, and requiring the owners of cattle, sheep, horses and "hawgs" to keep them in bounds. Buncombe was the pioneer county in adopting this economic reform; and Richmond Pearson the legislator who had the courage to secure its enactment. A quarrel grew out of this matter which resulted in the sending of a challenge to Mr. Pearson by Adjutant General Johnston Jones; but the day of duelling had passed forever, and the matter was adjusted.

Upon the election of Hon. Z. B. Vance as governor and a Democratic Legislature the magistrates were empowered to elect the county commissioners. This was done to enable the eastern counties to control their board of commissioners in counties where negro votes predominated. But it finally resulted in great dissatisfaction, and helped to defeat the Democratic Party in 1894. The Republicans changed the law, in 1895, making the county commissioners elective by the people.

SWAIN, GRAHAM AND AVERY. Not much was left to be done in the way of division of the mountain territory when the Civil War came to put a stop to legislation along this line. Swain county was formed in 1871 and in 1872 Graham was formed out of a portion of Cherokee because it was cut off from the rest of the State by two high ranges of mountains on the east and south and by the Little Tennessee river on the north. Its county seat is Robbinsville. The county seat of Swain is Bryson City, named for the late Col. Thad. D. Bryson who, as a member of the Legislature, secured its establishment as a county. Avery county was formed in 1911, and its county seat is Newland, named for Lieut. Gov. Newland of Caldwell. It is at the Old Fields of Toe, and the court house and jail are completed. In this county is some of the finest scenery in the South.

ONLY CRUMBS FOR THE WEST. Although Gen. Thomas Love had been in the Senate and the House from 1793 to 1828, except in 1797-98, and John and Elisha Calloway and George Bower from Ashe almost as long, it was not until Governor Swain was elected by the Legislature a Superior Court judge for one of the eastern circuits that there was the slightest breach in the wall of sectionalism. His election by the legislature to the governorship in 1832 and afterwards to to the presidency of the University followed; but up to his election to the bench there had never been a judge from west of the Ridge and there has never been a judge from this section elected to the Supreme Court, Judge Augustus S. Merrimon having moved from this locality long before his elevation to that office. And, with the exception of Judge Swain, there was never a Superior Court judge from the mountains till 1868, when Judges James L. Henry and Riley Cannon were elected under Reconstruction. Gov. Zebulon B. Vance of Buncombe was elected governor in 1862-64, and Gov. Locke Craig of the same county in 1912; but they and Governor Swain are the only governors this part of the State has ever had. Hon. James L. Robinson of Macon and Rufus A. Doughton of Alleghany have been presidents of the Senate, and James L. Robinson was elected speaker of the House in 1872 and 1874, but it was not till 1901 that Hon. Walter E. Moore of Jackson was elected speaker. In 1876 Dr. Samuel L. Love was elected State auditor from Haywood, and the Hon. Robert M. Furman in 1894. Hon. Theodore F. Davidson was elected attorney general in 1884 and 1888 and R. D. Gilmer in 1900. General Thomas L. Clingman of Buncombe was elected to the U. S. Senate in 1858, and Judge Jeter C. Pritchard in 1895 and 1897. Col. Allen T. Davidson was elected to the Provisional Congress of the Confederacy in 1861 and in 1862 by the people. In 1864 Judge George W. Logan of Rutherford county succeeded him. Hon. M. L. Shipman of Hendersonville has been labor commissioner for several years.

FELIX WALKER. [20] When the Missouri question was under discussion, Mr. Walker secured the floor, when some impatient member asked him to sit down and let a vote be taken. He refused, saying he must "make a speech for Buncombe," that is, for his constituents. Thus "bunkum," as it is usually spelt, has become part of our vocabulary. Mr. Walker was born in Hampshire county, Va., July 19, 1753, and became a merchant. His grandfather, John Walker, emigrated in 1720 from Derry, Ireland, to Delaware, where his father, also named John, was born. The younger John moved first to Virginia and afterwards to North Carolina, settling within four miles of Kings Mountain. He was a member of the first convention at Hillsboro, July, 1775, and of the Provincial Congress which met there, August 21, 1775, afterwards serving in the Revolutionary War. He died in 1796. Felix went with Richard Henderson to Kentucky (then called Louisa), 1774-1775, where he was badly wounded by Indians. He then joined the Watauga settlement and became the first clerk of the court of Washington county. While holding this office he went to Mecklenburg county, and was made captain of a company of State troops which was placed at Nollechucky to guard the frontier against the Indians. After serving four years as clerk he moved to Rutherford county, N. C., where in 1789 he was appointed clerk of the court of that county. He represented that county in the General Assembly in 1792, 1799, 1800, 1801, 1802, and 1806. In 1817 he was elected member of Congress, and for two succeeding Congresses. R. B. Vance succeeded him in 1823. Walker was a candidate again in 1827, but withdrew in favor of Sam. P. Carson, who defeated both Vance and James Graham. Walker then removed to Mississippi, where he died in 1828, at Clinton.

ISRAEL PICKENS was born in Cabarrus county, N. C., January 30, 1780; moved to Burke county, receiving limited schooling; State Senator in 1808 and 1809; elected as Democrat to 12th, 13th and 14th Congresses (March 4, 1811-March 3, 1817); appointed Register of Land Office of Mississippi territory in 1817; Governor of Alabama, 1821-1825; appointed from Alabama to United States Senate to fill vacancy caused by death of Henry Chambers, serving from February 17, 1826, to November 27, 1826; died near Matanzas, Cuba, April 24, 1827.[20]

JAMES GRAHAM was born in Lincoln county, January, 1793; graduated from University of North Carolina, 1814; admitted to bar and practiced; moved to Rutherford county, which he represented in the House of Commons 1822-1823, 1824, 1828-1829; elected to the 23d, 24th, 25th, 26th and 27th Congresses, and served from December 2, 1833, to March 3, 1843, excepting from March 25, 1836, to December 5, 1836, when a Democratic house declared the seat vacant, but at a new election Graham was again elected; defeated for the 28th Congress; elected as a Whig to the 29th Congress (March 4, 1845, to March 3, 1847); died in Rutherford county, September 25, 1851.[20]

THOMAS L. CLINGMAN was born at Huntersville, July 27, 1812; graduated from University of North Carolina, 1832; studied and practiced law; elected to House of Commons in 1835; moved to Asheville in 1836; elected State Senator in

1840; elected as a Whig to 28th Congress (March 4, 1843-March 3, 1845); defeated by James Graham to 29th Congress; reelected to 30th, 31st, 32d, 33d, 34th and 35th Congresses (March 4, 1847-December 6, 1858) when he resigned; appointed in 1858 United States Senator as a Democrat to fill vacancy caused by resignation of Asa Biggs; was elected to United States Senate and served from May 6, 1858, to January 21, 1861, when he withdrew; was formally expelled from United States Senate July 11, 1861; appointed May 17, 1862, brigadier general in the Confederate service, and commanded a brigade composed of the 8th, 31st, 51st, and 61st North Carolina infantry; delegate to the Democratic national convention of 1868; was a delegate to the State Constitutional convention of 1875; explored and measured mountain peaks and developed mineral resources of several regions; died November 3, 1897; buried in Asheville.

ZEBULON BAIRD VANCE, born in Buncombe county May 13, 1830, attended Washington College, Tennessee, was clerk at hotel, Hot Springs, North Carolina; attended University of North Carolina; admitted to bar in January, 1852, when he was elected county attorney of Buncombe; member of House of Commons, 1854; elected as a Democrat to 35th Congress to fill vacancy caused by resignation of Thomas L. Clingman; reelected to the 36th Congress, and served from December 7, 1858, to March 3, 1861; entered Confederate Army as captain in May, 1861, and made colonel in August, 1861; was elected governor August, 1862, and 1864; was member of Democratic national convention of 1868; elected to United States Senate November, 1870, but was refused admission, and resigned in January, 1872; he was defeated for United States Senate in 1872 by Hon. A. S. Merrimon; was elected governor over Hon. Thomas Settle in famous campaign of 1876; elected to United States Senate in 1879; reelected in 1884 and 1890, serving till his death in Washington, D. C., April 14, 1894 [20]

ALEXANDER HAMILTON JONES was born in Buncombe county July 21, 1822, was educated at Emory and Henry College; he was a merchant, a strong Union man during the Civil War, and in 1863 joined the Union Army and was captured in East Tennessee while raising a regiment and imprisoned at Asheville and at Camp Vance below Morganton, and at Camp Holmes and at Libby Prison at Richmond, Virginia. He made his escape November 14, 1864, and joined the Union Army at Cumberland, Maryland. After the war he returned to Hendersonville and was elected a delegate to the State Convention to frame a new constitution in 1865. He was elected a representative to the 39th Congress but was refused a seat. He was reelected to the 40th Congress and was admitted July 6, 1868. He was reelected to the 41st Congress and made his home in Washington, D. C., till 1876, and in Maryland till 1884, when he came to Asheville, where he resided till 1890, going thence to Oklahoma, where he remained till 1897, when he moved to Long Beach, California, where he died January 29, 1901. He married Sarah D. Brittain, daughter of William and Rachel Brittain of Mills river, in 1843, of which marriage five children were born: Col. Thad W. Jones, U. S. A., Otho M. Jones, and Mrs. J. P. Johnson, Mrs. Thomas J. Candler, and Miss Charlotte Jones, spinster. His widow died in January, 1913, aged 92.

GEN. ROBERT BRANK VANCE. He was born in Buncombe county, April 24, 1828, and was the eldest son of David and Mira Vance. When 21 years of age he was elected clerk of the county court, and reelected till 1858, when he retired voluntarily. He was a Union man and voted against secession, but went into the Confederate Army when war was declared. He was first captain, but soon afterwards elected colonel of the 29th North Carolina Infantry, becoming brigadier general in 1863, after the battle of Murfreesborough. He was captured at Cosby's creek, Tenn., in January, 1864, and kept a prisoner till the close of the war. He was elected to the 43d Congress in 1872, and thereafter till 1885. He succeeded in securing daily mails in every county in his district, and many money-order offices. He was appointed commissioner of patents in 1885, and obtained an appropriation for dredging the French Broad river between Brevard and Asheville, a small steamer having been operated there a short time in 1876. He was in the State Senate in 1893. He was a sincere Christian, and the most useful congressman who ever went from that district. He died at Alexander, ten miles below Asheville, November 28, 1899.

EDMUND SPENCER BLACKBURN, born in Watauga county, September 22, 1868; attended common schools and academies; admitted to the bar in May, 1890; was reading clerk of North

Carolina Senate, 1894-1895; representative in State Legislature, 1896-1897; was elected speaker pro tem of this Legislature; appointed assistant United States Attorney for western district in 1898, and assisted in the prosecution of Breese and Dickerson in the First National Bank case; elected as republican to 57th Congress (March 4, 1901-March 3, 1903); reelected March 4, 1905; and died at Elizabethton, Tenn., March 10, 1912. Interment at Boone, N. C. Edmund Blackburn was the first of his family to settle in Watauga, then Ashe county, and married a relative of Levi Morphew, who is still living on the New river, well up in the nineties. Edmund's children were Levi, Sallie, and Edmund, Levi having been the grandfather of E. Spencer and M. B. Blackburn of Boone. Levi Morphew is a son of Sallie Blackburn. Among the first Methodist churches in Watauga was the one built by the Blackburn family on Riddle's Fork of Meat Camp creek, called Hopewell, the Methodists having worshiped in Levi Blackburn's house prior to that time. Henson's chapel on Cove creek was probably the first Methodist church in Watauga. The first church built in Boone was built about 1880.

ROMULUS Z. LINNEY. He was born in Rutherford county December 26, 1841; was educated in the common schools of the country, at York's Collegiate Institute, and at Dr. Millen's school at Taylorsville; he served as a private in the Confederate army until the battle of Chancellorsville, where he was severely wounded, and was discharged. He then joined a class in Dr. Millen's school at Taylorsville, of which Hon. W. H. Bower was a member; studied law with the late Judge Armfield; was admitted to practice by the Supreme Court in 1868; was elected to the State Senate in 1870, 1872, 1874, and again in 1882; was elected to the 54th, 55th and 56th Congresses as a Republican, receiving 19,419 votes against 18,006 for Rufus A. Doughton, Democrat, and 640 for Wm. M. White, Prohibitionist. He married Dorcas Stephenson in Taylorsville. In 1880 he became interested in Watauga so much that he bought property there, and in September, 1902, he bought a tract of land he called Tater Hill on Rich mountain, where he built two rock houses. He was influential in getting a wagon road built along the top of the Rich mountain range from the gap above Boone to a gap just north of Silverstone. He contributed $500 to the Appalachian Training School. Above the front door of the chief building of this college is written in marble the following quotation from one of his speeches delivered July 4, 1903 : "Learning, the Handmaid of Loyalty and Liberty. A Vote Governs Better than a Crown." He died at Taylorsville, April 15, 1910. His mother was a sister of the late Judge John Baxter.

THOMAS DILLARD JOHNSTON was born at Waynesville, North Carolina, April 1, 1840. His father was William Johnston and his mother Lucinda Gudger, a daughter of the late James Gudger and a grand-daughter of Col. Robert Love of Waynesville. He went to school to the late Capt. James N. Terrell in a log school house in Waynesville, when about ten years of age. In 1853 he entered the school of the late Col. Stephen D. Lee, in Chunn's Cove, where he remained till the summer of 1857, when he entered the State University; but, his health failing, he returned to Asheville to which place his family had removed, and were living in a brick house that stood on the corner now occupied by the Drhumor Block. He began the study of law with the late Judge James L. Bailey at his law school near the foot of Black Mountain, where he remained till the summer of 1861, when he obtained license to practice in the County Court. In May, 1861, he enlisted as a private in the Rough and Ready Guards, the second Asheville company to enter the service of the Confederacy. He was desperately wounded three times at Malvern Hill, and for a long time his life was despaired of. Recovering, however, he became quartermaster to Col. W. C. Walker's battalion and Capt. J. T. Levy's battery of artillery. In 1866 he was admitted to practice by Chief Justice Pearson. He was defeated in 1867 for county solicitor by Col. V. S. Lusk, and in 1868 Col. Lusk defeated him for circuit solicitor. In 1869 he was elected mayor of Asheville, and in 1870 he was elected to the House of Representatives. He canvassed the Ninth Congressional District in 1871 in favor of a State convention to amend the Constitution, but the measure was defeated. He was a candidate for elector in 1872 on the Greeley ticket. In 1875 he again advocated a similar convention, which was called. He was elected to the Legislature again in 1872 and in 1876 to the State Senate. On the 10th of July, 1879, he married Miss N.

Leila Bobo of South Carolina. In 1884 he was elected to Congress, defeating H. G. Ewart, and again in 1886, defeating W. H. Malone. In 1888 he was defeated for Congress by H. G. Ewart. He died June 23, 1902. He gave the United States the site of the present postoffice in 1888, and assisted in the education of a number of worthy young men. Of him it has been said that "his word was better than his bond, and his bond was as good as gold."

JAMES MONTRAVILLE MOODY. He was born February 12, 1858, in Cherokee, now Graham, county, but while he was yet an infant his parents moved to and settled on Jonathan's creek, Haywood county. He attended the neighborhood schools and at seventeen years of age went to Waynesville Academy under the tutelage of John K. Boone, after which he went to the Collegiate Institute at Candler, Buncombe county. He was admitted to the bar in 1881, and in 1886 was Republican nominee for solicitor, and defeated Judge G. S. Ferguson for that position, serving four years. In 1894 he was elected to the State Senate from the 34th District, then composed of Haywood, Buncombe and Madison. He was appointed major and chief commissary and served on the staff of Major General J. Warren Keifer in the Spanish-American War of 1898. In 1900 he was elected from the Ninth District over W. T. Crawford, Esq., a member of Congress, and was renominated in 1902 by the Republicans, but was defeated by Mr. J. M. Gudger, Jr., two years later. On May 20, 1885, Mr. Moody married Miss Margaret E. Hawkins. He died February 5, 1903.

WILLIAM THOMAS CRAWFORD. He was born on Crabtree creek, Haywood county, N. C., June 1, 1856. He attended the public schools of this neighborhood, and in 1882 the old Waynesville Academy. In 1885 and 1887 he served as a member of the House of Representatives in the State legislature. In 1888 he was Presidential elector on the Democratic ticket, and in 1889 he served as engrossing clerk of the House. In 1889 and 1890 he studied law at the University of North Carolina. In 1890 he was elected to Congress. In 1891 he was admitted to the bar. On the 30th of November, 1892, he was married to Miss Inez Edna Coman, daughter of J. R. Coman and wife, Laura McCracken, daughter of David V. McCracken. J. R. Coman's father was that scholarly and eccentric gentleman, Matthew J. Coman, son of James Coman, of the city of Raleigh, N. C. Matthew J. Coman was a classmate of President James K. Polk at the University of North Carolina, was a fine classical scholar, and was born in Raleigh in 1802. In 1892 Mr. Crawford was again elected to Congress, defeating Hon. Jeter C. Pritchard. He was defeated for the 54th Congress. Was re-elected to the 56th Congress, but was unseated by Hon. Richmond Pearson by a majority of one vote. He was defeated for re-election to Congress in 1900. He was Presidential elector on the Democratic ticket in 1904. He was elected to the 60th Congress (1907 to 1909). He practised law in Waynesville till his death, November 16, 1913. Even his political rivals admitted that he had more strength before the people than any man since the death of his near kinsman, the late Col. William H. Thomas, for whom he was named. His widow and seven children survive.

JAMES LOWERY ROBINSON. He was a son of James and Matilda Lowery Robinson, was born September 17, 1838, married Miss Alice L. Siler, daughter of Julius T. and Mary Coleman Siler, October 12, 1864. He died July 8, 1887. On his mother's side he was descended from the Lanes and Swains, his mother having been a niece of Gov. D. L. Swain. He attended Emory and Henry College of Virginia, volunteered as a private in the Confederate army and was promoted to a captaincy, fighting gallantly till discharged because of a wound he carried all his life. He represented Macon in the House from 1868 to 1872, inclusive, when he was elected speaker, to which position he was reelected in 1873 and 1874. A silver service presented at the end of his service as speaker was inscribed : "From the Republicans and Democrats of the House : a testimonial of ability, integrity and impartiality." From 1876 to 1879, inclusive, he served as State Senator from the then 42d District, composed of Jackson, Swain, Clay, Macon, Cherokee and Graham counties; and on November 20, 1876, was elected president of the Senate by a vote of thirty-six to six. He was nominated for lieutenant governor by the Democrats in 1880 and elected, serving as governor in September, 1883, during the absence of Governor Jarvis from the State, and many important grants and State papers bear his signature as "Acting Governor." His first official act as governor was to pardon James

J. Penn, sentenced from Cherokee for perjury. But his great work was in his efforts to secure the construction of railroads through the western part of the State. He was appointed Inspector of Public Lands. From 1886 to 1887 he was Special Indian Agent. He was a good man as well as being a statesman.

NOTES.

[1]Constitution of the Watauga Association.
[2]From Asheville's Centenary.
[3]Hill, p. 43.
[4]Ibid., p. 152.
[5]Polk.
[6]Hill, 249.
[7]Col. Byrd, in his Writings, calls fire hunting driving game to a central point by means of fires set around a circumference,
[8]*Gazette News*, November 30, 1912.
[9]Handbook of North Carolina, by L. L. Polk, p. 22.
[10]Hill, 263.
[11]Address of Judge Walter Clark at Burnsville, July 5, 1909, unveiling statue to Captain Otway Burns.
[12]Hill, p. 264.
[13]Capt James W. Terrell in *The Commonwealth*, Asheville, June 1, 1893.
[14]From "Thirty-Ninth Regiment" by Lieut. Theo. F. Davidson in Vol. II, of "Histories of the Several Regiments and Battalions from North Carolina," p. 699.
[15]According to Wheeler's "History of North Carolina" there were only 4,669 slaves in 1850 in this entire mountain region.
[16]From Ch., 37, of Hill's "Young Peoples' History of North Carolina."
[17]In "The Last Ninety Days of the War," Ch. 16, when Federal General Gillam was approaching Swannanoa gap Love's regiment and Porter's battery went there and fortified it; and "Palmer's brigade was ordered to meet them there; but," Gen. Martin adds, "I regret to say the men refused to go."
[18]Hill, 357, 358.
[19]Polk, 22.
[20]The Biographical Congressional Directory states that he died in Asheville, which is erroneous.

APPENDIX

DAUGHTERS OF THE AMERICAN REVOLUTION

ARDEN CHAPTER. On the 31st of October, 1899, at Arden House, Arden, Buncombe county, was formed the Arden Chapter of the D. A. R. Mrs. Maria Beale, regent and acting historian; Mrs. Mary E. Child, vice-regent and secretary; Miss Bertha F. Beale, corresponding secretary; Mrs. Ella H. Morrison, treasurer; Mrs. Jane Banks Amiss, registrar.

DORCAS BELL LOVE CHAPTER, OF WAYNESVILLE, was organized by Miss Mary Love Stringfield, a great-granddaughter of Robert Love, and Miss Lucy Biddle Lewis, January 9, 1899. The first officers follow: Mary Love Stringfield, regent; Annie E. Gudger, secretary; Elizabeth Briscoe, treasurer; Nora Welch, historian; Bessie Love, registrar; Love B. Gilmer, vice-regent. The present officers (January, 1913) follow: Mrs. Marietta Welch Way, regent; Maria Love Mitchell, vice-regent; Florence V. Camp, secretary; Sarah Stringfield, treasurer; Jessie Howell Rogers, register; Love B. Gilmer, historian; Ella B. Atkins, treasurer. The first annual State Conference of the national society was held at Waynesville, July 2 to 5, 1901, upon invitation of the Dorcas Bell Love chapter. On the 23d of August, 1902, this chapter unveiled a bronze tablet to the memory of Robert Love, the son of Dorcas Bell Love, in the court house at Waynesville.

1760   1845

In Memory of
COL. ROBERT LOVE.
Founder of Waynesville.
Soldier, Statesman, Benefactor.
Erected by the
Dorcas Bell Love Chapter, D. A. R.,
August 23, 1902.

Dorcas Bell was the daughter of James Bell, of Augusta county, Va., and the wife of Samuel Love.

EDWARD BUNCOMBE CHAPTER OF ASHEVILLE was organized October 12, 1903, Mrs. Thomas Settle, regent; Mrs. J. M. Campbell, vice-regent; Miss Lelia May Johnston (now

Mrs. Duncan Cameron Waddell, Jr.,) secretary; Mrs. Theodore S. Morrison, treasurer; Miss Nan Erwin, registrar; Mrs. J. E. Ray, historian. Its officers in January, 1913, are: Mrs. Theodore S. Morrison, regent; Mrs. E. C. Chambers, vice-regent; Miss Hattie M. Scott, secretary; Miss Maria T. Brown, treasurer; Mrs. Chas. A. Moore, registrar; Mrs. M. E. Child, historian; Mrs. T. Woolridge, chaplain; Mrs. J. Edwin Ray, honorary chaplain. This chapter was named for

EDWARD BUNCOMBE, of whom Wheeler's History of North Carolina contains the following account: "Colonel Edward Buncombe was a native of St. Kitts, one of the West India islands. He inherited land in Tyrrell county and built a house, now in the possession of his descendants.

"With his regiment, he joined the army of the north under Washington; was wounded and taken prisoner at the battle of Germantown, in 1777. He died of wounds received in this battle, at Philadelphia, while on parole. He left one son, who died without issue, and two daughters; one, who married John Goelet, Esq., of Washington, N. C., and the other Mr. Clark, of Bertie, a daughter of whom is now the wife of John Cox, Esq., of Edenton.

"Edward Buncombe was distinguished for his manly appearance, indomitable bravery, unsullied patriotism, and open-hearted hospitality. Over his door was this distitch—

"To BUNCOMBE HALL,
Welcome All."

UNITED DAUGHTERS OF THE CONFEDERACY

ASHEVILLE CHAPTER. This was formed April 9, 1907, with Miss Fannie L. Patton, president; Mrs. E. C. Chambers, first vice-president; Mrs. Henry Redwood, second vice-president; Mrs. J. E. Dickerson, recording secretary; Miss Willie Ray, corresponding secretary; Mrs. W. D. Hilliard, treasurer.

MONUMENTS. A monument designed to honor the dead infantry of Buncombe county was erected in Newton cemetery in 1903. For the keeping of this plot and the annual decoration of the graves the chapter is chiefly indebted to Miss Julia Hatch and Miss Mary McDowell, as leaders.

GEN. THOMAS L. CLINGMAN's MONUMENT. This stands in the court house lot and is thus engraved: "Erected by Robert E. Lee Chapter, Children of the Confederacy, and

Friends; In Honor of Gen. Clingman, Colonel of the 25th
N. C. Reg.—Brig. Gen. Confederate army—U. S. Senator.
Clingman's Dome - Smoky Range, 6660 ft. — Next to Mt.
Mitchell 6714 ft., highest East of the Rockies."

THE ROBERT E. LEE CHAPTER was an auxiliary of this
chapter, and was organized in April, 1894, under the supervision of Mrs. Edward McDowell. Mrs. E. B. Glenn followed
Mrs. McDowell in fuller enlistment of interest as a study
circle and choir. The historical department is under the
direction of Mrs. J. E. Ray. Among those who have been
active and helpful from the organization are Mrs. J. P. Sawyer,
Mrs. Duffield, Mrs. Stockton, Mrs. W. W. West, Miss Mary
C. McDowell, Mrs. Betty Child, Mrs. William Breese, Miss
Carrie Furman, Mrs. Martha C. Kepler, president from January, 1899, to November, 1907; Mrs. Henry Redwood, president from 1907 till November, 1910; Mrs. C. E. Chambers,
who has served since as president. Mrs. Edith C. L. Cain,
Mrs. E. W. West, Mrs. Daisy S. Cleminger, Miss Pearl K.
Stevens, Mrs. B. K. Bassett, Miss Nancy Grant, Mrs. Eph-
raim Clayton, Mrs. Malcolm Platt, Miss Ethel Ray, Mrs.
F. B. Dickerson, Mrs. E. W. West.

THE MEN OF BUNCOMBE
By J. P. ARTHUR
(Read at Centennial Celebration of Buncombe County, August 11, 1892)

More than a hundred years ago, over the mountain walls,
Over the trackless forest-path, over the water-falls;
Over a hundred miles of swamp, over the sandy plain,
Our fathers came to this fair clime to build them homes again.
Away from the glistening sad sea-shore, away from the haunts of men,
Away from the busy marts of trade, away from brake and fen;
Away from the glare and grind of life, away from grasping greed,
Into this wilderness they came and planted deep their seed.
Driving their kind-eyed cows along, trusting their faithful dogs,
To Swannanoa's stream they came and built their home of logs;
With a Bible on the mantel-shelf and a rifle over the door,
The Men of Buncombe started life a hundred years ago.
Look out on these everlasting hills and towering mountains blue,
Look out on these verdant, smiling plains, bright rivers winding through;
Look up at the grand ethereal vault, the arching, heaven-kissed dome—
Look out, look up at land and sky our fathers chose for Home!
Italian lands with sunsets grand, bright noons and rosy morns,
Match not the gorgeous draperies of our opalescent dawns;
And famed Arcadia holds no nook one half so fair as this,
Nor the "Island Vale Avillion" airs which breathe so soft a kiss!

Kings Mountain's fight and Cowpens' fray, Guilford and Alamance
The story of their valor tell with halo of romance;
But now, their swords to ploughshares turned, their strife with man is o'er;
They battle with harsh nature's moods and conquer as before.
The forests girdled by their axe in burning log-heaps glow,
While, pulsing 'neath its brood of grain, the mother-earth smiles through!
Many an idle stream is bound and harnessed to a wheel,
And thousands herbs and weeds are made their secret balms to yield.
The martins, nesting in the gourd, like sentinels kept ward
For robber hawks, while timid fowl strutted the wide barn-yard;
Lithe, antlered red-deer roamed the hills, close followed by their fawns,
Cropping the dainty, crisp young grass in dew-bespangled dawns.
The anvil's clang, the saw's hoarse snore, the bellow's wheezing lay
The scythe's long swish, the hammer's ring made music all the day;
The furrow-scoured ploughshare bright, the sharp lip of the hoe,
The mattock, flail and reaping-hook were friends of the men of yore.
The wild deer furnished food and clothes; and, on a thousand hills,
Their cattle grazed knee-deep in grass, their sheep browsed by the rills;
Myriads of gold-enameled bees winged their swift flight in glee,
And, honey laden, homeward hummed to hives beneath the tree.

  .   .   .   .

Rude were these homes, but fairer far than many a palace grand,
For the love of God breathed everywhere—the love of God for man.
They manufactured all they used and, with their muscles strong,
They felled the woods, they sowed the fields with many an old-world song.
They had no artificial wants, no artificial airs,
No false conventions warped them from nature's sweet courtesies :
And what cared they for heraldry or long ancestral tree,
When Church and State for years had bound the world's best yeomanry?
Their eyes turned backward but to see the wrongs which they had flown;
And men were valued for their worth—not for their sires' renown;
And, though the lettered page was closed, and learning held in thrall,
Nature's grand university stood open to them all;
And many a useful art they knew and practiced far and wide;
Grew flax and hemp, made shoes and tools and tanned the raw cow-hide;
By lunar signs they sowed their seeds, reaped, threshed and garnered in;
Made spoons and cups of bone and horn, candles in molds of tin.
The hearth, the deep-mouthed fire-place, the look the old clock had;
The swinging crane, the steaming pots, the ovens ember-clad;—
The room ranged round with feather-beds, the fire-lighted wall,
The sweet home-faces round the board lapsed memories recall.
Outside, the soft, low murmurous wind, moving in stately stride,
Deep-toned, portentious, awful, grand, sobbed on the mountain-side;
Broke on life's sentient silences, spoke to the spirit's ear—
Hushed as the music of the stars, but speaking, weird and clear.

  .   .   .   .

Lonely the lot of those who first planted their roof-tree here,
With never a word from home or friends their lonely hearts to cheer :
Cold were the winter nights and long the short-lived winter days
Till spring, at last, broke into song with bird-note roundelays.

Far off in raptured solitudes and bosky mountain dells,
In fancy's footless wanderings, they heard home-chiming bells;
They heard the murmur of the sea in soughings of the pines
And traced again Ben Lomond's form in shadowy mountain lines.
Sometimes, by dimpled, purling streams—high in the spirit's noon—
They stood again on Shannon's shore, or by the banks of Doon;
Over the wolf's fierce howl there rose the spinning-wheels' low croon,
And the panther's curdling shriek was drowned in the click of the clack-
     ing loom.

     .   .   .   .

Still, not unlighted were their lives by mirth and homely wit—
Orlando wrestled in the groves and Touchstone made his hit :
Corn-shuckings, dances, tourneys, games, the wrestling match and race,
Won many a smile from Chloe's eyes for Strephons' skill and grace.
Vesta kept lit the glowing hearth, or, if its fire died,
Aeneas came with flint and steel and all her wants supplied :
The tallow-dip, with constant drip, gave light with fitful start,
While Orpheus's music won Eurydice's soft heart.
Bearing their own they still could bear each other's burdens then—
Their humble board was free to all the wandering sons of men.
Together by their brawn they reared each other's cabin walls,
Sat by the sick and ministered each to the other's calls.
And holy men of God were there whose lives were a hymn of praise—
Their altar by each fire-side, their temples 'neath the trees;
Statesmen and soldiers, judges, priests have gone from these lowly doors,
Their hearts alight with love they learned as they knelt on puncheon floors.

     .   .   .   .

Their crops laid-by, from cove and glen, from vale and sunny slope,
They gathered then as Druids did to feed the spirit's hope;
Camp-meeting lays the pillared aisles of forest swept along,
Soared to the fretted, leafy vault in ecstacy of song.
Sweet-throated Davids of the fane, rapt wild-bird psalmists true,
Joined in man's grand, triumphant strain and thrilled the woodlands
     through.
Anthems more glad did never melt cathedral solitudes
Than the sweet strains the song birds poured through these inspired woods.
Fair flowers swung by acolytes unseen their incense poured
From brimming censers, lavishly, to Him who was adored.
No need of robed priest or choir, nor shrill bell pealing clear—
God in His holy temple was, in word, in song, in prayer!
And, so, they lived from year to year, sequestered from the world;
Driving their herds to market oft through weary weeks of toil.
And when War's dreaded drum-beat rolled o'er mountain peak and crag,
Some fought for the cause of Home and Law, and some for Right and the
     Flag.

     .   .   .   .

If some of the sheeted dead could rise and be with us today;
Could see yon two bright lines of steel climbing their heavenward way;

Crossing the mountain passes high, bearing Steam's panting steeds,
They'd stand spell-bound, uncovered here, awed by our mighty deeds.
And time and distance they would see have almost passed away :
The league at last is but an ell, the long year but a day :
Our words, our music and our plays, though written years agone,
In phonograph arcanums live, as faces live in stone.
Lightning, the Arab of the sky, has been enslaved at last,
And bears our burdens, lights our homes and runs our errands fast;
Climbs the steep hill-sides, turns our wheels, plunges 'neath ocean's wave,
Flashes a signal over the seas the sinking ships to save.
But, ah, their eyes in pained surprise would note Wealth's lavish waste,
And weep at the shrunken forms of want and childhood's haggard face;
Would sigh at Fashion's furbelows, and Miss McFlimsey's moods,
And pity that excrescence, called the lah-de-dah-de doods.

.   .   .   .

No orison of poesy nor sculptured column's prayer
Pleads now to save from Lethe's wave the names we hold so dear;
But kind, remembering valleys keep some monuments they reared
In the rude forms of humble homes and hills of forests bared.
And we, their grandsons, honor now these men of kingly mold;
We glory in their poverty, their strife with want and cold;
We honor every mark and scar where stood a cabin-home,
And crumbling grave-stones on the hill that mark the rest of some.
Gone now is many a mountain home, the buck-skin suit is gone,
And stately piles to heaven rise where diamonds rare are worn;
But the frugal lives of honest toil the Men of Buncombe led
Have left their imprint on the soil tho' their hero-hearts be dead!
Our heritage?   An honest name, strong arms and healthy frames,
The evidence that virtue's thorns wound less than vice's chains;
The proof that, 'twixt ourselves and wealth, Conscience should ever stand,
Full-armed for justice, truth and right—a drawn sword in her hands!
Story has told and Song has sung the deeds of other climes,
And the record of men's victories is statued in their rhymes;
But, though the trump of Fame has missed their story, sad and true.
The Men of Buncombe builded well, ay, better than they knew!

VANCE'S MONUMENT AT ASHEVILLE

By J. P. ARTHUR

Deep bedded in his native soil it stands,
    Rugged and strong, like him of whom it speaks;
    Firm and inspiring as his mountain peaks,
Beautiful as the work of his kind hands,
This monument all reverence commands.
    What soul-enkindling memories it wakes!
    Almost the silence of the tomb it breaks!
Almost his clarion voice the scene commands!
Once more the wisdom of the sage unfolds
    As the true statesman wrests from War's grim chance

His prostrate State, and her bright future molds.
Read the inscription, telling at a glance
The briefest epic any language holds—
A patriot's story in that one word : VANCE!

POPULATION IN 1850

From Wheeler's History of North Carolina it appears
that in Ashe county there were 8,096 whites; 86 free
negroes; 595 slaves; 8,539 free population; 587 persons
over 20 who cannot read or write. Buncombe county contained 11,607 whites; 107 free negroes; 1,717 slaves; 12,738
federal population; 1,533 persons who cannot read or write.
Cherokee contained 6,493 whites; 337 slaves; eight free negroes; 6,703 representative population. Haywood county
contained 5,931 whites; 710 Indians; 418 slaves; 15 free negroes; 6,906 representative population. Henderson contained
5,892 whites; 924 slaves; 37 free negroes; 6,483 representative
population. Macon had 5,613 whites; 121 Indians; 549 slaves;
207 free negroes; 6,169 representative population. Watauga
contained 3,242 whites; 29 free negroes; 129 slaves; 3,348
representative population.

County	1910	1900	1890
Alleghany	7,745	7,759	6,523
Ashe	19,074	19,581	15,628
Avery			
Buncombe	49,798	44,288	35,266
Cherokee	14,136	11,860	9,976
Clay	3,909	4,532	4,197
Graham	4,749	4,343	3,313
Haywood	21,020	16,222	13,346
Henderson	16,262	14,104	12,589
Jackson	12,998	11,853	9,512
Macon	12,191	12,104	10,102
Madison	20,132	20,644	17,805
Mitchell	17,245	15,221	12,807
Swain	10,403	8,401	6,577
Transylvania	7,191	6,620	5,881
Watauga	13,556	13,417	10,611
Yancey	12,072	11,464	9,490

WILLIAM MITCHELL DAWSON

The reference on page 152 is to a narrative by J. M. Daw-
son which has been withdrawn.